Advanced Textbooks in Economics
Series Editors: C. J. Bliss *and* M.D. Intriligator

Currently Available:

DIFFERENTIAL EQUATIONS, STABILITY AND CHAOS IN DYNAMIC ECONOMICS

ADVANCED TEXTBOOKS IN ECONOMICS

VOLUME 27

Editors:

C.J. BLISS

M.D. INTRILIGATOR

Advisory Editors:

W.A. BROCK

D.W. JORGENSON

A.P. KIRMAN

J.-J. LAFFONT

L. PHLIPS

J.-F. RICHARD

NORTH-HOLLAND
AMSTERDAM • LONDON • NEW YORK • TOKYO

DIFFERENTIAL EQUATIONS, STABILITY AND CHAOS IN DYNAMIC ECONOMICS

W.A. BROCK
University of Wisconsin

A.G. MALLIARIS
Loyola University of Chicago

NORTH-HOLLAND
AMSTERDAM • LONDON • NEW YORK • TOKYO

ELSEVIER SCIENCE PUBLISHERS B.V.
Sara Burgerhartstraat 25
P.O. Box 1991, 1000 BZ Amsterdam, The Netherlands

First edition: 1989
2nd printing: 1992

Library of Congress Cataloging in Publication Data

Brock, W.A.
    Differential equations, stability and chaos in dynamic economics
    W.A. Brock,   A.G. Malliaris
        p.   cm.
    Includes index.
    ISBN 0-444-70500-7
    1. Economics, Mathematical.   2. Differential equations.
    I. Brock, W.A.   II. Title.
HB135.M3346 1989
330'.01'51—dc19

ISBN 0   444   70500   7

INTRODUCTION TO THE SERIES

The aim of the series is to cover topics in economics, mathematical economics and econometrics, at a level suitable for graduate students or final year undergraduates specializing in economics. There is at any time much material that has become well established in journal papers and discussion series which still awaits a clear, self-contained treatment that can easily be mastered by students without considerable preparation or extra reading. Leading specialists will be invited to contribute volumes to fill such gaps. Primary emphasis will be placed on clarity, comprehensive coverage of sensibly defined areas, and insight into fundamentals, but original ideas will not be excluded. Certain volumes will therefore add to existing knowledge, while others will serve as a means of communicating both known and new ideas in a way that will inspire and attract students not already familiar with the subject matter concerned.

The Editors

CONTENTS

PREFACE

> As a formal model of an economy
> acquires a mathematical life of its
> own, it becomes the object of an
> inexorable process in which rigor,
> generality and simplicity are
> relentlessly pursued.
>
> Debreu (1986, p. 1265)

Differential equations, stability and chaos in dynamic economics introduces the reader to three advanced mathematical methods by expositing both their theoretical underpinnings and their applications to a wide range of economic models.

As the title of the book indicates, the mathematical methods presented are ordinary differential equations, stability techniques and chaotic dynamics. The applications selected to illustrate these methods are numerous and include microeconomic dynamics, investment theory, macroeconomic policies, capital theory, business cycles, financial economics and many others.

The use of ordinary differential equations in economics, dates back, at least to L. Walras in 1874. However, it was Samuelson's (1947) *Foundations of Economic Analysis* which firmly established the appropriateness of using ordinary differential equations in dynamic economics. During the past forty years, ordinary differential equations have been employed extensively by economic researchers and such a use has created the need for an exposition of the fundamental notions and properties of these equations. This is done in chapters 1 and 2; an emphasis on existence, continuation of solutions, uniqueness, successive approximations and dependence on initial data and parameters is given in chapter 1. Chapter 2 discusses linear differential equations with a balanced approach between their properties and solutions. We note that although the classical approach to differential equations concentrates on methods and techniques for finding explicit solutions, the modern approach endeavors to obtain information about the whole class of solutions and their properties. Thus, the emphasis of chapter 1 is on properties while chapter 2 balances abstraction with concreteness and illustrates some problem solving techniques.

The notion of stability in economics, introduced by Walras and Cournot and later studied by Marshall, Hicks, Samuelson and others, was not completely formulated until the late 1950s in the papers of Arrow and his collaborators. The last thirty years have seen numerous papers on stability analysis applied to economic models. However, stability methods continue to remain under-utilized by economists partly because our profession has not been taught these methods in any detail and partly because the critical role played by stability analysis has not been fully appreciated outside theoretical circles. Chapter 3 gives numerous definitions and examples of stability notions, and discusses the stability properties of linear dynamic systems. It also gives a comprehensive presentation of two dimensional systems and their phase diagrams.

Chapter 4 continues on the topic of stability at a more advanced level. Liapunov theory for local stability and global asymptotic stability receive the bulk of our attention. In other words, chapter 3 illustrates the significance of linear systems, the linearization of nonlinear systems, the counting and examination of roots of characteristic equations while chapter 4 is more topological in nature. Furthermore, the recent results of several mathematicians, such as Hartman and Olech (1962), Markus and Yamabe (1960) and Olech (1963) on global asymptotic stability receive special attention in a unique way which has not previously been done by mathematical economics textbooks.

The above is not all we have to say on stability methods. An additional important contribution is chapter 5. This chapter surveys several important methods of stability analysis of optimal control problems. While chapters 3 and 4 are a collection of stability results contributed by mathematicians that were essentially completed prior to 1965, chapter 5 surveys the stability contributions of mathematical economists, all of which took place since the mid 1970s. This chapter unites the economic analyst and the mathematician at the forefront of stability research and is used as a foundation for later chapters.

Through the contents of this book we hope to show that the stability analysis of an economic model is an integral part of economic research. The stability properties of an economic model must be investigated and become understood before such a model is used to supply insights into the workings of the actual economic system. Although conditions of the existence and uniqueness of equilibrium are investigated almost automatically in economic model building, it is not always true that the same is done for stability. The many stability methods discussed in this book and the numerous illustrations are intended to persuade the economic theorist to become more comprehensive in his or her analysis of economic models. To encourage this methodological approach, stability is viewed as a property of the solution of the differential equation and chapter 3 makes explicit the connection between the property of dependence on initial data and the concept of stability.

Having argued that differential equations abound in economics and that stability methods form a limited subset of the former, what can we say about chaotic dynamics? Methods related to chaos and nonlinearity are very new to economics. As chapter 10 documents, the number of economic papers in this area, although growing very rapidly, remains limited, with most of these papers having been written in the 1980s. Chapter 10 attempts to give a mathematically precise version of recent tests on an observed time series for the presence of low dimensional deterministic chaos. A simple methodological connection between stability and chaos explains why chaos is introduced in this book. Chaos theory removes the emphasis from stability by stressing instabilities.

The exposition of differential equations, stability and chaos as a collection of important mathematical methods has not been made at the expense of illustrations. Fully one half of this book is devoted to applications. More specifically, chapter 6 is written to make two points. First, an infinite horizon two sector economy in which one sector is decreasing returns and the other is increasing returns may fail to achieve Pareto optimum, under decentralized institutions. This may occur even when the increasing returns sector is regulated in a *first best* fashion, efficient markets prevail, rational expectations obtain, and the necessity of the transversality condition at infinity for identical infinitely lived agents eliminate Hahn (1966) type problems. Second, there is a tendency for the increasing returns sector to overexpand although this is not always the case. The chapter also provides an analytically tractable framework where the impact of different modes of regulation upon economic development paths may be studied. Multiple optimal paths are also investigated.

Chapter 7 addresses stability issues in investment theory with primary emphasis on cost of adjustment models. Instead of just citing results, this chapter proposes a novel way of studying stability as a methodological consequence of a modified *Correspondence Principle*. The famous original Correspondence Principle of Paul Samuelson is discussed and a modification is proposed and utilized to obtain stability results in investment models.

Chapter 8 extends some of the recent macrodynamic models in two ways. First, it specifies a more complete corporate sector that such models usually contain and, second the relationships describing the private sector are derived from explicit optimizing procedures by households and firms. The equilibrium structure and dynamics of this model are studied in detail and the stability of a simplified case is analyzed.

Chapter 9 applies the results of chapters 1 through 5 to capital theory. A capital theory generates a capital-price differential equation by using the Pontryagin maximum principle to write the necessary conditions for an optimal solution. This process generates a system of differential equations that is called a *modified Hamiltonian dynamical system*. This chapter analyzes the stability properties of such modified Hamiltonian dynamical systems.

All chapters conclude with two sections on miscellaneous applications and exercises and further remarks and references. In total the reader will find a valuable guide to over 500 selected references that use differential equations, stability analysis and chaotic dynamics.

We are quite certain that this is the first economics monograph of its kind offering the economic theorist the opportunity to acquire new and important analytical tools. There are currently no books available covering all the methods presented here; nor are there any books with such a comprehensive coverage of applications. The primary audience of this book will include PhD students in economics with a special interest in economic theory. Furthermore, economic researchers should benefit from this book by developing expertise in the methods studied. Finally, applied mathematicians will find fresh mathematical ideas in chapter 5 relating to the stability of optimal control and can broaden the domain of their stability and chaos examples from chapters 6 through 10.

An attempt has been made to keep the mathematical background to a minimum. Many parts of this book can be understood by someone with a good background in analysis. The Appendix cites numerous definitions and theorems to help readers with insufficient mathematical background and gives references for further study.

ACKNOWLEDGEMENTS

We happily acknowledge an enormous intellectual debt to each of the mathematicians and economists cited in this book. They gave us the original, creative and valuable contributions which form the substance of this book.

The late W. T. Reid, Norman Lebovitz (Mathematics Department, University of Chicago) and Jerry Bona (Mathematics Department, Pennsylvania State University) gave valuable instruction on differential equations and stability. R. Becker (Indiana University), E. Burmeister (University of Virginia), F. R. Chang (Indiana University) and S. Turnovsky (University of Washington) wrote detailed comments that helped us improve our exposition.

Numerous individuals helped through insightful comments, suggestions, encouragement and interest in our work and among them we mention: N. Barron (Loyola University of Chicago), J. Benhabib (New York University), J. H. Boyd, III (Rochester University), G. Constantinides (University of Chicago), D. Dechert (University of Iowa), M. Hadjimichalakis (University of Washington), K. Judd (University of Chicago), M. Magill (University of Southern California), D. Meyer (Loyola University of Chicago), J. Scheinkman (University of Chicago), S. Stefani (University of Brescia, Italy), A. Takayama (University of Southern Illinois) and anonymous referees.

Several research assistants helped with proofreading, editing and bibliographical work. We are grateful to Carol Ross, Adrienne Colvert, John Potthast, Alexander Valvassori, Elizabeth Steber, John Gogniat and Hang Chang. Pamela Kellman made numerous editorial suggestions that improved the presentation of our ideas. Carmela Perno has shown outstanding patience and extraordinary skills in typing various versions during a period of five years.

M. Intriligator has supported us enthusiastically and Drs Ellen van Koten and Mr Joop Dirkmaat, former and current editors respectively of Elsevier Science Publishers B.V. (North-Holland), have been a pleasure to work with.

We are thankful to the Academic Press and the editors of the *Journal of Economic Theory*, to Springer-Verlag, to the North-Holland Publishing

Company and to the editors of the *International Economic Review* for giving us permission to use copyrighted papers authored and coauthored by W. A. Brock.

Parts of the book have been used by numerous students at the University of Wisconsin, Stanford University, Indiana University and Loyola University of Chicago and we are grateful to all students who have read and commented on the manuscript.

Finally, W. A. Brock dedicates his portion of this book to his wife Joan "who makes his work possible and his life fun" and A. G. Malliaris dedicates his portion to his wife Mary Elaine and their children Maryanthe and Steven for "their love, patience and joy".

CHAPTER 1

BASIC PROPERTIES OF DIFFERENTIAL EQUATIONS

> The importance of the ordinary differential equations vis à vis other areas of science lies in its power to motivate, unify and give force to those areas.
>
> Hirsch and Smale (1974, p. ix)

1. Introduction

The study of ordinary differential equations may be pursued from at least two broadly distinct approaches. On the one hand, one may endeavor to learn a large number of methods and techniques by which certain elementary equations can be solved explicitly. Alternatively, one may concentrate on obtaining information about the whole class of solutions and their properties, putting aside all endeavors to master skillfully a myriad of methods yielding closed form solutions.

In this chapter we select the latter approach to study the basic *properties* of ordinary differential equations and their solutions without expositing methods of solution. More specifically, we discuss in some detail the following topics: existence and uniqueness of solutions, dependence of solutions on initial data and parameters, differentiability of solutions and stability. Actually, the important property of stability is introduced in this chapter and then left to be treated in some detail in the following chapters.

There are at least three reasons justifying our approach in this chapter, with its emphasis on properties of solutions rather than on methods yielding explicit solutions. First, the notion of stability and its applications both seek to obtain information about a property of the whole class of solutions. In this sense, the present chapter's emphasis on properties will prepare the reader to view stability and its many applications as a fundamental property of certain ordinary differential equations. Second, almost all economic applications of stability exposited in this book or found in the general literature concentrate on the property of stability which is not dependent upon a specific and explicit solution of a differential equation. Thus most applications strive for generality and so does our analysis. Finally, our approach illustrates the modern inclination and interest of mathematicians with preference for abstraction and generality rather than amplification and specification. We note, however, that our approach is not carried to an extreme; in chapter 2 we supplement our theoretical analysis by showing how certain linear systems can be solved explicitly.

During the past three decades a modern approach has emerged which blends the theory of ordinary differential equations with techniques for solving them. This approach was pioneered by Coddington (1961) and Pontryagin (1962) and was followed by Plaat (1971), Roxin (1972), Arnold (1973), Birkhoff and Rota (1978), Braun (1978, 1983), and many others during the seventies and early eighties. Although in chapters 1 through 4 we concentrate primarily on the theoretical underpinnings of ordinary differential equations, this book viewed in its entirety blends in a unique way the theory with the many economic applications of ordinary differential equations.

2. Preliminaries

Let t be a real number on an open interval $I \subset R$ and denote by D an open and connected set in R^{n+1}. An open and connected set is called a *domain* and is denoted by D. An element of D is written as $(t, x) \in I \times R^n$. Suppose that f is a continuous function with domain the set $D \subset R^{n+1}$ and range the space R^n, that is, $f : D \to R^n$. An equation of the form

$$\frac{dx(t)}{dt} = f(t, x(t)) \tag{2.1}$$

is called an *ordinary differential equation*. Equation (2.1) may also be written as

$$\dot{x} = f(t, x), \tag{2.2}$$

where $\dot{x} = dx(t)/dt$. If there is a continuously differentiable function $\phi(t)$ defined on some open real interval I such that for $t \in I$ we have both that

$(t, \phi(t)) \in D$ and also

$$\dot{\phi}(t) = f(t, \phi(t)), \tag{2.3}$$

then we say that $\phi(t)$ is a *solution* of the differential equation (2.1) on *I*. The function f in (2.1) is called a *vector field* on *D* because it takes the vector $(t, x) \in R^{n+1}$ to the vector $\dot{x} \in R^n$. In R^2, geometrically, (2.1) prescribes a slope $f(t, x(t))$ at each point $(t, x) \in D$ and a solution $\phi(t)$, $t \in I$, is a function whose *graph* has the slope $f(t, \phi(t))$ for each $t \in I$. By graph we mean the set of all points $(t, \phi(t))$ for $t \in I$. In other words, a solution $\phi(t)$ is a curve whose direction at any point $t \in I$ coincides with the direction of the vector field.

A differential equation of the form

$$\dot{x} = f(x) \tag{2.4}$$

in which the right side does not include the independent variable *t* is called an *autonomous* or a *time independent* differential equation. Geometrically, the solutions $\phi(t)$ of (2.2) or (2.4) can be pictured as curves in the *x*-space with *t* as a curve parameter. Such a curve is called a *path*. In other words, the paths are the projections of the graphs on any hyperplane with *t* being a constant. The space of the variables *x* which contains the paths is called the *phase space* of (2.4). See also section 6 of chapter 3.

Let $(t_0, x_0) \in D$. An *initial value problem* for (2.1) consists of finding an interval *I* containing t_0 and a solution $\phi(t)$ of (2.1) such that $\phi(t_0) = x_0$. This problem is denoted by

$$\dot{x} = f(t, x), \quad x(t_0) = x_0, \quad t \in I. \tag{2.5}$$

We say that t_0 is the *initial point* or initial time and x_0 the *initial value*. The point (t_0, x_0) is called the *initial condition*. Geometrically, (2.5) means that we are searching for a solution passing through the point (t_0, x_0).

To illustrate the concepts of a solution to a differential equation and the initial value problem, we consider two examples.

Example 2.1. Consider the differential equation

$$\dot{x} = \alpha x, \tag{2.6}$$

where α is a real number. Here $f(t, x) = \alpha x$ so that the vector field depends only on the variable *x*. Integrating (2.6) we obtain a solution of the form

$$\phi(t) = c \, e^{\alpha t}, \quad t \in R, \tag{2.7}$$

where c is an arbitrary real number. Note that (2.7) is continuously differentiable for $t \in R$ and satisfies (2.6) because

$$\dot{x} = \dot{\phi}(t) = \alpha c\, e^{\alpha t} = \alpha \phi(t) = \alpha x.$$

For the initial value problem, in addition to (2.6), we need to specify a certain point t_0 and the corresponding value $x(t_0)$. As an illustration, assume that $t_0 = 0$ and $x(t_0) = x(0) = 1$. We write the initial value problem as

$$\dot{x} = \alpha x, \quad x(0) = 1, \tag{2.8}$$

and its solution is stated as

$$\phi(t) = 1\, e^{\alpha t}, \quad t \in R. \tag{2.9}$$

The solution in (2.9) is a specific solution passing through the point $(0, 1)$.

In the special case when $t \geq 0$ and $\alpha > 0$, (2.6) can be used to denote instantaneous interest earned by an x amount of dollars. Its solution in (2.7) denotes the current value of a sum of capital c with instantaneously compounded interest. In this special case, the initial value problem (2.8) specifies both the instantaneous interest earned by x dollars and the initial amount of capital; its solution in (2.9) yields at time t the total value of \$1 earning instantaneously compounded interest for t periods. Thus the 1 in (2.9) denotes the initial amount invested.

Example 2.2. Consider the differential equation

$$\dot{x} = x^2. \tag{2.10}$$

Here $f(t, x) = x^2$, so that the differential equation is autonomous. Assume that $x \neq 0$ and integrate (2.10) in the following manner,

$$\int (\dot{x}/x^2)\, dt = \int x^{-2} \dot{x}\, dt = \int dt.$$

We find that $-x^{-1} = t + c$, for c an arbitrary nonzero real constant and $\phi(0) = -1/c$. Assume that $c > 0$. Then

$$\phi(t) = -\frac{1}{t + c} \tag{2.11}$$

is a solution of (2.10) for $t \in (-c, \infty)$. Observe that (2.11) is a solution of (2.10) for $t \in (-c, \infty)$ because it is continuously differentiable in this interval and also

$$\dot{x} = \dot{\phi}(t) = \frac{1}{(t+c)^2} = \phi^2(t) = x^2.$$

If we assume that $c < 0$, then (2.11) is a solution of (2.10) for $t \in (-\infty, -c)$. Note that if $c = 0$, then (2.11) is not a solution for the differential equation for $t \in R$ because $\phi(t) = -1/t$ is not continuously differentiable on the real line. Actually at $t = 0$, $\phi(t) = -1/t$ is discontinuous and does not qualify as a solution. However, if $c = 0$, (2.11) is a solution for $t > 0$.

This example illustrates that, although $f(t, x) = x^2$ is a continuous function on the whole real line, its solution is restricted to a subset of the real line which depends on the value of the constant c. This observation suggests that existence of a solution is a local property. For an example of an initial value problem, consider

$$\dot{x} = x^2, \quad x(0) = -1. \tag{2.12}$$

From the preceding analysis, we conclude that

$$\phi(t) = -\frac{1}{1+t} \tag{2.13}$$

is a solution for $t \in (-1, \infty)$ since $c = 1$. If we change the initial value problem in (2.12) to

$$\dot{x} = x^2, \quad x(0) = 1, \tag{2.14}$$

then the solution becomes

$$\phi(t) = \frac{1}{1-t},$$

for $t \in (-\infty, 1)$ since now $c = -1$. This illustrates that a change in *initial values* may affect the interval of the *existence* of a solution.

In the two examples above, the continuity of $f(t, x)$ in (2.6) and (2.10) allows us to integrate in order to find a solution to the differential equation. In general, in order to establish the existence of solutions, the method usually followed consists of replacing the differential equation by an integral equation. Therefore, we conclude this section with a useful lemma. Assume that $f(t, x)$ is defined and continuous on some domain D for $t \in I$ and that

$(t_0, x_0) \in D$. From the continuity of f we know that its integral exists. By integrating (2.2) between the limits t_0 and t, that is,

$$\int_{t_0}^{t} \dot{x} \, ds = \int_{t_0}^{t} f(s, x) \, ds,$$

we obtain *Volterra's integral equation*

$$x(t) = x_0 + \int_{t_0}^{t} f(s, x) \, ds, \quad t \in I. \tag{2.15}$$

Note that $x(t)$ in (2.15) is a solution of the initial value problem in (2.5) since $x(t)$ is continuously differentiable and satisfies (2.5) on some open interval I including the point t_0. Conversely, for any continuously differentiable function $x(t)$ of the form (2.15), by putting $t = t_0$ we immediately obtain $x(t_0) = x_0$. Furthermore, we know that by differentiating (2.15), $\dot{x} = f(t, x)$ results and thus (2.15) yields the initial value problem. We summarize this analysis in

Lemma 2.1. If the function $f(t, x)$ is continuous, then the initial value problem $\dot{x} = f(t, x), x(t_0) = x_0, t \in I$ is equivalent to Volterra's integral equation

$$x(t) = x_0 + \int_{t_0}^{t} f(s, x) \, ds, \quad t \in I.$$

3. Existence

Consider the first order differential equation

$$\dot{x} = f(t, x), \tag{3.1}$$

where f is a real-valued continuous function on a domain $D \subset R^2$. The analysis in this section proceeds in terms of the first order differential equation. No loss of generality is suffered by treating this simple case; all theorems and proofs can be generalized by essentially replacing absolute values by vector norms.

In most applications, and specifically in the many economic applications of subsequent chapters, $f(t, x)$ is not explicitly stated. Even when $f(t, x)$ is explicitly stated, chances are that we will be unable to solve it explicitly. Therefore, it is prudent to ask the questions: how are we to know that (3.1) actually has a solution and how do we know that only one solution exists, instead of more than one or even infinitely many? To answer these questions, we must find a theorem which guarantees the existence of a unique function having certain properties in order to qualify as a solution, without actually having to write down this function explicitly. Note that assuming f to be continuous is an assumption without which we cannot go very far, for consider the simple case where $f(t, x)$ is a *Dirichlet* function which is not Riemann integrable, defined by

$$f(t, x) = \begin{cases} 1, & \text{if } t \text{ is rational} \\ 0, & \text{if } t \text{ is irrational.} \end{cases} \tag{3.2}$$

For $f(t, x)$, as in (3.2), there is no hope of finding a solution $\phi(t)$ satisfying (3.1). Furthermore, assuming $f(t, x)$ to be continuous does not guarantee the existence of a solution everywhere as the earlier example $\dot{x} = x^2$ suggested. Therefore, any general existence theorem must be of a *local* nature and an existence theorem for the whole space can be obtained only under additional conditions on f.

In this section we study the question of existence and leave the question of uniqueness for section 5. The analysis of local existence is done in two steps following Coddington and Levinson (1955). First, it is shown that an approximate solution to equation (3.1) exists, and second, it is shown that a sequence of such approximate solutions exists which converges to a solution. Thus we establish the existence of a solution without having to explicitly state the solution itself. We begin with the necessary definitions and theorems of the first step. Recall that $f(t, x)$ is assumed to be continuous on a domain $D \subset R^2$. An element of the set D is written as (t, x) for t belonging to an interval I.

We define an *ε-approximate solution* $\phi(t)$ of the ordinary differential equation $\dot{x} = f(t, x)$ in (3.1) on an interval I to be a continuous function satisfying:

(1) $(t, \phi(t)) \in D$ for $t \in I$,
(2) ϕ is continuously differentiable except for a finite set of points $S \subset I$ where $\dot{\phi}$ may have simple discontinuities. We say that $\dot{\phi}$ has a *simple discontinuity* at a point if the right and left limits of $\dot{\phi}$ at this point are finite but not equal.

(3) $|\dot{\phi}(t) - f(t, \phi(t))| \le \varepsilon$ for $t \in I - S$.

The first lemma establishes that an ε-approximate solution exists for the initial value problem

$$\dot{x} = f(t, x), \quad x(t_0) = x_0. \tag{3.3}$$

Lemma 3.1. Choose any two positive real numbers a and b and let R be the rectangle:

$$R = \{(t, x): |t - t_0| \le a \text{ and } |x - x_0| \le b\}.$$

Suppose that $f(t, x)$ is continuous on the rectangle R and let $\varepsilon > 0$ be given. Then there exists an ε-approximate solution $\phi(t)$ on some interval I that satisfies the initial value problem in (3.3).

Proof. From the assumed continuity of f in the rectangle R, we infer that f is bounded there. Let

$$M = \max|f(t, x)| \quad \text{for } (t, x) \in R$$

and set

$$\alpha = \min\left(a, \frac{b}{M}\right).$$

Furthermore, the rectangle R is closed and bounded, that is, R is compact and we know that a continuous function on a compact set is actually uniformly continuous. Thus given $\varepsilon > 0$ there is a δ, depending on ε, such that

$$|f(t, x) - f(s, y)| \le \varepsilon \tag{3.4}$$

if $(t, x) \in R$, $(s, y) \in R$, $|t - s| \le \delta$ and $|x - y| \le \delta$. Choose a partition for the interval $[t_0, t_0 + \alpha]$ of the form

$$t_0 < t_1 < \cdots < t_n = t_0 + \alpha$$

in such a way that

$$\max|t_k - t_{k-1}| \le \min\left(\delta, \frac{\delta}{M}\right). \tag{3.5}$$

An ε-approximate solution can now be constructed for the interval $[t_0, t_0 + \alpha]$. One can proceed in a similar manner to construct a solution for

$[t_0 - \alpha, t_0]$. The ε-approximate solution consists of a finite number of straight line segments joined end to end and sandwiched between the lines

$$x = x_0 + M(t - t_0) \quad \text{and} \quad x = x_0 - M(t - t_0) \tag{3.6}$$

for the interval $[t_0, t_0 + \alpha]$. Such a finite number of straight lines is called a *polygonal path* or an *Euler polygon*, or *Cauchy polygon*.

From the initial point and the initial value (t_0, x_0), construct a straight line with slope $f(t_0, x_0)$ until this intersects the line $t = t_1$. Then construct another straight line starting at (t_1, x_1), where the first line ends, with slope $f(t_1, x_1)$ up to its intersection with $t = t_2$. Repeating the same process a finite number of times, the resultant path $\phi(t)$ will meet the line $t = t_0 + \alpha$. The path will lie between the lines in (3.6) by definition of α and the fact that $|f(t, x)| \le M$. One can verify that $\phi(t)$ is the required ε-approximate solution. Furthermore, this construction specifies the interval of existence which is $|t - t_0| \le \alpha$. This concludes the proof of the lemma.

Let us move on to the second step towards establishing an existence theorem. Our goal now is to construct a sequence of ε-approximate solutions and show that these solutions converge to a solution of (3.3). Of course, we plan to use lemma 3.1 and we do so immediately. Let $\{\varepsilon_n\}$, $n = 1, 2, \ldots$ be a monotonically decreasing sequence of positive real numbers such that $\varepsilon_n \to 0$ as $n \to \infty$. For each ε_n, lemma 3.1 guarantees the existence of an ε_n-approximate solution, denoted as ϕ_n, for the initial value problem in (3.3) on $|t - t_0| \le \alpha$ such that $\phi_n(t_0) = x_0$. We wish to conclude that the sequence $\{\phi_n\}$ is equicontinuous. This follows immediately from the construction of ϕ_n because

$$|\phi_n(t) - \phi_n(s)| \le M|t - s| \tag{3.7}$$

for t and $s \in [t_0, t_0 + \alpha]$. Furthermore, applying (3.7) for $s = t_0$ we get

$$|\phi_n(t) - \phi_n(t_0)| \le M|t - t_0| \le M\frac{b}{M} \tag{3.8}$$

since $|t - t_0| \le b/M$. Note that (3.8) yields

$$|\phi_n(t)| \le |\phi_n(t_0)| + b = |x_0| + b,$$

which means that the sequence $\{\phi_n\}$ is uniformly bounded. Thus $\{\phi_n\}$ is a sequence of ε_n-approximate solutions that is both equicontinuous and uniformly bounded on a bounded interval $[t_0 - \alpha, t_0 + \alpha]$. By the *Ascoli lemma* in the appendix, deduce that there is a subsequence $\{\phi_{n_k}\}$, $k = 1, 2, \ldots$, of $\{\phi_n\}$, converging uniformly on $[t_0 - \alpha, t_0 + \alpha]$ to a limit function denoted by ϕ. Also, note that ϕ is continuous because each ϕ_n is continuous. To show that ϕ is a solution to (3.3) we let

$$\Delta_n(t) = \begin{cases} \dot{\phi}_n(t) - f(t, \phi_n(t)), & \text{where } \dot{\phi}_n \text{ exists} \\ 0, & \text{otherwise,} \end{cases}$$

and we write the ε_n-approximate solution as an integral equation of the form

$$\phi_n(t) = \phi_n(t_0) + \int_{t_0}^{t} \dot{\phi}_n(s) \, ds$$

$$= x_0 + \int_{t_0}^{t} [f(s, \phi_n(s)) + \dot{\phi}_n(s) - f(s, \phi_n(s))] \, ds$$

$$= x_0 + \int_{t_0}^{t} [f(s, \phi_n(s)) + \Delta_n(s)] \, ds$$

$$= x_0 + \int_{t_0}^{t} f(s, \phi_n(s)) \, ds + \int_{t_0}^{t} \Delta_n(s) \, ds. \tag{3.9}$$

Choose a subsequence $\{\phi_{n_k}\}$ of (3.9). Since f is uniformly continuous on R and $\phi_{n_k} \to \phi$ as $k \to \infty$ uniformly on $[t_0 - \alpha, t_0 + \alpha]$, it follows that $f(t, \phi_{n_k}(t)) \to f(t, \phi(t))$ uniformly as $k \to \infty$ on the same interval. Furthermore, by definition of $\Delta_n(t)$ for $t \in [t_0 - \alpha, t_0 + \alpha]$ we have

$$\left| \int_{t_0}^{t} \Delta_n(s) \, ds \right| \leq \varepsilon_n \alpha.$$

Therefore, in the limit (3.9) becomes

$$\phi(t) = x_0 + \int_{t_0}^{t} f(s, \phi(s)) \, ds$$

which verifies that $\phi(t)$ is a solution. We have proved an existence theorem.

Theorem 3.1. (Cauchy–Peano existence theorem.)   If $f(t, x)$ is a continuous function on the rectangle R, where

$$R = \{(t, x): |t - t_0| \leq a \text{ and } |x - x_0| \leq b\},$$

then there exists a continuously differentiable solution $\phi(t)$ on the interval $|t - t_0| \le \alpha$ that solves the initial value problem

$$\dot{x} = f(t, x), \quad x(t_0) = x_0.$$

Three clarifications seem appropriate about the last theorem. First, the existence theorem claims that, only under the stated assumptions a solution exists. Put differently, if more than one solution exists, the method of construction in the proof of theorem 3.1 cannot in general give *all* such solutions of the initial value problem. For an illustration, see exercise (4) in section 8. Second, there may exist polygonal paths $\{\phi_n\}$ which diverge everywhere; therefore, the choice of a converging subsequence is necessary to establish existence of a solution. Finally, theorem 3.1 is not helpful in showing how to construct a solution. We will see, however, in section 6 that if we know the solution is unique, then the sequence of ε_n-approximate solutions can be used to construct this solution.

4. Continuation of solutions

Theorem 3.1 assures us that a solution exists for the initial value problem on some interval *I*. It is mathematically interesting and in some applications it becomes important to know if solutions can be continued on an extended interval. Below we give a precise meaning to the concepts of a continuation of solutions and extended interval, and we explore the conditions under which such a continuation is possible.

Let $\phi(t)$, $t \in I$, be a solution of the initial value problem in (3.3). If $\psi(t)$ is also a solution of (3.3) on an interval *J*, where *J* contains properly *I*, and if $\psi(t) = \phi(t)$ for $t \in I$, then we say that $\psi(t)$ is a *continuation* of $\phi(t)$ and *J* is called an *extension* of *I*. If there is no such $\psi(t)$, then $\phi(t)$, $t \in I$ is called a *maximally* continued solution and *I* is a *maximal* interval of existence.

Example 4.1. To illustrate these concepts consider the initial value problem in (2.14) where $\dot{x} = x^2$ and $x(0) = 1$. Its solution $\phi(t) = 1/(1 - t)$ is maximally continued, with the maximal interval of existence being $(-\infty, 1)$. Note that at $t = 1$, $\phi(t)$ becomes unbounded and, therefore, it is impossible to extend it to $(-\infty, 1]$.

For the analysis in the remainder of this section we make use of *left* and *right limits* which we immediately define and indicate by the appropriate notation.

Consider the finite interval (a, b) of the real line. For $t \in (a, b)$, we write $t \to a + 0$ to denote that t approaches a from the right. Similarly we write $t \to b - 0$ to mean that t approaches b from the left. For a function $\phi(t), t \in (a, b)$, we define

$$\lim_{t \to a+0} \phi(t) = \phi(a+0),$$

$$\lim_{t \to b-0} \phi(t) = \phi(b-0).$$

We are now prepared to state the next theorem.

Theorem 4.1. (Continuation theorem.) Let $f(t, x)$ be continuous in a domain $D \subset R^2$ and suppose that $f(t, x)$ is bounded on D. If $\phi(t)$ is a solution of the initial value problem $\dot{x} = f(t, x), x(t_0) = x_0$ on an interval (a, b), then the limits $\phi(a+0)$ and $\phi(b-0)$ exist. Furthermore, if $(b, \phi(b-0)) \in D$, then ϕ can be continued to the right of b, and similarly if $(a, \phi(a+0)) \in D$, then ϕ can be continued to the left of a.

Proof. To show that $\phi(b-0)$ exists, we use Volterra's equation

$$\phi(t) = x_0 + \int_{t_0}^{t} f(s, \phi(s)) \, ds$$

for t_0 and $t \in (a, b)$. Note that if $a < u < v < b$, then

$$|\phi(u) - \phi(v)| \le \int_{u}^{v} |f(s, \phi(s))| \, ds$$

$$\le M|u - v|. \tag{4.1}$$

Here M is the bound of f on D, that is, $|f| \le M < \infty$. From (4.1) as u and v approach b from the left, then $\phi(u) - \phi(v) \to 0$ which implies by the *Cauchy convergence criterion* that

$$\lim_{t \to b-0} \phi(t) = \phi(b-0) < \infty.$$

A similar argument establishes the existence of $\phi(a+0)$.

Next, suppose that $(b, \phi(b-0)) \in D$. Define $\psi(t)$ as follows

$$\psi(t) = \begin{cases} \phi(t), & t \in (a, b) \\ \phi(b-0), & t = b. \end{cases}$$

Then $\psi(t), t \in (a, b]$, is a continuation of $\phi(t), t \in (a, b)$. Actually, the continuation can be extended by using $(b, \phi(b-0))$ as an initial condition, because by theorem 3.1 there is a solution $\chi(t)$, for $t \in [b, b+\beta]$, $\beta > 0$ such that $\chi(b) = \phi(b-0)$. Define $\theta(t)$ as

$$\theta(t) = \begin{cases} \psi(t), & t \in (a, b] \\ \chi(t), & t \in [b, b+\beta]. \end{cases}$$

It is easy to check that $\theta(t)$, $t \in (a, b+\beta]$ is a continuation of $\psi(t)$, $t \in (a, b]$ and $\theta(t)$ satisfies the initial value problem in (3.3). This concludes the proof.

5. Uniqueness

In economic applications and more generally in dynamic models described by a differential equation, it is of practical importance to know whether a solution of the equation is unique. Despite its great value, the existence theorem only asserts that a solution exists on some neighborhood of the initial point t_0. The continuation theorem specifies how far a solution can be extended. Having obtained such information about existence of solutions and their continuation, the applied researcher still does not know which one of the perhaps infinitely many solutions represents the true behavior of the dynamic model.

If uniqueness of the solution is to prevail, it is reasonable to expect $f(t, x)$ to satisfy some restriction in addition to continuity. The next example shows that continuity alone is not sufficient to guarantee uniqueness.

Example 5.1. Suppose that $f(t, x) = 3x^{2/3}$; here $f(t, x)$ is continuous. We want to find all solutions to the initial value problem

$$\dot{x} = 3x^{2/3}, \quad x(0) = 0. \tag{5.1}$$

By inspection we conclude that $x(t) = 0$, $t \in R$ is one solution. To search for other solutions, suppose that $x \neq 0$ and integrate

$$\int \dot{x} x^{-2/3} \, dt = 3 \int dt$$

to conclude that $x(t) = (t+c)^3$. Let c be a positive number and define ϕ_c by

$$\phi_c(t) = \begin{cases} 0, & t \in (-\infty, c] \\ (t-c)^3, & t \in (c, \infty). \end{cases}$$

We note that $\phi_c(t)$ is a solution of (5.1) for all real t and therefore conclude that this initial value problem has infinitely many solutions generated by arbitrary positive constants c.

The above example illustrates how a fairly simple initial value problem has infinitely many solutions. Dynamic models with nonunique solutions are unacceptable in applications because it is usually difficult to decide which solution represents the correct behavior of the model. It is therefore both necessary for applications and interesting mathematically to uncover restrictions that will guarantee uniqueness of solution. Example 5.1 can help us discover what is wrong with the initial value problem in (5.1). Upon reflection we conclude that the partial derivative $\partial f/\partial x$ does not exist at $x = 0$. For $f(t, x) = 3x^{2/3}$ we compute

$$\frac{\partial f}{\partial x} = 2x^{-1/3}$$

which becomes unbounded as $x \to 0$. To remove this difficulty and obtain the uniqueness property, we state and prove the next result.

Theorem 5.1. (Uniqueness.)   Let f and $\partial f/\partial x$ be continuous on the rectangle R,

$$R = \{(t, x): |t - t_0| \le a \text{ and } |x - x_0| \le b\}$$

with a and b positive and let

$$M = \max|f(t, x)| \quad \text{and} \quad \alpha = \min(a, b/M).$$

Then the initial value problem

$$\dot{x} = f(t, x), \quad x(t_0) = x_0$$

has a unique solution for $t \in [t_0, t_0 + \alpha]$.

Proof.   To show uniqueness we assume that $\phi(t)$ and $\psi(t)$ are two solutions. From the continuity of $f(t, x)$ and theorem 3.1, we conclude that at least one such solution exists. Our purpose is to use the added restriction about $\partial f/\partial x$ to show that $\phi(t) = \psi(t)$ for $t \in [t_0, t_0 + \alpha]$. Express

$$\phi(t) = x_0 + \int_{t_0}^{t} f(s, \phi(s)) \, ds \quad \text{and} \quad \psi(t) = x_0 + \int_{t_0}^{t} f(s, \psi(s)) \, ds.$$

Denote by L the maximum value of $|\partial f/\partial x|$ for t and x in the rectangle R and compute the difference of the two solutions. We obtain, using the *mean value theorem,*

$$|\phi(t) - \psi(t)| = \left| \int_{t_0}^{t} [f(s, \phi(s)) - f(s, \psi(s))] \, ds \right|$$

$$\leq \int_{t_0}^{t} |f(s, \phi(s)) - f(s, \psi(s))| \, ds$$

$$\leq L \int_{t_0}^{t} |\phi(s) - \psi(s)| \, ds. \tag{5.2}$$

We claim that this inequality implies that $\phi(t) = \psi(t)$. To verify this claim, set

$$U(t) = \int_{t_0}^{t} |\phi(s) - \psi(s)| \, ds \tag{5.3}$$

and rewrite (5.2) as

$$\frac{dU(t)}{dt} = |\phi(t) - \psi(t)| \leq L \int_{t_0}^{t} |\phi(s) - \psi(s)| \, ds = LU(t) \tag{5.4}$$

with $U(t_0) = 0$. Integrate (5.4) to get

$$e^{-L(t-t_0)} U(t) \leq U(t_0), \quad t \geq t_0. \tag{5.5}$$

In (5.5), $U(t_0) = 0$. This implies that $U(t) = 0$, which in turn implies that $|\phi(t) - \psi(t)| = 0$ because

$$0 \leq |\phi(t) - \psi(t)| \leq LU(t) = 0.$$

This completes the proof.

Actually, *uniqueness* of solutions can be established under a condition that is less restrictive than the existence and continuity of the partial derivative $\partial f / \partial x$. Such a condition is called a Lipschitz condition and is defined as follows. Let $f(t, x)$ be defined on a domain D of the (t, x) plane and suppose that there exists a positive constant k such that for every (t, x) and (t, y) in D

$$|f(t, x) - f(t, y)| \leq k|x - y|; \tag{5.6}$$

we then say that f satisfies a *Lipschitz condition with respect to x*, and k in (5.6) is called the *Lipschitz constant*. We immediately observe that if $f(t, x)$ is continuous on the rectangle R, given by

$$R = \{(t, x): |t - t_0| \leq a \text{ and } |x - x_0| \leq b\} \qquad (5.7)$$

with a and b positive and, furthermore, if $\partial f/\partial x$ exists and is continuous on the rectangle R in (5.7), then $f(t, x)$ satisfies a Lipschitz condition. This holds because the continuity of $\partial f/\partial x$ on the closed and bounded rectangle R implies that $\partial f/\partial x$ is bounded. We write

$$|\partial f(t, x)/\partial x| \leq k \qquad (5.8)$$

for some positive k and (t, x) in the rectangle R in (5.7). From the continuity of $\partial f/\partial x$ on the rectangle R, we have

$$f(t, x) - f(t, y) = \int_x^y \frac{\partial f}{\partial x}(t, u) \, du \qquad (5.9)$$

which implies by placing absolute values in (5.9) and using (5.8) that

$$|f(t, x) - f(t, y)| \leq \left| \int_x^y \left| \frac{\partial f}{\partial x}(t, u) \right| du \right|$$

$$\leq k|x - y| \qquad (5.10)$$

for all (t, x) and (t, y) in the rectangle R of (5.7). Therefore, we conclude that the hypotheses of theorem 5.1 are sufficient to imply that $f(t, x)$ satisfies a Lipschitz condition.

Example 5.2.   Consider the initial value problem

$$\dot{x} = tx^2, \quad x(0) = 0 \qquad (5.11)$$

and let the rectangle R be

$$R = \{(t, x): |t| \leq 1 \text{ and } |x| \leq 1\}.$$

We wish to show that $f(t, x) = tx^2$ satisfies a Lipschitz condition. This follows immediately because

$$|\partial f(t, x)/\partial x| = |2tx| \leq 2.$$

Therefore, by (5.10) for the initial value problem in (5.11), $f(t, x)$ satisfies a Lipschitz condition in the specified rectangle R with 2 as a Lipschitz constant.

Example 5.3. The function $f(t, x) = 3x^{2/3}$ of the initial value problem in (5.1) does not satisfy a Lipschitz condition on the rectangle R where

$$R = \{(t, x): |t| \le 1 \text{ and } |x| \le 1\}.$$

This is so because, if $x > 0$, then

$$\frac{|f(t, x) - f(t, 0)|}{|x - 0|} = \frac{3x^{2/3}}{x} = 3x^{-1/3}$$

becomes unbounded as $x \to 0$ and (5.6) is not satisfied.

Some additional remarks about the concept of the *Lipschitz condition* seem desirable. First, we have already shown that if $f(t, x)$ is continuous on the rectangle R in (5.7), and if $\partial f / \partial x$ exists and is continuous on the same rectangle R, then $f(t, x)$ satisfies a Lipschitz condition. Now we note that a Lipschitz condition can be deduced under slightly weaker hypotheses. Assuming that $f(t, x)$ is continuous on the rectangle R in (5.7) and that $\partial f / \partial x$ exists and is bounded on the same rectangle R with $|\partial f / \partial x| \le k$, k a positive constant, then a direct application of the *mean value theorem* of differential calculus shows that $f(t, x)$ satisfies a Lipschitz condition, with k as the Lipschitz constant. Specifically, for each fixed $t \in [t_0 - \alpha, t_0 + \alpha]$, the mean value theorem implies that

$$f(t, x) - f(t, y) = \frac{\partial f}{\partial x}(t, u)(x - y) \tag{5.12}$$

for some $u \in (x, y)$. Taking absolute values in (5.12) and using the assumption of the boundedness of $\partial f / \partial x$, we conclude that $f(t, x)$ satisfies a Lipschitz condition. It is worth pointing out that if the rectangle R is replaced by a closed domain D, we must require that D be *convex* in order to be able to use the mean value theorem. Such convexity guarantees that the point u in (5.12) lies in D.

Second, a rather simple example illustrates that even when a function $f(t, x)$ satisfies a *Lipschitz condition*, it does not necessarily follow that $\partial f / \partial x$ exists. Consider the function

$$f(t, x) = t^2 |x| \tag{5.13}$$

on $R = \{(t, x): |t| \le 1 \text{ and } |x| \le 1\}$. By inspection we see that $f(t, x)$ satisfies a Lipschitz condition with 1 as a Lipschitz constant because

$$\left| t^2 |x| - t^2 |y| \right| \le 1 \cdot |x - y|.$$

However, $\partial f(t, 0) / \partial x$ does not exist for $t \ne 0$.

Third, if a function $f(t, x)$ satisfies a *Lipschitz condition* with respect to its variable x, then for each $t, f(t, x)$ is uniformly continuous in x. This follows immediately from the definition of uniform continuity and (5.6) by choosing $\delta = \varepsilon / k$. Then for $|x - y| < \delta$, the Lipschitz condition in (5.6) implies

$$|f(t, x) - f(t, y)| \leq k|x - y| < k \cdot \frac{\varepsilon}{k} = \varepsilon,$$

which says that $f(t, x)$ is uniformly continuous with respect to x. Note that nothing is implied about the continuity of $f(t, x)$ with respect to t. Furthermore, one should remember that uniform continuity does not imply a *Lipschitz condition*. The function $f(x) = \sqrt{x}, 0 \leq x \leq 1$ is uniformly continuous but does not satisfy a Lipschitz condition.

More about the implications of Lipschitz conditions is presented in the sequel.

6. Successive approximations

An important existence and uniqueness theorem can be obtained by assuming that $f(t, x)$ is continuous and satisfies a Lipschitz condition. We know, of course, that the continuity of $f(t, x)$ is sufficient for the existence of a solution on some interval containing the initial point t_0; however, the result we are about to state also asserts the uniqueness of the solution which is obtained from the added hypothesis that $f(t, x)$ satisfies a Lipschitz condition.

The technique used in the proof of the next theorem is called the method of *successive approximations* and is attributed primarily to Picard (1890) and Lindelöf (1894), although mathematical historians suggest that this method had been used earlier by Liouville and Cauchy in certain special cases.

Consider the initial value problem

$$\dot{x} = f(t, x), \quad x(t_0) = x_0 \tag{6.1}$$

and suppose that f is continuous on the rectangle R, where

$$R = \{(t, x): |t - t_0| \leq a \text{ and } |x - x_0| \leq b\} \tag{6.2}$$

for positive a and b. The continuity of $f(t, x)$ on R implies that $f(t, x)$ is bounded. Let $|f(t, x)| \leq M$ on the rectangle R and, as before, set $\alpha = \min(a, b/M)$. The *successive approximations*, also called *Picard iterates*, for the initial value problem (6.1) are defined to be functions $\phi_0, \phi_1, \ldots$, given recursively as follows

$$\phi_0(t) = x_0,$$

$$\phi_{n+1}(t) = x_0 + \int_{t_0}^{t} f(s, \phi_n(s)) \, \mathrm{d}s, \qquad (6.3)$$

for $n = 0, 1, 2, \ldots$ and $t \in [t_0 - \alpha, t_0 + \alpha]$. The next theorem establishes that the successive approximations converge uniformly to the unique solution of (6.1).

Theorem 6.1. (Picard-Lindelöf existence and uniqueness.) Let $f(t, x)$ be continuous and satisfy a Lipschitz condition on the rectangle R as in (6.2). Let M be a bound for $|f(t, x)|$ on the rectangle R and set $\alpha = \min(a, b/M)$. Then the successive approximations $\phi_n(t)$, $n = 0, 1, 2, \ldots$ exist on $|t - t_0| \le \alpha$ as continuous functions and converge uniformly on this interval to the unique solution $\phi(t)$ of the initial value problem in (6.1).

Proof. We establish the theorem for the interval $[t_0, t_0 + \alpha]$. A similar proof holds for $[t_0 - \alpha, t_0]$. We first show that every $\phi_n(t)$ exists on $[t_0, t_0 + \alpha]$, and is continuously differentiable. Since $\phi_0(t) = x_0$, $\phi_0(t)$ is a constant and satisfies these conditions. If we assume that the same conditions hold for $\phi_n(t)$, then $f(t, \phi_n(t))$ is defined and continuous on $[t_0, t_0 + \alpha]$. This implies that $\phi_{n+1}(t)$ given by (6.3) also exists on $[t_0, t_0 + \alpha]$ and is continuously differentiable. Inductively, this establishes that $\phi_n(t)$, $n = 0, 1, 2, \ldots$ exist on $[t_0, t_0 + \alpha]$ as continuous functions. Furthermore, from (6.3) and the boundedness of $f(t, x)$, it follows that

$$|\phi_{n+1}(t) - x_0| \le \int_{t_0}^{t} |f(s, \phi_n(s))| \, \mathrm{d}s$$

$$\le M(t - t_0) \le M\alpha. \qquad (6.4)$$

Next, we establish that $\phi_n(t)$ converge uniformly on $[t_0, t_0 + \alpha]$. To do so we first need to show by induction that

$$|\phi_{n+1}(t) - \phi_n(t)| \le \frac{M}{k} \frac{k^{n+1}(t - t_0)^{n+1}}{(n+1)!}, \qquad t \in [t_0, t_0 + \alpha]. \qquad (6.5)$$

For $n = 0$, (6.5) follows immediately from (6.4). Assume that for $n \geq 1$, (6.5) holds, that is, assume

$$|\phi_n(t) - \phi_{n-1}(t)| \leq \frac{M}{k} \frac{k^n(t-t_0)^n}{n!}. \tag{6.6}$$

For the last step in the induction note that

$$\phi_{n+1}(t) - \phi_n(t) = \int_{t_0}^{t} [f(s, \phi_n(s)) - f(s, \phi_{n-1}(s))] \, ds, \tag{6.7}$$

which is obtained from (6.3) for $n \geq 1$. Use both the hypothesis that $f(t, x)$ satisfies a Lipschitz condition with a constant k and the induction assumption in (6.6) to get

$$|\phi_{n+1}(t) - \phi_n(t)| \leq \int_{t_0}^{t} |f(s, \phi_n(s)) - f(s, \phi_{n-1}(s))| \, ds$$

$$\leq k \int_{t_0}^{t} |\phi_n(s) - \phi_{n-1}(s)| \, ds$$

$$\leq \frac{M}{k} \frac{k^{n+1}}{n!} \int_{t_0}^{t} (s - t_0)^n \, ds$$

$$= \frac{M}{k} \frac{k^{n+1}(t - t_0)^{n+1}}{(n+1)!}.$$

This analysis verifies (6.5) which is used to conclude that the terms of the series

$$\sum_{0}^{\infty} |\phi_{n+1}(t) - \phi_n(t)| \tag{6.8}$$

are majorized by those of the power series for $(M/k) \, e^{k|t-t_0|}$, and thus (6.8) is uniformly convergent on $[t, t_0 + \alpha]$. Therefore, the series

$$\phi_0(t) + \sum_{0}^{\infty} (\phi_{n+1}(t) - \phi_n(t))$$

is absolutely and uniformly convergent on $[t_0, t_0 + \alpha]$ and the partial sum $\phi_n(t)$, where

$$\phi_n(t) = \phi_0(t) + \sum_{0}^{n-1} (\phi_{i+1}(t) - \phi_i(t)),$$

converges uniformly to a continuous function $\phi(t)$ on $[t_0, t_0 + \alpha]$. It is easy to verify that the limit function $\phi(t)$ is a solution since the uniform continuity of $f(t, x)$ on the rectangle R implies that $f(t, \phi_n(t))$ converges uniformly to $f(t, \phi(t))$ as $n \to \infty$. A term by term integration in (6.3) yields

$$\phi(t) = x_0 + \int_{t_0}^{t} f(s, \phi(s)) \, ds. \tag{6.9}$$

Finally, to prove uniqueness, let $\psi(t)$ be another solution of (6.1) on $[t_0, t_0 + \alpha]$ and write

$$\psi(t) = x_0 + \int_{t_0}^{t} f(s, \psi(s)) \, ds. \tag{6.10}$$

An induction similar to (6.5) shows that

$$|\phi_n(t) - \psi(t)| \le \frac{M}{k} \frac{k^{n+1}(t - t_0)^{n+1}}{(n+1)!} \tag{6.11}$$

for $t \in [t_0, t_0 + \alpha]$ and $n = 0, 1, 2, \ldots$. As $n \to \infty$ we know that $\phi_n(t) \to \phi(t)$ uniformly and (6.11) yields $|\phi(t) - \psi(t)| \le 0$, that is, $\phi(t) = \psi(t)$. This proves the theorem.

To show how the process of successive approximations works to produce a solution of the initial value problem, we provide two examples.

Example 6.1. Consider the initial value problem

$$\dot{x} = x, \quad x(0) = 1.$$

This initial value problem is equivalent to *Volterra's equation*

$$x(t) = 1 + \int_{0}^{t} x(s) \, ds$$

and yields $\phi_0(t) = 1$. Next, we compute $\phi_1(t)$ to get

$$\phi_1(t) = x_0 + \int_0^t \phi_0(s) \, ds = 1 + \int_0^t 1 \, ds = 1 + t.$$

For $\phi_2(t)$ we have

$$\phi_2(t) = x_0 + \int_0^t \phi_1(s) \, ds = 1 + \int_0^t (1+s) \, ds = 1 + t + \frac{t^2}{2!}.$$

In general,

$$\phi_n(t) = x_0 + \int_0^t \phi_{n-1}(s) \, ds = 1 + \int_0^t \left[1 + s + \cdots + \frac{s^{n-1}}{(n-1)!} \right] ds$$

$$= 1 + t + \frac{t^2}{2!} + \cdots + \frac{t^n}{n!}.$$

But as $n \to \infty$, $\phi_n(t) \to e^t$, which is the required solution for all real t.

Example 6.2.   Let the initial value problem be given by

$$\dot{x} = tx, \quad x(0) = 1.$$

The integral equation that is equivalent to this problem is

$$x(t) = 1 + \int_0^t sx \, ds.$$

The first three successive approximations now follow.

$$\phi_0(t) = 1,$$

$$\phi_1(t) = x_0 + \int_0^t s\phi_0(s) \, ds = 1 + \int_0^t s \, ds = 1 + \frac{t^2}{2},$$

$$\phi_2(t) = x_0 + \int_0^t s\phi_1(s) \, ds = 1 + \int_0^t s\left(1 + \frac{s^2}{2}\right) ds = 1 + \frac{t^2}{2} + \frac{t^4}{2 \cdot 4}.$$

In general, we have

$$\phi_n(t) = x_0 + \int_0^t s\phi_{n-1}(s)\, ds$$

$$= 1 + \int_0^t s\left[1 + \left(\frac{s^2}{2}\right) + \frac{1}{2!}\left(\frac{s^2}{2}\right)^2 + \cdots + \frac{1}{(n-1)!}\left(\frac{s^2}{2}\right)^{n-1} \right] ds$$

$$= 1 + \left(\frac{t^2}{2}\right) + \frac{1}{2!}\left(\frac{t^2}{2}\right)^2 + \cdots + \frac{1}{n!}\left(\frac{t^2}{2}\right)^n.$$

As $n \to \infty$, $\phi_n(t) \to e^{t^2/2}$, which is the required solution for all real t.

7. Dependence on initial data and parameters

Earlier sections analyzed the initial value problem

$$\dot{x} = f(t, x), \quad x(t_0) = x_0 \tag{7.1}$$

and established theorems about the existence and uniqueness of the solution $\phi(t)$. Assuming a solution existed, we clarified that such a solution $\phi(t)$ was really a function not only of the variable t but also a function of the initial data t_0 and x_0. We may recall example 2.1 and reconsider the initial value problem

$$\dot{x} = x, \quad x(t_0) = x_0 \tag{7.2}$$

whose solution is given by

$$\phi(t) = x_0 e^{t-t_0}, \quad t \in R. \tag{7.3}$$

Inspecting (7.3), we see that $\phi(t)$ is indeed a function of three variables: t, t_0 and x_0. Actually, we can go a step further and indicate that a solution may also depend on a parameter. A simple illustration is provided by the initial value problem

$$\dot{x} = \alpha x, \quad x(t_0) = x_0 \tag{7.4}$$

which is only slightly more general than (7.2) since it incorporates the parameter α. Here α is a real number. Its solution is given by

$$\phi(t) = x_0 e^{\alpha(t-t_0)} \tag{7.5}$$

and, it is clear that $\phi(t)$ in (7.5) depends not only on t but also on t_0, x_0 and α. The question then arises: how is the solution $\phi(t)$ affected when t_0, x_0 and α are slightly changed? To answer this question denote the initial value problem by

$$\dot{x} = f(t, x, p), \quad x(t_0) = x_0, \tag{7.6}$$

where p indicates that the function f depends on a parameter p. We consider here only one parameter for simplicity, but (7.6) can be generalized to denote a parameter vector. Let the general solution of (7.6) be written as

$$\phi = \phi(t, t_0, x_0, p) \tag{7.7}$$

to explicitly show its dependence on t, t_0, x_0 and p. Under rather mild assumptions, the next theorem establishes that ϕ in (7.7) is a continuous function of t, t_0, x_0 and p. The practical implication of this result is that small changes in initial data and/or a parameter do not cause large changes in the solution. This result is particularly useful in economic applications. Suppose that the dynamic behavior of an economic variable is described by the solution $\phi(t)$, but due to errors in statistical measurement we are not certain about the values of the initial data t_0 and x_0. The next theorem assures us that small statistical measurement errors do not significantly alter the results of the model and, therefore, $\phi(t)$ can be used as a close approximation of the true behavior.

Theorem 7.1. (Continuity of the solution on initial data and a parameter.) Assume first that the function $f(t, x, p)$ is continuous in all three arguments on a closed and bounded domain D and second, that, it satisfies a Lipschitz condition with respect to x on D. Then the solution $\phi(t, t_0, x_0, p)$ of the initial value problem

$$\dot{x} = f(t, x, p), \quad x(t_0) = x_0$$

is a continuous function of t, t_0, x_0 and p.

For a proof see Coddington and Levinson (1955, pp. 23–24).

The above theorem establishes the continuity of ϕ with respect to its arguments. Actually, if we make an additional assumption, we can conclude that $\partial\phi/\partial x_0$ exists and is a continuous function. This result is presented in the next theorem.

Theorem 7.2. (Differentiability of the solution.) Assume that the function $f(t, x)$ is continuous in both t and x on a closed and bounded domain D

and that $\partial f/\partial x$ exists and is continuous on D. Then the solution $\phi(t, t_0, x_0)$ of the initial value problem

$$\dot{x} = f(t, x), \quad x(t_0) = x_0$$

is also differentiable with respect to x_0, that is, $\partial\phi/\partial x_0$ exists and is continuous.

For a proof see Coddington and Levinson (1955, pp. 25-28).

8. Miscellaneous applications and exercises

(1)   Consider the autonomous differential equation

$$\dot{x} = \sqrt{x} \quad \text{for} \quad x \geq 0. \tag{8.1}$$

Integrate in the following manner

$$\int x^{-1/2}\dot{x}\, dt = \int dt$$

to obtain the function

$$\phi(t) = (t - c)^2/4, \quad t \geq c. \tag{8.2}$$

Verify that $\phi(t)$ is a solution of (8.1) and notice that $\phi(t) = x = 0$ is also a solution. This application illustrates the *nonuniqueness* property of this differential equation. Next, consider the initial value problem

$$\dot{x} = x^{1/2} \text{ for } x \geq 0, \quad x(0) = 0. \tag{8.3}$$

Verify that this initial value problem has $\phi(t) = 0$ for all real t as a solution and that

$$\phi(t) = \begin{cases} (t - c)^2/4, & 0 \leq c \leq t \\ 0, & c \geq t, \end{cases}$$

is also a solution. Conclude that the continuity of $f(t, x) = x^{1/2}$ is not sufficient for a unique solution.

(2)   Consider the nonautonomous differential equation

$$\dot{x} = \frac{2}{t^2 - 1}. \tag{8.4}$$

Note that $f(t, x) = 2/(t^2 - 1)$ has discontinuities at the points $t = 1$ and $t = -1$. To find a solution to this equation, divide the real line into three intervals, that is, $(-\infty, -1), (-1, 1)$ and $(1, \infty)$, and in each interval take the indefinite integral of $f(t, x)$. Note that $f(t, x)$ may be written as

$$f(t, x) = \frac{2}{t^2 - 1} = \frac{1}{t - 1} - \frac{1}{t + 1},$$

which simplifies the integration. Verify that

$$\phi(t) = \ln|t - 1| - \ln|t + 1| + c$$

$$= \ln\left|\frac{t - 1}{t + 1}\right| + c$$

defines three solutions of equation (8.4) corresponding to the three intervals.

(3) Consider the initial value problem

$$\dot{x} = t^2 + e^{-x^2}, \quad x(0) = 0$$

and let the rectangle R be given by

$$R = \{(t, x): t \in [0, \tfrac{1}{2}] \text{ and } x \in [-1, 1]\}.$$

Show that a solution $\phi(t)$ exists for this initial value problem for $t \in [0, \tfrac{1}{2}]$.

(4) Consider the initial value problem

$$\dot{x} = x^{1/3}, \quad x(0) = 0, \quad t \in [0, 1].$$

Show that there are an infinite number of solutions on $[0, 1]$ by verifying that, for any constant real number c such that $c \in [0, 1]$, the function ϕ_c is a solution on $[0, 1]$, where

$$\phi_c(t) = \begin{cases} 0, 0 \le t \le c \\ \left[\dfrac{2(t - c)}{3}\right]^{3/2}, & c < t \le 1. \end{cases}$$

Furthermore, note that if the construction of section 3 is applied in this example, the only polygonal path starting at $(0, 0)$ is ϕ_1. Conclude that the method of theorem 3.1 does not give all the solutions of this initial value problem.

(5) Assume that $f(t, x)$ is continuous on the closure of some domain D and that $\phi(t)$ is a right hand *maximal* solution of the initial value problem $\dot{x} = f(t, x)$, $x(t_0) = x_0$ on an interval (a, b). Verify that one of the following must hold:
1. $b = +\infty$
2. $\phi(t)$ becomes unbounded as $t \to b - 0$
3. $(t, \phi(t)) \to \partial D$ as $t \to b - 0$, where ∂D denotes the boundary of the domain D.

(6) Show whether the following functions satisfy a *Lipschitz condition* in the corresponding rectangle R and compute the Lipschitz constant when appropriate:
1. $f(t, x) = t^2 + x^2$ on $R = \{(t, x): |t| \leq 1 \text{ and } |x| \leq 1\}$
2. $f(t, x) = tx^{1/2}$ on $R = \{(t, x): |t| \leq 1 \text{ and } x \in [0, 1]\}$
3. $f(t, x) = t^2 e^{-xt}$ on $R = \{(t, x): |t| \leq 1 \text{ and } x \in [0, 1]\}$.

(7) Find the *successive approximations* and if applicable, the limit function for the following initial value problems:
1. $\dot{x} = 1 + x$, $x(0) = 0$
2. $\dot{x} = x^2$, $x(0) = 1$.

(8) Suppose that $f(t, x)$ is continuous in a domain $D \subset R^{n+1}$ and let f_x denote the matrix of partial derivatives. Suppose that f_x exists and is continuous in D. Let $U \subset D$ be a compact set and suppose that the set

$$U_t = \{x \in R^n : (t, x) \in U\}$$

is convex. Show that $f(t, x)$ satisfies a Lipschitz condition on U.

(9) Consider the scalar initial value problem

$$\dot{x} = px^2, \quad x(0) = 1,$$

where p denotes a positive parameter. Show by continuity in parameters that there exists a solution in any interval $[0, T]$ if p is small enough. Show also that there exists no solution in $[0, \infty)$ if $p > c$, with c being a positive constant. Finally, calculate the second approximation $\phi_2(t)$ in the sequence of successive approximations.

9. Further remarks and references

Although differential equations must have been introduced in one form or another by Newton, it was not until the beginning of the 19th century that the great French mathematician Cauchy proved for the first time an existence theorem. Mathematicians such as Lagrange and Laplace seem to have taken the existence of solutions for granted.

In this book we are interested in *ordinary* differential equations. The word ordinary refers to the fact that only ordinary, and not partial, derivatives enter into the equation. Furthermore, the independent variable in this book is *real* and is denoted by *t* to symbolize time. The literature in the field of ordinary differential equations is quite extensive. At an introductory level, the reader may consult Coddington (1961), Pontryagin (1962), Plaat (1971), Roxin (1972), Arnold (1973), Simmons (1972), Hirsch and Smale (1974), Boyce and Di Prima (1986), Birkhoff and Rota (1978), Braun (1978, 1983), McCann (1982), Martin (1983), Miller (1987), and Sanchez and Allen (1983). Among these books Coddington (1961), Pontryagin (1962), Plaat (1971) and Roxin (1972) constitute a welcome departure from the classical treatment with its preoccupation on methods for an explicit solution to the modern approach emphasizing the interplay between theory and techniques for solving equations. Braun (1978) follows the modern approach with a rather unique blend between theory and realistic applications to real world problems. Hirsch and Smale (1974) present the dynamical aspects of ordinary differential equations and the relationship between dynamical systems and certain applied areas.

The advanced theory of ordinary differential equations is skillfully presented in the classic books of Coddington and Levinson (1955), Hartman (1964) and W. T. Reid (1971), among others. Hale (1969) treats the subject from an advanced point of view and simultaneously devotes considerable space to specific analytical methods which are widely used in certain applications. Lefschetz (1962) and Arnold (1983) emphasize the geometric theory.

The books indicated above, either at the elementary or the more advanced level, do not treat any economic applications. Some books written primarily for economists interested in the use of differential equations in economic analysis are Benavie (1972), Gandolfo (1980) and Murata (1977). Differential equations with economic applications are treated among other topics in Intriligator (1971), Chiang (1984) and Takayama (1985).

The *order* of an ordinary differential equation is the maximal order of differentiation which appears in that equation. The analysis in section 2 is carried out in terms of a differential equation of the form (2.2), reproduced here for convenient reference

$$\dot{x} = f(t, x). \tag{9.1}$$

We note that this equation embraces not only the simple ordinary differential equation of the first order but also the *n*th order equation as well as systems of differential equations. For example, consider a system of *n* ordinary differential equations written as

$$\dot{x}_i = f_i(t, x_1, x_2, \ldots, x_n), \quad i = 1, 2, \ldots n, \tag{9.2}$$

where n is a positive integer and $f_1, f_2, \ldots, f_n$ are n real continuous functions defined on some domain $D \subset R^{n+1}$. If we regard the n dependent variables x_i as the coordinates of a single vector variable written as $x = (x_1, x_2, \ldots, x_n)$ and the n functions f_i as the coordinates of a single vector function $f = (f_1, f_2, \ldots, f_n)$, then (9.1) can be used to represent (9.2). The nth-order equation with one dependent variable of the form

$$x^{(n)} = f(t, x, \dot{x}, \ddot{x}, \ldots, x^{(n-1)}), \tag{9.3}$$

where n is a positive integer and f is a real continuous function defined on some domain $D \subset R^{n+1}$, can also be expressed by (9.1). To see the appropriateness of (9.1) in this case, consider the substitution

$$x = x_1, \qquad \dot{x} = x_2, \qquad \ddot{x} = x_3, \ldots, x^{(n-1)} = x_n \tag{9.4}$$

which transforms (9.3) into a system of equations

$$\dot{x}_1 = x_2$$
$$\dot{x}_2 = x_3$$
$$\cdots \tag{9.5}$$
$$\dot{x}_n = f(t, x_1, x_2, \ldots, x_n).$$

This system in (9.5) is equivalent to the nth-order equation in (9.3). Given what was said about (9.2), our claim is verified. In conclusion, there is no loss of generality in using (2.2) provided that *vector norms* replace absolute values whenever the order of the equation is higher than one.

It is of some historical significance to mention that the *Cauchy-Peano theorem* of section 3 can be traced back to Cauchy in the early part of the *19*th century and to Peano (1890) who offered a substantial generalization of Cauchy's work. Detailed historical remarks on various existence theorems are found in Hartman (1964, p. 23) and his detailed bibliographical references; see also Simmons (1972). The original ideas on uniqueness may be found in Lipschitz (1876).

Finally, note that existence can also be established using modern functional analysis techniques as is done in Coppel (1965), Hale (1969) and several other standard advanced differential equations books. Also, existence theorems have been established under assumptions weaker than the continuity of $f(t, x)$ using measure theoretic techniques that originate in Carathéodory (1927).

The main sources of the exercises in section 8 include Braun (1978), Coddington (1961), Coddington and Levinson (1955), Hale (1969), Pontryagin (1962) and Roxin (1972).

CHAPTER 2

LINEAR DIFFERENTIAL EQUATIONS

> Mathematical theories in the sciences,
> if they are to be realistic, must thus
> be built on the basis of differential
> equations, relations between the
> derivatives or differentials of varying
> quantities. It is then the business of
> the theories to deduce the functional
> equations between the variables
> which lie behind the differential
> equations, i.e. to express the general
> laws whose variations correspond to
> the given data.
>
> R. G. D. Allen (1938, p. 412)

1. Introduction

Linear differential equations are an important special case of ordinary differential equations. This chapter presents an analysis of linear equations, first, to illustrate the applicability of the general theorems obtained thus far and second, to supply some additional results that are needed in stability theory. Furthermore, some computational techniques are demonstrated to familiarize the reader with a number of available methods for solving linear differential equations. As was stated in chapter 1, we wish to emphasize the general theory of ordinary differential equations rather than accumulate an exhaustive list of computational methods. In this chapter we continue to be guided by the same motivation. The computational examples are appropriate illustrations which follow naturally from the general theory applied to the special case of linear systems.

2. Linear systems

Consider the linear system of n first order differential equations

$$\dot{x}_i = \sum_{j=1}^{n} a_{ij}(t)x_j + h_i(t), \quad i = 1, 2, \ldots, n, \tag{2.1}$$

where for $t \in [a, b]$, $a_{ij}(t)$ and $h_i(t)$ are continuous *real* valued functions with $i, j = 1, 2, \ldots, n$. In matrix notation (2.1) can be written as

$$\dot{x} = A(t)x + h(t), \tag{2.2}$$

where $A(t)$ is an $n \times n$ matrix whose elements are the $a_{ij}(t)$ functions for $i, j = 1, 2, \ldots, n$, $\dot{x}$ is a column vector with $\dot{x}_i$ elements and $h(t)$ is a column vector with elements $h_i(t)$, $i = 1, 2, \ldots, n$.

The system (2.2) is called a *linear nonhomogeneous system*; if $h(t) = 0$, then (2.2) is called a *linear homogeneous system*. Note that $h(t)$ is called the *forcing function* or the *input function*. Let

$$\dot{x} = A(t)x + h(t), \quad x(t_0) = x_0, \quad t_0 \in [a, b] \tag{2.3}$$

be an *initial value problem* for the nonhomogeneous linear system. By theorem 3.1 of chapter 1, the continuity of $A(t)$ and $h(t)$ on the rectangle R, where

$$R = \{(t, x): t \in [a, b], \quad x \in R^n\}$$

implies that a solution exists on some interval containing t_0. Actually, for linear systems, more can be said than existence on some interval containing t_0. Namely, a solution exists for all $t \in [a, b]$. This result is the consequence of the continuation theorem 4.1 of chapter 1 because a linear system is bounded in the rectangle R, and thus, a solution can be extended to $[a, b]$. In applications $[a, b]$ is usually taken to be $[0, \infty)$ or $(-\infty, \infty)$. Furthermore, because linear systems satisfy the Lipschitz condition, if a solution exists it is also unique. Therefore we can state

Theorem 2.1. Consider the initial value problem for the linear non-homogeneous system

$$\dot{x} = A(t)x + h(t), \quad x(t_0) = x_0, \quad t_0 \in [a, b]$$

and suppose that $A(t)$ and $h(t)$ are continuous for $t \in [a, b]$. Then, there exists a continuously differentiable unique solution $\phi(t)$ on the entire interval $[a, b]$ that solves (2.3).

Example 2.1. The second order homogeneous initial value problem

$$\ddot{y} + e^t\dot{y} + (1+t)y = 0; \quad y(1) = 0, \quad \dot{y}(1) = 0 \tag{2.4}$$

can be written in matrix form by making the substitutions (9.4) of chapter 1,

$$y = x_1, \quad \dot{y} = x_2.$$

These substitutions yield:

$$\dot{x}_1 = \dot{y} = x_2,$$

$$\dot{x}_2 = \ddot{y} = -e^t\dot{y} - (1+t)y = -e^t x_2 - (1+t)x_1.$$

Thus (2.4) can be written in matrix form as

$$\begin{bmatrix} \dot{x}_1 \\ \dot{x}_2 \end{bmatrix} = \begin{bmatrix} 0 & 1 \\ -(1+t) & -e^t \end{bmatrix} \begin{bmatrix} x_1 \\ x_2 \end{bmatrix}, \quad \begin{bmatrix} x_1(1) \\ x_2(1) \end{bmatrix} = \begin{bmatrix} 0 \\ 0 \end{bmatrix}. \tag{2.5}$$

Inspection of (2.5) indicates that the 0-solution satisfies (2.5). Since the functions of the matrix in (2.5) are continuous for $t \in (-\infty, \infty)$, it follows from theorem 2.1 that the 0-solution is the only solution for this initial value problem.

3. Basic results

In this section we state some definitions and theorems about the homogeneous system

$$\dot{x} = A(t)x. \tag{3.1}$$

An $n \times n$ matrix $\Phi(t)$ is said to be an $n \times n$ *matrix solution* of (3.1) if each column of $\Phi(t)$ satisfies (3.1). If a matrix solution $\Phi(t)$ is also *nonsingular*, it is called a *fundamental matrix solution*. In other words, a fundamental matrix solution of (3.1) is an $n \times n$ matrix with each column satisfying (3.1) and such that det $\Phi(t) \neq 0$. A *principal matrix solution* of (3.1) at initial time t_0 is a fundamental matrix solution such that $\Phi(t_0) = I$, with I being the identity $n \times n$ matrix.

Matrix solutions satisfy certain properties. These properties are presented after the notation used is introduced. $A(t) = [a_{ij}(t)]$ denotes the $n \times n$ matrix in (3.1); $\Phi(t) = [\phi_{ij}(t)]$ denotes the matrix solution or the fundamental matrix solution of (3.1); $X(t) = [x_{ij}(t)]$ denotes an $n \times n$ matrix; $\dot{\Phi}(t) = [\dot{\phi}_{ij}(t)]$ and $\dot{X}(t) = [\dot{x}_{ij}(t)]$ denote the derivatives of $\Phi(t)$ and $X(t)$. In all above cases $i, j = 1, 2, \ldots, n$.

Theorem 3.1. Consider the matrix differential equation

$$\dot{X} = A(t)X, \quad t \in [a, b]. \tag{3.2}$$

If Φ is a fundamental matrix solution of (3.1), then Φ satisfies (3.2) for $t \in [a, b]$.

Proof. Since Φ is a fundamental solution of (3.1) each of its columns satisfies (3.1). Denote the columns of Φ by $\phi_1, \ldots, \phi_n$. Then for $t \in [a, b]$,

$$\dot{\Phi} = [\dot{\phi}_1, \ldots, \dot{\phi}_n] = [A(t)\phi_1, \ldots, A(t)\phi_n]$$

$$= A(t)[\phi_1, \ldots, \phi_n] = A(t)\Phi.$$

Theorem 3.2. (Abel's formula.) Suppose that Φ is a matrix solution of

$$\dot{X} = A(t)X, \quad t \in [a, b]$$

and let $t_0 \in [a, b]$. Then

$$\det \Phi(t) = \det \Phi(t_0) \exp\left[\int_{t_0}^{t} \operatorname{tr} A(s) \, \mathrm{d}s \right] \tag{3.3}$$

for every $t \in [a, b]$.

Proof. We prove the theorem for the special case $n = 2$. The generalization is straightforward. Note that

$$\frac{\mathrm{d}}{\mathrm{d}t}[\det \Phi(t)] = \frac{\mathrm{d}}{\mathrm{d}t}(\phi_{11}\phi_{22} - \phi_{12}\phi_{21}) \cdot$$

$$= (\dot{\phi}_{11}\phi_{22} + \phi_{11}\dot{\phi}_{22} - \dot{\phi}_{12}\phi_{21} - \phi_{12}\dot{\phi}_{21})$$

$$= \begin{vmatrix} \dot{\phi}_{11} & \dot{\phi}_{12} \\ \phi_{21} & \phi_{22} \end{vmatrix} + \begin{vmatrix} \phi_{11} & \phi_{12} \\ \dot{\phi}_{21} & \dot{\phi}_{22} \end{vmatrix}$$

$$= \begin{vmatrix} a_{11}\phi_{11} + a_{12}\phi_{21} & a_{11}\phi_{12} + a_{12}\phi_{22} \\ \phi_{21} & \phi_{22} \end{vmatrix}$$

$$+ \begin{vmatrix} \phi_{11} & \phi_{12} \\ a_{21}\phi_{11} + a_{22}\phi_{21} & a_{21}\phi_{12} + a_{22}\phi_{22} \end{vmatrix}.$$

The last two determinants are not changed if: in the first determinant we subtract a_{12} times the second row from the first row; in the second determinant we subtract a_{21} times the first row from the second row. This operation results in

$$\begin{vmatrix} a_{11}\phi_{11} & a_{11}\phi_{12} \\ \phi_{21} & \phi_{22} \end{vmatrix} + \begin{vmatrix} \phi_{11} & \phi_{12} \\ a_{22}\phi_{21} & a_{22}\phi_{22} \end{vmatrix}$$

$$= a_{11}\det \Phi + a_{22}\det \Phi = [\text{tr } A(t)]\det \Phi(t).$$

Therefore, this calculation shows that

$$\frac{d}{dt}[\det \Phi(t)] = [\text{tr } A(t)]\det \Phi(t) \qquad (3.4)$$

and upon integration (3.3) follows. This completes the proof.

Theorem 3.3. Suppose that Φ is a matrix solution. Then, either $\det \Phi(t) \neq 0$ for all $t \in [a, b]$ or $\det \Phi(t) = 0$ for all $t \in [a, b]$.

Proof. This is an immediate consequence of (3.3) since $t_0 \in [a, b]$ is arbitrary.

Theorem 3.4. Let Φ be a fundamental matrix of the linear homogeneous system in (3.1) and let C be a nonsingular $n \times n$ constant matrix. Then ΦC is also a fundamental matrix of (3.1).

Proof. Calculate

$$\frac{d}{dt}[\Phi C] = \dot{\Phi}C = [A(t)\Phi]C = A(t)[\Phi C].$$

Thus ΦC is a matrix solution; furthermore,

$$\det(\Phi C) = \det \Phi \det C \neq 0,$$

which establishes the result.

Theorem 3.5. Suppose that $\Phi(t)$ and $\Psi(t)$ are two different fundamental matrix solutions for $t \in [a, b]$ of the linear homogeneous system in (3.1). There then exists a constant $n \times n$ nonsingular matrix C such that

$$\Psi = \Phi C. \qquad (3.5)$$

Proof. By hypothesis, Φ is a fundamental matrix solution which implies that det $\Phi(t) \neq 0$ for all $t \in [a, b]$. Therefore, Φ^{-1} exists for all $t \in [a, b]$ and $\Phi\Phi^{-1} = I$. Taking the time derivative on both sides of $\Phi\Phi^{-1} = I$ gives

$$\frac{d}{dt}(\Phi\Phi^{-1}) = \dot{\Phi}\Phi^{-1} + \Phi\frac{d}{dt}(\Phi^{-1}) = \dot{I} = 0,$$

from which we conclude that

$$\frac{d}{dt}(\Phi^{-1}) = -\Phi^{-1}\dot{\Phi}\Phi^{-1}. \tag{3.6}$$

The result in (3.6) is needed to show that $(d/dt)(\Phi^{-1}\Psi) = 0$. Specifically, note that

$$\begin{aligned}
\frac{d}{dt}(\Phi^{-1}\Psi) &= \Phi^{-1}\dot{\Psi} + \left(\frac{d}{dt}\Phi^{-1}\right)\Psi \\
&= \Phi^{-1}A(t)\Psi - (\Phi^{-1}\dot{\Phi}\Phi^{-1})\Psi \\
&= \Phi^{-1}A(t)\Psi - (\Phi^{-1}A(t)\Phi\Phi^{-1})\Psi \\
&= \Phi^{-1}A(t)\Psi - \Phi^{-1}A(t)\Psi = 0.
\end{aligned} \tag{3.7}$$

From (3.7) conclude that $\Phi^{-1}\Psi = C$ or that $\Psi = \Phi C$, where C is an $n \times n$ constant nonsingular matrix.

Example 3.1. Consider the linear system

$$\dot{x}_1 = x_1,$$

$$\dot{x}_2 = -x_2,$$

which is written in matrix notation as

$$\begin{bmatrix} \dot{x}_1 \\ \dot{x}_2 \end{bmatrix} = \begin{bmatrix} 1 & 0 \\ 0 & -1 \end{bmatrix} \begin{bmatrix} x_1 \\ x_2 \end{bmatrix}. \tag{3.8}$$

Note that $\phi_1 = \begin{bmatrix} e^t \\ 0 \end{bmatrix}$ and $\phi_2 = \begin{bmatrix} e^t \\ 0 \end{bmatrix}$ solve (3.8) and therefore

$$\Phi = \begin{bmatrix} e^t & e^t \\ 0 & 0 \end{bmatrix} \tag{3.9}$$

is a matrix solution. However (3.9) is not a fundamental matrix solution since det $\Phi = 0$ for all $t \in (-\infty, \infty)$. On the other hand, if we let $\phi_1 = \begin{bmatrix} e^t \\ 0 \end{bmatrix}$ and $\phi_2 = \begin{bmatrix} 0 \\ e^{-t} \end{bmatrix}$, then the matrix

$$\Phi = \begin{bmatrix} e^t & 0 \\ 0 & e^{-t} \end{bmatrix} \tag{3.10}$$

is a fundamental matrix solution because each of its columns solves (3.8) and det $\Phi = e^t e^{-t} = 1 \neq 0$ for all $t \in (-\infty, \infty)$.

This section concludes with a definition and two additional theorems. Given (3.1) where $\dot{x}$ and x are column vectors of dimension n, *the adjoint equation* is defined to be

$$\dot{y} = -yA(t), \qquad (3.11)$$

where $\dot{y}$ and y are row vectors of the same dimension n. The next theorem establishes that if Φ is a fundamental matrix solution of (3.1) then Φ^{-1} is a fundamental matrix solution of (3.11).

Theorem 3.6. If Φ is a fundamental matrix solution of $\dot{x} = A(t)x$, then the matrix Φ^{-1} is a fundamental matrix solution of *the adjoint equation*

$$\dot{y} = -yA(t).$$

Proof. Differentiate both sides of $\Phi\Phi^{-1} = I$ to obtain

$$\dot{\Phi}\Phi^{-1} + \Phi\frac{d}{dt}(\Phi^{-1}) = 0.$$

Therefore,

$$\frac{d}{dt}(\Phi^{-1}) = -\Phi^{-1}\dot{\Phi}\Phi^{-1} = -\Phi^{-1}A\Phi\Phi^{-1} = -\Phi^{-1}A,$$

which shows that Φ^{-1} is a solution of (3.11).

The next result is very important. It gives the solution of the non-homogeneous system and it will be used several times throughout the book.

Theorem 3.7. (Variation of constants.) If Φ is a fundamental matrix solution of the homogeneous linear system $\dot{x} = A(t)x$ then every solution of the nonhomogeneous system $\dot{x} = A(t)x + h(t)$ is given by

$$\phi(t) = \Phi(t)\left[\Phi^{-1}(t_0)\phi(t_0) + \int_{t_0}^{t} \Phi^{-1}(s)h(s)\,ds\right]$$

for any real $t_0 \in (-\infty, \infty)$.

Proof. Let Φ be a fundamental matrix solution of the homogeneous linear system. By theorem 3.4 the general solution of the homogeneous system can be written as

$$\phi(t) = \Phi(t)c, \qquad (3.12)$$

where c is an arbitrary constant vector. We wish to satisfy the non-homogeneous equation

$$\dot{x} = A(t)x + h(t)$$

by the same expression as (3.12) but allow c to be a function of t; this explains the name of the theorem as *variation of constants*. Rewrite (3.12) with c now being a variable, as

$$\phi(t) = \Phi(t)c(t) \tag{3.13}$$

and differentiate, to get

$$\dot{\phi} = \dot{\Phi}c + \Phi\dot{c} = A\Phi c + \Phi\dot{c} = A\phi + \Phi\dot{c}. \tag{3.14}$$

In order for (3.14) to satisfy the nonhomogeneous equation, it must be the case that $\Phi\dot{c} = h$. This follows from inspection of (3.14) and (2.2). Thus $\dot{c} = \Phi^{-1}h$ or equivalently, using (3.13)

$$\phi(t) = \Phi(t)c(t) = \Phi(t) \int \Phi^{-1}(s)h(s)\, ds. \tag{3.15}$$

In (3.15), if we integrate from t_0 to t, then the solution $\phi(t)$ will satisfy the initial condition $\phi(t_0) = 0$. If, instead, the initial condition is $\phi(t_0) = x_0$, then the solution of the nonhomogeneous equation becomes

$$\phi(t) = \Phi(t)\left[\Phi^{-1}(t_0)\phi(t_0) + \int_{t_0}^{t} \Phi^{-1}(s)h(s)\, ds \right], \tag{3.16}$$

which establishes the theorem.

4. Linear systems with constant coefficients

In this section we discuss the system

$$\dot{x} = Ax + h(t), \quad x(t_0) = x_0, \quad t_0 \in [a, b], \tag{4.1}$$

where A is an $n \times n$ constant matrix, that is, a matrix with n^2 numbers and $h(t)$ is a continuous n vector function. Even when $n = 2$, (4.1) is not trivial to solve. Although we do not wish to deviate from our methodology which emphasizes basic properties of differential equations, it is instructive to analyze linear systems with constant coefficients because of their importance in economic applications and in stability analysis. We first consider the homogeneous case when $h(t) = 0$ in (4.1).

To motivate the solution of the homogeneous case in (4.1), recall example 2.1 in chapter 1. This example is the simplest case of (4.1) with $h(t) = 0$ and $n = 1$. Its solution is given in (2.7) of chapter 1 as $\phi(t) = c\,e^{\alpha t}$, $t \in R = (-\infty, \infty)$, and so a good guess for the solution of $\dot{x} = Ax$ would be $\phi(t) = e^{At}c$, with c an arbitrary constant n vector. The next theorem establishes that this guess is correct.

Theorem 4.1. Let A be an $n \times n$ constant matrix, and consider the corresponding homogeneous system

$$\dot{x} = Ax. \tag{4.2}$$

A fundamental matrix Φ for (4.2) is given by

$$\Phi(t) = e^{At} \tag{4.3}$$

and the solution of the initial value problem

$$\dot{x} = Ax, \quad x(t_0) = x_0 \tag{4.4}$$

is given by

$$\phi(t) = e^{A(t - t_0)} x_0. \tag{4.5}$$

Remark 4.1. First note that t, t_0 and x_0 are finite; otherwise Φ and ϕ are not well defined.

Second, we must define e^{At} to avoid ambiguity. For an $n \times n$ constant matrix A, the definition $\exp(At)$ is:

$$e^{At} = I + \frac{1}{1!} At + \frac{1}{2!} A^2 t^2 + \cdots = \sum_{n=0}^{\infty} \frac{1}{n!} A^n t^n. \tag{4.6}$$

The infinite series (4.6) converges for every A and t, so that e^{At} is well defined for all square matrices. See Arnold (1973, pp. 97–107) or Hale (1969, p. 94).

Proof of theorem 4.1. To show that $\Phi(t) = e^{At}$ is a solution we must show that it satisfies (4.2), that is,

$$\frac{d}{dt}(e^{At}) = A\,e^{At}. \tag{4.7}$$

To establish (4.7) use the definition of a derivative and (4.6). Let $h > 0$ and compute

$$\frac{d}{dt}(e^{At}) = \lim_{h \to 0} \frac{e^{A(t+h)} - e^{At}}{h}$$

$$= \lim_{h \to 0} \frac{e^{At} e^{Ah} - e^{At}}{h} = e^{At} \left(\lim_{h \to 0} \frac{e^{Ah} - I}{h} \right) = e^{At} A = A e^{At}.$$

In the last step the limit is A because by (4.6)

$$\lim_{h \to 0} \frac{e^{Ah} - I}{h} = \lim_{h \to 0} \left(\frac{1}{h} \right) \left[I + Ah + \frac{1}{2!} A^2 h^2 + \cdots - I \right]$$

$$= A + \lim_{h \to 0} \left(\frac{1}{2!} A^2 h + \frac{1}{3!} A^3 h^2 + \cdots \right) = A.$$

Furthermore, using theorem 3.2 on Abel's formula obtain that

$$\det e^{At} = (\det e^{At_0}) e^{\operatorname{tr} A(t - t_0)} \neq 0.$$

Thus $\Phi(t)$ is fundamental and (4.5) is immediate. This concludes the proof.

Remark 4.2. Theorem 4.1 gives (4.5) as the solution of the differential system $\dot{x} = Ax$ for A being an $n \times n$ constant matrix. If $A(t)$ is an $n \times n$ nonconstant matrix, that is, if the elements or entries of $A(t)$ are functions of time, the reader should not assume that the solution of $\dot{x} = A(t)x$ is given by

$$\exp \int_{t_0}^{t} A(s) \, ds. \tag{4.8}$$

This last equation need not be a solution of $\dot{x} = A(t)x$ unless $A(t)$ and $\int_{t_0}^{t} A(s) \, ds$ commute. Note that they do commute if A is constant or if $A(t)$ is diagonal. See Coddington and Levinson (1955, p. 76).

The definition of e^{At} in (4.6) is not generally useful in computation. One method for computing e^{At} involves the following steps.

First, for A a constant $n \times n$ matrix express

$$e^{At} = a_0 I + a_1 At + a_2 A^2 t^2 + \cdots + a_{n-1} A^{n-1} t^{n-1}, \tag{4.9}$$

where $a_0, a_1, \ldots, a_{n-1}$ are functions of t which are determined in the next step.

Second, define

$$r(\lambda) = a_0 + a_1\lambda + a_2\lambda^2 + \cdots + a_{n-1}\lambda^{n-1}. \tag{4.10}$$

If λ_i is an eigenvalue of At of multiplicity 1 then use

$$e^{\lambda_i} = r(\lambda_i) \tag{4.11}$$

to solve for $a_0, a_1, \ldots, a_{n-1}$. If λ_i is an eigenvalue of At of multiplicity k, $k > 1$, then use

$$e^{\lambda_i} = \frac{dr(\lambda)}{d\lambda}; \quad e^{\lambda_i} = \frac{d^2r(\lambda)}{d\lambda^2}; \quad \ldots; \quad e^{\lambda_i} = \frac{d^{k-1}r(\lambda)}{d\lambda^{k-1}}; \tag{4.12}$$

with all derivatives in (4.12) being evaluated at λ_i to solve for the appropriate $a_0, a_1, \ldots, a_{n-1}$.

Example 4.1. Compute e^{At} for $A = \begin{bmatrix} 2 & 0 \\ 0 & 2 \end{bmatrix}$.

The eigenvalues of $At = \begin{bmatrix} 2t & 0 \\ 0 & 2t \end{bmatrix}$ are given by

$$\begin{vmatrix} 2t - \lambda & 0 \\ 0 & 2t - \lambda \end{vmatrix} = (2t - \lambda)(2t - \lambda) = 0,$$

which means that $\lambda = 2t$ is an eigenvalue of multiplicity 2. From (4.10) obtain

$$r(2t) = a_0 + a_1 2t,$$

and use (4.11) and (4.12) to get two equations that will determine a_0 and a_1. The two equations are

$$e^{2t} = a_0 + a_1 2t \quad \text{and} \quad e^{2t} = a_1,$$

and solving them for a_0 and a_1 yields

$$a_0 = e^{2t}(1 - 2t) \quad \text{and} \quad a_1 = e^{2t}.$$

Now that a_0 and a_1, as functions of t, have been found, (4.9) can be applied to give the final result

$$e^{At} = a_0 I + a_1 At = \begin{bmatrix} a_0 & 0 \\ 0 & a_0 \end{bmatrix} + \begin{bmatrix} a_1 2t & 0 \\ 0 & a_1 2t \end{bmatrix}$$

$$= \begin{bmatrix} e^{2t} - e^{2t}2t + e^{2t}2t & 0 \\ 0 & e^{2t} - e^{2t}2t + e^{2t}2t \end{bmatrix} = \begin{bmatrix} e^{2t} & 0 \\ 0 & e^{2t} \end{bmatrix} = e^{2t}I.$$

Example 4.2. Compute e^{At} for $A = \begin{bmatrix} 2 & 0 \\ 0 & -3 \end{bmatrix}$.

The eigenvalues of At are $\lambda_1 = 2t$ and $\lambda_2 = -3t$ and to find a_0 and a_1 use (4.11). The two equations are

$$e^{2t} = a_0 + a_1 2t \quad \text{and} \quad e^{-3t} = a_0 - a_1 3t.$$

Solving these equations yields

$$a_0 = \tfrac{3}{5} e^{2t} + \tfrac{2}{5} e^{-3t} \quad \text{and} \quad a_1 = \frac{1}{5t} (e^{2t} - e^{-3t}).$$

Put a_0 and a_1 in (4.9) to get the final result

$$e^{At} = a_0 I + a_1 At = \begin{bmatrix} a_0 + a_1 2t & 0 \\ 0 & a_0 - a_1 3t \end{bmatrix}$$

$$= \begin{bmatrix} \tfrac{3}{5} e^{2t} + \tfrac{2}{5} e^{-3t} + \dfrac{2t}{5t}(e^{2t} - e^{-3t}) & 0 \\ 0 & \tfrac{3}{5} e^{2t} + \tfrac{2}{5} e^{-3t} - \dfrac{3t}{5t}(e^{2t} - e^{-3t}) \end{bmatrix}$$

$$= \begin{bmatrix} e^{2t} & 0 \\ 0 & e^{-3t} \end{bmatrix}.$$

In examples 4.1 and 4.2, with A being diagonal, one may also use directly the definition in (4.6) because A^n is also diagonal.

Example 4.3. Compute e^{At} for $A = \begin{bmatrix} 0 & 1 \\ -1 & 0 \end{bmatrix}$.

The eigenvalues of $At = \begin{bmatrix} 0 & t \\ -t & 0 \end{bmatrix}$ are computed from

$$\begin{vmatrix} -\lambda & t \\ -t & -\lambda \end{vmatrix} = \lambda^2 + t^2 = 0$$

and they are $\lambda_1 = it$ and $\lambda_2 = -it$. Substitute these two eigenvalues into (4.11) to obtain

$$e^{it} = a_0 + a_1(it) \quad \text{and} \quad e^{-it} = a_0 + a_1(-it).$$

Solving these last two equations obtain

$$a_0 = \tfrac{1}{2}(e^{it} + e^{-it}) \quad \text{and} \quad a_1 = \frac{1}{2it}(e^{it} - e^{-it}).$$

Using *Euler's relations*

$$e^{it} = \cos t + i \sin t; \quad e^{-it} = \cos t - i \sin t$$

conclude that

$$a_0 = \cos t \quad \text{and} \quad a_1 = \sin t / t.$$

Finally,

$$e^{At} = a_0 I + a_1 At = \begin{bmatrix} \cos t & 0 \\ 0 & \cos t \end{bmatrix} + \begin{bmatrix} 0 & t \sin t / t \\ -t \sin t / t & 0 \end{bmatrix}$$

$$= \begin{bmatrix} \cos t & \sin t \\ -\sin t & \cos t \end{bmatrix}.$$

These three examples illustrate how to compute e^{At} in three representative cases: distinct roots, repeated roots and complex roots. Using theorem 4.1 we can immediately obtain the solution of the initial value problem (4.4) written as

$$\phi(t) = e^{A(t-t_0)} x_0.$$

Furthermore, the solution of the nonhomogeneous linear system with constant coefficients

$$\dot{x} = Ax + h(t), \quad x(t_0) = x_0, \quad t_0 \in [a, b],$$

is obtained from an application of theorem 3.7. The variation of constants theorem yields

$$\phi(t) = e^{A(t-t_0)} x_0 + e^{At} \int_{t_0}^{t} e^{-As} h(s) \, ds \qquad (4.13)$$

or, equivalently,

$$\phi(t) = e^{A(t-t_0)} x_0 + \int_{t_0}^{t} e^{A(t-s)} h(s) \, ds. \qquad (4.14)$$

We illustrate by solving a homogeneous and a nonhomogeneous initial value problem for a constant matrix A in the next examples.

Example 4.4. Solve the initial value problem

$$\ddot{x} + 2\dot{x} - 8x = 0; \quad x(1) = 2, \quad \dot{x}(1) = 3.$$

This initial value problem can be written in matrix notation as

$$\begin{bmatrix} \dot{x}_1 \\ \dot{x}_2 \end{bmatrix} = \begin{bmatrix} 0 & 1 \\ 8 & -2 \end{bmatrix} \begin{bmatrix} x_1 \\ x_2 \end{bmatrix}, \qquad \begin{bmatrix} x_1(1) \\ x_2(1) \end{bmatrix} = \begin{bmatrix} 2 \\ 3 \end{bmatrix}.$$

Using the same procedure as in the last three examples we find that the eigenvalues of At are $\lambda_1 = 2t$ and $\lambda_2 = -4t$. Next, solving

$$e^{2t} = a_0 + a_1 2t \quad \text{and} \quad e^{-4t} = a_0 - a_1 4t$$

we determine that

$$a_0 = \tfrac{1}{3}(2\,e^{2t} + e^{-4t}) \quad \text{and} \quad a_1 = \frac{1}{6t}(e^{2t} - e^{-4t}).$$

Therefore, after making the necessary simplifications, we conclude that

$$e^{At} = \frac{1}{6} \begin{bmatrix} 4e^{2t} + 2e^{-4t} & e^{2t} - e^{-4t} \\ 8e^{2t} - 8e^{-4t} & 2e^{2t} + 4e^{-4t} \end{bmatrix}. \tag{4.15}$$

Once e^{At} is obtained, the remaining is straightforward. Note that $t_0 = 1$ and

$$\phi(t) = e^{A(t - t_0)} x_0$$

$$= \frac{1}{6} \begin{bmatrix} 4\,e^{2(t-1)} + 2\,e^{-4(t-1)} & e^{2(t-1)} - e^{-4(t-1)} \\ 8\,e^{2(t-1)} - 8\,e^{-4(t-1)} & 2\,e^{2(t-1)} + 4\,e^{-4(t-1)} \end{bmatrix} \begin{bmatrix} 2 \\ 3 \end{bmatrix}$$

$$= \frac{1}{6} \begin{bmatrix} 11\,e^{2(t-1)} + e^{-4(t-1)} \\ 22\,e^{2(t-1)} - 4\,e^{-4(t-1)} \end{bmatrix}. \tag{4.16}$$

Example 4.5. Solve the nonhomogeneous initial value problem

$$\ddot{x} + 2\dot{x} - 8x = e^t; \quad x(0) = 1, \quad \dot{x}(0) = -4.$$

This problem can be written in matrix form as

$$\begin{bmatrix} \dot{x}_1 \\ \dot{x}_2 \end{bmatrix} = \begin{bmatrix} 0 & 1 \\ 8 & -2 \end{bmatrix} \begin{bmatrix} x_1 \\ x_2 \end{bmatrix} + \begin{bmatrix} 0 \\ e^t \end{bmatrix}, \qquad \begin{bmatrix} x_1(0) \\ x_2(0) \end{bmatrix} = \begin{bmatrix} 1 \\ -4 \end{bmatrix}.$$

Since $t_0 = 0$, $e^{A(t - t_0)} = e^{At}$, which is computed in (4.15). Matrix multiplication of (4.15) times $\begin{bmatrix} 1 \\ -4 \end{bmatrix}$ yields

$$e^{At} x_0 = \begin{bmatrix} e^{-4t} \\ -4\,e^{-4t} \end{bmatrix}. \tag{4.17}$$

Next, we need to compute

$$e^{-As} h(s) = \frac{1}{6} \begin{bmatrix} 4\,e^{-2s} + 2\,e^{4s} & e^{-2s} - e^{4s} \\ 8\,e^{-2s} - 8\,e^{4s} & 2\,e^{-2s} + 4\,e^{4s} \end{bmatrix} \begin{bmatrix} 0 \\ e^s \end{bmatrix}$$

$$= \frac{1}{6} \begin{bmatrix} e^{-s} - e^{5s} \\ 2\,e^{-s} + 4\,e^{5s} \end{bmatrix}. \tag{4.18}$$

Integrate (4.18) by integrating each element of the vector to obtain

$$\int_0^t e^{-As} h(s)\,ds = \begin{bmatrix} \int_0^t (\frac{1}{6}\,e^{-s} - \frac{1}{6}\,e^{5s})\,ds \\ \int_0^t (\frac{1}{3}\,e^{-s} + \frac{2}{3}\,e^{5s})\,ds \end{bmatrix}$$

$$= \frac{1}{30} \begin{bmatrix} -5\,e^{-t} - e^{5t} + 6 \\ -10\,e^{-t} + 4\,e^{5t} + 6 \end{bmatrix}. \tag{4.19}$$

Matrix multiplication of e^{At} times (4.19) gives

$$e^{At} \int_0^t e^{-As} h(s)\,ds = \frac{1}{30} \begin{bmatrix} -6\,e^t + 5\,e^{2t} + e^{-4t} \\ -6\,e^t + 10\,e^{2t} - 4\,e^{-4t} \end{bmatrix}. \tag{4.20}$$

Combining (4.17) and (4.20), the final result is

$$\phi(t) = e^{A(t-t_0)} x_0 + e^{At} \int_{t_0}^t e^{-As} h(s)\,ds$$

$$= \begin{bmatrix} e^{-4t} \\ -4\,e^{-4t} \end{bmatrix} + \frac{1}{30} \begin{bmatrix} -6\,e^t + 5\,e^{2t} + e^{-4t} \\ -6\,e^t + 10\,e^{2t} - 4\,e^{-4t} \end{bmatrix}$$

$$= \begin{bmatrix} \frac{31}{30}\,e^{-4t} + \frac{1}{6}\,e^{2t} - \frac{1}{5}\,e^t \\ -\frac{62}{15}\,e^{-4t} + \frac{1}{3}\,e^{2t} - \frac{1}{5}\,e^t \end{bmatrix}.$$

Example 4.6. The last example of this section involves a nonhomogeneous initial value problem with complex roots. Consider the problem

$$\ddot{x} + x = 1; \quad x(\pi) = 1, \quad \dot{x}(\pi) = 2, \tag{4.21}$$

and write it in matrix form as

$$\begin{bmatrix} \dot{x}_1 \\ \dot{x}_2 \end{bmatrix} = \begin{bmatrix} 0 & 1 \\ -1 & 0 \end{bmatrix} \begin{bmatrix} x_1 \\ x_2 \end{bmatrix} + \begin{bmatrix} 0 \\ 1 \end{bmatrix}; \quad \begin{bmatrix} x_1(\pi) \\ x_2(\pi) \end{bmatrix} = \begin{bmatrix} 1 \\ 2 \end{bmatrix}.$$

Note that $A = \begin{bmatrix} 0 & 1 \\ -1 & 0 \end{bmatrix}$ is the same as in example 4.3. Therefore, using the results of example 4.3, compute for $t_0 = \pi$ to find that

$$e^{A(t-\pi)} x_0 = \begin{bmatrix} \cos(t-\pi) & \sin(t-\pi) \\ -\sin(t-\pi) & \cos(t-\pi) \end{bmatrix} \begin{bmatrix} 1 \\ 2 \end{bmatrix}$$

$$= \begin{bmatrix} \cos(t-\pi) + 2\sin(t-\pi) \\ -\sin(t-\pi) + 2\cos(t-\pi) \end{bmatrix};$$

$$e^{A(t-\pi)} h(s) = \begin{bmatrix} \cos(t-\pi) & \sin(t-\pi) \\ -\sin(t-\pi) & \cos(t-\pi) \end{bmatrix} \begin{bmatrix} 0 \\ 1 \end{bmatrix} = \begin{bmatrix} \sin(t-\pi) \\ \cos(t-\pi) \end{bmatrix},$$

$$\int_{t_0}^{t} e^{A(t-s)} h(s) \, ds = \begin{bmatrix} \int_{\pi}^{t} \sin(t-s) \, ds \\ \int_{\pi}^{t} \cos(t-s) \, ds \end{bmatrix} = \begin{bmatrix} \cos(t-s)\big|_{s=\pi}^{s=t} \\ -\sin(t-s)\big|_{s=\pi}^{s=t} \end{bmatrix}$$

$$= \begin{bmatrix} 1 - \cos(t-\pi) \\ \sin(t-\pi) \end{bmatrix}.$$

Finally, combining the computations above, conclude that

$$\phi(t) = e^{A(t-t_0)} x_0 + \int_{t_0}^{t} e^{A(t-s)} h(s) \, ds$$

$$= \begin{bmatrix} \cos(t-\pi) + 2\sin(t-\pi) \\ -\sin(t-\pi) + 2\cos(t-\pi) \end{bmatrix} + \begin{bmatrix} 1 - \cos(t-\pi) \\ \sin(t-\pi) \end{bmatrix}$$

$$= \begin{bmatrix} 1 + 2\sin(t-\pi) \\ 2\cos(t-\pi) \end{bmatrix}.$$

5. Jordan decomposition

This section describes a second method of evaluating e^{At} and of solving the initial value problem (4.4), that is, $\dot{x} = Ax$, $x(t_0) = x_0$ for A a constant $n \times n$ matrix. This method uses the transformation of A into a Jordan canonical form and plays an important role in the stability analysis of linear systems with constant coefficients.

Consider the initial value problem

$$\dot{x} = Ax, \quad x(t_0) = x_0 \tag{5.1}$$

with A being an $n \times n$ constant matrix and let P be a real $n \times n$ nonsingular matrix. Consider the transformation $x = Py$ or equivalently $y = P^{-1}x$, and differentiate both sides to obtain

$$\dot{y} = P^{-1}\dot{x} = P^{-1}Ax = P^{-1}APy \equiv Jy; \quad y(t_0) = P^{-1}x_0. \tag{5.2}$$

Observe that the solution of (5.2) denoted by $\psi(t)$ is given by

$$\psi(t) = e^{J(t-t_0)} y(t_0) = e^{J(t-t_0)} P^{-1}x_0. \tag{5.3}$$

From the transformation $x = Py$ and (5.3) we conclude that the solution of (5.1) denoted by $\phi(t)$ is

$$\phi(t) = P\psi(t) = P e^{J(t-t_0)} P^{-1}x_0. \tag{5.4}$$

Consider the simplest case before studying the general expression for $\phi(t)$. Assume that the constant $n \times n$ matrix A in (5.1) has n distinct eigenvalues denoted by $\lambda_1, \lambda_2, \ldots, \lambda_n$, and choose eigenvectors $p_1, p_2, \ldots, p_n$ so that p_i corresponds to λ_i, $i = 1, 2, \ldots, n$. Let P denote the matrix having for columns the eigenvectors, that is let $P = [p_1, \ldots, p_n]$. Then the matrix $J = P^{-1}AP$ takes the form

$$J = \begin{bmatrix} \lambda_1 & 0 & \ldots & 0 \\ 0 & \lambda_2 & \ldots & 0 \\ \vdots & \vdots & & \vdots \\ 0 & 0 & \ldots & \lambda_n \end{bmatrix}. \tag{5.5}$$

Applying the definition of e^{Jt} we obtain

$$e^{Jt} = I + \sum_{n=1}^{\infty} \frac{1}{n!} J^n t^n = \begin{bmatrix} e^{\lambda_1 t} & 0 & \ldots & 0 \\ 0 & e^{\lambda_2 t} & \ldots & 0 \\ \vdots & \vdots & & \vdots \\ 0 & 0 & \ldots & e^{\lambda_n t} \end{bmatrix}. \tag{5.6}$$

Therefore $\phi(t)$ of (5.4) can be written as

$$\phi(t) = P \begin{bmatrix} e^{\lambda_1(t-t_0)} & \ldots & 0 \\ \vdots & & \vdots \\ 0 & \ldots & e^{\lambda_n(t-t_0)} \end{bmatrix} P^{-1}x_0. \tag{5.7}$$

Example 5.1. We solve the initial value problem

$$\begin{bmatrix} \dot{x}_1 \\ \dot{x}_2 \end{bmatrix} = \begin{bmatrix} 1 & 12 \\ 3 & 1 \end{bmatrix} \begin{bmatrix} x_1 \\ x_2 \end{bmatrix}; \quad \begin{bmatrix} x_1(0) \\ x_2(0) \end{bmatrix} = \begin{bmatrix} 0 \\ 1 \end{bmatrix} \tag{5.8}$$

using the method of this section and apply (5.7).

The characteristic polynomial of $A = \begin{bmatrix} 1 & 12 \\ 3 & 1 \end{bmatrix}$ is given by

$$p(\lambda) = \det \begin{bmatrix} 1 - \lambda & 12 \\ 3 & 1 - \lambda \end{bmatrix} = (1 - \lambda)^2 - 36 = 0. \tag{5.9}$$

Solving (5.9) we get two distinct eigenvalues: $\lambda_1 = 7$ and $\lambda_2 = -5$. Next, we need to choose eigenvectors corresponding to these two eigenvalues. For $\lambda_1 = 7$ solve

$$(A - 7I)p_1 = \left(\begin{bmatrix} 1 & 12 \\ 3 & 1 \end{bmatrix} - 7 \begin{bmatrix} 1 & 0 \\ 0 & 1 \end{bmatrix} \right) \begin{bmatrix} p_{11} \\ p_{12} \end{bmatrix} = \begin{bmatrix} -6 & 12 \\ 3 & -6 \end{bmatrix} \begin{bmatrix} p_{11} \\ p_{12} \end{bmatrix} = \begin{bmatrix} 0 \\ 0 \end{bmatrix}$$

to get that $p_{11} = 2p_{12}$ which means that $p_1 = \begin{bmatrix} 2 \\ 1 \end{bmatrix}$ is an eigenvector of A corresponding to $\lambda_1 = 7$. Similarly, for $\lambda_2 = -5$ solve

$$(A + 5I)p_2 = \left(\begin{bmatrix} 1 & 12 \\ 3 & 1 \end{bmatrix} + 5 \begin{bmatrix} 1 & 0 \\ 0 & 1 \end{bmatrix} \right) \begin{bmatrix} p_{21} \\ p_{22} \end{bmatrix} = \begin{bmatrix} 6 & 12 \\ 3 & 6 \end{bmatrix} \begin{bmatrix} p_{21} \\ p_{22} \end{bmatrix} = \begin{bmatrix} 0 \\ 0 \end{bmatrix}$$

to get $p_{21} = -2p_{22}$ which gives the vector $p_2 = \begin{bmatrix} -2 \\ 1 \end{bmatrix}$. Now note that $P = [p_1, p_2] = \begin{bmatrix} 2 & -2 \\ 1 & 1 \end{bmatrix}$ and compute its inverse to find that $P^{-1} = \begin{bmatrix} \frac{1}{4} & \frac{1}{2} \\ -\frac{1}{4} & \frac{1}{2} \end{bmatrix}$. The solution of (5.8) is given by (5.7), that is,

$$\phi(t) = \begin{bmatrix} 2 & -2 \\ 1 & 1 \end{bmatrix} \begin{bmatrix} e^{7t} & 0 \\ 0 & e^{-5t} \end{bmatrix} \begin{bmatrix} \frac{1}{4} & \frac{1}{2} \\ -\frac{1}{4} & \frac{1}{2} \end{bmatrix} \begin{bmatrix} 0 \\ 1 \end{bmatrix} = \begin{bmatrix} e^{7t} - e^{-5t} \\ \frac{1}{2} e^{7t} + \frac{1}{2} e^{-5t} \end{bmatrix}.$$

At this point, we wish to study the general case when the $n \times n$ matrix A of (5.1) has repeated eigenvalues. In this case it is not always possible to diagonalize A by using a similarity transformation P. However, we can generate n linearly independent vectors $p_1, \ldots, p_n$ and an $n \times n$ matrix $P = [p_1, \ldots, p_n]$ which transforms A into the *Jordan canonical form* with $J = P^{-1}AP$ where

$$J = \begin{bmatrix} J_0 & 0 & \ldots & 0 \\ 0 & J_1 & \ldots & 0 \\ \vdots & \vdots & & \vdots \\ 0 & 0 & \ldots & J_s \end{bmatrix}. \tag{5.10}$$

In (5.10), J_0 is a diagonal matrix with diagonal elements $\lambda_1, \ldots, \lambda_k$, which are *not* necessarily distinct, that is,

$$J_0 = \begin{bmatrix} \lambda_1 & 0 & \ldots & 0 \\ 0 & \lambda_2 & \ldots & 0 \\ \vdots & \vdots & & \vdots \\ 0 & 0 & \ldots & \lambda_k \end{bmatrix} \tag{5.11}$$

and each J_i, $i = 1, \ldots, s$ is an $n_i \times n_i$ matrix of the form

$$
J_i = \begin{bmatrix} \lambda_{k+i} & 1 & 0 & \cdots & & 0 \\ 0 & \lambda_{k+i} & 1 & \cdots & & 0 \\ \vdots & \vdots & & & & \\ 0 & 0 & 0 & \cdots & \lambda_{k+i} & 1 \\ 0 & 0 & 0 & \cdots & 0 & \lambda_{k+i} \end{bmatrix}. \tag{5.12}
$$

Note that in (5.12), λ_{k+i} need not be different from λ_{k+j} if $i \neq j$, and $k + n_1 + n_2 + \cdots + n_s = n$. Finally observe that the numbers λ_i, $i = 1, 2, \ldots, k+s$ denote the eigenvalues of A. If λ_i is a *simple* eigenvalue, it appears in the block J_0. The blocks $J_0, J_1, \ldots, J_s$ are called *Jordan blocks*.

Next use (5.10) and the power series representation of the exponential of a matrix to deduce for $t \in R$,

$$
e^{Jt} = \begin{bmatrix} e^{J_0 t} & \cdots & 0 \\ \vdots & & \vdots \\ 0 & & e^{J_s t} \end{bmatrix} \tag{5.13}
$$

and to conclude that the solution of the general initial value problem (5.1) is given by

$$
\phi(t) = P \begin{bmatrix} e^{J_0(t-t_0)} & & & 0 \\ 0 & e^{J_1(t-t_0)} & & \\ & & \ddots & \\ 0 & & & e^{J_s(t-t_0)} \end{bmatrix} P^{-1} x_0 = P \, e^{J(t-t_0)} P^{-1} x_0. \tag{5.14}
$$

Remark 5.1. Observe that for any matrix J_i in (5.12) we can write

$$
J_i = \lambda_{k+i} I_i + N_i, \tag{5.15}
$$

where I_i is the $n_i \times n_i$ identity matrix and N_i is the $n_i \times n_i$ nilpotent matrix, that is,

$$
N_i = \begin{bmatrix} 0 & 1 & & & 0 \\ 0 & 0 & 1 & & \\ & & \ddots & \ddots & \\ & & & & 1 \\ 0 & & & \ddots & 0 \end{bmatrix}.
$$

Since $\lambda_{k+i} I_i$ and N_i commute it follows that

$$
e^{J_i t} = e^{\lambda_{k+i} t} e^{N_i t}. \tag{5.16}
$$

Repeated multiplication of N_i by itself shows that $N_i^k = 0$ for all $k \geq n_i$. Therefore the series that defines $e^{N_i t}$ terminates and from (5.16) we conclude that

$$
e^{tJ_i} = e^{\lambda_{k+i} t}
\begin{bmatrix}
1 & t & \cdots & t^{n_i-1}/(n_i-1)! \\
0 & 1 & \cdots & t^{n_i-2}/(n_i-2)! \\
\vdots & \vdots & & \vdots \\
0 & 0 & \cdots & 1
\end{bmatrix}
\tag{5.17}
$$

for $i = 1, \ldots, s$.

Remark 5.2. The Jordan canonical form is a very useful theoretical tool but it is not always easy to apply to a specific matrix if there are multiple eigenvalues. To illustrate possible difficulties, consider the simplest case with $n = 2$ and suppose that $\lambda_1 = \lambda_2 = 5$ is a multiple root. Then according to the Jordan canonical form, J could be either $\begin{bmatrix} 5 & 0 \\ 0 & 5 \end{bmatrix}$ or $\begin{bmatrix} 5 & 1 \\ 0 & 5 \end{bmatrix}$ and it is unclear without further study which of the two possibilities is correct.

For a detailed presentation of a procedure for computing the Jordan canonical form, the reader is referred to Miller and Michel (1982, pp. 84–88) and Hale (1969, pp. 96–100).

6. Miscellaneous applications and exercises

(1) Indicate in which intervals the existence and uniqueness theorem 2.1 applies to the matrix differential equation $\dot{x} = A(t)x$ where:

    1. $A = \begin{bmatrix} 1 & t^2 \\ t & t^3 \end{bmatrix}$.

    2. $A = \begin{bmatrix} t & 1 \\ 2 & t^{-1} \end{bmatrix}$.

    3. $A = \begin{bmatrix} (1+t^2)^{-1} & 1 \\ 1 & t^{-2} \end{bmatrix}$.

(2) In each of the following cases, show that $\Phi(t)$ satisfies the matrix differential equation $\dot{X} = AX$. Indicate in which cases $\Phi(t)$ is a fundamental matrix:

    1. $A = \begin{bmatrix} 1 & 0 \\ 0 & 2 \end{bmatrix}$, $\Phi(t) = \begin{bmatrix} e^t & e^t \\ e^{2t} & -e^{2t} \end{bmatrix}$.

    2. $A = \begin{bmatrix} 0 & 1 \\ 1 & 0 \end{bmatrix}$, $\Phi(t) = \begin{bmatrix} e^{-t} & -e^{-t} \\ -e^{-t} & e^{-t} \end{bmatrix}$.

(3) Equation (4.6) defines e^{At} as an infinite series. For this definition to make sense, the infinite series must converge to a limit. Establish that convergence of the series holds.

(4) Compute e^{At} for the following matrices:

1. $A = \begin{bmatrix} 2 & 0 \\ 0 & 2 \end{bmatrix}$.

2. $A = \begin{bmatrix} 2 & 1 \\ 0 & 2 \end{bmatrix}$.

3. $A = \begin{bmatrix} 2 & 0 \\ 0 & -3 \end{bmatrix}$.

(5) Solve the initial value homogeneous linear system,

$$\dot{x}_1 = x_1 + x_2; \quad x_1(0) = 2,$$
$$\dot{x}_2 = x_1 + x_2; \quad x_2(0) = 0.$$

(6) Solve the initial value homogeneous linear system,

$$\dot{x}_1 = 2x_1; \quad\quad\quad\quad\quad x_1(0) = 1,$$
$$\dot{x}_2 = -2x_1 + x_2 - 2x_3; \quad x_2(0) = 2,$$
$$\dot{x}_3 = x_1 + 3x_3; \quad\quad\quad x_3(0) = -2.$$

(7) Solve the initial value nonhomogeneous linear system

$$\dot{x}_1 = 2x_1 + x_2; \quad\quad x_1(0) = \tfrac{31}{16},$$
$$\dot{x}_2 = 3x_1 + 4x_2 + e^t; \quad x_2(0) = \tfrac{29}{16}.$$

(8) Put in matrix form and solve the second order differential equation

$$\ddot{x} + 2\dot{x} - 8x = 9 e^{-t}; \quad x(0) = 0, \quad \dot{x}(0) = 0.$$

7. Further remarks and references

Linear differential equations play an important role both because of their intrinsic interest and because of their use in approximating nonlinear equations. The intrinsic interest of linear differential equations is demonstrated in this chapter where several theorems describe the nature and properties of solutions. The next chapter on stability methods illustrates the usefulness of linear equations in approximating nonlinear ones.

The basic bibliographical sources of this chapter are the standard texts of Coddington and Levinson (1955), Hartman (1964), Hale (1969) and Reid (1971). We have also used the comprehensive book of Miller and Michel (1982) and the rather specialized book of Harris and Miles (1980).

The discussion of linear systems with constant coefficients introduces the reader to only one method for solving such systems. Additional methods exist, such as, the method of Laplace transforms and Putzer's method, among a few others. A brief overview of various methods can be found in Apostol (1969a, 1969b).

Introductory books on ordinary differential equations treat linear equations rather exhaustively. The interested reader may consult: Roxin (1972), Bronson (1973), Hirsch and Smale (1974), Birkhoff and Rota (1978), Braun (1983), and Sanchez and Allen (1983). Our analysis in sections 4 and 6 relies heavily on numerous examples found in Bronson (1973), Plaat (1971) and Roxin (1974).

We close this chapter with the following:

Remark 7.1. In the special case of the linear system $\dot{x} = Ax$ when the matrix A is a 2×2 constant matrix, the transformation $x = Py$, where P is a constant nonsingular matrix, transforms the system $\dot{x} = Ax$ into $\dot{y} = P^{-1}APy \equiv Jy$. The purpose of the Jordan canonical form is to make the matrix $J = P^{-1}AP$ as simple as possible by choosing the transformation P appropriately. When A is a 2×2 matrix it is possible to list all of the canonical forms. More specifically, if A is a constant 2×2 matrix, then there exists a nonsingular 2×2 matrix P such that $P^{-1}AP$ is one of the following:

$$\begin{bmatrix} \lambda_1 & 0 \\ 0 & \lambda_2 \end{bmatrix}, \begin{bmatrix} \lambda & 0 \\ 0 & \lambda \end{bmatrix}, \begin{bmatrix} \lambda & 1 \\ 0 & \lambda \end{bmatrix}, \begin{bmatrix} \alpha & \omega \\ -\omega & \alpha \end{bmatrix};$$

the last case corresponds to the complex characteristic roots $\lambda_1 = \alpha + i\omega$, $\lambda_2 = \alpha - i\omega$. For a proof see Brauer and Nohel (1969, pp. 284–289). This classification will be helpful in the analysis of phase portraits for the two dimensional linear systems presented in chapter 3.

STABILITY METHODS: AN INTRODUCTION

> Traditionally, the philosopher-
> scientists judge the usefulness of a
> theory by the criterion of *adequacy*,
> that is, the verifiability of the
> predictions, or the quality of the
> agreement between the interpreted
> conclusions of the model and the
> data of the experimental domain. To
> this, Duhem (1954, pp. 138–143) adds
> the criterion of *stability*.
>
> Abraham and Marsden (1978, p. xix)

1. Introduction

Ordinary differential equations have proven to be a powerful tool in formu-
lating and analyzing continuous time dynamic economic models. This book
supplies numerous illustrations of the applicability of differential equations
to a broad spectrum of economic problems to demonstrate the usefulness
of these dynamic methods.

In general, there is only limited value in writing down a differential
equation describing a dynamic economic process. As emphasized earlier
the real usefulness is contained in the variety of properties that differential
equations can possess which, upon careful restatement in economic terms,
can supply the researcher with insightful understanding about the nature
of the economic problem. In chapter 1 several properties are exposed and
chapters 3 and 4 are devoted to the important property of stability. The
analysis proceeds along mathematical lines in order to lay an appropriate
methodological foundation. Subsequent chapters illustrate the use of stability methods in economic analysis.

To review the basic properties already presented and to motivate the notion of stability consider the initial value problem

$$\dot{x} = x^2, \quad x(0) = c, \quad c > 0. \tag{1.1}$$

The continuity of $f(t, x) = x^2$ guarantees the existence of a solution on some appropriate interval. Therefore it is justified to search for a solution by integrating (1.1),

$$\int_0^t x^{-2}\dot{x}\, ds = \int_0^t ds$$

to arrive immediately at

$$-x^{-1}(t) + x^{-1}(0) = t. \tag{1.2}$$

Solving (1.2) for $x(t)$ and using the initial data in (1.1), conclude that

$$\phi(t) = \frac{c}{1 - ct} \tag{1.3}$$

is a solution on $(-\infty, 1/c)$. Actually, this solution, passing through the point $(0, c)$, is unique. Moreover, the interval $(-\infty, 1/c)$ is the maximal interval and the solution cannot be continued to the right because $\phi(1/c)$ does not exist. Finally continuous dependence with respect to initial data $x(0) = c > 0$ holds since $\phi(t, 0, c)$ in (1.3) is unique and continuous in all arguments in its domain of definition.

Let us go a little further. Consider the interval $[0, T]$ with T a positive real number and let $\varepsilon > 0$ be given. We ask the question: can a restriction be placed on the initial value $x(0) = c > 0$ so that

$$|\phi(t, t_0, x_0)| \equiv |\phi(t, 0, c)| < \varepsilon\,? \tag{1.4}$$

Equation (1.4) suggests that some form of a boundedness property holds for the solution in its domain $[0, T]$. Actually (1.4) describes how close $\phi(t, t_0, x_0)$ is to the 0-solution denoted by $\phi(t, 0, 0) \equiv 0$. Inspection of the initial value problem $\dot{x} = x^2$, $x(0) = 0$, indicates that $\phi(t) = \phi(t, 0, 0) = 0$ is its solution. Using the 0-solution as a reference, the question can be reformulated: can a restriction be placed on the initial value so that

$$|\phi(t, t_0, x_0) - \phi(t, 0, 0)| = |\phi(t, 0, c) - \phi(t, 0, 0)|$$

$$= |\phi(t, 0, c) - 0| < \varepsilon\,? \tag{1.5}$$

Equation (1.5) is motivated by the researcher's interest in knowing the deviation of a solution from its 0-solution, where the latter is being used as a reference point. The source of change from $\phi(t, 0, 0)$ to $\phi(t, 0, c)$ is due to a change in the initial value at $t = 0$ from 0 to c. The purpose of the analysis is to determine the consequences that a disturbance in the initial value may have in reference to the equilibrium solution.

For the initial value problem in (1.1), the answer to the question asked is: for $T > 0$ and $\varepsilon > 0$, both given, there is a $\delta = \delta(\varepsilon, T) > 0$, depending on both T and ε, such that if $c < \delta$ then (1.4) holds. Actually, δ can be chosen such that

$$\delta < \varepsilon/(1 + \varepsilon T). \tag{1.6}$$

This estimate of δ follows from (1.3) with c replaced by δ and t replaced by T. Furthermore, for δ as in (1.6) it follows that if $|c| < \delta$ then

$$|\phi(t, 0, c)| = |c/(1 - ct)| < \varepsilon.$$

From (1.6) we conclude that as the length of the interval $[0, T]$ increases with $T \to \infty$, δ must approach zero. This implies that the continuity of the solution $\phi(t, 0, c)$ is not uniform with respect to t in the interval $[0, \infty)$.

This computation illustrates the importance of the *continuous dependence of solutions on initial data* on a finite interval $[0, T]$. While such information is useful we must now ask what happens to the continuous dependence of solutions on initial data as the interval is extended to become $[0, \infty)$.

In many applications the independent variable t denotes time, and the appropriate domain for this variable is $[0, \infty)$. The analysis of continuous dependence of solutions on initial data on an infinite interval of time is known as *stability analysis* which describes one more important property of differential equations. The above analysis of the initial problem $\dot{x} = x^2$, $x(0) = c > 0$ shows how the properties of existence, uniqueness and continuity with respect to initial data hold on a finite interval $[0, T]$ which is a subset of $(-\infty, 1/c)$, but that stability fails to hold on $[0, \infty)$. Actually for this initial value problem, no solution exists on $[0, \infty)$ let alone a stable solution.

2. Definitions

Consider the differential equation

$$\dot{x} = f(t, x) \tag{2.1}$$

with $f(t, x): [0, \infty) \times R^n \to R^n$ and assume that the function $f(t, x)$ satisfies the conditions ensuring existence, uniqueness and continuous dependence of solutions on initial conditions. The solution of (2.1) which at time t_0 passes through the initial point x_0 is denoted by $\phi(t, t_0, x_0)$ or by $\phi(t \mid t_0, x_0)$ or $x(t, t_0, x_0)$ or $x(t \mid t_0, x_0)$ so that

$$\phi(t_0, t_0, x_0) = x_0.$$

This notation is identical to the one used earlier and it suggests that we intend to examine *stability with respect to the initial conditions.*

A system of ordinary differential equations such as (2.1), has an infinite number of solutions. Therefore to find a certain solution, it is necessary to specify its initial conditions. Consider (2.1) and two initial conditions, namely $(0, c_1)$ and $(0, c_2)$ both in $[0, \infty) \times R^n$. To once again motivate the intuitive notion of stability, we ask the question: if c_1 and c_2 are close, how do the solutions $\phi(t, 0, c_1)$ and $\phi(t, 0, c_2)$ behave as $t \to \infty$? Do $\phi(t, 0, c_1)$ and $\phi(t, 0, c_2)$ remain very near to one another as $t \to \infty$, which is stability, or do they drift away from one another as $t \to \infty$, which is instability?

The mathematical treatment of the problem of stability becomes simpler, without loss of generality, by defining

$$y = \phi(t, 0, c_1) - \phi(t, 0, c_2), \tag{2.2}$$

that is, y denotes the difference between two solutions. Studying the stability properties of $\phi(t, 0, c_1)$ relative to $\phi(t, 0, c_2)$ is equivalent to studying the stability of y relative to the 0-solution. This is so because, from (2.2), by taking time derivatives and rearranging terms, it follows that

$$\dot{\phi}(t, 0, c_1) = \dot{y} + \dot{\phi}(t, 0, c_2). \tag{2.3}$$

Since $\phi(t, 0, c_1)$ is a solution of (2.1), then

$$\dot{\phi}(t, 0, c_1) = f(t, \phi(t, 0, c_1)). \tag{2.4}$$

Combining (2.3) and (2.4) gives

$$\dot{y} = f(t, \phi(t, 0, c_1)) - \dot{\phi}(t, 0, c_2) = f(t, y + \phi(t, 0, c_2)) - f(t, \phi(t, 0, c_2))$$

$$\equiv g(t, y). \tag{2.5}$$

Observe that the last step in (2.5) is a definition and that if $y = 0$ then $g(t, 0) = 0$.

In most, if not all applications, the researcher is not primarily interested in how close two arbitrary solutions remain as $t \to \infty$, as (2.2) suggests, but more importantly, in how close a solution remains to the equilibrium solution. An *equilibrium solution* or a *trivial solution* or a *rest point* is a solution, denoted by $\bar{x}$, that satisfies the equation

$$f(t, \bar{x}) = 0, \quad \text{for all } t \in [0, \infty). \tag{2.6}$$

One may repeat the analysis in equations (2.2)–(2.5) to conclude that there is no loss of generality in translating the equilibrium solution $\bar{x}$ to the 0-solution. Therefore, the various definitions of stability that follow are made with reference to the 0-equilibrium solution. Specifically let

$$\dot{x} = f(t, x) \text{ with } f(t, 0) = 0 \quad \text{for all } t \in [0, \infty) \tag{2.7}$$

and suppose that $f(t, x) : [0, \infty) \times R^n \to R^n$ satisfies the conditions ensuring existence, uniqueness and continuous dependence on initial data and parameters.

Definitions 2.1. The 0-solution is called *stable in the sense of Liapunov* if for every $\varepsilon > 0$ and $t_0 \geq 0$, there is a $\delta = \delta(\varepsilon, t_0) > 0$ such that $|x_0| < \delta$ implies that

$$|\phi(t, t_0, x_0)| < \varepsilon \quad \text{for all } t \in [t_0, \infty).$$

The 0-solution is *asymptotically stable in the sense of Liapunov* if it is stable and if $\phi(t, t_0, x_0) \to 0$ as $t \to \infty$. In other words, the 0-solution is asymptotically stable if it is stable and if for every $t_0 \geq 0$, there exists a $\delta_0 = \delta_0(t_0) > 0$ such that $|x_0| < \delta_0$ implies $|\phi(t, t_0, x_0)| \to 0$ as $t \to \infty$.

The 0-solution is *uniformly stable* if it is stable and if δ can be chosen independently of $t_0 \geq 0$. The 0-solution is *uniformly asymptotically* stable if it is uniformly stable, if $\delta_0(t_0)$ by the definition of asymptotic stability can be chosen independent of $t_0 \geq 0$, and also, if for every $\eta > 0$ there is a $T(\eta) > 0$ such that $|x_0| < \delta_0$ implies $|\phi(t, t_0, x_0)| < \eta$ if $t \geq t_0 + T(\eta)$.

Finally, the 0-solution is *unstable* if it is not stable.

Remark 2.1. The property of the 0-solution being *stable* can be visualized geometrically by considering the solutions of (2.7) as curves in a $(n+1)$-dimensional space. The inequality $|x_0| < \delta$ defines a ball in the hyperplane $t = t_0$ and the inequality $|\phi(t, t_0, x_0)| < \varepsilon$ determines a cylinder of radius ε about the t-axis. By choosing the initial points in a sufficiently small ball we can force the graph of the solution to remain for $t \geq t_0$ entirely inside a given cylinder of radius ε. See figure 3.1 and Hale (1969, p. 26).

This consideration also reveals an important property of the stability for differential equations. If the equilibrium solution is stable at t_0, then it is also stable at every initial time $t_1 > t_0$, possibly requiring a different value for δ.

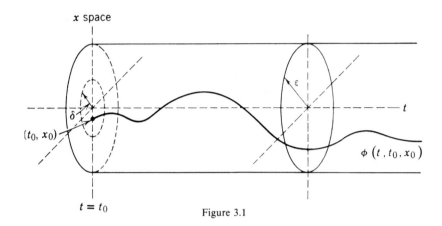

Figure 3.1

Example 2.1. Consider the equation $\dot{x} = 0$. The solutions of this equation are $x(t) = x_0$, where x_0 is an arbitrary constant. The 0-solution for $t \geq 0$ is stable, but it is not asymptotically stable. Furthermore, since the solutions are independent of time, the 0-solution is also uniformly stable.

Example 2.2. The equation $\dot{x} = x$ has solutions of the form $x(t) = x_0 \, e^t$ when x_0 is an arbitrary constant. The 0-solution is unstable because $x_0 \, e^t$ does not approach zero uniformly on $[0, \infty)$ as x_0 approaches zero.

Example 2.3. This example generalizes the previous two examples. Consider

$$\dot{x} = \lambda x$$

with $\lambda \in R$. The solutions are of the form $x(t) = x_0 \, e^{\lambda t}$. The 0-solution is stable, uniformly stable, asymptotically stable and uniformly asymptotically stable if $\lambda < 0$. The 0-solution is stable and uniformly stable if $\lambda = 0$; this is as example 2.1. Finally, the 0-solution is unstable if $\lambda > 0$, as example 2.2.

Example 2.4. The equation $\dot{x} = x^2$, analyzed in the previous section, has a 0-solution that is unstable because neighboring solutions are not defined for all $t \in [0, \infty)$.

Example 2.5. Consider the system

$$\dot{x} = y, \quad \dot{y} = -x,$$

and let $x(t)$ and $y(t)$ denote the corresponding solutions. Observe that

$$\frac{d}{dt}[x^2(t)+y^2(t)] = 2[x(t)\dot{x}(t)+y(t)\dot{y}(t)] = 2[x(t)\dot{x}(t)-x(t)\dot{x}(t)] = 0.$$

This means that, for r a positive real constant,

$$x^2(t)+y^2(t) = r^2,$$

that is, the solution paths are circles centered at the origin. The circles can be made arbitrarily small by choosing r to be small; thus the 0-solution is stable, but it is not asymptotically stable.

Example 2.6. Modify the previous example to consider

$$\dot{x} = -x, \quad \dot{y} = -y$$

with solutions $x(t) = x_0 e^{-t}$ and $y(t) = y_0 e^{-t}$. Observe that the ratio of the solution paths is constant, i.e., $y(t)/x(t) = y_0/x_0 = \text{constant}$. This means that the paths are rays through the origin. By choosing y_0/x_0 small, the 0-solution is shown to be uniformly asymptotically stable and therefore also uniformly stable.

Example 2.7. For the system

$$\dot{x} = x, \quad \dot{y} = y$$

the 0-solution is unstable since the solution paths are of the form $x(t) = x_0 e^t$ and $y(t) = y_0 e^t$.

3. Stability of linear systems

We begin the stability analysis of ordinary differential equations by studying the stability of linear equations of the form

$$\dot{x} = A(t)x, \tag{3.1}$$

assuming that $A(t)$ is an $n \times n$ continuous matrix, and $\dot{x}$ and x are n column vectors. The continuity of $A(t)$ implies the existence and uniqueness of a solution satisfying certain initial data. Note that $\phi(t) = 0$ is an equilibrium solution for (3.1) and therefore all the definitions of stability presented in the preceding section, with reference to the 0-solution, apply to the homogeneous linear system.

The stability analysis of the homogeneous linear system is a natural point of departure, not only because of the relative simplicity and usefulness of such a system, but also because nonlinear systems can be approximated by linear ones. It is instructive at this point to introduce the concept of *linearization*, which studies the linear approximation of a nonlinear system near the equilibrium.

Consider $\dot{x} = f(t, x)$, where $f : R^{n+1} \to R^n$ has at least two continuous partial derivatives with respect to its variable x. This assumption is needed because in linearizing $\dot{x} = f(t, x)$ we will need to apply Taylor's theorem. Let $\bar{x}(t)$, $t \in [0, \infty)$ be an equilibrium solution of $\dot{x} = f(t, x)$ and set

$$x(t) = z(t) + \bar{x}(t). \tag{3.2}$$

This is a translation of coordinates using $\bar{x}(t)$ as a reference-point and defining $z(t) = x(t) - \bar{x}(t)$. Taking the time derivative of $z(t)$, recalling that $f(t, \bar{x}) = 0$, and using (3.2) it follows immediately that

$$\dot{z}(t) = \dot{x}(t) - \dot{\bar{x}}(t) = f(t, x(t)) - f(t, \bar{x}(t)) = f(t, \bar{x}(t) + z(t)). \tag{3.3}$$

Observe that the solution $z(t) \equiv 0$ is an equilibrium solution of the system $\dot{z} = f(t, \bar{x} + z)$ in (3.3) and that the stability properties of the solution $\bar{x}(t)$ of $\dot{x} = f(t, x)$ are equivalent to the stability properties of the 0-solution of the system $\dot{z} = f(t, \bar{x} + z)$. Thus far, we have simply reviewed what was stated in the previous section.

Next, we wish to approximate $f(t, \bar{x} + z)$. Note that we can use Taylor's theorem to write

$$f(t, \bar{x} + z) = f(t, \bar{x}) + \frac{\partial f(t, \bar{x})}{\partial x} z + h(t, z). \tag{3.4}$$

Denote the Jacobian matrix of the first order partials by $A(t)$, that is, let $\partial f(t, \bar{x}) / \partial x \equiv A(t)$ where

$$A(t) = \begin{bmatrix} \dfrac{\partial f_1(t, \bar{x})}{\partial x_1} & \cdots & \dfrac{\partial f_1(t, \bar{x})}{\partial x_n} \\ \vdots & & \vdots \\ \dfrac{\partial f_n(t, \bar{x})}{\partial x_1} & \cdots & \dfrac{\partial f_n(t, \bar{x})}{\partial x_n} \end{bmatrix}.$$

Thus, using (3.3), (3.4) and the fact that $f(t, \bar{x}) = 0$, we conclude that

$$\dot{z}(t) = A(t)z + h(t, z), \tag{3.5}$$

with $h(t, 0) = 0$ and $\partial h(t, 0)/\partial z = 0$. Therefore, by using a translation of variables and Taylor's theorem, we can write $\dot{z} = f(t, \bar{x} + z)$ as the sum of a linear system and a residual nonlinear system. Since for fixed t, $|h(t, z)|/|z| \to 0$ it may be expected that the 0-solution of (3.5) shows the same stability behavior as the 0-solution of the linear variational system $\dot{z} = A(t)z$.

In summary, given a nonlinear system $\dot{x} = f(t, x)$ with an equilibrium solution $\bar{x}(t)$, the stability properties of $\bar{x}(t)$ can be studied by analyzing the stability properties of the 0-solution of the nonlinear system in (3.5). This system (3.5) consists of a linear term and a nonlinear term with higher polynomials of z. If the nonlinear term is small compared to $|z|$, uniformly in t, then the stability properties of the 0-solution of (3.5) can be deduced from the stability properties of the linear system $\dot{z} = A(t)z$. This suggests that the study of the linear homogeneous system should receive our primary attention and will lead us to theorem 4.2 in the next section.

Identically the same procedure of linearization can be applied to the autonomous differential equation $\dot{x} = f(x)$, where $f: R^n \to R^n$ is assumed to have two partial derivatives with respect to x. Let $\bar{x}$ be an equilibrium solution of $\dot{x} = f(x)$ and suppose that (3.2) holds. Using Taylor's theorem as in (3.4) write

$$f(\bar{x} + z) = f(\bar{x}) + Az + h(z).$$

In this last equation, $f(\bar{x}) = 0$, A is the Jacobian of the first order partials evaluated at $\bar{x}$, that is,

$$A = \begin{bmatrix} \dfrac{\partial f_1(\bar{x})}{\partial x_1} & \cdots & \dfrac{\partial f_1(\bar{x})}{\partial x_n} \\ \vdots & & \vdots \\ \dfrac{\partial f_n(\bar{x})}{\partial x_1} & \cdots & \dfrac{\partial f_n(\bar{x})}{\partial x_n} \end{bmatrix}$$

and $h(z)/|z|$ is a continuous function of z which vanishes for $z = 0$. Once again the approximate linearized system $\dot{z} = Az$ can be used to deduce, under certain conditions, the stability properties of the 0-solution of

$$\dot{z} = Az + h(z). \tag{3.6}$$

The next four theorems establish various stability properties of (3.1) for $A(t)$ being a continuous $n \times n$ matrix. In the next section we will study, among other things, the stability of $\dot{x} = Ax$ when A is an $n \times n$ constant matrix and then move on to study the stability or instability of the 0-solution

62 *Differential equations, stability and chaos in dynamic economics*

of the nonlinear system $\dot{x} = Ax + h(x)$. The various applications of subsequent chapters will make use repeatedly of the linearization method.

The first theorem below establishes that the 0-solution is stable if and only if the solutions of the linear homogeneous system (3.1) are bounded. Theorems 3.1–3.5 follow Hale (1969, pp. 84–89).

Theorem 3.1. Let $\Phi(t)$ be a fundamental matrix solution of (3.1). The system (3.1) is *stable* for any $t_0 \in R$ if and only if there is a positive constant $K = K(t_0)$ such that

$$|\Phi(t)| \leq K \quad \text{for all } t \geq t_0. \tag{3.7}$$

Proof. Let $t_0 \in R$ and suppose that $|\Phi(t)| \leq K$ for $t \geq t_0$. Recall from (3.12) of chapter 2 that any solution $\phi(t)$ of the linear homogeneous initial value problem $\dot{x} = A(t)x$, $x(t_0) = x_0$ can be written in the form $\phi(t) = \Phi(t)c$, where $\Phi(t)$ is a fundamental matrix solution and c is an arbitrary constant vector. Choose $c = \Phi^{-1}(t_0)x(t_0)$ and write the solution as

$$\phi(t) = \Phi(t)\Phi^{-1}(t_0)x(t_0).$$

Given $\varepsilon > 0$ choose $\delta = \delta(\varepsilon, t_0) \leq \varepsilon / K|\Phi^{-1}(t_0)|$. Stability follows because if $|x_0| < \delta$ then

$$|\phi(t)| = |\Phi(t)\Phi^{-1}(t_0)x_0| \leq |\Phi(t)||\Phi^{-1}(t_0)||x_0|$$

$$< |\Phi(t)||\Phi^{-1}(t_0)|\delta \leq K|\Phi^{-1}(t_0)| \frac{\varepsilon}{K|\Phi^{-1}(t_0)|} = \varepsilon.$$

Conversely, suppose that stability holds, that is, for any $\varepsilon > 0$ and t_0, there is a $\delta(\varepsilon, t_0) > 0$ such that, if $|x_0| < \delta$ then $|\Phi(t)\Phi^{-1}(t_0)x_0| < \varepsilon$. This means that

$$|\phi(t)|\delta^{-1} = |\Phi(t)\Phi^{-1}(t_0)x_0\delta^{-1}| < \varepsilon\delta^{-1}. \tag{3.8}$$

Use (3.8), let $K = \varepsilon\delta^{-1}|\Phi(t_0)|$ and compute

$$|\Phi(t)\Phi^{-1}(t_0)| = \sup_{|x_0| < \delta} |\Phi(t)\Phi^{-1}(t_0)x_0\delta^{-1}| < \varepsilon\delta^{-1}.$$

From this last step obtain

$$|\Phi(t)| = |\Phi(t)\Phi^{-1}(t_0)\Phi(t_0)| \leq |\Phi(t)\Phi^{-1}(t_0)||\Phi(t_0)| < \varepsilon\delta^{-1}|\Phi(t_0)| = K.$$

Theorem 3.2. Let $\Phi(t)$ be a fundamental matrix solution of (3.1) and let $\beta \in R$. The system (3.1) is *uniformly stable* for $t_0 \geq \beta$ if and only if there is a positive constant $K = K(\beta)$ such that

$$|\Phi(t)\Phi^{-1}(s)| \leq K \quad \text{for } t_0 \leq s \leq t < \infty. \tag{3.9}$$

Proof. Assume (3.9), let $\varepsilon > 0$ be given and choose $\delta = \delta(\varepsilon) \leq \varepsilon / K$. Then for any $t_0 \geq \beta$ if $|x_0| < \delta$ it follows that

$$|\phi(t)| = |\Phi(t)\Phi^{-1}(t_0)x_0| \leq K|x_0| < \varepsilon$$

and uniform stability holds. The converse follows in exactly the same way as the converse of theorem 3.1, with the remark that assuming uniform stability means that for a given $\varepsilon > 0$, δ is independent of t_0, that is, $\delta = \delta(\varepsilon)$.

Theorem 3.3. Let $\Phi(t)$ be a fundamental matrix solution of (3.1). The system (3.1) is *asymptotically stable* for any $t_0 \in R$ if and only if

$$|\Phi(t)| \to 0 \quad \text{as } t \to \infty. \tag{3.10}$$

Proof. Suppose that $|\Phi(t)| \to 0$ as $t \to \infty$. Then, for any $t_0 \in R$ there is a positive constant $K = K(t_0)$ such that $|\Phi(t)| \leq K$ for $t \geq t_0$ and by theorem 3.1, we deduce stability. Furthermore, since $\phi(t) = \Phi(t)\Phi^{-1}(t_0)x_0$ with $|\Phi(t)| \to 0$ and $|\Phi^{-1}(t_0)x_0|$ a constant, it follows that $|\phi(t)| \to 0$ and asymptotic stability holds. The converse is immediate because $|\phi(t)| = |\Phi(t)\Phi^{-1}(t_0)x_0| \to 0$ implies (3.10).

Theorem 3.4. Let $\Phi(t)$ be a fundamental matrix solution of (3.1) and let $\beta \in R$. The system (3.1) is uniformly asymptotically stable for $t_0 \geq \beta$ if and only if it is *exponentially asymptotically stable*, that is, there are constants $K = K(\beta) > 0$ and $\alpha = \alpha(\beta) > 0$ such that

$$|\Phi(t)\Phi^{-1}(s)| \leq K e^{-\alpha(t-s)}, \quad \beta \leq s \leq t < \infty. \tag{3.11}$$

Proof. Suppose that (3.11) holds. Then (3.9) follows from (3.11) and by theorem (3.2), uniform stability holds. Let $|x_0| \leq 1$ and note that for any $\eta > 0$ such that $0 < \eta < K$, we want to show that there is a $T(\eta) > 0$ such that

$$|\phi(t)| = |\Phi(t)\Phi^{-1}(t_0)x_0| \leq K e^{-\alpha(t-t_0)}|x_0| \leq \eta \tag{3.12}$$

if $t_0 \geq \beta$ and $t \geq t_0 + T(\eta)$. For (3.12) to hold, choose $T = -\alpha^{-1} \ln(\eta/K)$. This value of T establishes (3.12) and therefore (3.11) implies uniform asymptotic stability of the 0-solution of the linear system.

Conversely, suppose that the 0-solution is uniformly asymptotically stable for $t_0 \geq \beta$. There is a $\delta_0 > 0$ such that for any η, $0 < \eta < \delta_0$, there exists a $T = T(\eta) > 0$ such that by definition of uniform asymptotic stability

$$|\phi(t)| = |\Phi(t)\Phi^{-1}(t_0)x_0| < \eta, \quad t \geq t_0 + T \tag{3.13}$$

and all $t_0 \geq \beta$, $|x_0| \leq \delta_0$. From (3.13) deduce that

$$|\Phi(t)\Phi^{-1}(t_0)| < \eta/|x_0| < 1 \tag{3.14}$$

for $t_0 \geq \beta$, $t \geq t_0 + T$. In particular

$$|\Phi(t+T)\Phi^{-1}(t)| < 1 \tag{3.15}$$

for $t \geq \beta$. From theorem 3.2, uniform stability implies that there is a positive constant $M = M(\beta)$ such that

$$|\Phi(t)\Phi^{-1}(s)| \leq M, \quad \beta \leq s \leq t < \infty.$$

Let $\alpha = -\ln(\eta/\delta_0)/T$ and $K = M e^{\alpha T}$. Note that for any $t \geq t_0$, there is a positive integer k such that $kT \leq t - t_0 < (k+1)T$. Finally, use (3.15) to compute

$$
\begin{aligned}
|\Phi(t)\Phi^{-1}(t_0)| &\leq |\Phi(t)\Phi^{-1}(t_0+kT)| \cdot |\Phi(t_0+kT)\Phi^{-1}(t_0)| \\
&\leq M \cdot |\Phi(t_0+kT)\Phi^{-1}(t_0)| \\
&\leq M(\eta/\delta_0)|\Phi(t_0+(k-1)T)\Phi^{-1}(t_0)| \\
&\leq M(\eta/\delta_0)^k = M e^{-\alpha kT} = K e^{-\alpha(k+1)T} \\
&\leq K e^{-\alpha(t-t_0)}.
\end{aligned}
$$

This computation completes the proof.

So far, the stability analysis presented in the last four theorems deals with the homogeneous linear system $\dot{x} = A(t)x$ of (3.1), both because of its intrinsic importance and its use in linear approximations of the form (3.5). Finally, we present a theorem concerning the stability of the perturbed linear system, which is a generalization of theorem 4.2 in section 4.

Theorem 3.5. Suppose that $\dot{x} = A(t)x$ in (3.1) is uniformly asymptotically stable for $t_0 \geq \beta$, $\beta \in R$ and suppose that $h(t, x): R \times R^n \to R^n$ is continuous for (t, x). Also suppose that for any $\varepsilon > 0$, there is a $\delta > 0$ such that

$$|h(t, x)| < \varepsilon|x| \quad \text{for } \{(t, x): t \in R, |x| < \delta\}. \tag{3.16}$$

Then, the 0-solution

$$\dot{x} = A(t)x + h(t, x) \tag{3.17}$$

is *uniformly asymptotically stable* for $t_0 \geq \beta$.

Proof. Since $\dot{x} = A(t)x$ is uniformly asymptotically stable for $t_0 \geq \beta$ by theorem 3.4 there are constants $K = K(\beta)$ and $\alpha = \alpha(\beta)$ such that

$$|\Phi(t)\Phi^{-1}(s)| \leq K e^{-\alpha(t-s)}, \quad \beta \leq s \leq t < \infty. \tag{3.18}$$

Furthermore, recall that from the variation of constants theorem, any solution of the nonhomogeneous linear system (3.17) is of the form

$$\phi(t) = \Phi(t)\left[\Phi^{-1}(t_0)\phi(t_0) + \int_{t_0}^{t} \Phi^{-1}(s)h(s, \phi(s))\right] ds. \tag{3.19}$$

Choose ε so that $\varepsilon K < \alpha$ and let δ be such that (3.16) holds. For $t \geq t_0$ such that $|\phi(t)| < \delta$ use (3.18) and (3.19) to write

$$|\phi(t)| \leq K e^{-\alpha(t-t_0)}|\phi(t_0)| + \int_{t_0}^{t} \varepsilon K e^{-\alpha(t-s)}|\phi(s)| ds. \tag{3.20}$$

Make the transformation $z(t) = e^{\alpha t}|\phi(t)|$ and use it to rewrite (3.20) as

$$z(t) \leq Kz(t_0) + \int_{t_0}^{t} \varepsilon Kz(s) ds, \quad t \geq t_0. \tag{3.21}$$

Apply Gronwall's inequality to (3.21) to obtain

$$z(t) \leq Kz(t_0)\left[\exp \int_{t_0}^{t} \varepsilon K ds\right] \tag{3.22}$$

which implies

$$|\phi(t)| \leq K|\phi(t_0)| e^{-(\alpha - \varepsilon K)(t-t_0)} \tag{3.23}$$

for all values of $t \geq t_0$ for which $|\phi(t)| < \delta$. Since $\alpha - \varepsilon K > 0$ by choice of these constants, (3.23) implies $|\phi(t)| < \delta$ for all $t \geq t_0$ provided $|\phi(t_0)| < \delta/K$. Thus the 0-solution of (3.17) is uniformly asymptotically stable.

Example 3.1. Coppel (1965, p. 71) and Hale (1969, p. 87) report the following example to illustrate that extreme caution must be exercised in treating *perturbed linear systems* such as (3.17).

The second-order linear equation

$$\ddot{x} + x = 0 \tag{3.24}$$

has two solutions $\phi(t) = \sin t$ and $\phi(t) = \cos t$ and is *uniformly stable* but *not asymptotically stable*. Recall that (3.24) is a special case of (4.21) in chapter 2. However, the equation

$$\ddot{x} + 2t^{-1}\dot{x} + x = 0 \tag{3.25}$$

which can be considered as a perturbation of (3.24) has two solutions $\phi(t) = t^{-1} \sin t$ and $\phi(t) = t^{-1} \cos t$ and is *uniformly asymptotically stable*. On the other hand, the equation

$$\ddot{x} - 2t^{-1}\dot{x} + x = 0 \tag{3.26}$$

which can also be considered as a perturbation of (3.24) has two solutions $\phi(t) = \sin t - t \cos t$ and $\phi(t) = \cos t + t \sin t$ and is *unstable*.

4. Stability of linear systems with constant coefficients

Suppose that A is an $n \times n$ constant matrix and consider the linear autonomous homogeneous system

$$\dot{x} = Ax, \tag{4.1}$$

which is a special case of (3.1). Although the theorems presented in the preceding section can be used to study the stability properties of (4.1), the special nature of A allows us to obtain additional results. Note that $x = 0$ is an equilibrium solution of (4.1) and that its stability can be given in terms of the eigenvalues of A.

Theorem 4.1.

  (i) The 0-solution of (4.1) is *stable* if all eigenvalues of A have nonpositive real parts and if every eigenvalue of A which has a zero real part is a simple zero of the characteristic polynomial of A.
 (ii) The 0-solution is *asymptotically stable* if all eigenvalues of A have negative real parts.
(iii) The 0-solution is *unstable* if at least one eigenvalue of A has positive real part.

Proof. Without loss of generality, assume that the matrix A of (4.1) is in *Jordan canonical form*, as section 5 of chapter 2 describes it. Then the solution of (4.1) can be written as

$$\phi(t) = P e^{J(t - t_0)} P^{-1} x_0, \tag{4.2}$$

where J is as (5.10) of chapter 2. To establish stability we need to show that the solutions of (4.1) are bounded and then use theorem 3.1 of the previous section.

Consider separately the Jordan blocks J_0 and J_i, $i = 1, \ldots, s$. By construction, if an eigenvalue of A is simple, it appears in block J_0. Let $\lambda_1, \ldots, \lambda_k$ be the diagonal elements of J_0. By hypothesis $\text{Re } \lambda_i \leq 0$ for $i = 1, \ldots, k$. Therefore $|e^{J_0 t}|$ is bounded. For the other blocks, that is, J_i, $i = 1, \ldots, s$, note that $\text{Re } \lambda_{k+i} < 0$, $i = 1, \ldots, s$. Use (5.17) of chapter 2 to also conclude that $|e^{J_i t}|$, $i = 1, \ldots, s$, is bounded. Thus, there exists a positive constant K such that $|e^{J(t-t_0)}| \leq K$ for $t \geq t_0 \geq 0$. By theorem 3.1, the 0-solution of (4.1) is *stable*.

The second part of the theorem follows immediately since, by hypothesis, all eigenvalues of A have negative real parts. Actually, in this case, there are positive constants K and α such that $|e^{A(t-t_0)}| \leq K e^{-\alpha(t-t_0)}$, $t \geq t_0 \geq 0$, and by theorem 3.4 the 0-solution is *asymptotically stable*.

Finally, if at least one eigenvalue of A has positive real part, $\phi(t)$ in (4.2) is an increasing solution that becomes unbounded and stability does not hold.

Remark 4.1. Because (4.1) is time independent, stability implies *uniform stability* and asymptotic stability implies *uniform asymptotic stability*. For linear autonomous homogeneous systems such as (4.1), stability is equivalent to boundedness and asymptotic stability is equivalent to exponential asymptotic stability.

Furthermore, it is easy to prove that the condition that all eigenvalues of A in (4.1) have nonpositive real parts and every eigenvalue of A that has a zero real part is a simple zero, is not only sufficient but also necessary for stability. Finally, the condition that all eigenvalues of A in (4.1) have negative real parts is not only sufficient but also necessary for asymptotic stability as well.

Remark 4.2. It is important to emphasize that theorem 4.1 states sufficient conditions for stability and asymptotic stability for linear systems with constant coefficients. If the eigenvalues of a nonconstant matrix $A(t)$ satisfy the conditions of theorem 4.1, one *cannot* deduce stability for $\dot{x} = A(t)x$. Markus and Yamabe (1960) give a classic example showing that the eigenvalues of the matrix $A(t)$ cannot be used to determine the asymptotic behavior of the solutions of $\dot{x} = A(t)x$, where

$$A(t) = \begin{bmatrix} -1 + \frac{3}{2}\cos^2 t & 1 - \frac{3}{2}\cos t \sin t \\ -1 - \frac{3}{2}\sin t \cos t & -1 + \frac{3}{2}\sin^2 t \end{bmatrix}. \tag{4.3}$$

The eigenvalues of $A(t)$ are $\lambda_1(t) = [-1 + i\sqrt{7}]/4$ and $\lambda_2(t) = [-1 - i\sqrt{7}]/4$; that is, these two eigenvalues have negative real parts. However, the solution is given by

$$\phi(t) = e^{t/2} \begin{bmatrix} -\cos t \\ \sin t \end{bmatrix}$$

which is *not asymptotically stable* since it grows exponentially.

Remark 4.3. If an $n \times n$ matrix A is *negative definite*, then its eigenvalues are negative and the 0-solution of $\dot{x} = Ax$ is *asymptotically stable*. If A is positive definite, then its eigenvalues are positive and the 0-solution of $\dot{x} = Ax$ is *unstable*.

Remark 4.4. Consider the nth order homogeneous differential equation with constant coefficients given by

$$x^{(n)} + a_{n-1}x^{(n-1)} + \cdots + a_1\dot{x} + a_0 x = 0 \tag{4.4}$$

and define its *characteristic polynomial* to be

$$p(\lambda) = \lambda^n + a_{n-1}\lambda^{n-1} + \cdots + a_1\lambda + a_0. \tag{4.5}$$

Call $p(\lambda) = 0$ the *characteristic equation* of (4.4) and call the roots of $p(\lambda)$ the *characteristic roots* or *eigenvalues* of (4.4).

Suppose that (4.4) is transformed into a system $\dot{x} = Ax$ where

$$A = \begin{bmatrix} 0 & 1 & 0 & 0 & \cdots & 0 \\ 0 & 0 & 1 & 0 & \cdots & 0 \\ 0 & 0 & 0 & 1 & \cdots & 0 \\ \vdots & \vdots & \vdots & \vdots & & \vdots \\ 0 & 0 & 0 & 0 & \cdots & 1 \\ -a_0 & -a_1 & -a_2 & -a_3 & & -a_{n-1} \end{bmatrix}. \tag{4.6}$$

Observe that theorem 4.1 describes the stability or instability of $\dot{x} = Ax$ in terms of the eigenvalues of A. Since (4.4) and $\dot{x} = Ax$, with A as in (4.6), are equivalent, it can be shown by induction (see Miller and Michel (1982, p. 122)) that the characteristic polynomial of A in (4.6), that is $\det(A - \lambda I)$, is exactly the characteristic polynomial $p(\lambda)$ in (4.5). Therefore, the eigenvalues of A in (4.6) which are obtained by solving the characteristic equation $\det(A - \lambda I) = 0$, are the same as the roots of $p(\lambda) = 0$ in (4.5) which are obtained by solving the characteristic equation of the nth order equation in (4.4).

This means that, in practice, if an equation is given in the form of (4.4), one need not transform it into a system $\dot{x} = Ax$ and compute the eigenvalues of A in order to determine stability or instability. Rather, one can directly compute the roots of the characteristic equation $p(\lambda) = 0$, with $p(\lambda)$ as in (4.5), and apply theorem 4.1 to the characteristic roots.

Example 4.1. Consider the equation

$$\ddot{x} - \dot{x} - 2x = 0. \tag{4.7}$$

Let $x_1 = x$ and $x_2 = \dot{x}_1$; then (4.7) can be written as

$$\begin{bmatrix} \dot{x}_1 \\ \dot{x}_2 \end{bmatrix} = \begin{bmatrix} 0 & 1 \\ 2 & 1 \end{bmatrix} \begin{bmatrix} x_1 \\ x_2 \end{bmatrix}, \tag{4.8}$$

and the eigenvalues of the matrix are $\lambda_1 = -1$ and $\lambda_2 = 2$. Therefore, the 0-solution is *unstable*. In view of remark 4.4, note that you need not transform (4.7) into (4.8) in order to compute the eigenvalues of $\begin{bmatrix} 0 & 1 \\ 2 & 1 \end{bmatrix}$. One can compute the eigenvalues directly from the characteristic equation of (4.7) given by $\lambda^2 - \lambda - 2 = 0$.

Example 4.2. Determine the stability or instability of the 0-solution of

$$\ddot{x} + 4\dot{x} + 4x = 0. \tag{4.9}$$

The roots of the characteristic equation of (4.9) given by $\lambda^2 + 4\lambda + 4 = 0$ are $\lambda_1 = \lambda_2 = -2$. Therefore, the 0-solution is *asymptotically stable*.

Example 4.3. The 0-solution of

$$\ddot{x} + 4\dot{x} + 5x = 0$$

is *asymptotically stable* because the roots are $\lambda_1 = -2 + i$ and $\lambda_2 = -2 - i$.

Example 4.4. The 0-solution of

$$\ddot{x} + 4x = 0$$

is *stable*, but *not asymptotically stable*, because $\lambda_1 = 2i$ and $\lambda_2 = -2i$.

Example 4.5. Consider the system

$$\begin{bmatrix} \dot{x}_1 \\ \dot{x}_2 \\ \dot{x}_3 \end{bmatrix} = \begin{bmatrix} 2 & -3 & 0 \\ 0 & -6 & -2 \\ -6 & 0 & -3 \end{bmatrix} \begin{bmatrix} x_1 \\ x_2 \\ x_3 \end{bmatrix}$$

and compute the eigenvalues to find that $\lambda_1 = -7$, $\lambda_2 = \lambda_3 = 0$. Since zero is an eigenvalue of multiplicity 2, we must determine whether or not it is a simple zero. To do this we need to determine whether there are 2 linearly independent eigenvectors for the eigenvalue 0. Solve the equation

$$(A - \lambda I)p = \begin{bmatrix} 2 & -3 & 0 \\ 0 & -6 & -2 \\ -6 & 0 & -3 \end{bmatrix} \begin{bmatrix} p_1 \\ p_2 \\ p_3 \end{bmatrix} = \begin{bmatrix} 0 \\ 0 \\ 0 \end{bmatrix}$$

for $\lambda = 0$ to find that $p_1 = 3p_2/2$ and $p_3 = -3p_2$. This means that, although $\lambda = 0$ is of multiplicity 2, we only have one linearly independent eigenvector associated with $\lambda = 0$. This eigenvector is of the form

$$p = c \begin{bmatrix} \frac{3}{2} \\ 1 \\ -3 \end{bmatrix}$$

for c an arbitrary constant.

Thus, the eigenvalue zero is *not a simple zero* and the 0-solution is *unstable*.

Having analyzed in some detail the system $\dot{x} = Ax$ in (4.1), the next logical case to consider is the system

$$\dot{x} = Ax + h(x). \tag{4.10}$$

In (4.10), A is an $n \times n$ constant matrix, x and $\dot{x}$ are n column vectors and $h(x)$ is an n column vector with each element being a function of x. Unless we put some restrictions on $h(x)$, not much could be said about the stability or instability of the 0-solution of (4.10). Therefore assume that $h(0) = 0$ and also that $h(x)$ is very small compared to x. Note that this latter assumption is motivated by (3.16) of theorem 3.5 in the previous section.

If $h(0) = 0$ then $\phi(t) \equiv 0$ is an equilibrium solution of (4.10), for which we would like to know its stability properties. Theorem 4.1 states conditions for the stability or instability properties of the 0-solution of $\dot{x} = Ax$. Recall from the previous section that $\dot{x} = Ax$ is the approximate or linearized equation for (4.10). Therefore, is it possible to deduce stability or instability for the 0-solution of (4.10) from the stability properties of the 0-solution of the linearized system $\dot{x} = Ax$? The next theorem gives an answer to this question by specializing theorem 3.5.

Theorem 4.2. Consider $h(x)$ of (4.10) and suppose that $h(x)/|x|$ is a continuous function of x which vanishes for $x = 0$. Then

(i) if the 0-solution of the linearized system $\dot{x} = Ax$ is asymptotically stable, then the 0-equilibrium solution of (4.10) is also *asymptotically stable*;

(ii) if the 0-solution of $\dot{x} = Ax$ is unstable, then the 0-equilibrium solution of (4.10) is *unstable*.

Proof. The first part of this theorem can be proved in a way similar to theorem 3.5 of the previous section. We will present a proof after we have developed the Liapunov method in the next chapter.

Example 4.6. Consider the system

$$\dot{x}_1 = x_2 + 5x_1^3,$$
$$\dot{x}_2 = x_1 - 2x_2^2,$$

which can be expressed as in (4.10) by writing

$$\begin{bmatrix} \dot{x}_1 \\ \dot{x}_2 \end{bmatrix} = \begin{bmatrix} 0 & 1 \\ 1 & 0 \end{bmatrix} \begin{bmatrix} x_1 \\ x_2 \end{bmatrix} + \begin{bmatrix} 5x_1^3 \\ -2x_2^2 \end{bmatrix}.$$

Observe that the 0-solution is an equilibrium solution and that the nonlinear term $\begin{bmatrix} 5x_1^3 \\ -2x_2^2 \end{bmatrix}$ satisfies the conditions of theorem 4.2. The eigenvalues of the matrix are ± 1; therefore, the 0-solution of this system is *unstable*.

Example 4.7. Determine the stability of the 0-solution of the nonlinear system

$$\dot{x}_1 = -2x_1 + 3x_2^2,$$
$$\dot{x}_2 = -3x_2 - 4x_1^4.$$

Write this system as

$$\begin{bmatrix} \dot{x}_1 \\ \dot{x}_2 \end{bmatrix} = \begin{bmatrix} -2 & 0 \\ 0 & -3 \end{bmatrix} \begin{bmatrix} x_1 \\ x_2 \end{bmatrix} + \begin{bmatrix} 3x_2^2 \\ -4x_1^4 \end{bmatrix}$$

and note that the nonlinear term satisfies the hypotheses of theorem 4.2. Since the eigenvalues of the linear part are -2 and -3, the 0-equilibrium solution is *asymptotically stable*.

Remark 4.5. Theorem 4.2 is called the *Stability Theorem in the First Approximation* or the *Principle of Small Oscillations*. Note that this theorem does not tell us what happens when all the eigenvalues of A in (4.10) have a real part that is nonpositive with at least one eigenvalue of A having a zero real part. Recall that if the condition just stated holds, by theorem 4.1(i), the 0-solution of $\dot{x} = Ax$ is stable. This cannot be claimed for the 0-solution of (4.10). Thus, the stability of the 0-solution of (4.10) cannot be determined from the stability of the 0-solution of the linearized system, should all the eigenvalues of A have a nonpositive real part with at least one eigenvalue having a simple zero real part.

Example 4.8.   The standard example to illustrate remark 4.5 is the following system

$$\dot{x}_1 = x_2 - x_1(x_1^2 + x_2^2), \quad x_1(0) = c_1,$$
$$\dot{x}_2 = -x_1 - x_2(x_1^2 + x_2^2), \quad x_2(0) = c_2, \tag{4.11}$$

presented in Braun (1978, p. 364) and Hahn (1967, p. 77). The linearized system of (4.11) is given by

$$\begin{bmatrix} \dot{x}_1 \\ \dot{x}_2 \end{bmatrix} = \begin{bmatrix} 0 & 1 \\ -1 & 0 \end{bmatrix} \begin{bmatrix} x_1 \\ x_2 \end{bmatrix} \tag{4.12}$$

and the eigenvalues are $\pm i$. Therefore by part (i) of theorem 4.1, the system in (4.12) is *stable*. To study the behavior of the nonlinear part of (4.11) observe that

$$\frac{d}{dt}(x_1^2 + x_2^2) = 2x_1\dot{x}_1 + 2x_2\dot{x}_2 = 2[-x_1^2(x_1^2 + x_2^2) - x_2^2(x_1^2 + x_2^2)]$$

$$= -2(x_1^2 + x_2^2)^2.$$

Integrate this last equation to conclude that

$$x_1^2(t) + x_2^2(t) = \frac{c}{1 + 2ct}, \tag{4.13}$$

where $c = c_1^2 + c_2^2$. From (4.13) observe that $x_1^2(t) + x_2^2(t) \to 0$ as $t \to \infty$ and $x_1^2(t) + x_2^2(t) < c$. Therefore, the 0-solution of (4.11) is *asymptotically stable*, although the linearized part in (4.12) is only *stable*. This illustrates that *the nonlinear part of the system can influence the stability of the entire system.*

On the other hand, by slightly modifying the nonlinear part, the system can become unstable. Consider

$$\dot{x}_1 = x_2 + x_1(x_1^2 + x_2^2), \quad x_1(0) = c_1,$$
$$\dot{x}_2 = -x_1 + x_2(x_1^2 + x_2^2), \quad x_2(0) = c_2. \tag{4.14}$$

Note that (4.14) has the same linearized system as (4.11) given by (4.12); but

$$\frac{d}{dt}(x_1^2 + x_2^2) = 2(x_1^2 + x_2^2)^2$$

with solution

$$x_1^2(t) + x_2^2(t) = \frac{c}{1 - 2ct}, \tag{4.15}$$

where $c = c_1^2 + c_2^2$ is as before. From (4.15) conclude that every solution $x_1(t)$, $x_2(t)$ of (4.14), such that $x_1^2(t) + x_2^2(t) \neq 0$, approaches infinity in finite time. Therefore, the 0-solution of (4.14) is *unstable*, despite the fact that the linearized system in (4.12) is stable.

We close this section by connecting the stability results of $\dot{x} = Ax$ and $\dot{x} = Ax + h(x)$, presented in theorems 4.1 and 4.2 respectively, to the stability analysis of an arbitrary nonlinear system $\dot{x} = f(x)$.

Recall from section 3 that given a system $\dot{x} = f(x)$, with an equilibrium solution $\bar{x}$, Taylor's theorem can be used to transform $\dot{x} = f(x)$ into the system

$$\dot{z} = Az + h(z). \tag{4.16}$$

The stability properties of the equilibrium solution $\bar{x}$ of $\dot{x} = f(x)$ are equivalent to the stability properties of the 0-solution of $\dot{z} = Az + h(z)$ as presented in theorem 4.2. In turn, the equilibrium properties of the 0-solution of (4.16) are determined by the properties of the 0-solution of $\dot{z} = Az$ as presented in theorem 4.1. These ideas are illustrated in the next two examples.

Example 4.9. Consider the two dimensional nonlinear system

$$\dot{x}_1 = 1 - x_1 x_2,$$
$$\dot{x}_2 = x_1 - x_2^2, \tag{4.17}$$

and note that its equilibrium solution is found by solving the system

$$0 = 1 - x_1 x_2, \quad 0 = x_1 - x_2^2. \tag{4.18}$$

Solving (4.18) yields $\bar{x} = (\bar{x}_1, \bar{x}_2) = (1, 1)$ as a unique *equilibrium solution.* To study the stability properties of $\bar{x}_1(t) = 1$ and $\bar{x}_2(t) = 1$, set

$$z_1 = x_1 - 1, \quad z_2 = x_2 - 1 \tag{4.19}$$

and using (4.19), rewrite (4.17) as

$$\dot{z}_1 = 1 - (z_1 + 1)(z_2 + 1) = -z_1 - z_2 - z_1 z_2,$$
$$\dot{z}_2 = z_1 + 1 - (z_2 + 1)^2 = z_1 - 2z_2 - z_2^2.$$

The last system can be put in matrix form as

$$\begin{bmatrix} \dot{z}_1 \\ \dot{z}_2 \end{bmatrix} = \begin{bmatrix} -1 & -1 \\ 1 & -2 \end{bmatrix} \begin{bmatrix} z_1 \\ z_2 \end{bmatrix} + \begin{bmatrix} -z_1 z_2 \\ -z_2^2 \end{bmatrix}. \tag{4.20}$$

Observe that the 2×2 constant matrix in (4.20) is the Jacobian of partials of (4.17) evaluated at the equilibrium solution. Note also that the 0-solution is an equilibrium solution for (4.20) and that the nonlinear term of (4.20) satisfies the hypotheses of theorem 4.2. Computing the eigenvalues of the linear part of (4.20), obtain that $\lambda_1 = (-3 + i\sqrt{3})/2$, $\lambda_2 = (-3 - i\sqrt{3})/2$. Thus, the 0-solution is *asymptotically stable* and the equilibrium solution $\bar{x}_1(t) = 1$ and $\bar{x}_2(t) = 1$, is also *asymptotically stable*.

Example 4.10. This example is slightly more complicated than the previous one. Again, we combine the analysis on linearizing given in the previous section with the results of the two theorems in this section to study the stability properties of the equilibrium solutions of the nonlinear system

$$\dot{x}_1 = x_1^2 + x_2^2 - 1,$$
$$\dot{x}_2 = 2x_1 x_2. \tag{4.21}$$

Set $\dot{x}_1 = \dot{x}_2 = 0$ to compute the equilibrium solutions. There are four *equilibrium solutions*:

(a) $\bar{x}_1 = 0, \bar{x}_2 = 1$; (b) $\bar{x}_1 = 0, \bar{x}_2 = -1$; (c) $\bar{x}_1 = 1, \bar{x}_2 = 0$;

(d) $\bar{x}_1 = -1, \bar{x}_2 = 0$. $\tag{4.22}$

We first study the equilibrium solution $\bar{x}_1(t) = 0$, $\bar{x}_2(t) = 1$. Set

$$z_1 = x_1 - 0, \quad z_2 = x_2 - 1 \tag{4.23}$$

and using (4.23) rewrite (4.21) as

$$\dot{z}_1 = z_1^2 + (z_2 + 1)^2 - 1 = 2z_2 + z_1^2 + z_2^2,$$
$$\dot{z}_2 = 2z_1(z_2 + 1) = 2z_1 + 2z_1 z_2,$$

or equivalently, in matrix form, as

$$\begin{bmatrix} \dot{z}_1 \\ \dot{z}_2 \end{bmatrix} = \begin{bmatrix} 0 & 2 \\ 2 & 0 \end{bmatrix} \begin{bmatrix} z_1 \\ z_2 \end{bmatrix} + \begin{bmatrix} z_1^2 + z_2^2 \\ 2z_1 z_2 \end{bmatrix}. \tag{4.24}$$

The eigenvalues of the matrix $A = \begin{bmatrix} 0 & 2 \\ 2 & 0 \end{bmatrix}$ are ± 2 and therefore the 0-equilibrium solution of $\dot{z} = Az$ is *unstable*; by theorem 4.2 the 0-solution of (4.24) is unstable and finally the solution $\bar{x}_1(t) = 0$ and $\bar{x}_2(t) = 1$ is unstable.

Note that A is the Jacobian of partials evaluated at the equilibrium point. More specifically for (4.21), observe that the Jacobian is

$$\begin{bmatrix} 2\bar{x}_1 & 2\bar{x}_2 \\ 2\bar{x}_2 & 2\bar{x}_1 \end{bmatrix}. \tag{4.25}$$

Thus, putting the four equilibrium solutions of (4.22) in (4.25) we can determine the stability properties of the respective equilibria. We have already completed case (a) and concluded that it is unstable. For cases (b), (c) and (d), (4.25) becomes respectively

$$\begin{bmatrix} 0 & -2 \\ -2 & 0 \end{bmatrix}; \quad \begin{bmatrix} 2 & 0 \\ 0 & 2 \end{bmatrix}; \quad \begin{bmatrix} -2 & 0 \\ 0 & -2 \end{bmatrix},$$

with corresponding eigenvalues $\lambda = \pm 2$, $\lambda_1 = \lambda_2 = 2$ and $\lambda_1 = \lambda_2 = -2$. Therefore, the first three equilibrium solutions in (4.22) are *unstable* and the fourth equilibrium solution is *stable*.

5. Routh–Hurwitz criterion

This subsection briefly describes the Routh–Hurwitz stability criterion which applies to the nth order linear autonomous homogeneous ordinary differential equation with real coefficients of the form

$$a_0 x^{(n)} + a_1 x^{(n-1)} + \cdots + a_{n-1}\dot{x} + a_n x = 0, \tag{5.1}$$

where $a_0 \neq 0$. Using the substitution (9.4) of chapter 1, (5.1) is equivalent to the system $\dot{x} = Ax$ where A is given by

$$A = \begin{bmatrix} 0 & 1 & 0 & \cdots & 0 \\ 0 & 0 & 1 & \cdots & 0 \\ \vdots & \vdots & & & \vdots \\ -a_n/a_0 & -a_{n-1}/a_0 & & & -a_1/a_0 \end{bmatrix}. \tag{5.2}$$

The foregoing analysis, and particularly remark 4.4 in the previous section, can be used to determine the stability or instability of the 0-solution of the nth-order equation (5.1) by applying theorem 4.1 to $\dot{x} = Ax$ with A as in (5.2) or by finding the roots of the characteristic polynomial of (5.1).

The Routh–Hurwitz criterion describes a method for determining the stability of the nth order equation (5.1) without computing the eigenvalues of A in (5.2) or the roots of the characteristic polynomial of (5.1). More specifically we can state:

Theorem 5.1. (Routh–Hurwitz criterion.) Consider the nth-order polynomial $p(\lambda)$ with real coefficients given by

$$p(\lambda) = a_0 \lambda^n + a_1 \lambda^{n-1} + \cdots + a_{n-1}\lambda + a_n. \tag{5.3}$$

Assume without loss of generality that $a_0 > 0$. A necessary and sufficient condition that all the roots of $p(\lambda) = 0$ have negative real parts is that the following sequence of n determinants are all positive:

$$a_1 > 0; \quad \begin{vmatrix} a_1 & a_0 \\ a_3 & a_2 \end{vmatrix} > 0; \quad \begin{vmatrix} a_1 & a_0 & 0 \\ a_3 & a_2 & a_1 \\ a_5 & a_4 & a_3 \end{vmatrix} > 0;$$

$$\cdots \begin{vmatrix} a_1 & a_0 & 0 & 0 & \cdots \\ a_3 & a_2 & a_1 & a_0 & \cdots \\ a_5 & a_4 & a_3 & a_2 & \cdots \\ \vdots & \vdots & \vdots & \vdots & \vdots \\ 0 & 0 & 0 & 0 & a_n \end{vmatrix} > 0. \tag{5.4}$$

The proof of this theorem is very technical and can be found in Hahn (1967, pp. 16–22), or Gantmacher (1959).

It is of some historical interest to note that the problem of determining how many roots of the polynomial $p(\lambda)$ in (5.3) have negative real parts was initially solved by Sturm in 1836. In 1877, Routh used Sturm's method to obtain a simple algorithm and independently Hurwitz in 1895 solved the same problem using a method attributed to Hermite. A unified theory of this classical problem and its variants is found in Coppel (1965, pp. 142–158).

Example 5.1.   Determine the stability or instability of the 0-solution of

$$2\ddot{x} + 3\dot{x} + 2x = 0. \tag{5.5}$$

Using the Routh–Hurwitz criterion note that $a_1 = 3 > 0$ and $a_1 a_2 - a_0 a_3 = (3 \cdot 2) - (2 \cdot 0) = 6 > 0$. Thus the real parts of the roots of $2\lambda^2 + 3\lambda + 2 = 0$ are negative and the 0-solution of (5.5) is asymptotically stable. Solving $2\lambda^2 + 3\lambda + 2 = 0$ directly we verify the result since $\lambda_1 = (-3 + i\sqrt{7})/4$ and $\lambda_2 = (-3 - i\sqrt{7})/4$.

Remark 5.1.   Some results of the preceding analysis can be conveniently summarized as follows. The autonomous nth-order linear equation

$$a_0 x^{(n)} + a_1 x^{(n-1)} + \cdots + a_{n-1}\dot{x} + a_n x = 0$$

or the autonomous linear system

$$\dot{x} = Ax$$

is asymptotically stable if and only if every root of the characteristic polynomial

$$p(\lambda) = a_0\lambda^n + a_1\lambda^{n-1} + \cdots + a_{n-1}\lambda + a_n$$

or

$$p(\lambda) = \det(A - \lambda I)$$

has a negative real part. The Routh–Hurwitz criterion is an algebraic method of determining asymptotic stability without solving for the roots themselves.

6. Two dimensional linear systems

In section 2 of chapter 1 we indicated that, geometrically, a solution $\phi(t)$ of an ordinary differential equation is a curve whose direction at any point t coincides with the direction of the vector field. We also introduced the notion of the *phase space* for an autonomous differential equation of the form

$$\dot{x} = f(x), \tag{6.1}$$

with $f: R^n \to R^n$. Geometrically, the solutions $\phi(t)$ of (6.1) can be pictured as curves in the x space with t acting as a parameter. More specifically, if $\phi(t)$ is a solution of (6.1) on an interval I, we define the *trajectory* associated with this solution as the set in R^{n+1} given by $\{(t, \phi(t)): t \in I\}$. The *path* or *orbit* of a trajectory is the projection of the trajectory into R^n. The x space of dependent variables is called the *phase space* or the *state space*.

For example, when $n = 2$, the system

$$\dot{x}_1 = f(x_1, x_2), \quad \dot{x}_2 = g(x_1, x_2) \tag{6.2}$$

has solutions $\phi(t) = (\phi_1(t), \phi_2(t))$ which are curves in the three-dimensional space (t, x_1, x_2) and the trajectory is defined by $(t, \phi_1(t), \phi_2(t))$. On the other hand, if we let t take values in the parameter set $[0, \infty)$ and consider the set of points $(\phi_1(t), \phi_2(t))$ in the (x_1, x_2) plane, this (x_1, x_2) plane is the phase space and $(\phi_1(t), \phi_2(t))$ is the *path* or *orbit* of (6.2). Equivalently the path or orbit $(\phi_1(t), \phi_2(t))$ is the locus of points that the solution of (6.2) traverses in the (x_1, x_2) plane. Thus, the phase space of a system takes a *kinematic interpretation* because to every solution of a system of differential equations corresponds not only a trajectory in the (t, x) space, but, more importantly, the motion of a point along an orbit in the x space. This kinematic interpretation represented in the phase space is particularly expressive in studying the stability properties of a system's equilibrium.

Example 6.1.   The second-order linear equation

$$\ddot{x} + x = 0 \tag{6.3}$$

studied in example 3.1 of this chapter is equivalent to the system

$$\dot{x}_1 = x_2, \quad \dot{x}_2 = -x_1, \tag{6.4}$$

obtained by making the substitutions $x = x_1$, $\dot{x} = x_2$. The solution $\phi_1(t) = \sin t$, $\phi_2(t) = \cos t$ is easily verified to satisfy (6.4). In the three-dimensional space (t, x_1, x_2), the solution describes a helix, while in the (x_1, x_2) phase space, as t runs from 0 to 2π, the solution $(\phi_1(t), \phi_2(t)) = (\sin t, \cos t)$ traces out the unit circle $x_1^2 + x_2^2 = 1$. Furthermore, as t runs from 0 to ∞, the solution $(\sin t, \cos t)$ traces out this circle infinitely many times.

Having made the above preliminary remarks, we now proceed to study the *phase portraits* of two dimensional linear systems. Dynamic economic analysis relies heavily on such a phase analysis. More specifically consider the linear system

$$\dot{x} = Ax, \tag{6.5}$$

where A is a 2×2 matrix with constant coefficients a_{ij} with $i, j = 1, 2$ and x is a 2-dimensional column vector with elements x_1 and x_2. Throughout this section, assume that $\det A \neq 0$. This means that the origin $x = 0$ is the only equilibrium point of (6.5). Note that $x = 0$ is always a state of equilibrium of the system (6.5). This state is, furthermore, unique if and only if the determinant of A is different from zero, or, equivalently, if both eigenvalues of A are different from zero.

For two dimensional systems of the form of (6.5) with the assumption that $\det A \neq 0$, it is possible to give a fairly complete classification of the various representative phase portraits and to illustrate graphically the stability or instability of the 0-equilibrium.

Remark 6.1.   It is no loss of generality to study the phase portraits of the homogeneous system (6.5). The apparently more general case

$$\dot{x} = Ax + h, \tag{6.6}$$

where h is a constant two dimensional vector, can be reduced to (6.5) by translating the coordinates. The nonlinear case

$$\dot{x} = f(x) \tag{6.7}$$

can also be studied using the insights obtained from the linear case. More precisely, use the linearization method of sections 3 and 4 and recall that if $\phi(t)$ is an *equilibrium* solution of (6.7), then by letting $y = x - \phi(t)$, we can write (6.7) as

$$\dot{y} = Ay + h(y), \tag{6.8}$$

where A is a constant matrix and $h(y)$ is very small compared to y. Under these assumptions, the phase portraits of nonlinear systems such as (6.7) in the neighborhood of an equilibrium solution are very similar to the phase portraits of linear systems.

Remark 6.2.   Phase analysis is an additional tool in the study of stability of differential equations that supplements the theorems already stated. In particular, for two dimensional systems, phase analysis supplements the methods described previously for solving such systems explicitly. For systems that cannot be solved explicitly, as is the case with many economic models, phase analysis can be used to evaluate the qualitative properties of the model.

Remark 6.3.   In discussing the possible shape of the paths of the system $\dot{x} = Ax$, where A is a 2×2 constant matrix such that $\det A \neq 0$, we assume that the system has already been transformed into canonical form. Note that the phase portrait of the actual system $\dot{x} = Ax$ may differ from the one indicated below by the fact that the nonsingular transformation P distorts the portrait. However, the transformation P does not change the character and essential properties of these portraits. It can be shown mathematically that the transformation P amounts to, at most, a rotation about the origin, or a reflection in a line through the origin. This reflection is followed by a stretching of the plane away from, or compression toward, some line through the origin, and possibly another such stretching in a direction perpendicular to the first line. Thus, the effect of the transformation P is a distortion resulting from two mutually perpendicular expansions or contractions, which nevertheless preserves the essential properties of the phase diagrams.

Having made the above three remarks, suppose that we wish to study the stability or instability properties of the system $\dot{x} = Ax$ of (6.5). One way would be to solve explicitly this system by computing the exponential of the 2×2 matrix A, as was done in chapter 2, and to study the stability properties of its solution. Without solving $\dot{x} = Ax$ explicitly, we can also obtain important qualitative information by computing the eigenvalues of A and applying theorem 4.1 of this chapter. Or, as a third possibility, we can compute the eigenvalues of A and refer to the phase portraits presented below. This third method is the subject of the remainder of this section.

Consider $\dot{x} = Ax$ of (6.5) and recall the assumption that $\det A \neq 0$, which means that A does not have a zero eigenvalue and that the origin is the unique equilibrium point. From remark 7.1 of chapter 2, recall that A is similar to one of the four matrices

$$\text{(a)} \begin{bmatrix} \lambda_1 & 0 \\ 0 & \lambda_2 \end{bmatrix}, \quad \text{(b)} \begin{bmatrix} \lambda & 0 \\ 0 & \lambda \end{bmatrix}, \quad \text{(c)} \begin{bmatrix} \lambda & 1 \\ 0 & \lambda \end{bmatrix}, \quad \text{(d)} \begin{bmatrix} \alpha & \omega \\ -\omega & \alpha \end{bmatrix}. \quad (6.9)$$

Therefore, we distinguish the following cases.

Case 1. The matrix A of (6.5) has two real and distinct eigenvalues λ_1 and λ_2. In this case A is similar to the matrix (a) in (6.9) as was indicated in section 7 of chapter 2. The solution of this canonical form is

$$\begin{bmatrix} y_1 \\ y_2 \end{bmatrix} = \begin{bmatrix} e^{\lambda_1 t} & 0 \\ 0 & e^{\lambda_2 t} \end{bmatrix} \begin{bmatrix} c_1 \\ c_2 \end{bmatrix}. \quad (6.10)$$

Within this case we can further distinguish three subcases.

(i) Suppose $\lambda_2 < \lambda_1 < 0$: the origin is a *stable tangent node*. If $c_1 = c_2 = 0$ then (6.10) yields the origin. If $c_1 = 0$ and $c_2 \neq 0$ we obtain the y_2 axis with the origin deleted and observe that $y_2 \to 0$ as $t \to \infty$. Similarly, if $c_1 \neq 0$ and $c_2 = 0$ we obtain the y_1 axis with the origin deleted and conclude that $y_1 \to 0$ as $t \to \infty$. When $c_1 \neq 0$ and $c_2 \neq 0$ then for any point in the first quadrant, the motion along an arbitrary trajectory consists of an asymptotic approach of the point toward the origin, the trajectory in this case becoming tangent to the y_1 axis at the origin. See figure 3.2(a). If $\lambda_1 < \lambda_2 < 0$, then the trajectories would be tangent to the y_2 axis.

(ii) Suppose $0 < \lambda_1 < \lambda_2$: the origin is an *unstable tangent node*. This subcase is similar to subcase 1(i) with the orientation of the trajectories being reversed.

(iii) Suppose $\lambda_1 < 0 < \lambda_2$: the origin is a *saddle point*. If $c_1 = 0$ and $c_2 \neq 0$ in (6.10), then we obtain the y_2 axis with the origin deleted and note that $y_2 \to \pm\infty$ as $t \to \infty$. The motion along the positive y_1 semiaxis is directed toward the origin and the motion along the positive y_2 semiaxis is directed away from the origin. See figure 3.2(b). If $\lambda_2 < 0 < \lambda_1$, then the orientation of the trajectories in 3.2(b) would be reversed.

Case 2. The matrix A has a repeated real eigenvalue λ. This case can be divided into two subcases.

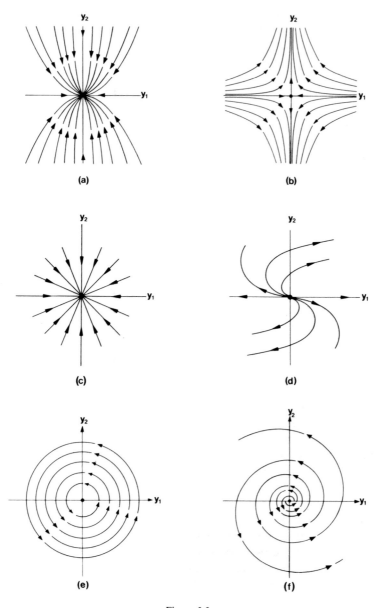

Figure 3.2

(i) Suppose the matrix A is diagonal. Then A is similar to matrix (b) in (6.9) and the solution of this canonical form is given by

$$\begin{bmatrix} y_1 \\ y_2 \end{bmatrix} = \begin{bmatrix} e^{\lambda t} & 0 \\ 0 & e^{\lambda t} \end{bmatrix} \begin{bmatrix} c_1 \\ c_2 \end{bmatrix}. \tag{6.11}$$

From (6.11) obtain immediately that $y_2/y_1 = (c_2/c_1)$, or equivalently, that $y_2 = (c_2/c_1)y_1$, provided $c_1 \neq 0$. This means that, in this subcase, the phase portrait consists of straight lines $y_2 = (c_2/c_1)y_1$ passing through the origin generated as c_1 and c_2 take arbitrary values. If $\lambda < 0$, then the motion moves towards the origin and the origin is called a *stable* (*stellar* or *isotropic*) *node* or *stable focus*; see figure 3.2(c). If $\lambda > 0$, then the motion moves away from the origin and the origin is called an *unstable node* or *unstable focus*.

(ii) If the matrix A is not diagonal, then its canonical form is like (c) of (6.9) which means that the system is of the form

$$\dot{y}_1 = \lambda y_1 + y_2,$$
$$\dot{y}_2 = \lambda y_2. \tag{6.12}$$

This system can be solved by integrating the second equation and by substituting this y_2 solution in the first equation. Since $y_2 = c_0 e^{\lambda t}$ then

$$\dot{y}_1 = \lambda y_1 + c_0 e^{\lambda t}.$$

Integrate this last equation to obtain the solution of (6.12) given by

$$y_1 = e^{\lambda t}(c_1 + c_2 t),$$
$$y_2 = c_1 e^{\lambda t}. \tag{6.13}$$

In this subcase, if $\lambda < 0$ the origin is called a *stable improper* (or *degenerate* or *one-tangent*) *node* and the phase portrait looks like 3.2(d) with the arrows reversed, since from (6.13) y_1 and y_2 tend to zero as $t \to \infty$. If $\lambda > 0$, then the origin is an *unstable improper node*. See figure 3.2(d).

Case 3. The final case occurs when the matrix A has complex eigenvalues. In this case its canonical form is matrix (d) in (6.9) and the system can be written as

$$\dot{y}_1 = \alpha y_1 + \omega y_2,$$
$$\dot{y}_2 = -\omega y_1 + \alpha y_2. \tag{6.14}$$

To study system (6.14), it is convenient to introduce polar coordinates. Let

$$y_1 = r \cos \theta, \quad y_2 = r \sin \theta \tag{6.15}$$

where $r > 0$ and $r = \sqrt{y_1^2 + y_2^2}$. Differentiate (6.15) with respect to time to obtain

$$\dot{y}_1 = \dot{r} \cos \theta - r \sin \theta \dot{\theta},$$

$$\dot{y}_2 = \dot{r} \sin \theta + r \cos \theta \dot{\theta}.$$

Solve this system of equations for $\dot{r}$ and $\dot{\theta}$, to get

$$\dot{r} = \cos \theta \dot{y}_1 + \sin \theta \dot{y}_2,$$
$$\dot{\theta} = (-\sin \theta \dot{y}_1 + \cos \theta \dot{y}_2)/r. \tag{6.16}$$

Substitute (6.14) in (6.16) using (6.15) to conclude

$$\dot{r} = \alpha r, \quad \dot{\theta} = -\omega. \tag{6.17}$$

The last system expresses the velocity of a representative point in the polar coordinates system (r, θ) in terms of $\dot{r}$ and $\dot{\theta}$; here $\dot{r}$ is the rate of change of the distance from the origin; $\dot{\theta}$ is the angular velocity about the origin. The solution of (6.14) is now given in polar coordinates by the solution of (6.17). The latter is

$$r = r_0 e^{\alpha t}, \quad \theta = \theta_0 - \omega t. \tag{6.18}$$

Two subcases arise immediately.

(i) If $\alpha = 0$, then r is a constant. The trajectories are circles centered at the origin. Furthermore, if $\omega > 0$ the arrows point in the clockwise direction and if $\omega < 0$, the phase diagram looks like 3.2(e). In this subcase, the origin is called a *center* or a *focal point*.

(ii) If $\alpha \neq 0$, then either $\alpha < 0$ or $\alpha > 0$. Suppose that $\alpha < 0$; then from (6.18) as $t \to \infty$, $r \to 0$ and the phase portrait looks like 3.2(f) with the arrows reversed. When $\alpha < 0$, the origin is called a *stable focus* or a *spiral sink* since the trajectories are spirals which approach the origin asymptotically as $t \to \infty$. If $\alpha > 0$ then the origin is called an *unstable focus* or a *source* and the phase diagram is like 3.2(f). Observe that in 3.2(f) we assumed that $\alpha > 0$ and $\omega < 0$.

We can summarize the above results and connect them with previous analysis in two remarks.

Remark 6.4. Stable nodes (tangent, stellar and improper) and foci are asymptotically stable. Saddle points and unstable nodes (tangent, stellar and improper) and foci are unstable. Finally, centers are stable but not asymptotically stable.

Remark 6.5. The analysis of sections 3 and 4 can naturally be applied here for the study of the stability properties of an equilibrium solution of a two dimensional nonlinear system $\dot{x} = f(x)$. If the nonlinear part satisfies the conditions of theorem 4.2, then the linearized part can be analyzed using not only theorem 4.2, but also the insights of phase portraits developed in this section.

7. Miscellaneous applications and exercises

(1) Suppose $f: [0, \infty) \times R^n \to R^n$ and consider $\dot{x} = f(t, x)$ such that $f(t, 0) = 0$ for $t \in [0, \infty)$. Furthermore, suppose that the 0-solution is stable at t_0. Show that the 0-solution is also stable at $t_1 \neq t_0, t_1 \in [0, \infty)$. See Hale (1969, p. 27).

(2) Consider $\dot{x} = f(t, x)$ such that $f: [0, \infty) \times R^n \to R^n$ and $f(t, 0) = 0$ for $t \in [0, \infty)$. The 0-solution is called *attractive* if there exists a number $\delta_0 = \delta_0(t_0) > 0$ such that $|x_0| < \delta_0$ implies $|\phi(t, t_0, x_0)| \to 0$ as $t \to \infty$. The 0-solution is *asymptotically stable* if it is stable and attractive.

Show that the concepts *stable* and *attractive* are independent of each other. See Hahn (1967, pp. 191-194) for the analysis of the following example of an autonomous system of differential equations of second order whose 0-solution is attractive but unstable:

$$\dot{x} = \frac{x^2(y-x) + y^5}{(x^2 + y^2)[1 + (x^2 + y^2)^2]},$$

$$\dot{y} = \frac{y^2(y - 2x)}{(x^2 + y^2)[1 + (x^2 + y^2)^2]}.$$

(3) Consider the system

$$\dot{x} = x^3 - xy^2, \quad \dot{y} = -y^3 - x^2 y.$$

Analyze the stability properties of the 0-solution of this system.

(4) There are systems that have no *equilibrium solutions*. An example of such a system is

$$\dot{x} = 2 + \sin(x + y) + x,$$
$$\dot{y} = 2 + \sin(x + y) - x.$$

(5) Determine the stability or instability of the 0-solution of the system $\dot{x} = Ax$ when A is as follows:

1. $A = \begin{bmatrix} 1 & 5 \\ 5 & 1 \end{bmatrix}$.
2. $A = \begin{bmatrix} 0 & -3 \\ 2 & 0 \end{bmatrix}$.
3. $A = \begin{bmatrix} -1 & 0 & 0 \\ -2 & -1 & 2 \\ -3 & -2 & -1 \end{bmatrix}$.

(6) Determine the stability or instability of the 0-solution of:

1. $x^{(3)} - 6\ddot{x} + 11\dot{x} - 6x = 0$,
2. $x^{(4)} - 4x^{(3)} + 7\ddot{x} - 4\dot{x} + 6x = 0$.

(7) Draw the phase diagram for the linear system

$$\begin{bmatrix} \dot{x}_1 \\ \dot{x}_2 \end{bmatrix} = \begin{bmatrix} 1 & -3 \\ -3 & 1 \end{bmatrix} \begin{bmatrix} x_1 \\ x_2 \end{bmatrix}$$

and determine the stability or instability of the 0-equilibrium solution.

(8) Draw the phase diagram for the linear system

$$\begin{bmatrix} \dot{x}_1 \\ \dot{x}_2 \end{bmatrix} = \begin{bmatrix} -1 & 1 \\ -1 & -1 \end{bmatrix} \begin{bmatrix} x_1 \\ x_2 \end{bmatrix}$$

and determine the stability or instability of the 0-equilibrium solution.

(9) Find all the equilibrium solutions of the nonlinear systems and study their stability properties.

1. $\dot{x}_1 = -2x_1 - x_2 + 2 + x_1 x_2$,
   $\dot{x}_2 = x_2 + x_1^2 x_2$.
2. $\dot{x}_1 = x_1 - x_1^2$,
   $\dot{x}_2 = x_2 - x_2^2$.

(10) Consider the system

$$\dot{x} = Ax + f(t, x), \tag{7.1}$$

where A is a constant $n \times n$ matrix and

$$|f(t, x)| \leq r(t)|x|$$

for $|x| < a$. Furthermore, assume that $\int_0^\infty r(t)\,dt < \infty$. Show that if the linear system $\dot{x} = Ax$ is stable then the 0-solution of (7.1) is also stable.

8. Further remarks and references

The stability and asymptotic stability definitions presented in 2.1 were originally introduced by Liapunov in 1893. They later reappeared in 1907 in the French translation of the original article. The French translation has been reproduced as Liapunov (1949). The original 1893 article and some other important subsequent papers of Liapunov have been translated into English and published as Liapunov (1966).

In his 1893 paper Liapunov studied stability using two distinct methods. The *first method* presupposes a known explicit solution and is only applicable to some special cases. His *second method* does not require the knowledge of solutions themselves and is therefore a method of great generality. This second method has found great applicability and is known as *Liapunov's direct method*. This chapter introduces fundamental notions of stability while chapter 4 presents the main results of Liapunov's method.

The definitions of uniform stability and uniform asymptotic stability, as well as several other definitions of various forms of stability, were introduced by several mathematicians during the past forty years. For a brief history on the subject of stability, see Coppel (1965, pp. 51-53), or Rouche et al. (1977, pp. 3-48).

One of the earlier books on stability in English is Bellman (1953). Hahn (1963) summarizes many important results, originally published in Russian, and Hahn (1967) remains one of the standard references on the topic of stability.

Unlike earlier treatises on differential equations which ignored the topic of stability, some current books such as Hartman (1964) and Hale (1969) give to the topic of stability a great deal of attention. Actually, even modern introductory books on differential equations familiarize the reader with the main concepts of stability. Such examples include: Pontryagin (1962), Sanchez (1968), Brauer and Nohel (1969), Plaat (1971), Roxin (1972), Arnold (1973) and Braun (1978, 1983).

The topic of stability has also been treated in the mathematical economics literature. Takayama (1985), Murata (1977) and Gandolfo (1980) are the standard references. Recently, F. Hahn (1982) has surveyed the main stability results of general equilibrium.

The analysis of this chapter has benefited greatly from several books, such as: Hale (1969), Coddington and Levinson (1955), Coppel (1965), and Miller and Michel (1982). The various examples, exercises and figure 3.2 presented follow the exposition of books such as Pontryagin (1962), Brauer and Nohel (1969), Plaat (1971), Roxin (1972), Braun (1978) and Hirsch and Smale (1974). See also Lehnigk (1966).

We emphasize once again that in this book, stability is studied with respect to changes in initial data. One could also study stability with respect to changes in the vector field $f(t, x)$: this is called *structural* stability and for an introductory survey the reader is referred to Hirsch and Smale (1974, chapter 16) or Peixoto (1962). R. Thom (1975) has applied structural stability to the natural and biological sciences and Fuchs (1975) uses structural stability in economics.

Finally, most introductory books on differential equations devote several pages to the *Poincaré-Bendixson Theory* which describes the geometry of phase portraits in two dimensions and could be used to supplement section 6. In nontechnical language the *Poincaré-Bendixson Theory* describes the behavior of a *bounded* trajectory and shows that as $t \to \infty$ such a trajectory either tends to an equilibrium point or spirals onto a simple closed curve. For general details see Plaat (1971, pp. 242-249) or Gandolfo (1980, pp. 433-448) and for proofs see Coddington and Levinson (1955, chapter 16). The original ideas may be found in Bendixson (1901). Schinasi (1982) gives an application of the Poincaré-Bendixson theory in economics.

For those interested in the study of differential equations through computer experiments, Koçak (1986) offers a manual and a diskette to help readers learn how to use a program called PHASER which runs on personal computers.

CHAPTER 4

ADVANCED STABILITY METHODS

> In his famous memoir, Liapunov gave
> some very simple geometric
> theorems ... for deciding the stability
> or instability of an equilibrium point
> of a differential equation. The idea is
> a generalization of the concept of
> energy and its power and usefulness
> lie in the fact that the decision is
> made by investigating the differential
> equation itself and not by finding
> solutions of the differential equation.
> Hale (1969, p. 291)

1. Preliminaries

In this chapter we continue to investigate the stability properties of ordinary differential equations. While the previous chapter presented some elementary stability methods, primarily for linear and linearized systems, this chapter exposits the Liapunov approach and some other recently developed mathematical methods that have been found useful by economists.

For methodological clarity, the theorems of the Liapunov approach can be classified as *local* and as *global* results. Local results report on stability, asymptotic stability and instability for initial values in a small neighborhood of the 0-equilibrium solution. The global results refer to asymptotic stability at large for initial values in the whole of R^n.

A further useful distinction is between autonomous and non-autonomous systems. This distinction has already been made on several earlier occasions. In this chapter, we concentrate essentially on the autonomous case because most economic applications deal with autonomous differential equations. However, for mathematical completeness and exposure of theoretical economists to new methods, several theorems are also stated for the non-autonomous case.

To begin with, consider an autonomous differential equation $\dot{x} = f(x), f: D \subset R^n \to R^n$; assume that f is continuously differentiable in an open set D. Further assume that the open set D contains the origin and that $f(0) = 0$. For future reference we write

$$\dot{x} = f(x); \quad f: D \subset R^n \to R^n; \quad f(0) = 0; \quad 0 \in D \subset R^n. \tag{1.1}$$

Recall from chapter 1, that assuming f to be continuously differentiable implies that a unique solution exists through any initial value. Also assume that the 0-solution is the only equilibrium solution in D.

Liapunov in his original 1893 article proposed two distinct methods for studying stability. The first method consisted of expanding analytic solutions in series and studying their stability. The second method does not require any knowledge of the solutions themselves but it does rely heavily on the existence of a certain function. This function measures a *distance* between a given solution and the 0-equilibrium solution. The time derivative of such a function can be used to infer whether the distance between a solution and the 0-equilibrium solution decreases or increases and consequently whether stability or instability holds.

With this intuitive motivation, we make the next definitions that allow us to embark on the details of Liapunov's second method, also called Liapunov's *direct* method.

Definitions 1.1. Let D be an open subset of R^n containing the origin. A scalar function $V(x): D \to R$ is *positive semidefinite* on $D \subset R^n$ if it is continuous on D and $V(x) \geq 0$ for $x \in D$. A scalar function $V(x)$ is *negative semidefinite* on D if $-V(x)$ is positive semidefinite. A scalar function $V(x)$ is *positive definite* on D if it is continuous on D, $V(x) > 0$ for $x \neq 0$ and $V(0) = 0$. In other words, $V(x)$ is positive definite if it is positive semidefinite with $V(0) = 0$ and $V(x) > 0$ for $x \neq 0$. Finally, a scalar function $V(x)$ is *negative definite* if $-V(x)$ is positive definite. A continuous scalar function $V(x)$ is *indefinite* if $V(0) = 0$ and in every neighborhood of the origin it takes both positive and negative values.

Example 1.1. The function

$$V(x_1, x_2, x_3, x_4) = x_1^2 + x_2^2 + x_3^2$$

is positive definite on R^3 and positive semidefinite on R^4. The function

$$V(x_1, x_2, x_3) = x_1^2 + (x_2 + x_3)^2$$

is positive semidefinite on R^3 because for $x_1 = 0$ and $x_2 = -x_3 \neq 0$, it becomes zero. The function

$$V(x_1, x_2) = x_1^2 + x_2^2 - (x_1^4 + x_2^4)$$

is positive definite inside the unit circle but indefinite on R^2 because it becomes negative for x outside the unit circle.

It is helpful to describe the geometric meaning of the function $V(x)$. For concreteness, take $n = 2$ and assume that $V(x_1, x_2)$ is positive definite. The curves $V(x_1, x_2) = $ constant, represent a set of ovals or *level curves* surrounding the origin. Thus, for a positive definite $V(x)$ on D, there is a neighborhood U of the origin $x = 0$, with the closure of U contained in D and a constant $k > 0$, such that any continuous curve from the origin to the *boundary* of U, denoted by ∂U, must intersect the level curve described by the set $\{x : V(x) = c\}$ for $0 \leq c \leq k$.

Let us take one step further. Assume that $V(x)$ is positive definite on $D \subset R^n$ and further assume that $V(x)$ is continuously differentiable. In other words, we assume not only that $V(x)$ is continuous on D but also that its partial derivatives of all arguments exist and are continuous themselves on D. Since $V(x)$ has continuous partials, it has a gradient usually denoted by V_x or $\nabla V(x)$ or grad V. Recall that such a *gradient* is defined as a vector valued function of partial derivatives given by

$$\nabla V(x) = \left(\frac{\partial V}{\partial x_1}, \dots, \frac{\partial V}{\partial x_n} \right). \tag{1.2}$$

A fundamental concept in Liapunov's method is the time derivative of $V(x)$ along solutions of the autonomous differential equation. For f as in (1.1) define

$$\dot{V}(x) \equiv \nabla V(x) \cdot \dot{x} = \nabla V(x) \cdot f(x) = \sum_{k=1}^{n} \frac{\partial V(x)}{\partial x_k} \cdot f_k(x). \tag{1.3}$$

If we let $\phi(t, t_0, x_0) \equiv \phi(t) \equiv x(t)$ be a solution of $\dot{x} = f(x)$ in (1.1), then use of the chain rule in calculus yields,

$$\frac{d}{dt} V(x(t)) = V_x(x(t)) \cdot \dot{x}(t) = \nabla V(x(t)) \cdot f(x(t)) = \dot{V}(x(t)). \tag{1.4}$$

The function $\dot{V}(x(t))$ is called the *trajectory derivative* or the *time derivative* along a solution $x(t)$.

The functions $V(x)$ and $\dot{V}(x)$ play an important role in Liapunov theory. Actually, a positive definite function $V(x)$, $x \in D$ with a negative semi-definite $\dot{V}(x)$ is usually called a *Liapunov function*. We have already given an intuitive geometric meaning of a positive definite $V(x)$.

To supplement this geometric meaning for $n = 2$, suppose that $V(0) = 0$, $V(x_1, x_2) > 0$ for x_1, x_2 in a neighborhood D of the origin and furthermore that $\dot{V}(x_1, x_2) \leq 0$ for x_1, x_2 in D. The surface $y = V(x_1, x_2)$ has the general shape of a parabolic mirror pointing upward or, put in plain English, of a cup on a table. How can this help us with issues of the stability of the 0-equilibrium of $\dot{x} = f(x)$? To answer this question, let $y_1, y_2, \ldots$ be a decreasing sequence of real numbers approaching 0 such that the level

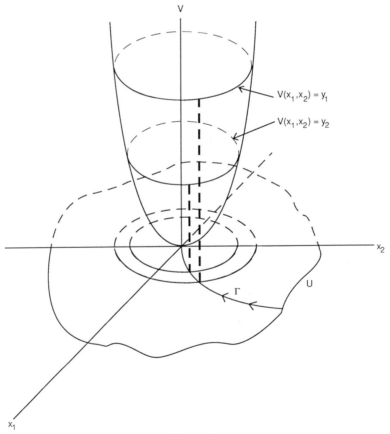

Figure 4.1

curves, $y_1 = V(x_1, x_2)$, $y_2 = V(x_1, x_2)$, ... shrink towards the origin. Furthermore let $\phi(t, t_0, x_0) \equiv x(t)$ be a solution of $\dot{x} = f(x)$ in (1.1) and consider, in the special case of $n = 2$, a continuous curve Γ from the origin to the boundary of a set U containing the origin with $U \subset D$. Such a curve may represent the path or orbit of the solution $x(t)$ in the phase space as $t \to \infty$. Since we assume that $\dot{V}(\phi(t, t_0, x_0)) \equiv \dot{V}(x(t)) < 0$ for $x \neq 0$ and $x \in D$ it follows that as $t \to \infty$, $V(x(t))$ decreases monotonically and that the level curves $y_1 = V(x_1, x_2)$, $y_2 = V(x_1, x_2), \ldots$, are crossed by the continuous curve Γ from the exterior and toward the interior. Therefore, since the motion in the phase space along the curve Γ is toward the origin, as $t \to \infty$, we conclude that the 0-equilibrium solution is *asymptotically stable*. See figure 4.1.

2. Local stability and instability for autonomous systems

This section collects several local stability and instability theorems for autonomous systems that make the intuitive ideas presented above more precise. For autonomous systems, recall that stability of the 0-solution implies, automatically uniform stability and asymptotic stability implies uniform asymptotic stability. Our analysis follows Hale (1969, pp. 292–299) and LaSalle and Lefschetz (1961, pp. 37–40).

Theorem 2.1. (Liapunov stability for autonomous systems.) Suppose that there is a continuously differentiable positive definite function $V(x): D \subset R^n \to R$, where D is an open set containing the origin, and $\dot{V}(x)$ is negative semidefinite for $x \in D$. Then the 0-solution of $\dot{x} = f(x)$ in (1.1) is *stable*.

Proof. We need to show that given an $\varepsilon > 0$ and $t_0 \geq 0$, there is a $\delta > 0$ such that for $|x_0| < \delta$ the solution $x(t, t_0, x_0)$ of $\dot{x} = f(x)$ satisfies $|x(t, t_0, x_0)| < \varepsilon$ for all $t \geq 0$. Let $\varepsilon > 0$ be given such that the closed ball of radius ε is contained in D; that is, let $\{x: |x| \leq \varepsilon\} \subset D \subset R^n$. Define

$$V_0 = \min_{|x| = \varepsilon} V(x). \tag{2.1}$$

Choose $\delta > 0$ such that if $|x| \leq \delta$ then $V(x) < V_0$. Such a $\delta, 0 < \delta \leq \varepsilon$, exists because $V(0) = 0$ and $V(x)$ is continuous on D. Then if $|x_0| < \delta$, the hypothesis that $\dot{V}(x) \leq 0$ implies that

$$V(x(t, t_0, x_0)) \leq V(x_0) < V_0. \tag{2.2}$$

From (2.2) conclude that $|x(t, t_0, x_0)| < \varepsilon$ for $t \geq 0$ and thus the 0-solution is stable.

Theorem 2.2. (Liapunov asymptotic stability for autonomous systems.)   Suppose that there is a continuously differentiable positive definite function $V(x)$: $D \subset R^n \to R$, with D an open set containing the origin, and let $\dot{V}(x)$ be negative definite for $x \in D$. Then the 0-solution of $\dot{x} = f(x)$ in (1.1) is *asymptotically stable*.

Proof.   Assume the hypothesis that $\dot{V}$ is negative definite on D. The stability of the 0-solution follows from the previous theorem so that for $|x_0| < \delta$ we have that $|x(t, t_0, x_0)| < \varepsilon$ for all $t \geq 0$. Here, we need to show that $|x(t, t_0, x_0)| \to 0$ as $t \to \infty$ or equivalently that $V(x(t, t_0, x_0)) \to 0$ as $t \to \infty$.

Suppose that $V(x(t, t_0, x_0)) \to V_0 > 0$ as $t \to \infty$. In other words, we suppose that $V(x(t, t_0, x_0))$ does not approach zero as $t \to \infty$ and hope to get a contradiction. If it is true that $V(x(t)) \to V_0 > 0$ as $t \to \infty$, then there is some $\alpha > 0$ such that for $|x| < \alpha$ it follows that $V(x) < V_0$. Consider β defined by

$$\beta = \max_{\alpha \leq |x| \leq \varepsilon} [\dot{V}(x(t))] < 0. \tag{2.3}$$

For $x \in \{x: \alpha \leq x \leq \varepsilon\}$ note that

$$\frac{d}{dt} V(x(t)) = \dot{V}(x(t)) \leq \beta \tag{2.4}$$

which upon integration, with respect to t, yields

$$V(x(t, t_0, x_0)) \leq V(x(t_0, t_0, x_0)) + \beta t,$$

written simply as

$$V(x(t)) \leq V(x_0) + \beta t \tag{2.5}$$

for all $t \geq 0$. Observe that (2.5) is a contradiction of the hypothesis that V is positive definite because as t becomes large and is multiplied by $\beta < 0$ it forces $V(x(t)) < 0$. Therefore $V_0 = 0$ and $|x(t, t_0, x_0)| \to 0$ as $t \to \infty$.

Remark 2.1.   The previous two theorems demonstrate the usefulness of *Liapunov functions* in determining the stability of an autonomous system. The existence of a Liapunov function is sufficient for establishing the stability of the 0-solution of $\dot{x} = f(x)$, $f(0) = 0$, without solving such a system.

The ingenuity of A. M. Liapunov cannot be overemphasized. The voluminous literature on this subject is partial evidence of the significance of his method. The key notion of a Liapunov function is that V, by being positive definite, is a generalized measurement of the distance between a solution and the 0-solution. Furthermore, $\dot{V}$ by being either negative semi-definite or negative definite, tells us whether such a distance does not increase or whether it strictly decreases as time increases.

Assuming the existence of a *Liapunov function* makes the stability and asymptotic stability proofs simple. Ultimately, the critical question to be answered is how to construct such Liapunov functions. In some special cases, such as for linear systems, a methodology is available to guide us in constructing a Liapunov function. The topic is addressed later in this section. However, constructing Liapunov functions is in general a rare skill that is acquired, partially, by having seen many Liapunov functions corresponding to specific systems. The examples in this chapter and the applications in subsequent chapters will familiarize the reader with several useful techniques.

Remark 2.2. Liapunov theory remains valid by assuming that V is only continuous in D instead of continuously differentiable provided that $\dot{V}$ is defined for $x_0 \in D$ as

$$\dot{V}(x_0) = \limsup_{h \to 0} \frac{1}{h} [V(x(t_0 + h, t_0, x_0)) - V(x(t_0, t_0, x_0))]. \tag{2.6}$$

Since, in most of the applications, V is continuously differentiable, this book uses the definition of $\dot{V}$ in (1.3) instead of (2.6). See Hale (1969, p. 293).

Theorem 2.3. (Liapunov instability for autonomous systems.)   Let $D \subset R^n$ be an open, connected set that contains the origin. Let U be an open set which contains in its closure the 0-equilibrium solution. Suppose that V is continuously differentiable on D, that V and $\dot{V}$ are positive definite on $D \cap U$, and also that $V = 0$ on $\partial U \cap D$, that is on that part of the boundary of U inside D. Then the 0-solution of $\dot{x} = f(x)$ in (1.1) is unstable.

Proof.   Choose an open and bounded set D_0 containing the origin such that $\bar{D}_0 \subset D$. Given $\delta > 0$, choose $x_0 \in D_0 \cap U$ with $0 < |x_0| < \delta$. From the hypothesis we infer that $V(x_0) > 0$. Define

$$S = \{x : x \in \overline{D_0 \cap U} \text{ with } V(x) \geq V(x_0)\}.$$

Note that S is closed and bounded which makes it compact. Let

$$\alpha = \min_{x \in S} \dot{V}(x).$$

Observe that $\alpha > 0$ since $\partial U \cap S$ is empty. Let $x(t) \equiv x(t, t_0, x_0)$ be a solution which implies that $\dot{V}(x(t)) \geq \alpha$ for $x(t) \in S$. Integrating, we conclude that

$$V(x(t)) = V(x_0) + \int_0^t \dot{V}(x(s)) \, ds \geq V(x_0) + \alpha t \quad \text{for } x(t) \in S. \tag{2.7}$$

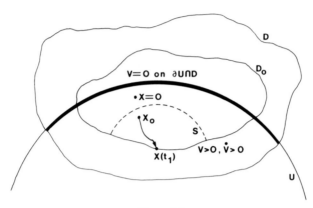

Figure 4.2

This last equation says that as t increases $V(x(t))$ eventually becomes unbounded. However, since V is continuous and S is compact, V cannot become unbounded for $x \in S$. Therefore, $x(t)$ must eventually leave $\overline{D_0 \cap U}$. Since $\overline{D_0 \cap U}$ is compact and V is continuous, there is a t_1 such that $x(t)$ leaves $\overline{D_0 \cap U}$ at time t_1. Let $x(t_1) \in \partial(\overline{D_0 \cap U})$. But $x(t_1)$ cannot be on the part of the boundary of U inside D because by hypothesis $V = 0$ there. Thus $x(t_1)$ is on the boundary of D_0 inside U. Since x_0 is chosen arbitrarily close to the origin, we conclude that the 0-solution is unstable because no matter how close to the origin we start, solutions escape a bounded set D_0 in finite time. See figure 4.2.

Example 2.1.   Consider the system

$$\dot{x} = y - xf(x, y),$$
$$\dot{y} = -x - yf(x, y),$$
                                                                    (2.8)

with $f(0, 0) = 0$. To discuss the stability properties of this system let

$$V(x, y) = \tfrac{1}{2}(x^2 + y^2)$$
                                                                    (2.9)

and compute

$$\dot{V}(x, y) = x\dot{x} + y\dot{y} = xy - x^2 f(x, y) - xy - y^2 f(x, y)$$
$$= -(x^2 + y^2)f(x, y).$$
                                                                    (2.10)

To determine the stability properties of the 0-solution we need to make an assumption about $f(x, y)$. Some independent possibilities include:

First, assume that $f(x, y)$ is positive semidefinite on an open neighborhood $D \subset R^2$ of the origin. Then V is positive definite on D, $\dot{V}$ is negative semidefinite on D and by theorem 2.1, the 0-solution is stable. Note that if $f(x, y)$ is positive semidefinite, the 0-solution need not be asymptotically stable. For example, if $f(x, y) \equiv 0$ on D, then this example reduces to example 2.5 of chapter 3. It is shown there that with $f(x, y) = 0$ on D, that the 0-solution is stable but it is not asymptotically stable.

Second, assume that $f(x, y)$ is positive definite on D. Then, V is positive definite, $\dot{V}$ is negative definite and by theorem 2.2 the 0-solution is asymptotically stable. A special case is reported in example 4.8 of chapter 3 where $f(x, y) = x^2 + y^2$ is positive definite. In example 4.8 it is shown that the 0-solution is asymptotically stable using a specialized analysis. The analysis of this chapter illustrates the generality of the Liapunov approach.

Third, suppose that $f(x, y)$ is negative definite in a neighborhood D of the origin. To apply theorem 2.3 let $U = R^2$ and conclude that the 0-solution is unstable.

This example illustrates the generality of the Liapunov method in deciding stability or instability. The nonlinear system in (2.8) cannot be studied conclusively by computing the eigenvalues of its linearization. It is clear from (2.10) that the nonlinear part $f(x, y)$ plays a critical role. More specifically, the eigenvalues of the linearization of (2.8) can be computed to be $\pm i$ from which we can only conclude the stability of the 0-solution of the linear system. However, the three cases discussed here illustrate that, in general, stability cannot be decided by examining only the linear system because the nonlinearities of the system may play a critical role in determining the stability of the whole system.

Example 2.2. Let $g(x)$ be a continuously differentiable real valued function on a neighborhood $D = (-\delta, \delta)$ of zero. Consider the autonomous system

$$\dot{x} = g(x), \quad g(0) = 0 \tag{2.11}$$

and make appropriate assumptions to study the stability properties of (2.11).
First, assume that $g'(0) < 0$. Let

$$V(x) = \tfrac{1}{2}x^2; \quad \dot{V}(x) = x\dot{x} = xg(x). \tag{2.12}$$

Since $g'(0) < 0$ and $g(0) = 0$ it follows that g is decreasing through the origin with $g(x) < 0$ for $x \in (0, \delta)$ and $g(x) > 0$ for $x \in (-\delta, 0)$. For $x \in (-\delta, \delta)$ observe that $V(x)$ is positive definite and $\dot{V}(x)$ is negative definite and conclude from theorem 2.2 that the 0-solution is asymptotically stable.

Second, assume that $g'(0) > 0$. Using (2.12) and the assumption that $g'(0) > 0$, conclude by theorem 2.3 that the 0-solution is unstable.

Example 2.3. Consider the second-order equation

$$\ddot{x} + f(x) = 0,$$

which can be rewritten in system form as

$$\dot{x} = y,$$
$$\dot{y} = -f(x).$$

(2.13)

Assume that $xf(x) > 0$ for $x \neq 0$ and $f(0) = 0$. Let

$$V(x, y) = \tfrac{1}{2} y^2 + \int\limits_0^x f(s) \, ds.$$

Then

$$\dot{V}(x, y) = y\dot{y} + f(x)\dot{x} = -yf(x) + yf(x) = 0.$$

Therefore by theorem 2.1, the 0-solution of (2.13) is stable.

Example 2.4. In this example we establish the stability of the equilibrium solution of the neoclassical economic growth model. In a later chapter, stability issues of economic growth are presented in greater detail.

Consider a production function

$$Y(t) = F(K(t), L(t)),$$

(2.14)

where $Y(t)$ denotes units of output, $K(t)$ denotes units of capital stock and $L(t)$ denotes units of labor force, all at time t. It is assumed that (2.14) satisfies the property: if each of the independent variables in (2.14) is multiplied by a positive constant λ, then the dependent variable is also multiplied by the same constant. If this property is satisfied, (2.14) is called homogeneous of degree 1. From the homogeneity assumption obtain (note that the variable t is dropped)

$$F\left(\frac{K}{L}, 1\right) = f\left(\frac{K}{L}\right) = f(k),$$

(2.15)

where $k = K/L$ is the capital–labor ratio. Assume that $f(0) = 0, f'(k) > 0, f''(k) < 0, \lim_{k \to 0^+} f'(k) = \infty, \lim_{k \to \infty} f'(k) = 0$. Investment is defined to be the time derivative of $K(t)$, denoted by $\dot{K}$, and saving is defined to be $sF(K, L)$, with $0 < s < 1$. Equilibrium requires that investment must equal saving, that is,

$$\dot{K} = sF(K, L).$$

(2.16)

Assume that labor grows exponentially given by

$$L(t) = L(0) e^{nt}, \quad L(0) > 0, \quad 0 < n < 1. \tag{2.17}$$

Under the above differentiability and concavity assumptions about (2.14), Solow (1956) used equations (2.15) through (2.17) to derive the one-sector neoclassical differential equation of economic growth for the certainty case:

$$\dot{k} = \frac{d}{dt}\left(\frac{K}{L}\right) = \frac{\dot{K}L - \dot{L}K}{L^2} = \frac{\dot{K}}{L} - \frac{\dot{L}}{L}\frac{K}{L} = sf(k) - nk. \tag{2.18}$$

Equation (2.18) has been the subject of much research in economics. A useful reference on this subject is the book of Burmeister and Dobell (1970). Assume that

$$0 < n/s < f'(0)$$

and set $\dot{k} = 0$ in (2.18) to obtain a unique positive equilibrium solution. Denote the equilibrium solution by k^* and use the Liapunov function

$$V(x) = \tfrac{1}{2}x^2, \tag{2.19}$$

where $x = k - k^*$. Compute:

$$\dot{V}(x) = x\dot{x} = x\dot{k} = x[sf(x + k^*) - n(x + k^*)]$$
$$\leq x[sf(k^*) + xsf'(k^*) - n(x + k^*)]$$
$$= x^2[sf'(k^*) - n] = x^2\left[\frac{nk^*f'(k^*)}{f(k^*)} - n\right]$$
$$= \frac{x^2 n}{f(k^*)}[k^*f'(k^*) - f(k^*)] < 0. \tag{2.20}$$

In (2.20) note that the inequality follows from the strict concavity property of $f(k)$. Also, $\dot{V}(x)$ is negative definite because $k^*f'(k^*) < f(k^*)$. By theorem 2.2 the k^*-equilibrium solution is asymptotically stable for k in a neighborhood of k^*. Actually k^* is asymptotically stable for $k > 0$. This concludes example 2.4.

The next logical step in the study of the Liapunov method is the analysis of the linear autonomous system with constant coefficients. The importance of this system has already been emphasized in the previous two chapters. The purpose of revisiting this topic is to illustrate a method for constructing a Liapunov function for an autonomous linear system with constant coefficients.

Consider the system

$$\dot{x} = Ax, \tag{2.21}$$

with A being an $n \times n$ constant matrix. To apply theorems 2.1, 2.2 and 2.3 we need a Liapunov function. Set

$$V(x) = x^T Bx, \tag{2.22}$$

where B is some $n \times n$ constant positive definite matrix and compute its time derivative

$$\dot{V}(x) = \frac{d}{dt}(x^T Bx) = \dot{x}^T Bx + x^T B\dot{x} = x^T (A^T B + BA)x. \tag{2.23}$$

The next lemma gives necessary and sufficient conditions for $V(x)$ to be a Liapunov function.

Lemma 2.1. Suppose A in (2.21) is a real $n \times n$ constant matrix such that $\det A \neq 0$. The matrix equation

$$A^T B + BA = -C \tag{2.24}$$

has a positive definite solution B for every positive definite matrix C if and only if all the eigenvalues of the matrix A have negative real parts.

Proof. Let C be a positive definite matrix and suppose that B is a positive definite solution of (2.24). Then $V(x)$ in (2.22) is positive definite and $\dot{V}(x)$ in (2.23) is negative definite. Therefore, by theorem 2.2, the 0-solution of $\dot{x} = Ax$ is asymptotically stable and from remark 4.1 of chapter 3 we conclude that the eigenvalues of the matrix A have negative real parts.

Conversely, suppose that the eigenvalues of A have negative real parts and let C be a given positive definite matrix. Recall that A^T denotes the transpose of A and define

$$B = \int_0^\infty e^{A^T t} C e^{At} dt. \tag{2.25}$$

Since, by hypothesis, A has negative real parts there are positive constants K and α such that $|e^{At}| \leq K e^{-\alpha t}$, $t \geq 0$. Thus the integral in (2.25) converges and thus B is well defined. Also, from its definition in (2.25), B is positive definite because by hypothesis C is positive definite, so that for any vector $y \in R^n$, $y \neq 0$,

$$y^T By = \int_0^\infty y^T e^{A^T t} C e^{At} y \, dt = \int_0^\infty (e^{At}y)^T C(e^{At}y) \, dt > 0.$$

Finally, B satisfies (2.24) since

$$A^T B + BA = \int_0^\infty \frac{d}{dt}[e^{A^T t} C e^{At}]\,dt = e^{A^T t} C e^{At}|_{t=0}^{t=\infty} = -C.$$

This completes the proof.

Example 2.5. Consider the linear system

$$\begin{bmatrix} \dot{x}_1 \\ \dot{x}_2 \end{bmatrix} = \begin{bmatrix} 0 & 1 \\ -1 & -2 \end{bmatrix}\begin{bmatrix} x_1 \\ x_2 \end{bmatrix},\tag{2.26}$$

which represents the second order homogeneous differential equation

$$\ddot{x} + 2\dot{x} + x = 0.$$

To study the stability properties of the 0-solution we have various techniques available. Consider, for instance, the eigenvalues of the matrix in (2.26). They are $\lambda_1 = \lambda_2 = -1$. Therefore, by theorem 4.1 of chapter 3, the 0-solution is asymptotically stable.

Next, consider the Routh–Hurwitz criterion of theorem 5.1 of chapter 3. Since $a_1 = 2 > 0$ and $a_1 a_2 - a_0 a_3 = (2 \cdot 1) - (1 \cdot 0) = 2 > 0$ we also conclude that the 0-solution is asymptotically stable.

To apply the Liapunov approach let $C \equiv I$, that is, let C be the identity matrix and use (2.24) to solve for $B = \begin{bmatrix} b_{11} & b_{12} \\ b_{21} & b_{22} \end{bmatrix}$

$$\begin{bmatrix} 0 & -1 \\ 1 & -2 \end{bmatrix}\begin{bmatrix} b_{11} & b_{12} \\ b_{21} & b_{22} \end{bmatrix} + \begin{bmatrix} b_{11} & b_{12} \\ b_{21} & b_{22} \end{bmatrix}\begin{bmatrix} 0 & 1 \\ -1 & -2 \end{bmatrix} = \begin{bmatrix} -1 & 0 \\ 0 & -1 \end{bmatrix}.$$

Carrying out the two multiplications and the addition in the above equation we get four equations to solve for four unknowns. The solution is

$$B = \begin{bmatrix} \frac{3}{2} & \frac{1}{2} \\ \frac{1}{2} & \frac{1}{2} \end{bmatrix}.\tag{2.27}$$

Therefore, for B as above $V(x) = x^T B x > 0$ and $\dot{V}(x) = -x^T C \dot{x} < 0$ for $x \in R^2$ and $x \neq 0$ and by theorem 2.2 the 0-solution is asymptotically stable. Note that since I is symmetric, B in (2.27) is also symmetric.

In this example we reviewed two methods exposited in chapter 3 and the Liapunov method. The purpose of presenting all three methods is to show that the Liapunov approach is more complicated when applied to linear systems with constant coefficients than either the eigenvalue method or the

Routh-Hurwitz criterion. The advantage of the Liapunov method becomes evident when, instead of considering a linear system as (2.21), we apply the Liapunov method of lemma 2.1 to the equation

$$\dot{x} = Ax + h(x). \tag{2.28}$$

Recall that (2.28) is the same as (4.10) of the previous chapter. Furthermore, recall that a proof of theorem 4.2 is pending. Our immediate purpose now is to illustrate the usefulness of the Liapunov method in determining the stability properties of a linearized system such as (2.28). Actually, the following analysis is more than an illustration; it is a proof for theorem 4.2 of the previous chapter.

Suppose that $h(x)$ in (2.28) has continuous first derivatives in R^n with $h(0) = 0$ and $\partial h(0)/\partial x = 0$. Let I be the identity matrix which is positive definite and suppose that the eigenvalues of A have negative real parts. Then, there is a positive, symmetric, definite matrix B such that $A^T B + BA = -I$. Put $V(x) = x^T Bx$ and compute $\dot{V}(x)$ for (2.28), using the definition in (1.3) of the previous section

$$\dot{V}(x) = \nabla V(x) \cdot \dot{x} = 2x^T B(Ax + h(x)) = 2x^T BAx + 2x^T Bh(x)$$

$$= x^T(A^T B + BA)x + 2x^T Bh(x) = -x^T x + 2x^T Bh(x). \tag{2.29}$$

To determine that $\dot{V}(x)$ in (2.29) is negative definite we need the following lemma. Note that $W(x) = o(|x|^p)$ as $|x| \to 0$ means that $(W(x)/|x|^p) \to 0$ as $|x| \to 0$.

Lemma 2.2.   Let $V_p(x)$ be a homogeneous positive definite polynomial of degree p, and also let $W(x) = o(|x|^p)$ as $|x| \to 0$ be continuous. Then

$$V(x) = V_p(x) + W(x) \tag{2.30}$$

is positive definite in a neighborhood of the origin.

Proof.   Let $k = \min_{|x|=1} V_p(x)$. Since $V_p(x)$ is positive definite $k > 0$ and since $V_p(x)$ is homogeneous of degree p, for any $x \neq 0$,

$$V_p(x) = V_p\left(\frac{|x|x}{|x|}\right) = V_p\left(\frac{x}{|x|}\right)|x|^p \geq k|x|^p.$$

From the hypothesis about $W(x)$ for any given $\varepsilon > 0$, there is a $\delta(\varepsilon) > 0$ such that if $|x| < \delta(\varepsilon)$ we have $|W(x)| < \varepsilon|x|^p$. Choose $\delta(k/2)$ and for $0 < |x| < \delta(k/2)$ conclude that

$$V(x) \geq V_p(x) - |W(x)| \geq k|x|^p - (k/2)|x|^p = (k/2)|x|^p = \varepsilon|x|^p.$$

Thus $V(x)$ is positive definite in a neighborhood of the origin.

With the help of lemma 2.2, we conclude that $-\dot{V}(x)$ in (2.29) is positive definite in a neighborhood of the 0-solution of (2.28). Therefore for the 0-solution of (2.28), $V(x) = x^T B x$ is positive definite and $\dot{V}(x)$ in (2.29) is negative definite and by theorem 2.2 the 0-solution is asymptotically stable.

If, on the other hand, no eigenvalue of A has a zero real part and an eigenvalue of A has positive real part, then we conclude, as in theorem 4.2 part (ii) of the previous chapter, that the 0-solution of (2.28) is unstable. To establish this result without loss of generality, assume that the matrix A is in Jordan canonical form, as in section 5 of chapter 2, with two blocks. The first block A_1 consists of all the eigenvalues having negative real part and the second block A_2 consists of all the eigenvalues having positive real part. This way we can apply lemma 2.1 twice in the following manner. Let B_1 be a positive definite solution of $A_1^T B_1 + B_1 A_1 = -I$ and let B_2 likewise be a positive definite solution of $(-A_2^T) B_2 + B_2 (-A_2) = -I$. Define the Liapunov function

$$V(x) = -x_1^T B_1 x_1 + x_2^T B_2 x_2, \tag{2.31}$$

where $x = (x_1, x_2)$ with x_1 and x_2 having the same dimensions as B_1 and B_2 respectively. Computing $\dot{V}(x)$ of $V(x)$ as in (2.31) for $\dot{x}$ as in (2.28) obtain that

$$\dot{V}(x) = -x^T x + o(|x|^2) \quad \text{as } |x| \to 0.$$

By lemma 2.2, $\dot{V}(x)$ is positive definite in a neighborhood of the 0-solution of (2.28) and by theorem 2.3 the 0-solution is unstable.

Thus, the analysis beginning after (2.28) establishes theorem 4.2 of the previous chapter. Since (2.28) arises from the linearization of the nonlinear autonomous system $\dot{x} = f(x)$, we can restate theorem 4.2, which has just been proved, as follows.

Theorem 2.4. Consider the autonomous system $\dot{x} = f(x)$ and suppose that $f(x)$ is continuously differentiable on a set D containing the origin and also $f(0) = 0$. Then

(i) if all the real parts of the eigenvalues of the Jacobian $f_x(0)$ are negative, the 0-solution is asymptotically stable.

(ii) if some eigenvalue of the Jacobian $f_x(0)$ has positive real part, the 0-solution is unstable.

Example 2.6. Consider the nonlinear system

$$\begin{aligned} \dot{x}_1 &= x_2 - x_1^2, \\ \dot{x}_2 &= -x_1 - 2x_2 - x_2^2, \end{aligned} \tag{2.32}$$

and study its stability properties. Note that (2.32) can be put immediately
in the form of (2.28)

$$\begin{bmatrix} \dot{x}_1 \\ \dot{x}_2 \end{bmatrix} = \begin{bmatrix} 0 & 1 \\ -1 & -2 \end{bmatrix} \begin{bmatrix} x_1 \\ x_2 \end{bmatrix} + \begin{bmatrix} -x_1^2 \\ -x_2^2 \end{bmatrix}. \tag{2.33}$$

From the analysis in example 2.5 we conclude that we can apply the
Liapunov approach with $C \equiv I$ to solve for B given by (2.27). Therefore,
for system (2.32) choose as $V(x)$ the following:

$$V(x_1, x_2) = [x_1 \quad x_2] \begin{bmatrix} \frac{3}{2} & \frac{1}{2} \\ \frac{1}{2} & \frac{1}{2} \end{bmatrix} \begin{bmatrix} x_1 \\ x_2 \end{bmatrix} = \frac{3}{2}x_1^2 + x_1 x_2 + \frac{1}{2}x_2^2. \tag{2.34}$$

To compute $\dot{V}(x)$ use (2.29) to obtain

$$\dot{V}(x_1, x_2) = -[x_1 \quad x_2] \begin{bmatrix} x_1 \\ x_2 \end{bmatrix} + 2[x_1 \quad x_2] \begin{bmatrix} \frac{3}{2} & \frac{1}{2} \\ \frac{1}{2} & \frac{1}{2} \end{bmatrix} \begin{bmatrix} -x_1^2 \\ -x_2^2 \end{bmatrix}$$

$$= -(x_1^2 + x_2^2) - (3x_1^3 + x_1^2 x_2 + x_1 x_2^2 + x_2^3). \tag{2.35}$$

From lemma 2.1 observe that B in (2.27) is positive definite so that (2.34)
is $V(x) > 0$ for $x \neq 0$ and $V(0) = 0$. Also from lemma 2.2 conclude that
$\dot{V}(x) < 0$ for $x \neq 0$ and $\dot{V}(0) = 0$. Therefore, the 0-solution of (2.32) is
asymptotically stable by theorem 2.2. The same conclusion is also obtained
from theorem 2.4(i).

This example illustrates the usefulness of the Liapunov method in determining the stability properties of a nonlinear system, by using a Liapunov
function obtained from the linearized part of the system via lemma 2.1. The
same example can be worked out using theorem 4.2 of the previous chapter
to obtain the eigenvalues of A and to check the properties of $h(x)$. Although
it is usually easier to compute the eigenvalues of A and use theorem 4.2,
the Liapunov approach provides the researcher with a second option and
indeed it is by the help of the Liapunov approach that theorem 4.2 is proved.
Of course, both the eigenvalue method and the Liapunov method for systems
such as (2.21) or (2.28) are connected by lemma 2.1.

Remark 2.3. Hahn (1963, p. 27) uses the concept of *significant* or *noncritical
behavior* to describe the case when the matrix A of the linear system $\dot{x} = Ax$
has either all eigenvalues with negative real part or at least one eigenvalue
with positive real part. Using this terminology, we can rephrase theorem
4.2 of the previous chapter or theorem 2.4 by saying that if the stability
behavior of $\dot{x} = Ax$ is significant then for $h(x) = o(|x|)$ the stability behavior

of $\dot{x} = Ax + h(x)$ is also significant. When the behavior of A is not *significant*, often times, it is called *critical*. That is, A has critical behavior when none of its eigenvalues have a positive real part with some having zero real part and some negative real part. As was pointed out earlier, when A has a critical behavior we cannot automatically deduce the stability properties of $\dot{x} = Ax + h(x)$. Recall example 2.1 in this section where the nonlinear part plays a critical role in determining the stability properties of the entire system.

Example 2.7. We close this section by studying the stability properties of the Lotka-Volterra system which represents population changes for two competing species:

$$\dot{x}_1 = k_1 x_1 (1 - c_{11} x_1 - c_{12} x_2),$$
$$\dot{x}_2 = k_2 x_2 (1 - c_{21} x_1 - c_{22} x_2). \tag{2.36}$$

Assume that all six constants are positive, $c_{11} > c_{21}$, $c_{22} > c_{12}$, $x_1 > 0$ and also that $x_2 > 0$.

Before we can determine the stability properties of this system we need to find the equilibrium states. Set $\dot{x}_1 = \dot{x}_2 = 0$ in (2.36) to obtain four equilibria: $(0, 0)$; $(0, 1/c_{22})$; $(1/c_{11}, 0)$ and $([c_{22} - c_{12}]/[c_{11}c_{22} - c_{12}c_{21}], [c_{11} - c_{21}]/[c_{11}c_{22} - c_{12}c_{21}])$.

First, for $(0, 0)$ consider

$$V(x_1, x_2) = \tfrac{1}{2}(x_1^2 + x_2^2),$$

$$\dot{V}(x_1, x_2) = x_1 \dot{x}_1 + x_2 \dot{x}_2 = x_1 [k_1 x_1 (1 - c_{11} x_1 - c_{12} x_2)]$$
$$+ x_2 [k_2 x_2 (1 - c_{21} x_1 - c_{22} x_2)].$$

Note that for small values of $x_1, x_2, (x_1, x_2) \neq (0, 0)$, V and $\dot{V}$ are positive definite and therefore $(0, 0)$ is unstable.

Second, for the equilibrium $(0, 1/c_{22})$ apply the translation $y_2 = x_2 - (1/c_{22})$. By assumption $x_1 \geq 0$, $0 < c_{12} < c_{22}$; therefore, for all (x_1, y_2) sufficiently close to the origin we get that $\dot{x}_1 > 0$. Let $V(x_1, y_2) = x_1$, D is a neighborhood of the origin,

$$D = \{(x_1, y_2) : \dot{x}_1 > 0\} \cup \{(x_1, y_2) : x_1 = 0\} \quad \text{and} \quad U = \{(x_1, y_2) : x_1 > 0\}.$$

Then the closure of U contains the origin, $V(x_1, y_2)$ and $\dot{V}(x_1, y_2)$ are positive on $U \cap D - \{0\}$, $V(x_1, y_2) = 0$ on the boundary of U inside D. Thus, the equilibrium $(0, 1/c_{22})$ is unstable.

Third, the equilibrium $(1/c_{11}, 0)$ is unstable using an analysis similar to the second case. For the fourth equilibrium point denote

$$z_1 = [c_{22} - c_{12}]/[c_{11}c_{22} - c_{12}c_{21}]; \quad z_2 = [c_{11} - c_{21}]/[c_{11}c_{22} - c_{12}c_{21}]$$

and apply the translation

$$y_1 = x_1 - z_1; \quad y_2 = x_2 - z_2. \tag{2.37}$$

Using (2.37), rewrite (2.36) as

$$\begin{aligned}
\dot{y}_1 &= -k_1(y_1 + z_1)(c_{11}y_1 + c_{12}y_2), \\
\dot{y}_2 &= -k_2(y_2 + z_2)(c_{21}y_1 + c_{22}y_2),
\end{aligned} \tag{2.38}$$

with equilibrium $(y_1, y_2) = (0, 0)$. Put (2.38) in matrix form as in (2.28) by writing

$$\begin{bmatrix} \dot{y}_1 \\ \dot{y}_2 \end{bmatrix} = \begin{bmatrix} -k_1 z_1 c_{11} & -k_2 z_1 c_{12} \\ -k_2 z_2 c_{21} & -k_2 z_2 c_{22} \end{bmatrix} \begin{bmatrix} y_1 \\ y_2 \end{bmatrix} + \begin{bmatrix} -k_1 y_1(c_{11}y_1 + c_{12}y_2) \\ -k_2 y_2(c_{21}y_1 + c_{22}y_2) \end{bmatrix}.$$

Note that in this last equation the nonlinear term approaches zero as $(y_1, y_2) \rightarrow (0, 0)$. Also, solving $\det(\lambda I - A)$, with A being the linear part of this last equation we obtain that the eigenvalues of A have negative real parts. Therefore the equilibrium (z_1, z_2) is stable.

3. Local stability for nonautonomous systems

Theorems 2.1, 2.2 and 2.3 of the previous section can be extended easily to nonautonomous systems. This section collects the appropriate definitions and states theorems on the stability properties of nonautonomous systems. The proofs are similar to the ones presented earlier, the only difference being that some attention is required to see that things happen uniformly in the time variable t.

Consider the nonautonomous system

$$\dot{x} = f(t, x), f(t, 0) = 0 \quad \text{for } t \geq 0, \tag{3.1}$$

where $f:[0, \infty) \times R^n \rightarrow R^n$ is continuously differentiable so that solutions exist, are unique and also depend continuously upon initial data. Several useful definitions are collected below.

Definitions 3.1. Let D be an open subset of R^n that contains the origin. A function $V(t, x):[0, \infty) \times D \rightarrow R$ is *positive definite* if $V(t, x)$ is continuous in (t, x), $V(t, 0) = 0$ for all $t \geq 0$ and there is a positive definite function

$W(x): D \to R$ such that $V(t, x) \ge W(x)$ for all $(t, x) \in [0, \infty) \times D$. A continuous function $V(t, x):[0, \infty) \times D \to R$ is *positive semidefinite* if $V(t, 0) = 0$ for all $t \ge 0$ and $V(t, x) \ge 0$ for $(t, x) \in [0, \infty) \times D$. A function $V(t, x):[0, \infty) \times D \to R$ is *decrescent* if it is continuous in (t, x) and there exists a positive definite function $U(x): D \to R$ such that $|V(t, x)| \le U(x)$ for all $(t, x) \in [0, \infty) \times D$. Assuming that $V(t, x)$ is continuously differentiable so that it has continuous partial derivatives with respect to both (t, x), we define the *time derivative along the trajectories* of (3.1) as

$$\dot{V}(t, x) = \frac{\partial V(t, x)}{\partial t} + \frac{\partial V(t, x)}{\partial x} f(t, x) = \frac{\partial V(t, x)}{\partial t} + \nabla V(t, x) f(t, x). \quad (3.2)$$

Note, once again, that the time derivative of $V(t, x)$ given in (3.2) is computed without having to solve the ordinary differential equation in (3.1).

Example 3.1. Let $D \subset R^2$ be a small neighborhood of the origin. The function

$$V(t, x) = x_1^2(1 + \sin^2 t) + x_2^2(1 + \cos^2 t)$$

is positive definite and decrescent for $(t, x) \in [0, \infty) \times D$. On the other hand, the function

$$V(t, x) = e^t(x_1^2 + x_2^2)$$

is positive definite but it is not decrescent for $(t, x) \in [0, \infty) \times D$. Finally the function

$$V(t, x) = (x_1 - x_2)^2/(1 + t)$$

is positive semidefinite but it is not decrescent for $(t, x) \in [0, \infty) \times D$.

Remark 3.1. It is helpful in the analysis of the stability properties of a nonautonomous system to have equivalent definitions for positive definite and decrescent. To formulate such equivalent definitions the key idea is the notion of a strictly increasing continuous function. More specifically, for some real $r > 0$ let $g(x):[0, r] \to [0, \infty)$ denote an arbitrary continuous function that is strictly increasing on $[0, r]$ with $g(0) = 0$. It is easy to show that a continuous $V(t, x):[0, \infty) \times D \to R$ is *positive definite* if and only if $V(t, 0) = 0$ for all $t \ge 0$, and that for some $r > 0$ it follows that $V(t, x) \ge g(|x|)$ for all $(t, x) \in [0, \infty) \times D$. Note that $D \subset \{x \in R^n : |x| < r\}$. Also, a continuous function $V(t, x):[0, \infty) \times D \to R$ is *decrescent* if and only if $|V(t, x)| \le g(|x|)$ for all $(t, x) \in [0, \infty) \times D$ for some $r > 0$ with $D \subset \{x \in R^n : |x| < r\}$.

Next we state theorem 3.1.

Theorem 3.1.   (Liapunov stability for nonautonomous systems.)   Suppose
that there is a continuously differentiable positive definite function
$V(t, x):[0, \infty) \times D \to R$ such that $\dot{V}(t, x) \leq 0$. Then the 0-solution of $\dot{x} =$
$f(t, x)$ in (3.1) is stable.

Proof.   The proof is similar to the proof of theorem 2.1 in the preceding
section with additional attention paid to the variable t. Using remark 3.1,
let $g(x):[0, r] \to [0, \infty)$ be a continuous function that is strictly increasing
with $g(0) = 0$, such that $V(t, x) \geq g(|x|)$ for $0 \leq |x| < r$ and $t \geq 0$.
  Let $\varepsilon > 0$ and $t_0 \geq 0$ be given with $\varepsilon < r$. We need to show that there is a
$\delta = \delta(\varepsilon, t_0)$ such that if $|x_0| < \delta$ then $|x(t, t_0, x_0)| < \varepsilon$ for all $t \geq t_0$. Since
$V(t, x)$ is continuous with $V(t, 0) = 0$ for all $t \geq 0$ we can choose δ to be so
small that if $|x_0| < \delta$ then $V(t_0, x_0) < g(\varepsilon)$. For δ thus chosen we conclude
that $|x(t, t_0, x_0)| < \varepsilon$ because $\dot{V}(t, x) \leq 0$ so that $V(t, x(t, t_0, x_0))$ is nonin-
creasing with $V(t, x(t, t_0, x_0)) < g(\varepsilon)$ for $t \geq t_0$. This completes the proof.

  The following three theorems summarize the stability and instability
properties of the *nonautonomous* systems. Proofs are similar to the ones
presented in the previous section and are omitted. The interested reader
can find these proofs in Hahn (1967, pp. 198–204).

Theorem 3.2.   (Uniform stability.)   Suppose that there is a continuously
differentiable, positive definite, decrescent function $V(t, x):[0, \infty) \times D \to R$
with $\dot{V}(t, x) \leq 0$. Then the 0-solution of $\dot{x} = f(t, x)$ in (3.1) is *uniformly stable*.

Theorem 3.3.   (Uniform asymptotic stability.)   Suppose that there is a
continuously differentiable, positive definite, decrescent function $V(t, x):$
$[0, \infty) \times D \to R$ with $-\dot{V}(t, x)$ positive definite. Then the 0-solution of $\dot{x} =$
$f(t, x)$ in (3.1) is *uniformly asymptotically stable*.

Theorem 3.4.   (Instability for nonautonomous systems.)   Suppose that
there is a continuously differentiable decrescent function $V(t, x):[0, \infty) \times$
$D \to R$ such that in every neighborhood of the origin there are points x such
that $V(t, x) > 0$ with $\dot{V}(t, x) > 0$. Then the 0-solution is *unstable*.

  To illustrate these theorems we present three examples.

Example 3.2.   For the nonautonomous system

$$\dot{x}_1 = x_2,$$
$$\dot{x}_2 = -x_2 - e^{-t}x_1, \tag{3.3}$$

consider the Liapunov function

$$V(t, x_1, x_2) = x_1^2 + e^t x_2^2 \tag{3.4}$$

and compute the time derivative of (3.4) using (3.2). It is given by

$$\dot{V}(t, x_1, x_2) = 2x_1\dot{x}_1 + e^t x_2^2 + 2x_2\dot{x}_2 e^t$$

$$= 2x_1 x_2 + e^t x_2^2 + 2x_2 e^t(-x_2 - e^{-t}x_1) = -x_2^2 e^t.$$

Since $V(t, x_1, x_2)$ in (3.4) is positive definite and $\dot{V}(t, x_1, x_2) \leq 0$, we conclude by theorem 3.1 that the 0-solution of (3.3) is stable. Furthermore, observe that although $V > 0$ and $\dot{V} \leq 0$ we cannot use theorem 3.2 to conclude the uniform stability of the 0-solution because V in (3.4) is not decrescent.

It may be instructive to note that the stability of the 0-solution of (3.3) can also be established using exercise 10 of the previous chapter. The linear part of (3.3) is

$$\begin{bmatrix} \dot{x}_1 \\ \dot{x}_2 \end{bmatrix} = \begin{bmatrix} 0 & 1 \\ 0 & -1 \end{bmatrix} \begin{bmatrix} x_1 \\ x_2 \end{bmatrix} \tag{3.5}$$

with eigenvalues $\lambda_1 = 0$ and $\lambda_2 = -1$. Therefore (3.5) is stable. Furthermore since the nonlinear part of (3.3) is bounded and $\int_0^\infty e^{-t} \, dt = 1$ we conclude by exercise 10 that the 0-solution of (3.3) is stable.

Example 3.3. Suppose that $a(t) > 0$ and $\dot{a}(t) > 0$ for $t \in [0, \infty)$. We want to show that the 0-solution of the second order nonlinear equation

$$\ddot{x} + a(t)x = 0 \tag{3.6}$$

is stable. Let

$$V(x) = x^2 + \frac{\dot{x}^2}{a} \geq 0$$

and compute

$$\dot{V}(x) = 2x\dot{x} + [(2\ddot{x}\dot{x}a - \dot{x}^2\dot{a})/a^2]$$

$$= 2x\dot{x} + [(2a\dot{x}(-ax) - \dot{x}^2\dot{a})/a^2] = -\dot{x}^2\dot{a}/a^2 \leq 0.$$

Therefore by theorem 3.1, the 0-solution is stable for x in a small neighborhood of the origin.

Example 3.4.   Consider the system reported in Hahn (1967, p. 204)

$$\dot{x} = a(t)y + b(t)x[x^2 + y^2],$$
$$\dot{y} = -a(t)x + b(t)y[x^2 + y^2]. \qquad (3.7)$$

Note that (3.7) generalizes example (4.8) of the previous chapter and is related to example 2.1 of the previous section. Use

$$V(t, x, y) = \tfrac{1}{2}(x^2 + y^2)$$

and compute

$$\dot{V}(t, x, y) = x\dot{x} + y\dot{y} = x\{a(t)y + b(t)x[x^2 + y^2]\}$$
$$+ y\{-a(t)x + b(t)y[x^2 + y^2]\}$$
$$= b(t)(x^2 + y^2)^2.$$

If $b(t) \leq 0$ then the 0-equilibrium is uniformly stable. If $b(t) > 0$ then the 0-equilibrium is unstable. If $b(t) < 0$ then the 0-equilibrium is uniformly asymptotically stable.

4. Global asymptotic stability

The previous chapter and the preceding sections have presented several theorems on *local* stability and asymptotic stability for both autonomous and nonautonomous systems. The exposition of these theorems has been mathematical in scope and no emphasis has been given to an evaluation of the various stability properties. Actually, the numerous books that treat stability from a strictly mathematical point of view consider it beyond their scope to express any nonmathematical opinions about the relative appropriateness of the stability notions in applications.

As is mentioned elsewhere in this book, our study of stability is motivated by reasons that go beyond its intrinsic mathematical interest. Our goal is to illustrate that the analysis of dynamic economic models benefits from the methods of stability theory. Actually, unless dynamic economic models are analyzed for the existence, uniqueness and stability properties of the equilibrium solution, how could such models be helpful in guiding the theorist's deductions and the policy maker's recommendations? Therefore, it is relevant for the economic theorist to reflect on the relative importance of the various stability concepts.

In economic applications it is not difficult to find reasons to argue that asymptotic stability is more important than stability. For example, suppose that a dynamic macroeconomic model has a unique equilibrium rate of inflation of 5%. Stability means that inflation will fluctuate around 5%, assuming the system starts with an inflation rate close to 5%; asymptotic stability means that inflation will actually converge to 5%, instead of just closely fluctuating around it. If the goal of economic policy is to reduce inflation fluctuations, then a preference may be expressed for the asymptotic stability property of the equilibrium solution.

Although asymptotic stability may be moderately more important than stability, it still remains a narrow concept for economic applications. In practice, it may not be possible to adjust a system initially to be very close to its equilibrium. The desirable notion of stability in such cases is *global asymptotic stability*. This notion describes the property of a dynamic system that converges to its equilibrium, independent of its initial state. The terms *asymptotic stability in the large* or *complete stability* are also used by some authors. This section is devoted to this important kind of stability. We first discuss the autonomous case.

As in earlier sections, consider

$$\dot{x} = f(x), \quad f(0) = 0 \quad \text{for } t \geq 0, \tag{4.1}$$

where $f(x): R^n \to R^n$ is assumed to be continuously differentiable with a unique equilibrium at the origin. We say that the 0-solution of (4.1) is *globally asymptotically stable* (also *stable in the large* or *completely stable*) if for any $x_0 \in R^n$ the solution $\phi(t, t_0, x_0)$ exists for $t \geq 0$ and $\phi(t, t_0, x_0) \to 0$ as $t \to \infty$. Recall that we denote the solution $\phi(t, t_0, x_0)$ also as $\phi(t)$ or $x(t)$ by suppressing the initial data. Usually we take $t_0 = 0$ and global asymptotic stability describes the notion that any solution will converge to the 0-solution independent of the x_0 where it starts.

Example 4.1. The simplest example of a globally asymptotically stable 0-solution is the equation

$$\dot{x} = \lambda x$$

which has a solution, obtained by integration and given by,

$$\phi(t, 0, x_0) \equiv x(t) = x_0 e^{\lambda t}, \quad x(0) = x_0, \quad t \geq 0. \tag{4.2}$$

If λ is a negative real number then we conclude from (4.2) that the 0-solution is globally asymptotically stable because for any $x_0 \in R$, $x(t) \to 0$ as $t \to \infty$. If $\lambda = 0$ then (4.2) becomes $x(t) = x_0$, $t \geq 0$ and the 0-solution *is stable* for small x_0 but it *is not globally asymptotically stable*. If $\lambda > 0$ then the 0-solution is unstable.

Example 4.2.   Here we give an example of an ordinary differential equation in which the 0-solution is locally asymptotically stable but not globally asymptotically stable. Consider

$$\dot{x} = -x + x^2 \tag{4.3}$$

which upon integration becomes

$$\int \frac{1}{-x + x^2} \, dx = \int dt.$$

Use the method of partial fractions from the theory of integration in elementary calculus to rewrite the last equation as

$$\int \frac{1}{-x + x^2} \, dx = \int \left[\frac{-1}{x} + \frac{1}{x-1} \right] dx = \int dt.$$

Integrate this last equation from 0 to t, to obtain

$$-\ln x(t) + \ln x(0) + \ln[x(t) - 1] - \ln[x(0) - 1] = t$$

which yields the solution for $t = 0$ and $x(0) = x_0$

$$x(t) = \frac{1}{1 + [(1/x_0) - 1] \, e^t}. \tag{4.4}$$

From (4.3) conclude that $x = 0$ and $x = 1$ are the two equilibrium solutions of that equation. From (4.4) observe that as x_0 is chosen close to the 0-solution, then $x(t) \to 0$ as $t \to \infty$ and thus conclude that the 0-solution is *asymptotically stable*. However, the 0-solution is *not globally asymptotically stable*; for example, if we choose $x_0 = 1$ then it is not true that $x(t)$ in (4.4) will approach zero as $t \to \infty$. For $x_0 = 1$ obtain from (4.4) that $x(t) = 1$ as $t \to \infty$. Therefore, *local stability does not imply global stability*.

It is also true that global stability need not imply local stability. For example imagine, in the simple two dimensional space (t, x), solution curves that are defined for all $x_0 \in R$ and $t \geq 0$ which have the following property: no matter how small x_0 is chosen the solution $\phi(t, 0, x_0)$ grows rapidly before it decays approaching zero as $t \to \infty$. This behavior implies that the 0-solution is globally asymptotically stable but not stable, because for any given $\varepsilon > 0$, no matter how small an x_0 we choose, the solution $|\phi(t, 0, x_0)| > \varepsilon$ for values of t in some subinterval of $[0, \infty)$.

To proceed with various results on global asymptotic stability we need some topological definitions and a lemma about the limit properties of orbits.

Definitions 4.1. Consider the autonomous differential system

$$\dot{x} = f(x), \tag{4.5}$$

where $f(x): D \subset R^n \to R^n$ is continuous and D is an open set in R^n. Assume that for any point $p \in D$, there exists a unique solution $\phi(t, t_0, p)$ of (4.5) going through p at time t_0. It is no loss of generality to let $t_0 = 0$ and to write $\phi(t, 0, p)$ as $\phi(t, p)$. The solution $\phi(t, p)$ of (4.5) going through p at $t_0 = 0$ can be viewed as a function of (t, p) which has certain properties. More specifically, let G be an open subset of $(-\infty, \infty) \times R^n$ and consider the function

$$\phi(t, p): G \subset (-\infty, \infty) \times R^n \to R^n. \tag{4.6}$$

This function $\phi(t, p)$ satisfies three properties:

1. $\phi(0, p) = p$;
2. $\phi(t, p)$ is continuous on $G \subset R^{n+1}$;
3. $\phi(t + s, p) = \phi(t, \phi(s, p))$ for any real number s on $G \subset R^{n+1}$.

For the purpose of analyzing the global asymptotic stability property of (4.5) we assume that $f: R^n \to R^n$ satisfies enough conditions to ensure that the solution $\phi(t, p)$ going through p at $t_0 = 0$ is defined for all $t \in (-\infty, \infty)$, all $p \in R^n$ and properties 1, 2 and 3 hold. For a given point p, the *path* or *orbit* associated with it is denoted by $\gamma(p)$ and defined as

$$\gamma(p) = \{x \in R^n : x = \phi(t, p), t \in (-\infty, \infty)\}. \tag{4.7}$$

From the uniqueness property of solutions we deduce that for a given p there is a unique orbit $\gamma(p)$ going through this point. Put differently, no two orbits can intersect. The reader may recall that the notion of an orbit as trajectory into R^n is introduced in section 6 of the previous chapter. Here we review this notion by defining an orbit as the range of the solution $\phi(t, p)$ in the x-space.

The *positive semiorbit* through p is denoted by $\gamma^+(p)$ and defined as

$$\gamma^+(p) = \{x \in R^n : x = \phi(t, p), t \geq 0\} \tag{4.8}$$

and, similarly, we define

$$\gamma^-(p) = \{x \in R^n : x = \phi(t, p), t \leq 0\} \tag{4.9}$$

to be the *negative semiorbit* through the point p. We denote γ, γ^+ or γ^- the orbit, positive semiorbit or negative semiorbit with no reference to a specific point p.

The *positive limiting* or ω-*limit set* of an orbit of (4.5) is denoted by $\omega(\gamma^+)$ and defined as

$$\omega(\gamma^+) = \{y \in R^n : \text{there exists an increasing sequence of times}$$
$$\{t_k\}, t_k \to \infty \text{ as } k \to \infty, \text{ such that } \phi(t_k, p) \to y \text{ as } k \to \infty\}. \quad (4.10)$$

Similarly, the negative limiting or α-*limit set* is defined in the same way as (4.10) with the only exception that t is replaced by $-t$.

Finally, a set $M \subset R^n$ is called an *invariant set* for (4.5) if for any $p \in M$, then $\phi(t, p) \in M$ for all $t \in (-\infty, \infty)$. Observe from the definitions given that any orbit is an invariant set. In other words, an invariant set M is characterized by the property that if a point p is in M then its whole forward and backward path lies in M. The properties of the ω-limit set are summarized in the following lemma.

Lemma 4.1. The ω-limit set of an orbit γ of an autonomous system (4.5) is closed and invariant. Also, if the positive semiorbit, γ^+, is bounded, then the ω-limit set is nonempty, compact, connected and the distance between $\phi(t, p)$, and $\omega(\gamma^+)$ approaches 0 as $t \to \infty$.

For a proof see Hale (1969, p. 47).

Having introduced the concept of global asymptotic stability and made several essential definitions we are now ready to state and prove a few theorems. These theorems follow either the Liapunov methodology or state conditions involving the Jacobian matrix $J(x)$ of $\dot{x} = f(x)$ in (4.5). The theorems that follow the Liapunov methodology rely on the concept of the Liapunov function. Recall from section 1, that a scalar function $V(x): D \subset R^n \to R, 0 \in D$, is a *Liapunov function* if $V(x)$ is positive definite and its trajectory derivative $\dot{V}(x)$ is negative semidefinite for $x \in D$. For the theorems that state conditions involving the Jacobian of $f(x)$ we note that the Jacobian matrix is the matrix of first-order partial derivatives, that is, $J(x) \equiv [\partial f(x)/\partial x] \equiv [\partial f_i(x)/\partial x_j]$, where $i, j = 1, 2, \ldots, n$. The criteria for global asymptotic stability that make use of the Jacobian, reduce to conditions involving one of the two inequalities

$$J(x)f(x) \cdot f(x) \leq 0, \quad (4.11)$$

or

$$\text{if } y \cdot f(x) = 0 \quad \text{then } J(x)y \cdot y \leq 0, \quad (4.12)$$

where a dot in (4.11) and (4.12) denotes scalar multiplication. Recall that if $x = [x_1, \ldots, x_n] \in R^n$ and $y = [y_1, \ldots, y_n] \in R^n$ are n-vectors then the *dot product* or *inner product* or *scalar multiplication* is given by

$$x \cdot y = \sum_1^n x_i y_i.$$

Most of the results that follow are relatively recent and have appeared in Hartman (1961), Hartman and Olech (1962), and Markus and Yamabe (1960). This section draws heavily from Hartman (1964, pp. 537-555), Hale (1969, pp. 296-299) and LaSalle and Lefschetz (1961, pp. 56-71).

Theorem 4.1. Let $f(x)$ of (4.5) be continuously differentiable on an open set $D \subset R^n$ and let $V(x)$ be a continuously differentiable real valued function on D such that $V(x) \geq 0$ and $\dot{V}(x) \leq 0$ for $x \in D$. Suppose that $\phi(t)$ is a solution of (4.5) for all $t \geq 0$ and suppose that x_0 is a point of the ω-limit set of $\phi(t)$ that lies in D. Then $\dot{V}(x_0) = 0$.

Proof. We need to show that if $x_0 \in \omega(\gamma^+)$ then $x_0 \in \{x : \dot{V}(x) = 0\}$. Since x_0 is an ω-limit point there exists a sequence $\{t_k\}$, $t_k \to \infty$, with $\phi(t_k) \to x_0$ as $k \to \infty$. Without loss of generality suppose that $t_k < t_{k+1}$. From the continuity of the Liapunov function obtain that $V(\phi(t_k)) \to V(x_0)$ as $k \to \infty$ and from the fact that $\dot{V} \leq 0$ conclude that

$$V(\phi(t_k)) \geq V(x_0) \quad \text{for } t_k \geq 0. \tag{4.13}$$

To show that $\dot{V}(x_0) = 0$, suppose that $\dot{V}(x_0) < 0$ and consider the solution $\phi(t, x_0)$ for $0 \leq t \leq \varepsilon$, where $\varepsilon > 0$ is small. From the assumption that $\dot{V}(x_0) < 0$ conclude that

$$V(\phi(t, x_0)) < V(x_0) \quad \text{for } 0 < t \leq \varepsilon. \tag{4.14}$$

The continuity of solutions on initial data theorem 7.1 of chapter 1 implies that if $|\phi(t_k) - x_0| \to 0$ as $k \to \infty$, then $|\phi(t, \phi(t_k)) - \phi(t, x_0)| \to 0$ uniformly for $t \in [0, \varepsilon]$. From the continuity of the Liapunov function we get that

$$|V[\phi(t, \phi(t_k))] - V[\phi(t, x_0)]| \to 0 \tag{4.15}$$

uniformly for $t \in [0, \varepsilon]$ as $k \to \infty$. In particular as $\phi(t_k) \to x_0$ for $k \to \infty$, (4.14) and (4.15) yield

$$V(\phi(\varepsilon + t_k)) < V(x_0),$$

for $t_k \geq 0$. However, this last equation is a contradiction to (4.13). Thus it is proved that $x_0 \in \{x : \dot{V}(x) = 0\}$.

Theorem 4.2. (Global asymptotic stability.) Let $f(x)$ of (4.5) be continuously differentiable on the whole R^n space and let $V(x)$ be a continuously differentiable real-valued function on R^n such that $V(x) \geq 0$, $\dot{V}(x) \leq 0$ for $x \in R^n$ and $V(x) \to \infty$ as $|x| \to \infty$. Then all solutions of $\dot{x} = f(x)$ exist on $[0, \infty)$ and are bounded, and if there exists a unique point x_0 such that $\dot{V}(x_0) = 0$, this x_0 is *globally asymptotically stable*.

Proof. Let $\phi(t, p)$ be a solution of $\dot{x} = f(x)$ for $p \in R^n$. The hypothesis that $V(x) \to \infty$ as $|x| \to \infty$ implies that $V[\phi(t, p)]$ exists and because $\dot{V}(x) \leq 0$ we conclude that $V[\phi(t, p)] \leq V[\phi(0, p)]$. Thus, all solutions exist on $[0, \infty)$ and are bounded. The boundedness of solutions means that there exists an ω-limit set in R^n which by the preceding theorem 4.1 is a subset of $\{x: \dot{V}(x) = 0\}$. However, by hypothesis there exists only one unique point x_0 such that $\dot{V}(x_0) = 0$, that is, $\{x: \dot{V}(x) = 0\} = \{x_0\}$. Therefore, we conclude that independent of the initial point $p \in R^n$ all solutions $\phi(t, p) \equiv \phi(t, 0, p) \to x_0$ which proves that x_0 is *globally asymptotically stable*.

Remark 4.1. Under the stated assumptions about f, V and $\dot{V}$ in theorem 4.2, the global asymptotic stability of x_0 can be restated using the notion of an invariant set M as follows: if the largest invariant set M consists only of the singleton $\{x_0\}$, that is, if $M = \{x_0\}$ then x_0 is globally asymptotically stable. This is true because as in the proof of theorem 4.2, the hypothesis that $V(x) \to \infty$ as $|x| \to \infty$ for $x \in R^n$ implies the boundedness of solutions independent of where they start in R^n, and the other assumptions about f and V imply that these bounded solutions approach the singleton $\{x_0\}$ as $t \to \infty$.

Remark 4.2. In the preceding theorem without loss of generality, assume that $\{x_0\} = \{0\}$, and strengthen the hypotheses by assuming that $V(x)$ is a Liapunov function, that is, by requiring that V is positive definite instead of positive semi-definite. Then we could conclude that the 0-solution is not only *globally* asymptotically stable but also *locally* stable from theorem 2.1 of this chapter. Furthermore, under this added assumption, we can also conclude that the 0-solution is *locally asymptotically stable* because *both* the local stability (from the assumption that V is a Liapunov function) and the global asymptotic stability (from theorem 4.2) imply local asymptotic stability.

Remark 4.3. Again with reference to theorem 4.2, assume that $\{x_0\} = \{0\}$, f and V are continuously differentiable on the whole R^n space and let $V(x) > 0$

for $x \neq 0$, $\dot{V}(x) < 0$ for $x \neq 0$ and $V(x) \to \infty$ as $|x| \to \infty$. Then the 0-solution of $\dot{x} = f(x)$ is *globally asymptotically stable*. This is true because here we have strengthened the assumption by requiring V to be a Liapunov function with $\dot{V}(x)$ negative definite for $x \neq 0$; this implies local asymptotic stability and the assumption $V(x) \to \infty$ as $|x| \to \infty$ implies boundedness of solutions; all together these hypotheses imply that, independent of the initial condition $x_0 \in R^n$ at $t = 0$, the solution $\phi(t, 0, x_0) \to 0$. Thus, the 0-solution is globally asymptotically stable.

Remark 4.4. We can also reason in the language of remark 4.1 as follows: assuming V to be a Liapunov function such that $V(x) \to \infty$ as $|x| \to \infty$ with $\dot{V}(x) < 0$, $x \neq 0$, $\dot{V}(0) = 0$, imply that all solutions are bounded and converge to the largest invariant singleton set $M = \{0\}$; therefore the 0-solution is *globally asymptotically stable*.

Example 4.3. Consider the Lienard equation

$$\ddot{x} + f(x)\dot{x} + g(x) = 0,$$

which can be written equivalently in system form as

$$\dot{x} = y,$$
$$\dot{y} = -g(x) - f(x)y. \tag{4.16}$$

Following LaSalle and Lefschetz (1961, pp. 67–68) or Hale (1969, p. 298) let the Liapunov function $V(x, y)$ be given by

$$V(x, y) = \tfrac{1}{2}y^2 + \int_0^x g(s)\, ds, \tag{4.17}$$

and its trajectory derivative is obtained immediately by

$$\dot{V}(x, y) = y\dot{y} + g(x)\dot{x} = y[-g(x) - f(x)y] + g(x)y = -f(x)y^2. \tag{4.18}$$

Assume that

(1) $xg(x) > 0$ for all $x \neq 0$;
(2) $f(x) > 0$ for all $x \neq 0$, and
(3) $\int_0^x g(s)\, ds \to \infty$ as $|x| \to \infty$.

These three assumptions imply that

(1) $V(x, y) \to \infty$ as $|x| \to \infty$;

(2) $V(x, y) > 0$ for all $(x, y) \neq (0, 0)$ with
      $V(0, 0) = 0$, and
(3) $\dot{V}(x, y) \leq 0$, and vanishing only on the axes
      $x = 0$ and $y = 0$.

Therefore, from theorem 2.1 we conclude that the 0-solution $(x, y) = (0, 0)$ is locally stable; from theorem 4.2 we conclude that the 0-solution is *globally* asymptotically stable and from remark 4.2 we also conclude that the 0-solution is *locally* asymptotically stable.

The next two theorems make use of the Jacobian of $f(x)$ and involve trivial generalizations of conditions (4.11) and (4.12). Specifically, assume that A is a $n \times n$ constant, real, symmetric, positive definite matrix. Conditions (4.11) and (4.12) can be replaced by

$$AJ(x)f(x) \cdot f(x) \leq 0 \tag{4.19}$$

or by

$$\text{if } Ay \cdot f(x) = 0 \quad \text{then } AJ(x)y \cdot y \leq 0. \tag{4.20}$$

The theorems below make use of (4.19) and (4.20) in the calculation of $\dot{V}(x)$ and afterwards appeal to theorem 4.2 to conclude the global asymptotic stability of the 0-solution of $\dot{x} = f(x)$.

Theorem 4.3.   (Global asymptotic stability.)   Suppose that $f(x)$ of (4.5) is continuously differentiable on the whole R^n space and $f(0) = 0$. Let A be an $n \times n$ constant, real, symmetric positive definite matrix and let the Jacobian matrix $J(x)$ satisfy for all points $x \neq 0$ and for all vectors $y \neq 0$,

$$AJ(x)y \cdot y < 0. \tag{4.21}$$

Then the 0-solution is *globally asymptotically stable*.

Proof.   Put

$$V(x) = Ax \cdot x \tag{4.22}$$

and observe that such V is positive definite and $V(x) \to \infty$ as $|x| \to \infty$. If it can be shown that $\dot{V}$ is negative definite using (4.21) we can conclude from theorem 4.2, or remark 4.3 that the 0-solution is globally asymptotically stable. Observe that for V as in (4.22),

$$\dot{V}(x) = 2Ax \cdot f(x). \tag{4.23}$$

To go from (4.23) to the desired result that $\dot{V}(x) < 0$ for $x \neq 0$ and $\dot{V}(0) = 0$, observe the following: for $0 \leq s \leq 1$ use the chain rule to write

$$\frac{d}{ds} f(sx) = J(sx)x,$$

which by integration yields

$$f(x) = \int_0^1 J(sx)x \, ds \tag{4.24}$$

because $f(0) = 0$. Put (4.24) into (4.23) and use the hypothesis (4.21) and the properties of the matrix A to conclude that

$$\dot{V}(x) = 2Ax \cdot f(x) = 2Ax \cdot \int_0^1 J(sx)x \, ds$$

$$= 2\int_0^1 [Ax \cdot J(sx)x] \, ds = 2\int_0^1 [AJ(sx)x \cdot x] \, ds < 0$$

if $x \neq 0$ and $\dot{V}(0) = 0$. Thus the 0-solution is *globally asymptotically stable*.

Theorem 4.4. (Global asymptotic stability.) Suppose that $f(x)$ of (4.5) is continuously differentiable on the whole R^n space and furthermore suppose that $|f(x)| \to \infty$ as $|x| \to \infty$. Let A be an $n \times n$ constant, real, symmetric positive definite matrix and let the Jacobian matrix $J(x)$ satisfy for $x \neq 0$

$$AJ(x)f(x) \cdot f(x) < 0. \tag{4.25}$$

Then $f(0) = 0$ and the 0-solution is *globally asymptotically stable*.

Proof. Use as a Liapunov function

$$V(x) = Af(x) \cdot f(x) \tag{4.26}$$

and compute

$$\dot{V}(x) = 2Af(x) \cdot J(x)f(x) = 2[AJ(x)f(x) \cdot f(x)] < 0$$

for $x \neq 0$ and $\dot{V}(0) = 0$. From (4.26) conclude that V is positive definite and $V \to \infty$ as $|x| \to \infty$ because $|f(x)| \to \infty$ as $|x| \to \infty$. Since $\dot{V}$ vanishes at zero then $f(0) = 0$, and from theorem 4.2 the 0-solution is globally asymptotically stable. Actually, the 0-solution is also locally asymptotically stable.

120   *Differential equations, stability and chaos in dynamic economics*

To state the next global asymptotic stability theorems we need a definition and a lemma from Hartman (1964, pp. 548–554). The *domain of attraction* of the 0-solution of $\dot{x} = f(x)$, where f is continuously differentiable on a domain D, means the set of points $x_0 \in D$ such that the solutions $\phi(t, 0, x_0)$ exist for $t \geq 0$ and $\phi(t, 0, x_0) \to 0$ as $t \to \infty$. From the continuity of solutions with respect to initial data and the assumed asymptotic stability of the 0-solution we note that the domain of attraction is an open set.

The next lemma and the theorem are due to Hartman and Olech (1962) and are reported in Hartman (1964). Both lemma 4.2 and theorem 4.5 have found many applications in capital theory and several results are presented in chapter 9.

Lemma 4.2.   Let $f(x) \neq 0$ be continuously differentiable on an open and connected set E and suppose that

$$J(x)y \cdot y \leq 0 \quad \text{if } f(x) \cdot y = 0.$$

Let $\phi(t)$ be a solution of $\dot{x} = f(x)$ remaining in the set E on its right maximal interval $[0, b)$ with the property that there exists a positive number α such that the distance between $\phi(t)$ and the boundary of E denoted ∂E, satisfies $d[\phi(t), \partial E] > \alpha$. Then there are positive constants δ and K such that for any solution $\psi(t)$ of $\dot{x} = f(x)$ with $|\psi(0) - \phi(0)| < \delta$ there is an increasing function $s(t), t \in [0, b), s(0) = 0$ and for the right maximal interval of existence of $\psi(t), t \in [0, s(b))$ the following holds

$$|\psi(s(t)) - \phi(t)| \leq K|\psi(0) - \phi(0)|, \quad t \in [0, b). \tag{4.27}$$

For a proof see Hartman (1964, pp. 550–554).

Theorem 4.5.   Suppose that $f(x)$ of (4.5) is continuously differentiable on the whole R^n space with $f(0) = 0$ and $f(x) \neq 0$ if $x \neq 0$. Suppose also that the 0-solution of $\dot{x} = f(x)$ is locally asymptotically stable. Let $\mu > 0$ be so small that the set $B_\mu = \{x : |x| \leq \mu\}$ is in the domain of attraction of the locally asymptotically stable 0-solution. Also, let $D_\mu = \{x : |x| \geq \mu\}$ and assume that

$$J(x)y \cdot y \leq 0 \quad \text{if } f(x) \cdot y = 0 \tag{4.28}$$

holds for $x \in D_\mu$ and all $y \in R^n$. Then the 0-solution is *globally asymptotically stable*.

Proof. The proof makes use of lemma 4.2. Since the domain of attraction of the locally asymptotically stable 0-solution is open, it contains both the set $B(\mu) = \{x\colon |x| \le \mu\}$ and also there exists an $\alpha > 0$ such that the set $B(\mu + \alpha) = \{x\colon |x| \le \mu + \alpha\}$ is also contained in the domain of attraction. Let E^* denote the open set obtained by deleting $B(\mu)$ from the set E in lemma 4.2, that is $E^* = E - B(\mu)$. From hypothesis, $f(x) \ne 0$, $x \in E^*$ and (4.28) holds for $x \in E^*$.

Suppose that the 0-solution is not globally asymptotically stable. Then there exists a point $x_0 \in E^*$ on the boundary of the domain of attraction of the 0-solution. Let $\phi(t, 0, x_0)$ of $\dot{x} = f(x)$ be such that $d[\phi(t, 0, x_0), \partial E^*] > \alpha$ on the right maximal interval $[0, b)$. Using lemma 4.2 with E replaced by E^* conclude that all solutions $\psi(t)$ starting at $\psi(0)$ near $\phi(0) = x_0$ remain close to $\phi(t)$ in the sense of (4.27). In particular $\psi(t) \in E^*$ on its right maximal interval of existence. This is a contradiction of the fact that x_0 is on the boundary of the domain of attraction of the 0-solution.

The next theorem is due to Markus and Yamabe (1960).

Theorem 4.6. Suppose that $f(x)$ of (4.5) is continuously differentiable in the whole R^n space. Assume that each eigenvalue of

$$M(x) = J(x) + J^{\mathrm{T}}(x) \tag{4.29}$$

is negative and also that there are positive constants c_1, c_2 such that

$$|\text{Trace } M(x)| < c_1, \tag{4.30}$$

$$|\det M(x)| > c_2. \tag{4.31}$$

Then each solution $\phi(t)$ of $\dot{x} = f(x)$ is bounded in R^n and it approaches the critical point as $t \to \infty$.

Proof. See Markus and Yamabe (1960, pp. 309–310).

Example 4.4. Markus and Yamabe (1960, p. 310) use the following example to illustrate theorem 4.6. Consider the system

$$\dot{x} = -2x + \cos y,$$
$$\dot{y} = \sin^2 x - y, \tag{4.32}$$

for $(x, y) \in R^2$. To compute (4.29) for (4.32) start with

$$J(x, y) = \begin{bmatrix} f_{11} & f_{12} \\ f_{21} & f_{22} \end{bmatrix} = \begin{bmatrix} -2 & -\sin y \\ 2\sin x \cos x & -1 \end{bmatrix}$$

and obtain

$$M(x, y) = J(x, y) + J^{\mathrm{T}}(x, y)$$

$$= \begin{bmatrix} f_{11} & f_{12} \\ f_{21} & f_{22} \end{bmatrix} + \begin{bmatrix} f_{11} & f_{21} \\ f_{12} & f_{22} \end{bmatrix} = \begin{bmatrix} 2f_{11} & f_{12}+f_{22} \\ f_{21}+f_{12} & 2f_{22} \end{bmatrix}$$

$$= \begin{bmatrix} -4 & 2\sin x \cos x - \sin y \\ 2\sin x \cos x - \sin y & -2 \end{bmatrix}, \tag{4.33}$$

where as before J^{T} denotes transpose of J. From (4.33) conclude that

$$|\text{trace } M| = 6; \quad |\det M| \geq 4. \tag{4.34}$$

Therefore, there exist constants c_1 and c_2 so that (4.30) and (4.31) are satisfied. Furthermore, computing the characteristic polynomial of $M(x, y)$ observe that

$$|M(x, y) - \gamma I| = \begin{vmatrix} 2f_{11} - \lambda & f_{12}+f_{21} \\ f_{21}+f_{12} & 2f_{22} - \lambda \end{vmatrix}$$

$$= \lambda^2 - 2\lambda(f_{11}+f_{22}) + [4f_{11}f_{22} - (f_{12}+f_{21})^2]$$

$$= \lambda^2 - \lambda(\text{trace } M) + (\det M) = 0. \tag{4.35}$$

Use the computations of (4.33) in (4.35) and apply the Routh–Hurwitz criterion to conclude that the eigenvalues of M are negative. Therefore, by theorem 4.6 every solution approaches the unique critical point as $t \to \infty$.

Remark 4.5.   Markus and Yamabe (1960) state and prove a theorem that is more general than theorem 4.6. They use a condition more general than (4.29) which considers a constant, positive definite, symmetric matrix B so that (4.29) is generalized to $M = J^{\mathrm{T}}B + BJ$. Hartman (1961) further generalizes $J^{\mathrm{T}}B + BJ$ by considering a nonconstant matrix B. The interested reader is referred to these two papers for further details.

Remarks 4.6.   All the results in this section refer to global asymptotic stability of an autonomous system. Economists have used these results as subsequent chapters illustrate. Numerous theorems exist that establish the global asymptotic stability of nonautonomous systems. Actually, Russian mathematicians such as Krasovskii (1963), Barbashin (1970), Chetaev (1961) and Zubov (1964) summarize these theorems which follow the Liapunov methodology and appeared in Russian journals during the 1950s. For detailed bibliographical references see Hahn (1963). Here we present one typical result that is the direct analogue of theorem 4.2 and remark 4.3.

In addition to the definition given in the previous section about $V(t, x)$ being *positive definite* and *decrescent*, and $\dot{V}(t, x)$ given in (3.2), we also need the equivalent of $V(x) \to \infty$ as $|x| \to \infty$ used in this section. We define a continuous function $V(t, x):[0, \infty) \times R^n \to R$ to be *radially unbounded* if $V(t, 0) = 0$ for all $t \geq 0$ and there exists a continuous function $U(x): R^n \to R^n$ with $U(0) = 0$, $U(x) > 0$ for $x \neq 0$, $U(x) \to \infty$ as $|x| \to \infty$ such that $V(t, x) \geq U(x)$ for all $t \geq 0$ and all $x \in R^n$.

Theorem 4.7. Suppose that the 0-solution is the only equilibrium of the nonautonomous system $\dot{x} = f(t, x)$ in (3.1) and suppose that $f:[0, \infty) \times R^n \to R^n$ is continuously differentiable. Also suppose that there exists a continuously differentiable, positive definite, decrescent, and radially unbounded function $V(t, x):[0, \infty) \times R^n \to R$ such that $\dot{V}(t, x)$ is negative definite. Then the 0-solution is globally asymptotically stable.

Proof. From theorem 3.3 of the previous section we conclude that the 0-solution is locally uniformly asymptotically stable. So it remains to be shown that the domain of attraction of the 0-solution is the whole R^n space. To do this, use the property that $V(t, x)$ is radially unbounded to show the boundedness of solutions, and use the fact that $\dot{V}$ is negative definite to conclude that bounded solutions converge to the 0-solution.

We close this section with two theorems about the global asymptotic stability in the plane. The first one is due to Markus and Yamabe (1960) and the second is due to Olech (1963).

Theorem 4.8. Consider the two dimensional system

$$\dot{x} = f_1(x, y),$$
$$\dot{y} = f_2(x, y),$$
(4.36)

and assume that f_1, f_2 are continuously differentiable for all $(x, y) \in R^2$. Suppose that the origin is the unique equilibrium solution and also suppose that the Jacobian

$$J(x, y) = \begin{bmatrix} f_{11} & f_{12} \\ f_{21} & f_{22} \end{bmatrix}$$
(4.37)

has eigenvalues which have negative real parts everywhere in R^2. Finally, assume that one of the four partials $f_{11}, f_{12}, f_{21}, f_{22}$ vanishes identically in R^2. Then the 0-solution is *globally asymptotically stable*.

Proof. See Markus and Yamabe (1960, pp. 311–314).

Theorem 4.9.   Consider the two dimensional system in (4.36) and assume that f_1, f_2 are continuously differentiable for all $(x, y) \in R^2$. Suppose that $f_1(0, 0) = f_2(0, 0) = 0$ and also suppose that the Jacobian matrix $J(x, y)$ in (4.37) satisfies

$$\text{trace } J(x, y) = f_{11} + f_{22} < 0 \qquad \text{on } R^2, \tag{4.38}$$

$$\det J(x, y) = f_{11}f_{22} - f_{12}f_{21} > 0 \quad \text{on } R^2. \tag{4.39}$$

Furthermore, assume that *either*

$$f_{11}f_{22} \neq 0 \quad \text{on } R^2 \tag{4.40}$$

or

$$f_{12}f_{21} \neq 0 \quad \text{on } R^2. \tag{4.41}$$

Then, the 0-solution is *globally asymptotically stable.*

Proof. See Olech (1963, pp. 390–394).

Olech uses conditions (4.38) and (4.39) to obtain that the Jacobian of (4.36) has, at each point in R^2, characteristic roots with negative real parts (as assumed in theorem 4.8) and then employs (4.40) or (4.41) to establish that the 0-equilibrium solution is unique. Together these facts imply global asymptotic stability.

Observe also that theorems 4.8 and 4.9 are closely related. Indeed, if any of the four partials $f_{11}, f_{12}, f_{21}, f_{22}$ vanishes for all $(x, y) \in R^2$ as assumed by Markus and Yamabe, then this assumption with (4.38) and (4.39) implies (4.40) or (4.41). Thus, Olech's theorem 4.9 contains theorem 4.8 by Markus and Yamabe. For an extension of Olech's theorem see Meisters and Olech (1988).

Example 4.5.   To determine the global asymptotic stability of the 0-solution of

$$\dot{x} = -x + y^2,$$

$$\dot{y} = -y,$$

compute (4.38), (4.39), (4.40) or (4.41):

$$f_{11} + f_{22} = -1 - 1 = -2 < 0;$$

$$f_{11}f_{22} - f_{12}f_{21} = (-1)(-1) - (2y)(0) = 1 > 0;$$

$$f_{11}f_{22} = (-1)(-1) = 1 \neq 0.$$

Thus, the 0-solution is globally asymptotically stable.

5. Stable manifold

In this section we return to *local* stability to introduce the reader to the notion of stable manifold. To provide a geometric motivation of the theorem to be stated shortly let us refer to the two dimensional portrait 3.2(b). The reader may recall that figure 3.2(b) is a *saddle* and the origin is a *saddle point* with the motion along the y_1 axis being directed towards the origin while the motion along the y_2 axis is being directed away from the origin. Therefore, one could say that solutions, starting in one dimensional linear subspace given by the y_1 axis, tend to the 0-solution as $t \to \infty$, and call the y_1 axis the stable manifold of this saddle. By implication, the y_2 axis is an unstable manifold because any solution that starts in y_2 moves away from the 0-solution as $t \to \infty$. With this pictorial motivation one can understand that if local stability cannot be established for a given system, then the property of the stable manifold may be worth investigating. In other words for a given system, even if it is not true that local stability of an equilibrium holds, it may be true that a certain subset of solutions starting from a given subspace converge to this equilibrium. To make these remarks more precise we need to first, explain the notion of a manifold, second, write the system of differential equations and third, state the stable manifold theorem. We take these three steps in order.

First, to explain the notion of a manifold we need to define a *diffeomorphism*. If U and V are open sets in R^n, a differentiable function $h: U \to V$ with a differentiable inverse $h^{-1}: V \to U$ is called a diffeomorphism. A subset S of R^n is called a k-dimensional *manifold* in R^n if for every point $x \in S$, there is an open set U containing x, an open set $V \subset R^n$, and a diffeomorphism $h: U \to V$ such that

$$h(U \cap S) = V \cap (R^k \times \{0\}) = \{y \in V: y^{k+1} = \cdots = y^n = 0\}.$$

In other words, a k-dimensional (differentiable) manifold is a space which is locally diffeomorphic to the euclidean k-space.

Second, the system of differential equations considered is given by

$$\dot{x} = Ax + h(t, x). \tag{5.1}$$

Note that A is a real $n \times n$ matrix that is assumed to be *noncritical* as described earlier in remark 2.3. Recall that this means that the matrix A has either all eigenvalues with negative real part or at least one eigenvalue with positive real part. The function $h(t, x):[0, \infty) \times D \to R^n$ is assumed to be continuous in both $(t, x) \in [0, \infty) \times D$, where D is an open subset of R^n containing the origin; also, $h(t, 0) = 0$ for $t \ge 0$ and finally, given any $\varepsilon > 0$, there exists a $\delta > 0$ and $T > 0$ such that

$$|h(t, x) - h(t, y)| \le \varepsilon|x - y|,$$

for $t \ge T, |x| \le \delta$ and $|y| \le \delta$.

Although the system described by (5.1) with the assumptions just stated seems more general than the two dimensional phase portrait 3.2(b), the intuition is similar. To repeat, what we want to show is the existence of stable and unstable manifolds when such manifolds become slightly distorted due to the influence of $h(t, x)$. The analysis is local, around a small neighborhood of the 0-solution. Having assumed A in 5.1 to be an $n \times n$ *noncritical*, real matrix we distinguish between k eigenvalues with negative real parts and $n - k$ eigenvalues with positive real parts and show that there is a $(k+1)$-dimensional stable manifold and an $(n-k+1)$-dimensional unstable manifold, in the (t, x) space, in a sufficiently small neighborhood of the 0-solution. The special cases $k = n$ or $k = 0$ refer to asymptotic stability and instability. More specifically the following holds.

Theorem 5.1. (Stable manifold.) Suppose that the $n \times n$ matrix A and the function $h(t, x)$ of (5.1) satisfy the assumptions stated above and let k eigenvalues of A have negative real parts and $n - k$ have positive real parts. Then there exists a real k-dimensional manifold S containing the origin and having the following properties:

(i) any solution $\phi(t) = x(t)$ of (5.1) starting on S at $t = t_0$ for t_0 sufficiently large, satisfies $x(t) \to 0$ as $t \to \infty$;

(ii) there exists an $\eta > 0$, sufficiently small such that any solution $x(t)$ near the origin but not on S at $t = t_0$ cannot satisfy $|x(t)| \le \eta$ for $t \ge t_0$.

Proof. See Coddington and Levinson (1955, pp. 330–333).

The books by Carr (1981), Guckenheimer and Holmes (1983), and Irwin (1980) discuss in detail the stable manifold theory.

6. Miscellaneous applications and exercises

(1) For the system

$$\dot{x} = x^3,$$

use the Liapunov function $V(x) = x^2$ to determine the stability properties of the 0-solution. See Brauer and Nohel (1969, p. 205).

(2) Consider the system

$$\dot{x}_1 = -x_1 - x_2,$$

$$\dot{x}_2 = x_1 - x_2^3,$$

and investigate the stability properties of the 0-solution by using the Liapunov function $V(x_1, x_2) = x_1^2 + x_2^2$. Can you use theorem 2.4 to verify your answer? See Brauer and Nohel (1969, p. 200).

(3) Given the system

$$\dot{x}_1 = x_2,$$

$$\dot{x}_2 = -\sin x_1,$$

use the Liapunov function

$$V(x_1, x_2) = \tfrac{1}{2}x_2^2 + \int_0^{x_1} \sin u \, du = \tfrac{1}{2}x_2^2 + (1 - \cos x_1)$$

to show that the 0-equilibrium solution is stable. Can you use the theorem 2.4 to verify your answer?

(4) For the system

$$\dot{x}_1 = x_2(1 + x_1),$$

$$\dot{x}_2 = -x_1(1 + x_2),$$

show that the Liapunov function $V(x_1, x_2) = x_1^2 + x_2^2$ is *not* helpful in deciding the stability properties of the 0-solution. Also note that the Jacobian of this system evaluated at the origin is *critical* and therefore theorem 2.4 cannot be applied. One way to decide the stability properties of this system is to construct a Liapunov function by taking the ratio of $\dot{x}_1$ and $\dot{x}_2$ as follows:

$$\dot{x}_1/\dot{x}_2 = -[x_2(1 + x_1)/x_1(1 + x_2)], \tag{6.1}$$

or equivalently

$$x_1 \, dx_1/(1 + x_1) = -x_2 \, dx_2/(1 + x_2) \tag{6.2}$$

which upon integration yields

$$[x_2 - \ln(1 + x_2)] + [x_1 - \ln(1 + x_1)] = \text{constant}.$$

Define

$$V(x_1, x_2) = [x_1 - \ln(1 + x_1)] + [x_2 - \ln(1 + x_2)] \tag{6.3}$$

for $x_1, x_2 > -1$. Such a V is continuous for x_1 and x_2 and for $e^{x_1} \geq 1 + x$, $e^{x_2} \geq 1 + x_2$, V is positive definite because $x_1 - \ln(1 + x_1) \geq 0$ and $x_2 - \ln(1 + x_2) \geq 0$. Finally, $V(0) = 0$ and $\dot{V} = 0$. Thus the 0-solution is *stable*.

(5) Let a, b, c, d be real constants and consider the system

$$\dot{x} = ax^3 + by,$$

$$\dot{y} = -cx + dy^3.$$

Use the Liapunov function $V(x, y) = cx^2 + by^2$ to study the stability properties of the 0-equilibrium solution in each of the cases:

1. a, b, c, d are all positive.
2. a, b, c, d are all negative.
3. $a < 0, b > 0, c > 0, d < 0$.
4. $a = 0, b > 0, c > 0, d < 0$.

(6) Find an appropriate Liapunov function to study the stability properties of

$$\dot{x}_1 = x_1(a^2 - x_1^2 - x_2^2) + x_2(x_1^2 + x_2^2 + a^2),$$

$$\dot{x}_2 = -x_1(a^2 + x_1^2 + x_2^2) + x_2(a^2 - x_1^2 - x_2^2),$$

when $a = 0$ and when $a \neq 0$. See Hahn (1967, p. 105).

(7) Let D be an open subset that contains the origin and suppose that the function $V(t, x): [0, \infty) \times D \to R$ satisfies $V(t, 0) = 0$ for all $t \geq 0$ and also $V(t, x)$ has bounded partial derivatives with respect to x. Then $V(t, x)$ is *decrescent* in $[0, \infty) \times D$.

(8) Which of the following $V(t, x): [0, \infty) \times D \to R$ are decrescent?

1. $(x_1^2 + x_2^2)/(1 + t)$.
2. $(x_1^2 + x_2^2)(1 + t^2)$.
3. $x_1^2 \sin^2 t + x_2^2 \cos^2 t + x_3^2 \sin^2 t$.
4. $(x_1^2 + x_2^2)/e^t$.

(9) Find an appropriate Liapunov function to determine if the 0-solution of the following system is *globally* asymptotically stable.

$$\dot{x} = y,$$

$$\dot{y} = -x^3 - (1 + x^2)y.$$

(10) Suppose that there is a positive definite matrix Q such that

$$J^T(x)Q + QJ(x) \tag{6.4}$$

is negative definite for all $x \neq 0$, where as before $J(x)$ is the Jacobian of $f(x)$. Show that (6.4) implies that the 0-solution of $\dot{x} = f(x), f(0) = 0$ is *globally* asymptotically stable.

7. Further remarks and references

The standard reference for Liapunov stability is Hahn (1967). This book contains most of the material presented in Hahn (1963) with a detailed documentation of Liapunov's original work and the subsequent scientific discoveries up to the late fifties. Every serious student of stability is encouraged to consult W. Hahn (1967).

LaSalle and Lefschetz (1961) describe Liapunov's direct method at a level accessible to persons without an advanced mathematical background. Rouche et al. (1977) is a rigorous monograph on Liapunov's direct method.

The extensive contributions to stability theory made by Russian mathematicians are reported in several books which appeared originally in Russian and later translated into English. Some representative examples are: Chetaev (1961), Krasovskii (1963), Zubov (1964) and Barbashin (1970).

Liapunov's stability methods have also been reported in review articles. Among such review articles, the reader is referred to Antosiewicz (1958), LaSalle (1964, 1968) and Bushaw (1969). See also Massera (1949, 1956) and Mangasarian (1963).

Several books discuss Liapunov's method as well as other related methods of stability. In this category, it is worth mentioning the books of Cesari (1963), Hartman (1964), Halanay (1966), Coppel (1965), Hale (1969) and Harris and Miles (1980). A recent book on ordinary differential equations with a major emphasis on stability with engineering applications is Miller and Michel (1982). Another book that introduces the reader to the dynamical aspects of the theory of ordinary differential equations with an emphasis on the stability of equilibria in dynamical systems is Hirsch and Smale (1974). Finally, Bhatia and Szegö (1967, 1970) use topological methods to present various stability results for dynamical systems first introduced by Birkoff (1927) and recently reviewed by Smale (1967). See also the classic book by Nemytskii and Stepanov (1960).

There exist numerous stability concepts beyond the ones treated in this chapter. For example, some authors use the notion of *weakly stable* to describe a solution that is stable but not asymptotically stable. *Lagrange stability* describes the notion of boundedness of all solutions. *Practical stability* characterizes a system which may be mathematically unstable and

yet the system may oscillate sufficiently near its equilibrium that its perform-
ance is empirically acceptable. Finally, a trajectory which is contained in
a limit set is called *Poisson stable*. For details about these notions see Hahn
(1967), LaSalle and Lefschetz (1961), Michel (1970) and Bushaw (1969).

In addition to the major references on global asymptotic stability given
in section 4 we also mention Markus (1954), Levin (1960), Levin and Nohel
(1960), Brauer (1961), Mufti (1961), Datko (1966), Burganskaya (1974),
and Shub (1986). Two economic applications of Olech's theorem are found
in Garcia (1972) and Desai (1973).

Furthermore, the saddle-type stability and instability described in section
5 has been treated by economists such as Kurz (1968a), Samuelson (1972a),
Levhari and Liviatan (1972), Heller (1975), and Kuga (1977) among others.
The typical example of the existence of a stable manifold in a saddle point
equilibrium is the optimal economic growth model of Cass (1965). For a
discussion of this model and its graphical illustration of the saddle point
equilibrium and the existence of a stable manifold see Burmeister and
Dobell (1970, p. 395), Neher (1971, p. 228) or Intriligator (1971, p. 411).
Burmeister (1980, chapter 5) explains both the intuitive meaning and
economic interpretation of saddle point equilibrium. See also the mathematical papers of Hirsch and Pugh (1970) and Rockafellar (1973, 1976).

The reader who wishes to go beyond the topics covered in this chapter
may consider the topic of *orbital stability* presented in Halanay (1966),
Yoshizawa (1975) and Burton (1985) and the related topic of *bifurcation*
presented in Andronov et al. (1973), Sattinger (1973), Martin (1973), Coppel
(1978) and Iooss and Joseph (1980). Benhabib and Nishimura (1979) apply
the Hopf bifurcation theory in optimal economic growth. Finally, *stochastic
stability* is presented in Kushner (1967), Malliaris and Brock (1982) and
Ladde and Lakshimkantham (1980). Unlike orbital stability and bifurcation
theory which build on the theory of ordinary differential equations, stochastic stability requires the methodology of Itô's calculus presented in some
length in Malliaris and Brock (1982) or briefly in Malliaris (1983, 1984).

CHAPTER 5

STABILITY OF OPTIMAL CONTROL

> A real system is subject to
> perturbations and it is never possible
> to control its initial state exactly. This
> raises the question of stability: under
> a slight perturbation will the system
> remain near the equilibrium state or
> not?
> LaSalle and Lefschetz (1961, p. 30)

1. Introduction

This chapter surveys various stability results of optimal control and indicates some possible areas of their application. Unlike previous chapters where most of the results reported have been obtained by mathematicians several decades ago, this chapter presents results obtained primarily by mathematical economists since the early 1970s.

The chapter relies on Brock (1977a) and its emphasis is on basic ideas and not on technical details in order for the basic structure of the analysis to remain clear. Without further ado, consider the following optimal control problem

$$\max_{v(\cdot)} \int_0^T e^{-\rho t} U[x(t), v(t)] \, dt, \tag{1.1}$$

subject to

$$\dot{x} = T[x(t), v(t), t], \tag{1.2}$$

$$x(0) = x_0, \quad \text{given } x(t) \in R^n, \quad v(t) \in R^m, \tag{1.3}$$

$$v(\cdot) : [0, T] \to R^m \text{ measurable,}$$

where U is the instantaneous utility, t is time, T is the planning horizon, $x(t)$ is the *state* vector at time t, $v(t)$ is the *instrument* vector at time t, $T[\cdot]$ is the technology which relates the rate of change of the state vector $\dot{x} \equiv dx/dt$ to the state $x(t)$ and instruments $v(t)$ at time t, $\rho \geq 0$ is the discount in future utility, and x_0 is the initial position of the state vector at time 0. The choice of T to denote the terminal time, the technology function and transpose should not cause any difficulty because it is rather standard in the literature. The objective is to maximize

$$\int_0^T U \, dt,$$

subject to equations (1.2) and (1.3) over some set θ of instrument functions,

$$v(t):[0, T] \to R^m,$$

which is usually taken to be the set of all measurable $v(\cdot)$ or the set of all piecewise continuous $v(\cdot)$.

Problem (1.1) is chosen as the vehicle of explanation of the results in this chapter because it is described in Arrow and Kurz (1970, chapter 2). To specialize problem (1.1) somewhat, let

$$T = \infty, \quad \rho > 0. \tag{1.4}$$

Then, the problem becomes:

$$W(x, t_0) = \sup \int_{t_0}^{\infty} e^{-\rho(t-t_0)} U[x(t), v(t)] \, dt \tag{1.5}$$

subject to

$$\dot{x} = T[x(t), v(t)], \quad x(t_0) = x, \quad v(\cdot) \in \theta.$$

Note that sup in (1.5) denotes supremum which is taken over all instrument functions $v(\cdot) \in \theta$.

As pointed out by Arrow and Kurz, W is independent of t_0, and, under strict concavity assumptions on $U(\cdot)$ and $T(\cdot)$, the optimal $v(t)$, denoted by $v^*(t)$, is of the time stationary feedback form; that is, there is a function $h(x)$ such that

$$v^*(t) = h(x^*(t)). \tag{1.6}$$

Thus optimal paths $x^*(t)$ satisfy

$$\dot{x}^*(t) = T[x^*(t), h(x^*(t))] \equiv F(x^*(t)), \quad x^*(t_0) = x, \tag{1.7}$$

which is an autonomous set of differential equations.

The basic problem addressed in this chapter may now be stated.

Basic problem (P). Find sufficient conditions for the utility function $U[\cdot]$, the technology $T[\cdot]$, and the discount ρ such that there exists a steady state of equation (1.7). Call it x^* such that (i) x^* is locally asymptotically stable (L.A.S.), and (ii) x^* is globally asymptotically stable (G.A.S.). We recall the definitions of L.A.S. and G.A.S.

Definition. The steady state solution x^* of equation (1.7) is L.A.S. if there is $\varepsilon > 0$ such that

$$|x^* - x_0| < \varepsilon \text{ implies } x(t, x_0) \to x^* \text{ as } t \to \infty,$$

where $x(t, x_0)$ is the solution of equation (1.7) with initial condition $x(0) = x_0$. The steady state solution x^* is G.A.S. if for all $x_0 \in R^n$, $x(t, x_0) \to x^*$ as $t \to \infty$.

Here $|y|$ denotes the norm of vector y defined by

$$|y| = \left(\sum_{i=1}^{n} y_i^2 \right)^{1/2}.$$

It will be useful to write down some specializations of the general problem (1.5). Put $t_0 = 0$, $x = x_0$, and suppress t_0 in W, henceforth. The neoclassical theory of investment as stated by Mortensen (1973) is

$$W(x_0) = \sup \int_0^{\infty} e^{-\rho t}[f(x(t), v(t)) - w^T x(t) - g^T v(t)]\, dt, \tag{1.8}$$

subject to

$$\dot{x} = v(t), \quad x(0) = x_0, \quad v(\cdot): [0, \infty) \to R^n \text{ measurable.}$$

Here $f(x, v)$ is a generalized production function which depends upon the vector of n factors $x(t)$, and the rate of adjustment of the factors $v(t)$. The cost of obtaining factor services in each instant of time is $w^T x(t)$, where w^T denotes the transpose of the vector w, and the cost of adding to the stock of factors (which may be negative) is $g^T v(t)$. It is assumed that a stationary solution $x_0 = x^*$ exists for equation (1.8), so that the optimal plan exists and is unique for each $x_0 \gg 0$ (note that for $x \in R^n$, $x \gg 0$ means that $x_i > 0$ for $i = 1, 2, \ldots, n$) and is interior to any natural boundaries (this means that $x_i^*(t) > 0$ for all $t \geq 0$, $i = 1, 2, \ldots, n$). Furthermore, it is assumed that f is twice continuously differentiable and that the optimal plan is one with piecewise continuous time derivatives. These assumptions are placed on problem (1.5) to avoid many tangential technicalities and are maintained throughout this chapter.

The next few pages summarize the fundamental work of Magill (1977a) on the stability of the linear quadratic approximation around a steady state solution of (1.5). These results go far beyond the simple checking of eigenvalues that most people associate with a local analysis. Furthermore, the local results of Magill lead naturally to the global results of Cass-Shell, Rockafellar, and Brock-Scheinkman, which are discussed below.

The linear quadratic approximation of equation (1.8) at a steady state x^* is

$$W(\xi_0) = \sup \int_0^\infty e^{-\rho t} [(\xi(t), \eta(t))^T A^* (\xi(t), \eta(t))] \, dt, \qquad (1.9)$$

subject to

$$\dot{\xi} = \eta(t), \quad \xi(0) = x_0 - x^* = \xi_0,$$

$$\eta(\cdot) : [0, \infty) \to R^n \text{ measurable},$$

where

$$\xi(t) = x(t) - x^*, \quad \eta(t) = v(t) - v^* = v(t), \qquad (1.10)$$

$$A^* = \begin{bmatrix} f_{xx}^* & f_{xv}^* \\ f_{vx}^* & f_{vv}^* \end{bmatrix}.$$

The symbols $f_{xx}^*, f_{vx}^*, f_{xv}^*, f_{vv}^*, f_x^*, f_v^*$ denote

$$\frac{\partial^2 f}{\partial x^2}, \quad \frac{\partial^2 f}{\partial v \partial x}, \quad \frac{\partial^2 f}{\partial x \partial v}, \quad \frac{\partial^2 f}{\partial v^2}, \quad \frac{\partial f}{\partial x}, \quad \frac{\partial f}{\partial v},$$

all evaluated at $(x^*, v^*) = (x^*, 0)$, respectively.

The linear quadratic approximation at a steady state (x^*, v^*) for the general problem (1.5) is presented in the next section.

2. Linear quadratic approximation to general problem (Magill (1977a))

Consider

$$W(\xi_0) = \sup \int_0^\infty e^{-\rho t} \left[(\xi(t), \eta(t))^T \begin{bmatrix} U_{xx}^* & U_{xv}^* \\ U_{vx}^* & U_{vv}^* \end{bmatrix} (\xi(t), \eta(t)) \right] dt,$$

$$(2.1)$$

subject to

$$\dot{\xi} = T_x^* \xi(t) + T_v^* \eta(t),$$

$$\xi(0) = x_0 - x^* = \xi_0,$$

$$\eta(\cdot):[0, \infty) \to R^m \text{ measurable,}$$

where

$$U_{xx}^*, \ U_{xv}^*, \ U_{vx}^*, \ U_{vv}^*, \ T_x^*, \ T_v^*$$

are the appropriate matrices of partial derivatives evaluated at (x^*, v^*). The quadratic approximation (2.1) can be expected to hold only in the neighborhood of x_0. The validity of the linear quadratic approximation for the infinite horizon problem (1.5) has not been studied yet. The finite horizon case is studied, for example, by Breakwell et al. (1963) (see also Magill (1977a)).

A problem studied extensively in the engineering literature and closely related to equation (2.1) is the *time stationary optimal linear regulator problem* (OLRP):

$$-W(\xi_0) = \inf \int_0^\infty e^{-\rho t} \left[(\xi(t), \eta(t)) \begin{bmatrix} Q & S \\ S^T & R \end{bmatrix} (\xi(t), \eta(t)) \right] dt, \qquad (2.2)$$

subject to

$$\dot{\xi} = F\xi(t) + G\eta(t),$$

$$\xi(0) = \xi_0,$$

$$\eta(\cdot):[0, \infty) \to R^m \text{ measurable.}$$

Clearly, by putting

$$Q = -U_{xx}^*, \quad S = -U_{xv}^*, \quad S^T = -U_{vx}^*,$$

$$R = -U_{vv}^*, \quad F = T_x^*, \quad G = T_v^*,$$

becomes the same problem as equation (2.1). The importance of observing
that equations (2.1) and (2.2) are the same problem is that it enables us to
carry the extensive set of results derived by engineers on OLRP (see
Anderson and Moore (1971) and Kwakernaak and Sivan (1972) for
example) to linear quadratic approximations (2.1) to economic problems.

Such an approach would virtually resolve the local asymptotic stability
question for problem (1.5) if the engineers had focused on the case $\rho > 0$
instead of the case $\rho \leq 0$. Fortunately, the paper by Magill (1977a) fills this
gap. Results on the OLRP are applicable, provided that the question of
sufficient conditions for the validity of the linear quadratic approximation
is resolved for problem (1.5) to the L.A.S. problem for economic problems
with $\rho > 0$ for two reasons.

First, $\xi(t)$, $\eta(t)$ may be replaced by

$$\xi(t) = e^{(\rho/2)t}\hat{\xi}(t), \quad \eta(t) = e^{(\rho/2)t}\hat{\eta}(t)$$

in equation (2.2). The constraint in equation (2.2) becomes

$$\dot{\hat{\xi}} = (F - (\rho/2)I)\hat{\xi}(t) + G\hat{\eta}(t), \quad \hat{\xi}(0) = \xi_0, \tag{2.3}$$

where I denotes the $n \times n$ identity matrix. This transformation of variables,
used by Magill (1977a) and Anderson and Moore (1971, p. 53), allows
results for the case $\rho = 0$ (the bulk of results on the OLRP) to be carried
over directly to the case $\rho > 0$. Second, the OLRP suggests an important
class of Liapunov functions upon which several theorems below will be
based, viz. the minimum from ξ_0 itself (Anderson and Moore (1971, p. 41)).
The minimum is a positive definite quadratic form $\xi_0^T P \xi_0$ under general
assumptions (see Anderson and Moore (1971)).

Before plunging into statements of formal theorems, let us use the OLRP
to explore the determinants of L.A.S. The following is based upon Magill
(1977a), but brevity demands that many of his results be passed over.
Assume that the matrix

$$\begin{bmatrix} Q & S \\ S^T & R \end{bmatrix}$$

is positive definite in order to reflect the concavity of $U(x, v)$, leading to
the negative definiteness of the matrix

$$\begin{bmatrix} U_{xx}^* & U_{xv}^* \\ U_{vx}^* & U_{vv}^* \end{bmatrix}$$

in economic problems.

When is the OLRP equation (2.2) unstable? First, put $S = 0$. Then in the one dimensional case, we see that instability is more likely the larger F is, the smaller $|G|$ is, the larger R is, the smaller Q is, and the larger ρ is. The intuition behind this is quite compelling for, if F is positive, the system

$$\dot{\xi} = F\xi(t), \quad \xi(0) = \xi_0$$

is unstable. If $|G|$, the absolute value of G, is small then a lot of input $\eta(t)$ must be administered in order to have much impact on $\xi(t)$. However, inputs $\eta(t)$ cost $\eta^T(t)R\eta(t)$ to administer. If $\eta(0)$ is administered today, then $\xi(t)Q\xi(t)$ will be smaller in the next instant. But the future is discounted by ρ. To sum up in words: why stabilize a highly unstable system (large F) when control input is ineffective (small $|G|$), when control input is expensive (R is large) when deviation of the state from the origin is not very costly (Q is small) and the future is not worth much (ρ is large)?

Now assume that $S \neq 0$. Change units to reduce the problem to the case $S = 0$. Following Anderson and Moore (1971, p. 47), and Magill (1977a).

$$(\xi, \eta)^T \begin{bmatrix} Q & S \\ S^T & R \end{bmatrix} (\xi, \eta) = \eta^T R \eta + 2\xi^T S \eta + \xi^T Q \xi$$

$$= (\eta + R^{-1}S^T\xi)^T R(\eta + R^{-1}S^T\xi)$$

$$+ \xi^T (Q - SR^{-1}S^T)\xi. \tag{2.4}$$

Note that since the left hand side of (2.4) is positive definite, R, Q, and $Q - SR^{-1}S^T$ are all positive definite. Defining

$$\eta_1 = \eta + R^{-1}S^T\xi,$$

the OLRP (2.2) with $S \neq 0$ becomes

$$\inf \int_0^\infty e^{-\rho t} [\eta_1^T R \eta_1 + \xi^T (Q - SR^{-1}S^T)\xi] \, dt \tag{2.5}$$

subject to

$$\dot{\xi} = (F - GR^{-1}S^T)\xi + G\eta_1, \quad \xi(0) = \xi_0.$$

Clearly, equation (2.5) is unstable if and only if equation (2.2) is unstable.

Let us use equation (2.5) to explore when instability may be likely. Consider the one dimensional case. Without loss of generality we may assume $G \geq 0$. For if $G \leq 0$, put $\eta_2 = -\eta_1$ and stability will not be affected.

It is clear from equation (2.5) that when $S < 0$ a decrease in S is destabilizing, because a decrease in S makes $F - GR^{-1}S^{\mathrm{T}}$ larger and makes

$$Q - SR^{-1}S^{\mathrm{T}}$$

smaller. For $S > 0$, an increase in S makes the underlying system matrix,

$$F - GR^{-1}S^{\mathrm{T}}$$

smaller (a stabilizing force), but

$$Q - SR^{-1}S^{\mathrm{T}}$$

becomes smaller (a destabilizing force). Hence, ambiguity is obtained in this case.

It is known that instability in the multidimensional case is related to the amount of *asymmetry* in the underlying system matrix,

$$A = F - GR^{-1}S^{\mathrm{T}}.$$

This is so because, roughly speaking, instability of A which is related to its lack of symmetry makes instability of the optimal path more likely.

In the multidimensional case when $\rho \le 0$, G.A.S. is intuitive from the existence of a finite value to the integral and the positive definiteness of the matrix

$$\begin{bmatrix} Q & S \\ S^{\mathrm{T}} & R \end{bmatrix}.$$

Roughly speaking, $(x^*(t), v^*(t))$ must converge to 0 as $t \to \infty$, or else the integral will blow up. Sufficient conditions for G.A.S. of the OLRP are covered in detail in Anderson and Moore (1971, chapter 4) for the case $\rho \le 0$. The paper by Magill (1977a) develops a rather complete set of results for all ρ.

Let us apply our intuitive understanding of the determinants of G.A.S. gained from the OLRP to the linear quadratic approximation (1.9) to the neoclassical model of investment (1.8). Here

$$Q = -f_{xx}^*, \quad R = -f_{vv}^*, \quad S = -f_{xv}^*, \quad G = I, \quad F = 0.$$

By the reasoning above from equation (2.5), in the one dimensional case, provided that $A > 0$, instability at x^* is likely when ρ is large, $-f_{vv}^*$ is large (it is positive by concavity of f in (x, v)), and $-f_{xx}^* + f_{xv}^* f_{vv}^{*-1} f_{xv}^*$ is small (it is positive by concavity of f). Note that when $F = 0$ and $S = 0$, since 0 is not a stable matrix, the underlying system matrix is not stable. If $S = 0$, however, a theorem to be proved below will show that G.A.S. still holds.

3. The general nonlinear nonquadratic problem

In searching for sufficient conditions on U, T for G.A.S. to hold it turns out to be convenient to form the *current* value Hamiltonian (following Arrow and Kurz (1970, p. 47)) for equation (1.5)

$$H(q, x, v) = U[x, v] + qT[x, v].$$
$$(3.1)$$

Let $v^*(\cdot)$ be a choice of instruments that maximizes

$$\int_0^\infty e^{-\rho t} U[x(t), v(t)] \, dt,$$

subject to

$$\dot{x} = T[x(t), v(t)], \quad x(0) = x_0,$$

over all measurable $v(\cdot)$. Then Arrow and Kurz (1970, p. 48) show that there exists costate variables $q^*(t)$, expressed in current value, such that on each interval of continuity of $v^*(t)$,

$$\dot{q}^* = \rho q^*(t) - H_x^0(q^*(t), x^*(t)),$$
$$(3.2)$$

$$\dot{x}^* = H_q^0(q^*(t), x^*(t)), \quad x^*(0) = x_0,$$
$$(3.3)$$

where $v^*(t)$ solves

$$\max_{v \in R^m} H(q^*(t), x^*(t), v) \equiv H^0(q^*(t), x^*(t)).$$

Arrow and Kurz (1970, p. 35) have also shown that if W_x exists,

$$q^*(t) = W_x(x^*(t)),$$

where $W(x)$ is the current value state valuation function. Note further that W_{xx} exists almost everywhere and is negative and is negative semi-definite when U and T are concave. This is so because $W(x)$ is concave in this case.

We are now in a position to state the G.A.S. results of Cass and Shell (1976a), Rockafellar (1976), and Brock and Scheinkman (1976, 1977a). These results are based on two Liapunov functions. The first is given by

$$V_1 = -(q - q^*)^\mathrm{T}(x - x^*),$$
$$(3.4)$$

where (q^*, x^*) is a steady state solution of the system equations (3.2) and (3.3).

It is important to interpret the meaning of V_1 for the OLRP. Here, since the state–costate equations (3.2) and (3.3) are linear, $x^* = q^* = 0$. The minimum cost, $C(\xi_0) = -W(\xi_0)$, given by equation (2.2), is quadratic in ξ_0 and is 0 when $\xi_0 = 0$. Thus, there is a matrix P such that

$$C(\xi_0) = \xi_0^{\mathrm{T}} P \xi_0.$$

Also, P is positive semi-definite when the integrand is convex in (ξ, η). Furthermore, the costate $q^*(t)$ in equations (3.2) and (3.3) for the OLRP is given by

$$q^*(t) = W_x(\xi^*(t)) = -2P\xi^*(t).$$

Thus,

$$V_1 = -2\xi^{*\mathrm{T}}(t) P \xi^*(t),$$

and asking that $\dot{V}_1 > 0$ is simply asking that the minimal cost fall as time increases when the minimal cost is calculated at $\xi^*(t)$ for each t. See Anderson and Moore (1971), Kwakernaak and Sivan (1972), and Magill (1977a) for a more complete discussion of why V_1 is the basic Liapunov function in the OLRP literature.

The second Liapunov function is given by

$$V_2 = -\dot{q}^{\mathrm{T}}\dot{x}.$$

The next two sections report stability results based on these two Liapunov functions.

4. Stability results based on V_1

Cass and Shell (1976a) and Rockafellar (1976) were the first to recognize that V_1 is of basic importance for G.A.S. analysis in economics. Such a Liapunov function was used earlier by Samuelson (1972a) to eliminate limit cycles in the case $\rho = 0$. More specifically, Cass and Shell formulate a general class of economic dynamics in price–quantity space which includes both descriptive growth theory and optimal growth theory. Here we are concerned only with their stability analysis. Roughly speaking, they take the time derivative of V_1 along solutions of equations (3.2) and (3.3) that satisfy

$$\lim_{t \to \infty} q^*(t) x^*(t) \, \mathrm{e}^{-\rho t} = 0, \tag{4.1}$$

and interpret the economic meaning of the assumption

$$0 \geq \dot{V}_1(q^*(t), x^*(t)) = -\{[\rho q^*(t) - H_x^0(q^*(t), x^*(t))]^T(x^*(t) - x^*)$$
$$+ (q^*(t) - q^*)^T H_q^0(q(t), x^*(t))\}. \tag{4.2}$$

They show that equation (4.2) implies

$$V_1(q^*(t), x^*(t)) \geq 0. \tag{4.3}$$

Thus, only a slight strengthening of equation (4.2) and assumptions sufficient to guarantee that $x^*(t)$ is uniformly continuous of $[0, \infty)$ allow them to prove that the steady state solution x^* is G.A.S. in the set of all solutions of equations (3.2) and (3.3) that satisfy equation (4.1). More precisely:

Theorem 4.1. (Cass and Shell (1976a).) For the case $\rho \geq 0$ assume that for every $\varepsilon > 0$, there is a $\delta > 0$ such that $|x - x^*| > \varepsilon$ implies

(S) $\quad (q - q^*)^T H_q^0(q, x) - (H_x^0)^T(q, x)(x - x^*) + \rho q^{*T}(x - x^*)$
$$> -\rho(q - q^*)^T(x - x^*) + \delta.$$

Then if $(q^*(t), x^*(t))$ solves equations (3.2) and (3.3) and if equation (4.1) holds, then

$$|x^*(t) - x^*| \to 0, \quad \text{as } t \to \infty.$$

Proof. See Cass and Shell (1976a).

It should be noted that (S) is only required to hold on the set of (q, x) such that $(q, x) = (q^*(t), x^*(t))$ for some $t \geq 0$. Also (S) is the same as

$$-\dot{V}_1(q, x) > \delta.$$

Cass and Shell (1976a) also prove the following useful theorem.

Theorem 4.2. Assume that $H^0(q, x)$ is convex in q and concave in x. Then

$$\frac{d}{dt}[e^{-\rho t}(q(t) - q^*)^T(x(t) - x^*)] \geq 0, \tag{4.4}$$

for any solution $(q(t), x(t))$ of equations (3.2) and (3.3).

Proof. See Cass and Shell (1976a).

Note that if U, T are concave in (x, v), then it is trivial to show that $H^0(q, x)$ is concave in x. Convexity in q follows from the very definition of H^0. That is,

$$H^0(q, x) = \max_v [U(x, v) + q^T T(x, v)],$$

regardless of whether U, T are concave. The proof uses the definition of convexity and the definition of maximum. See Rockafellar (1976) and its references for a systematic development of properties of the function H^0. Here we give a simple overview of Rockafellar's work.

Rockafellar (1976) studies the case in which $U(x, v)$ is concave in (x, v) and $T(x, v) = v$. He points out, however, that the restriction $(x, \dot{x}) \in X$, X convex, may be treated by defining U to be equal to $-\infty$ when $(x, \dot{x})$ is not in X. Thus a very general class of problems may be treated by his methods. The paper and its references develop the following ideas assuming $U(x, v)$ to be concave but not necessarily differentiable: (1) a dual problem that the optimal costate $q^*(t)$ must solve; (2) duality theory of the Hamiltonian function $H^0(q, x)$; (3) existence and uniqueness theory for optimum paths; (4) theorems on the differentiability of $W(x)$ under assumptions sufficient for G.A.S. of the stationary solution x^*; (5) relations between $W(x)$ and its analogue for the dual problem; (6) theorems on the monotonicity of the expression

$$V = -(q_1(t) - q_2(t))^{\mathrm{T}}(x_1(t) - x_2(t))$$

for any pair of solutions $(q_1(t), x_1(t))$, $(q_2(t), x_2(t))$ of equations (3.2) and (3.3) starting from any set of initial conditions; and (7) the notion of (α, β) convexity-concavity for the H^0 function and its relation to G.A.S. of the stationary solution x^*. To present the main G.A.S. theorem of Rockafellar a definition is needed.

Definition. Let $h: C \to R$ be a finite function on a convex set $C \subset R^n$. Then h is α-convex, $\alpha \in R$, if the function

$$h(x) - \tfrac{1}{2}\alpha|x|^2$$

is convex on C. If C is open and h is twice continuously differentiable, then α-convexity is equivalent to: for all $x_0 \in C$, for all $w \in R^n$,

$$w^{\mathrm{T}} h_{xx}(x_0) w \geq \alpha w^{\mathrm{T}} w$$

must hold. Here $h_{xx}(x_0)$ is the matrix of second-order partial derivatives of h evaluated at x_0. A function $g: C \to R$ is β-concave if $-g$ is β-convex.

Theorem 4.3. (Rockafellar (1976).) Assume that $H^0(q, x)$ is finite and β-convex-α-concave on $R^n \times R^n$. Also assume that a stationary solution (q^*, x^*) to equations (3.2) and (3.3) exists and that optimum paths exist from the initial condition x_0. Then the stationary solution x^* is G.A.S. provided that

$$(R) \quad 4\alpha\beta > \rho^2.$$

Proof. See Rockafellar (1976).

A more precise statement of theorem 4.3 is given in Rockafellar (1976) who works with a more general system. The basic idea of the proof is just to show that (R) implies

$$\dot{V}_1 < 0$$

along solutions of equations (3.2) and (3.3) that correspond to optimal paths.

5. Stability results based on V_2

In this section we summarize the stability results of Brock and Scheinkman (1976, 1977a) based on the Liapunov function V_2. These results are developed rapidly with primary emphasis on contrasting them with the other theorems reported in this chapter. We will return to some of the Brock and Scheinkman results in the next chapter where their applicability to capital theory is demonstrated.

Differentiate the Liapunov function $V_2 = -\dot{q}(t)^{\mathrm{T}}\dot{x}(t)$ along solutions of equations (3.2) and (3.3) to yield

$$\dot{V}_2(q(t), x(t)) = -(\dot{q}(t), \dot{x}(t))^{\mathrm{T}}B(q(t), x(t))(\dot{q}(t), \dot{x}(t)), \qquad (5.1)$$

where

$$B(q(t), x(t)) = \begin{bmatrix} H^0_{qq} & (\rho/2)I \\ (\rho/2)I & -H^0_{xx} \end{bmatrix}, \qquad (5.2)$$

and where I denotes the $n \times n$ identity matrix and the matrices of partial derivatives

$$H^0_{qq}, \ -H^0_{xx},$$

(which are positive semi-definite since H^0 is convex in q and concave in x) are evaluated at $(q(t), \dot{x}(t))$. The following sequence of theorems summarize the results in Brock and Scheinkman (1976, 1977a).

Theorem 5.1. Let $(q^*(0), x^*(0))$ be a solution of equations (3.2) and (3.3). Then

$$\dot{V}_2(q^*(t), x^*(t)) < 0 \qquad (5.3)$$

provided that

$$z^*(t)^{\mathrm{T}}B(q^*(t), x^*(t))z^*(t) > 0 \quad \text{for all } t \geq 0,$$

where

$$z^*(t) = [\rho q^*(t) - H_x^0(q^*(t), x^*(t)), H_q^0(q^*(t), x^*(t))]. \tag{5.4}$$

Furthermore, if $(q^*(\cdot), x^*(\cdot))$ is bounded independently of t or if

$$\lim_{t \to \infty} \sup - \dot{V}_2(q^*(t), x^*(t)) < \infty, \tag{5.5}$$

then there is a stationary solution (q^*, x^*) of (3.2) and (3.3) such that

$$(q^*(t), x^*(t)) \to (q^*, x^*) \quad \text{as } t \to \infty. \tag{5.6}$$

Proof. Inequality (5.3) is obvious from equation (5.1). The second part of the theorem is just a standard application of results on G.A.S. by means of Liapunov functions.

Remark. Here, given a function $y(\cdot): [0, \infty) \to R$, lim sup $y(t)$ denotes the largest cluster point of the function values $y(t)$ as $t \to \infty$. Assumption (5.5) is quite natural for optimal paths because if $W_{xx}(\cdot)$ exists it will be negative semidefinite since $W(\cdot)$ is concave for U and T concave. Thus,

$$\dot{q}^{*T}\dot{x}^* = \dot{x}^*(t)^T W_{xx}(x^*(t))\dot{x}^*(t) \le 0,$$

and equation (5.5) holds automatically.

Theorem 5.2. If (a) (q^*, x^*) is the unique stationary solution of equations (3.2) and (3.3); (b) For all $(q, x) \ne (q^*, x^*)$,

$$(q - q^*)^T H_q^0(q, x) + (x - x^*)^T(\rho q - H_x^0(q, x)) = 0,$$

implies

$$(q - q^*, x - x^*)^T B(q, x)(q - q^*, x - x^*) > 0;$$

(c) For all $w \ne 0$, $w^T B(q^*, x^*)w > 0$. Then all solutions of (3.2) and (3.3) that are bounded for $t \ge 0$ converge to (q^*, x^*) as $t \to \infty$.

Proof. Put $V_1(q, x) = -(q - q^*)^T(x - x^*)$ and use (b) and (c) to show that $\dot{V}_1(q, x) < 0$ for $(q, x) \ne (q^*, x^*)$. The rest is a standard Liapunov function stability exercise.

Note that theorem 5.2 gives a set of sufficient conditions for the Cass and Shell hypothesis,

$$\dot{V}_1(q, x) < 0,$$

to hold. Also note that boundedness of $(q^*(t), x^*(t))$ may be dispensed with provided that one assumes

$$\lim_{t \to \infty} q^*(t) x^*(t) e^{-\rho t} = 0, \tag{5.7}$$

and refines the Liapunov analysis or one assumes that $W_x(\cdot)$ exists. Benveniste and Scheinkman (1979) provide a set of very general conditions on equation (1.5) that imply that W_x exists and that (5.7) holds for optimal paths. For if $W(\cdot)$ is concave and $W_x(\cdot)$ exists, then

$$(q^*(t) - q^*)^{\mathrm{T}}(x^*(t) - x^*) = [W_x(x^*(t)) - W_x(x^*)]^{\mathrm{T}}(x^*(t) - x^*) \le 0.$$

The use of $W_x(\cdot)$ in the last line exposes why the Liapunov function, $-(q - q^*)^{\mathrm{T}}(x - x^*)$ is natural.

Theorems 5.1 and 5.2 are, in some sense, complementary since each asks that Q be positive definite in directions which are transversal to each other.

Theorem 5.3. Assume that $W_{xx}(\cdot)$ exists and is negative definite on R_+^n. Let $(q^*(t), x^*(t))$ be a solution of equations (3.2) and (3.3) that corresponds to an optimal path. Assume (a) H^0 is twice continuously differentiable; (b) (q^*, x^*) is the unique stationary solution of (3.2) and (3.3); (c) x^* is a locally asymptotically stable solution of the reduced form system

$$\dot{x}(t) = H_q^0(W_x(x(t)), x(t)); \tag{5.8}$$

(d) $H^0(q, x)$ is locally α-convex-β-concave at (q^*, x^*); and (e) $H^0(q, x)$ is locally α-quasi-convex and $H^0(q, x) - \rho q x$ is β-quasi-concave along $(q^*(t), x^*(t))$ where $4\alpha\beta > \rho^2$. Then (q^*, x^*) is G.A.S.

We define a twice continuously differentiable function $f: R^n \to R$, to be locally β-quasi-concave at $x_0 \in R^n$ if for all $w \in R^n$, $w \ne 0$, we have

$$w^{\mathrm{T}} f_{xx}(x_0) w \le -\beta w^{\mathrm{T}} w,$$

for all w such that

$$w^{\mathrm{T}} f_x(x_0) = 0.$$

$g: R^n \to R$ is locally α-quasi-convex at $x_0 \in R^n$ if $-g$ is locally α-quasi-concave at x_0.

Proof. This is an adaptation of Hartman–Olech's theorem in Hartman (1964, p. 548) to the system equation (5.8) with their $G(\cdot) = -W_{xx}(\cdot)$.

Theorem 5.3 allows a weak form of increasing returns to the state variable. For β-quasi-concavity in x of the imputed profit function, the Hamiltonian function $H^0(q, x) - pqx$ amounts to allowing increasing returns to x provided that the isoquants for each fixed q have enough curvature. We say that theorem 5.3 allows a *weak* form of increasing returns because we assume $W_{xx}(\cdot)$ is negative definite which implies a form of long run *decreasing* returns. In particular, the state valuation function is concave. Note that concavity of W does not imply concavity of U or T.

Theorem 5.3 is in an unsatisfactory state of affairs at the moment since it requires $W_{xx}(\cdot)$ to exist and to be negative definite, but we do not have a useful set of sufficient conditions on U and T for this to happen. Both this question and the question of stability analysis under increasing returns seem to be wide open and important fields of research. Systematic study of economic dynamics under increasing returns is likely to change our view of how a dynamic economy functions. See next chapter.

The last six theorems are all unified by the fact that they represent results that can be obtained from the Liapunov functions,

$$V_1 = -(q - q^*)^{\mathrm{T}}(x - x^*) \quad \text{and} \quad V_2 = -\dot{q}^{\mathrm{T}}\dot{x},$$

and their analogues. These results lead us intuitively to expect that G.A.S. is likely when $H^0(q, x)$ has a lot of convexity in q and a lot of concavity in x relative to the discount rate ρ. More specifically, the Rockafellar condition,

$$(R) \quad 4\alpha\beta > \rho^2,$$

or its analogues, are sufficient for G.A.S.

To sharpen our understanding of functions U and T that satisfy the hypotheses of the preceding G.A.S. theorems, it is useful to look at the OLRP or the linear quadratic approximation to problem (1.5) as given in equation (2.1). This we do in the next section. However, we record here the Hamiltonians for OLRP obtained by converting the OLRP into a maximization problem. They are

$$H(q, x, v) = x^{\mathrm{T}}(-Q)x + 2x^{\mathrm{T}}(-S)v + v^{\mathrm{T}}(-R)v + q^{\mathrm{T}}[F_x + G_v], \qquad (5.9)$$

$$H^0(q, x) = x^{\mathrm{T}}[SR^{-1}S^{\mathrm{T}} - Q]x + q^{\mathrm{T}}[F - GR^{-1}S^{\mathrm{T}}]x$$

$$+ \tfrac{1}{4}q^{\mathrm{T}}GR^{-1}G^{\mathrm{T}}q. \qquad (5.10)$$

Brock (1977a, p. 224) derives in detail equation (5.10).

6. Linear quadratic approximation

Let the Hamiltonians be given by

$$H(\eta, \xi, \gamma) = \xi^{\mathsf{T}}(U^*_{xx})\xi + 2\xi^{\mathsf{T}}(U^*_{xv})\gamma + \gamma^{\mathsf{T}}(U^*_{vv})\gamma$$
$$+ \eta^{\mathsf{T}}[T^*_x\xi + T^*_v\gamma], \tag{6.1}$$

$$H^0(\eta, \xi) = \xi^{\mathsf{T}}[U^*_{xx} - U^*_{xv}(U^*_{vv})^{-1}U^{*\mathsf{T}}_{xv}]\xi + \eta^{\mathsf{T}}[T^*_x - T^*_v U^{*-1}_{vv} U^{*\mathsf{T}}_{xv}]\xi$$
$$- \tfrac{1}{4}\eta^{\mathsf{T}}[T^*_v U^{-1}_{vv} T^{*\mathsf{T}}_v]\eta. \tag{6.2}$$

Substitute the formula

$$v^0 = -R^{-1}S^{\mathsf{T}}x + \tfrac{1}{2}R^{-1}G^{\mathsf{T}}q$$

to obtain the system

$$\dot{x} = Fx + Gv^0 = (F - GR^{-1}S^{\mathsf{T}})x + \tfrac{1}{2}GR^{-1}G^{\mathsf{T}}q = H^0_q(q, x). \tag{6.3}$$

Similarly,

$$\dot{\xi} = T^*_x\xi + T^*_v\eta = (T^*_x - T^*_v U^{*-1}_{vv} U^{\mathsf{T}}_{xv})\xi + T^*_v\eta. \tag{6.4}$$

Let us use these formulas to build some understanding of the meaning of the G.A.S. tests in the first five theorems, and to obtain at the same time some of the Magill (1977a) G.A.S. results for the OLRP. The Cass and Shell test requires that

$$\frac{\mathrm{d}}{\mathrm{d}t} V_1 = -\frac{\mathrm{d}}{\mathrm{d}t}(q - q^*)^{\mathsf{T}}(x - x^*) = -[(\rho q - H^0_x)^{\mathsf{T}}x + q^{\mathsf{T}}H^0_q] < 0, \tag{6.5}$$

for all q, x. Note the existence of the stationary solution $(q^*, x^*) = (0, 0)$ for the OLRP. From equations (5.10) and (6.5)

$$-\frac{\mathrm{d}}{\mathrm{d}t} V_1 = [\rho q - 2(SR^{-1}S^{\mathsf{T}} - Q)x]^{\mathsf{T}}x + q^{\mathsf{T}}[\tfrac{1}{2}GR^{-1}G^{\mathsf{T}}]q$$

$$= (q, x)^{\mathsf{T}}B(q, x), \tag{6.6}$$

where

$$B = \begin{bmatrix} H^0_{qq} & (\rho/2)I \\ (\rho/2)I & -H^0_{xx} \end{bmatrix} = \begin{bmatrix} \tfrac{1}{2}GR^{-1}G^{\mathsf{T}} & (\rho/2)I \\ (\rho/2)I & 2(Q - SR^{-1}S^{\mathsf{T}}) \end{bmatrix}, \tag{6.7}$$

which is the negative of the Magill (1977a) K^ρ matrix. Now it is easy to see that the Rockafellar condition (R) is basically the same as B positive definite. Thus in the case of the OLRP, all five G.A.S. tests developed in the first five theorems of this chapter amount to the same thing. This will not be true for nonquadratic problems.

When is B positive definite? To get some understanding for this put $G = I, S = 0$. Then in the one dimensional case, we require

$$(\tfrac{1}{2}R^{-1})(2Q) = R^{-1}Q > \rho^2/4. \tag{6.8}$$

Inequality equation (6.8) holds if Q is large, R is small and ρ is small. This is in accord with our earlier heuristic discussion of the stability of the OLRP. However, one source of stability or instability is ignored by equation (6.8) and indeed by all six theorems. That is the matrix F, which is the very law of motion of the system. We shall say more about F later.

In general, as is easy to see, B will be positive definite when

$$\underline{\lambda}[\tfrac{1}{2}GR^{-1}G^{\mathrm{T}}]\underline{\lambda}[2(Q - SR^{-1}S^{\mathrm{T}})]$$

$$= \underline{\lambda}[GR^{-1}G^{\mathrm{T}}]\underline{\lambda}[Q - SR^{-1}S^{\mathrm{T}}] > \rho^2/4, \tag{6.9}$$

where $\underline{\lambda}(A)$ is the smallest eigenvalue of $(A + A^{\mathrm{T}})/2$. Inequality (6.9) is the same as (R) since α-convexity of $H^0(q, x)$ means α equals the smallest eigenvalues of H^0_{qq} and, in this case,

$$H^0_{qq} = \tfrac{1}{2}GR^{-1}G^{\mathrm{T}}.$$

Similarly for β-concavity.

Return now to the role of the matrix F. Any information on F is wasted by the last six theorems. Indeed, it is pointed out by Magill (1977a) that a fruitful way to view G.A.S. tests based on the six theorems is that they give sufficient conditions for G.A.S. no matter *how stable or unstable the matrix F*. A test needs to be developed that uses information on F, for intuition suggests that, for the OLRP, if F has all eigenvalues with negative real parts, that is, F is a stable matrix, then it seems odd that it would be optimal to destabilize the system. This seems plausible because it costs $v^{\mathrm{T}}Rv$ to administer control; and one would think that in view of the cost $x^{\mathrm{T}}Qx$ of x being away from zero it would be sensible to use v to speed up the movement of x to zero when F is a stable matrix. However, there are two state variable examples in which the underlying system matrix is stable, but it is optimal to administer control to destabilize the system! See problem 7 in section 9 for an outline of how to construct such an example.

Now there is one test for G.A.S. of the OLRP that wastes no information at all. That is to count the eigenvalues of the linear system

$$(L) \quad \begin{aligned} \dot{q} &= \rho q - H^0_{xx}x - H^0_{xq}q, \\ \dot{x} &= H^0_{qx}x + H^0_{qq}q, \end{aligned}$$

and check whether half of them have negative real parts. Then, provided that the corresponding eigenvectors in (q, x) space generate a linear space whose projection on x space is all of R^n, G.A.S. holds. The problem posed by Harl Ryder of finding a neat set of conditions on (L), making full use of its structure, for half of the eigenvalues of (L) to have negative real parts and for the projection property to hold seems to be open. However, there are Routh–Hurwitz-type tests for $k \leq n$ of the eigenvalues to have negative real parts, but the problem appears to be in developing a test that is efficient in the use of the structure of (L).

Let us call this kind of test the *ideal OLRP test*. This sort of test has not been generalized in an interesting and useful way to nonquadratic problems, however. This is another research problem of some importance.

The tests proposed in the six theorems, wasteful relative to the ideal test for the OLRP though they may be, provide adequate results for nonlinear problems and generalize easily to the case of uncertainty. For example, they indicate that G.A.S. follows from just convexo-concavity of H^0 for the case $\rho = 0$, which is the famous no discounting case in optimal growth theory. Brock and Majumdar (1978) and also Chang (1982) develop stochastic analogues of theorems 4.1, 4.2, 4.3, 5.1 and 5.2 and obtain G.A.S. results for a highly nonlinear multisector model under uncertainty. The objective of the work being surveyed in this chapter is to develop G.A.S. tests on U and T that work for *nonlinear, nonquadratic problems*, and that generalize easily to uncertainty. Turn now to the development of a test that uses information on F.

7. Results based upon the Liapunov function V_3

Brock and Scheinkman (1977a) consider the class of Liapunov functions

$$V_3 = \dot{x}^\mathsf{T} G(q, x)\dot{x}, \tag{7.1}$$

where the matrix $G(q, x)$ is positive definite. Look at

$$\dot{x} = H_q^0(q, x), \quad x(0) = x_0. \tag{7.2}$$

Evaluate $\dot{V}_3$ along solutions of equation (7.2). One obtains

$$\dot{V}_3 = \ddot{x}^\mathsf{T} G\dot{x} + \dot{x}^\mathsf{T} G\ddot{x} + \dot{x}^\mathsf{T} \dot{G}\dot{x}$$
$$= [H_{qq}^0 \dot{q} + H_{qx}^0 \dot{x}]^\mathsf{T} G\dot{x} + \dot{x}^\mathsf{T} G[H_{qq}^0 \dot{q} + H_{qx}^0 \dot{x}] + \dot{x}^\mathsf{T} \dot{G}\dot{x}. \tag{7.3}$$

Here $\dot{G}(q, x)$, the trajectory derivative of G, is defined by

$$\dot{G}_{ij} = \sum_s (\dot{G}_{ijq_s} \dot{q}_s + \dot{G}_{ijx_s} \dot{x}_s) = \sum_s [G_{ijq_s}(\rho q_s - H_{x_s}^0) + G_{ijx_s} H_{q_s}^0]. \tag{7.4}$$

Assuming $W_{xx}(\cdot)$ exists and is negative semi-definite, so that $\dot{q}^T\dot{x} \le 0$ along solutions of equations (3.2) and (3.3) that correspond to optimal paths, equation (7.3) suggests choosing

$$G = H_{qq}^{0-1}. \tag{7.5}$$

Thus,

$$\dot{V}_3 = 2\dot{q}^T\dot{x} + \dot{x}^T\{H_{qq}^{0-1}H_{qx}^0 + (H_{qq}^{0-1}H_{qx}^0)^T + (H_{qq}^{0-1})'\}\dot{x}. \tag{7.6}$$

We may now state the following theorem.

Theorem 7.1. Let $q(\cdot)$, $x(\cdot)$ be a solution of equations (3.2) and (3.3) such that

$$\dot{q}^T\dot{x} \le 0 \quad \text{on } [0, \infty).$$

Assume

$$\dot{x}^T\{H_{qq}^{0-1}H_{qx}^0 + (H_{qq}^{0-1}H_{qx}^0)^T + (\dot{H}_{qq}^0)^{-1}\}\dot{x} \le 0 \tag{7.7}$$

along $x(\cdot)$. Also assume that $W_x(\cdot)$ exists. Then $x(t)$ converges to the largest future invariant set contained in

$$\{\bar{x}: \dot{V}_3(W_x(\bar{x}), \bar{x}) = 0\}.$$

The proof is just a standard application of Liapunov theory to the function V_3. See Brock and Scheinkman (1977a) for details and some extensions of theorem 7.1. Recall from chapter 4 that M is *future invariant* under $\dot{x} = f(x)$ if for each $x_0 \in M$ the solution $x(t, x_0)$ starting from x_0 stays in M for $t \ge 0$. Many times the special structure of the Liapunov function V and the law of motion f can be used to show that the largest future invariant set contained in $\{x_0: \dot{V}(x_0) = 0\}$ is a point. Obviously, theorems 4.1, 4.2, 4.3, 5.1 and 5.2 may be sharpened in this way.

Theorem 7.1 would be very nice if the term $\dot{H}_{qq}^{0-1}$ did not appear. This term is hard to grasp. However, for quadratic problems, and especially for problems where H_{qq}^0 is independent of (q, x), the G.A.S. test (7.7) is useful. Problems where H_{qq}^0 is independent of (q, x) arise in neoclassical investment models in which the adjustment cost function is quadratic, but the *production function* is not necessarily quadratic. See Brock and Scheinkman (1977a) for a wide class of investment models where equation (7.7) is applicable.

Let us apply equation (7.7) to the OLRP. Here

$$H_{qq}^{0-1}H_{qx}^0 = (\tfrac{1}{2}GR^{-1}G^T)^{-1}(F - GR^{-1}S^T). \tag{7.8}$$

To get some understanding for negative quasi-definiteness of equation (7.8) put $G = I$, $S = 0$. Then

$$H_{qq}^{0-1} H_{qx}^0 = 2RF. \qquad (7.9)$$

If R and F are one dimensional, then since $R > 0$ by convexity of the objective, we see that $F < 0$ implies G.A.S. by theorem 7.1 regardless of the size of ρ and Q. This is in accord with our intuition that, if F is a stable matrix, then the OLRP should be G.A.S. independently of ρ.

None of the G.A.S. tests mentioned above make use of H_{xx}^0 in a way that parallels H_{qq}^0 in theorem 7.1. This brings us to one of Magill's (1977a) nice results for the OLRP. We state it for the case of certainty only.

Theorem 7.2. (Magill (1977a).)   Assume that

$$-H_{qq}^0, \, H_{xx}^0$$

are negative definite. Furthermore, assume that

$$M^\rho = [\rho I - H_{xq}^0]^{\mathrm{T}}(-H_{xx}^0)^{-1} + (-H_{xx}^0)^{-1}[\rho I - H_{xq}^0]$$

is nonpositive definite. Then G.A.S. holds for the OLRP.

Proof.   Put

$$V = \eta^{\mathrm{T}}(-H_{xx}^0)^{-1}\eta.$$

Then, Magill (1977a) shows that

$$\dot{\eta} = \rho\eta(t) - H_{xx}^0\xi(t) - H_{xq}^0\eta(t), \quad \xi(t)^{\mathrm{T}}\eta(t) < 0$$

implies the following

$$
\begin{aligned}
\dot{V} &= \dot{\eta}^{\mathrm{T}}(-H_{xx}^0)^{-1}\eta + \eta^{\mathrm{T}}(-H_{xx}^0)^{-1}\dot{\eta} \\
&= [\rho\eta - H_{xx}^0\xi - H_{xq}^0\eta]^{\mathrm{T}}(-H_{xx}^0)^{-1}\eta \\
&\quad + \eta^{\mathrm{T}}(-H_{xx}^0)^{-1}[\rho\eta - H_{xx}^0\xi - H_{xq}^0\eta] \\
&= 2\xi^{\mathrm{T}}\eta + \eta^{\mathrm{T}}(\rho I - H_{xq}^0)^{\mathrm{T}}(-H_{xx}^0)^{-1}\eta + \eta^{\mathrm{T}}(-H_{xx}^0)^{-1}(\rho I - H_{xq}^0)\eta < 0.
\end{aligned}
$$

The rest is standard, since $\xi^{\mathrm{T}}\eta = 2\xi^{\mathrm{T}}W_{xx}\xi < 0$ under Magill's hypotheses.

8. The Liapunov function V_4

Consider the Liapunov function,

$$V_4 = a\dot{q}^{\mathrm{T}}\dot{x} + b\dot{x}^{\mathrm{T}}H_{qq}^{0-1}(q, x)\dot{x},$$

which leads to the following: find sufficient conditions on $H^0(q, x)$ such that $\dot{V}_4 \leq 0$ holds along $(q(t), x(t))$, $t \in [0, \infty)$, for particular choices of a, $b \in R$. One useful sufficient condition for $\dot{V}_4 \leq 0$ that emerges from this approach is

$$\rho \bar{\lambda}[H_{qq}^{0-1}H_{qx}^0 + (H_{qq}^{0-1}H_{qx}^0)^\mathsf{T} + (\dot{H}_{qq}^{0-1})] \leq 2\underline{\lambda}q[-H_{xx}^0] \qquad (8.1)$$

holds along the solution $(q(t), x(t))$ to equations (3.2) and (3.3). Here $\bar{\lambda}(A)$ denotes the largest eigenvalue of $(A + A^\mathsf{T})/2$ and $\underline{\lambda}$ the smallest.

Relationship (8.1) is derived by differentiating V_4 along solutions to equations (3.2) and (3.3),

$$\dot{V}_4 = \rho a \dot{q}^\mathsf{T} \dot{x} + a\dot{x}^\mathsf{T}(-H_{xx}^0)\dot{x} + a\dot{q}^\mathsf{T}H_{qq}^0\dot{q}$$

$$+ b\dot{x}^\mathsf{T}[H_{qq}^{0-1}H_{qx}^0 + (H_{qq}^{0-1}H_{qx}^0)^\mathsf{T} + (\dot{H}_{qq}^{0-1})]\dot{x} + 2b\dot{q}^\mathsf{T}\dot{x}.$$

Note that the first line of $\dot{V}_4$ is just

$$(\dot{q}, \dot{x})^\mathsf{T}B(q, x)(\dot{q}, \dot{x}),$$

so if B is positive semi-definite along $(q(t), x(t))$, just put $b = 0$, $a < 0$ to get $\dot{V}_4 < 0$ for all $t \geq 0$. Similarly, if $A \equiv H_{qq}^{0-1}H_{qx}^0 + (H_{qq}^{0-1}H_{qx}^0)^\mathsf{T} + (\dot{H}_{qq}^{0-1})$ is negative definite along $(q(t), x(t))$ and if we assume that $\dot{q}^\mathsf{T}\dot{x} \leq 0$ along optimal paths, we then get $\dot{V}_4 \leq 0$ for all $t \geq 0$ by putting $a = 0$, $b > 0$. The only case where we can get a new theorem, therefore, is when B is not positive semi-definite and A is not negative quasi semi-definite for all $t \geq 0$. Suppose that $\bar{\lambda}(A) > 0$, for $t \geq 0$. Grouping the terms common to $\dot{q}^\mathsf{T}\dot{x}$ in $\dot{V}_4$, choose $a < 0$, $b > 0$ such that $2b + a\rho \geq 0$. Then

$$\dot{V}_4 \leq a\dot{x}^\mathsf{T}(-H_{xx}^0)\dot{x} + b\dot{x}^\mathsf{T}A\dot{x} \leq a\underline{\lambda}(-H_{xx}^0)|\dot{x}|^2 + b\bar{\lambda}(A)|\dot{x}|^2, \qquad (8.2)$$

since $\dot{q}^\mathsf{T}\dot{x} \leq 0$. The right hand side of (8.2) is nonpositive provided that

$$\bar{\lambda} \leq (-a)\underline{\lambda}.$$

However,

$$(-a)\underline{\lambda} \leq \frac{2b}{\rho}\underline{\lambda}.$$

Therefore,

$$b\bar{\lambda} \leq \frac{2}{\rho}\underline{\lambda},$$

which is equation (8.1).

9. Miscellaneous applications and exercises

(1)   If the Hamiltonian $H^0(q, x)$ is separable, that is,

$$H^0(q, x) = F_1(q) + F_2(x), \tag{9.1}$$

for some pair of functions $F_1(\cdot)$, $F_2(\cdot)$, then Scheinkman (1978) shows that G.A.S. holds under convexo-concavity of H^0 by setting $V_5 = F_1(q)$, and using $\dot{q}^T\dot{x} \le 0$ to show that $\dot{V}_5 \le 0$ along optimal paths. Scheinkman has also generalized the above result to discrete time. Note that stability does not depend on the size of ρ. Separable Hamiltonians arise in adjustment cost models where the cost of adjustment is solely a function of net investment.

(2)   Araujo and Scheinkman (1977) have developed notions of dominant diagonal and block dominant diagonal that take into account the saddle point character of equations (3.2) and (3.3), and have obtained interesting G.A.S. results. The Araujo and Scheinkman paper also relates l_∞ continuity of the optimal path in its initial condition, in discrete time, to G.A.S. They show that l_∞ continuity plus L.A.S. of a steady state x^* implies G.A.S. of that steady state. Thus l_∞ continuity is not an assumption to be taken lightly. They also show the converse result that if G.A.S. is true, then l_∞ differentiability of the optimal paths with respect to both initial conditions and discount factor must hold. This establishes, in particular, that both the policy function and the value function are differentiable if G.A.S. holds.

(3)   Magill (1972, 1977b) has formulated a linear quadratic approximation to a continuous time stochastic process versions of problem (P), and has established the stochastic stability of this approximation. His paper (1972) was the first to point out the correct Liapunov function to use, namely the minimal expected value of the objective as a function of the initial condition x_0. Magill's stability result is the first one for the multisector optimal growth model driven by a continuous time stochastic process. Brock and Majumdar (1978) treat the discrete time stochastic case. See also Brock and Magill (1979) or Chang and Malliaris (1987) for the continuous time stochastic case. Malliaris (1987a) discusses some modelling issues in continuous uncertainty. This is a promising area for future research that is largely undeveloped.

(4)   Scheinkman (1976) shows the important result that G.A.S. is a continuous property in $\rho > 0$ at $\rho = 0$. This result was generalized for any $\rho > 0$ in Araujo and Scheinkman (1977). Burmeister and Graham (1973) present the first set of G.A.S. results for multisector models

under adaptive expectations. This looks like a promising area for future investigation.

(5)   Another particularly promising area of research is to apply the program of results surveyed in this chapter to noncooperative equilibria generated by N-player differential games, where the objective of player i is to solve

$$\sup \int_0^\infty e^{-\rho_i t} U_i(x_i(t), \hat{x}_i(t), v_i(t), \hat{v}_i(t)) \, dt$$

subject to

$$\dot{x}_i(t) = T_i(x_i(t), \hat{x}_i(t), v_i(t), \hat{v}_i(t)),$$

$$x_i(0) = x_{i0} \text{ given},$$

$$v_i(\cdot):[0, \infty) \to R^m \text{ measurable}.$$

Here $x_i(t) \in R^n$ denotes the vector of state variables under the control of player i; $v_i(t) \in R^m$ denotes the vector of instrument variables under control by i; and $\hat{x}_i(t)$, $\hat{v}_i(t)$ denote the state and instrument variables under control by all players but i. A discussion of the economic basis for these games and some very preliminary results is given in Brock (1977b).

(6)   The relationship between L.A.S. and G.A.S. is not well understood at this point. In particular, suppose that equations (1.5), (1.6) and (1.7) had only one rest point x^* and assume it is L.A.S. What additional assumptions are needed on the Hamiltonian to ensure G.A.S.? A nonlinear version of the OLRP suggests that this problem may be difficult. For example, consider the problem

$$\min \int_0^\infty e^{-\rho t}(x^T Q x + u^T R u) \, dt \tag{9.2}$$

subject to

$$\dot{x} = F(x) + Gu, \quad x_0 \text{ given}.$$

Note that only $F(x)$ is nonlinear. Now, arguing heuristically, if we let $|G| \to 0$, $|R| \to \infty$, $|Q| \to 0$, $\rho \to \infty$, then the optimal solution of equation (9.2), call it $\bar{x}(t, x_0)$, should converge to the solution $x(t, x_0)$ of

$$\dot{x} = F(x), \quad x(0) = x_0. \tag{9.3}$$

Here $|A|$ denotes a norm of the matrix A. In other words, given any differential equation system (9.3) we should be able to construct a problem (9.2) that generates optimum paths that lie arbitrarily close to the solution trajectories of equation (9.3). This suggests that any behavior that can be generated by systems of the form (9.3) can be generated by optimum paths to problems of the form (9.2). There are many systems $\dot{x} = F(x)$ that possess a unique L.A.S. rest point but are not G.A.S. An obvious example in the plane is concentric limit cycles surrounding a unique L.A.S. rest point.

In economic applications more information on F is available. We may assume $F(x)$ is concave in x, for example. Still, a lot of phenomena may be generated by systems of the form $\dot{x} = F(x)$ with F concave.

An important research project would be to classify the class of optimal paths generated by problem (1.5) for all concave U, T. The heuristic argument given above suggests that anything generated by equation (9.3) for F concave is possible. Thus, it appears that strong additional hypotheses must be placed on the Hamiltonian, above and beyond convexo-concavity, to get G.A.S. even when the rest point is L.A.S. and unique. It should be pointed out that there is a close relationship between uniqueness of the rest point and G.A.S. Obviously, G.A.S. cannot hold when there is more than one rest point. The uniqueness of rest points is comprehensively studied in Brock (1973) and Brock and Burmeister (1976).

(7) Without loss of generality, assume that $S = 0$ in equation (2.2). For the one dimensional case, it is fairly easy to show that $F < 0$ implies $\xi(t, \xi_0) \to 0$, $t \to \infty$ for all ξ_0, where $\xi(t, \xi_0)$ denotes the optimum solution of equation (2.2) starting from ξ_0. Thus we must go to the two dimensional case in order to construct a counter-example. Put $\xi = x$, $\eta = q$ to ease the notation.

The Hamilton–Jacobi equation

$$\rho W(x) = H^0(W_x(x), x), \tag{9.4}$$

generates, letting $W(x_0) = x_0^T W x_0$ be the state valuation function of equation (2.2), the matrix equation

$$\rho W = -Q + F^T W + WF + WGR^{-1}G^T W. \tag{9.5}$$

See Magill (1977a) for this easy derivation and a discussion of the properties of the Riccati quadratic matrix equation (9.5).

Now the system

$$\dot{x} = Fx + Gu^0 \tag{9.6}$$

becomes

$$\dot{x} = Fx + \tfrac{1}{2}GR^{-1}G^{\mathrm{T}}q = [F + GR^{-1}G^{\mathrm{T}}W]x \equiv Ax, \qquad (9.7)$$

using

$$q = W_x = 2Wx$$

and the formula for the optimal control,

$$u^0 = \tfrac{1}{2}R^{-1}G^{\mathrm{T}}q.$$

The task is to construct a matrix F that has all eigenvalues with negative real parts and to construct ρ, Q, R, G so that $F + GR^{-1}G^{\mathrm{T}}W$ is unstable. The easiest way to do this is to divide both sides of (9.5) by ρ, let $\rho \to \infty$, and change Q so that $Q/\rho = \bar{Q}$, where $\bar{Q}$ is a fixed positive definite matrix. Thus for ρ large, W is approximately given by $W = -\bar{Q}$ and

$$A = F - GR^{-1}G^{\mathrm{T}}\bar{Q}.$$

Our task now is to construct a stable matrix F and two positive definite matrices

$$B \equiv GR^{-1}G^{\mathrm{T}}, \; \bar{Q}$$

so that A is unstable. Put

$$B = \begin{bmatrix} b_1 & 0 \\ 0 & b_2 \end{bmatrix}, \quad \bar{Q} = I,$$

so that $BQ = B$ and $A = F - B$.

Pick stable F and positive diagonal B so that the determinant of $F - B$ is negative:

$$|F - B| = (F_{11} - b_1)(F_{22} - b_2) - F_{12}F_{21} < 0. \qquad (9.8)$$

To do this set $F_{11} + F_{22} < 0$,

$$F_{11} < 0, \quad F_{22} > 0, \quad F_{11}F_{22} - F_{12}F_{21} > 0.$$

Obviously, if b_1 is large enough and b_2 is small enough, then the right hand side of (9.8) is negative. This ends the sketch of the counter-example.

What causes this odd possibility that it may be optimal to destabilize a stable system when more than one dimension is present? To explain, let us call

$$B = GR^{-1}G^{\mathrm{T}}$$

the control gain. It is large when control cost, R, is small and Gu is effective in moving x. Now, the discount ρ is high on the future, but the state disequilibrium cost $Q = \rho I$ is large. For $i = 1, 2$, the cost of x_i disequilibrium is weighted equally by Q. But if b_1 is large and b_2 is small, then control gain is larger for x_1 than for x_2. Therefore, the optimizer administers more control to x_1 relative to x_2. But $-F_{12}F_{21} > 0$ in order that $F_{11} < 0$, $F_{22} > 0$, $|F| > 0$, so that the sign of the impact of an increase of x_2 on $\dot{x}_1$ is opposite to the sign of the impact of an increase of x_1 on $\dot{x}_2$. Thus the optimizer is led to destabilize the system.

The economic content of our example shows that optimal stabilization policy may be destabilizing when there is a high cost of state disequilibrium, a high discount on the future, and differential control gains or differential state costs.

10. Further remarks and references

It is appropriate to discuss why the results reported in this chapter are useful. In brief, their usefulness depends on their applicability in several areas of economic analysis as was indicated in section 9.

A first area is the neoclassical theory of investment associated with the names of Eisner-Strotz, Lucas, Mortensen, Jorgenson, Treadway, and others. A version of this theory was used by Nadiri and Rosen (1969) in a well-known article on estimating interrelated factor demand functions. The Nadiri-Rosen work culminated in their book (1973) which ended with a plea for useful results on problem (P).

The paper by Mortensen (1973) obtains a set of empirical restrictions on dynamic interrelated factor demand functions derived from the neoclassical theory of investment *provided that the stability hypothesis is satisfied*. Mortensen's paper can be viewed as *Samuelson's Correspondence Principle* done right in the context of the neoclassical theory of investment. Thus, there is no doubt that stability results are of great importance to the neoclassical theory of investment. More on this topic is presented in chapter 7.

A second area of applications of stability results is economic growth theory. Fortunately, this area is well covered in the papers by Cass and

Shell (1976a, 1976b), so we will not spend time on it here. It is, basically, the extension of the well-known turnpike theory of McKenzie, Gale, Radner, Samuelson, and others to the case $\rho > 0$. For an illustration of the importance of stability in economic growth see chapter 9.

A third area of applications of the results reported here is the dynamic oligopoly games of J. Friedman (1971), Prescott (1973), and others. These games represent important new efforts to dynamize the field of industrial organization. Indeed, this area is wide open for new researchers.

A fourth area of applications is the optimal regulator problem of engineering reported in Anderson and Moore (1971), the optimal filtering problem reported in Kwakernaak and Sivan (1972), and the integral convex cost problem of operations research discussed in Lee and Markus (1967, chapter 3). This application is developed by Magill (1977a). No doubt there are many more applications, but this should be enough to convince the reader that the stability problem is of basic importance in a number of areas.

Finally, the role of the transversality condition given in (4.1) or (5.7) is discussed in Benveniste and Scheinkman (1982) and Araujo and Scheinkman (1983). The mathematical analysis of deterministic optimal control with numerous applications in economics is presented in Kamien and Schwartz (1981) or Seierstad and Sydsaeter (1987). Fleming and Rishel (1975), Bensoussan (1982) and LaSalle (1986) give a rigorous mathematical presentation of deterministic and stochastic optimal control. Brock (1987a) and Malliaris (1987b) offer a brief introduction to the deterministic and stochastic optimal control in economics respectively. The specialized topic of the stability of optimal control is treated mathematically in Lefschetz (1965) and Roxin (1965a, 1965b).

CHAPTER 6

MICROECONOMIC DYNAMICS

> When one considers the equation,
> supply equals demand for several
> interdependent markets, the
> mathematical problem already takes
> on some sophistication.
>
> Smale (1976, p. 288)

1. Introduction

The previous chapter studies the question of locating sufficient conditions on the Hamiltonian of an infinite horizon optimal control problem for the optimal dynamics to be globally asymptotically stable. The hypothesis of joint concavity of the Hamiltonian in the state and the control factor was maintained throughout chapter 5.

The concavity hypothesis does not allow increasing returns. In this chapter we relax the hypothesis of concavity of the Hamiltonian. Increasing returns in the state variable are allowed. This leads to hard mathematical problems. To keep the analysis tractable and to focus on important economic issues of decentralization and stability that arise when increasing returns are present, we conduct the exposition in the context of a two sector economy. The reader is forewarned that we are entering unchartered terrain. Perhaps, the gaps in this chapter will stimulate badly needed research in the area of increasing returns. For recent work on increasing returns see Majumdar and Mitra (1982), Dechert (1983), Dechert and Nishimura (1983), Brock and Dechert (1985), Romer (1986a, 1986b, 1987), and Mitra (1987).

This chapter is written to make three points. First an infinite horizon two sector economy in which one sector is decreasing returns and the other is increasing returns may fail to achieve Pareto optimum, under decentralized institutions. This may occur even when the increasing returns sector is regulated in a *first best* fashion, efficient markets prevail, rational expectations obtain, and the necessity of the transversality condition at infinity for identical infinitely lived agents eliminate F. Hahn (1966) type problems. Second, there is a tendency for the increasing returns sector to overexpand although this is not always the case. Third, we illustrate the nature of stability analysis when increasing returns are present.

The chapter also provides an analytically tractable framework where the impact of different modes of regulation upon economic development paths may be studied. The framework presented here leads one to decompose the dynamic decentralization problem into a sequence of static decentralization problems.

Consider a two sector economy. Sector one is described by a one output, two input neoclassical production function. It provides consumption goods and capital goods which are perfect substitutes. Inputs are capital goods and energy. Energy is produced by a one output, one input increasing returns production function. Capital goods are input to the energy sector. Capital is shiftable across the two sectors. Welfare is measured by the discounted sum of utility of consumption over time.

Conditions may be located on the technologies so that the Pareto optimum problem is equivalent to the problem of one sector optimal growth under a convexo-concave technology treated by Skiba (1978).

Skiba shows that there are two trajectories I, II that satisfy the Euler equations and transversality conditions at infinity. The economy stagnates along II and grows along I. The optimum is found by calculating value functions $V_I(x_0)$, $V_{II}(x_0)$ along I, II for each level of capital stock x_0. Skiba shows that there is x_s such that $V_I(x_0) > V_{II}(x_0)$, for $x_0 > x_s$ and vice versa for $x_0 < x_s$. We come to our subject.

To study of decentralized regulatory institutions in the framework laid out above becomes a parable, intended to capture the main features of regulation of public utilities in the U.S. In the U.S., a state commission regulates public utilities in the state. National commissions such as the Federal Communications Commission regulate interstate business. It seems reasonable to assume that all of these commissions are so small relative to the U.S. capital market that they treat the cost of capital as parametric. The assumption of price taking public utilities and price taking commissions in the capital market is the key assumption that drives our results.

Consider the following parable. Imagine that production of goods takes place in a large number of regions. Each region is inhabited by a large number of identical neoclassical firms who all buy energy from one energy company. Energy production is a natural monopoly in each region. Each region has a regulatory commission that regulates its natural monopoly. Each firm buys capital input in the interregional capital market. Capital is mobile across regions and firms, and there are a large number of identical price taking consumers in each region.

Neoclassical firms are price takers in the goods market, the energy market and the capital market. Energy firms are price takers in the capital market. Since there are a lot of regions, each commission also acts like a price taker in the capital market. Call such an economy a *decentralized regulated* economy.

We will examine two classes of modes of regulation of energy firms. *First best* modes set the price of the last unit sold equal to the marginal cost of the last unit sold of energy at each point in time, such as an efficient multipart tariff. *Second best* modes impose a wedge between price and marginal cost. We define an α-competitive equilibrium to be a *decentralized regulatory competitive equilibrium* where all commissions use mode α of regulation.

The conclusions of the analysis are fourfold. First, if mode α is a first best mode of regulation then the first order necessary conditions (F.O.N.C.) of an α-competitive equilibrium are not satisfied by a rest point or one of Skiba's trajectories I, II. Second, first best α-competitive equilibrium may not exist when Pareto optimum is II. In other words suppose one accepts the decentralized institutions described above as reasonable abstractions of observed regulatory institutions. Then perfect capital markets, necessity of identical consumers' transversality condition at infinity, and rational expectations are not enough market forces to achieve a Pareto optimum – contrary to the case in which both sectors are neoclassical as in Brock (1982) or Prescott and Mehra (1980).

Third, we exhibit a class of examples where static first best regulatory institutions realize a social optimum even though commissions and their firms act as price takers in the capital market. In the examples, this state of affairs occurs when the output elasticities of capital and energy in the neoclassical sector are relatively small and economies of scale in energy production are not too large. In general, concavity of the aggregate production function as a function of raw capital input is sufficient.

Fourth, if all commissions follow a second best mode of regulation such as Ramsey (maximize surplus subject to breakeven constraint), then under general conditions on technology the F.O.N.C. of an α-competitive equilibrium are satisfied by two trajectories $\bar{I}, \bar{II}$. Moreover, the economy as a whole may follow $\bar{I}$ when $\bar{II}$ yields more welfare. Trajectory $\bar{II}$ cannot be supported by an α-competitive equilibrium.

The central finding that the decentralized regulatory institutions fail to generate Pareto optimal competitive equilibria, is likely to remain in more complicated setups with heterogeneous consumers, overlapping generations, multiproducts and uncertainty since these complications require even more markets to achieve the same degree of coordination.

The central cause of the failure of decentralized institutions is easy to explain. It is the assumption that commissions and their firms face interest rates parametrically. Even though the equilibrium interaction between interest rates and increasing returns generates F.O.N.C. satisfied by the same two trajectories and rest points as the optimum planning problem, it does not generate the correct mechanism for choosing between them. Hence, economic actors must engage in some type of joint centralized approach to the control of investment in order to achieve a Pareto optimum. They must coordinate their planned paths of investment. But this requires a degree of centralized planning that does not prevail in mixed economies.

2. First best regulatory modes in a two sector model

This section proceeds rapidly because we reinterpret existing literature. We analyze a two sector abstraction that is analytically tractable and generates a Skiba-like phase diagram under plausible assumptions. The optimum planning problem is

$$\text{maximize} \int_0^\infty e^{-\rho t} u[g_1(x_1, y_1) - \dot{x}] \, dt, \tag{2.1}$$

$$y_1 = g_2(x - x_1). \tag{2.2}$$

Here, g_1 is output of capital and consumables. The function g_1 is neoclassical, that is, it is jointly concave, increasing in both arguments and satisfying right and left hand Inada conditions. Function g_2 produces power which is needed as input into g_1. Power production is convex increasing, that is, increasing returns prevail in the power industry.

The economy's freely shiftable capital stock x is allocated between power production and capital goods-consumption goods production. Put

$$g(x) = \max_{x_1} g_1(x_1, g_2(x - x_1)). \tag{2.3}$$

We assume

A2.1. $g(x)$ is convexo-concave, $g(0) = 0$, $g'(0) = 0$, $g'(\infty) \le 0$, $g'(x) > 0$ for $x > 0$, and g is twice differentiable.

Function $g(\cdot)$ is graphed in figure 6.1.

Obviously the planning problem is a Skiba problem. Hence the Skiba (1978) results on optimal one sector growth under a convexo-concave production function may be applied to our problem. We digress to describe Skiba's results.

2.1. Digression on optimal growth under convexo-concave technology

Using the definition of $g(x)$ given in (2.3) the optimal planning problem (2.1) may be restated thus:

$$\text{maximize} \int_0^\infty e^{-\rho t} u(c)\, dt \tag{2.4}$$

$$\text{s.t.} \quad c + \dot{x} = g(x), \quad x(0) = x_0.$$

Put

$$p \equiv u'(c), \quad c \equiv C(p). \tag{2.5}$$

The Euler equation and material balance equation are given by

$$\dot{p} = p(\rho - g'(x)), \tag{2.6}$$

$$\dot{x} = g(x) - C(p). \tag{2.7}$$

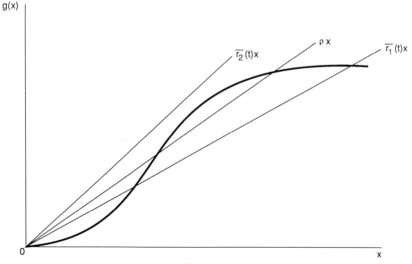

Figure 6.1

Let x_1^0 denote the value of x_1 that solves (2.3). Then g' is given by

$$g'(x) \equiv dg/dx = g_{1x_1}(x_1^0, g_2(x - x_1^0)),\tag{2.8}$$

where subscripts denote partial derivatives.

Define average product, $AP(x)$, and marginal product $MP(x)$ by

$$AP(x) \equiv g(x)/x; \quad MP(x) \equiv g'(x).\tag{2.9}$$

The convexo-concavity of g implies the relationship between AP and MP which is depicted in figure 6.2. Steady states of (2.6), (2.7) are given by the two points $\underline{x}$, $\bar{x}$. The system (2.6), (2.7) is phase diagrammed as in Skiba (1978, p. 536). The phase diagram is depicted in figure 6.3.

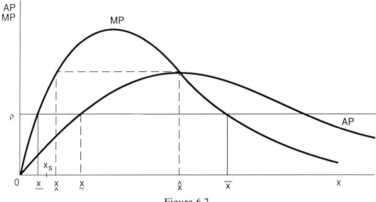

Figure 6.2

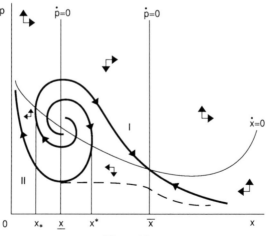

Figure 6.3

Skiba's result is:

Theorem 2.1. (Skiba (1978).)   Assume $\rho < \max AP(x)$. Assume A2.1 and suppose that trajectory II cuts $\dot{x} = 0$ at x^*. Then there is a cutoff point x_s such that $\underline{x} < x_s < \bar{x}$, and such that II is optimal for $x_0 < x_s$ and I is optimal for $x_0 > x_s$.

Proof.   See Skiba (1978) and Dechert and Nishimura (1983) for continuous time. Majumdar and Mitra (1982), and Dechert and Nishimura (1983) prove this result also for discrete time.

Notice that both trajectories I, II satisfy the transversality condition at infinity (TVC_∞),

$$\lim_{t \to \infty} p \, e^{-\rho t} = 0 \tag{2.10a}$$

as well as the Euler equation.

In order to avoid concern with technical tangentialities we will assume

A2.2.   (Nondegeneracy.)   The Skiba trajectories I, II and the steady states $\underline{x}$, $\bar{x}$ are the only trajectories that satisfy the Euler equation and the TVC_∞ (2.10a).

A useful tool in comparing values along different trajectories is

Lemma 2.2.   (Skiba (1978, p. 537).)   Let V_I, V_{II} denote the discounted sum of utility along two trajectories I, II starting at x_0 that satisfy the Euler equation and

$$\lim_{t \to \infty} e^{-\rho t} H(t) = 0, \quad H(t) \equiv u(\widehat{c(t)}) + u'(c(t))(g(x(t)) - c(t)). \tag{2.10b}$$

Then $V_{II} > V_I$ provided that

(i) $\dot{x}_1(0) \geq 0$, $u'(c_1(0)) < u'(c_2(0))$,

or,

(ii) $\dot{x}_1(0) \leq 0$, $u'(c_1(0)) > u'(c_2(0))$.

Proof.   Skiba shows that (2.10b) implies

$$\rho V_i = \int\limits_0^\infty e^{-\rho t} u(c_i)\, \mathrm{d}t = H_i(0). \tag{2.10c}$$

Apply (2.10c) to write, by putting $c_i(0) \equiv c_i$

$$\rho(V_{II} - V_I) = u(c_2) - u(c_1) + u'(c_2)(g(x_0) - c_2) - u'(c_1)(g(x_0) - c_1)$$

$$\geq u'(c_2)(c_2 - c_1) + u'(c_2)(g(x_0) - c_2) - u'(c_2)(g(x_0) - c_1) = 0.$$

The inequality follows from concavity of u and application of (i) or (ii). This ends the proof.

Corollary 2.3.   Let $\underline{V}$, $V_I(x_0)$, $V_{II}(x_0)$ denote values computed at the steady state $\underline{x}$, along I starting at x_0, and along II starting at x_0, respectively. Then $x_* < x_s < x^*$ and

(i) $V_I(x_*) < V_{II}(x_*)$,
(ii) $\underline{V} < V_{II}(\underline{x})$,
(iii) $V_{II}(x^*) < V_I(x^*)$.

If there is no point x^* where II cuts $\dot{x} = 0$ then

(iv) $V_I(x_0) < V_{II}(x_0)$,

for all x_0 where both I, II are defined.

Proof.   Apply lemma 2.2.

Let $\underline{x}$ be the smallest positive solution of the equation $g(x) = \rho x$. One can show that $x_s < \underline{x}$ by using a lemma of Dechert and Nishimura (1983).

Lemma 2.4.   (Dechert and Nishimura (1983).)   If $x(\cdot)$ is an optimal trajectory then

$$(DN) \quad g(x_0) \leq \rho \int\limits_0^\infty (g(x(t)) - \dot{x}(t))\, e^{-\rho t}\, \mathrm{d}t.$$

Proof. By Jensen's inequality

$$\rho \int_0^\infty e^{-\rho t} u(g(x(t)) - \dot{x}(t))\, dt \le u\left[\int_0^\infty \rho\, e^{-\rho t}(g(x(t)) - \dot{x}(t))\, dt\right].$$

Suppose by way of contradiction that

$$\int_0^\infty \rho\, e^{-\rho t}(g(x(t)) - \dot{x}(t))\, dt < g(x_0).$$

Hence, the constant path defined by $x(t) = x_0$, $t \ge 0$ generates more utility. This contradiction to the optimality of $x(\cdot)$ completes the proof.

Theorem 2.5. (Dechert and Nishimura (1983).) If $x_0 \ge \underline{x}$, where $\underline{x}$ is the smallest positive solution of $g(x) = \rho x$, then I is optimal.

Proof. We find a contradiction to (DN) if II is optimal. In view of corollary 2.3 we need only to examine the case $x_0 < x^*$. Notice that $\dot{x} \le 0$ along II. Therefore along II since $x_0 < x^* < \bar{x}$, we have

$$(\alpha) \quad g(x_0) - \rho x_0 \ge g(x(t)) - \rho x(t), \quad t \ge 0.$$

Multiply both sides of (α) by $e^{-\rho t}$ and integrate to get $(g(x_0) - \rho x_0)/\rho > \int_0^\infty (g(x) - \rho x)\, e^{-\rho t}\, dt = \int_0^\infty (g(x) - \dot{x})\, e^{-\rho t}\, dt - x_0$. Hence,

$$g(x_0) > \int_0^\infty e^{-\rho t}(g(x) - \dot{x})\, dt.$$

This contradicts (DN) and the proof is finished.

To understand the Skiba-Dechert-Nishimura results look at figure 6.4. The slope of V_i is given by the corresponding value of p_i, $i = $ I, II. The interval $[x_*, x^*]$ is the common domain of definition of V_i, $i = $ I, II. Look at Skiba's phase diagram to see that

$$V_I'(x_0) = p_I(x_0) > p_{II}(x_0) = V_{II}'(x_0), \quad x_0 \in [x_*, x^*].$$

Furthermore, we know that

$$V_I(x_*) < V_{II}(x_*),$$
$$V_I(x^*) > V_{II}(x^*).$$

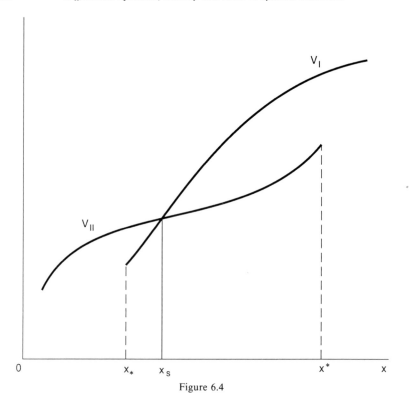

Figure 6.4

The conclusion that there is a unique cutoff point $x_s \in [x_*, x^*]$ follows. The cases where g is convex increasing and concave increasing are easy to analyze given the above background. Take the convex case first. The phase diagram is qualitatively the same as that obtained from figure 6.3 by pushing the large steady state $\bar{x}$ off to $+\infty$. Figure 6.4 still describes the qualitative features of the solution. Notice that if $x_0 < x_s$ it is still optimal to stagnate and run the capital stock down to the origin.

Turn now to the concave case. The phase diagram for this case is obtained from figure 6.3 by pushing $\underline{x}$ to zero. Doing this we obtain the standard phase diagram of the neoclassical growth model.

2.2. First best decentralization in a regulated economy

Let there be a large finite number of identical price taking consumers that act as if they are infinitely long-lived and let there be a large number of regions. Each region is populated by a large number of consumers, one public utility firm which produces power using technology g_2, one regulatory commission, and a large number of identical price taking firms who produce consumer-capital goods using technology g_1. Each consumer lives off income from equity in firms. In order to avoid notational clutter we will assume there is one region, one consumer and one firm of each type. Due care will be taken to differentiate between the individual and the aggregate.

The representative consumer solves (for the all equity financed, no tax case):

$$\text{maximize} \int_0^\infty e^{-\rho t} u(c)\, dt \tag{2.11}$$

$$\text{s.t.} \quad c + q_1 \dot{E}_1 + q_2 \dot{E}_2 = d_1 E_1 + d_2 E_2, \quad E_i(0) = E_{i0}, \quad i = 1, 2.$$

Here $q_1, q_2, E_1, E_2, d_1, d_2$ denote price of an equity share in firm i, quantity of equity held in firm i, and dividends per share in firm i, respectively. The consumer faces q_1, q_2, d_1, d_2 parametrically and chooses E_1, E_2, c to solve (2.11). Firm 1 will denote the representative consumer goods producer and firm 2 will denote the representative power producer. Turn now to describing the firm side of the economy.

Firms of both types are assumed to be initial equity value maximizers that face the cost of capital parametrically. Valuation formulae are developed below. The cost of capital is generated by the consumer's first order necessary conditions of optimality as in chapter 8.

Put $p \equiv u'(c)$. Then the consumer's first order conditions for optimality are given by

$$r \equiv \rho - \dot{p}/p = \dot{q}_i/q_i + d_i/q_i, \quad i = 1, 2. \tag{2.12}$$

Here r is the cost of capital. Following the analysis in chapter 8, apply the Benveniste and Scheinkman (1982) theorem to conclude that the following transversality condition at infinity (TVC_∞) is necessary for the consumer optimum:

$$\lim_{t \to \infty} p V_i\, e^{-\rho t} = 0. \tag{2.13}$$

Here

$$V_i \equiv q_i E_i, \tag{2.14}$$

denotes the equity value of firm i.

The accounting identities

$$P_i g_i - \dot{x}_i + q_i \dot{E}_i = d_i E_i, \quad i = 1, 2 \tag{2.15}$$

may be written in terms of equity value as

$$\dot{V}_i + \gamma_i = rV_i, \quad \gamma_1 \equiv g_1(x_1, y_2) - P_2 y_1 - \dot{x}_1, \quad \gamma_2 \equiv P_2 g_2(x_2) - \dot{x}_2. \quad (2.16)$$

Here P_2 denotes the price, possibly nonlinear, of good 2 in terms of good 1 as numeraire. Unlike chapter 8 there are no tax issues here that may effect the firm's policy of issuing shares. Therefore, we shall put $E_i = 1$. This simplification makes the asset pricing side of our model equivalent to the model of Lucas (1978).

Integrate (2.16) from 0 to T to get the valuation formulae

$$V_i(0) = \int_0^T e^{-\Gamma(t)} \gamma_i(t) \, dt + e^{-\Gamma(t)} V_i(T), \quad i = 1, 2, \quad (2.17)$$

where

$$\Gamma(t) \equiv \int_0^t r(z) \, dz. \quad (2.18)$$

It is easy to show as in chapter 8 that (2.13) implies

$$\lim_{T \to \infty} e^{-\Gamma(T)} V_i(T) = 0. \quad (2.19)$$

In other words, the necessity of the consumer's TVC_∞ prevents divergence between equity value and capitalized value of earnings in equilibrium.

Integrate the first term of (2.17) by parts to obtain

$$V_i(0) = \int_0^T e^{-\Gamma(t)} \pi_i(t) \, dt + x_i(0) - e^{-\Gamma(T)} x_i(T) + e^{-\Gamma(T)} V_i(T) \quad (2.20)$$

where

$$\pi_1 \equiv g_1 - P_2 y_1 - rx_1, \quad \pi_2 \equiv P_2 g_2 - rx_2,$$
$$\pi_1^0 \equiv \underset{x_1}{\text{maximum}} \, (g_1 - rx_1). \quad (2.21)$$

In order to insure well defined optima for firms we place the following restriction on paths of capital acquisition,

$$\underline{\lim_{T \to \infty}} \, e^{-\Gamma(T)} x_i(T) \geq 0. \quad (2.22)$$

Here $\underline{\lim}$ denotes limit inferior – the smallest cluster point of the sequence $\{x_i(T)\}_{T=0}^\infty$. Condition (2.22) is needed to prevent the firm from choosing borrowing strategies that asymptotically never pay off the loan.

In view of (2.19) we shall postulate that firms face $r(\cdot)$ parametrically and solve

$$\text{maximize} \int_0^\infty e^{-\Gamma(t)} \pi_i \, dt. \tag{2.23}$$

Notice that (2.21) defines static profit maximization problems from static microeconomic theory. If g_2 were concave we could just postulate static profit maximization and calculate a static general equilibrium of the static economy (2.21) at each point of time. The path of the interest rate would be determined via (2.21) by the additional requirement that the consumption the consumers are willing to forego add up to the total capital demanded by firms via (2.21). We will assume that the economy starts off in equilibrium. Namely the values of $x_i(0)$ are compatible with the values dictated by (2.21).

But g_2 is *not* concave. If firm 2 faces P_2 parametrically no optimum x_2 will exist since g_2 is convex. If firm 2 is regulated by the commission in its region so that, facing r parametrically, the static first best problem

$$\text{maximize} \int_0^{g_2(x_2)} D_2(y, r) \, dy - rx_2$$

$$\equiv \text{maximize} \ \pi_1^0(g_2(x_2), r) - rx_2, \tag{2.24}$$

is solved then firms of type 2 fail to break even with linear pricing schedules.

Here $D_2(y, r)$ denotes the demand curve generated by firms of type 1, facing P_2, r parametrically via (2.21). The demand curve $D_2(y, r)$ is just the marginal product schedule of power derived from π_1, that is, $D_2(y, r) = \partial \pi_1^0 / \partial y$.

Let us explain the breakeven problem. The first order necessary conditions for (2.24) are

$$D_2 g_2' \equiv P_2 g_2' = r. \tag{2.25}$$

But profits are

$$P_2 g_2 - rx_2 < 0 \tag{2.26}$$

because g_2 is convex. Hence, the firm will always run a deficit charging P_2 per unit. Later, we show that the firm may even run a deficit if it is allowed to extract the entire surplus (2.24).

The breakeven problem is well known and exhaustively studied in the literature on public utility pricing. First best modes of solving it are, for example, (i) lump sum taxes, (ii) appropriately designed multipart tariffs, (iii) contractual bidding for the market a la Demsetz (1968) where a contract is a multipart tariff schedule.

Assume that the static problem is solved in a first best manner for this section. Next we define the notion of first best decentralized regulatory competitive equilibrium.

Definition 2.1. *A first best decentralized regulatory competitive equilibrium* is an allocation $(\bar{x}_1(t), \bar{x}_2(t), \bar{y}_1(t), \bar{c}(t))$, an interest rate function $\bar{r}(t)$, a possibly multipart tariff schedule $T(y_1, r)$, stock price functions $\bar{q}_1(t)$, $\bar{q}_2(t)$ such that

(i) The solution of:

$$\underset{x_2}{\text{maximize}} \int_0^{g_2(x_2)} T(y, \bar{r}(t))\, \mathrm{d}y - \bar{r}(t)x_2$$

is $\bar{x}_2(t)$ for $t \geq 0$.

(ii) The solution of:

$$\underset{x_1, y_1}{\text{maximize}} \; g_1(x_1, y_1) - \int_0^{y_1} T(y, \bar{r}(t))\, \mathrm{d}y - \bar{r}(t)x_1$$

is $(\bar{x}_1(t), \bar{y}_1(t))$, for $t \geq 0$.

(iii) The solution functions $c(\cdot)$, $E_1(\cdot)$, $E_2(\cdot)$ of (2.11) facing $\bar{q}_1(\cdot)$, $\bar{q}_2(\cdot)$,

$$\bar{d}_1(\cdot) \equiv g_1(\bar{x}_1(\cdot), \bar{y}_1(\cdot)) - \int_0^{\bar{y}_1(\cdot)} T(y, \bar{r}(\cdot))\, \mathrm{d}y - \dot{\bar{x}}_1(\cdot);$$

$$\bar{d}_2(\cdot) \equiv \int_0^{\bar{y}_1(\cdot)} T(y, \bar{r}(\cdot))\, \mathrm{d}y - \dot{\bar{x}}_2(\cdot)$$

parametrically and initial conditions $E_{i0} = 1$, $i = 1, 2$, satisfy $c(t) = \bar{c}(t)$, $\bar{E}_i(t) = 1$, $t \geq 0$, $i = 1, 2$.

(iv) Let $x = x_1 + x_2$, $g(x) \equiv \text{maximum}_{x_1} g_1(x_1, g_2(x - x_1))$. Then $\bar{c}(t) + \dot{x}(t) = g(\bar{x}(t))$ for $t \geq 0$.

(v) The last unit of energy is sold at the demand price, that is, the multipart tariff schedule T is such that the solutions of (i), (ii), $\bar{y}_1(t) = g_2(\bar{x}_2(t))$, satisfy

$$T(\bar{y}_1(t), \bar{r}(t)) = \frac{\partial \pi_1^0}{\partial y_1}(\bar{y}_1(t), \bar{r}(t)),$$

where π_1^0 is the maximum of the function π_1 in (2.21) over x_1.

Theorem 2.6. (First order equivalence.)

(i) Both of Skiba's trajectories I, II and $\underline{x}$, $\bar{x}$ may be realized as the first order necessary conditions (F.O.N.C.) for a first best regulatory mode competitive equilibrium.

(ii) The F.O.N.C. for first best mode competitive equilibrium are the same as the F.O.N.C. for Skiba's trajectories I, II, $\underline{x}$, or $\bar{x}$.

Proof. In order to prove part (i) define $r(\cdot)$ by the formula

$$\bar{r}(t) = \rho - \dot{p}/\bar{p}, \tag{2.27}$$

where the right hand side is calculated along one of Skiba's trajectories, say I. It is easy to check that the Skiba values $\bar{x}_1(t)$, $\bar{y}_1(t)$ satisfy the F.O.N.C. for (2.21) and (2.24). Notice that a solution of the F.O.N.C. may not be a maximum.

With respect to consumers, since there is one perfectly divisible equity share outstanding for each firm, the consumer's budget constraint (2.11) becomes

$$c + q_1 \dot{E}_1 + q_2 \dot{E}_2 = \bar{y}_1 E_1 + \bar{y}_2 E_2. \tag{2.28}$$

Consumers face q_i, γ_i parametrically and choose E_i to solve (2.11). We have placed bars over γ_i because the F.O.N.C. for equity value maximization by firms facing $\bar{r}(\cdot)$ are satisfied by γ_i values equal to their Skiba values $\bar{y}_i$.

The values of q_i are determined as in Lucas (1978). Specifically, they are determined by the requirement that the demand for equity in firm i be equal to the supply of equity in firm i which is unity. Hence, for each t,

$$\bar{q}_i(t) = \int_t^\infty \exp\left[-\int_t^s \bar{r}(t)\, dt\right] \bar{y}_i(s)\, ds, \quad i = 1, 2, \tag{2.29}$$

$$\bar{c} = \bar{y}_1 + \bar{y}_2 = g_1(\bar{x}_1, \bar{y}_1) - \pi_1^0(\bar{y}_1, \bar{r}) - \dot{x}_1 + \pi_1^0(\bar{y}_1, \bar{r}) - \dot{x}_2$$

$$= g_1(\bar{x}_1, \bar{y}_1) - \dot{x} \equiv g(\bar{x}) - \dot{x}. \tag{2.30}$$

This ends the proof of part (i).

For part (ii) let $\bar{q}_1(\cdot), \bar{q}_2(\cdot), \bar{x}_1(\cdot), \bar{x}_2(\cdot), \bar{c}(\cdot)$ satisfy the F.O.N.C. of a first best regulated competitive equilibrium. We claim that an equilibrium satisfies the same Euler equations and TVC$_\infty$ as the Skiba paths I, II. The Euler equations and the necessity of TVC$_\infty$ for the consumer imply (dropping upper bars to ease notation)

$$r \equiv \rho - \dot{p}/p = \dot{q}_i/q_i + \gamma_i/q_i, \quad i = 1, 2, \tag{2.31}$$

$$\lim_{t\to\infty} q_i E_i p \ e^{-\rho t} = 0. \tag{2.32}$$

Equilibrium requires

$$E_i = 1. \tag{2.33}$$

Look at the firm side. Firms face $r(\cdot)$ parametrically and maximize (2.23) subject to (2.22). Matching up the firms' first order necessary conditions, the budget equation of the consumer, and the accounting identities of the firms, with (2.31) generates the same Euler equation and material balance equation as a Skiba trajectory I, II. The TVC$_\infty$ remains.

If firm 2 runs deficits we assume that either stockholders have unlimited liability or lump sum taxes are imposed on consumers to remove the deficits. If lump sum taxes render each $\pi_2(t) \geq 0$ in (2.20) then (2.34) is valid. If the capitalized value of $\pi_2(t)$ is negative then the argument given in the text for necessity of (2.35) breaks down. In this case we simply assume (2.35) in order to bypass more complicated arguments concerning necessity of transversality conditions at infinity.

Since g_1 is concave and if firm 2 is regulated at each point in time so that it breaks even, $E_i = 1$ and (2.20) implies

$$q_i = V_i \geq x_i. \tag{2.34}$$

Therefore (2.32) implies

$$\lim_{t\to\infty} p \ e^{-\rho t} = 0 \tag{2.35}$$

which is the TVC$_\infty$ satisfied by a Skiba trajectory I, II. Application of the nondegeneracy assumption A2.2 finishes the proof.

The main conclusion of this section is: more market and regulatory institutions are needed to get the economy onto the optimal Skiba trajectory. The problem seems basic for two reasons. First, F. Hahn (1966) type problems have been eliminated by necessity of the consumer's TVC$_\infty$. Second, distortions between marginal cost and price have been eliminated by first best regulatory institutions that seem operational under ideal conditions. Yet there is still not enough coordination to get a Pareto optimum.

It is known from Guesnerie (1975) and Brown and Heal (1980) that nonconvexities cause problems for decentralized markets in achieving Pareto optimality. Their framework is a finite dimensional commodity space Arrow–Debreu economy with nonconvex production sets. Our framework has an infinite dimensional commodity space but only one consumer type and a recursive structure. The work of Brown and Heal (1980) suggests searching for a general Brown and Heal marginal cost pricing equilibrium. This necessitates abandoning our institutional framework of decentralized commissions facing interest rates parametrically. The intent of this chapter is to show how *static first best* regulation schemes like theories used in practice can go awry when interest rates are treated parametrically. Therefore, it is not appropriate to use the Brown and Heal concept in this context. What may be surprising to public utility economists is the failure of the imposition of static *Brown–Heal–Guesnerie* first best decentralization schemes at each point in time together with imposition of TVC_∞ to correct the problem.

Notice however, if $g(x)$ defined by (2.3) is *concave* and increasing in x then there is no problem. That is to say $\pi_1 + \pi_2 > 0$ even though π_2 may be negative. Hence, a multipart tariff like that of (2.24) can be designed to price the last unit of energy at marginal cost but yet assure both firms non-negative profits at a given interest rate. Thus one can show that a first best competitive equilibrium is *Pareto Optimum* and vice versa when g is concave.

The problem of supporting the socially optimal trajectory I or II with a first best decentralized regulatory competitive equilibrium may be easily explained with the aid of figures 6.1 and 6.2. Four points may be made.

First, it is easy to see that

$$\bar{r}(t) = g'(\bar{x}(t)), \ \bar{x}(t) = \arg \max_x \ (g(x) - \bar{r}(t)x)$$

in any equilibrium. This requirement is the heart of the problem. Let us see why. Suppose for example that the stagnation trajectory II is socially optimal. Look at the line $\bar{r}_1(t)x$ drawn in figure 6.1. Interest rates $r(t) = g'(\bar{x}(t))$ eventually fall on II. But a small interest rate like $\bar{r}_1(t)$ in figure 6.1 causes each commission and its firm to select the large root of the equation $\bar{r}(t) = g'(x)$ rather than the correct small root. Hence, no trajectory which, at some point of time, satisfies $g''(\bar{x}_1(t)) > 0$ can be supported by a first best decentralized regulatory competitive equilibrium (FBCE).

Second, any part $\bar{x}_2(t)$ of a trajectory such that $\bar{x}_2(t) \in (\underline{x}, \check{x})$, that is, such that

$$\bar{r}_2(t) \equiv g'(x_2(t)) > \text{maximum } g(x)/x$$

can be supported by a FBCE. This is so because for interest rate $\bar{r}_2(t)$ the natural monopoly runs a deficit even though it captures all the surplus from the firms to which it sells.

Third, even though all points of Skiba's trajectories I, II satisfy the F.O.N.C. of a FBCE only the part of I that lies in the interval $[\hat{x}, \infty)$ may be supported by a FBCE.

Fourth, in the case where $g(x)$ is globally concave with $[\hat{x}, \infty) = [0, \infty)$, the amount of coordination necessary to correct the problem seems to require that the government choose the correct path of the rate base, x_2.

In any event the problem of two trajectories persist when we turn to second best modes of regulation.

3. Second best modes of regulation

The *Ramsey* and the *rate of return on rate base* model of Averch and Johnson (1962) are analyzed as two second best modes of regulation. In our framework the Ramsey problem is: Choose x_2 to solve

$$\text{maximize} \int_0^{g_2(x_2)} D_2(y, r) \, dy - rx_2 \tag{3.1}$$

$$\text{s.t.} \quad D_2(g_2, r)g_2 \geq rx_2. \tag{3.2}$$

Refer to (2.24) for the construction of demand curve D_2. Here the regulator is treated as facing r parametrically. Recall the parable in which each identical region contains a public utility commission that treats r as beyond its control because there are a large number of regions. Hence, each region is a small part of the capital market which is interregional.

The solution is given by

$$P_2 \equiv D_2(y_1, r) = rx_2(y_1)/y_1 \equiv AC(y_1, r). \tag{3.3}$$

Compare this with first best marginal cost pricing

$$P_2 \equiv D_2(y_1, r) = r/g_2' \equiv MC(y_1, r). \tag{3.4}$$

The solutions are graphed below.

Notice that convexity of g_2 implies $MC < AC$ for any level of r. Hence, marginal cost pricing induces a deficit which is removed by Ramsey pricing at the social cost of surplus foregone.

Turn now to rate of return on rate base regulation. In our framework rate of return regulation solves the problem

$$\text{maximize } D_2(g_2, r)g_2 - rx_2 \tag{3.5}$$

$$\text{s.t.} \quad D_2(g_2, r)g_2 \le (r + v)x_2. \tag{3.6}$$

Here $v \ge 0$ is the premium allowed on the rate base x_2. We call this type of regulation $AJ(v)$ after Averch and Johnson (1962). We assume that v is small enough that the AJ constraint is binding. Therefore, the solution is given by

$$P_2 \equiv D_2(g_2, r) = (r + v)x_2/g_2 = ((r + v)/r)AC(y_1, r)$$

$$\equiv (1 + \delta)AC(y_1, r). \tag{3.7}$$

It is clear from figure 6.5 that for the case as drawn we may parameterize different $AJ(v)$ modes of regulation by v with Ramsey being the limiting case $v = 0$. There is no room in a one input, one output production process for the familiar input distortions of AJ type to appear.

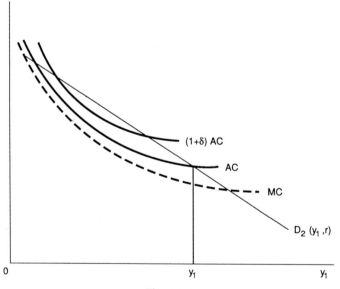

Figure 6.5

Next, we analyze the dynamics for each mode of regulation ν. The only thing that is changed from the decentralization in section 2 is equation (2.25). This becomes, for mode ν,

$$P_2 g_2 = (r + \nu) x_2. \tag{3.8}$$

Therefore, the dynamics are given by

$$r \equiv \rho - \dot{p}/p = g_{1x_1}[x_1(\nu, x), g_2(x - x_1(\nu, x))] \equiv MP_1(x, x_1(\nu, x)), \tag{3.9}$$

$$\dot{x} = g_1[x_1(\nu, x), g_2(x - x_1(\nu, x))] - c(p) \equiv g_1(x, \nu) - c(p). \tag{3.10}$$

Here $x_1(\nu, x)$ denotes the solution of

$$g_{1y_1}[x_1, g_2(x - x_1)](g_2(x - x_1)/(x - x_1)) - \nu = MP_1(x, x_1). \tag{3.11}$$

It is straightforward to locate assumptions on $g_1[x_1, g_2(x - x_1)]$ that will enable us to compare steady states. Recall that x_1^0 denotes the solution to

$$\text{maximize } g_1[x_1^0, g_2(x - x_1^0)] \equiv g(x). \tag{3.12}$$

The first order condition for (3.12) is given by

$$g_{1y_1} g_2' = g_{1x_1} = MP_1(x, x_1^0). \tag{3.13}$$

Notice that

$$g_{1x_1}[x_1^0, g_2(x - x_1^0)] = g'(x) = MP_1(x, x_1^0). \tag{3.14}$$

Since x_1^0 is the optimal choice of x_1 given x, it follows that

$$g_1(x, \nu) \le g(x). \tag{3.15}$$

Sufficient conditions on g_1 and g_2 are needed so that the relationship between $MP_1(x, x_1(\nu))$ and $MP_1(x, x_1^0)$ satisfies the natural condition

$$MP_1(x, x_1^0) > MP_1(x, x_1(\nu_1)) > MP_1(x, x_1(\nu_2)) \quad \text{for } \nu_2 < \nu_1. \tag{3.16}$$

Inequality (3.16) captures the idea that the marginal product of capital in the consumer–capital goods sector falls as the wedge between the second and first best allocations of capital across sectors widens. We assume (3.16) and bypass the routine job of locating sufficient conditions for (3.16) to hold.

A3.1. Inequality (3.16) is assumed to hold.

Let us phase diagram the second best dynamics and compare them with the first best (see figure 6.6).

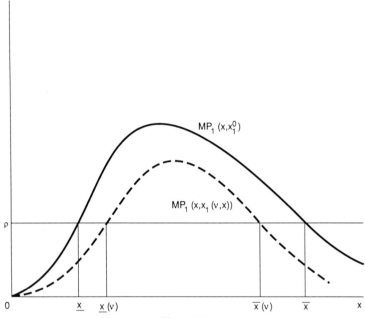

Figure 6.6

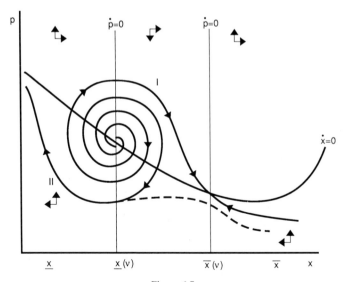

Figure 6.7

It is easy to explain intuitively what happens to the dynamics as we move from first best (marginal cost pricing of power) to second best (a form of average cost pricing of power) (see figure 6.7). Since marginal cost lies below average cost then, at any level of total capital stock, too little power is produced in second best. Under A3.1 a smaller input of power causes a drop in MP_1 at each level of total capital stock x. Since output of consumables drops, then the curve $\dot{x} = 0$ rises. Furthermore, the steady states move toward each other with $\underline{x}(\nu)$ rising and $\bar{x}(\nu)$ falling as ν rises. The vertical lines $\dot{p} = 0$ are pushed closer together as ν increases. They may pass in which case only II remains. This corresponds to $MP_1(x, x_1(\nu, x))$ falling below the horizontal line $p = \rho$ in figure 6.6.

Analysis of the second best dynamics is not easy. Skiba's argument (1978, p. 533) that there is no limit cycle around the steady state $(\underline{x}(\nu), \underline{p}(\nu))$ is no longer valid. Furthermore, his lemma 2.2 that is so useful in comparing values along I, II and steady states is no longer valid. We may still, however, draw three conclusions.

First, the fundamental problem of steering the economy onto the welfare maximizing path still remains. There are three trajectories that satisfy the F.O.N.C. of regulatory equilibria: (i) the steady state $(\underline{x}(\nu), \underline{p}(\nu))$, (ii) the trajectory I, and (iii) the trajectory II. No apparent mechanism other than central coordination will suffice to get the economy onto the welfare maximizing equilibrium.

Second, the *Klevorick problem* (1971) of the optimal choice of ν may be posed for each x_0 as

$$\underset{\nu \geq 0}{\text{maximize }} W(\nu, x_0),$$

where

$$W(\nu, x_0) \equiv \text{maximum}\, \{V_I(x_0, \nu), V_{II}(x_0, \nu)\}.$$

Another choice appears when $x_0 = \underline{x}(\nu)$, with respect to the steady state $(\underline{x}(\nu), \underline{p}(\nu))$. This problem is much more difficult to solve and operationalize than the original partial equilibrium Klevorick problem.

Third, the problem of multiple equilibrium paths of development is surely worse in multiproduct, multi-input, heterogeneous consumer extensions of our model. The conclusion is that the fine tuning suggested by the Ramsey-Baumol-Bradford-Diamond-Mirrlees optimal tax theory may be self defeating unless the economy is on the correct development path in the first place.

4. Multiple optimal paths

Here we analyze cases where the aggregate production function g has multiple zones of convexo-concavity. Call a zone of convexo-concavity a *development stage*, that is, a stage of economic growth. The terminology is motivated by Rostow's famous metaphor. The model of the previous two sections has only one development stage. The model analyzed below has only two for ease of exposition. The analysis of first best follows section two and is embodied in figures 6.8, 6.9, and 6.10.

In order to focus attention we assume the relationship between MP and ρ that is depicted in figure 6.9.

We see from figure 6.10 that there are several trajectories that satisfy the Euler equation and the TVC_∞. The same decentralization analysis developed in section two may be used to show that each trajectory α, $\alpha = I, II, III, IV$ as well as the four rest points satisfy the F.O.N.C. of first best regulatory institutions. The difficulty in decentralization discovered in section two emerges with a vengeance when there are multiple development stages. Turn now to determination of the optimum.

Judicious use of Skiba's lemma 2.2 will allow us to determine the optimum. Since there are so many possibilities to screen out, it is useful to state the

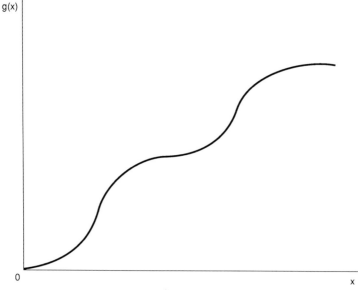

Figure 6.8

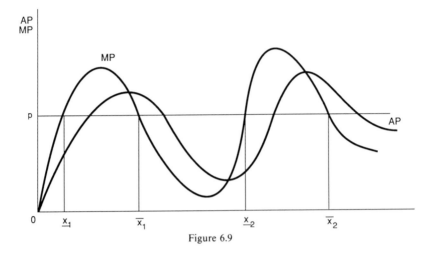

Figure 6.9

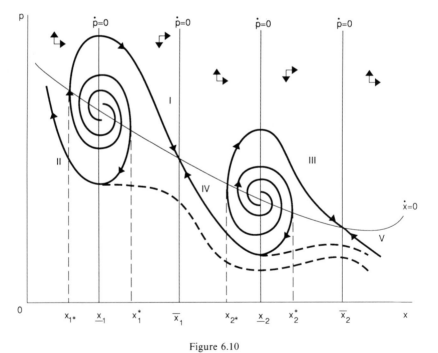

Figure 6.10

basic principle of Skiba's lemma 2.2 intuitively. If at x_0 you have two trajectories α, β where (i) initial investment on α is nonnegative and the initial price of investment $(u'(c_\beta(0)))$ on β is bigger than on α; or (ii) initial investment on α is nonpositive and the initial price of investment on β is smaller than on α then

$$\beta > \alpha \text{ at } x_0. \tag{4.1}$$

Hence, $\beta > \alpha$ at x_0 means the value of the discounted sum of consumption along β is bigger than α starting at x_0. Notice that initial investment on β is positive in case (i) and negative in case (ii).

We need to dispose of some degenerate cases. Skiba's lemma shows that I, II $> (\underline{x}_1, \underline{p}_1)$, at $\underline{x}_1$ and III, IV $> (\underline{x}_2, \underline{p}_2)$ at $\underline{x}_2$. Hence, we ignore $\underline{x}_1, \underline{x}_2$. Suppose that II follows the dotted path in figure 6.10, that is, there is no $x_1^* > 0$ such that II cuts $\dot{x} = 0$. Skiba's lemma immediately implies that II $>$ V at $x_0 \geq \bar{x}_2$, II $>$ III $=$ V at $\bar{x}_2$, II $>$ IV at x_2^*, II $>$ III at x_{2*}, II $>$ I $=$ IV at $\bar{x}_1$, II $>$ I, at x_{1*}. Since the initial price, $p_i(0)$, satisfies $p_i(0) = V_i'(x_0)$, at x_0, then the chain of inequalities derived above shows that II $> i, i = 1, \ldots,$ V. In order to avoid this degeneracy we assume II cuts $\dot{x} = 0$ at x_1^* as depicted in figure 6.10. Turn to the dotted portion of IV.

As in the analysis of II, Skiba's lemma implies IV $>$ V at $x_0 > \bar{x}_2$, IV $>$ III $=$ V at $\bar{x}_2$, and IV $>$ III at x_{2*}. Hence, on (x_{2*}, ∞), IV $>$ III, V. Since there is no point in discussing two development phases when one is dominant, we assume that there is x_2^* such that IV cuts $\dot{x} = 0$ at x_2^*. Call the case depicted in continuous lines in figure 6.10 *regular*.

Definition 4.1. The dynamics are said to be *regular* if there exist points $x_{1*}, x_1^*, x_{2*}, x_2^*$ such that I, II, III, IV cut $\dot{x} = 0$ at $x_{1*}, x_1^*, x_{2*}, x_2^*$ respectively.

We may now prove

Theorem 4.1. If the dynamics are regular then the optimum is constructed from figure 6.10 as follows: Let $V^0(x_0)$ be the optimum value starting at x_0. Then

(i) There are cutoff points $x_{1s} \in (x_{1*}, x_1^*), x_{2s} \in (x_{2*}, x_2^*)$ such that $V^0(x_0) = V_{II}(x_0), x_0 \in (0, x_{1s})$.

(ii) $V^0(x_0) = V_I(x_0), x_0 \in [x_{1s}, \bar{x}_1]$.

(iii) $V^0(x_0) = V_{IV}(x_0), x_0 \in [\bar{x}_1, x_{2s}]$.

(iv) $V^0(x_0) = V_{III}(x_0), x_0 \in [x_{2s}, \bar{x}_2]$.

(v) $V^0(x_0) = V_V(x_0), x_0 \in [\bar{x}_2, \infty)$.

Proof. The logic of the proof is contained in figure 6.11.

Apply Skiba's lemma to verify that the relationship between the value functions at x_{i*}, x_i^*, $i = 1, 2$ is as depicted. Then use $p_i(0) = V_i'(x_0)$ to fill in the rest of the values of V_i as graphed in figure 6.11.

The values at steady states $\underline{x}_i$, $i = 1, 2$ are represented by open circles. Skiba's lemma shows that they are dominated as shown in figure 6.11. This ends the proof.

The method of construction outlined above may be applied to economies with any number of stages of growth. In the n stage regular case there will be cutoff values $x_{is} \in (x_{i*}, x_i^*)$, $i = 1, 2, \ldots, n$ that determine when to switch from one trajectory to another. Furthermore, for all i, the steady state $\underline{x}_i \in (x_{i*}, x_i^*)$ will be dominated by both choices.

We conclude that all of the possibilities depicted in figure 6.11, including the steady states $\underline{x}_i$, $i = 1, 2$ may be realized by first best decentralization schemes. The *upper envelope* will not be attained unless some centralized authority coordinates rate bases. Recall that in this model the rate base is just x_2. The problem of the possible inefficiency of the first best mode regulatory equilibrium is worse.

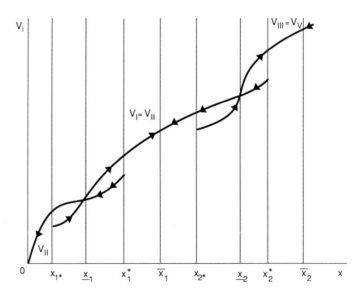

Figure 6.11

5. Examples

It is useful to have some worked examples to illustrate the phenomena presented. Let

$$g_1(x_1, y_1) = x_1^{\alpha_1} y_1^{\beta_1};$$

$$0 < \alpha < 1, 0 < \beta_1 < 1, \alpha_1 + \beta_1 < 1, g_2(x_2) = x_2^{a_2}, a_2 > 1. \tag{5.1}$$

Then

$$g(x) \equiv \max_{0 \le x_1 \le x} g_1(x_1, g_2(x - x_1))$$

$$= (\alpha_1(\alpha_1 + \beta_1 a_2)^{-1})^{\alpha_1} (\beta_1 a_2(\alpha_1 + \beta_1 a_2)^{-1})^{\beta_1 a_2} x^{\alpha_1 + \beta_1 a_2}$$

$$\equiv A x^{\alpha_1 + \beta_1 a_2}. \tag{5.2}$$

Notice that $g(x)$ may be convex or concave. In order to have a solution to the optimum planning problem we assume concavity of g, that is,

$$\alpha_1 + \beta_1 a_2 < 1. \tag{5.3}$$

Under assumption 3.1 the planning problem (2.1) is a standard textbook Ramsey optimal growth problem with concave production function.

For the decentralization case, find the inverse demand curve $P_2 \equiv D_2(y_1, r)$ by solving the F.O.N.C. of (2.21),

$$\alpha_1 x_1^{\alpha_1 - 1} y_1^{\beta_1} = r, \ \beta_1 x_1^{\alpha_1} y_1^{\beta_1 - 1} = P_2. \tag{5.4}$$

Doing so we obtain

$$x_1 = r^{1/(\alpha_1 - 1)} \alpha_1^{1/(1-\alpha_1)} y_1^{\beta_1/(1-\alpha_1)};$$

$$P_2 = \beta_1 x_1^{\alpha_1} y_1^{\beta_1 - 1} = \beta_1 \alpha_1^{\alpha_1/(1-\alpha_1)} r^{\alpha_1/(\alpha_1 - 1)} y_1^{\alpha} \equiv D_2(y_1, r), \tag{5.5}$$

where

$$\alpha \equiv \beta_1 - 1 + \frac{\beta_1 \alpha_1}{1 - \alpha_1} = \frac{\alpha_1 + \beta_1 - 1}{1 - \alpha_1} < 0. \tag{5.6}$$

Put

$$B(x_2, r) \equiv \int_0^{g_2(x_2)} D_2(y, r) \, dy = (1 - \alpha_1) \alpha_1^{\alpha_1/(1-\alpha_1)} r^{\alpha_1/(\alpha_1-1)} g_2^{\beta_1/(1-\alpha_1)}$$

$$\equiv (1 - \alpha_1) L(r) x_2 \frac{a_2 \beta_1}{1 - \alpha_1}. \tag{5.7}$$

From (5.7) *social benefits* B falls in r and rises in x_2. The main point is that B is concave in x_2 when the exponent

$$\beta \equiv a_2\beta_1/(1-\alpha_1) \tag{5.8}$$

is less than unity and B is convex when β is greater than unity. Notice that (5.3) is equivalent to $\beta < 1$. Let us look at decentralization.

Let $\bar{x}_1(t)$, $\bar{y}_1(t)$ solve the optimum planning problem (2.1). Define $\bar{r}(t)$ by

$$\bar{r}(t) = g'(x(t)) = p - \dot{p}/\bar{p} \tag{5.9}$$

as in (2.27). From facing $\bar{r}(t)$ parametrically it follows that $\bar{x}_2(t)$ is the unique solution of (2.24) when $\beta < 1$ and $x_2^0(t) = +\infty$ is the solution of (2.24) when $\beta > 1$.

The conclusion is that the *global social optimum* may be realized by regulated utilities and atomistic firms solving (2.24) and (2.20), (2.21) facing $\bar{r}(t)$ parametrically *provided* that $\beta < 1$. If $\beta > 1$, regulated utilities will expand their rate bases x_2 to infinity facing *any* interest rate $\bar{r}(t)$ parametrically. In this case there is no equilibrium.

For the Ramsey regulation problem (3.1) becomes, recalling that β denotes $a_2\beta_1/(1-\alpha_1)$

$$\text{maximize } (1-\alpha_1)L(r)x_2^\beta - rx_2 \tag{5.10}$$

$$\text{s.t. } \beta_1 L(r)x_2^\beta \geq rx_2. \tag{5.11}$$

Since $1-\alpha_1 > \beta_1$, therefore, in the case $\beta > 1$ the Ramsey problem is unbounded and $x_2 = +\infty$ is the solution.

For the $AJ(\nu)$ regulation problem (3.5) becomes

$$\text{maximize } \beta_1 L(r)x_2^\beta - rx_2 \tag{5.12}$$

$$\text{s.t. } \beta_1 L(r)x_2^\beta \leq (r+\nu)x_2. \tag{5.13}$$

The conclusion is that the much maligned $AJ(\nu)$ regulation performs better than Ramsey and first best in this *general* equilibrium economy in a certain sense. To explain, let x_2^ν denote the positive rate base that solves (5.13) with equality. The marginal incentive to expand x_2^ν is ν. Since $\beta > 1$ the marginal incentive rises with the rate base for Ramsey and first best. In the case $\beta < 1$, $AJ(\nu)$ regulation induces choice of x_2 nearer to the social optimum than private profit maximizing monopoly. The reader is encouraged to reflect on this problem and to read Dechert (1984) which shows that the Averch-Johnson effect has not been theoretically justified under the assumptions that are relevant in regulation.

Next, we turn to several microeconomic applications before we conclude the chapter with further remarks. Actually, since the last section continues the discussion on what has been said so far, it can be read before section 6.

6. Miscellaneous application and exercises

(1) Following Gaudet (1977), suppose that a competitive firm's production function is of the Cobb-Douglas form

$$F(K, L) = K^\alpha L^\beta,$$

where $0 < \alpha, \beta < 1$. Let $\varepsilon = \alpha + \beta$ take on any positive value. K denotes capital units, L denotes labor units, p is the output price and w is the real wage. Investment expenditures, at the rate of gross investment I, are $qI + pC(I)$, where $pC(I)$ represents adjustment costs and q is the supply price of investment goods. The firm maximizes the sum of discounted future net cash flows

$$PV = \int_0^\infty e^{-rt} \{ pK^\alpha L^\beta - wL - qI - pC(I) \}\, dt$$

subject to

$$\dot{K} = I - \delta K, \quad K(0) = K_0$$

where $\delta > 0$ denotes rate of depreciation. The Euler–Lagrange equations for this problem are

$$\dot{I} = \{ (r+\delta)[q + pC'(I)] - paK^{(1-\varepsilon)/(\beta-1)} \}/pC''(I), \tag{6.1}$$

$$\dot{K} = I - \delta K. \tag{6.2}$$

Note that L has been solved as a function of K and the real wage from the marginal productivity of labor, and $a = \alpha w/p(\beta - 1)$. The first and second derivatives of $C(I)$ are denoted by $C'(I)$ and $C''(I)$ respectively. $C'(I) > 0$ as $I > 0$; $C'(I) < 0$ as $I < 0$; $C''(I) > 0$.

Let $(\bar{K}, \bar{I})$ denote an arbitrary equilibrium of (6.1)–(6.2). That is,

$$(r+\delta)[q + pC'(\bar{I})] - pa\bar{K}^{(1-\varepsilon)/(\beta-1)} = 0,$$

$$\bar{I} - \delta\bar{K} = 0.$$

Linearizing system (6.1)-(6.2) around $(\bar{K}, \bar{I})$, we find that its characteristic roots are

$$\theta = r/2 \pm \left[(r/2)^2 + (r+\delta)\delta - \frac{a(1-\varepsilon)\bar{K}^b}{(\beta-1)C''(\bar{I})} \right]^{1/2},$$

where $b = [2(1-\beta) - \alpha]/(\beta-1)$. If

$$(r+\delta)\delta > [a(1-\varepsilon)\bar{K}^b]/[(\beta-1)C''(I)] \tag{6.3}$$

then both roots are real and of opposite signs and $(\bar{K}, \bar{I})$ is a *saddle point* equilibrium. If (6.3) does not hold, then the roots are either real and both positive or complex with positive real parts and $(\bar{K}, \bar{I})$ is locally *unstable*.

To study the role of returns to scale on the stability of the equilibrium $(\bar{K}, \bar{I})$ note that if decreasing returns, $\varepsilon < 1$, or constant returns, $\varepsilon = 1$, hold then inequality (6.3) is satisfied and as already noted saddle point stability holds and the optimal investment path is the stable manifold of the saddle equilibrium. Furthermore, notice that (6.3) imposes no restriction on the sign of $(1-\varepsilon)$ and therefore we may have a saddle point stable equilibrium even with increasing returns to scale, $\varepsilon > 1$. Gaudet (1977) concludes that although an unstable equilibrium can occur only with increasing returns to scale, the existence of increasing returns does not rule out the possibility of a saddle point stability. For a stability analysis under increasing returns see Brock and Dechert (1985).

(2) A fundamental problem in corporate finance is the optimal determination of the amount and mix of equity and debt capital to allocate to net investment, and the subsequent decision concerning the firm's growth and divident policy.

Assume that capital markets are purely competitive, investors prefer more wealth to less and the investment decision process leaves the firm's business risk-class unchanged. Denote by

$W(\tau) = $ the value of the firm to its equity holders at τ,
$B(t) = $ the stock of debt capital,
$E(t) = $ the stock of equity capital,
$k_j(B/E) = $ the equity investors' market-determined opportunity rate for a dollar of expected return of a firm in risk-class j as a function of the firm's financial risk or debt-to-equity ratio,
$\bar{X}(t) = $ the level of expected net earnings available to all equity owners,
$b(t) = $ the net change in debt financing,

$i(t)$ = the net change in internal equity financing,

$s(t)$ = the net change in external equity financing,

$\sigma(s)$ = the average per dollar flotation costs of new equity as a function of the dollar amount of external equity issued,

y, z = constant interest rate and corporate tax rates,

θ, ϕ = earnings functions.

The firm's investment financing, dividend and growth decision model can be stated as

$$\max_{\{b,i,s\}} W(0) = \int_0^\infty [\bar{X}(t) - i(t) - s(t)] \exp\{-k_j[B(t)/E(t)]t\} \, \mathrm{d}t,$$

$$\dot{B}(t) = b(t),$$

$$\dot{E}(t) = i(t) + [1 - \sigma(s)]s(t), \quad 0 < \sigma \le 1, \ t > 0,$$

$$\dot{X}(t) = \theta[\bar{X}(t)]\phi[b(t), i(t), (1-\sigma)s(t), y, z],$$

$$i(t) \le \bar{X}(t), \ B(0), \ E(0), \ X(0) \text{ given.}$$

Senchack (1975), who develops this problem in detail, states necessary and sufficient conditions for the firm's optimal earnings and dividend time sequences and determines conditions for the existence and stability of the firm's equilibrium paths. Senchack (1975, p. 551) concludes that in the initial high-growth stage of a firm's life cycle, when $\theta_X > 0$, the equilibrium growth path will be locally *unstable* while in the declining growth period when $\theta_X < 0$, the firm's path will be locally *stable*.

(3) Turnovsky et al. (1980) study the question of whether or not consumers benefit from price stability using a more general utility criterion than the concept of consumer surplus. They show that the consumer's preference for price instability depends upon four parameters: (i) the income elasticity of demand for the commodity, (ii) the price elasticity of demand, (iii) the share of the budget spent on the commodity in question, and (iv) the coefficient of relative risk aversion. The desirability of price instability increases with the magnitudes of the two elasticities, it decreases with the degree of risk aversion and its response to an increase in the budget share is indeterminate. For details see Turnovsky et al. (1980) and Baye (1985). For a brief review of the literature on the topic of price instability and

economic welfare see Waugh (1944), Oi (1961), Massel (1969), and Samuelson (1972b).

Craine (1987), has recently shown, in the context of general equilibrium models of asset pricing with production, that these results of price stability and economic welfare disappear once general equilibrium feedback facts are taken into account. We refer the reader to Craine (1987) for an understanding of the relationship between relative price stability and economic welfare.

(4) The stability properties of the Cournot model of oligopoly have been studied by several economists. F. Hahn (1962) states two sufficient conditions for stability under the standard adjustment system. These are (i) the marginal cost curve for individual firms should not fall faster than market demand and, (ii) marginal revenue of each producer should fall, at given output of his, were the remaining producers to expand their collective output. Seade (1980) extends the analysis of these two conditions for local instability. Al-Nowaihi and Levine (1985) study local and global stability conditions and correct the well known proof of Hahn (1962). For an extensive analysis of the stability of oligopoly see Okuguchi (1976). Cartel stability is studied by Donsimoni et al. (1986).

(5) Walras, Hicks and Samuelson have made important contributions to the stability of general competitive equilibrium. Walras (1954) as early as 1874 analyzed the problem of stability for the two-commodity exchange economy. Hicks (1946) extended the stability analysis to the multi-market economy by distinguishing two types of stability: *imperfect stability* and *perfect stability.*

According to Hicks, a competitive equilibrium is *imperfectly stable* if excess demand for any commodity is negative when its price is above equilibrium, given that all other prices are adjusted so that the markets for all other commodities are cleared. A competitive equilibrium is *perfectly stable* or *Hicksian stable* if excess demand for any commodity is negative when its price is above the equilibrium level, given that any arbitrary set of prices may be adjusted, the others being held fixed, as long as the markets for those commodities whose prices are adjusted are cleared. Hicks shows that the only source of instability of a competitive equilibrium is asymmetric income effects.

Samuelson (1947, p. 261) defines the general competitive equilibrium to have *perfect stability of the first kind if from* any initial conditions all the variables approach their equilibrium values in the limit as time approaches infinity. Note that this is the same definition as global asymptotic stability. Samuelson (1947, p. 261) also defines *stability of the first kind in the small* to hold if for sufficiently small displacements the equilibrium is stable and investigates this stability for the general competitive equilibrium and its relationships to perfect and imperfect stability in Hicks' sense.

In a little more detail, Samuelson (1947) observes that one cannot consider the stability problem of the general competitive equilibrium without specifying a dynamic adjustment process. He formulates the problem as a set of ordinary differential equations and gives conditions for the convergence to its equilibrium. One such dynamic adjustment process is the one in which the instantaneous rate of change of the price of any good is proportional to its excess demand with excess demand being expressed as a function of all prices. Samuelson approximates linearly the excess demand equations at equilibrium and sets the speeds of adjustment equal to one to conclude that stability holds if the real part of all the characteristic roots of the matrix of the linear approximation are negative. This condition is neither necessary nor sufficient for stability in Hicks' sense.

The interested reader can review these ideas in Hicks (1946) and Samuelson (1947) or in books such as Quirk and Saposnik (1968), Arrow and Hahn (1971), or Takayama (1985). Negishi (1962) surveys the main stability results up to 1962 while F. Hahn (1982) gives a comprehensive survey of both local and global stability of competitive equilibrium up to 1982.

In chapter 7, we shall provide a revised version of Samuelson's Correspondence Principle that attempts to deal with some of the criticism of Samuelson's previous version. But at the same time, the revised version of Samuelson's Correspondence Principle, will illustrate how the stability methods in this book are put to use.

(6) Of particular importance in economic theory is the notion of D *stability* and *total stability*. A real $n \times n$ matrix A is said to be D *stable* if the product DA is a matrix having characteristic roots with negative real parts for any positive diagonal matrix D. Recall that a matrix D is positive diagonal if its elements $d_{ii} > 0$ for all i and $d_{ij} = 0$ for $i \neq j$. Arrow and McManus (1958) give sufficient conditions for D stability.

Related to D stable matrices are *totally stable* matrices. A real $n \times n$ matrix A is said to be *totally stable* if every submatrix of A whose determinant is a principal minor of A is D stable. Metzler (1945) shows that if a matrix A is totally stable then A is a *Hicksian matrix*, that is, every even order principal minor of A is positive and every odd order principal minor of A is negative.

McKenzie (1960) shows that if a real $n \times n$ matrix $A = [a_{ij}]$, $i, j = 1, \ldots, n$, has a negative diagonal and is quasi-dominant diagonal, then A is totally stable. Note that an $n \times n$ matrix A is *quasidominant diagonal* if there exist positive numbers $c_1, c_2, \ldots, c_n$ such that $c_i|a_{ii}| > |\sum_{j \neq i} c_j|a_{ij}|$ for every $i =$ 1, 2, \ldots n, or if there exist positive numbers $b_1, b_2, \ldots, b_n$ such that $b_i|a_{ii}| > \sum_{j \neq i} b_j|a_{ji}|$ for every $i = 1, 2, \ldots, n$. In words an $n \times n$ matrix A is quasidominant, if positive weights can be found so that the absolute value of every weighted diagonal element exceeds the weighted sum of the absolute values of the off diagonal elements in the same column or same row.

Takayama (1985), Nikaido (1968, 1970) and Murata (1977) discuss the stability properties of various matrices that arise in economics and give examples from competitive general equilibrium and the dynamic Leontief model. The mathematical theory of such matrices is presented in Gant-macher (1959). Khalil (1980) gives a new test for D stability.

(7) The two classic papers of Arrow and Hurwicz (1958) and Arrow et al. (1959) investigate systematically for the first time the problem of stability of a competitive general equilibrium.

In the first paper, Arrow and Hurwicz (1958) construct a dynamic economic model described by differential equations whose characteristics reflect the general nature of the competitive process and examine its stability properties under certain assumptions. Two kinds of the dynamic adjustment process called tâtonnement are considered: instantaneous and lagged. Also, three specific cases of the model are analyzed: (i) no trade at equilibrium; (ii) case of two commodities, one of which is a numéraire both in a one-individual and the n-individual case; and (iii) all goods are *gross substitutes* at all prices that is, if the price of one commodity goes up while all other prices remain the same, then there will be an increase in demand for every commodity whose price has remained constant. The overall con-clusion of this paper is that in none of the cases studied has the system been found to be unstable under the perfectly competitive adjustment process whether instantaneous or lagged, that is, they show that *local* stability holds.

The second paper extends the results of the first by establishing *global stability* when all goods are gross substitutes.

(8) Scarf (1960) and Gale (1963) indicate some limitations to the scope of stability of the tâtonnement mechanism in competitive general equili-brium by constructing examples of *global instability*.

Scarf's instability example makes full use of the perfect complementarity case and supports, in general, the traditional view that the phenomenon of instability is due either to the income effect or to the complementarity of goods. Scarf states that his instability example does not depend on a delicate assignment of values of initial stocks. Hirota (1981) studies whether or not the instability of Scarf's system is robust against changes in the assignment of initial stocks. By perturbing the assignment of initial holdings, Hirota (1981) shows that most assignment patterns are stable, while the globally unstable case emerges only in an extreme limited situation. See also Scarf (1981) who points out the significance of Hirota's example.

The results of Sonnenschein (1972, 1973), Debreu (1974) and Mantel (1974, 1976) which lead to the conclusion that almost any market excess demand function is possible also suggest that there is a large class of economies which have *unstable* equilibria under the *tâtonnement* price adjustment process. See also Balasko (1975), Keenan (1982) and Hirota (1985). More specifically, Hirota (1985) gives an estimate of the fraction of initial endowment distributions which result in global stability of a tâtonnement process, for a class of economies which includes Scarf's instability example as a limiting case.

(9) Arrow and Nerlove (1958) study the role of expectations on stability. They show that in a continuous time general competitive economic equilibrium model if all commodities, both present and future are gross substitutes, then stability with *static expectations* is equivalent to stability with *adaptive expectations*. Tarr (1978) extends the Arrow and Nerlove analysis by showing that the stability property of the system is unaffected by the selection of the more sophisticated adaptive expectations over static expectations, provided the substitute-complement relationship of commodities, both present and future, fits into the Morishima (1952) matrix pattern. Tarr also gives a counterexample to illustrate that the Arrow and Nerlove result does not hold in general and that the choice of adaptive versus static expectations can affect stability. See also Burmeister and Graham (1973, 1974, 1975).

(10) In two papers, Bewley (1980a, 1980b) studies the role of the *permanent income hypothesis* on short run and long run stability. Bewley defines the permanent income hypothesis to be, roughly, that demand is determined by constancy of the marginal utility of money. That is, a consumer spends money on a good up to the point at which the utility derived from the marginal purchase equals the utility of the money spent on it. This marginal utility of money is approximately independent of current income and prices provided that the planning horizon is large and the variability of the uncertainty is small relative to the size of the initial holdings of cash. This formulation of the permanent income hypothesis leads to a definition of demand functions different from the usual one appearing in general competitive economic equilibrium. Such a modification of demand function eliminates the income effects which can cause the *tâtonnement* price adjustment process to be unstable. Since the permanent income hypothesis makes sense only in the short run Bewley (1980b) shows that short run global stability

holds for the tâtonnement process. However, perverse income effects reappear as a source of instability, when consumers' notions of their average real income vary over the long run and Bewley (1980a) shows that the long run adjustment process may be unstable. In fact, Bewley (1980a) shows that an analogue of the results of Sonnenschein (1972, 1973), Debreu (1974) and Mantel (1974, 1976) applies to the long run adjustment process assuming the permanent income hypothesis.

(11) According to the now famous *Hotelling rule* established in Hotelling (1931), the price of an exhaustible resource must grow at a rate equal to the rate of interest, both along an efficient extraction path and in a competitive resource industry equilibrium. If we denote by $p(0)$ the initial period price and by $p(t)$ the price at period t we can write that

$$p(t) = p(0) \, e^{rt},$$

where r is the rate of interest. If we assume that this interest rate r is equal to society's optimal discount rate between future and present, Hotelling showed that the competitive resource owner would deplete at the socially optimal rate.

The intuition behind the Hotelling rule is simple. The present value of a unit of resource extracted must be the same in all periods if there is to be no gain from shifting extraction among periods. For the present value of price, or price net of extraction cost, to be the same in all periods, the undiscounted value must be growing at precisely the rate of interest. Put differently, suppose that price, or price net of extraction cost, is expected by producers to be rising too slowly, say below the interest rate r. Then resource deposit is not a good way to hold wealth. Producers will try to liquidate their resource deposits by increasing current production and by investing their revenues at the higher $r\%$. But as production increases, the current price must decrease along the demand curve. Thus, initial pessimistic price expectations lead to current price decreases. Similar reasoning suggests that if prices are expected to grow faster than the interest rate r, then the value of resource deposits would grow faster than any other form of wealth which may cause speculative withholding of production and higher current prices.

There is an extensive literature on this subject and it would be interesting to use the stability methods of this book to analyze appropriate dynamic models of exhaustible resources. For an introduction to the economics of exhaustible resources see DasGupta and Heal (1979) and their references.

(12) Urban economics is a fertile field for the application of the methods of dynamic analysis and stability. For an introductory survey of the

numerous dynamic urban economics models on industrial location, residential location, dynamic stability of the interaction between industrial and residential locations, instability of a mixed city, urban growth and unemployment and rural-urban migration see the book of T. Miyao (1981) and its references.

(13) Losses from unexpected changes in interest rates have become an increasing problem at depository institutions over the past decade, as interest rates have become more volatile and have climbed to unprecedented levels. Such losses occur when unexpected increases in interest rates decrease the market value of an institution's assets more quickly than the market value of its liabilities. This differential change in market values occurs if the institution's assets are more price sensitive but less *interest sensitive* than its deposits. Interest sensitivity means that the coupon or contract interest rates change with market rates of interest. Under the same balance sheet condition, the institution experiences a gain when interest rates decline unexpectedly.

The more quickly an asset or liability adjusts to market rate changes, the more interest sensitive it is said to be. Institutions expose themselves to interest rate risk whenever the interest sensitivity of the two sides of their balance sheet is not equal.

The problems of interest rate risk are well known, but accurate measurement of risk exposure is not easy. And, without such measurements, reliable management of this risk is not possible. Malliaris and Kaufman (1984) describe the use of *duration* as a technique for measuring in one number the degree of risk exposure an institution assumes, and develop simple hypothetical examples to demonstrate the implications of various interest rate changes for depository institutions. Malliaris and Kaufman (1984) also present a dynamic notion of duration in continuous time models both for the deterministic and the stochastic case. See also their numerous bibliographical references.

(14) One of the more controversial notions in the *economics of information* is the concept of *informational equilibrium*. In a world of incomplete markets an informational equilibrium is one where, either the observed actions of better informed agents or the resulting equilibrium prices, yield valuable information to worse informed agents. Riley (1979) explores the viability of such signaling or informational equilibria and discusses the instability of informationally consistent price functions. Miller and Rock (1985) extend the standard finance model of the firm's dividend-investment-financing decisions by allowing the firm's managers to know more than outside investors about the true state of the firm's current earnings.

(15) The *cash balances* problem of the firm concerns the management of the timing of cash receipts and payments. This problem has been an active area of research during the past few decades and numerous techniques have been used to solve numerous variations of this microeconomic problem. Malliaris (1988a) presents three approaches to this problem and surveys numerous references.

7. Further remarks and references

This chapter formulates an analytically tractable model that captures the striving of independent regional regulatory commissions to achieve first or second best regulation of regional natural monopolies in a rational expectations economy with perfect capital markets. To the extent our abstraction captures aspects of reality we have shown there is serious danger that the system will follow the wrong path. It seems that only control of rate bases will correct the problem.

The piece meal recommendations to commissions made by devotees of Ramsey pricing are stimulated by partial equilibrium analysis. Such recommendations may be counterproductive if the economy follows a suboptimal path of development. It is disturbing that the difficulty emerges in a model with so much plausible structure. There would be less cause for concern if we had to go to a heterogeneous consumer multigoods general equilibrium model to generate the difficulty. The paucity of structure of such models naturally leads to few restrictions on the set of equilibria.

The problem uncovered here seems to be *economic* rather than *mathematical* because we have imposed so much structure that if any of it is relaxed the difficulty would become worse. Let us attempt to explain what we think the relevance of this exercise is to practical problems of regulatory policy.

We designed our abstract model to show what may happen to development paths in an economy where decentralized commissions regulated natural monopolies in an attempt to efficiently resolve the break even problem but facing interest rates or the *cost of capital* parametrically. We found that no problem emerges when the aggregate production function maximum $g_1(x_1, g_2(x - x_1)) \equiv g(x)$ is concave increasing in x.

If, however, $g(x)$ has a convex zone then utilities and their commissions have an incentive to expand beyond the socially optimum level for certain initial stocks. How might such a situation reveal itself in practice? Take the case of $g(x)$ everywhere convex which is worked out in the examples.

Suppose that $r(t)$ is the current interest rate. A regional natural monopoly sees that if it can charge a multipart tariff to capture most of the potential surplus from the firms in its region then it can turn an ever increasing profit from expansion. It plans to do this by exploiting scale economies to get the unit cost of energy down to a low level but use multipart tariffs to scoop ever increasing revenue from the firms in its domain. It convinces both the commission that regulates it and the neoclassical firms in its domain to accept this plan because (i) the multipart tariff can be designed so that the profits of the neoclassical firms and the utility both increase, (ii) the commission sees higher utility stock prices, lower unit costs of energy, and higher profits to energy using firms. Hence everyone is happier in the region under discussion.

But what one region can do, all can do. The expansion occurring in all regions puts upward pressure on the cost of capital. The cost of capital rises. This causes each utility in each region to push for even more expansion of its rate base to produce energy at the same or even lower unit cost as before.

As more and more resources are drawn from consumption into capital formation the interest rate that consumers demand to forego current consumption continues to rise.

One might think that ever rising interest rates would choke off the profits of neoclassical firms and this would put a brake on the runaway process of expansion that is under scrutiny. However, in the case where $g(x)$ is convex the economies of scale in $g_2(\cdot)$ allow energy to be produced so much cheaper that the combined positive effects of productivity of energy and scale economies outweigh the negative effect on the profits of neoclassical firms. Hence neoclassical firms keep favoring more expansion. The process continues.

Future research should investigate the seriousness of the difficulty uncovered here in more disaggregated models. If the problem is found to be present under plausible assumptions then future research should look into decentralized schemes with low information requirements and nice incentive properties to fix the problem. Perhaps an adaptation of a Brown and Heal (1980) equilibrium using the recursive structure present in our type of model may be fruitful.

CHAPTER 7

STABILITY IN INVESTMENT THEORY

> It is the central task . . . to show how
> the problem of stability of
> equilibrium is intimately tied up with
> the problem of deriving fruitful
> theorems in comparative statics. This
> duality constitutes what I have called
> the *Correspondence Principle.*
>
> Samuelson (1947, p. 258)

1. Introduction

The purpose of this chapter is to show how some recent results on the *global* and *local asymptotic stability* of optimal control problems may be used in comparing long run equilibria in various economic models with emphasis in investment theory. The problem of comparing long run equilibria, known by most economists as *comparative statics* or *comparative dynamics*, is the main concern of this chapter. In such an exercise, a revised version of Samuelson's famous *Correspondence Principle* plays an important role. This chapter relies on Brock (1986b).

In this section we formulate a general class of optimal control problems which have found many applications in economics as has already been demonstrated in chapter 5. The various definitions and results which are needed are stated next.

Consider the problem

$$\max \int_0^\infty e^{-\rho t} \pi(x(t), \dot{x}(t), \alpha) \, dt, \tag{1.1}$$

s.t. $x(0) = x_0$.

Here $\pi(x(t), \dot{x}(t), \alpha)$ is instantaneous payoff at time t which is assumed to be a function of the state of the system at time t, $x(t)$, the rate of change of the state, $dx/dt \equiv \dot{x}(t)$, and a vector of parameters α. Observe that $x(t) \in R^n$, $\dot{x}(t) \in R^n$, $\alpha \in R^m$ and $\rho \geq 0$ with ρ being the discount rate. As in Rockafellar (1976), the maximum in (1.1) is taken over the set of absolutely continuous functions $x(t)$ such that $x(0) = x_0$. Recall that a function $x(\cdot)$ is absolutely continuous if dx/dt exists almost everywhere. Define the Hamiltonian function, H, as

$$H(x, \dot{x}, \alpha, q) \equiv \max_{\dot{x}} \{\pi(x, \dot{x}, \alpha) + q^{\mathsf{T}}\dot{x}\}, \tag{1.2}$$

where q is an auxiliary variable, also called a costate variable, whose existence is claimed by the maximum principle in Hestenes (1966) and Pontryagin et al. (1962). As before superscript T denotes the transpose of a vector or a matrix. If $\pi(\cdot, \cdot, \alpha)$ is strictly concave in $(x, \dot{x})$, then there is at most one optimal path $x(t, x_0, \alpha)$ for each x_0 and α. If an optimum exists for each (x_0, α), then there exists a function $h : R^n \times R^m \rightarrow R^n$, called the *optimal policy function,* such that

$$\dot{x}(t, x_0, \alpha) = h[x(t, x_0, \alpha), \alpha]. \tag{1.3}$$

Furthermore, h does not depend upon x_0 or on t because (1.1) is time independent. In this chapter we discuss a set of sufficient conditions on π and ρ which imply that there is a unique steady state $\bar{x}(\alpha)$ such that for all x_0, $x(t, x_0, \alpha) \rightarrow \bar{x}(\alpha)$ as $t \rightarrow \infty$.

When the Hamiltonian of (1.2) is evaluated at the optimum we use the notation H^0, that is,

$$H^0(q, x, \alpha) = H(x, h[x(t, x_0, \alpha), \alpha], \alpha, q), \tag{1.4}$$

where $x(t, x_0, \alpha)$ is the optimal path corresponding to x_0 and α.

Using (1.4) we write down the necessary conditions for an optimal solution

$$\dot{q} = \rho q - \frac{H^0}{\partial x}(q, x, \alpha), \tag{1.5}$$

$$\dot{x} = \frac{\partial H^0}{\partial q}(q, x, \alpha); \quad x(0) = x_0. \tag{1.6}$$

In section 2 the system of differential equations (1.5) and (1.6) is used to obtain an important abstract result in comparing optimal steady states.

Chapter 5 surveys various sufficient conditions on the instantaneous payoff function π and the discount rate ρ of (1.1) such that there exists a steady state solution, denoted by $\bar{x}(\alpha)$, which is *locally asymptotically* stable

(L.A.S.) or globally *asymptotically stable* (G.A.S.). It is worth repeating that $\bar{x}(\alpha)$ is L.A.S. if there is an $\varepsilon > 0$ such that $|\bar{x}(\alpha) - x_0| < \varepsilon$ implies $x(t, x_0, \alpha) \to \bar{x}(\alpha)$ as $t \to \infty$, where $x(t, x_0, \alpha)$ is an optimal solution with $x(0, x_0, \alpha) = x_0$. Also, we say that $\bar{x}(\alpha)$ is G.A.S. if for all $x_0 \in R^n$, it follows that $x(t, x_0, \alpha) \to \bar{x}(\alpha)$ as $t \to \infty$.

We are now in a position to state our

Problem: What restrictions do the various sufficient conditions for L.A.S. or G.A.S. of a steady state solution $\bar{x}(\alpha)$ of (1.3) together with the natural structure of $\pi(x, \dot{x}, \alpha)$ impose on $\partial \bar{x}(\alpha)/\partial \alpha$?

To provide some answers to this important problem we proceed as follows. In the remainder of this section we state some recent results on G.A.S. and give some additional definitions. In section 2 we discuss Samuelson's Correspondence Principle and offer a reformulation motivated by our problem. Section 3 states an abstract result which is subsequently applied to economic models in section 4, 5, 6 and 7.

Let $(\bar{x}, \bar{q})$ be a steady state of (1.3), where $\bar{q}$ is the costate variable at steady state $\bar{x}$. Consider the three hypotheses,

(i) $H_{qx}^0 = 0$ at $(\bar{q}, \bar{x})$;

(ii) $Q \equiv \begin{bmatrix} H_{qq}^0 & \frac{\rho}{2}I_n \\ \frac{\rho}{2}I_n & -H_{xx}^0 \end{bmatrix}$ is positive definite at $(\bar{q}, \bar{x})$;

(iii) $R \equiv (H_{qq}^0)^{-1}H_{qx}$ is negative quasi-definite at $(\bar{q}, \bar{x})$, where H_{qx}^0, H_{qq}^0, H_{xx}^0 is the usual notation for second order partial derivatives and I_n denotes the $n \times n$ identity matrix.

Chapter 5 reports that any of these three hypotheses is sufficient for the G.A.S. of $\bar{x} = \bar{x}(\alpha)$. These three hypotheses will be used in this chapter along with some structural assumptions to obtain results on $\partial \bar{x}/\partial \alpha$.

Recall that an $n \times n$ matrix A is *negative quasi-definite* if $x^T A x < 0$ for all $x \neq 0$. We use the terms *negative definite* for the case when A is symmetric and $x^T A x < 0$ for all $x \neq 0$. We denote by A^{-1} the inverse of a matrix A which we assume exists.

2. Samuelson's Correspondence Principle

Samuelson (1941, 1942, 1947), in two articles and in his *Foundations*, was the first economist to recognize the importance of relating the problem of stability of equilibrium to the problem of comparative statics. This duality

was called by Samuelson the *Correspondence Principle* and its main purpose
is to provide useful empirical information "concerning the way in which
equilibrium quantities will change as a result of changes in the parameters
taken as independent data". See Samuelson (1947, p. 257).

Samuelson (1947) considered the system of equations

$$E(p, \alpha) = 0, \tag{2.1}$$

where $E: R^n \times R^m \to R^n$ is a system of excess demand functions for $n+1$
goods as a function of the price vector $(p_1, \ldots, p_n)$ and the parameter vector
$(\alpha_1, \ldots, \alpha_m)$. Note that there are only n independent equations by Walras
Law. The $n+1$ good is the numéraire. Equation (2.1) describes competitive
equilibrium where excess demand equals zero, assuming there are no free
goods. Equation (2.1) tells us what the equilibrium price is but does not
tell us how the economic system arrives at equilibrium. Samuelson proposed
the adjustment mechanism

$$\dot{p}_i = g_i(E_i(p, \alpha)), \quad i = 1, 2, \ldots, n, \tag{2.2}$$

such that $p_i(0) = p_{i_0}$ given, $i = 1, 2, \ldots, n$, where $g_i(0) = 0$, $g_i(E_i) > 0$, for
$E_i > 0$, and $g_i(E_i) < 0$, for $E_i < 0$. Mechanism (2.2) corresponds to the intuitive idea that price increases when excess demand is positive and vice versa.

After introducing (2.2) Samuelson studied its asymptotic stability and
enunciated his *Correspondence Principle*: the hypothesis of asymptotic
stability of (2.2) together with a priori information on $\partial E/\partial \alpha$ gives rise to
useful restrictions on $\partial \bar{p}/\partial \alpha$, where $\bar{p}(\alpha)$ is the equilibrium price as a function
of α which is assumed locally unique. Samuelson applied his principle to
other problems as well as general equilibrium but we shall concentrate on
the equilibrium problem here for illustrative purposes. Note that the essence
of this principle is, given a complex system with certain properties, how to
infer its qualitative changes analytically.

We have deliberately stated the Correspondence Principle as a *methodological principle* rather than as a precise theorem in order to capture Samuelson's basic idea. Research reported in Quirk and Saposnik (1968) shows
that it is not possible *in general* to use the hypothesis of asymptotic stability
of (2.2) together with sign information on $\partial E/\partial \alpha$ to get comparative statics
information on $\partial E/\partial \alpha$. For example, look at the case where α is one
dimensional. Without loss of generality, assume $g_i(E_i) = E_i$. Differentiate
(2.1) totally with respect to α and solve for $\partial \bar{p}/\partial \alpha$,

$$\partial \bar{p}/\partial \alpha = -\left(\frac{\partial E}{\partial p}\right)^{-1} \frac{\partial E}{\partial \alpha}. \tag{2.3}$$

The hypothesis that all eigenvalues of $\partial E/\partial p$ have negative real parts contains n restrictions, and also, a priori sign restrictions on $\partial E / \partial \alpha$ contain n more restrictions. But there are n^2 elements in $\partial E / \partial p$. Since Sonnenschein's theorem (1972) shows that the axioms of Arrow–Debreu–McKenzie general equilibrium theory are general enough to allow *any continuous function* from $R^n \to R^n$ to be an excess demand function for some $n + 1$ goods general equilibrium system, then it comes as no surprise that examples of higher dimensional systems satisfying all of the restrictions listed above could be created that give arbitrary sign to $\partial \bar{p} / \partial \alpha$. Yet, in such examples, $\partial E / \partial p$ is a stable matrix and $\partial E / \partial \alpha$ has a priori sign restrictions.

These findings led to a lot of research on the Correspondence Principle, reported in Quirk and Saposnik (1968), with the conclusion that a priori sign information on $\partial E / \partial \alpha$ plus stability assumed on $\partial E / \partial p$ give sign restrictions on $\partial \bar{p} / \partial \alpha$ from (2.3) if this system is either one dimensional or if $\partial E / \partial p$ has a lot of zeroes in it.

This was discouraging enough but while this type of research was going on the very mechanism (2.2) came under attack as a description of an adjustment process. The papers by Gordon and Hynes (1970) and Phelps and Winter (1970) come to mind. Gordon and Hynes (1970) argue that speculative activity would destroy any such mechanism as (2.2); they also ask, "Whose maximizing behavior does such a mechanism describe?" They remark that it is mechanical and not based on rational behavior. Phelps and Winter (1970) develop the beginnings of an alternative disequilibrium dynamics.

After Phelps et al. (1970) was published, there were several attempts in the literature to rationalize mechanisms of type (2.2) but no consensus seems in sight. Hence, the epitaph of the Correspondence Principle was written by Arrow and Hahn (1971, p. 321) in their chapter on comparing equilibria.

Shortly after Arrow and Hahn (1971) was published, the Sonnenschein (1972)–Mantel (1974)–Debreu (1974) theorem appeared. This result shows that any continuous function $E(p)$ could be an excess demand function for some economy populated by people with perfectly well-behaved utility functions.

In view of the Sonnenschein–Mantel–Debreu result, it seems certain that the Correspondence Principle will fail to be of much use if one insists on the generality of abstract general equilibrium theory. Nevertheless, this principle in some form lurks in the underworld of economists of a more practical bent.

Turn now to a closely related idea. Arrow and Hahn (1971) in their chapter on comparing equilibria gave little credence to the hope that the hypothesis of L.A.S. of equilibria of (2.2) alone would yield useful restrictions on $\partial \bar{p}/\partial \alpha$. They did show, however, how *sufficient conditions* for L.A.S. or G.A.S. of (2.2) such as *all goods are gross substitutes* yield useful restrictions on $\partial \bar{p}/\partial \alpha$. This is some kind of a Correspondence Principle in that stability hypotheses are closely linked to the problem of getting useful restrictions on $\partial \bar{p}/\partial \alpha$.

A version of the Correspondence Principle is offered below which is somewhat immune to the cirticisms listed above. Return now to the optimal control problem (1.1) together with the dynamics of the solution (1.3). Many intertemporal equilibrium systems studied in the literature, such as Cass and Shell (1976a) on optimal economic growth; Lucas (1967), Treadway (1971) and Mortensen (1973) on adjustment cost models in the neoclassical theory of investment; and Lucas and Prescott (1971) and Brock (1972) on perfect foresight models, to name a few, can be fit into (1.1). By the device of describing general intertemporal equilibrium as the solution to a problem of maximizing a discounted sum of consumer surplus an economically interesting class of equilibrium models in modern capital theory is covered by (1.1). Let

$$h(\bar{x}(\alpha), \alpha) = 0 \qquad (2.4)$$

play the role of (2.1) and let (1.3) play the role of (2.2) in the Correspondence Principle. We have a

Revised Correspondence Principle.   For problems of type (1.1), whose solution generates the *equilibrium-disequilibrium* adjustment process (1.3), the hypotheses of stability of the solution $\bar{x}(\alpha)$ of (2.4) with respect to (1.3) together with a priori structural assumptions which are economically meaningful on $\pi(x, \dot{x}, \alpha)$ lead to useful comparative statics information on $\partial \bar{x}/\partial \alpha$.

Observe that the Revised Correspondence Principle is stated as a methodological notion unlike Burmeister and Long's (1977) Correspondence Principle which is a theorem.

3. Abstract results on comparing optimal steady states

Here we develop some mathematical results which are used in economic applications in later sections.

Consider the system mentioned in the introduction, that is,

$$\dot{q} = \rho q - H_x^0(q, x, \alpha), \qquad (3.1)$$

$$\dot{x} = H_q^0(q, x, \alpha), \qquad (3.2)$$

with initial condition $x(0) = x_0$. The differential equations (3.1) and (3.2) are necessary for optimality in a large class of problems. The transversality condition

$$\lim_{t \to \infty} q(t)^T x(t) e^{-\rho t} = 0 \qquad (3.3)$$

has been shown by Benveniste and Scheinkman (1982) to be *necessary* as well as sufficient for a general class of problems.

A steady state $\bar{x}(\alpha)$ with its associated costate $\bar{q}(\alpha)$ must solve the equations below

$$\rho \bar{q}(\alpha) - H_x^0(\bar{q}(\alpha), \bar{x}(\alpha), \alpha) = 0, \qquad (3.4)$$

$$H_q^0(\bar{q}(\alpha), \bar{x}(\alpha), \alpha) = 0. \qquad (3.5)$$

The transversality condition (3.3) is automatically satisfied at a steady state. Hence equations (3.4) and (3.5) characterize optimal steady states.

Totally differentiate both sides of (3.4) and (3.5) with respect to α and drop upper bars to ease the notation; we obtain

$$\rho q_\alpha - H_{xq}^0 q_\alpha - H_{xx}^0 x_\alpha - H_{x\alpha}^0 = 0, \qquad (3.6)$$

$$H_{qq}^0 q_\alpha + H_{qx}^0 x_\alpha + H_{q\alpha}^0 = 0. \qquad (3.7)$$

Premultiply (3.6) and (3.7) by the matrix $[x_\alpha^T, q_\alpha^T]$ to obtain

$$[x_\infty^T, q_\infty^T] \begin{bmatrix} H_{x\alpha}^0 - \rho q_\alpha \\ -H_{q\alpha}^0 \end{bmatrix} = -x_\alpha^T H_{xx}^0 x_\alpha + q_\alpha^T H_{qq}^0 q_\alpha$$

$$- x_\alpha^T H_{xq}^0 q_\alpha + q_\alpha^T H_{qx}^0 x_\alpha. \qquad (3.8)$$

The right hand side of (3.8) is nonnegative quasi-definite because H^0 is convex in q and concave in x, and the cross product terms cancel. This can be seen immediately by premultiplying and postmultiplying the right hand side of (3.8) by a vector $a \in R^m$. Recall that $\alpha \in R^m$. Add to both sides of (3.8) $\rho x_\alpha^T q_\alpha$ to get for $a \in R^m$,

$$a^T [x_\alpha^T, q_\alpha^T] \begin{bmatrix} H_{x\alpha}^0 \\ -H_{q\alpha} \end{bmatrix} a = a^T [q_\alpha, x_\alpha]^T Q(\alpha) [q_\alpha, x_\alpha] a, \qquad (3.9)$$

where, for notational convenience, we define

$$Q(\alpha) \equiv \begin{bmatrix} H_{qq}^0 & \frac{\rho}{2} I_n \\ \frac{\rho}{2} I_n & -H_{xx}^0 \end{bmatrix}. \qquad (3.10)$$

The matrix $Q(\alpha)$ plays a central role in the stability hypotheses of Magill (1977a), Rockafellar (1976), and Brock and Scheinkman (1976) as reported in chapter 5. Magill (1977a), for example, shows that if $Q(\alpha)$ is positive definite at the steady state $(\bar{x}(\alpha_0), \bar{q}(\alpha_0))$, then $\bar{x}(\alpha_0)$ is locally asymptotically stable. In chapter 5 the function $V = \dot{q}^T \dot{x}$ is differentiated with respect to t along solutions of (1.1) and (1.2) to obtain $\dot{V} = (\dot{q}, \dot{x})^T Q(\alpha)(\dot{q}, \dot{x})$, so that the positive definiteness of $Q(\alpha)$ implies that V acts like a Liapunov function. Hence the global positive definiteness of Q implies G.A.S.

In the spirit of the Correspondence Principle we have an abstract *comparative statics* result:

Theorem 3.1. If $Q(\alpha)$ is positive semidefinite at $x(\alpha_0)$, $q(\alpha_0)$, then for all $y \in R^m$,

$$y^T[x_\alpha^T, q_\alpha^T] \begin{bmatrix} H_{x\alpha}^0 \\ -H_{q\alpha}^0 \end{bmatrix} y \geq 0 \tag{3.11}$$

at $x(\alpha_0)$ and $q(\alpha_0)$.

Proof. The proof follows immediately from (3.9).

This theorem will be useful when we turn to a problem where α enters the Hamiltonian with a specific structure. Also, note that except for hairline cases $Q(\alpha)$ is always positive definite when $\rho = 0$.

Next we present another abstract result. Solve (3.7) for q_α in terms of x_α,

$$q_\alpha = -(H_{qq}^0)^{-1} H_{qx}^0 x_\alpha - (H_{qq}^0)^{-1} H_{q\alpha}^0. \tag{3.12}$$

Insert (3.12) into (3.6) to obtain

$$-(\rho - H_{xq}^0)(H_{qq}^0)^{-1} H_{qx}^0 x_\alpha - (\rho - H_{xq}^0)(H_{qq}^0)^{-1} H_{q\alpha}^0$$
$$- H_{xx}^0 x_\alpha - H_{x\alpha}^0 = 0. \tag{3.13}$$

Equation (3.13) plays a central role in the comparative dynamics analysis of the Lucas–Treadway–Mortensen model of optimal accumulation of capital by a profit maximizing firm under adjustment cost. This will be presented in the next section. Note that for the interesting special case when the Hamiltonian is *separable* in q and x, that is, when $H_{xq}^0 = H_{qx}^0 = 0$, equations (3.12) and (3.13) become

$$q_\alpha = -(H_{qq}^0)^{-1} H_{q\alpha}^0, \tag{3.14}$$

$$-\rho(H_{qq}^0)^{-1} H_{q\alpha}^0 - H_{xx}^0 x_\alpha - H_{x\alpha}^0 = 0. \tag{3.15}$$

4. Applications to adjustment cost models

Consider a model of the type (1.1) where

$$\pi(x, \dot{x}, \alpha) = f(x, \dot{x}) - \alpha_1^T x - \alpha_2^T \dot{x}, \tag{4.1}$$

with $x(0) = x_0$ given. This model was studied by Lucas (1967), Treadway (1971) and Mortensen (1973) among others. The original literature includes Eisner and Strotz (1963) and Treadway (1969) who show that the existence of a demand function for investment goods can be explained in terms of costs of adjustment.

In this application we need to calculate the quantities H_{qq}^0, H_{qx}^0, H_{xx}^0, etc., for this model. The function π is assumed to be twice continuously differentiable, concave in $(x, \dot{x})$, and all optimum paths are assumed to be interior to all natural boundaries. Let $\alpha \equiv (\alpha_1, \alpha_2)$ and define

$$H^0(q, x, \alpha) \equiv \max_{u \in R^n} \{ f(x, u) - \alpha_1^T x - \alpha_2^T u + q^T u \}. \tag{4.2}$$

Let $u^0(q, x, \alpha_2)$ denote the optimum choice of u in (4.2) and note that u^0 does not depend upon α_1. Since $f_u(x, u^0) = \alpha_2 - q$ defines u^0, we obtain immediately that

$$f_{ux} + f_{uu} u_x^0 = 0, \quad u_x^0 = -f_{uu}^{-1} f_{ux}, \tag{4.3}$$

$$f_{uu} u_q^0 = -I_n, \quad u_q^0 = -f_{uu}^{-1}, \tag{4.4}$$

$$f_{uu} u_{\alpha_2}^0 = I_n, \quad u_{\alpha_2}^0 = f_{uu}^{-1}, \tag{4.5}$$

$$u_{\alpha_1}^0 = 0. \tag{4.6}$$

From these equations the formulae below follow quickly.

$$H_x^0 = f_x(x, u^0) - \alpha_1, \quad H_{xx}^0 = f_{xx} + f_{xu} u_x^0 = f_{xx} - f_{xu} f_{uu}^{-1} f_{ux}, \tag{4.7}$$

$$H_{x\alpha_1}^0 = f_{xu} u_{\alpha_1}^0 - I_n = -I_n, \quad H_{x\alpha_2}^0 = f_{xu} u_{\alpha_2}^0 = f_{xu} f_{uu}^{-1}, \tag{4.8}$$

$$H_{xq}^0 = f_{xu} u_q^0 = -f_{xu} f_{uu}^{-1}, \tag{4.9}$$

$$H_q^0 = u^0, \quad H_{qq}^0 = u_q^0 = -f_{uu}^{-1}, \tag{4.10}$$

$$H_{qx}^0 = u_x^0 = -f_{uu}^{-1} f_{ux}, \tag{4.11}$$

$$H_{q\alpha_1}^0 = u_{\alpha_1}^0 = 0, \quad H_{q\alpha_2}^0 = u_{\alpha_2}^0 = f_{uu}^{-1}. \tag{4.12}$$

Let us examine some of the abstract results obtained in the previous section. We record (3.13) here for convenience and analyze it first.

$$-(\rho I_n - H_{xq}^0)(H_{qq}^0)^{-1} H_{qx}^0 x_\alpha - (\rho I_n - H_{xq}^0)(H_{qq}^0)^{-1} H_{q\alpha}^0$$
$$- H_{xx}^0 x_\alpha - H_{x\alpha}^0 = 0. \tag{4.13}$$

Examine (4.13) for $\alpha = \alpha_1$. By (4.8) and (4.12) we get

$$-(\rho I_n - H^0_{xq})(H^0_{qq})^{-1}H^0_{qx}x_{\alpha_1} - H^0_{xx}x_{\alpha_1} + I_n = 0. \tag{4.14}$$

Premultiply both sides of (4.14) by $x^{\mathrm{T}}_{\alpha_1}$ and manipulate to get

$$-\rho x^{\mathrm{T}}_{\alpha_1}(H^0_{qq})^{-1}H^0_{qx}x_{\alpha_1} + x^{\mathrm{T}}_{\alpha_1}H^0_{xq}(H^0_{qq})^{-1}H^0_{qx}x_{\alpha_1}$$
$$- x^{\mathrm{T}}_{\alpha_1}H^0_{xx}x_{\alpha_1} + x^{\mathrm{T}}_{\alpha_1} = 0. \tag{4.15}$$

Since x_{α_1} is an $n \times n$ matrix equation (4.15) is an $n \times n$ matrix equation. Pre- and postmultiply (4.15) by the $n \times 1$ vector y to get

$$-\rho(x_{\alpha_1}y)^{\mathrm{T}}(H^0_{qq})^{-1}H^0_{qx}(x_{\alpha_1}y) + (H^0_{qx}x_{\alpha_1}y)^{\mathrm{T}}(H^0_{qq})^{-1}(H^0_{qx}x_{\alpha_1}y)$$
$$(?) \qquad\qquad\qquad\qquad (+)$$
$$-(x_{\alpha_1}y)^{\mathrm{T}}H^0_{xx}(x_{\alpha_1}y) + y^{\mathrm{T}}x^{\mathrm{T}}_{\alpha_1}y = 0. \tag{4.16}$$
$$(+) \qquad\qquad (?)$$

Notice that we used $(H^0_{qx})^{\mathrm{T}} = H^0_{xq}$. The signs in parentheses are the signs of each term in equation (4.16). We now arrive at

Theorem 4.1. If $\rho \geq 0$ and $(H^0_{qq})^{-1}H^0_{qx}$ is negative quasi-semidefinite at the steady state $x(\alpha)$, then x_{α_1} is negative quasi-semidefinite.

Proof. We must show that for all vectors y, $y^{\mathrm{T}}x_{\alpha_1}y \leq 0$. But $(x_{\alpha_1}y)^{\mathrm{T}}(H^0_{qq})^{-1}H^0_{qx}(x_{\alpha_1}y) \leq 0$ by hypothesis. The other two terms of (4.16) are nonnegative by convexity of H^0 in q and concavity of H^0 in x. Hence $y^{\mathrm{T}}x^{\mathrm{T}}_{\alpha_1}y \leq 0$. But

$$y^{\mathrm{T}}x^{\mathrm{T}}_{\alpha_1}y = y^{\mathrm{T}}x_{\alpha_1}y,$$

which completes the proof.

Theorem 4.1 is a typical example of a comparative statics result derived from a G.A.S. hypothesis. Consider the quantity

$$R \equiv (H^0_{qq})^{-1}H^0_{qx}$$

and assume that R is negative quasi-definite. We digress in order to sketch how R negative quasi-definite implies L.A.S. It was noted in the introduction that this is a sufficient condition for G.A.S. as shown in Brock and Scheinkman (1977a) and Magill (1977a). To verify this claim, Brock and Scheinkman (1977a) use as a Liapunov function $V = \dot{x}^{\mathrm{T}}G\dot{x}$, with $G \equiv (H^0_{qq})^{-1}$, and calculate

$$\dot{V} = \ddot{x}^{\mathrm{T}}G\dot{x} + \dot{x}^{\mathrm{T}}G\ddot{x} + \dot{x}^{\mathrm{T}}\dot{G}\dot{x}$$
$$= 2\dot{q}^{\mathrm{T}}\dot{x} + \dot{x}^{\mathrm{T}}[R + R^{\mathrm{T}}]\dot{x} + \dot{x}^{\mathrm{T}}\dot{G}\dot{x} < 2\dot{q}^{\mathrm{T}}\dot{x} + \dot{x}^{\mathrm{T}}\dot{G}\dot{x} < 0.$$

Note that $\dot{V} < 0$ because $\dot{G} = 0$ at steady states and $\dot{q}^T \dot{x} \leq 0$. The latter follows from the fact that

$$q(x(t)) = W_x(x(t)), \quad \dot{q}(x(t)) = W_{xx}(x(t))\dot{x}(t),$$

where

$$W(x_0) \equiv \max \int_0^\infty e^{-\rho t} \pi(x, \dot{x}, \alpha) \, dt,$$

such that $x(0) = x_0$ is concave in x_0 because we assumed that π is concave in $(x, \dot{x})$. Hence

$$\dot{q}^T \dot{x} = \dot{x}^T W_{xx} \dot{x} \leq 0,$$

if it exists. Thus $\dot{V} < 0$ and, therefore, V is a Liapunov function. Thus, the negative quasi-definiteness of R plays a central role as a sufficient condition for L.A.S. It turns out to be very powerful in analyzing a large class of adjustment cost models reported in Brock and Scheinkman (1977a).

We return to discuss x_α. Notice that the $n \times n$ matrix x_{α_1} is not necessarily symmetric but our result gives sufficient conditions for it to be negative *quasi*-semidefinite, that is,

$$y^T x_{\alpha_1} y \leq 0 \tag{4.17}$$

for all $y \in R^n$. Since α_1 is the vector of wage rates for x, (4.17) says that the long run factor demand curve $x(\alpha)$ is *downward sloping* in a generalized sense. Turn now for similar results on x_{α_2}.

Replace α by α_2 in (4.13) and use (4.8) and (4.12) to obtain

$$-(\rho I_n - H_{xq}^0)(H_{qq}^0)^{-1}H_{qx}^0 x_{\alpha_2} - (\rho I_n - H_{xq}^0)(H_{qq}^0)^{-1}f_{uu}^{-1}$$
$$-H_{xx}^0 x_{\alpha_2} - f_{xu}f_{uu}^{-1} = 0. \tag{4.18}$$

But by (4.10), $(H_{qq}^0)^{-1} = -f_{uu}$ so that

$$(\rho I_n - H_{xq}^0)(H_{qq}^0)^{-1}f_{uu}^{-1} = -(\rho I_n - H_{xq}^0). \tag{4.19}$$

Also,

$$-f_{xu}f_{uu}^{-1} = H_{xq}^0 \tag{4.20}$$

by (4.11). Hence by (4.19) and (4.20),

$$-(\rho I_n - H_{xq}^0)(H_{qq}^0)^{-1}f_{uu}^{-1} - f_{xu}f_{uu}^{-1} = \rho I_n - H_{xq}^0 + H_{xq}^0 = \rho I_n. \tag{4.21}$$

We conclude that (4.18) simplifies down to

$$-\rho(H_{qq}^0)^{-1}H_{qx}^0 x_{\alpha_2} + H_{xq}^0(H_{qq}^0)^{-1}H_{qx}^0 x_{\alpha_2} + \rho I_n - H_{xx}^0 x_{\alpha_2} = 0. \tag{4.22}$$

Follow the same argument which leads from equation (4.14) to theorem 4.1 to obtain

Theorem 4.2. If $\rho > 0$ and $(H^0_{qq})^{-1}H^0_{qx}$ is negative quasi-semidefinite then x_{α_2} is negative quasi-semidefinite.

It is worthwhile and instructive to verify theorem 4.2 in a different manner. Look at the steady state equations,

$$\rho q - H^0_x = \rho q + \alpha_1 - f_x = 0, \tag{4.23}$$

$$H^0_q = u^0 = 0, \tag{4.24}$$

$$\alpha_2 - q - f_u = 0. \tag{4.25}$$

From these last three equations we obtain that the steady state x must satisfy

$$\rho \alpha_2 + \alpha_1 - \rho f_u(x, 0) - f_x(x, 0) = 0. \tag{4.26}$$

Put $\beta = \rho \alpha_2 + \alpha_1$ and differentiate totally with respect to β to get

$$I_n - \rho f_{ux} x_\beta - f_{xx} x_\beta = 0, \tag{4.27}$$

$$x_\beta = (f_{xx} + \rho f_{ux})^{-1}. \tag{4.28}$$

Now obviously,

$$x_{\alpha_1} = x_\beta \text{ and } x_{\alpha_2} = \rho x_\beta. \tag{4.29}$$

Hence if x_{α_1} is negative quasi-semidefinite and $\rho > 0$, then so is x_{α_2} which gives another verification of theorem 4.2.

We close this discussion of the implications of the negative quasi-definiteness of $(H^0_{qq})^{-1}H^0_{qx}$ with the problem of comparing long run equilibria in the Lucas–Treadway–Mortensen model. Notice how equations (4.14)–(4.16) utilize the special structure of H^0 as a function of α to force the discovery of $(H^0_{qq})^{-1}H^0_{qx}$ as the central quantity to determine the sign of $y^T x_{\alpha_1} y$.

It is fascinating to note that the negative quasi-definiteness of $(H^0_{qq})^{-1}H^0_{qx}$ is a very expeditious G.A.S. hypothesis for the Lucas–Treadway–Mortensen model as well as playing a central role in determining the sign of x_{α_1} and x_{α_2}.

Turn now to the comparative statics implications of the separability of the Hamiltonian in (q, x). Separability of H^0 occurs when $H^0_{xq} = 0 = H^0_{qx}$ for all (q, x) and α. Replace α by α_1 in (3.15), use (4.8) and (4.12) to obtain

$$-H^0_{xx} x_{\alpha_1} + I_n = 0. \tag{4.30}$$

Hence we have

Theorem 4.3. If $\rho > 0$ and $H^0_{xq} = 0$ for all x, q, α, then x_{α_1}, x_β, x_{α_2} are all negative quasi-semidefinite and symmetric.

Proof. The theorem follows because x_{α_1} is negative quasi-semidefinite and symmetric from (4.30). With x_{α_1} negative quasi-semidefinite and (4.29) we get the other results.

The separability of the Hamiltonian is Scheinkman's (1978) G.A.S. hypothesis. Again we see a close connection between a G.A.S. hypothesis and strong comparative statics results.

Before we complete the analysis in this section, we use the abstract results of section 3. Use equations (3.6) and (3.7) to write them in matrix form

$$\begin{bmatrix} H^0_{x\alpha} - \rho q_\alpha \\ -H^0_{q\alpha} \end{bmatrix} = \begin{bmatrix} -H^0_{xq} & -H^0_{xx} \\ H^0_{qq} & H^0_{qx} \end{bmatrix} \begin{bmatrix} q_x \\ x_\alpha \end{bmatrix}. \tag{4.31}$$

Premultiply (4.31) by $[x^T_\alpha, q^T_\alpha]$ and rearrange terms to get

$$x^T_\alpha H^0_{x\alpha} - q^T_\alpha H^0_{q\alpha} = \rho x^T_\alpha q_\alpha - x^T_\alpha H^0_{xx} x_\alpha + q^T_\alpha H^0_{qq} q_\alpha$$
$$- x^T_\alpha H^0_{xq} q_\alpha + q^T_\alpha H^0_{qx} x_\alpha. \tag{4.32}$$

Replace α by α_1 in (4.32), use $H^0_{x\alpha_1} = -I_n$, $H^0_{q\alpha_1} = 0$ from (4.8) and (4.12) for the Lucas–Mortensen–Treadway model to obtain

$$-x^T_{\alpha_1} - \rho x^T_{\alpha_1} q_{\alpha_1} = -x^T_{\alpha_1} H^0_{xx} x_{\alpha_1} + q^T_{\alpha_1} H^0_{qq} q_{\alpha_1}$$
$$- x^T_{\alpha_1} H^0_{xq} q_{\alpha_1} + q^T_{\alpha_1} H^0_{qx} x_{\alpha_1}. \tag{4.33}$$

Pre- and postmultiply both sides of (4.33) by $y \in R^n$ to obtain

$$-y^T x^T_{\alpha_1} y - \rho y^T x^T_{\alpha_1} q_{\alpha_1} y = -y^T x^T_{\alpha_1} H^0_{xx} x_{\alpha_1} y + y^T q^T_{\alpha_1} H^0_{qq} q_{\alpha_1} y. \tag{4.34}$$

Notice that the cross product terms cancel to give the right-hand side of (4.34). From (4.34)

$$-y^T x^T_{\alpha_1} y = [q_{\alpha_1} y, x_{\alpha_1} y]^T Q(\alpha) [q_{\alpha_1} y, x_{\alpha_1} y], \tag{4.35}$$

where $Q(\alpha)$ is defined in (3.10). We can now state

Theorem 4.4. (i) The matrix $x^T_{\alpha_1} + \rho x^T_{\alpha_1} q_{\alpha_1}$ is negative quasi-semidefinite, (ii) if $Q(\alpha)$ is positive semidefinite, then x_{α_1}, x_β and x_{α_2} are all negative quasi-semidefinite.

Proof. Part (i) follows from (4.34) because H^0 is convex in q and concave in x. Part (ii) follows from (4.35) and the hypothesis that $Q(\alpha)$ is positive semidefinite. That x_β and x_{α_2} are negative quasi-semidefinite follows from (4.29).

Once again we see that a G.A.S. hypothesis, that is $Q(\alpha)$ being positive semidefinite, yields strong comparative statics results. Furthermore, when $\rho = 0$, theorem 4.4 (ii) shows that $x_{\alpha_1}, x_\beta, x_{\alpha_2}$ are all negative quasi-semidefinite.

Remark. When $\pi = pf(x, \dot{x}) - \alpha_1^T x - \alpha_2^T \dot{x}$, where p is product price, we may obtain comparative statics results on p by noticing that the choice of optimum path is homogeneous of degree 0 in (p, α_1, α_2). Put $\bar{\alpha}_1 = p^{-1}\alpha_1$, $\bar{\alpha}_2 = p^{-1}\alpha_2$. Then use the results obtained above to deduce qualitative results for $\partial x / \partial p$.

Next examine the impact on steady state x when the discount ρ is increased.

5. Generalized capital deepening

Consider the steady state equations

$$\rho q - H_x^0(q, x) = 0, \tag{5.1}$$

$$H_q^0(q, x) = 0. \tag{5.2}$$

Burmeister and Turnovsky (1972) introduce the measure of capital deepening $B(\rho) \equiv q^T x_\rho$ where x_ρ is the derivative of the steady state with respect to ρ: an economy is called *regular* at ρ_0 if $B(\rho_0) \leq 0$. The motivation for introducing $B(\rho)$ is discussed in detail in Burmeister and Turnovsky (1972). It is a measure in a growth model for the impact of the interest rate ρ changes on the steady state capital stock constellation. It turns out that the following theorem holds.

Theorem 5.1. All of the following G.A.S. hypotheses at $q(\rho_0)$, $x(\rho_0)$ are sufficient for $B(\rho) \leq 0$ at $\rho = \rho_0 \geq 0$: (i) Q is positive semidefinite, (ii) $(H_{qq}^0)^{-1} H_{qx}^0$ is negative quasi-semidefinite, or (iii) $H_{xq}^0 = 0$.

Proof. We demonstrate (i) first. Differentiate totally (5.1)–(5.2), with respect to ρ, to obtain

$$\rho q_\rho + q - H_{xq}^0 q_\rho - H_{xx}^0 x_\rho = 0, \tag{5.3}$$

$$H_{qq}^0 q_\rho + H_{qx}^0 x_\rho = 0. \tag{5.4}$$

Premultiply (5.3) by x_ρ^T to get

$$\rho x_\rho^T q_\rho + x_\rho^T q - x_\rho^T H_{xq}^0 q_\rho - x_\rho^T H_{xx}^0 x_\rho = 0. \tag{5.5}$$

Premultiply (5.4) by q_ρ^T to get

$$q_\rho^T H_{qq}^0 q_\rho + q_\rho^T H_{qx}^0 x_\rho = 0. \tag{5.6}$$

Combine (5.5) and (5.6) to get

$$\rho x_\rho^T q_\rho + x_\rho^T q - x_\rho^T H_{xx}^0 x_\rho + q_\rho^T H_{qq}^0 q_\rho$$

$$= [q_\rho, x_\rho]^T Q(q_\rho, x_\rho)[q_\rho, x_\rho] + x_\rho^T q = 0. \tag{5.7}$$

It follows immediately from (5.7) that (i) implies

$$x_\rho^T q = q^T x_\rho \le 0.$$

In order to derive the second result solve (5.4) for q_ρ in terms of x_ρ and insert the solution into (5.3) to get

$$q_\rho = -(H_{qq}^0)^{-1} H_{qx}^0 x_\rho, \tag{5.8}$$

$$-\rho (H_{qq}^0)^{-1} H_{qx}^0 x + q + H_{xq}^0 (H_{qq}^0)^{-1} H_{qx}^0 x_\rho - H_{xx}^0 x_\rho = 0. \tag{5.9}$$

Premultiply both sides of (5.9) by x_ρ^T to obtain

$$-\rho x_\rho^T (H_{qq}^0)^{-1} H_{qx}^0 x_\rho + x_\rho^T q + x_\rho^T H_{xq}^0 (H_{qq}^0)^{-1} H_{qx}^0 x_\rho$$

$$- x_\rho^T H_{xx}^0 x_\rho = 0. \tag{5.10}$$

Now,

$$x_\rho^T H_{xq}^0 (H_{qq}^0)^{-1} H_{qx}^0 x_\rho = (H_{qx}^0 x_\rho)^T (H_{qq}^0)^{-1} (H_{qx}^0 x_\rho) \ge 0$$

since H^0 is convex in q. Also $-x_\rho^T H_{xx}^0 x_\rho \ge 0$ because H^0 is concave in x. Hence from (5.10) either (ii) or (iii) is sufficient for $q^T x_\rho \le 0$.

Remark. Parts (i) and (ii) of this theorem are due to Brock and Burmeister (1976) and Magill (1977a) respectively.

As we note in the last section of this chapter a fascinating discussion of the implications of the L.A.S. hypothesis in comparing equilibria when ρ changes and the relation of this problem to the Cambridge Controversy and the *Hahn Problem* is contained in Burmeister and Long (1977).

This concludes the presentation of results we have obtained on the implications of sufficient conditions on $\pi(x, \dot{x}, \alpha)$ and ρ for the G.A.S. of optimal paths for qualitative results on steady states. Notice that all of the results are of the following character: A G.A.S. hypothesis and a hypothesis about how α enters H^0 is placed upon the Hamiltonian $H^0(q, x, \alpha)$ of the system to obtain results on comparing steady states. This suggests that a general theory of comparing steady states is waiting to be discovered. This is so because Hamiltonian constructs are very general. For example, such a construct can be invented for dynamic games in which some arguments enter in a passive way and are determined by equilibrium forces in much the same way as competitive prices are determined; and, other arguments enter in an active way and are determined in much the same way as Cournot oligopoly models determine output levels. See Brock (1977b) for a development of games in terms of a general Hamiltonian approach. Dechert (1978) locates sufficient conditions for dynamic games to be represented by the Euler equation of some variational problem.

Furthermore, the analysis of Cass and Shell (1976a) succinctly develops the Hamiltonian formalism of modern growth theory for both descriptive and optimal growth models. A Hamiltonian formalism underlies virtually any dynamic model that has a recursive structure. Hence results such as those obtained in this chapter which depend upon hypotheses placed upon the *Hamiltonian alone* should extend to more general models.

Turn now to the development of results on comparing equilibria that depend only on the L.A.S. hypothesis of the steady state x.

6. More on the adjustment cost model

This section presents a simplified proof of a theorem of Mortensen (1973). Return to the adjustment cost model of Lucas, Treadway and Mortensen.

$$\max \int_0^\infty e^{-\rho t}(pf(x, \dot{x}) - \alpha_1^T x - \alpha_2^T u) \, dt, \tag{6.1}$$

subject to $x(0) = x_0$ with $\dot{x} = u$.

Assume that p, α_1 and α_2 are time independent. Write the necessary conditions for optimality in Euler equation form,

$$\frac{d}{dt}(f_u - \alpha_2) = f_x - \alpha_1 + \rho(f_u - \alpha_2). \tag{6.2}$$

Let $\bar{x}$ be a steady state and let $x_0 = \bar{x} + \Delta x_0$. Under very general conditions stated in Magill (1977a), equation (6.2) may be approximated for small Δx_0 as

$$\frac{d}{dt}(f_{uu}\Delta u + f_{ux}\Delta x) = f_{xu}\Delta u + f_{xx}\Delta x + \rho f_{ux}\Delta x + \rho f_{uu}\Delta u, \tag{6.3}$$

$$\Delta \dot{x} = \Delta u, \ \Delta x(0) = \Delta x_0. \tag{6.4}$$

Here (6.3) was obtained from (6.2) by expansion in a Taylor series at $(\bar{x}, 0)$ and using the equations of steady state to cancel out the first order terms. All second derivatives are evaluated at the steady state $(x, u) = (\bar{x}, 0)$.

Now if f is strictly concave in $(x, \dot{x})$, there is a policy function $h(x, p, \alpha)$ such that optimum trajectories satisfy

$$\dot{x} = h(x, p, \alpha), \quad x(0) = x_0. \tag{6.5}$$

Linearize h around the steady state $\bar{x}$ to get

$$\Delta \dot{x} = h_x(\bar{x}; p, \alpha)\Delta x, \quad \Delta x(0) = \Delta x_0. \tag{6.6}$$

Equations (6.3), (6.4) and (6.6) describe the same trajectory and, therefore, the matrix $M \equiv h_x(\bar{x}; p, \alpha)$ must solve a quadratic matrix equation that is generated by (6.3). That is,

$$BM^2 + (C - C^{\mathrm{T}} - \rho B)M = A + \rho C, \tag{6.7}$$

where $B = f_{uu}$, $C = f_{ux}$, $C^{\mathrm{T}} = f_{xu}$ and $A = f_{xx}$. Equation (6.7) is obtained by putting $\Delta \dot{x} = M \Delta x$ and $\Delta \ddot{x} = M \Delta \dot{x} = M^2 \Delta x$ into (6.3) and equating coefficients.

Equation (6.7) is difficult to solve for the optimal adjustment matrix M except in the one dimensional case. Nonetheless, we can say a good deal about M in terms of A, B, C, ρ. For instance, we know that for $f(x, \dot{x})$ strictly concave there is only one steady state $\bar{x}$ and it is G.A.S. for the case $\rho = 0$ where the maximum is interpreted in the sense of the overtaking ordering as in Brock and Haurie (1976). Scheinkman's (1976) result tells us that, except for hairline cases, if $\rho > 0$ and ρ is small enough, then G.A.S. will hold. Hence we know, except for hairline cases, that M is a stable matrix when ρ is small. We also may employ the G.A.S. hypotheses listed above to find conditions on A, B, C, ρ that guarantee that M is a stable matrix.

In this section we are interested in the following: What restrictions does the stability of M imply on the comparison of steady states? This question is more in the spirit of the original Samuelson Correspondence Principle which asserted that stability of M would generate comparative statics results. This brings us to Mortensen's theorem.

Theorem 6.1. (Mortensen (1973).) Assume that B is negative definite. If M is a stable matrix, then $\bar{x}_\beta$ and $(\partial h/\partial \beta)(\bar{x}; p, \alpha_1, \alpha_2)$, where $\beta \equiv \alpha_1 + \rho \alpha_2$, are both symmetric and negative definite if and only if C is symmetric. Moreover, the characteristic roots of M are all real if C is symmetric.

For a proof see Mortensen (1973).

We next develop formulae for later use. First, by direct use of the steady state equations, obtain

$$\bar{x}_\beta = (A+\rho C)^{-1}, \quad \frac{\partial h}{\partial \beta}(\bar{x}; p, \alpha_1, \alpha_2) = -M(A+\rho C)^{-1}. \tag{6.8}$$

Second, we need a lemma.

Lemma 6.1. At any steady state, if the quadratic approximation (6.3) is valid, then

$$M^T B - BM = C - C^T, \tag{6.9}$$

$$A + \rho C = (M^T - \rho I_n)BM. \tag{6.10}$$

Proof. To prove this lemma note that equation (6.10) follows directly from (6.9) and (6.7). So we need establish (6.9) only. Write the necessary conditions of optimality in Hamiltonian form,

$$\dot{q} = \rho q - H_x^0(q, x), \tag{6.11}$$

$$\dot{x} = H_q^0(q, x), \, x(0) = x_0, \tag{6.12}$$

$$\lim_{t\to\infty} e^{-\rho t} q(t)^T x(t) = 0. \tag{6.13}$$

In order to see that (6.13) is necessary for optimality and is the correct transversality condition in general, see Benveniste and Scheinkman (1982).

Following Magill (1977a), look at the necessary conditions for optimality of the linear quadratic approximation to (1.1) written in Hamiltonian form.

$$\Delta\dot{q} = \rho\Delta q - H_{xq}^0 \Delta q - H_{xx}^0 \Delta x, \tag{6.14}$$

$$\Delta\dot{x} = H_{qx}^0 \Delta x + H_{qq}^0 \Delta q, \tag{6.15}$$

$$\lim_{t\to\infty} e^{-\rho t}\Delta q^T(t)\Delta x(t) = 0. \tag{6.16}$$

The matrices in (6.14) and (6.15) are evaluated at steady state $(\bar{q}, \bar{x})$ and $\Delta x, \Delta q$ denote deviations from the steady state. Now, suppose that

$$\Delta q = W\Delta x \tag{6.17}$$

for some matrix W. The intuition behind this is compelling.
If

$$R(x_0) \equiv \max \int_0^\infty e^{-\rho t}\pi(x, u, \alpha)\,dt,$$

subject to $x(0) = x_0$, $\dot{x} = u$, and if R is twice continuously differentiable at $x_0 = \bar{x}$, then (6.17) holds where $W = (\partial^2 R / \partial x^2)(\bar{x})$. This is so because by definition $q \equiv \partial R / \partial x$ and hence, $\Delta q = (\partial^2 R / \partial x^2) \Delta x = W \Delta x$ for the linear approximation. Turn back to (6.15) and get

$$\Delta \dot{x} = H_{qx}^0 \Delta x + H_{qq}^0 \Delta q = H_{qx}^0 \Delta x + H_{qq}^0 W \Delta x = M \Delta x. \tag{6.18}$$

Hence $M = H_{qx}^0 + H_{qq}^0 W$. Next calculate $M^T B - BM$ to obtain

$$M^T B - BM = (H_{xq}^0 + W H_{qq}^0) B - B (H_{qx}^0 + H_{qq}^0 W). \tag{6.19}$$

But,

$$B \equiv f_{uu}, \quad H_{qq}^0 = -f_{uu}^{-1}, \quad H_{xq}^0 = -f_{xu} f_{uu}^{-1}, \quad H_{qx}^0 = -f_{uu}^{-1} f_{ux}$$

from (4.9)–(4.11). Thus

$$M^T B - BM = H_{xq}^0 f_{uu} - f_{uu} H_{qx}^0 = -f_{xu} + f_{ux} = C - C^T. \tag{6.20}$$

This ends the proof of the lemma.

Observe that the proof of the lemma did not assume that $\bar{x}$ is L.A.S. or G.A.S. What is needed for the proof of the lemma is that the linear quadratic approximation to (1.1) be valid and that $R(x)$ be twice continuously differentiable. A sufficient condition for both is that $f(x, \dot{x})$ be quadratic in $(x, \dot{x})$. Magill (1977a) discusses the linear quadratic approximation. Hence, in particular, equation (6.20) holds for all problems, where $f(x, \dot{x})$ is quadratic and concave in $(x, \dot{x})$. Mortensen does not need to assume that $\bar{x}$ is L.A.S. to obtain (6.20) when $f(x, \dot{x})$ is quadratic in $(x, \dot{x})$.

Examine the following quantities obtained directly from (6.10)

$$A + \rho C = M^T BM - \rho BM, \tag{6.21}$$

$$-(A + \rho C) M^{-1} = \rho B - M^T B. \tag{6.22}$$

Notice that by (6.10), both $A + \rho C$ and $(A + \rho C) M^{-1}$ are symmetric, provided that $C = C^T$. Hence by (6.8) it follows that $\bar{x}_\beta$ and $\partial h / \partial \beta$ are both symmetric since the inverse of a symmetric matrix is symmetric.

It is important to note that the only part of Mortensen's theorem that needs the L.A.S. of $\bar{x}$ is the negative definiteness of $\bar{x}_\beta$ and $\partial h / \partial \beta$. The symmetry of $\bar{x}$ and $\partial h / \partial \beta$ as well as the characteristic roots of M being real require the symmetry of C alone.

Mortensen's theorem is a good example of how the structure of the adjustment cost model interplays with the L.A.S. hypothesis to produce strong qualitative results.

Corollary 6.1. (i) $(H^0_{qq})^{-1} H^0_{qx} = f_{ux} \equiv C^{\mathrm{T}}$ and (ii) if C is negative quasi-definite, then $\bar{x}$ is L.A.S. and both $\bar{x}_\beta$, $(\partial h/\partial \beta)(\bar{x}; p, \alpha_1, \alpha_2)$ are negative quasi-definite.

Proof. To prove this corollary note that the first formula follows directly from

$$H_{qq} = -f^{-1}_{uu}, \quad H^0_{qx} = -f^{-1}_{uu} f_{ux}, \tag{6.23}$$

and $C \equiv f_{xu}$. Here equation (6.23) is recorded from (4.10) and (4.11) for convenience.

Now C is negative quasi-definite if and only if C^{T} is. Hence the negative quasi-definiteness of C is simply the sufficient condition for G.A.S. reported in Brock and Scheinkman (1976) and Magill (1977a). Turn now to the task of showing that $\bar{x}_\beta$ and $\partial h/\partial \beta$ are negative quasi-definite. Look at (6.21) and (6.22). Since for any $y \in R^n$,

$$y^{\mathrm{T}}(M^{\mathrm{T}} B - BM)y = y^{\mathrm{T}}(C - C^{\mathrm{T}})y = 0,$$

and $\bar{x}_\beta$, $\partial h/\partial \beta$ are negative quasi-definite if and only if $A + \rho C$ and $-(A + \rho C)M^{-1}$ are negative quasi-definite; therefore, by (6.21) and (6.22) we need only show that BM is positive quasi-definite in order to finish the proof. Recall that

$$\bar{x}_\beta = (A + \rho C)^{-1}; \quad \partial h/\partial \beta = -((A + \rho C)M^{-1})^{-1}. \tag{6.24}$$

In order to see that BM is positive quasi-definite calculate

$$BM = f_{uu}(H^0_{qq} W + H^0_{qx}) = -W - (H^0_{qq})^{-1} H^0_{qx}. \tag{6.25}$$

The first equality follows from (6.23) and the second follows because $f_{uu} = -(H^0_{qq})^{-1}$.

Now, W is negative semidefinite by concavity of the state valuation function of the associated linear quadratic approximation of the original problem around the steady state $\bar{x}$. See Magill (1977a). Hence the right-hand side of (6.14) is positive quasi-definite. This ends the proof.

We close this section by remarking that some additional structure on the problem above and beyond the stability of M is needed in order to get the negative quasi-semidefiniteness of $\bar{x}_\beta$. This is so because Mortensen (1973, p. 663) provides a two dimensional example where M is stable, C is not symmetric, and $\partial \bar{x}_2/\partial \beta_2 > 0$.

. The reader is advised to look at Magill and Scheinkman (1979) where for the case of (6.1) a complete characterization of the local behavior of

(6.5) near steady states is given under the assumption that the matrix f_{xx} is symmetric.

Furthermore if p, α_1, α_2 in (6.1) were determined *endogenously* by the device of maximizing a discounted sum of consumer net producer surplus, the revised correspondence principle could be developed in price space rather than in quantity space as is done here. In that way an *equilibrium-disequilibrium* price adjustment process is derived that replaces the ad hoc Walrasian tâtonnement. The methods developed in this chapter can be used to show how structural properties of the Hamiltonian of the discounted consumer net producer surplus problem translates into a correspondence principle for the equilibrium price adjustment process. This question has been studied by Magill–Scheinkman (1979), and Magill (1979).

7. Miscellaneous applications and exercises

(1) *Rational expectations.* In this application we illustrate once again the Correspondence Principle and we contrast the comparative statics results obtained by the static theory of the firm versus the dynamic cost of adjustment theory of Lucas, Treadway and Mortensen. Furthermore, to partially differentiate the analysis from the one in the preceding section, we assume *rational expectations* and we use the technique of *consumer surplus* employed by Lucas and Prescott (1971).

Consider an industry with $N \geq 1$ firms, each producing the same industry good by employing $K \geq 1$ capital goods, x, and investing $\dot{x}$. Each firm forms identical expectations about the product price path denoted by $p(t)$ with $p(t): [0, \infty) \to R^+$. The instantaneous flow of profit of the ith representative firm is the difference between its revenue $p(t)f(x(t), \dot{x}(t))$ and its costs $\alpha_1^T x(t) + \alpha_2^T \dot{x}(t)$. The firm's problem may be stated as

$$\max_{\dot{x}} \int_0^\infty e^{-\rho t}(pf(x, \dot{x}) - \alpha_1^T x - \alpha_2^T \dot{x})\, dt, \tag{7.1}$$

subject to $x(0) = x_0 \in R^+$, which is identical to (6.1). Denote by $Q_S(t)$ the *market supply* which is defined by

$$Q_S(t) = Nf(x(t), \dot{x}(t)). \tag{7.2}$$

There is no loss of generality to assume that $N = 1$. The market supply depends on $p(t)$, which in turn depends on the solution of the maximum problem in (7.1). The *market demand* also depends on $p(t)$ and we denote it by

$$Q_D(t) = d^{-1}(p(t)), \tag{7.3}$$

for $p(t) \geq 0$, $t \in [0, \infty)$, with $d(Q) > 0$ and $d'(Q) < 0$ for $Q \geq 0$.

Next, we define a *rational expectations equilibrium* for the product market of the industry as a price path $p(t)$: $[0, \infty) \to R^+$ such that

$$Q_D(t) = Q_S(t) \tag{7.4}$$

for almost all $t \in [0, \infty)$. Note that the firm's expectations are rational in Muth's (1961) sense; that is, anticipated price is equal, for almost all times, to actual price, the latter being determined by the market. The integral of the demand function, denoted by $D(Q)$, is given by

$$D(Q) = \int_0^Q d(y)\, dy \tag{7.5}$$

for $Q \geq 0$, so that $D'(Q) = d(Q)$, $D''(Q) = d'(Q) < 0$. The problem of finding a continuous vector function $\dot{x}(t)$ such that

$$\max_{\dot{x}} \int_0^\infty e^{-\rho t}[D(Q) - \alpha_1^T x - \alpha_2^T \dot{x}]\, dt \tag{7.6}$$

is called the *extended integrand problem.* Brock and Magill (1979) show sufficient conditions under which the price path $p(t)$ is a rational expectations equilibrium. This result is useful because it reduces the study of problem (7.1) to an analysis of (7.6).

Write the integrand in (7.6) in the consumer surplus form

$$F(x, \dot{x}) - \alpha_1^T x - \alpha_2^T \dot{x} \equiv D(Q) - \alpha_1^T x - \alpha_2^T \dot{x}$$

$$= \int_0^{Q = f(x, \dot{x})} d(y)\, dy - \alpha_1^T x - \alpha_2^T \dot{x}, \tag{7.7}$$

and let us check to discover sufficient conditions so that

$$F_{x\dot{x}} = F_{\dot{x}x}. \tag{7.8}$$

From (7.7) we compute

$$F_x = d(f(x, \dot{x}))f_x,$$

$$F_{xx} = d'(f(x, \dot{x}))f_x f_x + d(f(x, \dot{x}))f_{xx}, \tag{7.9}$$

$$F_{\dot{x}} = d(f(x, \dot{x}))f_{\dot{x}},$$

$$F_{\dot{x}x} = d'(f(x, \dot{x}))f_x f_{\dot{x}} + d(f(x, \dot{x}))f_{\dot{x}x}. \tag{7.10}$$

From (7.9) and (7.10) we conclude that if $f_{x\dot{x}} = f_{\dot{x}x}$, then (7.8) will hold. Suppose that $f_{x\dot{x}} = f_{\dot{x}x}$, or equivalently, suppose that the matrix C of section 6 is symmetric. Furthermore, let $\bar{x}$ be the optimal path of the extended integrand problem in (7.6) and suppose that $\bar{x}$ is L.A.S. Then by Mortensen's theorem we conclude that both $\partial \bar{x}/\partial(\alpha_1 + \rho\alpha_2)$ and $\partial \dot{x}/\partial(\alpha_1 + \rho\alpha_2)$ are symmetric and negative definite. Thus we have sketched a proof of

Theorem 7.1. Assume that the optimal path of the extended integrand problem is L.A.S. and that the matrix C is symmetric. Then both $\partial \bar{x}/\partial(\alpha_1 + \rho\alpha_2)$ and $\partial \dot{x}/\partial(\alpha_1 + \rho\alpha_2)$ are symmetric and negative definite.

The above result illustrates, once again, the usefulness of the Correspondence Principle in obtaining comparative statics results in the cost of adjustment theory with rational expectations. Although this application is similar to the one in the preceding section, it differs in one significant aspect, that is, $p(t)$ here is a rational expectations equilibrium instead of a *constant* vector as Lucas, Treadway and Mortensen assume. Despite this extension, comparative statics results hold as theorem 7.1 shows and are obtained easily because of the powerful technique of consumer surplus.

(2) *Static vs dynamic theory.* It might be informative to compare the results in theorem 7.1 to the results of static theory. Reducing (4.1) to the static case we want to maximize

$$\pi(x, \alpha) = f(x) - \alpha_1^T x - \rho\alpha_2^T x. \tag{7.11}$$

Carrying out the maximization, we obtain the necessary conditions

$$f_x(\bar{x}) = \alpha_1 + \rho\alpha_2$$

and $f_{xx}(\bar{x})$ is negative quasi-definite. Following Hicks (1946, pp. 320–323), we conclude that $\partial \bar{x}/\partial(\alpha_1 + \rho\alpha_2)$ is symmetric and negative definite. Therefore, theorem 7.1 is a generalization of the early literature on the subject as presented by Hicks (1946), Samuelson (1947) and later made popular by Henderson and Quandt (1971). Note that in the static case, $f_{\dot{x}} = 0$ with no meaningful information available about $\partial \dot{x}/\partial(\alpha_1 + \rho\alpha_2)$. The reader,

however, must be cautioned that the dynamic theory is not just a straightforward generalization of the static theory of the firm. When C is not symmetric
as we have assumed, Treadway (1971) and Mortensen (1973) show that the
dynamic theory yields results that are dissimilar to those of the static theory.

(3) We close this section with an illustration of the usefulness of our
comparative statics results in theorem 7.1. Consider the simple case with
$x = (x_1, x_2)$ as the output vector and $\alpha = (\alpha_1, \alpha_2)$ as the parameter vector
denoting input prices. Then, for an increase in the input price i, where $i = 1$
or 2, denoted by $\Delta\alpha_i > 0$, theorem 7.1 yields

$$\Delta\alpha_i \frac{\partial \bar{x}_i}{\partial \alpha_i} \Delta\alpha_i < 0, \tag{7.12}$$

which means that an increase in the input price causes a decrease in the
output production due to a decrease in the quantity of the input employed.
More generally, if $\Delta\alpha_1 = \Delta\alpha_2 > 0$, then

$$[\Delta\alpha_1, \Delta\alpha_2] \begin{bmatrix} \dfrac{\partial \bar{x}_1}{\partial \alpha_1} & \dfrac{\partial \bar{x}_1}{\partial \alpha_2} \\ \dfrac{\partial \bar{x}_2}{\partial \alpha_1} & \dfrac{\partial \bar{x}_2}{\partial \alpha_2} \end{bmatrix} \begin{bmatrix} \Delta\alpha_1 \\ \Delta\alpha_2 \end{bmatrix} < 0. \tag{7.13}$$

What is the economic content of (7.13)? The negative definiteness of $\partial \bar{x}/\partial \alpha$,
which in our special case is the 2×2 matrix in (7.13), yields

$$\frac{\partial \bar{x}_1}{\partial \alpha_1} \frac{\partial \bar{x}_2}{\partial \alpha_2} - \frac{\partial \bar{x}_1}{\partial \alpha_2} \frac{\partial \bar{x}_2}{\partial \alpha_1} > 0. \tag{7.14}$$

While carrying out the multiplication in (7.13) we get

$$\frac{\partial \bar{x}_1}{\partial \alpha_1} + \frac{\partial \bar{x}_1}{\partial \alpha_2} + \frac{\partial \bar{x}_2}{\partial \alpha_1} + \frac{\partial \bar{x}_2}{\partial \alpha_2} < 0. \tag{7.15}$$

From (7.14) and (7.15) we conclude that *complementarity* is likely to be
dominant in the production process. Substitution between inputs is possible
but it could not prevail. Therefore, our comparative statics results of the
dynamic theory of the firm are consistent with the results of the Hicksian
static analysis. Hicks (1946, p. 98) points out, "there is a tendency for
products jointly produced in the same firm to be complementary, and for
factors jointly employed in the same firm to be complementary".

8. Further remarks and references

In this section we offer a few comments on the literature related to this chapter. Some of the relevant papers are Mortensen (1973), Burmeister and Long (1977), Araujo and Scheinkman (1979), Magill and Scheinkman (1979), Magill (1979) and McKenzie (1983). In particular, Mortensen (1973) and Burmeister and Long (1977) are the first to explicitly formulate questions of the type: What are the implications of the L.A.S. hypothesis on the optimal steady states of a control problem for the question of comparing steady states?

Burmeister and Long (1977) are interested in studying the basic aspect of the *Cambridge Controversy* in capital theory, namely, the paradoxical consumption behavior associated with alternative steady states when the interest rate changes as an exogenous parameter. The behavior is paradoxical because if the interest rate is above the exogenous rate of labor growth, then it is possible that a decrease in the interest rate will decrease, instead of increase, per capita consumption.

Another unresolved issue in capital theory is the *Hahn problem*, which originated in F. Hahn's (1966) paper, and which is concerned with whether or not a general equilibrium model of capital theory is stable. Burmeister and Long (1977) note a similarity between the Cambridge Controversy and the Hahn problem and they conjecture a Correspondence Principle to study these issues. Indeed, they conjecture that a paradoxical steady state is in some sense unstable, and vice versa. Their conclusion is that the Conjecture Correspondence Principle holds only in some very special cases. However, their Correspondence Principle proves to be a useful tool in studying these two important issues in capital theory.

The Correspondence Principle of section 2 is different but the purpose is the same, namely, to be used as a methodological tool to get comparative statics results. Furthermore, we focus on the formulation of equilibrium-disequilibrium mechanisms (1.5)–(1.6) and the extension of Samuelson's Correspondence Principle to such mechanisms.

Magill and Scheinkman (1979) present a complete characterization of the L.A.S. of regular steady states for a class of optimal control problems similar to ours. Their results depend upon an assumption of *symmetry* on the integrand of the variational problem and their technique involves the use of an equilibrium potential function. In the spirit of Samuelson's Correspondence Principle, Magill and Scheinkman (1979) are able, under the assumption of symmetry and L.A.S., to obtain comparative statics results by means of the equilibrium potential function. We continue to be interested in similar questions with more emphasis on G.A.S. and using different techniques. We note that Magill and Scheinkman (1979) is extended to the *asymmetric* case in Magill (1979).

Furthermore, Araujo and Scheinkman (1979) and McKenzie (1983) present important results on comparative statics and dynamics for a *discrete* time optimal model and Epstein (1982) reports comparative dynamics results in the adjustment cost model of the firm.

An effort to rehabilitate Samuelson's Correspondence Principle was implicit in Lucas (1967) and Mortensen (1973) in the context of an adjustment cost model of the dynamic investment theory of the firm and also in Liviatan and Samuelson (1969) in the context of an aggregate one-sector growth model with joint production. Recently, Bhagwati, Brecher and Hatta (1987) have generalized Samuelson's (1971) *Global Correspondence Principle* with an application to international trade.

CHAPTER 8

MACROECONOMIC POLICIES

Let me start by posing what I like to
call "the fundamental problem of
equilibrium theory": *how is economic
equilibrium attained?* A dual question
more commonly raised is: *why is
economic equilibrium stable?* Behind
these questions lie the problem of
modeling economic processes and
introducing dynamics into
equilibrium theory.

Smale (1980, p. 113)

1. Introduction

This book stresses the theme that the stability analysis of optimal control
is a useful tool in economics. Chapter 8 shows how to analyze economic
models where, due to tax distortions, there is no optimal control problem
that describes the equilibrium dynamics of the system. Yet the methods
discussed in this book can still be applied. For example, equilibrium
dynamics can be phased diagrammed and stability analysis conducted. Turn
now to the substance of the chapter.

Several developments in macroeconomic theory have stressed what one
might call the intrinsic dynamics of the system; that is, the dynamics arising
from the creation of assets required to finance certain current activities.
Blinder and Solow (1973), Tobin and Buiter (1976), Turnovsky (1977) and
others have placed an emphasis on analyzing the short-run, and more
particularly the long-run effects of various government policies, as well as,
insofar as this is feasible, on considering the transitional dynamic adjustments in response to such policies. This literature, like most of macroeconomic theory which precedes it, suffers from two major deficiencies.

The first is its simplistic treatment of the corporate sector. The traditional textbook macro model typically assumes that all private investment is financed through borrowing. More recently, authors such as Tobin (1969) and Mussa (1976) have introduced very crude stocks markets into their models by identifying one unit of equity with one unit of physical capital. Yet this typically is not how real world stock markets operate. Physical capital on the one hand, and the paper claims to these physical assets on the other, are distinct entities, the relative prices of which are continually changing, thereby invalidating the one-to-one relationship assumed by these authors and others. Recent attempts to differentiate explicitly between physical capital and the corresponding paper claims in a macroeconomic context are contained in Turnovsky (1977, 1978), although his analysis is based on the extreme case of all-equity financing.

The second major shortcoming is that these analyses are all based on arbitrary behavioral relationships. Despite the increasing awareness by economists of the need to ground macroeconomic theory on the firm microeconomic foundations, in practice in many cases they don't and thus the underlying behavioral relationships remain arbitrarily specified. The deficiencies of following this procedure become particularly severe when one wishes to augment the model to include a corporate sector embodying rational behavior. Indeed, as will become clear below, the effects of alternative government policies depend critically upon the capital structure employed by firms, which in turn is a function of the tax structure and the differential tax treatments of different securities. To incorporate this aspect adequately requires an explicit model of optimizing behavior.

Moreover, the policy implications derived from models based on ad hoc behavioral relationships may be misleading. Accordingly, the purpose of this chapter is to introduce a more complete corporate sector into a contemporary dynamic macro model, embedding it in an explicit optimizing framework. The approach we shall adopt is an extension of the general equilibrium framework developed by Brock (1974, 1975) and follows Brock and Turnovsky (1981). It includes the following key features: (a) all demand and supply functions of households and firms are derived from maximizing behavior; (b) expectations are determined simultaneously with perfect foresight continually holding; (c) all markets are continually cleared. Under these conditions, all expectations will be *self-fulfilling* and for this reason an equilibrium characterized by (a), (b) and (c) has been termed a *perfect foresight equilibrium.*

The earlier Brock analysis essentially abstracted from the government and corporate sectors and it is these aspects (particularly the latter) which we wish to emphasize here. More specifically we shall assume that the government can finance its deficit either by issuing bonds or by the creation of money. Similarly, firms may finance their investment plans by issuing debt, or equities, or out of retained earnings. Government bonds and both types of private securities are assumed to be perfect substitutes for one another. We shall introduce corporate and personal taxes on various forms of income. In doing so, we shall specify the tax rates so as to approximate what might be considered to be real world tax structures as in Feldstein, Green, and Sheshinski (1979) and Auerbach (1979).

The question of the impact of various corporate and personal taxes on real and financial decisions of the firm continues to be widely discussed in the literature such as Stiglitz (1973, 1974), Feldstein et al. (1979) and Auerbach (1979). These taxes impinge on the firm primarily through the cost of capital and hence it is important to make sure that this is defined appropriately. It would not be entirely unfair to say that traditionally the literature has been less than fully lucid on the appropriate definition of the cost of capital in the presence of taxes.

The approach taken here is to derive the appropriate cost of capital facing firms and hence determining their decisions, from the optimizing decisions of households. The basic idea is that, beginning with the budget constraint for firms, a differential equation determining the market value of firms may be derived. This equation is then manipulated to determine a cost of capital for firms, expressed in terms of market yields. Using the optimality conditions for consumers, these market yields can be related to consumers' rate of return on consumption and the various tax parameters. The expression for the cost of capital thereby obtained embodies the underlying optimizing behavior of consumers. The resulting objective function for firms separates into two parts. First, financial decisions are made to minimize the cost of capital; second, having determined the minimized cost of capital, real productive decisions may then be made to maximize discounted net after tax cash flow. The implications of our approach turn out to be fully consistent with the existing treatments of taxes in the corporate finance literature such as Modigliani and Miller (1958) and Miller (1977).

Except for special circumstances in which the debt to equity ratio is indeterminate, the optimal financial structure will consist of all bond financing or all equity financing depending upon relevant tax rates. While the conclusions of this methodology are not particularly novel, following Brock and Turnovsky (1981) for the derivation of the cost of capital from underlying consumer behavior and within an intertemporal general equilibrium framework, does appear to be new and in any event seems to be particularly instructive. We should emphasize that our primary objective is the development of an integrated framework, rather than any detailed manipulations of such a model. To do this, we shall assume that perfect certainty holds throughout. While this is obviously a restriction, it seems that the construction of a consistent and more complete macro model under certainty is a necessary prerequisite for proceeding further to an analysis in a world characterized by uncertainty.

2. The macroeconomic structure

The model contains three basic sectors – households, firms, and the government – all of which are interrelated through their respective budget constraints. We shall consider these sectors in turn, in all cases expressing their behavioral constraints directly in *real* terms.

2.1. Household sector

We assume that households can be aggregated into a single consolidated unit. The objective of this composite unit is to choose its consumption demand, its supply of labor, the rates at which it wishes to add to its real holdings of money balances, government bonds, corporate bonds, and equities, to maximize the intertemporal utility functions

$$\int_0^\infty e^{-\beta t} U(c, g, l^s, m^d)\, dt; \quad U_c > 0,\ U_g > 0,\ U_l > 0 \tag{2.1a}$$

subject to

$$c + \dot{b}_g^d + \dot{b}_p^d + \dot{m}^d + q\dot{E}^d$$
$$= wl^s + r_g b_g^d + r_p b_p^d - p^*(b_g^d + b_p^d + m^d) + iqE^d - T_h \tag{2.1b}$$

$$M(0) = M_0, \quad B_g(0) = B_{g_0}, \quad B_p(0) = B_{p_0}, \quad E(0) = E_0 \tag{2.1c}$$

$$\lim_{t \to \infty} \exp\left[-\int_0^t \theta(s)\, ds \right] b_g \geq 0, \quad \lim_{t \to \infty} \exp\left[-\int_0^t \theta(s)\, ds \right] b_p \geq 0;$$

$$\lim_{t \to \infty} \exp\left[-\int_0^t \theta(s)\, ds \right] qE \geq 0, \tag{2.1d}$$

where

c = real private consumption plans by households,

g = real government expenditure, taken to be fixed exogenously,

l^s = real supply of labor by households,

$m^d = M^d/P$ = demand for real money balances,

M = nominal stock of money,

P = nominal price of output,

b_g^d = demand for real government bonds,

B_g = nominal stock of government bonds,

b_p^d = demand for real corporate bonds,

B_p = nominal stock of corporate bonds,

E = number of shares outstanding,

q = relative price of equities in terms of current output,

$i = D/qE$ = dividend yield, taken to be parametrically given to the household sector,

D = real dividends,

qE^d = real stock demand for equities,

w = real wage rate,

r_g = nominal interest rate on government bonds,

r_p = nominal interest rate on private bonds,

p^* = instantaneous anticipated rate of inflation,

T_h = personal income tax in real terms, specified more fully below,

β = consumers' rate of time preference,

$\theta(s)$ = instantaneous rate of return on consumption at time s, to be determined endogenously below.

Note that lower case letters denote partial derivatives. The utility function is assumed to be concave in its four arguments c, g, l, and m. The introduction of c and g as separate arguments reflects the assumption that consumers view private and public goods as imperfect substitutes. At appropriate places below, it is convenient to focus on the case where they are perfect substitutes, in which case they enter additively as $c + g$. This corresponds to the assumption of *ultrarationality* in the sense discussed by Buiter (1977). Labor affects utility of leisure. The introduction of real money balances into the utility function is a convenient device for capturing the reasons for holding money in a certainty world. As Brock (1974) has shown, one can justify the inclusion of money in the utility function by means of transactions costs arguments. We assume that for given values of c, g, l, the marginal utility of money balances satisfies

$$\text{sgn } U_m = \text{sgn}(m^* - m)$$

so that m^* denotes the corresponding satiation level of real money balances, such as in Friedman (1969). For the real stock of money less than this level, the marginal utility of money is positive; for real stocks of money in excess of m^*, the holding costs outweigh the benefits and the net marginal utility of money becomes negative. While most of our discussion will focus on the general utility function U, it is expositionally convenient at appropriate places below to assume that it is *additively separable* in m, enabling us to separate out the real part of the system from the monetary part.

The household sector's budget constraint is given by (2.1b), which we have expressed in real flow terms. At each point of time the households are assumed to acquire income from a variety of sources. They supply labor to firms, at a real wage rate w; they earn interest income on their holdings of real private and government bonds; they suffer instantaneous capital gains or losses on their holdings of financial wealth denominated in nominal terms (money and bonds); they receive dividend payments at a rate i on their holding of equities. This rate is taken as parametrically given to households, but is one of the decision variables of the corporate sector. This income can be used in a variety of ways. They may use it to purchase real consumption goods, to add to their real holdings of money, government bonds, corporate bonds, and equities (the relative price of which is q), and to pay taxes to the government.

It is important to note that the decisions derived from this optimization procedure are planned demands (or supply in the case of labor). We have recorded this fact explicitly by the inclusion of the superscripts $d(s)$. Finally, the restraints (2.1d) must be added if borrowing is allowed, in order to prevent the present value of debt from becoming unbounded as $t \to \infty$; lim denotes limit inferior.

2.2. Corporate sector

As noted in the introduction, the corporate sector is driven by households in the sense that the optimizing decisions of the households determine the appropriate cost of capital facing the firms, which in turn governs their real and financial decisions. Thus, before the firm's optimization problem can be explicitly formulated and solved, it is first necessary to solve the optimization problem for the household sector. At this stage we shall simply record the financial and production constraints facing the firm and note the general form of the objective function which we shall derive.

The constraints facing the firm are summarized as follows

$$y^s = f(k^d, l^d), \tag{2.2a}$$

$$\pi = y^s - wl^d, \tag{2.2b}$$

$$\pi = r_p b_p + D + RE + T_f, \tag{2.2c}$$

$$k^d = RE + q\dot{E}^s + \dot{b}_p^s + p^* b_p^s, \tag{2.2d}$$

$$k(0) = k_0, \ E(0) = E_0, \ B_p(0) = B_{p_0}, \tag{2.2e}$$

where

l^d = real demand for labor by firms,
k^d = real demand for physical capital by firms,
y^s = real output,
π = real gross profit,
b_p^s = supply of corporate bonds by firms, in real terms,
E^s = quantity of equities, issued by firms,
RE = retained earnings, in real terms,
T_f = corporate profit taxes in real terms, specified more fully below,

and all other symbols are as defined earlier.

Equation (2.2a) describes the production function, which is assumed to have the usual neoclassical properties of positive but diminishing marginal productivities and constant returns to scale. Equation (2.2b) is the conventional definition of gross profits in real terms as being revenue less payments to labor. Equation (2.2c) describes the allocation of gross profits. After paying corporate income taxes, this may be used to pay interest to bond holders, to pay dividends to stockholders, or retained within the firm. Equation (2.2d) expresses the firm's financial constraint. Any additions to capital stock must be financed out of retained earnings, by issuing additional equities, or by issuing additional bonds. The final term $p^* b_p$ is essentially the revenue on private bonds accruing to the firm by virtue of the fact that these bonds are presumed to be denominated in nominal terms. It is precisely analogous to the inflation tax generated on financial wealth issued by the government and which also appears in the household sector's budget constraint. Finally, equations (2.2e) are initial conditions on the real stock of capital, the number of equities outstanding, and the nominal stock of corporate bonds.

We define the market value of the firm's securities outstanding at time t by

$$V(t) = b_p(t) + q(t)E(t), \tag{2.3}$$

(where we suppress superscripts) and shall assume that the firm's objective is to maximize the initial real market value of its securities, $V(0) = b_p(0) + q(0)E_0$. Given the constraints in (2.2a)-(2.2e) and the optimality conditions for households, we shall show in section 5 below that this objective function leads to the following optimization problem for firms. Their problem is to choose production decisions k^d, l^d, and financial decisions b_p^s, E^s, i to maximize an objective function of the form

$$V(0) = \int_0^\infty \exp\left[-\int_0^t \theta^*(\tau)\, d\tau\right] \gamma(t)\, dt, \qquad (2.4)$$

where $\gamma(t) =$ real net cash flow, $\theta^*(t) =$ instantaneous cost of capital at time t.

The precise forms of the functions $\gamma(t)$, $\theta^*(t)$, will be developed in section 5 below. At this point we wish to emphasize that $\gamma(t)$ is a function of *real* production decision variables, k, l; the *financial* decision variables are all embodied in the cost of capital $\theta^*(\tau)$. As a result, the two sets of decisions can be obtained in a convenient, sequential manner.

There is a technical point here which should be noted. In general, the interests of bondholders may conflict with those of stockholders. Hence maximizing the market value of all claims against the firm is not the same as maximizing the market value of equity. Later we shall see that the value maximizing firm will specialize in either all debt or all equity financing, depending upon the tax treatment. It will want to jump to the optimal level of debt or equity immediately at date zero. Therefore it may not be possible to satisfy the initial conditions on $b_p(0)$, E_0 in any equilibrium. There are two natural ways around this. One is to impose exogenous bounds on the rate of change of debt or equity. Then the equilibrium would involve eliminating the non-optimal security at the most rapid rate. This introduces a lot of messy mathematical detail. The second is to allow jumps in the appropriate variables directly. More will be said about this problem as we proceed.

The choice of the maximization of the market value of the firm as the objective function requires further comment. Auerbach (1979) has developed a model in which this objective is inappropriate from the viewpoint of maximizing the welfare of existing stockholders. In fact, the appropriateness or otherwise of the value maximization criterion depends upon the dividend policy adopted by the firm. In the Auerbach model, at the margin all equity based investment is financed through retained earnings. By contrast, in the present model, dividend policy is assumed to follow a fixed payout rule, so that at the margin, all equities come through new issues. Under the present assumption, it can be shown that value maximization is indeed appropriate from the viewpoint of maximizing the welfare of existing stockholders.

2.3. The government

The government is assumed to provide real goods and services g, which it finances out of real tax receipts or by issuing some form of government debt. Its budget constraint is described in real terms by

$$\dot{m}^s + \dot{b}_g^s = g + r_g b_g^s - T_h - T_f - (m^s + b_g^s)p^*, \tag{2.5}$$

where the superscript s denotes the planned supply by the government. This equation defines the real deficit net of the inflation tax by the right hand side of (2.3) and asserts that this is financed either by increasing the real money supply or by increasing the real stock of government bonds. The choice between these two alternatives, or any other monetary policy for that matter, represents a policy decision which needs to be specified in order to close the model.

Finally, we specify the tax functions T_h, T_f. These are hypothesized as follows

$$T_h = \tau_y (wl^s + r_g b_g^d + r_p b_p^d + iqE^d) + \tau_c (\dot{q} + qp^*)E, \tag{2.6a}$$

$$T_f = \tau_p (y^s - wl^d - r_p b_p^s), \quad 0 \le \tau_y \le 1, \quad 0 \le \tau_c \le 1, \quad 0 \le \tau_p \le 1, \tag{2.6b}$$

where for simplicity all tax structures are assumed to be linear. According to (2.6a), ordinary personal income – income from wages, interest, and dividends – are taxed at the flat rate τ_y. Nominal capital gains on equities are assumed to be taxed at the rate τ_c, which may, or may not, equal τ_y, and indeed in many economies $\tau_c = 0$. Notice that (2.6a) implies that capital gains are realized at each point in time; that is, the portfolio is continuously rolled over. Alternatively, one may view (2.6a) as representing taxes on unrealized capital gains. Turning to corporate income taxes, gross profit is assumed to be taxed at the proportional rate τ_p, with the interest payments to bondholders being fully deductible. In all cases full loss offset provisions are assumed.

We have specified these tax functions as reasonable approximations to real world tax structures. As we shall demonstrate below, this generally implies non-neutrality of the various tax rates. In order to restore neutrality, it would be necessary to introduce appropriate tax deductions for the capital losses arising from inflation on the holdings of money and bonds as well as appropriate offset provisions for firms. Since such taxes do not generally characterize real world tax structures, we do not incorporate them, although it would be straightforward to do so.

3. Perfect foresight equilibrium

The *perfect foresight equilibrium* (PFE) we shall consider is defined as follows. First consider the household sector's maximization problem defined by (2.1a), (2.1b) subject to (2.1c) with T_h defined by (2.6a). Carrying out this maximization yields a set of demand functions for consumption and various securities together with a labor supply function, in terms of p^*, w, r_b, r_g, etc, and other parameters which consumers take as given. Likewise, the corporate sector's optimization problem defined by (2.2a)–(2.2e) and (2.4), with T_f defined by (2.6b) yields a set of demand functions for capital and labor, and a set of supply functions for various securities together with output, which are also functions of w, r_b, etc, which firms also treat as parametrically given. Thirdly, the government policy decisions constrained by (2.5) generate supplies of money and government bonds and a demand for goods.

The *perfect foresight equilibrium* is defined as a situation in which the planned demands for output, labor, and the various securities in the economy all equal their corresponding real supplies, and in addition all anticipated variables are correctly forecast. In this case $m^d = m^s$, etc, and where no confusion can arise we shall simply drop the superscript. Thus, the quantity m, say, will denote the real money supply in a perfect foresight equilibrium. Henceforth, we shall focus our attention on these equilibrium quantities. Nothing will be done regarding the question of existence of equilibrium. In fact, equilibrium may not exist under all tax structures – especially when borrowing, lending, and new security creation is allowed.

4. Determination of optimality conditions for households

As indicated above, the household sector's optimization problem is to choose c, m, b_g, b_p, E to maximize its utility function (2.1a), subject to the budget constraint (2.1b), with T_h defined by (2.6a), and subject to the initial conditions (2.1c). Substituting for T_h enables us to define the Hamiltonian function

$$H \equiv e^{-\beta t} U(c, g, l, m)$$
$$- v\{c + (\dot{b}_g + \dot{b}_p) + \dot{m} + q\dot{E} - (1 - \tau_y)[wl + r_g b_g + r_b b_p + iqE]$$
$$+ [b_g + b_p + m]p + \tau_c(\dot{q} + qp)E\}. \tag{4.1}$$

Since we are dealing with a perfect foresight equilibrium we have set $p^* = p$, the actual rate of inflation. Also, for notational convenience, all superscripts have been dropped.

We shall assume that $[c(t), m^{\mathrm{d}}(t), b_g^{\mathrm{d}}(t), b_p^{\mathrm{d}}(t), E^{\mathrm{d}}(t)] \geq 0$ for all t. The assumption that financial stock variables are non-negative rules out short selling. The Hamiltonian H is observed to be linear in the financial decision variables b_p, b_g, E. In view of this, depending upon the precise tax structure assumed, some of these securities may or may not appear in strictly positive quantities in the equilibrium demands of the household sector. To allow for the possibility that some securities may be zero in equilibrium, it is necessary to solve the optimization problem by using Euler inequalities rather than in terms of the more familiar Euler equations. These are simply the analogues to the Kuhn–Tucker conditions in conventional non-linear programming. Performing the optimization yields the following conditions

$$e^{-\beta t} U_c \leq v, \tag{4.2}$$

$$c(e^{-\beta t} U_c - v) = 0, \tag{4.3}$$

$$e^{-\beta t} U_l \leq -vw(1 - \tau_y), \tag{4.4}$$

$$l[e^{-\beta t} U_l + vw(1 - \tau_y)] = 0, \tag{4.5}$$

$$e^{-\beta t} U_m - vp \leq -\dot{v}, \tag{4.6}$$

$$m(e^{-\beta t} U_m - vp + \dot{v}) = 0, \tag{4.7}$$

$$v[r_i(1 - \tau_y) - p] \leq -\dot{v}, \quad i = p, g, \tag{4.8}$$

$$b_p\{v[r_b(1 - \tau_y) + p] + \dot{v}\} = 0, \tag{4.9}$$

$$b_g\{v[r_g(1 - \tau_y) - p] + \dot{v}\} = 0, \tag{4.10}$$

$$v\left[i(1 - \tau_y) + \frac{\dot{q}}{q}(1 - \tau_c) - \tau_c p\right] \leq -\dot{v}, \tag{4.11}$$

$$E\left\{v\left[i(1 - \tau_y) + \frac{\dot{q}}{q}(1 - \tau_c) - \tau_c p\right] + \dot{v}\right\} = 0, \tag{4.12}$$

where $v > 0$ is the Lagrange multiplier associated with the household sector budget constraint.

Inequalities (4.2), (4.4), (4.6), (4.8), (4.11) are the Euler inequalities with respect to c, l, m, b_p and b_g (which are identical) and E respectively. If any of these inequalities are met *strictly*, then the corresponding decision variable is set equal to zero. Conversely, if any of the decision variables are strictly positive in equilibrium, the corresponding constraint is satisfied with equality. These dualistic type relationships are reflected in the equations (4.3), (4.5), (4.7), (4.9), (4.10), and (4.12).

Throughout the analysis, we shall assume in equilibrium $c > 0, l > 0$, $m > 0$, so that (4.2), (4.4), (4.7) all hold with equality. The strict positivity of these quantities seems reasonable on economic grounds and can be ensured by imposing appropriate Inada conditions on the utility function of consumers. Introducing the above equality conditions, the optimality conditions (4.1)–(4.12) can be simplified and interpreted more readily. The Lagrange multiplier is simply the discounted marginal utility of consumption, so that

$$\frac{-\dot{\nu}}{\nu} = \beta - \frac{\dot{U}_c}{U_c} \equiv \theta \quad \text{say,} \tag{4.13}$$

represents the rate of return on consumption. The optimality conditions for consumers thus may be written

$$U_l / U_c = -w(1 - \tau_y), \tag{4.14}$$

$$U_m / U_c = p + \theta, \tag{4.15}$$

$$r_i(1 - \tau_y) - p \le \theta; \quad i = p, g, \tag{4.16}$$

$$b_i[r_i(1 - \tau_y) - p - \theta] = 0; \quad i = p, g, \tag{4.17}$$

$$i(1 - \tau_y) + \frac{\dot{q}}{q}(1 - \tau_c) - \tau_c p \le \theta, \tag{4.18}$$

$$E\left[i(1 - \tau_y) + \frac{\dot{q}}{q}(1 - \tau_c) - \tau_c p - \theta\right] = 0. \tag{4.19}$$

These optimality conditions will now be used to explicitly derive the objective function for the firms.

5. Determination of optimality conditions for firms

To derive the objective function for firms, we begin by eliminating RE from the firm's financial constraints (2.2c), (2.2d) to yield

$$\pi + q\dot{E} + \dot{b}_p + pb_p = r_p b_p + D + T_f + \dot{k},$$

where, because we are dealing with PFE, the superscripts have been dropped. Adding $\dot{q}E$ to both sides of this equation and noting the definition of V given in (2.3) (and hence $\dot{V}$), we obtain

$$\dot{V} + \pi = (r_p - p)b_p + D + T_f + \dot{k} + \dot{q}E. \tag{5.1}$$

We now define the firm's real net cash flow $\gamma(t)$ to be

$$\gamma(t) \equiv (1 - \tau_p)\pi - \dot{k} = (1 - \tau_p)[f(k, l) - wl] - \dot{k}. \tag{5.2}$$

That is, $\gamma(t)$ equals the gross profit after tax, less the cost of the additional capital purchased. Now using the definition of T_f together with (5.2), and recalling the definitional relation $D/qE = i$, equation (5.1) becomes

$$\dot{V} + \gamma = [r_p(1 - \tau_p) - p]b_p + iqE + \dot{q}E. \tag{5.3}$$

We now define the firm's debt-to-equity ratio

$$\lambda = b_p/qE \tag{5.4}$$

enabling us to write (5.3) in the form

$$\dot{V} + \gamma = \left\{ [r_p(1 - \tau_p) - p]\frac{\lambda}{1+\lambda} + \left(i + \frac{\dot{q}}{q}\right)\frac{1}{1+\lambda} \right\} V. \tag{5.5}$$

Next, letting

$$\theta^*(\lambda, i, r_p, \dot{q}/q) \equiv [r_p(1 - \tau_p) - p]\frac{\lambda}{1+\lambda} + \left(i + \frac{\dot{q}}{q}\right)\frac{1}{1+\lambda}$$

(5.5) can be written more conveniently as

$$\dot{V}(t) + \gamma(t) = \theta^*(\lambda, i, r_p, \dot{q}/q)V(t), \tag{5.6}$$

where θ^* is in general a function of t, but is independent of V. Equation (5.6) can now be readily integrated to yield a general solution

$$V(s) = \exp\left[\int_0^s \theta^*(t)\,dt\right]\left\{ A - \int_0^s \gamma(t)\exp\left[-\int_0^t \theta^*(\tau)\,d\tau\right]dt \right\},$$

where A is an arbitrary constant. Suppose for the moment that $\theta^* > 0$ (an assumption which will be justified below and certainly holds in steady state) and assume that $\lim_{s\to\infty}\int_0^s \theta^*\,dt = \infty$. Then, in order for $V(s)$ to remain finite as $s \to \infty$, we require

$$A = \int_0^\infty \gamma(t) \exp\left[-\int_0^t \theta^*(\tau)\, d\tau \right] dt$$

and hence the value of the firm at any arbitrary time s is

$$V(s) = \exp \int_0^s \theta^*(t)\, dt \int_s^\infty \gamma(t) \exp\left[-\int_0^t \theta^*(\tau)\, d\tau \right] dt.$$

The *initial* value of the firm, which we assume the firm seeks to maximize, is therefore

$$V(0) = \int_0^\infty \exp\left[-\int_0^t \theta^*(\tau)\, d\tau \right]\{(1-\tau_p)[f(k,l)-wl]-\dot{k}\}\, dt, \qquad (5.7)$$

where we have substituted for $\gamma(t)$. Thus, we have derived the objective function (2.4) and shown that $V(0)$ is an appropriately discounted integral of the future net real cash flows.

The fact that $\gamma(t)$ depends only upon the real production variables (k, l), while the discount rate depends upon the financial variables $(\lambda, i, r_p, \dot{q}/q)$ means that the firm's optimization can be conducted sequentially. First it chooses its financial decisions to minimize θ^*; having determined the optimal θ^*, it then chooses the optimal production decisions.

The critical factor in the firm's objective function is θ^*. Using the definitions of λ and V it may be written as

$$\theta^* = [r_p(1-\tau_p)-p]\frac{b_p}{V} + \left(i+\frac{\dot{q}}{q}\right)\frac{qE}{V}. \qquad (5.8)$$

In other words, θ^* is simply a weighted average of the real costs of debt capital and equity capital to the firm, and hence will surely be positive. The real cost of debt capital is the after-corporate income tax nominal interest rate, less the rate of inflation; the real cost of equity capital to firms is the dividend payout ratio plus the real rate of capital gains on equity. Hence (5.8) is an expression which turns out to be familiar from basic corporate finance theory.

However, the expression for θ^* given in (5.8) is inappropriate from the viewpoint of determining the firm's financial decisions. The reason is that these decisions are themselves constrained by the preferences of households.

These preferences, embodied in the optimality conditions (4.17) and (4.19), impose constraints on the components of the financial rates of return. To obtain an appropriate expression for θ^*, we invoke the optimality conditions (4.17), (4.19) for consumers to eliminate r_p and $\dot{q}E$

$$r_p b_p = \frac{(\theta + p)b_p}{1 - \tau_y}, \tag{5.9}$$

$$\dot{q}E = \frac{(\theta + \tau_c p)qE}{1 - \tau_c} - \frac{(1 - \tau_y)iqE}{1 - \tau_c}. \tag{5.10}$$

Substituting these expressions into (5.8), we may express θ^* as

$$\theta^*(\lambda, i) = \theta + \frac{(\tau_y - \tau_p)(\theta + p)}{1 - \tau_y} \frac{\lambda}{1 + \lambda}$$
$$+ \frac{(\theta + p)\tau_c + i(\tau_y - \tau_c)}{1 - \tau_c} \frac{1}{1 + \lambda}. \tag{5.11}$$

It becomes evident from this expression how the cost of capital θ^* provides the means whereby consumers drive the firms. As written in (5.11), the relevant cost of capital is equal to the consumer's rate of return on consumption θ, adjusted by the various corporate and personal income tax rates, the adjustments themselves being weighted by the share of bonds and equities in the firm's financial structure. But (5.11) may also be written in the form

$$\theta^* = \left[\theta + \frac{(\tau_y - \tau_p)(\theta + p)}{1 - \tau_y} \right] \frac{\lambda}{1 + \lambda} + \left[\frac{\theta + \tau_c p + i(\tau_y - \tau_c)}{1 - \tau_c} \right] \frac{1}{1 + \lambda}. \tag{5.12}$$

The expression (5.11) or (5.12), being expressed in terms of the firm's financial decision variables, together with other variables parametric to the firm is now suitable for determining the firm's optimal financial policies. This is done by calculating the partial derivatives with respect to λ, i

$$\operatorname{sgn} \frac{\partial \theta^*}{\partial i} = \operatorname{sgn}\left(\frac{\tau_y - \tau_c}{1 - \tau_c}\right), \tag{5.13}$$

$$\operatorname{sgn} \frac{\partial \theta^*}{\partial \lambda} = \operatorname{sgn}\left[\frac{(\tau_y - \tau_p)(\theta + p)}{1 - \tau_y} - \frac{(\theta + p)\tau_c + i(\tau_y - \tau_c)}{1 - \tau_c}\right]. \tag{5.14}$$

The optimal dividend policy and the optimal capital structure will therefore involve corner solutions. Note that in the absence of taxes, θ^* is independent of i. Dividend policy is therefore irrelevant, confirming the well known Miller and Modigliani (1961) proposition for this case. Given that the capital gains in the model really reflect accruals, whereas tax rates in reality apply to realized capital gains, it seems reasonable to assume $\tau_c < \tau_y$; see Auerbach (1979). Thus if the firm is to minimize its cost of capital, it should minimize the dividend payout ratio i. In the absence of any constraints this would involve the repurchase of shares, as long as D were positive. In fact such behavior is discouraged, at least in the U.S. by section 302 of the Internal Revenue Code. To model the legal constraints included in this code fully would be rather complicated and we do not attempt to do so here. Rather, we shall simply argue that the firm minimizes its dividend payments by setting $i = \bar{i}$, where $\bar{i}$ is the legal minimum payout rate, which we take to be exogenous. Thus setting $i = \bar{i}$, the optimal financial mix (λ) is determined as follows

$$\frac{(\tau_y - \tau_p)(\theta + p)}{1 - \tau_y} < \frac{(\theta + p)\tau_c + \bar{i}(\tau_y - \tau_c)}{1 - \tau_c} \quad \text{set } \lambda = \infty \tag{5.15}$$

that is all bond financing ($E = 0$)

$$\frac{(\tau_y - \tau_p)(\theta + p)}{1 - \tau_y} > \frac{(\theta + p)\tau_c + \bar{i}(\tau_y - \tau_c)}{1 - \tau_c} \quad \text{set } \lambda = 0 \tag{5.16}$$

that is all equity financing ($b_p = 0$). Defining the average tax rate on income from stock τ_s, to be a weighted average of the tax rates on income from dividends and income from capital gains,

$$\tau_s = \frac{\bar{i}\tau_y + (\dot{q}/q + p)\tau_c}{(\bar{i} + \dot{q}/q + p)}$$

and using the optimality condition (4.19), the criterion for determining the optimal financial mix can be rewritten as follows

$$(1 - \tau_y) > (1 - \tau_p)(1 - \tau_s) \quad \text{set } \lambda = \infty, \tag{5.17}$$

$$(1 - \tau_y) < (1 - \tau_p)(1 - \tau_s) \quad \text{set } \lambda = 0. \tag{5.18}$$

Thus, written in this way, we see that our criterion is identical to that of Miller (1977). This is true for the case of a single agent. See Miller (1977) and also Miller and Scholes (1978) for the multi-agent case. In effect, (5.17) asserts that if the net after tax income on bonds exceeds the net after tax income from equity, where the latter are taxed twice, first as corporate profits, secondly as personal income to stockholders, no investor will wish to hold equities and the firm must engage in all bond financing. The opposite applies if the inequality is reversed as in (5.18). A simple sufficient condition for (5.17) to hold, not uncharacteristic of some real world tax structures, is that the corporate profit tax rate τ_p exceed the personal income tax rate τ_y. No such simple condition for (5.18) to hold exists. Loosely speaking it requires τ_y to exceed τ_p by an amount which suffices to take account of the double taxation of income from stock.

If $(1 - \tau_y) = (1 - \tau_p)(1 - \tau_s)$, then the optimal debt to equity ratio is indeterminate. One special case of this arises when all tax rates are zero, when the conditions (5.15)-(5.16) simply reduce to a statement of the familiar Modigliani and Miller (1958) no-tax case. Our results are also consistent with Miller's (1977) extension of this proposition, again in the case of a single agent. He shows that the value of any firm in equilibrium will be independent of the amount of debt in its capital structure, provided that the marginal rate of tax payable by stockholders on income from shares is sufficiently far below the marginal rate of tax on personal income. This result follows immediately from the equality $(1 - \tau_y) = (1 - \tau_p)(1 - \tau_s)$. Thus while our conclusions for the firm's financial policy turn out to be familiar, we feel that the derivation we have given for the cost of capital, in terms of the underlying optimality conditions for consumers, has merit in making explicit the role played by consumers in determining the optimality conditions for value maximizing firms.

Thus using (5.17) and (5.18), the firm's minimum cost of capital may be expressed as

$$\theta^*_{min} = \theta + min\left[\frac{(\tau_y - \tau_p)(\theta + p)}{1 - \tau_y}, \frac{(\theta + p)\tau_c + \bar{i}(\tau_y - \tau_c)}{1 - \tau_c}\right] \tag{5.19}$$

with all bond financing this reduces to

$$\theta^*_{min} = \frac{\theta(1 - \tau_p) + (\tau_y - \tau_p)p}{1 - \tau_y} = r_p(1 - \tau_p) - p \tag{5.20}$$

while with all equity financing it becomes

$$\theta^*_{min} = \frac{\theta + \tau_c p + \bar{i}(\tau_y - \tau_c)}{1 - \tau_c} = \bar{i} + \dot{q}/q. \tag{5.21}$$

In deriving the second equalities in these two equations, use has been made of (5.9) and (5.10). These expressions are generally similar to those given by Auerbach (1979), although there is one difference. Instead of (5.21), he finds that with all equity financing, the cost of capital (expressed in our notation and invoking his assumption of zero inflation) is

$$\theta^*_{min} = \frac{\theta}{1 - \tau_c}. \tag{5.22}$$

This is seen to be independent of the payout rate i and the rate at which dividends are taxed, and furthermore is less than (5.21). The reason for the difference in this respect again stems from the difference in assumptions made with respect to dividend policy. The fact that in the Auerbach analysis, all equity comes from retentions means that it comes from before tax funds, thereby making it cheaper.

We are finally in a position to state and solve the real part of the firm's optimization problem. Having chosen i, λ, to minimize the cost of capital and determined θ^*_{min}, it must next choose k, l, to maximize

$$\int_0^\infty \exp\left(-\int_0^t \theta^*_{min} \, d\tau\right)\{(1 - \tau_p)[f(k, l) - wl] - \dot{k}\} \, dt \qquad (5.23)$$

subject to the initial condition $k(0) = k_0$. The optimality conditions to this problem are simply

$$(1 - \tau_p)f_k(k, l) = \theta^*_{min}, \qquad (5.24)$$

$$f_l(k, l) = w. \qquad (5.25)$$

That is, the after tax marginal physical product of capital should be equated to the minimized cost of capital while the marginal physical product of labor should be equated to the real wage.

Moreover, substituting (5.24) and (5.25) back into (5.7), we are able to use the transversality condition at infinity for the above optimization problem to establish the familiar balance sheet constraint

$$V = b_p + qE = k. \qquad (5.26)$$

This condition requires that the capitalized value of the state variables be zero in the limit, which in effect rules out the possibility of the values of the claims becoming divorced from the underlying sources of earnings. The proof of the assertion just made is as follows. For notational ease denote θ^*_{min} by θ^*. From (5.7) we may write

$$V(t) = \lim_{T \to \infty} \exp\left[\int_0^t \theta^*(s) \, ds\right] \int_t^T \exp\left[-\int_0^s \theta^*(\tau) \, d\tau\right]$$

$$\times [(1 - \tau_p)[f - wl] - \dot{k}] \, ds.$$

Using the linear homogeneity of the production function and the optimality conditions (5.24), (5.25), this expression may be simplified to yield

$$V(t) = \lim_{T \to \infty} \exp\left[\int_0^t \theta^*(s) \, ds\right] \int_t^T \exp\left[-\int_0^s \theta^*(\tau) \, d\tau\right][\theta^* k - \dot{k}] \, ds.$$

Now integrating by parts and cancelling, we obtain

$$V(t) = k(t) - \exp\left[\int_0^t \theta^*(s)\,ds\right] \lim_{T\to\infty} \exp\left[-\int_0^T \theta^*(\tau)\,d\tau\right] k(T).$$

But the limit of the second term is zero, by the necessity of the transversality condition at infinity for infinite horizon concave programming problems of this type; see Weitzman (1973) for the discrete time case and Benveniste and Scheinkman (1982) for the continuous time version. Hence we deduce $V(t) = k(t)$. Thus we may conclude by noting that if (5.17) holds $b_p = k$; if (5.18) applies $qE = k$; while in the knife edge case where (5.17)-(5.18) holds with equality, b_p and qE are indeterminate. This completes the formal optimization of the firm.

6. Equilibrium structure and dynamics of system

The optimality conditions for the households and firms, together with the government budget constraint can now be combined to describe the perfect foresight equilibrium in the economy and to determine its dynamic evolution.

Combining the optimality conditions in (4.14)-(4.19), (5.24) and (5.25) we may write

$$U_c(c, g, l, m) = \alpha, \tag{6.1}$$

$$\frac{U_l(c, g, l, m)}{U_c(c, g, l, m)} = -f_l(k, l)(1 - \tau_y), \tag{6.2}$$

$$\frac{U_m(c, g, l, m)}{U_c(c, g, l, m)} = \theta + p, \tag{6.3}$$

$$(1 - \tau_p)f_k(k, l) = \theta^*_{\min}, \tag{6.4}$$

$$\theta^*_{\min} = \theta + \min\left[\frac{(\tau_y - \tau_p)(\theta + p)}{1 - \tau_y}, \frac{(\theta + p)\tau_c + \bar{i}(\tau_y - \tau_c)}{1 - \tau_c}\right], \tag{6.5}$$

$$\dot{\alpha} = \alpha(\beta - \theta), \tag{6.6}$$

$$\dot{k} = f(k, l) - g - c, \tag{6.7}$$

$$\dot{m} + \dot{b}_g = g + \theta b_g - \tau_y f - mp + [\theta - (1 - \tau_y)f_k]k. \tag{6.8}$$

Equation (6.1) simply defines a short hand notation for the marginal utility of consumption. Equation (6.2) equates the marginal rate of substitution between consumption and leisure to the after-tax real wage, while (6.3) requires that the marginal utility derived from holding a dollar in cash balances must equal the marginal utility that would be derived from spending the dollar on consumption. Equations (6.4) and (6.5) restate the marginal productivity condition for capital, and the minimum cost of capital respectively.

These five equations may be used to solve for the short-run solutions for the five variables l, c, p, θ, $\theta^*_{\min}$, in terms of the dynamically evolving variables α, k, m, b_g. The dynamics governing these latter variables are expressed in equations (6.6)-(6.8). The first of these is a restatement of (4.13), in terms of the new notation, while (6.7) describes the rate of capital accumulation required to maintain product market equilibrium. The final equation (6.8) is the government budget constraint. The derivation of this form of the equation involves several steps. Essentially it is obtained by first substituting the tax functions (2.6a), (2.6b) into (2.5); then using the optimality conditions for consumers and the optimality conditions for firms, together with the linear homogeneity of the production function and the balance sheet constraint (5.26), to simplify the resulting expression for the real deficit, one obtains (6.8).

As part of the specification of the dynamics of the system, something must be said about government financial policy. There are various policies which are traditionally chosen in dynamic macro models of this kind. They included pegging the real money supply; pegging the real stock of government bonds; pegging the rate of nominal monetary growth, etc. Once such a policy is chosen, the dynamics is fully determined.

To complete the description of the system we must consider the initial conditions, $k(0)$, $E(0)$, $m(0)$, $b_p(0)$, $b_g(0)$. The first two of these are exogenously determined, being given by $k(0) = k_0$, $E(0) = E_0$. In the case of money and bonds, the initial nominal stocks are assumed to be given, with the initial real stocks being endogenously determined by an initial jump in the price level. The size of this initial jump, and therefore the initial values $m(0)$, $b_p(0)$, $b_g(0)$ are obtained from the transversality conditions at infinity for households and firms. Unfortunately, given the dimensionality of the system, a full dynamic analysis of the system turns out to be rather complex and not very enlightening. Rather than pursue it further with the model specified at the present level of generality, we shall proceed directly to a discussion of the steady state. Then in section 9 below, we shall analyze a simplified version of the dynamics, which arises when labor is supplied exogenously. This simplification suffices to give a good indication of the nature of the transitional dynamics for the general case.

But before concluding the present discussion, we should also explain how the equilibrium stocks of bonds and equities and their respective rates of return are determined. In the case where firms find it optimal to engage in all bond financing, the balance sheet constraint (5.26) implies $b_p = k$. Note that with the nominal stocks of bonds given, a jump may occur at time zero, through the price level, so that $k_0 = b_p(0) = B_{p_0}/P(0)$. The nominal rate of interest can then be determined by inserting the known values into the consumers' optimality condition (4.16), which holds as an equality. Obviously this implies that the rates of interest on private and public bonds must be equal, that is, $r_p = r_g$. Similarly, with all equity financing, the price of equities can be obtained by substituting known values into (4.18) and integrating. Again an initial jump may be required in q, in order to satisfy the balance sheet constraint (5.26), which is now $qE = k$. With both the value of equities and their price determined, the quantity of shares outstanding can be immediately inferred. In this case the rate of interest on government bonds will again be given by (4.16), with their after tax real rate of return now equaling that on equities, but now exceeding that on private bonds.

7. Steady state

The steady state of the system is attained when

$$\dot{\alpha} = \dot{k} = \dot{m} = \dot{b}_g = 0. \tag{7.1}$$

The fact that steady state requires $\dot{k} = \dot{m} = \dot{\alpha} = 0$ is readily apparent. The requirement that $\dot{b}_g = 0$ is less immediate, since b_g is determined residually by (6.8). However, the need for bond accumulation to cease in steady state can be established by integrating the government budget constraint and imposing the transversality condition at infinity for consumers, $\lim_{t \to \infty} U_c(t) b_g(t) \exp(-\beta t) = 0$. The argument may be sketched as follows.

First integrate (4.13) to yield

$$U_c(t) = U_c(0) \exp\left[\int_0^t \theta(\tau)\,d\tau\right] e^{\beta t}.$$

Next, integrate the government budget constraint (6.8), to obtain

$$b_g(t) = \exp\left[\int_0^t \theta(s)\,ds\right]\left\{B + \int_0^t x(s)\exp\left[-\int_0^s \theta(\tau)\,d\tau\right]ds\right\},$$

where $x(s) \equiv g - \tau_y f - mp + [\theta - (1 - \tau_y)f_k]k - \dot{m}$ and is independent of b_g, while B is an arbitrary constant. Inserting these solutions for $U_c(t), b_g(t)$ into the transversality condition and taking the limit we require (with $U_c(0)$ finite)

$$B = -\int_0^\infty x(s) \exp\left[-\int_0^s \theta(\tau)\, d\tau\right] ds$$

so that the implied time path for real government bonds is

$$b_g(t) = -\exp\left[\int_0^t \theta(s)\, ds\right] \int_t^\infty x(s) \exp\left[-\int_0^s \theta(\tau)\, d\tau\right] ds$$

which converges to (7.5) in steady state.

The implied endogenous initial value $b_g(0)$ is not necessarily equal to $B_{go}/P(0)$, even after allowing for the initial jump in the price level. Thus, in order to ensure an equilibrium we require the monetary authorities to undertake an initial open market exchange of money for bonds in order to ensure that the solution for $b_g(t)$ is consistent with the consumers' optimality conditions.

From (7.1) obtain that $\theta = \beta$, and $f(k, l) = c + g$. Accordingly, the long-run equilibrium of the system can be reduced to the following four equations

$$\frac{U_l[f(k, l) - g, g, l, m]}{U_c[f(k, l) - g, g, l, m]} = -f_l(k, l)(1 - \tau_y), \tag{7.2}$$

$$\frac{U_m[f(k, l) - g, g, l, m]}{U_c[f(k, l) - g, g, l, m]} = \beta + p, \tag{7.3}$$

$$(1 - \tau_p)f_k(k, l)$$
$$= \beta + \min\left[\frac{(\tau_y - \tau_p)(\beta + p)}{1 - \tau_y}, \frac{(\beta + p)\tau_c + \bar{i}(\tau_y - \tau_c)}{1 - \tau_c}\right], \tag{7.4}$$

$$g + \beta b_g - \tau_y f(k, l) - mp + [\beta - (1 - \tau_y)f_k]k = 0. \tag{7.5}$$

The first three equations involve the four variables k, l, m, and p. Thus, if for given exogenous values of g and the tax rates, one specifies an independent government financial policy in terms of the real stock of money or the inflation, then these three equations, together with the policy specification, will determine the four variables k, l, m, p. Inserting these stationary values into the steady-state government budget constraint determines the required real stock of government bonds to maintain the budget in balance. On the other hand, if the policy is specified in terms of the real stock of government bonds, then for given g and rates, the four equations determine the equilibrium values of k, l, m, p.

It is of interest to note that, in general, the system summarized by (7.2)–(7.5) is interdependent; real production decisions and financial decisions are jointly determined. This is in part a consequence of the fact that only the nominal component of the real interest rate is taxed and the tax deductibility provisions assumed. It is also in part a consequence of the interdependence between real money balances m on the one hand, and capital and labor on the other, in the consumers' utility function. Under certain conditions, however, the system dichotomizes into two recursive subsystems. The first determines the real decisions k and l while the second determines the financial variables m and p, conditional on these initially chosen real variables. Finally, the equilibrium rates of return on the financial securities can be obtained by substituting the solutions from (7.2)–(7.5) into the appropriate arbitrage condition for consumers (4.17) and (4.19).

8. Characterizations of alternative steady states

In order to discuss the steady state of the system in further detail, it is necessary to introduce some government financial policy. We shall restrict most of our attention to the case in which the monetary authorities maintain a constant rate of the nominal money supply, namely

$$\dot{M}/M = \mu. \tag{8.1}$$

The real money supply $m = M/P$ therefore evolves in accordance with

$$\dot{m} = m(\mu - p)$$

so that in steady state we have

$$p = \mu.$$

It is evident from previous sections that the steady state will be dependent on the capital structure employed by the firms. This is determined by the inequality conditions (5.15)–(5.16) and the corresponding minimized cost of capital. Thus, for the government monetary policy specified by (8.1), the following steady states may be characterized.

8.1. All bond financing by firms

In this case inequality (5.15) holds and the steady state reduces to the following

$$\frac{U_l[f(k,l)-g,g,l,m]}{U_c[f(k,l)-g,g,l,m]} = -f_l(k,l)(1-\tau_y), \tag{8.2}$$

$$\frac{U_m[f(k,l)-g,g,l,m]}{U_c[f(k,l)-g,g,l,m]} = \beta + \mu, \tag{8.3}$$

$$(1-\tau_p)f_k(k,l) = \frac{\beta(1-\tau_p)+(\tau_y-\tau_p)\mu}{1-\tau_y}, \tag{8.4}$$

$$g + b_g - \tau_y f(k,l) - \mu m + [\beta - (1-\tau_y)f_k]k = 0. \tag{8.5}$$

Thus the steady state in the case where firms engage in all bond financing can be obtained in the following recursive manner. First, given the parameters β, μ, τ_p, τ_y, (8.4) yields the marginal physical product of capital. With the linear homogeneity of the production function, this establishes the capital–labor ratio, which in turn determines the real wage $f_l(k,l)$. Having determined k/l, the two marginal rate of substitution conditions (8.2), (8.3), together determine the employment of labor l, and the real stock of money balances m. With k/l and now l fixed, the real stock of capital k is known, while the level of output y immediately follows from the production function. The government budget then determines the real stock of government bonds necessary to balance the budget.

Being a perfect foresight equilibrium, equations (8.2)–(8.5) have important implications for the debate concerning the effectiveness of fully anticipated government policies under *rational expectations*. It is seen from these equations that the real productive decisions, k, l, are in general dependent upon the rate of growth of the nominal money supply, as well as upon both the corporate and personal income tax rates. Also, to the extent that public and private goods are viewed as imperfect substitutes by households, so that c and g enter as separate arguments in the utility function, an expansion in real government expenditure will have real effects on output and employment. This confirms the argument advanced by Fair (1978) that in a fully rational expectations model generated from underlying optimizing behavior, anticipated government policies are indeed able to have real effects. On the other hand, the range of effective government policies may be restricted. For example, if public and private goods are perfect substitutes, so that c

and g enter additively in U, g disappears from the expressions U_c, etc. It can then be easily seen that an increase in government expenditure will cease to have any effect on the real part of the system. It will simply displace an equal volume of private activity, resulting in complete *crowding out*. This result is in agreement with the analogous property obtained by Buiter (1977), although his analysis was not conducted within an optimizing framework. Also, real activity will be neutral with respect to the monetary growth rate μ if: (i) the corporate and personal income tax rates are equal, and (ii) the utility function is separable in real money balances, so that the marginal rate of substitution U_l / U_c is independent of m. This form of neutrality in a full employment model such as this is often referred to as super-neutrality. In this case the only government policy parameter able to influence real activity is the personal income tax rate, which does so by affecting the consumption–leisure choice.

To preserve simplicity, we shall restrict our analysis of the comparative static properties of (8.2)–(8.5) to the effects of tax rates and the monetary growth rate on the capital–labor ratio. These effects have been discussed extensively in the literature over the years and are among the more interesting. They operate through the cost of capital, which therefore provides the critical channel through which alternative tax structures impinge on the system. Also, when the results are compared to those we shall derive in section 8.2 below, they serve to highlight very clearly how comparative static effects depend upon the equilibrium financial structure employed by firms and emphasize again the need to derive equilibria from underlying optimizing procedures.

From equation (8.4) we may derive

$$\operatorname{sgn} \frac{\partial(k/l)}{\partial \mu} = \operatorname{sgn}(\tau_p - \tau_y), \tag{8.6}$$

$$\partial(k/l)/\partial \tau_y < 0, \tag{8.7}$$

$$\partial(k/l)/\partial \tau_p > 0. \tag{8.8}$$

To understand these results it is useful to recall the expression for the nominal rate of interest (5.9), which in steady state is $r_p = (\beta + \mu)/(1 - \tau_y)$. An increase in the rate of nominal monetary growth raises the nominal before tax interest rate by $1/(1 - \tau_y)$. The effect on the after-tax real rate of interest to firms, which with all bond financing is their effective cost of capital, is thus equal to $[(1 - \tau_p)/(1 - \tau_y) - 1]$, so that the effect on the capital–labor ratio depends upon $(\tau_p - \tau_y)$. In order for all bond financing to be optimal, (5.15) imposes a lower bound on this quantity. Thus for example, if the rate of taxation on capital gains and the required minimum rate of dividend payments are both zero, then $\tau_p > \tau_y$ and k/l will rise. But the reverse cannot be ruled out. An increase in the personal income tax rate raises the nominal interest rate s and hence the after-tax interest rate to firms, thereby inducing them to lower their capital–labor ratio. On the other hand, an increase in the corporate tax rate τ_p has no effect on the nominal interest rate. It therefore leads to a reduction in the after-tax real interest rate for firms, inducing them to increase their capital–labor ratio. Given the effects summarized in (8.6)–(8.8), the implications for the other endogenous variables can be easily obtained by taking appropriate differentials of (8.2)–(8.5).

8.2. All equity financing by firms

With all equity financing, (5.16) now applies and the steady state becomes

$$\frac{U_l[f(k, l) - g, g, l, m]}{U_c[f(k, l) - g, g, l, m]} = -f_l(k, l)(1 - \tau_y), \tag{8.9}$$

$$\frac{U_m[f(k, l) - g, g, l, m]}{U_c[f(k, l) - g, g, l, m]} = \beta + \mu, \tag{8.10}$$

$$(1 - \tau_p)f_k(k, l) = \frac{\beta + \tau_c\mu + \bar{i}(\tau_y - \tau_c)}{1 - \tau_c}, \tag{8.11}$$

$$g + \beta b_g - \tau_y f(k, l) - \mu m + [\beta - (1 - \tau_y)f_k]k = 0. \tag{8.12}$$

The steady state is obtained in much the same way as with bond financing described in section 8.1, though the relevant cost of capital determining the capital–labor ratio is now given by (8.11). With k/l so given, the marginal rate of substitution conditions (8.9), (8.10) determine l, m and hence k, with the government budget constraint determining b_g. The exogenous government policy parameters μ, τ_y, τ_p, τ_c, all have real effects, again confirming the proposition of Fair. In this case neutrality with respect to the monetary rate will pertain if and only if $\tau_c = 0$ and the utility function is separable in m. Finally, the previous comments made with respect to the crowding out effects of increases in government expenditure continue to hold.

The effects of changes in the rate of monetary growth and the various tax rates on the capital–labor ratio are obtained from (8.11) and have the following general characteristics

$$\partial(k/l)/\partial\mu < 0, \tag{8.13}$$

$$\partial(k/l)/\partial\tau_y < 0, \tag{8.14}$$

$$\partial(k/l)/\partial\tau_p < 0, \tag{8.15}$$

$$\mathrm{sgn}\left[\frac{\partial(k/l)}{\partial\tau_c}\right] = \mathrm{sgn}[\,\bar{i}(1-\tau_y)-(\mu+\beta)]. \tag{8.16}$$

It will be observed that the effects of a change in τ_p and also probably that of an increase in μ are opposite to those obtained under bond financing. The reason for these results can be understood by considering the expressions for the equilibrium rate of capital gains, which from (5.10) is

$$\frac{\dot{q}}{q} = \frac{\beta + \tau_c\mu - \bar{i}(1-\tau_y)}{1-\tau_c}.$$

Thus an increase in either the rate of monetary growth or the rate of personal income tax τ_y will raise the equilibrium rate of capital gain on equities and hence the equilibrium rate of equity costs $(\bar{i}+\dot{q}/q)$, inducing firms to reduce their capital–labor ratio. On the other hand, an increase in the corporate profit tax rate τ_p leaves equity costs unchanged. The after-tax marginal physical product of capital must remain fixed, so that as τ_p increases, k/l must fall. Finally, the effect of an increase in the capital gains tax on the rate of capital gains is ambiguous, depending upon the expression in (8.16).

The effects of an increase in the rate of inflation (steady-state monetary growth) on the real after-tax yield on bonds and equities has recently been studied by Feldstein (1976) and Feldstein et al. (1978). In the latter, more general analysis, the authors (FGS) show that if one abstracts from induced changes in the debt–equity ratio and assumes that the rate of depreciation is zero (the assumption made here), then the effect of an increase in the inflation rate upon the steady state net yield on bonds equals $(\tau_p - \tau_y)/(1 - \tau_p)$ while that on equities is $-\tau_c$. In our analysis, on the other hand, we find that under both modes of corporate financing, these two rates of return equal β in steady state and therefore are independent of the inflation rate. The difference in the result stems from the fact that the FGS result abstracts from changes in the capital–labor ratio and therefore is associated with a much shorter time horizon. In fact, it corresponds to our short-run value of θ. With the capital–labor ratio and therefore $\theta^*_{\min}$ fixed in the short run, it follows from (6.5) that under bond financing $d\theta/dp = (\tau_p - \tau_y)/(1 - \tau_p)$, while with equity financing $d\theta/dp = -\tau_c$, exactly as in the FGS analysis.

8.3. Both bonds and equities in firms' financial structure

The third possible steady state equilibrium is one in which both bonds and equities appear in the firms' capital structure. This will arise only in the *knife edge* case where (5.15)–(5.16) is satisfied with equality, in which case λ will be indeterminate.

9. Dynamics in a simplified case

Finally, we turn to a brief analysis of the dynamics of the system where labor is assumed to remain fixed at an exogenously set level $\bar{l}$ say. To keep things simple we shall assume that $\tau_y = \tau_p (= \tau)$, in which case firms find it optimal to engage in all bond financing. The monetary authorities maintain a fixed rate of growth of the nominal money supply, as specified by (8.1). Also, in order to simplify the dynamics as much as possible, we assume that the government maintains the real stock of government bonds fixed, financing its deficit with an endogenous lump sum tax.

With labor supplied exogenously, the marginal rate of substitution condition determining the labor supply is no longer applicable. Thus omitting $\bar{l}$ from the relevant functions, the dynamics of the system (6.1)–(6.8), corresponding to the present set of assumptions becomes

$$U_c(c, g, m) = \alpha, \tag{9.1}$$

$$\frac{U_m(c, g, m)}{U_c(c, g, m)} = \theta + p, \tag{9.2}$$

$$(1 - \tau_p)f_k(k) = \theta, \tag{9.3}$$

$$\dot{\alpha} = \alpha(\beta - \theta), \tag{9.4}$$

$$\dot{k} = f(k) - c - g, \tag{9.5}$$

$$\dot{m} = (\mu - p)m, \tag{9.6}$$

$$g + \theta \bar{b}_g = \tau_y f + \mu m + \mu. \tag{9.7}$$

The first three equations determine c, θ, p, in terms of α, k, m the dynamics of which are then determined by equations (9.4)–(9.6). Given the tax rates, monetary growth rate, and g, the final equation determines the endogenous lump sum tax μ required to meet the government deficit. Since this equation is a residual, it can henceforth be ignored.

The solutions for c, p may be written in the form

$$c = c^0(\alpha, m, g), \tag{9.8}$$

$$p = \frac{1}{\alpha} U_m[c^0(\alpha, m, g), g, m] - (1 - \tau_p) f_k(k), \tag{9.9}$$

while θ is given explicitly by (9.3). From (9.8) we have $c^0_\alpha = 1/U_{cc} < 0$. In addition, introducing the mild restriction that consumption and money balances are complementary in utility, that is, $U_{cm} > 0$, we also have $c^0_m = -U_{cm}/U_{cc} > 0$. Now substituting (9.8), (9.9), (9.3) into (9.4)-(9.7), the dynamics of the system becomes

$$\dot{\alpha} = \alpha(\beta - (1 - \tau_p) f_k(k)), \tag{9.10}$$

$$\dot{k} = f(k) - c^0(\alpha, m, g) - g, \tag{9.11}$$

$$\dot{m} = m[\mu + (1 - \tau_p) f_k(k) - \frac{1}{\alpha} U_m[c^0(\alpha, m, g), g, m]]. \tag{9.12}$$

Linearizing the system about its steady state equilibrium, we find that its local stability depends upon the eigenvalues of the matrix

$$\begin{bmatrix} 0 & -\alpha(1 - \tau_p) f_{kk} & 0 \\ -c^0_\alpha & f_k & -c^0_m \\ -m I_\alpha & m(1 - \tau_p) f_{kk} & -m I_m \end{bmatrix}, \tag{9.13}$$

where all derivatives are evaluated at steady state and

$$I_\alpha = (U_{mc} U_c - U_m U_{cc})/U^2_c U_{cc} < 0,$$

$$I_m = (U_{mm} U_{cc} - U^2_{mc})/U_{cc} < 0.$$

Denoting the roots of (9.13) by λ_i, and using properties of cubic equations, the sign restrictions we have imposed suffice to ensure that

$$\lambda_1 + \lambda_2 + \lambda_3 > 0,$$

$$\lambda_1 \lambda_2 \lambda_3 < 0.$$

Thus we may deduce that there are two unstable roots, possibly complex, and just one stable root. By invoking the transversality conditions, we may argue that in response to any disturbance, the system will jump so as to be always on the stable locus associated with the stable eigenvalue. Thus for example, the capital stock will evolve in accordance with the stable first order adjustment process

$$\dot{k} = \Delta_1(k - \bar{k}),$$ (9.14)

where $\bar{k}$ denotes the steady state value and Δ_1 is a function of the single stable root $\lambda_1 < 0$; likewise for the other variables in the system. It is apparent that λ_1 will be a function of the various government policy parameters. In particular, the rate of monetary growth μ will affect the speed of adjustment of the capital stock, as well as its steady state level. To calculate the response of the adjustment speed λ_1 explicitly involves solving the cubic characteristic equation to (9.13) and is rather tedious.

The same kind of analysis can be carried out for the case of equity financing. One can also use the above method to consider the case where labor supply is endogenous. In all cases the strategy is the same, namely to invoke the transversality conditions to eliminate unstable adjustment paths. One would expect that this will lead to stable first order adjustment paths similar to (9.14), although the extent to which this is in fact the case remains an open question.

10. Miscellaneous applications and exercises

(1) The incidence of taxes has been a central issue in public finance for a long time. The standard framework for conducting incidence analysis has been the two-sector general equilibrium model of Harberger (1962) which, despite its importance, suffers from several limitations pointed out by McLure (1975). Recently, several authors have considered the question of tax incidence using a dynamic growth model. See, for example Homma (1981) and his references. One of the general conclusions to emerge from these authors is that the incidence of a particular tax in the long run may be very different from what it is in the short run. However, the existing dynamic models suffer from at least three limitations: (i) they are variants of the traditional neoclassical one-sector growth model, (ii) they abstract from issues related to the corporate sector and corporate finance, and (iii) the savings behavior is specified arbitrarily, and the firm's production decisions are derived from static optimization. Turnovsky (1982) uses the intertemporal optimizing framework presented in this chapter to show that the effects of tax changes: (i) vary between the short run and the long run, (ii) depend critically upon the financial structure adopted by firms, and (iii)

may also depend upon government financial policy. See Turnovsky (1982) for details and also Becker (1985) and Pohjola (1985).

(2) The question of optimal aggregate monetary and fiscal policy making is a very broad one and many strands of literature can be identified. Perhaps most attention, at least recently, has been devoted to investigating the optimal rate of monetary growth. This question has been considered from a number of perspectives. First, it has been analyzed from the viewpoint of government revenue maximization, with the general conclusion that the optimal monetary growth rate is critically dependent upon the interest elasticity of the demand for money; see M. Friedman (1971). Secondly, other authors have focused on the consumption maximizing rate of monetary growth and have shown that this involves choosing the rate so that the economy is driven to its golden rule capital–labor ratio; see Turnovsky (1978). Thirdly, extensive literature has determined the optimal rate of monetary growth in terms of a more general utility maximizing framework; see, for example, Friedman (1969), and Brock (1974, 1975). The most important proposition to emerge from this last group of studies is the Friedman full liquidity rule, which concludes that the optimal rate of monetary growth is to contract the money supply at a rate equal to the rate of consumer time preference.

Secondly, there is a body of literature focusing on the optimal differential tax rates on different commodities. While the traditional public finance approach examines the trade-offs between such taxes within a general equilibrium microeconomic context, recent contributions by Phelps (1972) analyze the problem within a macroeconomic context. Specifically, once one realizes that the steady-state rate of inflation associated with the steady-state rate of monetary growth acts as a tax on real money balances, the optimal rate of monetary growth is equivalent to determining the optimal rate of inflation tax. And while inflation is recognized as being one way a government may finance its expenditure, other sources of revenue, most notably the conventional income tax, are also available. Thus, it is natural to analyze the question of optimal monetary growth in conjunction with the optimal choice of income tax, investigating the possible trade-offs between these two forms of taxation. To undertake this, is the essence of Phelp's important contributions.

There is also a third extensive literature dealing with optimal monetary and fiscal policy from the standpoint of a stabilization objective. While most of this literature is concerned with determining the optimal adjustment of the system about a given long-run equilibrium, this aspect is generally regarded as a weakness of these models. It is often argued that the long-run targets should be chosen optimally, in conjunction with the corresponding short-run adjustment paths.

Turnovsky and Brock (1980) develop a framework which is capable of analyzing the kinds of issues we have noted above in an integrated manner. To some extent this is undertaken by Phelps, although his analysis is purely static. Their aim is to analyze these questions within a dynamic framework, where the objective is the maximization of some intertemporal utility function. Thus their paper can be viewed as an attempt to present an integrated, albeit simplified, theory of optimal policy decisions within a conventional macroeconomic context.

The Turnovsky and Brock (1980) model relies on the critical concept of *perfect foresight equilibrium*, in which all plans and expectations are realized and all markets are cleared. As Calvo (1978a, 1978b) has shown, optimal policies in an economy characterized by perfect foresight may be *time inconsistent*. That is, policies which are optimal from the viewpoint of time t say, are no longer optimal at some other point $t+h$ say, even though ostensibly nothing has changed. This consideration turns out to be central to the Turnovsky and Brock (1980) analysis who discuss at some length the problem of time inconsistency of alternative policies.

The question of the time inconsistency of optimal policies as discussed by Calvo can be viewed as an example of the time inconsistency of optimal policies arising out of the more general dynamic framework considered by Kydland and Prescott (1977). As these authors have shown in the framework of a rational expectations equilibrium, the optimal policy will be time inconsistent if the agents' current decisions depend upon their expectations of future events, which are in turn affected by the selected policy. On the other hand, an appropriate stationary policy may be time consistent, though in general it will be nonoptimal. Thus a time consistent optimal policy will in general hold only if the underlying dynamics is somehow eliminated in the course of the optimization. In the cases discussed by Calvo, this is achieved by having the system jump instantaneously to steady state, so that the government and private sector are continuously solving the same intertemporal optimization. Accordingly, the issue of the time consistency or otherwise of optimal policies reduces to the question of whether or not such policies may drive the system instantaneously to a consistent steady-state equilibrium.

The general proposition to emerge from the Turnovsky and Brock (1980) analysis is that time consistency will prevail with respect to the optimization of any single policy instrument which does not appear explicitly in the indirect utility function, but which may be used to drive the money supply instantaneously to its constant steady-state level. The proposition would also seem to generalize to the case where many assets subject to initial jumps appear in the utility function, provided the number of linearly independent instruments not appearing in the utility function, but appearing in the dynamic relationships is at least as great as the number of such assets. In effect this is the Tinbergen static controllability condition. Finally, the phenomenon of time inconsistency can in general be expected to exist in the presence of sluggishly evolving variables, such as capital. The main point is that time consistency in effect imposes an additional constraint on costate variables, which only in special circumstances will be consistent with the structure of the system. The nature of these circumstances in an economy with capital goods deserves further investigation. See also Hillier and Malcomson (1984), Lucas and Stokey (1983), M. Persson et al. (1987), and Calvo and Obstfeld (1988).

(3) The stability of Keynesian and classical macroeconomic systems is studied by Siegel (1976) who synthesizes the work of Metzler and Cagan to produce more general models which include asset and commodity markets out of equilibrium as well as inflationary expectations. Siegel divides his models into two classes: one describing the adjustment process in the spirit of Keynes, and another in the style of the monetary classicist, Irving Fisher. It is shown that the dynamics of these extended models, both Keynesian and classical are very similar to the Cagan model, and actually, Cagan's derived stability condition holds for all models.

A similar topic is studied by Uzawa (1974) who investigates the stability properties of the Keynesian versus the neoclassical dynamic macroeconomic models. Uzawa shows that, under certain assumptions, the economic growth path is dynamically stable in the neoclassical model and dynamically unstable in the Keynesian model, unless certain stabilizing monetary and fiscal policies are adopted in the latter case.

(4) Development economists Aghevli and Khan (1977), present a dynamic macroeconomic model to study the policy consequences of financing government expenditures by the creation of money. Such a monetary policy of deficit financing has been attractive to numerous countries which are unable to enact adequate tax programs, or administer them effectively, to gain the required revenue. Such a form of deficit financing causes inflationary pressures by increasing the money supply and as inflation rates increase, government expenditures, at times, increase even faster than tax revenues, forcing the government authorities to increase money supply even further. Aghevli and Khan study the stability properties of their model and show that depending upon the numerical values of certain parameters such

as, the adjustment coefficients for inflation, real government expenditures and taxes, among others, the self-perpetuating process of inflation converges to a steady state equilibrium or it becomes explosive. Their model applied to Indonesia explains well the self-perpetuating process of inflation which occurred in that country. Batavia et al. (1986) apply the same model and suggest that inflation is not self-perpetuating in the case of the Greek economy.

(5) Tobin (1975) studies the local stability of two dynamic macro-economic models: the Walras–Keynes–Phillips model and the Marshall model. For the Walras–Keynes–Phillips model it is found that (i) a strong negative price level effect on aggregate demand, (ii) a weak price expectation effect and (iii) a slow response of price expectations to experience, are conducive to stability. The Marshallian model is separable into output and price equations. The output equation is stable and the stability of the price equation is similar to the stability of the Walras–Keynes–Phillips model. Some of Tobin's conclusions include: the Walras–Keynes–Phillips adjustment model allows the distinct possibility that lapses from full employment will not be automatically remedied by market forces. Also even with stable monetary and fiscal policy combined with price and wage flexibility, the adjustment mechanisms of the economy may be too weak to eliminate persistent unemployment.

See also Tobin (1986) who develops a dynamic macroeconomic model to analyze, both algebraically and by numerical simulations, long run *crowding out* generated by an easy fiscal and tight monetary policy mix. Tobin (1986) shows that in some cases an unstable vicious circle can lead fairly quickly to a dramatic crisis.

(6) An important macroeconomic question is this: suppose that fiscal policies are implemented which increase the savings rate; what will the dynamic effects on output and capital accumulation be? There are two well known but partly conflicting answers. The first emphasizes aggregate demand effects and claims the possible paradox of savings. The second claims that larger savings imply a higher sustainable capital stock. Obviously, the first answer is addressed to the short run and the second to the long run dynamic effects. To study this problem, Blanchard (1983) develops a dynamic macroeconomic model to emphasize the role of firms in the transmission mechanism of a shift towards savings. Blanchard considers the dynamics of the adjustment process, the stability properties of the steady state and concludes that even with rational forward looking firms, a shift towards savings may lead a temporary decrease in investment and savings before leading to more capital accumulation.

(7) Tobin (1965) introduced money in a deterministic, continuous-time, neoclassical economic growth model. Several economists, such as Sidrauski (1967), Nagatani (1970), Hadjimichalakis (1971a, 1971b, 1973, 1979) and Hadjimichalakis and Okuguchi (1979) have studied the saddle point stability of the Tobin model. In general, it is often claimed that versions of the Tobin (1965) model which assume perfect foresight are dynamically unstable. If the system is initially in a steady state with zero inflation, it is claimed that a once and for all increase in the money supply will set off a process of ever accelerating deflation. Sargent and Wallace (1973) proposed an alternative view, according to which, such an increase in the money supply produces a once and for all increase in the price level that is just sufficient to keep the system at its steady state and therefore to keep the system stable. What makes the equilibrium stable in the Sargent and Wallace (1973) model is that the price level rises, that is, the price of money falls instantaneously when at an initial price level the supply of real balances exceeds the demand, thereby eliminating the excess supply of real balances without affecting the expected rate of inflation. Calvo (1977) comments that the conditions proposed by Sargent and Wallace (1973) to remove the dynamic instability of monetary perfect foresight models are not sufficient to ensure uniqueness in any of the possible configurations of the money supply path allowed in their paper. Calvo (1977) shows that uniqueness can be recovered in some cases if a continuity condition on the price level path is added to the Sargent and Wallace (1973) assumptions. See also Stein and Nagatani (1969), Fischer (1972, 1979), Black (1974), Benhabib (1980), Benhabib and Miyao (1981), Malliaris (1982) and Hartman (1987).

(8) Shane (1974) extends Tobin's (1965) model by introducing an equity security into money and growth analysis. The model is developed explicitly in terms of securities and capital, instead of the more traditional treatment in terms of money and capital. Such an approach has two distinct advantages. First, in a model that considers only money and capital, saving is merely a decision to invest directly in real capital or money balances, whereas the introduction of a financial market allows one to analyze directly the mechanism by which saving and investment are separated. Second, in terms of developing a policy tool, this approach also provides a basis for directly relating policy actions which are financial in nature to the effects on real variables such as income and capital intensity. Shane's (1974) model consists of three differential equations in capital intensity, the wealth ratio and price expectations, and its global asymptotic stability is found to depend on whether the direct interest rate effect was greater than the offsetting wealth effect and whether the rate of forced saving was greater than the adjustment

in the rate of inflation. The model illustrates that the crucial role of financial markets in general, and security markets in particular, is to take the short run impact of economic disturbances and allow the rate of inflation to adjust slowly to changes in the economic environment. See also Purvis (1973, 1978) and Smith (1978).

(9) Brock (1974) examines a perfect foresight monetary growth model that consists of the following. Firms maximize one period profits which determine demand functions for capital and labor services as functions of the real rental and real wage. Consumers forecast the price level, real wage, real rental, income from profits, and income from Milton Friedman's (1969) famous helicopter. The consumers who obtain utility from consumption, real balances and leisure then solve their infinite horizon optimization problems to produce demand for goods, demand for money, supply of capital, and supply of labor. Equilibrium obtains when all markets clear. Thus all variables, including the price level, are determined, by explicitly specified maximizing behavior of agents, as a function of the quantity of money.

For various specifications of the utility function Brock (1974) establishes existence of equilibrium, studies uniqueness, and examines the impact of changes in the rate of growth of the money supply. Multiple equilibria may exist if the marginal utility of consumption falls with an increase in real balances, and since welfare increases as real balances increase along the set of equilibria, equilibrium may be inefficient. This possibility of two equilibria, one preferred by everyone to the other, is due to external effects translated through real balances as an argument in the utility function.

Calvo (1979) uses Brock's (1974, 1975) model to check local uniqueness for cases not studied by Brock. Calvo (1979) shows that there are perfectly plausible cases where nonuniqueness is the rule as well as others where uniqueness can always hold. Uniqueness prevails in some cases where capital enters in production, and money and consumption are Edgeworth-complementary while nonuniqueness arises where money is a factor of production. Calvo also notes that nonuniqueness and instability can in principle be corrected by government policy.

Benhabib and Bull (1983) and Brock (1974) attempt to formalize Milton Friedman's (1969) optimum quantity of money and to study the properties of dynamic equilibrium paths in monetary growth models. Benhabib and Bull show that, although the difficulty of multiple equilibrium paths complicates welfare comparisons, a strengthened version of M. Friedman's optimum quantity of money theorem can be proved. See also Hadjimi-chalakis (1981). J. A. Gray (1984) motivated by Brock's (1974) paper explores the conditions under which the procedure of specifying a dynamically unstable macroeconomic model and then arbitrarily selecting the stable path of that model may be justified.

Finally, Obstfeld (1984) demonstrates the possibility of multiple convergent equilibrium paths in a modified version of Brock's (1974) model. See also Obstfeld and Rogoff (1983).

(10) Obstfeld and Stockman (1984) review an extensive literature of dynamic exchange rate models. These models attempt to explain certain facts about floating exchange rates using several common features such as (i) the assumption of rational expectations, that is, individuals know the structure of the economy and use all available information to make optimal forecasts of future variables, and (ii) the assumption of saddle-path stability which requires that there must also be market forces that present the emergence of self-fulfilling speculative bubbles, so that the exchange rate is tied to its economic fundamentals. For details see Obstfeld and Stockman (1984). A balance of payments analysis is found in Michener (1984). Additional references are Lucas (1982), Mussa (1982), Helpman and Razin (1982), Gray and Turnovsky (1979), Dornbusch (1976) and Mundell (1968).

11. Further remarks and references

This chapter is taken from Brock and Turnovsky (1981) and its purpose is to extend some of the recent macrodynamic models in two directions. First, it has specified a more complete corporate sector than such models usually contain; second, the relationships describing the private sector are derived from explicit optimizing procedures by households and firms.

While much of our attention has been on the development of the model, we have discussed its steady-state structure in detail for one particular form of monetary policy. Probably the most important general conclusion to emerge from this analysis is the need to ground such models in an optimizing framework. It is shown how this will lead to three possible equilibrium capital structures, the choice of which depends upon relevant tax rates, and that these equilibria have very different implications for the effectiveness of various monetary and fiscal instruments. These differences are highlighted most clearly when one considers the effects of an increase in the monetary growth rate on the capital-labor ratio. If all bond financing is optimal for firms, the capital-labor ratio will most probably (but not necessarily) rise; if all equity financing is optimal, it will definitely fall. The difference is even more clear-cut with respect to an increase in the corporate profit tax rate.

The equilibrium capital-labor ratio will rise with all bond financing and fall with all equity financing. These results confirm Fair's (1978) view that in a complete rational expectations model – one in which the underlying behavioral relations are obtained from optimizing behavior and fiscal policy is precisely specified – anticipated government policies are able to generate real output effects.

But the model is capable of dealing with many other kinds of issues. For instance, more attention could be devoted to considering the comparative static properties of alternative monetary and fiscal policies under alternative tax structures. Furthermore, it is apparent from our analysis that currently popular policy discussions of pegging the monetary growth rate at say 4% are seriously incomplete. The predictions of such policies are indeterminate in the model until fiscal policy is specified. This is another reason why a richer model such as the one in this chapter is essential for understanding the *full* implications of policies of this type.

Perhaps more interestingly, one has a framework capable of evaluating the welfare effects of alternative government policies. To take one example, one can look at questions concerning tradeoffs among alternative tax rates. Specifically, the choice of monetary expansion can be viewed as representing the choice of an inflation tax rate. If one can also choose the various income tax rates, this raises the question of the optimal mix between these two forms of taxation. This issue turns out to be extremely complicated to analyze. It is considered in Turnovsky and Brock (1980) using a much simpler version of the present model, which abstracts from the corporate sector and the issues being stressed here.

The model we have developed is capable of providing a framework within which important issues can be discussed. For example, view the debt to equity ratio λ and the dividend payoff ratio i in (5.12) as fixed, in the short run, and look at the pricing equation (5.6) reproduced here for convenience

$$\dot{V}(t) + \gamma(t) = \theta^*(\lambda, i, r_p, \dot{q}/q) V(t). \tag{5.6}$$

Equation (5.6) may be used to discuss real world phenomena of the 1980s like: (i) the extraordinary bull market in stocks; (ii) complaints that the quality of corporate debt is deteriorating; and (iii) the massive influx of foreign capital into the U.S.A.

Equation (5.12) reveals a plausible partial explanation for such disparate phenomena. Look at how the disinflation and the tax cuts of the 1980s have cut the value of θ^*. This helps explain (i). Also, note how the gains to issuing corporate debt have increased. In other words the cost of debt capital has dropped relative to the cost of equity capital. To put it another way formula (5.12) reveals that a drop in the personal tax rate relative to the corporate tax rate cuts the cost of debt capital relative to the cost of equity capital. This increases the gains to leverage. Since firms would want to lever more, the quality of corporate debt will tend to fall. This is so because the same capital stock is backing a larger stock of corporate debt. This helps explain (ii).

If foreign countries, such as Japan, have not experienced as sharp a drop in θ^* as has the U.S. (which casually seems to be the case), then this helps explain (iii).

We are not saying that taxes explain everything. We are only saying that models and techniques like those exposited in this chapter help the economist explain the real world.

The model can be extended in different directions. Alternative assets such as rented capital, can be introduced. But undoubtedly the most important extension relates to uncertainty. Problems of corporate financing really become interesting only in a world of uncertainty. Recent developments in stochastic calculus indicate that it might be possible to extend our framework to include various forms of stochastic disturbances. For a comprehensive text on dynamic equilibrium macroeconomics that stresses uncertainty see Sargent (1987).

Having made the above remarks about this chapter's model we next offer general comments on stability notions in rational expectations analysis and related topics.

11.1. Stability notions in rational expectations analysis

Early examples of a type of stability analysis in the rational expectations literature that we shall exposit here are in Brock (1974), Sargent and Wallace (1973), Burmeister and Turnovsky (1977, 1978), Turnovsky and Burmeister (1977) and others. Although the Sargent and Wallace (1973) analysis was not in the context of a fully specified rational expectations equilibrium model it illustrates the role of the price of a stock variable like capital stock as a fast moving market equilibrator. That is, the price will jump very fast in response to a change in the expected capitalized payoffs from a unit of capital. This behavior of asset prices leads to notions of stability and to solution theory that is different than much of that in the natural sciences. Asset markets are asymptotically stable if in response to a parameter change the prices jump in such a way that the system hops to a new solution manifold such that along that manifold the system converges to a new steady state. The literature on this kind of rational expectations model has grown rapidly in the last few years. For example, see Buiter (1984), Judd (1985), Tillman (1985) and their references. We shall briefly describe some of the main principles that have emerged from this literature in this section of the book.

Consider an equilibrium dynamical system which is defined by the following pair of differential equations:

$$dx/dt = F(x, p, \alpha), \quad dp/dt = G(x, p, \alpha);$$ (11.1)

where F, G are smooth (at least twice continuously differentiable) and x, p lie in n-dimensional Euclidean space. The variable x will be called the state or stock variable and p will be called the jump or price variable. Let the pair $(\bar{x}, \bar{p})$ denote the steady state and note that it is a function of the shift parameters α. You should think of each component of x as a stock, asset, or capital stock variable and the corresponding component of p as a jump or price variable that can equilibrate rapidly in the very short run in order to equilibrate supply and demand for the stock. For example if one component of x is fiat money stock then the matching jump variable is the *real price of money*, i.e., $1/P$ where P is the nominal price level (Brock (1974)). In models where fiat money is perfectly inelastically supplied by government the equilibrium dynamics can be rewritten in terms of real balances and the pair (11.1) can be reduced to one differential equation in real balances. This reduction simplifies the analysis in such cases.

An example of (11.1) is the Brock–Turnovsky model (1981) treated in this chapter. To keep things simple suppose that the firm is all equity financed and there are no taxes but corporate taxes. Furthermore, all taxes are redistributed lump sum back to households. In this case the dynamical system that describes equilibrium is given by:

$$dx/dt = f(x) - C(p);$$ (11.2)(a)

$$dp/dt = p(\beta - (1 - T)f'(x)), \quad x(0) = x_0,$$ (11.2)(b)

where T denotes the corporate tax rate, $C(p)$ is the inverse function of $u'(c)$, $p = u'(c)$, $f(x)$ is the production function, and β is the subjective rate of time discount on future utility. In the general case of the Brock–Turnovsky model treated in this chapter the equation (11.2)(b) will be replaced by,

$$\theta^* = (1 - T)f'(x),$$ (11.3)(b)

where θ^* is the cost of capital. It is a function of parameters such as the rate of monetary growth (the rate of inflation), the capital gains tax rate, the personal tax rate, and the debt/equity ratio. It is also a function of the *rate of return on consumption* $\theta = \beta - (\mathrm{d}p/p \; \mathrm{d}t)$. If the proceeds of taxes are redistributed lump sum back to households then (11.2)(a) remains the same. If taxes go to finance government goods g, then g must be subtracted off the RHS (11.2)(a). In this case because taxes collected in equilibrium are a function of x and tax parameters, the RHS of (11.2)(a) will have parameters in it. We stick to the simple case (11.2) because it will be clear how to generalize the principles that we will set forth here.

In chapter 7 of this book we presented a modified form of Samuelson's Correspondence Principle that included systems (11.1) where the dynamics were derived from the primitives of economic analysis such as tastes and technology. More specifically, the dynamics (11.1) were derived from equilibrium problems that could be reduced to solutions of optimal control problems. That is to say, the RHS (11.1) was the state–costate equation in current value units of an optimal control system. In this special case we know that, near the steady state $(\bar{x}, \bar{p})$, solutions that are optimal, i.e., *equilibria* lie on the n-manifold generated by the eigenspaces of the n smallest real part eigenvalues of the Jacobian matrix evaluated at the steady state. Call this the *local solution manifold* (Brock and Scheinkman (1976) and chapter 9). In *regular stable* cases, i.e., cases where n of the eigenvalues of J have negative real parts, all the eigenvalues are distinct, and the projection of the local solution manifold on n-space is all of n-space we know that there is a function $p(x)$ such that $p = p(x)$ along this manifold. In general, except for hairline cases, there will be a manifold $EM = \{(x, p(x))\}$ of points such that if you solve (11.1) starting at $(x, p(x))$ you will generate an equilibrium. We will call EM the *equilibrium manifold*. The local solution manifold LEM is tangent to the EM at the steady state.

11.2. Examples where the equilibrium manifold is not the stable manifold

Most of the examples in the published literature are examples where the equilibrium manifold is the stable manifold. Recall that the stable manifold generated by a steady state of (11.1) is the set of all pairs (x, p) such that if you solve (11.1) you converge to the steady state as time goes to infinity. It is easy to modify the Brock and Turnovsky (1981) setup to exhibit unstable steady states and the equilibrium manifold not being the stable manifold. To do this let all taxes be zero so that the solution of the equilibrium problem is the same as the solution to the optimal growth problem. Then either put capital into the utility function as does Kurz (1968b) or replace the material balance equation, $c + \mathrm{d}x/\mathrm{d}t = f(x)$ by $c = G(\mathrm{d}x/\mathrm{d}t, x)$ as do

Liviatan and Samuelson (1969). Kurz and Liviatan and Samuelson show that examples of growth problems with multiple steady states can be constructed. Now turn one of these examples into an equilibrium rational expectations model as do Brock and Turnovsky. For specificity take the Liviatan and Samuelson model. The firm's balance sheet equation is given by $dV/dt + G(dx/dt, x) = \theta V$. Follow the same procedure as for the case $G(dx/dt, x) = f(x) - dx/dt$ to study equilibria and focus on an unstable steady state. The linearization of the system about an unstable steady state has two roots both real and positive. To get the local solution manifold take the eigenspace generated by the smallest root. The global solution manifold is tangential to this eigenspace at the unstable steady state. See Liviatan and Samuelson (1969, p. 464) for the phase portrait in (c, x) space.

If you follow the revised correspondence principle in chapter 7, the unstable steady state can be ignored for the purposes of comparative statics. This is so because, for the same reason as in the Samuelson *Correspondence Principle*, one can argue that the unstable steady state will never be observed.

In chapter 7 and in Brock (1986b) it was pointed out that when $dx/dt = F(x, p(x), \alpha) \equiv h(x, \alpha)$ was globally asymptotically stable (G.A.S.) at steady state $\bar{x}(\alpha)$, then standard Samuelsonian comparative statics and dynamics could be done. But in our case, unlike that of Samuelson, the dynamics are *derived* from primitives like tastes and technology. Hence, we may expect to obtain a more powerful analysis given a smaller number of free parameters. Recall that in Samuelson's formulation of his correspondence principle and his dynamics were ad hoc in the sense that they were not derived from maximizing behavior of economic agents. This ad hocery introduces free parameters which robs the analysis of empirical content in that the analysis does not lead to the formulation of econometric models with strong restrictions. For this reason, perhaps, the rational expectations approach of Lucas replaced the earlier Samuelson–Hicks approach to economic dynamics. This came at a price, however – we gave up as a profession on the task of modelling out of equilibrium behavior. In any event let us explain the analysis.

There are two main forms of analysis of rational expectations models that we want to stress here. The first question is: what happens if at date zero the parameter α changes to α_1 and remains at α_1 forever? This is called *unanticipated event analysis*. Good examples of this technique are Wilson (1979) and Judd (1985) among others. The second type of analysis is: what happens if at date zero it is announced that at date $T > 0$ the parameter α will change to α_1? This is called *anticipated event analysis*. More generally one can study questions such as: What happens if α is changed to α_1 on

$(0, T_1]$, α_2 on $(T_1, T_2]$, ... in order to make this latter kind of problem analytically tractable assume that α has the value α_n on (T_n, ∞). Then the analyst pieces together the comparative dynamics by working backwards.

11.3. Unanticipated event analysis

To get into the spirit of unanticipated event analysis consider the following parable. The economy is at (x_0, p_0) at date zero. It is announced that parameter α has now changed from its old value α to a new value α_1 that will reign forever. What happens? The economy was on the old equilibrium manifold $EM(\alpha)$. The new equilibrium manifold is now $EM(\alpha_1)$. The state variable x cannot change much in a short unit of time; but prices, i.e., jump variables can. Hence the price of x, $p(x, \alpha)$ changes abruptly to $p(x, \alpha_1)$ so that $(x_0, p(x_0, \alpha_1))$ is in $EM(\alpha_1)$. The equilibrium solution solves (11.1) with α set equal to α_1 on $(0, \infty)$. Judd (1985) uses this kind of technique to analyze changes in tax policy and shows how to extend linearization analysis for small changes in parameters. Basically you jump from $LEM(\alpha)$ to $LEM(\alpha_1)$ to get the dynamics for dx and dp in response to a change dα that holds forever, i.e., on $(0, \infty)$. We refer the reader to Judd (1985) for the details.

Apply this type of analysis to the tax model (11.2) above. Draw the phase diagram for (11.2). Draw the stable manifold, i.e., the set of (x, p) such that starting at (x, p) and following the dynamics (11.2) you will converge to the unique steady state $(\bar{x}, \bar{p})$. Now let the corporate tax rate increase from T_1 to T_2 at date zero. There is now a new stable manifold lying below the old one. The initial value of p must drop instantly to get on the new stable manifold since the stock variable x cannot change in the very short run. If the initial value of x is at the old steady state value then p will plummet but eventually rise to a higher level. This is called *overshooting*. The same thing will happen to the stock market value, V, of the firm. What is going on here is that prices must give the signal to decrease capital stock to a lower level in the long run. But the only variable that can adjust in the short run is price. Therefore, the burden of the entire adjustment must fall on price at first. Therefore, in the beginning of the adjustment period price sinks below its ultimate value. But if initial capital stock is so small that it is still smaller than the new steady state value overshooting will not occur. This is so because capital stock will still be increasing but not as urgently as before. Therefore, price will drop from its old value in order to discourage the speed of accumulation but it doesn't drop below its new long run value.

This is all easy to see by drawing the phase diagram. See Judd (1985) and his references.

Judd's article also shows the limitations of graphical analysis for many policy questions and develops a Laplace transform technique to get around these limitations. For details see Judd (1985).

11.4. Anticipated event analysis

Consider a change in the parameter α from α_0 to α_1 that is to take place T periods from now and to be permanent over $[T, \infty)$. Working backwards as in dynamic programming we know that to be in equilibrium the system must be on $EM(\alpha_1)$ on $[T, \infty)$. It must start at x_0 at date zero and follow the dynamics (11.1) where the RHS is evaluated at α_0 over $[0, T)$. Hence p must change from the old value, $p(x_0, \alpha_0)$ to a new value $\tilde{p}$ so that starting from $(x_0, \tilde{p})$ and following the dynamics (11.1) at value α_0 over $[0, T)$ we arrive at $EM(\alpha_1)$ at *exactly* date T. Again Judd (1985) shows how to apply this methodology to economic problems such as change in tax policy and shows how to extend it to the analysis of small changes $d\alpha$.

We conclude this section with some additional references. Attfield et al. (1985) provide an introduction to the theory and evidence of rational expectations in macroeconomics. An earlier standard reference is Shiller (1978). Conditions for unique solutions in stochastic macroeconomic models with rational expectations are given in Taylor (1977), while McCallum (1983) argues that the nonuniqueness of many macroeconomic models involving rational expectations is not properly attributable to the rationality hypothesis but, instead, is a general feature of dynamic models involving expectations. Taylor (1986) reviews rational expectations models in macroeconomics; see also McCallum (1977, 1978, 1980).

We close with a comment about disequilibrium behavior and learning. Learning and disequilibrium is an important research area in economics despite the fact that this book focuses almost entirely upon rational expectations models. Although it is beyond our scope to study learning and disequilibrium, the stability techniques exposited here will help researchers in this area. For example, Marcet and Sargent (1988) draw heavily upon recent work in optimal control theory in their paper on learning. Also, the papers of Bray (1982), Blume et al. (1982) and Lucas (1986) contain references on learning where stability analysis is stressed. See also Malliaris (1988b, 1988c) for learning illustrations related to the quantity theory of money.

There is a basic economic reason why the techniques of this book will be valuable in the area of learning and disequilibrium dynamics. This is so, because there is one parameter that plays a central role in the stability analysis of optimal dynamics. This is the rate of discount, i.e., the rate of interest that agents place upon the future. One can argue that this same parameter should play a central role in any sensible economic model of learning and disequilibrium. After all, learning imposes costs that must be borne today in return for gains tomorrow. The optimal rate of learning, and hence the adjustment rate to equilibrium, must depend on the discount rate of the future in any sensible economic model of learning. See DeCanio (1979) and his references for details.

CHAPTER 9

STABILITY IN CAPITAL THEORY

Finally, there is the problem of
stability. Does the economy converge
to balanced growth?
Stiglitz and Uzawa (1969, p. 406)

1. Introduction

The previous chapter analyzed the dynamics of a one sector economy that
was distorted by taxes. In this chapter we analyze the much harder case of
many sectors. In order to make progress, tax and other distortions will not
be treated. Furthermore, we will only treat the case of the optimal growth
model. This is not restrictive. The optimal growth model may be turned
into a market model by following the methods of the previous chapter. Of
course, if one wants to introduce tax distortions, the methods of the current
chapter will have to be modified.

A general formulation of capital theory or optimal growth problem is

$$\max \int_0^\infty e^{-\rho t} u[k(t), \dot{k}(t)] \, \mathrm{d}t$$

subject to

$$k(0) = k_0.$$

Here $u : B \subset \mathring{R}_+^n \times R^n \to R$ is usually assumed to be twice continuously
differentiable and concave, $\mathring{R}_+^n = \{x \in R^n : x_i > 0; i = 1, \ldots, n\}$, and B is convex with nonempty interior.

$$R(k) = \max \int_0^\infty e^{-\rho t} u[k(t), \dot{k}(t)] \, \mathrm{d}t$$

is called the *value of the initial stock* k_0.

A capital theory model generates a capital-price differential equation by using the maximum principle reported in Hestenes (1966) and Pontryagin et al. (1962) to write down necessary conditions for an optimal solution. This process generates a type of differential equation system that Brock and Scheinkman (1976) call a *modified Hamiltonian dynamical system*. The adjective modified appears because it is a certain type of perturbation, peculiar to economics, of the standard Hamiltonian system. This chapter reports the Brock and Scheinkman (1976) approach to capital theory.

A definition is needed. A *modified Hamiltonian dynamical system*, call it an MHDS for short, is a differential equation system of the form

$$\dot{q}_j = \rho q_j - \frac{\partial H}{\partial k_j}(q, k), \quad H(q, k) \equiv \underset{\dot{k};(k,\dot{k})\in B}{\text{maximum}}\{u(k, \dot{k}) + q\dot{k}\},$$

$$\dot{k}_j = \frac{\partial H}{\partial q_j}(q, k), \quad j = 1, 2, \ldots, n. \tag{1.1}$$

Here $H : \mathring{R}^n_+ \times \mathring{R}^n_+ \to R$, and $\rho \in R_+$. In economics, k_j is stock of capital good j and q_j is the price of capital good j. The function H is called a *Hamiltonian*, and it is well defined on $\mathring{R}^n_+ \times \mathring{R}^n_+$ for many economic problems. However, what follows only depends on H being defined on an open convex subset of R^{2n}, provided the obvious changes are made. H turns out to be the current value of national income evaluated at prices q. The number ρ is a discount factor on future welfare arising from the structure of social preferences. See Cass and Shell (1976a) for a complete interpretation of (1.1).

Clearly not all solutions of (1.1) which satisfy $k(0) = k_0$ will, in general, be optimal. We call a solution $[q(t), k(t)]$ of (1.1) optimal if $k(t)$ is the optimal solution of the optimal growth problem when $k(0) = k_0$.

The problem that we address in this chapter may now be defined.

Problem 1.   Find sufficient conditions on optimal solutions ϕ_t of (1.1) such that $\phi_t \to (\bar{q}, \bar{k})$ as $t \to \infty$. Also find sufficient conditions such that the steady state $(\bar{q}, \bar{k})$ is independent of the initial condition (q_0, k_0).

The literature on problem 1 has two main branches: (i) analysis of the local behavior of (1.1) in a neighborhood of a steady state, and (ii) analysis of global behavior of solutions of (1.1).

The first branch of the literature is fairly complete and a brief survey is presented at the end of this chapter. Concerning the second branch, until the mid-1970s, no general results on the convergence of optimal solutions of (1.1) were available. In fact, little was known about sufficient conditions for the uniqueness of steady states of (1.1). Papers of Brock (1973) and Brock and Burmeister (1976) gave a fairly general set of sufficient conditions for uniqueness of the steady state. However, there was nothing done in the Brock (1973) paper on convergence.

In this chapter we present results that build on the work of Cass and Shell (1976a), Rockafellar (1976), Magill (1977a), and Hartman and Olech (1962). We start by discussing the three basic types of results presented and their relation to the literature.

The following problem has been analysed extensively in the differential equations literature and has been reviewed in chapter 3. Let

$$\dot{x} = f(x), \quad x(0) = x_0$$

be a differential equation system. Let $\bar{x}$ satisfy $f(\bar{x}) = 0$. Under what conditions is the solution $x(t) \equiv \bar{x}$ globally asymptotically stable for all x_0? We recall two definitions.

Definition 1.1. The solution $x(t) \equiv \bar{x}$ of $\dot{x} = f(x)$ is *globally asymptotically stable* (G.A.S.) if for all x_0 the solution $\phi_t(x_0) \to \bar{x}$ as $t \to \infty$.

Definition 1.2. The solution $x(t) \equiv \bar{x}$ of $\dot{x} = f(x)$ is *locally asymptotically stable* (L.A.S.) if there is $\varepsilon > 0$ such that $|x_0 - \bar{x}| < \varepsilon$ implies $\phi_t(x_0) \to \bar{x}$ as $t \to \infty$.

However, if f is a modified Hamiltonian, new problems arise. In this case, $x(t) = \bar{x}$ is usually never even locally asymptotically stable in a neighborhood of $\bar{x}$. This is so because if λ is an eigenvalue of the linear approximation so also is $-\lambda + \rho$. See Kurz (1968a). Thus, a natural question to pose is our problem 1 for MHDS.

Definition 1.3. $\phi_t(q_0, k_0)$ will be called *a bounded solution* of (1.1) if there exists a compact set $K \subset \mathring{R}_+^n \times \mathring{R}_+^n$ such that $\phi_t(q_0, k_0) \subset K$ for all t.

Note that our definition of bounded solutions requires not only boundedness on the (q, k) space, but also requires that there exists $\varepsilon > 0$ such that

$$q_i(t) \geq \varepsilon, \quad k_i(t) \geq \varepsilon \quad i = 1, \ldots, n; \quad 0 \leq t < \infty.$$

In many optimal growth problems, Inada-type conditions guarantee that in fact optimal solutions will satisfy our boundedness condition. For this reason we concentrate on the convergence of bounded solutions.

Definition 1.4.   The steady state solution $(q, k) = (\bar{q}, \bar{k})$ of (1.1) is said to be *globally asymptotically stable* for bounded solutions of (1.1), that is, those who satisfy definition 1.3, if for all (q_0, k_0) such that $\phi_t(q_0, k_0)$ is bounded, we have

$$\phi_t(q_0, k_0) \to (\bar{q}, \bar{k}) \quad \text{as } t \to \infty.$$

Definition 1.5.   The steady state solution $(q, k) = (\bar{q}, \bar{k})$ of (1.1) is said to be *locally asymptotically stable* for bounded solutions of (1.1) if there is $\varepsilon > 0$ such that

$$|(q_0, k_0) - (q, k)| < \varepsilon \text{ implies } \phi_t(q_0, k_0) \to (\bar{q}, \bar{k}) \text{ as } t \to \infty,$$

provided that $\phi_t(q_0, k_0)$ is bounded.

For MHDS the words G.A.S. and L.A.S. will always apply to bounded solutions alone in this chapter. We will sometimes call MHDS *saddle-point* systems when we want to emphasize their saddle-point structure.

Denote by $(\bar{q}, \bar{k})$ some rest point of (1.1) and rewrite (1.1) as

$$\dot{z}_1 = F_1(z_1, z_2),$$
$$\dot{z}_2 = F_2(z_1, z_2), \tag{1.2}$$

where $F_i : A \subset R^{2n} \to R^n$ where A is open and convex, by letting

$$q - \bar{q} = z_1, k - \bar{k} = z_2, \quad F_1(z) \equiv -H_2[z + (\bar{q}, \bar{k})] + \rho(z_1 + \bar{q}),$$
$$F_2(z) \equiv H_1[z + (\bar{q}, \bar{k})].$$

Here again a bounded solution means a solution which is contained in a compact set $K \subset A$.

Most of the assumptions in this chapter refer to the *curvature* matrix

$$Q(z) = \begin{bmatrix} H_{11}(z) & (\rho/2)I_n \\ (\rho/2)I_n & -H_{22}(z) \end{bmatrix},$$

where $H_{11}(z) \equiv (\partial H_1 / \partial z_1)(z + (\bar{q}, \bar{k}))$, $H_{22}(z) \equiv (\partial H_2 / \partial z_2)(z + (\bar{q}, \bar{k}))$, and I_n is the $n \times n$ identity matrix.

In section 2 we show that if $F(z)Q(z)F(z) > 0$ for all z such that $F(z) \neq 0$, then every bounded trajectory converges to a rest point. This is the Hamiltonian version of the well-known result in differential equations which states that if $f: R^n \to R$ and $J(x) = (\partial f(x)/\partial x)$, then $f^T(x)J(x)f(x) < 0$, for all x with $f(x) \neq 0$, implies that all solutions of $\dot{x} = f(x)$ converge to a rest point. The result is obtained by using the Liapunov function $F_1^T(z)F_2(z)$.

In section 3 we show that if $z_1^T F_2(z) + z_2^T F_1(z) = 0$ implies $z^T Q(z)z > 0$ and if $Q(0)$ is positive definite, then all bounded trajectories of (1.2) converge to the origin. This is related to a result by Hartman and Olech (1962) which states that if $w^T J(x)w < 0$ for all w such that $|w| = 1$ and $w^T f(x) = 0$, then every solution to $\dot{x} = f(x)$ converges to the origin provided that 0 is L.A.S. The proof is inspired by the elegant proof of a Hartman–Olech type of result obtained by Mas–Colell (1974). As a by-product of the proof, we show that the above conditions are sufficient for the function $z_1^T z_2$ to be monotonically increasing along trajectories, which is the Cass and Shell hypothesis. Note that the assumptions of sections 2 and 3 are somewhat complementary.

The method of proof of section 3 does not, unfortunately, generalize to prove results analogous to Hartman and Olech's (1962) most general results. For this reason, in section 4 we outline the method of proof of a more general theorem. This method is similar to the method used by Hartman and Olech of constructing an orthogonal field of trajectories to the trajectories generated by a system of differential equations $\dot{z} = F(z)$, and placing conditions on the Jacobian matrix of F so that all trajectories of the original field come together monotonically as $t \to \infty$, in the metric induced by the arc length measure along the orthogonal field of trajectories.

Furthermore, the results in section 4 have a nice geometrical interpretation in terms of quasi-convexity and quasi-concavity. In particular, we show that for the case $\rho = 0$, if the Hamiltonian is quasi-concave in the state variable, then G.A.S. holds, although in this case optimality may not make sense. A notion of α-quasi-convexity is introduced to provide a geometric interpretation for the case where $\rho > 0$.

The curvature matrix Q is a natural economic and geometric quantity. As Cass and Shell (1976a) point out, the Hamiltonian is convex in q and concave in k for optimal control problems with a concave objective function. Hence $H_{11}, -H_{22}$ are positive semidefinite matrices.

Geometric Content of Q. For the one-dimensional case, Q is positive definite provided that

$$(H_{11})(-H_{22}) > \rho^2/4.$$

This suggests that if the smallest eigenvalue α of H_{11} and the smallest eigenvalue β of $-H_{22}$ satisfy

$$\alpha\beta > \rho^2/4, \qquad (R)$$

then Q is positive definite. It is easy to show that (R), which is Rockafellar's

(1976) basic stability hypothesis, does indeed imply that Q is positive definite.

Economic Content of Q. It is well-known that the Hamiltonian $H(q, k)$ can be interpreted as shadow profit when q is the shadow price of investment, all with utility as numéraire. Cass and Shell develop in detail the economic meaning of the Hamiltonian. They show, in particular,

$\partial H/\partial q = $ optimum investment level,

and

$\partial H/\partial k = $ marginal value product of k.

Thus, $\partial H/\partial q$ is an *internal supply curve for investment*, and $\partial H/\partial k$ is a *Marshallian demand curve for capital services*. Therefore,

$$H_{11} = \partial^2 H/\partial q^2, \quad H_{22} = \partial^2 H/\partial k^2$$

are generalized slopes of supply and demand curves for investment and capital services. The matrix Q is just a convenient way of tabulating information on supply, demand, and the interest rate ρ, that is important for stability analysis.

More specifically, a sufficient condition for stability is that

$$Q = \begin{bmatrix} H_{11} & (\rho/2)I_n \\ (\rho/2)I_n & -H_{22} \end{bmatrix}$$

be positive definite. An intuitive way of putting this is that the slopes of the supply curves for investment and the demand curves for capital services are large relative to the interest rate ρ, and that cross terms are small relative to own terms.

Let us expand upon the economics here. Along an optimum path, $q(t)$ is the current value of the demand price for capital goods. Thus, $q(t)$ is a Marshallian demand curve for capital equipment; that is,

$$q(t) = \frac{\partial}{\partial k} \left\{ \max \int_t^\infty e^{-\rho(s-t)} u(y, \dot{y}) \, ds, \quad \text{subject to } y(t) = k(t) \right\}$$

$$= \partial R[k(t)]/\partial k \equiv R'[k(t)],$$

if $\partial R/\partial k$ exists. Like any demand curve, the demand for k should be downward-sloping. For $u(y, \dot{y})$ concave the Hessian of R, $R''(k)$, is a negative semidefinite matrix which exists for almost every k. See Karlin (1959, p. 405).

Look at the reduced form and its equation of first variation,

$$\dot{k}(t) = H_1(R'[k(t)], k(t)), \tag{1.3}$$

$$\ddot{k} = (H_{11}R'' + H_{12})\dot{k}. \tag{1.4}$$

Stabilizing forces are forces that lead to increased negative feedback in (1.3). An increase in H_{11} is stabilizing because R'' is negative semidefinite. It is a little more difficult to explain why an increase in $-H_{22}$ is stabilizing. For an increase in $-H_{22}$ is clearly a destabilizing force for q, as can be seen intuitively by examining

$$\dot{q} = \rho q - H_2.$$

But since along an optimum path, q decreases in k, a destabilizing force for q is stabilizing for k.

It is also intuitively clear that moving ρ closer to 0 is stabilizing. This is so because if $\rho = 0$, the system strives to maximize long-run static profit since the future is worth as much as the present.

Inspection of (1.4) hints that an increase in H_{12} is destabilizing. This source of instability is not exposed by the Q matrix. The quantity H_{12} represents a shift in the internal supply curve of investment when capital stock is increased. Therefore an increase in H_{12} represents a type of increase of non-normality; that is, since H_{12} is the derivative of the internal supply curve with respect to k, it is likely that H_{12} will be negative in some sense. For an increase in the number of machines, that is an increase in k, is likely to lead to a decrease in new machines supplied by the firm to itself when q increases, if some sort of diminishing returns to capital services and substitutability between investment goods and capital goods is present.

We would expect an increase in H_{12} to contribute to instability because an increase in k leads to more new machines, which leads to yet larger k. See Brock and Scheinkman (1977a) for stability results that focus on the role of H_{12}, and that are based on a different class of Liapunov functions than those presented here.

2. A first result on G.A.S.

The work in this section is closely related to work by Cass and Shell (1976a), Rockafellar (1976), Magill (1977a), Arrow and Hurwicz (1958), Arrow et al. (1959), Hartman (1961), and Markus and Yamabe (1960). Consider the modified Hamiltonian system

$$\dot{q} - \rho q = -H_k(q, k), \quad \dot{k} = H_q(q, k), \quad k(0) = k_0, \quad q(0) = q_0. \tag{2.1}$$

Let $(\bar{q}, \bar{k})$ be a rest point of (2.1) and let

$$z_1 = q - \bar{q}, \; z_2 = k - \bar{k},$$

$$F_1(z) = \rho(z_1 + \bar{q}) - H_2, \qquad F_2(z + (\bar{q}, \bar{k}))(z) = H_1(z + (\bar{q}, \bar{k})).$$

Then (2.1) becomes

$$\dot{z}_1 = F_1(z),$$
$$\dot{z}_2 = F_2(z). \tag{2.2}$$

Markus and Yamabe (1960) and Arrow and Hurwicz (1958) present sufficient conditions for global stability of differential equations of the form $\dot{x} = f(x)$. Let $J(x) \equiv \partial f / \partial x$. Arrow and Hurwicz and Markus and Yamabe prove, roughly speaking, that the negative definiteness of $J^T + J$ is sufficient for global stability of $\dot{x} = f(x)$, by differentiating $(\dot{x})^T \dot{x} = W$ with respect to t and showing, thereby, that $x(t) \to 0$ as $t \to \infty$ along trajectories. Here x^T denotes x transposed. We present an analog of this type of result for Hamiltonian systems.

Consider a trajectory $z(t) \equiv \phi_t(q_0, k_0)$ of (2.1) where q_0 is chosen so that $\phi_t(q_0, k_0)$ is bounded. Optimal growth paths will have this boundedness property under reasonable conditions. Cass and Shell (1976a) prove global stability of such a trajectory by differentiating the Liapunov function $V \equiv z_1^T z_2$ with respect to t. Cass and Shell are the first to obtain G.A.S. results for (2.1) by use of the Liapunov function $V \equiv z_1^T z_2$ for the discounted case. Their methods provided inspiration for many of the Brock and Scheinkman (1976) results. Rockafellar (1973) and Samuelson (1972a) have used the same function to investigate stability for the case $\rho = 0$. Magill (1977a) used V to obtain G.A.S. results for a discounted linear quadratic problem. It is, therefore, natural to ask what may be obtained by differentiating the closely related Liapunov function $F_1^T F_2$.

We will make use of the result in Hartman (1964, p. 539) which is also theorem 4.1 of chapter 4, rephrased for our current need.

Lemma 2.1. Let $F(z)$ be continuous on an open set $E \subset R^m$, and such that solutions of

$$\dot{z} = F(z) \tag{*}$$

are uniquely determined by initial conditions. Let $W(z)$ be a real-valued function on E with the following properties:

(a) W is continuously differentiable on E,
(b) $0 \le \dot{W}(z)$, where $\dot{W}(z)$ is the trajectory derivative of $W(z)$ for any $z \in E$.

Let $z(t)$ be a solution of (*) for $t \geq 0$. Then the limit points of $z(t)$ for $t \geq 0$, in E, if any, are contained in the set $E_0 = \{z : \dot{W}(z) = 0\}$.

Proof. Let $t_n < t_{n+1} \to \infty$, $z(t_n) \to z_0$ as $n \to \infty$, and $z_0 \in E$. Then $W[z(t_n)] \to W(z_0)$ as $n \to \infty$, and by (b) $W[z(t)] \leq W(z_0)$ for $t \geq 0$. Suppose $z_0 \notin E_0$ so that $\dot{W}(z_0) > 0$ by (b). Let $z_0(t)$ be a solution of (*) satisfying $z_0(0) = z_0$. Since W is continuously differentiable and $\dot{W}(z_0) > 0$, there exists by the mean value theorem $\varepsilon > 0$ and $\delta > 0$ such that for $0 \leq t \leq \varepsilon$

$$W[z_0(t)] - W(z_0) > \delta t,$$

and, in particular,

$$W[z_0(\varepsilon)] - W(z_0) > \delta \varepsilon. \tag{2.3}$$

Since $z(t_n) \to z_0$, and solutions are continuously dependent on initial values, given any $\eta > 0$, there exists $N(\eta)$ such that for $n \geq N(\eta)$,

$$|z(t + t_n) - z_0(t)| < \eta \quad \text{for } 0 \leq t \leq \varepsilon.$$

And in particular,

$$|z(\varepsilon + t_n) - z_0(\varepsilon)| < \eta \quad \text{for } n \geq N(\eta).$$

The continuity of W guarantees that for η sufficiently small,

$$|W[z(\varepsilon + t_n)] - W[z_0(\varepsilon)]| < \delta\varepsilon/2. \tag{2.4}$$

Inequalities (2.3) and (2.4) imply that $W[z(\varepsilon + t_n)] > W(z_0)$, and this contradicts $W[z(t)] \leq W(z_0)$. This completes the proof.

We can now prove

Theorem 2.1. Let

$$Q(z) = \begin{bmatrix} H_{11}(z) & (\rho/2)I_n \\ (\rho/2)I_n & -H_{22}(z) \end{bmatrix},$$

where $H_{11} = \partial F_2/\partial z_1$, $H_{22} = -\partial F_1/\partial z_2$, and I_n denotes the $n \times n$ identity matrix. If $F^{\mathrm{T}}(z)Q(z)F(z) > 0$ for all z with $F(z) \neq 0$, and if the rest points of (2.2) are isolated, then given any z_0 such that $\phi_t(z_0)$ is bounded, there exists a rest point $\bar{z}$, which may depend on z_0, such that $\lim \phi_t(z_0) \to \bar{z}$ as $t \to \infty$.

Proof. Let $\gamma^+ = \{z \in R^n : z = \phi_t(z_0) \text{ for some } t \geq 0\}$, and $\omega(\gamma^+) = \{z \in R^n : \text{there exists an increasing sequence } \{t_n\}_{n=0}^{\infty} \text{ such that } \lim_{n \to \infty} \phi_{t_n}(z_0) = z\}$.

Since γ^+ has compact closure on the domain of F, $\omega(\gamma^+)$ is nonempty, compact and connected. See Hartman (1964, p. 145).

Let $W(z) = F_1^{\mathrm{T}}(z) F_2(z)$. Then

$$\dot{W}(z) = \dot{F}_1^{\mathrm{T}}(z) F_2(z) + F_1^{\mathrm{T}}(z) \dot{F}_2(z)$$

$$= \rho F_1^{\mathrm{T}}(z) F_2(z) + F_1^{\mathrm{T}}(z) H_{11}(z) F_1(z) - F_2^{\mathrm{T}}(z) H_{22}(z) F_2(z)$$

$$= F^{\mathrm{T}}(z) Q(z) F(z) \geq 0.$$

By the previous lemma, if $\bar{z} \in \omega(\gamma^+)$, then $F^{\mathrm{T}}(\bar{z}) Q(\bar{z}) F(\bar{z}) = 0$, and, hence, $F(\bar{z}) = 0$; that is, $\bar{z}$ is a rest point. Since the rest points are isolated and $\omega(\gamma^+)$ is connected, $\omega(\gamma^+) = \{\bar{z}\}$. Thus, $\lim \phi_t(z_0) \to \bar{z}$ as $t \to \infty$.

Remark 2.1. For MHDS derived from optimal growth problems, it would be useful to replace the condition that $\phi_t(z_0)$ is bounded with the condition $\phi_t(z_0)$ is optimal, since it is possible to find models in which optimal paths are not bounded. One can, however, bound the Liapunov function W by assuming regularity and concavity conditions on the so-called value function. In fact, consider an optimal growth problem

$$\max \int_0^\infty \mathrm{e}^{-\rho t} u[k(t), \dot{k}(t)]\, \mathrm{d}t \tag{2.5}$$

given $k(0) = k_0$.

Here $u: R^{2n} \to R$ is usually assumed concave and twice continuously differentiable.

Let $k^*(t, k_0)$ be the optimal solution and

$$R(k_0) = \int_0^\infty \mathrm{e}^{-\rho t} u[k^*(t, k_0), \dot{k}^*(t, k_0)]\, \mathrm{d}t;$$

that is, R is the value of the objective function along the optimal path (the value function).

If we assume that R is twice continuously differentiable, then one can show that $R'(k) = q$ where (q, k) solve the MHDS corresponding to (2.5). Benveniste and Scheinkman (1979) provide a general set of conditions on u that imply that R' exists.

Hence, $\dot{q} = (\mathrm{d}/\mathrm{d}t) R'(k) = R''(k)\dot{k}$. The concavity of u implies that R is concave, and so, $R''(k)$ is seminegative definite. If one assumes that in fact $R''(k)$ is negative definite, then $\dot{k}^{\mathrm{T}}\dot{q} = \dot{k}^{\mathrm{T}} R''(\dot{k})\bar{k} < 0$ along any optimal path provided $\dot{k} \neq 0$. Thus, $W \equiv \dot{k}^{\mathrm{T}}\dot{q}$ is bounded above on optimal paths.

Remark 2.2. The Liapunov function $V \equiv z_1^T z_2 = (q - \bar{q})^T (k - \bar{k})$ amounts to

$$(q - \bar{q})^T (k - \bar{k}) = [R'(k) - R'(\bar{k})]^T (k - \bar{k}).$$ (i)

Since the value function $R(\cdot)$ is concave,

$$[R'(k) - R'(\bar{k})](k - \bar{k}) \leq 0$$ (ii)

for all k. Inequality (ii) is well-known for concave functions. It holds with strict inequality for strictly concave functions. Thus, it is natural to search for sufficient conditions on the Hamiltonian that imply V is increasing on trajectories; and the matrix Q plays an important role in such sufficient conditions.

3. Convergence of bounded trajectories

In this section we shall present a general theorem closely related to Hartman and Olech's basic theorem (1962, p. 157). Theorem 3.1 below and many other results will follow as simple corollaries. Furthermore, the general theorem is stated and proved in such a way as to highlight a general Liapunov method that is especially useful for the stability analysis of optimal paths generated by optimal control problems arising in capital theory.

Theorem 3.1. Let $f : E \subset R^m \to R^m$ be twice continuously differentiable, E open and convex. Consider the differential equation system

$$\dot{x} = f(x).$$ (3a.1)

Assume there is x such that $f(x) = 0$ (without loss of generality put $x = 0$) such that there is $V : E^m \to R$ satisfying:

(a) for all $x \neq 0$, $x^T \nabla^2 V(0)[J(0)x] < 0$,
(b) $\nabla V(0) = 0$,
(c) for all $x \neq 0$, $[\nabla V(x)]^T f(x) = 0$ implies $x^T \nabla^2 V(x) f(x) = 0$,
(d) for all $x \neq 0$, $x^T \nabla^2 V(x) f(x) = 0$ implies $[\nabla V(x)]^T J(x)x < 0$.

Then

(α) $[\nabla V(x)]^T f(x) < 0$ for all $x \neq 0$,
(β) all trajectories that remain bounded, that is, are contained in a compact set $k \subset E$, for $t \geq 0$ converge to 0.

Proof. Let $x \neq 0$, and put

$$g(\lambda) \equiv [\nabla V(\lambda x)]^T f(\lambda x). \tag{3a.2}$$

We shall show that $g(1) < 0$ in order to obtain (α). We do this by showing that $g(0) = 0$, $g'(0) = 0$, $g''(0) < 0$, and $g(\bar{\lambda}) = 0$ implies $g'(\bar{\lambda}) < 0$ for $\bar{\lambda} > 0$. (At this point, the reader will do well to draw a graph of $g(\lambda)$ in order to convince himself that the above statements imply $g(1) < 0$.) Calculating, we get

$$g'(\lambda) = x^T \nabla^2 V(\lambda x) f(\lambda x) + [\nabla V(\lambda x)]^T J(\lambda x) x, \tag{3a.3}$$

$$g''(\lambda) = x^T \left[\frac{\mathrm{d}}{\mathrm{d}\lambda} \nabla^2 V(\lambda x) \right] f(\lambda x) + x^T \nabla^2 V(\lambda x) [J(\lambda x) x]$$

$$+ x^T \nabla^2 V(\lambda x) [J(\lambda x) x] + [\nabla V(\lambda x)]^T \left[\frac{\mathrm{d}}{\mathrm{d}\lambda} J(\lambda x) \right] x. \tag{3a.4}$$

Now $\lambda = 0$ implies $f(\lambda x) = 0$, so $g(0) = 0$. Also $g'(0) = 0$ from $f(0) = 0$, and (b). Furthermore, $f(0) = 0$, and (b) imply

$$g''(0) = 2x^T \nabla^2 V(0) [J(0) x]. \tag{3a.5}$$

But this is negative by (a). By continuity of g'' in λ, it must be true that there is $\varepsilon_0 > 0$ such that $g(\lambda) < 0$ for $\lambda \in [0, \varepsilon_0]$. Suppose now that there is $\lambda > 0$ such that $g(\lambda) = 0$. Then there must be a smallest $\bar{\lambda} > 0$ such that $g(\bar{\lambda}) = 0$. Also, $g'(\bar{\lambda}) \geq 0$. Let us calculate $g'(\bar{\lambda})$, show that $g'(\bar{\lambda}) < 0$, and get an immediate contradiction. From (3a.3),

$$g'(\bar{\lambda}) = x^T \nabla^2 V(\bar{\lambda} x) f(\bar{\lambda} x) + [\nabla V(\bar{\lambda} x)]^T J(\bar{\lambda} x) x. \tag{3a.6}$$

Now $g(\bar{\lambda}) = 0$ implies $[\nabla V(\bar{\lambda} x)]^T f(\bar{\lambda} x) = 0$. But this, in turn, implies that $\bar{\lambda} x^T \nabla^2 V(\bar{\lambda} x) f(\bar{\lambda} x) = 0$ by (c). Finally, (d) implies that $[\nabla V(\bar{\lambda} x)]^T \times J(\bar{\lambda} x) \times (\bar{\lambda} x) < 0$. Thus $g'(\bar{\lambda}) < 0$, a contradiction to $g'(\bar{\lambda}) \geq 0$. Therefore,

$$[\nabla V(x)]^T f(x) < 0 \quad \text{for all } x \neq 0. \tag{3a.7}$$

By lemma 2.1, all the rest points of $\phi_t(x_0)$ satisfy $[\nabla V(x)]^T f(x) = 0$, and so, $x = 0$ is the only candidate. But if $\phi_t(x_0)$ is bounded, $\phi_t(x_0)$ must have a limit point. Hence $\phi_t(x_0) \to 0$ as $t \to \infty$. This completes the proof.

Note that to get global asymptotic stability results for bounded trajectories, all one needs to do is find a V that is monotone on bounded trajectories and assume that $E_0 = \{x: [\nabla V(x)]^T f(x) = 0\} = \{0\}$. This result is important for global asymptotic stability analysis of optimal paths generated by control problems arising in capital theory. Also, Hartman and Olech

(1962) type results emerge as simple corollaries. We demonstrate the power of the theorem by extracting few corollaries, some already mentioned in chapter 4.

Corollary 3.1. Let $f: R^m \to R^m$. Consider the ordinary differential equations $\dot{x} = f(x), f(0) = 0$. If $J(x) + J^T(x)$ is negative definite for each x, then 0 is globally asymptotically stable.

Proof. Put $V = x^T x$. Then $\nabla V(x) = 2x\nabla^2 V(x) = 2I_n$ where I_n is the $n \times n$ identity matrix. Assumption (a) becomes

$$x^T J(0)x < 0 \quad \text{for all } x \neq 0.$$

But this follows because

$$2x^T J(0)x = x^T[J(0) + J^T(0)]x < 0.$$

Assumption (b) trivially holds since $\nabla V(x) = 2x$. Assumption (c) amounts to $2xf(x) = 0$ implies $x^T(2I_n)f(x) = 0$ which obviously holds. Assumption (d) obviously holds because $2x^T J(x)x < 0$ for all $x \neq 0$. Thus all bounded trajectories converge to 0 as $t \to \infty$. It is easy to use $V = x^T x$ decreasing in t in order to show that all trajectories are bounded. This ends the proof.

The following corollary is a stronger result than Hartman and Olech (1962) in one way and weaker in another. We explain the difference in more detail below.

Corollary 3.2. (Mas–Colell (1974).) Consider $\dot{x} = f(x), f(0) = 0$. Assume that $x^T[J(0) + J^T(0)]x < 0$ for all $x \neq 0$, and

$$x^T f(x) = 0 \text{ implies } x^T[J(x) + J^T(x)]x < 0 \quad \text{for all } x \neq 0. \tag{3a.8}$$

Then 0 is globally asymptotically stable.

Proof. Let $V = x^T x$. We show that

$$dV/dt = 2x^T f(x) < 0 \quad \text{for } x \neq 0. \tag{3a.9}$$

Assumptions (a)-(d) of the theorem are trivially verified. Therefore, $dV/dt < 0$, and the rest of the proof proceeds as in corollary 3.1.

Remark 3.1. The condition

$$x^T f(x) < 0 \quad \text{for } x \neq 0 \tag{3a.10}$$

has a natural geometric interpretation when $\dot{x} = f(x)$ is a gradient flow; that is, there is a potential $F: R^n \to R$ such that

$$\nabla F(x) = f(x)$$

for all x. A function $F: R^n \to R$ is said to be *pseudoconcave* at x_0 if

$$F(x_0) > F(x_1) \quad \text{implies} \quad \nabla F(x_1)^T (x_0 - x_1) > 0. \tag{3a.11}$$

Put $x_0 = 0$, assume that F is maximum at $x_0 = 0$, and note that (3a.11) is just

$$x_1^T f(x_1) < 0.$$

Thus, condition (3a.10) amounts to pseudoconcavity of the potential F.

A result similar to corollary 3.2 is reported in Hartman and Olech (1962) and in Hartman (1964) where 0 is assumed to be the only rest point, and it is assumed to be locally asymptotically stable. On the one hand, Mas-Colell puts the stronger assumption: $x[J(0) + J^T(0)]x < 0$ for $x \neq 0$ on the rest point. It is well-known that negative real parts of the eigenvalues of $J(0)$ do not imply negative definiteness of $J(0) + J^T(0)$, but negative definiteness of $J(0) + J^T(0)$ does imply negative real parts for $J(0)$.

But on the other hand, Hartman and Olech (1962) make the assumption: for all $x \neq 0$, $w^T f(x) = 0$ implies $w^T[J(x) + J^T(x)]w \leq 0$ for all vectors w. Note that Mas-Colell only assumes $x^T f(x) = 0$ implies $x^T[J(x) + J^T(x)]x < 0$. So he places the restriction on a much smaller set of w, but he requires the strong inequality. Furthermore, the proof of the Mas-Colell result is much simpler than that of Hartman and Olech.

It is possible to obtain general results of the Hartman and Olech type from the theorem. For example,

Corollary 3.3. Let G be a positive definite symmetric matrix, and let 0 be the unique rest point of $\dot{x} = f(x)$. Assume that

$$x^T[GJ(0)]x < 0 \quad \text{for all } x \neq 0,$$

and

$$x^T G f(x) = 0 \quad \text{implies} \quad x^T[GJ(x)]x < 0 \quad \text{for all } x \neq 0.$$

Then $x = 0$ is globally asymptotically stable for bounded trajectories.

Proof. Let $V(x) = x^T G x$. Then,

$$\nabla V(x) = 2Gx.$$

Also,

$$\nabla^2 V(x) = 2G.$$

The rest of the proof is now routine.

Corollary 3.3 is closely related to a theorem of Hartman and Olech (1962, theorem 2.3, p. 157) and to a theorem in Hartman's book (1964, theorem 14.1, p. 549). Hartman and Olech also treat the case of G depending on x. We have not been able to obtain their result for nonconstant G as a special case of our theorem. Thus, their different methods of proof yield theorems that the methods presented in this section are unable to obtain. This leads us to believe that the method of proof outlined above is necessary for developing Hartman and Olech type generalizations for nonconstant G for modified Hamiltonian dynamical systems. We turn now to an application of the general theorem 3.1 to modified Hamiltonian dynamical systems. Assume that the MHDS has a singularity $(\bar{q}, \bar{k})$, and rewrite it as

$$\dot{z}_1 = \rho(z_1 + \bar{q}) - H_2 z + (\bar{q}, \bar{k}) \equiv F_1(z), \quad z \equiv (q, k) - (\bar{q}, \bar{k}),$$

$$\dot{z}_2 = H_1(z + (\bar{q}, \bar{k})) \equiv F_2(z). \tag{3b.1}$$

We now state and prove

Theorem 3.2. Let

$$Q(z) = \begin{bmatrix} H_{11}(z) & (\rho/2)I_n \\ (\rho/2)I_n & -H_{22}(z) \end{bmatrix}, \tag{3b.2}$$

where I_n is the $n \times n$ identity matrix. Assume

(a) $0 = F(0)$ is the unique rest point of $\dot{z} = F(z)$,

(b) for all $z \neq 0$,

$$z_1^T F_2(z) + z_2^T F_1(z) = 0 \quad \text{implies } z^T Q(z) z > 0, \tag{3b.3}$$

(c) for all $w \neq 0$, $w^T Q(0) w > 0$.

Then all trajectories that are bounded for $t \geq 0$ converge to 0 as $t \to \infty$.

Proof. Let $V = z^T A z$ where

$$A = -\begin{bmatrix} 0 & I_n \\ I_n & 0 \end{bmatrix},$$

where I_n is the $n \times n$ identity matrix. Note that $z^T A z = -2z_1^T z_2$. Since $\nabla^2 V(0) = A + A^T = 2A$ and $(w^T A)^T (J(0)w) = -w^T Q(0) w$, we have that (c) implies (a) of theorem 3.1. Also $[\nabla V(z)]^{\mathrm{T}} = z^{\mathrm{T}}(A + A^{\mathrm{T}}) = 2z^{\mathrm{T}}A$, and hence, $\nabla V(0) = 0$. Therefore, (b) of theorem 3.1 follows. Now (c) of theorem 3.1 amounts to $[\nabla V(z)]^{\mathrm{T}}F(z) \equiv 2z^{\mathrm{T}}AF(z) = 0$ implies $z^{\mathrm{T}}\nabla^2 V(z)F(z) \equiv 2z^{\mathrm{T}}AF(z) = 0$, which is trivially true. Furthermore, (d) amounts to

$$2z^{\mathrm{T}}AF(z) = 0 \quad \text{implies} \quad 2(z^{\mathrm{T}}A)J(z)z > 0. \tag{3b.4}$$

But (3b.4) is identical to (3b.3), as an easy calculation will immediately show. Thus, $\dot{V} < 0$ except at the rest point 0. The rest of the proof is routine by now.

The proof of theorem 3.2 also yields the result that the Liapunov function $z_1^{\mathrm{T}}z_2 = (q - \bar{q})^{\mathrm{T}}(k - \bar{k})$ is monotonically increasing along trajectories. Theorem 3.2 is a *local* sufficient condition for the hypothesis of the Cass and Shell stability theorem to hold. This is so because theorem 3.2 gives conditions for the trajectory derivative of $V = z_1^{\mathrm{T}}z_2$ to be positive for all $z \neq 0$, and that is the Cass and Shell hypothesis.

Remark 3.2. It is worth pointing out here that the hypothesis

$$\dot{V}(z) > 0 \quad \text{for } z \neq 0$$

has a geometric interpretation for the case $\rho = 0$. It implies pseudoconvexity, pseudoconcavity at $(\bar{q}, \bar{k})$ of $H(q, k)$ in q, k respectively. For the special case

$$H(q, k) = f_1(q) + f_2(k),$$

$\dot{V}(z) > 0$ for $z \neq 0$ is equivalent to pseudoconcavity at $(\bar{q}, \bar{k})$ of

$$G(q, k) \equiv -f_1(q) + f_2(k).$$

These statements may be easily checked by referring to the definition of pseudoconcavity in Mangasarian (1969, p. 147).

Sufficient conditions, of local form such as the Q condition of theorem 3.2, for positive trajectory derivative are useful for computations. Applications and economic interpretations of local conditions for stability to the adjustment cost literature are discussed in Brock and Scheinkman (1977b).

There is a neat sufficient condition for the positive definiteness of Q. If H is convexo-concave, the matrix Q is clearly positive semidefinite for $\rho = 0$. Furthermore, if the minimum eigenvalue of H_{11} is larger than α and the maximum eigenvalue of H_{22} is less than $-\beta$ where $\alpha\beta > \rho^2/4$, then Q is positive definite. The hypothesis $\alpha\beta > \rho^2/4$ is the basic curvature assumption in Rockafellar's (1976) analysis.

The positive definiteness of Q is also related to the Burmeister and Turnovsky (1972) regularity condition. Let $[\bar{q}(\rho), \bar{k}(\rho)]$ be the steady state associated with ρ. It solves

$$0 = \rho q - H_2(q, k),$$

$$0 = H_1(q, k).$$

Differentiate this last system with respect to ρ to obtain

$$0 = \bar{q} + \rho\bar{q}' - H_{21}\bar{q}' - H_{22}\bar{k}',$$

$$0 = H_{11}\bar{q}' + H_{12}\bar{k}',$$

where

$$[\bar{q}', \bar{k}'] = \left[\frac{\mathrm{d}\bar{q}}{\mathrm{d}\rho}, \frac{\mathrm{d}\bar{k}}{\mathrm{d}\rho}\right].$$

Rewrite this as

$$-\begin{bmatrix} \bar{q} \\ 0 \end{bmatrix} = \begin{bmatrix} \rho - H_{21} & -H_{22} \\ H_{11} & H_{12} \end{bmatrix}\begin{bmatrix} \bar{q}' \\ \bar{k}' \end{bmatrix}.$$

Multiply both sides of this by the row vector $[\bar{k}', \bar{q}']$ to get

$$-\bar{q}^{\mathrm{T}}\bar{k}' = [\bar{k}', \bar{q}']\begin{bmatrix} \rho - H_{21} & -H_{22} \\ H_{11} & H_{12} \end{bmatrix}\begin{bmatrix} \bar{q}' \\ \bar{k}' \end{bmatrix} = [\bar{q}', \bar{k}']^{\mathrm{T}}Q[\bar{q}(\rho), \bar{k}(\rho)][\bar{q}', \bar{k}'].$$

But the quantity

$$\theta \equiv \bar{q}^{\mathrm{T}}\bar{k}'$$

is the Burmeister–Turnovsky (1972) *regularity* quantity. Burmeister and Turnovsky use the quantity θ as an aggregate measure of capital deepening response. Thus, the positive definiteness of Q in the directions $[\bar{q}', \bar{k}']$ as ρ varies is equivalent to capital deepening response in the Burmeister–Turnovsky sense for each value of ρ.

4. A more general result

In this section we present a result, theorem 4.2 below, on convergence of bounded trajectories of MHDS that is related to a theorem of Hartman and Olech (1962). We start by presenting a sketch of the proof of a result, theorem 4.1, that is, in fact, almost contained in theorem 3.2. Furthermore, corollary 4.1 below gives a nice geometric interpretation of the hypothesis in terms of quasi-convexity and quasi-concavity of the Hamiltonian function. Reconsider the system (3b.1),

$$\dot{z}_1 = F_1(z),$$

$$\dot{z}_2 = F_2(z).$$

Put

$$F(z) = [F_1(z), F_2(z)]. \tag{4.1}$$

Assume $F(0) = 0$, $F(z) \neq 0$ for $z \neq 0$, F is continuously differentiable. Let $\phi_t(z_0)$ be the solution of (4.1) given z_0; let W_s be the stable manifold of (4.1), that is, $W_s = \{\bar{z}_0 : \phi_t(\bar{z}_0) \to 0 \text{ as } t \to \infty\}$; and let Λ be the bounded manifold of (4.1), that is, $\Lambda = \{\bar{z}_0 : \text{there is } M > 0 \text{ such that for all } t \geq 0, |\phi_t(\bar{z}_0)| \leq M\}$. Assume that for each $z_{20} \in R^n$ there is a unique z_{10} such that $(z_{10}, z_{20}) \in \Lambda$. Write

$$z_{10} = g(z_{20}) \tag{4.2}$$

for this functional relation, and assume that g is differentiable. We are after sufficient conditions to guarantee that $\phi_t[g(z_{20}), z_{20}] \to 0$ as $t \to \infty$ for all $z_{20} \in R^n$.

We could just apply the Hartman-Olech result to the reduced form

$$\dot{z}_2 = F_2[g(z_2), z_2], \tag{4.3}$$

but this requires knowledge of $\partial g / \partial z_2$. In most problems not much is known about g other than its existence and differentiability and other general properties. In some problems g is badly behaved, but we shall ignore those here. Thus, we formulate a sufficient condition involving $\partial F / \partial z$ alone.

Let us proceed in a way that uncovers a natural set of sufficient conditions for the global asymptotic stability of (4.1) on bounded trajectories. Assume the solution $z_2 = 0_2$ is locally asymptotically stable for (4.3). Here $F_2[g(0_2), 0_2] = 0_2$. This means that there is an open neighborhood $N_2(0_2) \subset R^n$ such that $z_{20} \in N_2$ implies $\phi_t[g(z_{20}), z_{20}] \to 0$ as $t \to \infty$. Let $A_2(0_2) = \{z_{20} : \phi_t[g(z_{20}), z_{20}] \to 0 \text{ as } t \to \infty\}$. If $A_2(0_2)$ is the whole of R^n, we have global asymptotic stability. So suppose that z_{20} is in the boundary of $A_2(0_2)$. Let $u_2 \in R^n$ have unit norm. Consider the vector

$$z_0(p, u_2) \equiv [g(z_{20} + pu_2), z_{20} + pu_2], \quad p \in [0, \beta].$$

Put

$$y(t, p) \equiv \phi_t[z_0(p, u_2)].$$

Let $y_p(t, p) \equiv \partial \phi_t[z_0(p, u_2)]/\partial p$. Consider the following differential equation (we drop transpose notation except when needed for clarity).

$$T_p \equiv \frac{dT}{dp} = -\frac{y_{1p}F_2[y(T, p)] + y_{2p}F_1[y(T, p)]}{2F_1[y(T, p)]F_2[y(T, p)]} \equiv h(T, p), \tag{4.4}$$

$$T(0, q) = q.$$

Let $y[T(p, q), p] \equiv x(q, p)$ be a solution, if a solution exists, and denote $(\partial/\partial p)x(q, p)$ by x_p. Note that

$$x_p = \frac{\partial y}{\partial T} T_p + y_p = F[x(q, p)]T_p + y_p[T(p, q), p]. \tag{4.5}$$

Also note that

$$x_{1p}F_2[x(q, p)] + x_{2p}F_1[x(q, p)] = 0. \tag{4.6}$$

The latter follows from

$$(F_1 T_p + y_{1p})F_2 + (F_2 T_p + y_{2p})F_1 = 2T_p F_1 F_2 + y_{1p}F_2 + y_{2p}F_1 = 0. \tag{4.7}$$

But (4.7) is identical to (4.4).

We call the system of trajectories satisfying (4.6) *Hamiltonian orthogonal* trajectories. They are not the same kind of orthogonal trajectories as in the original Hartman-Olech result. We shall see, however, that it is natural to construct trajectories of type (4.6) for our type of problem.

Consider

$$w(q, p) \equiv x_{1p}(q, p) \cdot x_{2p}(q, p). \tag{4.8}$$

It is natural to look at w of (4.8) in light of the previous results and the Hartman-Olech technique. Observe that

$$\frac{\partial w}{\partial q} = T_{pq}[F_1 x_{2p} + F_2 x_{1p}] + T_q x_p Q x_p = T_q x_p Q x_p. \tag{4.9}$$

The last follows from the definition of Hamiltonian orthogonal trajectories in (4.6). The reader will recall

$$Q(x) \equiv \begin{bmatrix} H_{11}(x) & (\rho/2)I_n \\ (\rho/2)I_n & -H_{22}(x) \end{bmatrix}, \quad x = x(q, p), \tag{4.10}$$

$$z_q = F(x)T_q, \quad x_{pq} = T_{pq}F(x) + T_q J(x)x_p, \quad T_q > 0.$$

Notice here that both the Liapunov function (4.8) and the method of constructing the transverse trajectories (4.4) are different from Hartman-Olech. The method of proof is also different.

A theorem may now be stated.

Theorem 4.1.   Assume that (a) F is continuously differentiable, (b) $F(0) = 0$, $F(z) \neq 0$ for $z \neq 0$, (c) $z_2 = 0_2$ is a locally asymptotically stable solution of $\dot{z}_2 = F_2[g(z_2), z_2]$, and (d) for all bounded trajectories $z(t)$, for all vectors $c \in R^{2n}$ such that $|c| = 1$, $c = (c_1, c_2)$, $c_1 = J_g c_2$ where $J_g = g'(z_2)$, $c_1 F_2[z(t)] + c_2 F_1[z(t)] = 0$ hold, we have

$$c^T Q[z(t)]c > 0. \tag{4.11}$$

Then $z_2 = 0_2$ is G.A.S. for $\dot{z}_2 = F_2[g(z_2), z_2]$. That is, all bounded trajectories of $\dot{z} = f(z)$ converge to 0 as $t \to \infty$.

   Notice that although in hypothesis (d) of the theorem we used information on the Jacobian matrix of g, we could have stated the stronger hypothesis that for all $z \in R^{2n}$, for all $c \in R^{2n}$ with $|c| = 1$, $c_1^T F_2[z(t)] + c_2^T F_1[z(t)] = 0$ implies $c^T Q[z(t)]c > 0$, which does not use any properties of J_g. The reason theorem 4.1 is stated in the form above is that one can obtain the following corollary.

Corollary 4.1.   Given a MHDS like (3b.1) under hypotheses (a)-(c) of theorem 4.1, suppose J_g is symmetric and that the Hamiltonian function satisfies for all $z = (g(z_2), z_2)$

 (i) $c_1^T H_{11}(z)c_1 > \alpha |c_1|^2$ for all $c_1 \neq 0$ such that $c_1^T H_1(z) = 0$,
(ii) $c_2^T [-H_{22}(z)]c_2 > \beta |c_2|^2$ for all $c_2 \neq 0$ such that $c_2^T [H_2(z) - \rho(z_1 + \bar{q})] = 0$
       for some $(\alpha, \beta) \in R^2$ with $\alpha\beta \geq \rho^2/4$.

Then global asymptotic stability of bounded trajectories holds.

Proof.   Since in theorem 4.1, $z(t)$ is a bounded trajectory and (4.2) holds, we have

$$F_1(z) \equiv \rho(z_1 + \bar{q}) - H_2(z + (\bar{q}, \bar{k})) = J_g F_2(z) \equiv J_g H_1(z + (\bar{q}, \bar{k})).$$

Since

$$c_1 = J_g c_2, \quad c_1^T F_2[z(t)] + c_2^T F_1[z(t)] = 0$$

if and only if $(J_g c_2)^T F_2 + c_2^T J_g F_2 = 0$. Hence, (d) of theorem 4.1 holds if and only if $c_2^T F_1 = c_1^T F_2 = 0$. By (i) and (ii), $c^T Q[z(t)]c > 0$ for all c satisfying (d) of theorem 4.1. Consequently G.A.S. must hold.

Remark 4.1.   In corollary 4.1 only the fact that J_g is symmetric was used. As in remark 2.1, if a value function R exists and is twice continuously differentiable, $J_g = R''$, and is, thus, symmetric.

Remark 4.2. For $\rho = 0$, (i) and (ii) can be interpreted as quasi-concavity of the Hamiltonian function H. The Hamiltonian is, in fact, always a convex function of q. Therefore, the equivalent bordered matrix conditions so beloved by economists may be written down in place of (i) and (ii). This generalizes the result of Rockafellar (1970a) on the G.A.S. of convexo-concave Hamiltonians to the quasi-convex-quasi-concave case.

Remark 4.3. Given a function $F: R^n \to R$ we say that F is α-*quasi-convex* at x if for any $c \neq 0$, $c^\mathsf{T} Df(x) = 0$ implies $c^\mathsf{T} D^2 f(x) c > \alpha |c|^2$. Define α-quasi-concavity in the obvious way. Inequality (i) of corollary 4.1 simply says that the Hamiltonian is α-quasi-convex in z_1. Let $\tilde{H}(z) = H(z + (\bar{q}, \bar{k})) - \rho(z_1 + \bar{q})^\mathsf{T} z_2$. Then (ii) says that $\tilde{H}$ is β-quasi-concave in z_2. Note that ρ introduces a distortion that vanishes at $\rho = 0$.

The general result is now stated. Let $G: R^{2n} \to M[R^{2n}, R^{2n}]$ (the set of all $2n \times 2n$ real matrices) be such that $G(z)$ is positive definite for all z. In what follows $G(z)$ will be assumed to be continuously differentiable. Let

$$j \equiv \begin{bmatrix} 0 & I_n \\ I_n & 0 \end{bmatrix},$$

where I_n is the $n \times n$ identity matrix. Put $\alpha(z) \equiv jG + (jG)^\mathsf{T}$. Let

$$D(z) \equiv [(\alpha(z)J(z))^\mathsf{T} + \alpha(z)J(z)] + \alpha'(z)$$

where $\alpha'(z) \equiv \sum_{r=1}^{2n} (\partial \alpha / \partial z_r) F_r$, the trajectory derivative of the matrix $\alpha(z)$. Now consider the system

$$\dot{z} = F(z). \tag{4.12}$$

We now state the following theorem.

Theorem 4.2. Suppose that (4.12) obeys assumptions

(a) 0 is the unique rest point of (4.12),
(b) 0 is L.A.S. in the sense that the linearization of $\dot{z}_2 = F_2[g(z_2), z_2]$ at $z_2 = 0$ has all eigenvalues with negative real parts,
(c) Let K be a compact subset of the bounded manifold.

Then, $\bigcup_{z \in K} \bigcup_{t \geq 0} \phi_t(z)$ is bounded, and, furthermore, the following basic property holds.

Assumption 1. For all $w \in R^{2n}$, $w \neq 0$ for all $z \neq 0$, we have

$$w^\mathsf{T} \alpha(z) F(z) = 0 \tag{4.13}$$

implies

$$w^{\mathrm{T}}D(z)w > 0. \tag{4.14}$$

Then all trajectories in the bounded manifold converge to 0 as $t \to \infty$.

The proof of this theorem is long and involved, and is done in a sequence of lemmas. For a proof see Brock and Scheinkman (1975).

Hartman and Olech's basic result in Hartman (1964, theorem 14.1) is closely related to this theorem. To see this, put $\alpha(z) = -2G(z)$. Assumption 1 then becomes Hartman and Olech's (H–O) assumption.

Theorem 4.2 would not be interesting if all it did was restate Hartman and Olech. Its interest lies in applicability to systems where the stable manifold W (where $W \equiv \{z_0 : \phi_t(z_0) \to 0$ as $t \to \infty\}$) is not all of R^{2n}. In particular, the important special case of MHDS that we are interested in generates systems where W is n-dimensional.

For example, let $G(z) \equiv I_{2n}$, the $2n \times 2n$ identity matrix. Assumption 1 becomes

$$w^{\mathrm{T}}jF(z) = 0 \quad \text{implies} \quad w^{\mathrm{T}}[jJ(z) + J^{\mathrm{T}}(z)j]w > 0. \tag{4.15}$$

Note that

$$w^{\mathrm{T}}[jJ(z) + J^{\mathrm{T}}(z)j]w = 2w^{\mathrm{T}}Q(z)w, \tag{4.16}$$

where

$$Q(z) = \begin{bmatrix} H_{11}(z) & (\rho/2)I_n \\ (\rho/2)I_n & -H_{22}(z) \end{bmatrix}. \tag{4.17}$$

We have reported in this chapter some recent progress toward providing a comprehensive analysis of G.A.S. of optimal controls generated by MHDSs. Several topics for future research follow in the next section.

5. Miscellaneous applications and exercises

(1) A more general notion of long-run behavior needs to be formulated. There is really no economic reason to rule out limit cycles, for example. It is, therefore, necessary to build a theory that allows more general limit sets than rest points, and find sufficient conditions on preferences and technology for a minimal limit set to be stable in some sense. This kind of theory where sets more general than points, cycles and tori can be attractors, will be treated in the next chapter.

(2) Both our results and the Cass-Shell-Rockafellar (CSR) results are *small ρ* theorems. In other words, the sufficient conditions for G.A.S. are most likely to hold when ρ is small. However, the Cass-Koopmans' one good model is G.A.S. independent of the size of ρ. Intuition suggests that if we perturb such an economy slightly, it will still be G.A.S. This suggests development of a notion of block dominant diagonal for MHDSs to parallel the development of dominant diagonal notions in the study of the Walrasian tâtonnement. See McKenzie (1960). Perhaps a more fruitful approach will build on Pearce's (1974) notion of block dominance.

(3) It is natural to extend our findings and the CSR results to uncertainty. Some results in this area are reported in Magill (1977b), Brock and Majumdar (1978), Brock and Magill (1979), and Bhattacharya and Majumdar (1980), but much more remains to be done.

(4) One of the original motivations for introducing positive definite matrices, $G(x)$, into the Hartman-Olech framework was that this is needed to obtain their result. Consider the differential equations

$$\dot{x} = f(x), f(0) = 0.$$

Let

$$\Gamma(x) = \underset{1 \leq i < j \leq n}{\text{maximum}} \{\lambda_i(x) + \lambda_j(x)\},$$

where $\lambda_r(x)$ is an eigenvalue of the symmetric matrix $[J^{\mathrm{T}}(x) + J(x)]/2$.

Theorem 5.1. (Hartman and Olech in Hartman (1964, p. 549).) If $\Gamma(x) \leq 0$ for all $x \neq 0$ and 0 is L.A.S. then 0 is G.A.S.

See Hartman (1964, p. 549) in order to be convinced that matrices of the form $G(x) = p(x)I_n, p(x) > 0$ for all $x, p : R^n \to R$ must be introduced into the basic Hartman and Olech method in order to obtain the above theorem. The above theorem is important because Γ is an easy quantity to interpret.

It is worth searching for an analog of theorem 5.1 for MHDS.

(5) Burmeister and Graham (1973) have exhibited a class of models where G.A.S. holds under conditions not sensitive to the size of ρ. Furthermore, their G.A.S. models do not satisfy either the CSR hypotheses or the hypotheses in this chapter. Therefore, a general stability hypothesis that covers the one good model, the Burmeister-Graham models and the CSR-Brock-Scheinkman models, remains to be developed. Further evidence to support this proposition is the Ryder-Heal (1973) experience. Some of their G.A.S. results are not dependent on the size of ρ.

Results reported in Brock and Scheinkman (1977a) on adjustment cost models indicate the existence of a large class of models where the CSR-Brock-Scheinkman small ρ conditions do not hold, but G.A.S. does hold. This class is basically the class where the Liapunov function $V = \dot{k}^T H_{qq}^{-1} \dot{k}$ together with concavity of the value function yields $\dot{V} < 0$.

(6) Araujo and Scheinkman (1977) obtain conditions for G.A.S. for discrete time models that are independent of the discount rate, except around the steady state.

(7) Kurz (1968a, 1969) studies the general instability of a class of competitive growth and the inverse optimal control problem respectively. Kurz points out that a solution of the inverse optimal control problem for a given competitive path may provide valuable information regarding the *stability* properties of the path under consideration. Chang (1988) extends the inverse optimal problem to the stochastic case.

6. Further remarks and references

The qualitative study of optimal economic growth has attracted the attention of economic theorists for a number of years. One major focus of this research has been to find sufficient conditions on models of economic growth for the convergence of growth paths to a steady state. Cass and Shell (1976a) present the Hamiltonian formulation of competitive dynamical systems that arise in capital theory. In this chapter we present a set of conditions on the Hamiltonian for such dynamical systems to converge to a steady state as time tends to infinity.

We refer the reader to the Cass and Shell (1976a) paper for an introduction to competitive dynamical systems and a complete survey of the literature.

The first branch of the literature on problem 1 is fairly complete. It studies the linear approximation of (1.1) in a neighborhood of a rest point. Eigenvalues have a well-known symmetric structure that determines the local behavior. Kurz (1968a), Samuelson (1972a) and Levhari and Liviatan (1972) are some representative references. See also the paper by Liviatan and Samuelson (1969) which is an important study of the limits of linear analysis and the relevance of multiple steady states stability and instability.

Although the amount of literature on problem 1 is extensive there are no general results on global stability. The simplest case with $n = 1$, that is, the one good optimal growth model, is well understood. Standard references are Cass (1965), Koopmans (1965) and Burmeister and Dobell (1970). Ryder and Heal (1973) analyze a case of (1.1) for $n = 2$. They generate a variety of examples of different qualitative behavior of optimal paths. Burmeister and Graham (1973) present an analysis of a model where there is a set S containing the steady state capital $\bar{k}$ such that for $k \in S$, the value of q along an optimal path is independent of k. See Burmeister and Graham (1973, p. 149).

The case $\rho = 0$ is the famous Ramsey problem, studied first by Ramsey (1928) for the one good model, then by Gale (1967), McKenzie (1968), McFadden (1967) and Brock (1970) for the n goods model in discrete time and by Rockafellar (1970a) for continuous time. These results state, roughly speaking, that if $H(q, k)$ is strictly convex in q and strictly concave in k and $\rho = 0$, then all solution paths of (1.1) that are optimal converge to a unique steady state $(\bar{q}, \bar{k})$ as $t \to \infty$ independently of (q_0, k_0).

Scheinkman (1976) has proved a result that shows that the qualitative behavior for $\rho = 0$ is preserved for small changes in ρ near $\rho = 0$.

Some additional recent references are Becker (1980), Benhabib and Nishimura (1981), McKenzie (1982), Feinstein and Oren (1983), DasGupta (1985), Boyd (1986a, 1986b), Chang (1987, 1988), Epstein (1987) and Becker et al. (1987). Burmeister (1980) gives a comprehensive exposition of dynamic capital theory.

CHAPTER 10

INTRODUCTION TO CHAOS AND OTHER ASPECTS OF NONLINEARITY

> Again I saw that under the sun the race is not to the swift nor the battle to the strong, nor bread to the wise, nor riches to the intelligent, nor favor to the men of skill; but *time* and *chance* happen to them all.
>
> Ecclesiastes 9.11,
> Revised standard version.

1. Introduction

The previous chapters did not spend much time on understanding sources of *instability* in economics. The main focus was on sufficient conditions for convergence to stationary states, i.e., global asymptotic *stability* of the optimum or equilibrium dynamics. In contrast, the present chapter focuses on systems that generate complex time series behavior that ranges from toroidic trajectories to a form of instability known as deterministic chaos.

Recently there has been a lot of interest in nonlinear deterministic economic models that generate highly irregular trajectories. Some representative references include Benhabib and Day (1981, 1982), Benhabib and Nishimura (1985), Grandmont (1985, 1986), Day (1982, 1983), Stutzer (1980), Day and Shafer (1983), Deneckere and Pelikan (1986), Boldrin and Montrucchio (1986).

Grandmont (1986) and the survey paper by Baumol and Benhabib (1988) can be used as initial reading. Eckmann and Ruelle (1985) is a nice review of the ergodic theory of chaos and strange attractors. This chapter relies on Grandmont (1986), Baumol and Benhabib (1988), Eckmann and Ruelle (1985) and their references.

Mathematical interest in deterministic dynamical systems that generate apparently random (at least to the naked eye and to some statistical tests) trajectories has dated, at least, back to Poincare's work in the late 1800s. Interest by the natural sciences was piqued by the seminal and controversial (at the time) paper by Ruelle and Takens (1971) who argued that the traditional model of fluid flow turbulence was structurally unstable and that a dynamical system that converged to a low dimensional deterministic chaotic attractor was a better model of certain types of fluid flow turbulence than the traditional one.

Ruelle and Takens also proposed that a useful way of looking at transitions to turbulence was to first write down a differential equation model of the system, $dx/dt = F(x, \mu)$, where x is the *state* of the system and μ denotes a vector of *slow moving parameters*. The state may be a finite dimensional vector, or, in the case of a fluid, a point in an infinite dimensional space. The second step was to study the long run behavior of the system. The idea was that the long run behavior would converge to some attractor set $A(\mu)$ and the long run behavior may change (go through phases) as you change μ. For example, the parameter, μ, might be the Reynolds number in a fluid flow experiment. As you increase the parameter μ, the long run behavior of the system becomes more complex in many cases.

An example is the difference equation,

$$x(t+1) = \mu x(t)(1 - x(t)).$$

As you increase the parameter, μ, the long run behavior progressively passes from a fixed point, to a two-cycle, to a four-cycle, ..., to a 2^n, cycle, ..., to chaos. This is the *period doubling* route to chaos. In Grandmont (1985) it was the risk aversion of the old agents in a two period overlapping generations model that played the role of μ in his example of a period doubling route to chaos in an economic model. It was the discount rate on future utility in the Boldrin and Montrucchio and Deneckere and Pelikan models published in Grandmont (1986).

The Ruelle and Takens (1971) proposal was radical. After all, if anything looks stochastic it is turbulence. The idea that a system with only a few active modes could generate such complex behavior *actually observed* in nature was rather controversial. Experimental work discussed by Roux et al. (1983) and Swinney (1983) has documented the existence of chaos in nature. After this experimental evidence appeared, interest in the study of chaos was greatly increased.

We remark that when studying the natural science literature in this area it is important for the economic theorist brought up in the tradition of abstract general equilibrium theory to realize that many natural scientists are not impressed by mathematical arguments showing that "anything can happen" in a system loosely disciplined by general axioms. Just showing existence of logical possibilities is not enough for such skeptics. The parameters of the system needed to get the erratic behavior must conform to parameter values established by empirical studies or the behavior must actually be documented in nature.

To expand upon this point, a style of research in macroeconomics that many natural scientists may find congenial is that exemplified in the debate on rational expectations business cycle models. Recall that Lucas, Barro, Sargent, Prescott and others (see for example Lucas (1981) on monetary misperception models, McCallum's (1986) review and other papers in Barro) opened a debate by showing that a class of tightly specified, parsimoniously parameterized *stochastic* economic models built on rational economic behavior, rather than postulated reduced forms of the IS/LM type, can account for a collection of stylized facts about business cycles. This caused the ground rules of debate to change towards theorizing disciplined by empirical regularities that show up in data (such as the observed structure of estimated vector autoregressions in Litterman and Weiss (1985) and their references, especially to Sims). To put it another way, consider an obvious fact such as Keynes' remark that labor will resist a real wage cut of equal size much more if it is activated by a cut in nominal wages rather than by a rise in the rate of inflation. Such common sense claim will not be accepted today unless one can produce a data set where it is shown that this effect leaves an empirical trace in that data set.

The criteria of what constitutes a successful direct argument and what is a rebuttal have changed. For example, to rebut the new neoclassicals such as Lucas, Sargent, Barro, Prescott, and others, the critics have to produce models based on plausible purposive economic behavior that can better account for empirical regularities in aggregative macroeconomic time series data than the neoclassical models. An example of this style of rebuttal is Summers' (1986a) attack on real business cycle models. Successful attacks in this area replace the target model with another model, that is a priori, reasonable theoretically but accounts for a much wider spectrum of facts by paying a low price in terms of additional parameters. A good example in finance is the *excess volatility debate* (Kleidon (1986b) and references).

Another example of the style of rebuttal of classical theory is Shiller (1984) and Summers' (1986b) attack on the *efficient markets hypothesis.* They propose alternative models of stock returns that lead to the prediction of negative autocorrelations in returns over 3 to 5 year periods of time. This prediction has been supported by evidence in papers by Poterba and Summers (1987) and Fama and French (1986). We attempt to follow the same research style in this chapter.

To return to the mathematical literature, Ruelle and Takens (1971) studied carefully the theoretical properties of equations of fluid flow during transition to turbulence. Also the equations themselves came from tightly reasoned physics – not some loosely constrained axiom system. Still, natural scientists were skeptical.

Interest in the Ruelle and Takens scenario and chaos theory exploded when experimentalists documented evidence supporting the existence of low dimensional chaotic attractors in nature.

1.1. Elementary notions of chaos

Recall the dynamical systems studied in the earlier chapters and the emphasis on locating sufficient conditions on tastes and technology so that the optimum or equilibrium dynamics were globally asymptotically stable. That is to say, the dynamics are described by a factor of differential equations, $dx/dt = F(x(t))$, where the steady state is globally asymptotically stable (G.A.S.). Notice that such a system has the property that trajectories starting from two distinct initial conditions converge together as time goes to ∞. Notice also that if you know the initial conditions and the law of motion, F, you can retrocede the history of the system and predict the future. In the G.A.S. system if you make a small error in measuring today's state, the error shrinks away to zero as time moves forward. Hence, the error melts away as $t \to \infty$, in a t-step ahead forecast based on knowledge of the law of motion, F, and a slightly erroneous measure of today's state. The reverse is the case for a t-backcast. If, knowing the law of motion, F, and making a small error in measuring today's state of the system, you backcast t periods into the past in an attempt to find out what the state of the system was t periods ago, your ignorance about where the system was grows with t.

Contrast this behavior with the behavior of a deterministic chaos: (i) trajectories locally diverge away from each other, and (ii) small changes in initial conditions build up exponentially fast into large changes in evolution. The impact of small measurement errors in today's system state on t period ahead forecasts and t period behind backcasts are exactly the opposite. It is as if you turned your views of science, measurement, history, and evolution upside down.

At the risk of repeating, we explain why such a contrast raises important issues in macroeconomic modelling. The dominant approach to macro-economic modelling (see the earlier references as well as many Keynesian approaches) assumes a G.A.S. system buffeted by exogenous stochastic shocks. If the shocks are small enough relative to trend levels, the system may be approximated by a linear (possibly in logs) stochastic time series model. See for example Kydland and Prescott (1982) or King et al. (1987). Writers such as Blatt (1980) attack such modelling as being unable to capture fundamental nonlinearity in economic nature. Blatt argues that nonlinearity is so fundamental that it cannot be handled by a mere changing of units, detrending, and deseasonalization as in conventional macroeconomics.

Obviously, even a nonlinear changing of units cannot change an unstable system such as a chaotic system into a G.A.S. system. For example, if $x(t+1) = F(x(t))$, and $y = G(x)$, with G assumed to be smooth, one to one, with a smooth inverse, then $y(t+1) = G \circ F \circ G^{-1}(y(t))$, is G.A.S. if and only if $x(t+1) = F(x(t))$ is G.A.S. Here $\circ$ denotes composition. If the underlying system is so nonlinear that the best attempt to transform to linearity after astutely changing units, deseasonalizing, and detrending before fitting linear models will not give a good fit, then the basic nonlinearity should show up as temporal dependence in the residuals of the best linear fit.

We plan to report on some attempts to test for the existence of low dimensional chaotic attractors in economics next. Before going further into detail let us set out some basic ideas and concepts of chaos theory.

1.2. Preview of chaos and its empirical tests

Look at the following difference equation, $x(t+1) = f(x(t))$, studied by Sakai and Tokumaru (1980). They show that most trajectories of the *tent maps*

$$f(x) = x/a, \quad 0 \le x \le a, \quad f(x) = (1-x)/(1-a),$$
$$a \le x \le 1, \quad 0 < a < 1,$$

(1.1)

generate the same autocorrelation coefficients as the first-order auto-regressive $(AR(1))$ process

$$v(t+1) = (2a-1)v(t) + u(t+1),$$

(1.2)

where $\{u(t)\}$ are independent and identically distributed (IID) random variables. The maps (1.1) are a good example of what is called *low dimensional deterministic chaos*, a concept which is explained below.

The case $a = \frac{1}{2}$ is especially striking. In this case the autocorrelation function and the spectrum generated by most trajectories are the same as that of white noise, i.e., the IID sequence $\{u(t)\}$. Bunow and Weiss (1979) display results of calculation of empirical spectra for several examples of low dimensional deterministic chaos including the case $a = \frac{1}{2}$ of (1.1).

Two basic properties of deterministic chaos are well illustrated by the simple tent map recursion (1.1). First, this recursion generates, for almost all in the sense of Lebesgue measure, initial conditions $x_0 \in (0, 1)$, trajectories such that

$$\#\{x(t), \quad 1 \le t \le T \colon x(t) \in [a, b]\}/T \to b - a; \quad a, b \in [0, 1], a < b. \quad (1.3)$$

That is to say the map (1.1) has a nondegenerate invariant measure μ (not the same as μ in the explanation of the Ruelle and Takens scenario) just like the stochastic growth models of Brock and Mirman (1972), Kydland and Prescott (1982), and others that are used in macroeconomics.

The measure μ is an *invariant measure* for map f if $\mu(f^{-1}(S)) = \mu(S)$ for all measurable sets S. Almost all trajectories converge (in the sense of (1.3)) to it. In the case of (1.1), an invariant measure of the map f turns out to be the uniform measure on $[0, 1]$, i.e., the ordinary Lebesgue measure on $[0, 1]$. This is the meaning of (1.3): the long run fraction of $x(t)$ contained in $[a, b]$ is just $b - a$. In general the long run fraction of $x(t)$ in some set S converges to $\mu(S)$.

Care must be taken with invariant measures in chaos theory. In general, for a given map f, there are many of them. Eckmann and Ruelle (1985) discuss criteria for selecting particular ones and conditions for convergence of time averages to that particular one. For simplicity, we will assume that we have a unique ergodic, invariant measure in the sense that we have a unique μ such that for all measurable sets S, and for almost all initial conditions x_0 in $[0, 1]$, the long run fraction of $x(t)$ in S is $\mu(S)$. Collet and Eckmann (1980) discuss sufficient conditions on maps for the existence of a unique, ergodic, absolutely continuous with respect to Lebesgue, invariant measure.

Second, suppose one makes a small error in measuring the initial state so that it is only known that the initial state lies in the interval

$$I = [a - \varepsilon, a + \varepsilon], \quad \varepsilon > 0. \quad (1.4)$$

Now imagine that at date 1, one must forecast $x(t)$ based on the knowledge (1.4). The loss of precision in the forecast (the length of the interval where one knows that $x(t)$ lies) grows exponentially fast as t grows in the short term until one knows nothing, i.e., one only knows that $x(t)$ lies in $[0, 1]$.

This property means that we have the *potential* ability, if we could measure x_0 with infinite accuracy, to forecast $x(t)$ perfectly.

A third property of deterministic chaos (redundant given the two properties listed but repeated for emphasis) is that the time series $\{x(t)\}$ appears stochastic even though it is generated by a deterministic system (1.1). More precisely, in the case of (1.1), the empirical spectrum and autocovariance function is the same as that of white noise, i.e., the same as that generated by independently and identically distributed uniform $[0, 1]$ random variables.

Example (1.1) illustrates the need for a test for stochasticity beyond spectral and autocovariance analysis. Simply plotting $x(t+1)$ against $x(t)$ will not do because examples like

$$x(t+1) = F(x(t), \dots, x(t-q)), \quad q \geq 1 \tag{1.5}$$

can be generated that are chaotic.

Intuitively one would think that a time series is generated by a deterministic chaotic generator rather than a random generator if the dimension of the time series is low. After all if the time series $\{x(t)\}$ is generated by (1.1) then the sequence of ordered pairs, $\{(x(t), x(t+1))\}$, lies on a one dimensional set embedded in a two dimensional space. In general, if $\{x(t)\}$ is generated by deterministic chaos then the sequence of ordered m-tuples, $\{(x(t), \dots, x(t+m-1))\}$, lies in an r dimensional space for all embedding dimensions m, big enough. Thus, as a matter of pure theory, a test for deterministic chaos is simple: calculate the dimension of $\{x(t)\}$ and examine if it is small.

Unfortunately, it is not easy to come up with a notion of dimension that is easy to calculate and gives reliable results. A popular notion of dimension used in natural science is the notion of correlation dimension due to Grassberger and Procaccia (1983a, b) and Takens (1983) which is discussed in what follows.

An efficient way to test for chaos is to consider the following quantity

$$C_m(e, T) = \#\{(t, s), \quad 1 \leq t, \quad s \leq T: \|x_t^m - x_s^m\| < e\}/T_m^2, \tag{1.6}$$

where $T_m = T - (m-1)$, $x_t^m = (x(t), \dots, x(t+m-1))$.

Brock and Dechert (1987) show that

$$C_m(e, T) \to C_m(e), \quad T \to \infty, \tag{1.7}$$

for almost all initial conditions. They prove (1.7) for noisy chaotic systems also.

The correlation dimension is estimated by physicists (see the surveys of Eckmann and Ruelle (1985), and Brock (1986a)) by plotting $\ln(C_m(e, T))$ against $\ln(e)$ for large T and looking for constant slope zones of this plot that appear independent of m for large enough m. Here ln denotes the natural logarithm.

The definition of *correlation dimension* in embedding dimension m is

$$d_m = \lim \lim \ln[C_m(e, T)]/\ln(e), \quad T \to \infty, \quad e \to 0, \tag{1.8}$$

where the limit is taken w.r.t. T first and w.r.t. e second.

The correlation dimension itself is given by,

$$d = \lim d_m, \quad m \to \infty. \tag{1.9}$$

Brock (1986a), Brock and Sayers (1988), and Scheinkman and LeBaron (1987) estimate various measures of dimension that were stimulated by the theoretical quantities above. More specifically, Brock (1986a) and Brock and Sayers (1988) estimate several measures of dimension for macroeconomic time series data. Two of them are:

$$SC_m(e, f, T) = [\ln(C_m(e, T)) - \ln(C_m(f, T))]/[\ln(e) - \ln(f)], \tag{1.10}$$

$$\alpha_m(e, T) = \ln(C_m(e, T))/\ln(e). \tag{1.11}$$

The quantity, SC_m is an estimate of the slope of the plot of $\ln(C_m)$ against $\ln(e)$, i.e.,

$$\text{slope at } e = C'_m(e, T)e/C_m(e, T). \tag{1.12}$$

Note that the slope at e is just the elasticity of C_m at e. It measures the percentage change in new neighbors that a typical m-history x_t^m gets when e is increased to $e + de$. Hence, dimension is a crude measure of the level of parsimony (the minimal number of parameters) needed in a dynamic model to fit the data.

However, interpretation of dimension estimates from data is tricky. A low estimated dimension does *not* indicate the presence of deterministic chaos. It is shown in Brock (1986a) that the near unit root processes which are ubiquitous in macroeconomics and finance, such as in Nelson and Plosser (1982), generate low dimension estimates by this method. For example the $AR(1)$,

$$y(t+1) = by(t) + n(t+1), \quad \{n\} \text{ IID},$$

will generate low dimension estimates, indeed, the estimated dimension will approach unity as $b \to 1$.

Brock (1986a) proposes a way to avoid this problem by fitting an $AR(q)$ by Box-Jenkins methods to the data $\{x(t)\}$. If the data was generated by deterministic chaos then the dimension of the data would be the same as the dimension of the $AR(q)$ residuals for any q.

It is explained in Brock (1986a) that this diagnostic may reject deterministic chaos too many times when in fact it is true. The reason is that the estimated residuals consist of an approximately linear combination of q iterates (and lower order iterates) of a chaotic map. For large q this puts in so many "wiggles" that the estimated dimension will approach that of an IID process. Hence, the estimated dimension of the residuals will be so much larger than the estimated dimension of the data that you will reject deterministic chaos even if it is true. This problem is likely to be especially acute in actual applications in trying to detect the presence of deterministic chaos when the dimension of the underlying chaos is of intermediate size, say between 3 and 6.

Before going further it is worthwhile to explain why anyone should care about testing for the presence of deterministic chaos rather than stochasticity in economic data. In reality we doubt that anyone (including writers such as Day, Benhabib, and Grandmont) believes that *strictly* deterministic models like those discussed in Grandmont (1985) and references generate observed macroeconomic time series. Study, for example, the views of Granger (1987) who has done substantial work in nonlinear time series analysis. A potentially serious issue is whether actual data is generated by a stochastic model of the form, for example,

$$y(t+1) = G(y(t), \quad u(t+1)), y \in R^n, u \in R^p, \{u\} \text{ IID},$$

G is chaotic when u is fixed at its mean, a, and the randomness in u is small relative to the apparent randomness in trajectories generated by $G(\cdot, a)$. This is aptly called *noisy chaos*.

Generalizing, the most serious issue is whether the data under scrutiny is generated (after transformation to stationarity by detrending and deseasonalization) by a process G that is so nonlinear that a linear quadratic approximation to the parent optimal control problem, i.e., a linear approximation to G, like that used by Kydland and Prescott (1982) and formally justified by the method of Fleming (1971) as used by Magill (1977a) is completely misleading.

We do not think anyone in macroeconomics needs to be convinced of the drastic difference in policy implications of a view that macroeconomic fluctuations are generated in the main by endogenous propagation mechanisms rather than exogenous shocks. Theories that support the existence of endogenous propagation mechanisms typically suggest strong government stabilization policies. Theories that argue that business cycles are, in the main, caused by exogenous shocks suggest that government stabilization policies are, at best, an exercise in futility and, at worst, harmful. See Lucas (1981) for a strong statement of the exogenous shock view.

The vast bulk of econometric methods in macroeconomics use linear models after appropriate units changes and detrendings. Exceptions are bilinear models (Granger and Andersen (1978)), semi nonparametric models (Gallant and Tauchen (1986)), time deformations models (Stock (1985, 1986, 1987), ARCH models (Engle (1982)), GARCH models (Bollerslev 1986)), and modelling nonlinearity with normal polynomial expansions (Geweke (1987)).

The next section of this chapter explains tests for nonlinearity that were inspired by concepts in chaos theory. These tests for nonlinearity, low dimensional deterministic chaos, and temporal dependence in residuals of best fit linear models (after units changes and detrending) will be applied in macroeconomics and finance later in this chapter.

2. Statistical theory for nonlinear dynamics

We begin with a definition.

Definition 2.1.   The series $\{a_t\}$ has a C^2 *deterministic chaotic explanation* if there exists a system, (h, F, x_0), such that $h \in C^2$ maps R^n to R, $F \in C^2$ maps R^n to R^n, $a_t = h(x_t)$, $x_{t+1} = F(x_t)$, and x_0 is the initial condition at $t = 0$. The map F is chaotic in the sense that there is a unique, indecomposable chaotic attractor A for F such that the trajectory $\{x_t\}$ lies in A. We shall also assume that F has a unique, ergodic, invariant measure on A.

We need to expand on the meaning of this definition. Here C^2 denotes the set of twice continuously differentiable functions. Think of h as being a measuring apparatus and F as an unknown, to the observer, law of motion. The scientist is trying to learn about F by taking observations using a measuring apparatus, h. Here the map F is deterministic and the state space is n-dimensional. In order to make statistical analysis valid it is required that all trajectories lie on an indecomposable attractor A, and to get the property of chaos it is required that any two nearby trajectories generated by F on A locally diverge.

The local divergence property is formalized by requiring that the largest *Liapunov exponent, L,* be positive (Brock (1986a)); where L is given by

$$L = \lim \ln[\,\|DF^t(x) \cdot v\|\,]/t. \tag{2.1}$$

Under the regularity conditions in Eckmann and Ruelle (1985) the limit in
(2.1) as $t \to \infty$ is independent of almost all initial conditions x and almost
all direction vectors v. D denotes derivative, and $F'(x)$ is t applications of
the map F to x. This is a measure of the average local rate of spread between
two nearby trajectories. It is positive for chaos and is $\ln(2)$ for the tent map
(1.1). The term *chaos* is used to express this notion of sensitive dependence
on initial conditions which is captured by the requirement that the largest
Liapunov exponent be positive.

There are several algorithms that are used by natural scientists to estimate
the spectrum of Liapunov exponents as explained in Eckmann and Ruelle
(1985) and their references. The largest Liapunov exponent has been estimated for some economic data by Barnett and Chen (1987) and Brock and
Sayers (1988). But no *statistical* theory of inference seems to exist for
Liapunov estimation. Some mathematical theory for the Wolf et al. (1985)
algorithm was provided by Brock and Dechert (1987).

The following proposition is needed. *Residual Diagnostic* (Brock
(1986a)): Fit any time series model of the form $G \in C^2$, $G(a_t, \ldots, a_{t-L}, \beta) =$
ε_t to your data $\{a_t\}$. Here β denotes the parameter vector to be estimated
and $\{\varepsilon_t\}$ is an IID stochastic process with zero mean and finite variance.
Then the theoretical dimension and largest Liapunov function are (generically) independent of the functional form of G and the number of lags, L.

For details of this proof see Brock (1986a) and references. Outlining the
proof, let $\{e_t\}$ and b denote the sequence of estimated residuals and the
estimated value of β respectively. Then

$$e_t = G(a_t, \ldots, a_{t-L}, b) \equiv M(x_{t-L}).$$

The function M is just an observer of $\{x_m\}$. Since the largest Liapunov
exponent and the correlation dimension are independent of the observer
(generically), therefore the dimension and largest Liapunov exponent of
$\{e_t\}$ is the same as for $\{a_t\}$. This completes the outline.

The word *generic* means except for hairline cases. In practice it is
treacherous to give precise meaning to this concept and there is more than
one way to do it. We want to exclude, for example, observers, $h: R^n \to R$
that map all points of R^n to a constant, such as zero. Obviously in such a
case, $\{a_t\}$ will be a constant sequence and will have dimension zero independent of the underlying dynamics, $x(t+1) = F(x(t))$. But, intuitively, such
observers are hairline cases relative to the space of all observer functions;
i.e., that such observers are not generic. See Eckmann and Ruelle (1985)
and Takens (1980) for concepts of genericity that are adequate to exclude
these degenerate cases.

Chaos is quantified by another measure besides positivity of the largest Liapunov exponent. This concept is called *Kolmogorov entropy*. The idea is simple. Imagine that you are an observer who cannot tell that two states within distance $e > 0$ of each other are different. For example you may be an 8-bit computer. Two states have to be $d > e$ units apart before you can tell that they are distinct. Entropy is a measure of how fast F produces information in the sense of how many iterations of F on the two indistinguishable states are necessary before we can tell that their images under iteration by F are different. See Eckmann and Ruelle (1985) for the details. It turns out that one of the statistical concepts that we shall talk about here is closely related to Kolmogorov entropy.

A useful lower bound to Kolmogorov entropy (Grassberger and Procaccia (1983b)) is defined as follows:

$$K = \lim \lim \lim K(e, m, T), \quad T \to \infty, \ m \to \infty, \ e \to 0, \quad \text{where,} \qquad (2.2)$$

$$K(e, m, T) = \ln\{C_m(e, T)/C_{m+1}(e, T)\}. \qquad (2.3)$$

Here the limit is taken first w.r.t. T, second w.r.t. m, third w.r.t. e.

K can be looked at from another perspective. Brock and Dechert (1987) show for $T = \infty$ that

$$C_{m+1}(e) = \text{Prob}\{|x(t+m) - x(s+m)| < e : \|x_t^m - x_s^m\| < e\}C_m(e). \qquad (2.4)$$

Equation (2.4) captures a measure of how well the m-past helps to predict the future at likeness of the past e. From (2.2)–(2.3) we see directly that $K(e, m, \infty)$ is a measure of how poorly the m-past helps to predict the future at likeness of the past e. Note that if $\{x\}$ is IID, $K(e, m, \infty) = -\ln\{C_1(e)\} \to \infty$, $e \to 0$. These considerations lead naturally to a new statistical test for temporal dependence.

2.1. Size and power characteristics of the BDS test

Brock et al. (1987) create a family of statistics based upon the correlation integral C_m. This is calculated by first putting

$$C_m(e, T) = \#\{(t, s), \quad 1 \le t, s \le T : \|x_t^m - x_s^m\| < e\}/T_m,$$
$$T_m \equiv T - (m - 1). \qquad (2.5)$$

·Second, the limit of (2.5) exists almost surely under modest stationarity and ergodicity assumptions on the stochastic process under scrutiny (Brock and Dechert (1987)). Call this limit $C_m(e)$.

Brock et al. (1987) consider tests based upon the statistic,

$$W_m(e, T) \equiv T^{1/2} D_m(e, T)/b_m(e, T), \quad D_m \equiv C_m - [C_1]^m, \tag{2.6}$$

where b_m is an estimate of the standard deviation under the IID null. Brock, Dechert and Scheinkman show, under the null of IID, that $W_m \to N(0, 1)$, as $T \to \infty$. The W statistic is shown to have higher power against certain alternatives than the tests of independence based upon the bispectrum. The reason is that the bispectrum is zero for the class of processes with zero third-order cumulants. There are many dependent processes with zero third-order cumulants.

Given an IID stochastic process $\{X_t\}$ consider the formula

$$b_m = (1, -mC_{m-1})' \Sigma (1, -mC_{m-1}), \quad \text{where,} \tag{2.7}$$

$$\Sigma_{11} = 4(Q - C^2), \tag{2.8}$$

$$\Sigma_{22} = 4(Q^m - C^{2m}) + 8 \sum_{j=1}^{m-1} (Q^{m-j} C^{2j} - C^{2m}),$$

$$\Sigma_{12} = 2(Q + Q^m + 2QC^{m-1} - (C + C^m)^2)$$

$$+4 \sum_{j=1}^{m-1} (QC^{m-1} + Q^{m-j} C^{2j} - C^{1+m} - C^{2m})$$

$$-0.5(\Sigma_{11} + \Sigma_{22}), \quad \text{where,} \tag{2.9}$$

$$C = E\{I_e(X_i, X_j)\} \equiv C_1(e), \tag{2.10}$$

$$Q = E\{I_e(X_i, X_j) I_e(X_j, X_k)\}. \tag{2.11}$$

Here $I_e(X, Y)$ is just the indicator function of the event $\{|X - Y| < e\}$.

This formula for the standard deviation, b_m, used in the W statistic, is adapted from Brock, Dechert and Scheinkman by Scheinkman and LeBaron (1987).

Look at table 10.1, which displays results from Brock and Sayers (1988). Brock and Sayers fit best linear models, after transformation of units and detrending, in the usual manner. Recall that under the null hypothesis of correct fit the estimated residuals are asymptotically IID. If the residuals were actually IID the W statistics reported below would be asymptotically $N(0, 1)$. Of course the estimation process induces extra variance. Based on our own computer experiments and those reported in Scheinkman and LeBaron (1987) we do not believe that the correction is very large for most

Table 10.1
W statistics for residuals of linear models

Dim	#prs	*W*	Series	*N*
2	902	−0.63	ed	147
3	272	0.16	ed	147
4	92	1.44	ed	147
2	12 554	5.10	dsear1pd	433
3	5 176	6.52	dsear1pd	433
4	2 310	8.34	dsear1pd	433
2	12 555	5.21	dsear4pd	430
3	5 216	6.61	dsear4pd	430
4	2 338	8.35	dsear4pd	430
2	1 173	0.94	dsegpdi1	147
3	423	1.77	dsegpdi1	147
4	152	1.88	dsegpdi1	147
2	1 087	1.61	dsegpdi4	144
3	391	2.53	dsegpdi4	144
4	148	3.21	dsegpdi4	144
2	970	−0.50	dsegpdi8	140
3	344	1.40	dsegpdi8	140
4	121	1.79	dsegpdi8	140
2	54 848	15.97	edpig	715
3	32 072	20.09	edpig	715
4	19 519	24.10	edpig	715
2	1 617	5.19	edsun	170
3	642	6.90	edsun	170
4	239	6.47	edsun	170
2	990	3.24	edunemp	130
3	404	4.94	edunemp	130
4	163	5.32	edunemp	130
2	1 345	1.21	egpdid	147
3	506	1.57	egpdid	147
4	191	1.60	egpdid	147
2	841	4.21	empar2	130
3	316	5.94	empar2	130
4	128	7.64	empar2	130

Code for table 10.1 of W statistics
ed = residuals of $AR(2)$ fit to detrended U.S. real gnp; *dsear1pd* = residuals from an $AR(1)$ fit to the first difference of ln U.S. Industrial Production. The Industrial Production series is for U.S. post war quarterly data and is taken from Litterman and Weiss (1985); *dsear4pd* = residuals from an $AR(4)$ fit to the first difference of ln U.S. Industrial Production; *dsegpdi1, dsegpdi4, dsegpdi8*, are residuals from an $AR(1)$, $AR(4)$, $AR(8)$ fit to the first difference of ln real U.S. quarterly gross domestic investment (GPDI); *edpig* = residuals of an $AR(2)$ fit to detrended U.S. pigiron production; *edsun* = residuals of an $AR(2)$ fit to the Wolfer sunspot series; *edunemp* = residuals of an $AR(2)$ fit to U.S. unemployment rate; *egpdid* = residuals of an $AR(2)$ fit to linearly detrended ln real U.S. GPDI; *empar2* = residuals of an $AR(2)$ fit to linearly detrended ln U.S. employment. This table is drawn from Brock (1986a) and Brock and Sayers (1988) and we are thankful to Blake LeBaron for the computations.

cases in practice. Brock (1988b) has shown that the correction does not affect the first order asymptotics. In any event the reader is advised to keep this in mind while reading table 10.1.

Evidence is strong for nonlinearity in (a) industrial production, (b) civilian employment, (c) unemployment rate, (d) pigiron production, (e) Wolfer's sunspot numbers. Brock and Sayers (1988) also perform symmetry tests on many of these same series. Symmetry testing confirms the presence of nonlinearity.

While the evidence from the residual diagnostic did not favor the hypothesis of deterministic chaos we hope that we have made it clear that the residual diagnostic may falsely reject the hypothesis of deterministic chaos when in fact it is true. This problem of false rejection is likely to become more serious as the number of lags increases in the autoregressive linear time series models fitted to the data. It is worthwhile to amplify the argument in Brock (1986a) to explain why the residual diagnostic rejects deterministic chaos too often in short time series.

Let us use the tent map sequence, $x(t+1) = F(x(t))$, as a vehicle of exposition. Recall that $F(x) = 2x$, $x \le 0.5$, $F(x) = 2 - 2x$, $x \ge 0.5$. Two effects increase the estimated correlation dimension. First, as the embedding dimension, m, is increased, the estimated correlation dimension will increase. The reason for this is simple. Fix an m-history, x_t^m. Look at the fraction of m-histories, $\mu(e, x_t, m) = \#\{x_e^m: \|x_s^m - x_t^m\| < e\}$ for a fixed value of e. Relax e to $e + de$ and ask how many new neighbors of x_t^m are obtained. In a series of length T we can build $T_m = T - (m-1)$ m-histories. We know from Brock and Dechert (1987), that

$$\#\{x_e^m: \|x_s^m - x_t^m\| < e\}/T_m \to \int I_e(z_m, w_m)\mu_m(dw_m), \quad \text{as } T \to \infty, \quad (2.12)$$

where $z_m \equiv x_t^m$, $w_m \in R^m$, μ_m is the measure on R^m by the invariant measure μ for F, and $I_e(z_m, w_m)$ is the indicator function for the event, $\{w_m: \|w_m - z_m\| < e\}$.

If we use (2.12) to approximate $\mu(e, x_t, m)$, then an increase in m causes $\mu(e, x_t, m)$ to fall. So, for a fixed T, we will run out of comparable points as we increase m. But this is not the worst of it. The main problem is that x_t^m contains iterates F^q for $q \le m - 1$. For a fixed value of e, as we increase e to $e + de$ and count the extra neighbors of x_t^m that we get, the number of wiggles in F^q that cross the e-neighborhood of x_t^m increases as m increases. Hence for a large m, and a fixed value of e, this effect causes the number of new neighbors of x_t^m that we get to scale faster than the power 1 – the true dimension. Hence the estimated dimension is biased upward. To put it another way, we must decrease e as we increase m in order to keep the iterates F^q, $q \le m - 1$, from wiggling across the e-neighborhood of x_i^m. But then for fixed T we run out of data even faster as we increase m. This effect is amplified when the residual diagnostic is applied.

The estimated residuals of an $AR(p)$, say, fitted to data generated by the tent map contain tent map iterates, F^i, $i \le p$. When these residuals are embedded in m dimensions for correlation dimension estimation and for comparison with the estimated correlation dimension of the rough tent map data then the upward bias effect is compounded. That is to say, the estimated dimension of the $AR(p)$ residuals will tend to be larger than the theoretical value of 1. Or, to put it another way, you will need even a smaller value of e to get a range of scaling of unity for the $AR(p)$ residuals. As you increase p the upward bias in estimated dimension will tend to increase. This can be verified by computer experiments. Ramsey and Yuan (1987) have conducted computer experiments on some deterministic chaotic maps. These experiments show that dimension estimates as well as estimated standard deviations of dimension are biased in short samples.

The highest number of lags that Brock and Sayers (1988) fit to their data was 2. But computer experiments on the residual diagnostic using the tent map and the logistic, $x(t+1) = 4x(t)(1 - x(t))$, indicate that on sample sizes similar to those of Brock and Sayers (1988), the estimated correlation dimension of the estimated residuals of $AR(2)$'s fit to tent and logistic data range between 2 and 3, whereas the theoretical value is 1. Therefore, we are inclined to interpret the Brock and Sayers (1988) results as evidence against the hypothesis that low dimensional deterministic chaos is responsible for macroeconomic fluctuations about trend. This evidence is supplemented by the application of the W test to the estimated residuals of best fit linear models as in table 10.1. Turn now to theoretical arguments that shed light on the likelihood of macroeconomic chaos.

3. Roads to chaos in macroeconomics

In the last section we explained how time series data can be used to test for the presence of low dimensional deterministic chaos. The evidence adduced for deterministic chaos in the macroeconomic data analyzed above was weak. Evidence did exist for nonlinearity however. We warned that evidence of low correlation dimension does not make the case for deterministic chaos. Even evidence of a positive estimated largest Liapunov exponent does not make the case for chaos as Brock (1986a) explains.

Ruelle and Takens (1971) argue that in physics there are certain instances where one could make a fairly strong theoretical argument that chaos might be likely. Can we make a plausible theoretical case for the presence of chaos in macroeconomics? In this section we briefly examine and evaluate some theoretical arguments that have been presented for the presence of chaos in macroeconomics.

Recall that the Ruelle and Takens (1971) setup was a differential or a difference equation model, $x(t+1) = F(x(t), \mu)$, where x is an n dimensional state vector and μ is an r dimensional parameter vector. Different values of μ can give you different long run limiting behavior of the sequence $\{x(t)\}$. We saw a famous example of a map $F:[0, 1] \to [0, 1]$, i.e., $x(t+1) = \mu x(t)(1 - x(t))$, where as you keep increasing μ from smaller values to larger ones, the long run limiting behavior of $\{x(t)\}$ goes from a stable rest point, to a stable two-cycle, to a stable four-cycle, . . . , to a stable 2^n cycle, to chaos (Eckmann and Ruelle (1985)). This sequence of period doubling bifurcations is sometimes called the *Feigenbaum scenario* or *Feigenbaum cascade*. Under surprisingly modest sufficient conditions the same type of behavior occurs for general maps F when F humps up more and more as you increase the tuning parameter μ. This robustness of the Feigenbaum scenario to the form of map F is what makes the scenario important.

Another closely related idea is *Li and Yorke's theorem* that a value of μ large enough to give a nondegenerate period three steady state of F indicates that there are smaller values of μ that give chaos. The Li and Yorke theorem is easy to use because all that is needed to show that chaos exists is find a μ value for which a nondegenerate solution exist to: $a = F(b, \mu)$, $b = F(c, \mu)$, $c = F(a, \mu)$. See the papers by Saari, Grandmont, and references to others such as R. Day, J. Benhabib, R. Dana, and P. Malgrange in H. Sonnenschein (1986) where use of the Li and Yorke theorem, as well as the related *Sarkovskii sequence*, appears in economics.

The long and detailed paper of Grandmont (1985) contains a wealth of references and techniques of chaos theory. He applies these techniques to locate sufficient conditions on tastes and technology to get low dimensional deterministic chaotic rational expectations paths in an overlapping generations model.

Let us briefly outline how Grandmont (1985) gets chaos and why it matters to macroeconomists. He uses chaos theory to challenge the conventional neoclassical macroeconomic models that argue that the macroeconomy is asymptotically stable about trend in the absence of exogenous stochastic shocks (see Grandmont's references to Lucas, Prescott, Sargent and others). The argument is that one does not need to introduce what Grandmont calls ad hoc exogenous shocks in order to get equilibrium fluctuations that look like business cycles. He uses a variation of the offer curve diagram of Gale (1973) to display the dynamics of the set of rational expectations equilibria in an overlapping generations (OG) model consisting of identical two period lived agents. We give a simplified treatment here that draws partly on the paper of Brock (1988a).

3.1. Offer curve depiction of Gale equilibria

Equilibria in this model are easy to depict. Draw, at each date t the offer curve of the young born at date t. That is, consider the problem

$$\text{maximize } U(c_y(t), c_0(t+1)) \tag{3.1}$$

subject to

$$p(t)c_y(t) + p(t+1)c_0(t+1) = p(t)w_y + p(t+1)w_0.$$

Here $p(t)$, $p(t+1)$, $c_y(t)$, $c_0(t+1)$ denote price of goods at date t, price of goods at date $t+1$, consumption while young, and consumption while old respectively. The utility function is denoted by $U(\cdot, \cdot)$.

The offer curve 0 is the locus of solutions to (3.1) as $p(t)$, $p(t+1)$ vary. We need to specify initial conditions to start up the model. Do this by supposing that the representative old person at date 1 faces the constraint

$$p(1)c_0(1) = p(1)w_0 + M. \tag{3.2}$$

Here M denotes the initial stock of nominal money balances which is held by the old at date 1. Now draw the Ricardian production possibility frontier

$$R = \{(c_y, c_0): c_y + c_0 = w_y + w_0\}.$$

We shall, like the bulk of the literature including Gale (1973), use the concept of *perfect foresight* or *rational expectations equilibrium*. Such equilibria are described by the set,

$$\{(p(t), p(t+1); c_y(t), c_0(t+1))\},$$

where $(c_y(t), c_0(t+1))$ solves (3.1) facing $(p(t), p(t+1))$, $t = 1, 2, \ldots$; $c_y(t) + c_0(t) = w_y + w_0$, $t = 1, 2, \ldots$; and $p(1)$, $c_0(1)$ satisfy (3.2).

In order to get a set of equilibria where money has value in Gale's model and to display the dynamics of monetary equilibria (in order to locate sufficient conditions for chaotic dynamics) draw an offer curve 0 through the endowment point (w_y, w_0) in 2-space such that 0 cuts R but with slope less than one in absolute value. Notice the positive steady state L in figure 10.1. This is a steady state equilibrium where fiat money has positive value. Notice the sequence $(c_y(t), c_0(t+1))$ that converges to autarchy (w_y, w_0). This is a monetary equilibrium where fiat money loses its value asymptotically. This is the situation depicted in Gale (1973, figure 3, p. 24) in the analysis of his "Samuelson" case.

This method of analysis, used also by Grandmont (1985), illustrates several features of the class of OG models most commonly exploited by macroeconomists.

First, if there is a steady state equilibrium where money has value then there is a continuum of equilibria where money has value. This is sometimes called *indeterminacy*. Second, there are steady state competitive equilibria where money has value, for example the equilibrium denoted by L, and steady state equilibria (autarchy in our case) where money does not have value. Third, the presence of money moves the economy to Pareto optimality at the steady state with valued fiat money in this setup. This leads to the general presumption that the presence of valued fiat money in an equilibrium is associated with Pareto optimality. This general presumption is not true in all OG setups (Cass et al. (1980)).

It is obvious that arbitrarily small policy perturbations, such as convertibility of each unit of fiat money to e units of real goods, no matter how small e is, will get rid of the hyperinflationary equilibria that converge to autarchy. Figure 10.2 depicts equilibria that cannot be disposed of so easily. The work

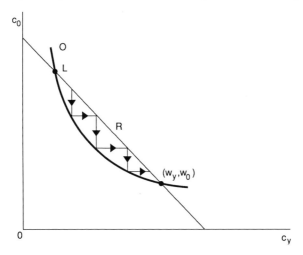

Figure 10.1

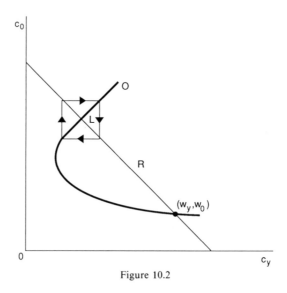

Figure 10.2

of Azariadis and Guesnerie (1986) shows that there are *sunspot equilibria,*
that is, equilibria that are random, even though the model is deterministic,
whenever cycles like those in figure 10.2 are present. We are not concerned
with sunspot equilibria here.

Notice how cycles appear when the offer curve is bowed out to the left
more than in figure 10.1 so that you get the situation in figure 10.2. This
suggests that if you can find a parameter of the model to play the role of
μ in the Ruelle and Takens (1971) setup then you could generate a Feigenbaum period doubling cascade as you increase μ. Indeed Grandmont (1985,
figure 4, p. 1030) displays a period doubling cascade generated by letting
the relative risk aversion parameter, α_2, of the representative old person
play the role of Ruelle and Takens' parameter, μ. (Caution: Grandmont's
μ is our limiting value of $\{x(t)\}$ and his α_2 is our μ.) Let us explain how
Grandmont generates the Feigenbaum scenario, and, hence, deterministic
chaos.

3.2. Difference equation depiction of Gale equilibria

The Gale equilibria can be depicted alternatively by a difference equation
analysis as in Brock and Scheinkman (1980) and Scheinkman (1980).

Put $x(t) = M(t)/p(t)$ where $M(t)$ is nominal money supply at date t. Observe that along any candidate equilibrium path of real balances, $\{x(t)\}$, we must have by the first order condition for optimality of the young:

$$U_c(w_y - x(t), w_0 + x(t+1))x(t)$$

$$= U_0(w_y - x(t), w_0 + x(t+1))x(t+1). \qquad (3.3)$$

Call the LHS of (3.3) $A(\cdot)$ and the RHS $B(\cdot)$. When U is separable in consumption today and consumption tomorrow, that is, $U(c_y, c_0) = u(c_y) + v(c_0)$, then (3.3) can be written as a difference equation in the form:

$$u'(w_y - x(t))x(t) \equiv A(x(t)) = B(x(t+1)), \qquad (3.4)$$

where $v'(w_0 + x(t+1))x(t+1) \equiv B(x(t+1))$.

Solutions of this difference equation that can be continued forever are equilibria. Note that $B = 0$ at $x = 0$ when $w_0 > 0$. Note also that $u' > 0$, $u'' < 0$ implies that $A(\cdot)$ is strictly increasing. Assume positive endowment while young which implies $A(0) = 0$.

As in the offer curve analysis one may locate the conditions for a positive steady state to exist. Since A and B intersect at 0 when $w_0 > 0$, the condition needed for a positive steady state to exist is that A cut B from below. This is equivalent to Gale's condition in his "Samuelson" case that the offer curve of the young cut the PPF from below.

Following Grandmont (1985) write, since A is invertible,

$$x(t) = A^{-1}(B(x(t+1))) \equiv \Theta(x(t+1)).$$

Now run time backwards: $y(t) = \Theta(y(t-1), \mu)$. All we have to do to generate a Feigenbaum cascade is to find a parameter to play the role of μ so that $\Theta(y, \mu)$ becomes more humpy as μ increases. To put it another way, we want $\Theta(y, \mu)$ to have the same qualitative behavior as the function $\mu y(1-y)$. Grandmont achieves this by putting the old person's utility $v(y) = y^{1-b}/(1-b)$. Here b is the relative risk aversion, $v''(y)y/v'(y)$, of the old agent. He then shows that a parameterization by μ, exists such that a Feigenbaum cascade occurs. Intuitively, increasing b makes Θ humpier but there is more to it than this. See Grandmont (1985) for the details.

This argument shows that it is not necessary to introduce exogenous stochastic shocks into macroeconomic models in order to get random looking behavior of equilibrium time series output. This argument did not convince critics like Sims (1984) who argued that this kind of model, and argument where the time scale is on the order of human lifetimes, cannot explain business cycle fluctuations where the modal length is three to three and a half years. The critics were basically using results like those in chapters

5, 7, and 9 of this book to argue that optimizing agents, facing discount rates (like those discount rates implicit in observed bond prices) on future utilities would indulge in optimal smoothing behavior to such an extent that cycles of modal length of three to four years could not exist.

The most recent paper on global asymptotic stability of rational expectations equilibria in deterministic general equilibrium models with long lived agents is that of Epstein (1987). Epstein's results show that when markets are complete (so that for a given competitive equilibrium, *E*, a set of positive weights exist, one for each agent such that the allocation for *E* maximizes the weighted sum of discounted utilities) low discounting by consumers or low rates of return to production by firms leads to global asymptotic stability much along the lines of chapters 5, 7, and 9 of this book. The message is that in order to get chaotic intertemporal equilibria there must be substantial obstructions to the basic intertemporal smoothing behavior that does so much to stabilize fluctuations that are deterministic and forecastable. One way to do this is to introduce restraints on borrowing and lending. This strategy was pursued by Bewley's paper in Sonnenschein (1986).

In order to counter the critics' argument that the parameter values and time scale used in previous examples of chaotic equilibrium paths did not agree well with the range of values established by empirical studies, Woodford (1987) has built a class of models where one type of agent is liquidity constrained and the other type is not. He constructs examples where equilibrium trajectories are chaotic. However, to our knowledge, no one has constructed examples of economic models that generate chaotic paths where the parameters of the tastes and technology are constrained by the range of parameter values established by empirical studies. Hence, skepticism still exists among writers such as Sims (1984) and Granger (1987) whether low dimensional deterministic chaos is a phenomenon that is likely to exist in actual economic time series. Turn now to the question whether introduction of a stock market or commodity money has any effect on the theoretical likelihood of deterministically chaotic equilibria.

3.3. Commodity money, stock market assets and productive land

Introduce real assets into the model along the lines of Lucas (1978) by replacing the budget constraints of the young and old in Gale's model with

$$c_y(t) + q(t)z(t) = w_y,$$
$$c_0(t+1) = w_0 + (q(t+1)+y)z(t),$$

where $q(t)$ denotes the price of the asset that pays constant real earnings y at date t, $z(t)$ denotes the quantity of the asset demanded by the young at date t. There is one perfectly divisible share of the asset outstanding at each point of time.

A *perfect foresight equilibrium* is defined as previously in the Gale case except that $z(t) = 1$ at each t (demand for the asset = supply of the asset). For the separable case, the first order necessary conditions for a perfect foresight equilibrium are:

$$U_y(w_y + q(t))q(t) = U_0(w_0 + q(t+1))(q(t+1) + y).$$

In the same manner as earlier, paths $\{q(t)\}$ are equilibria provided they can be continued indefinitely. However, a new twist now appears. Think of changing y from 0 to a positive value in Gale's model. Then the set of hyperinflationary equilibria that converge to a real balance level of 0 moves to a set of equilibria that converge to a negative steady state q_n. This brings us to

Proposition.   Free disposal of the asset, i.e., limited liability eliminates equilibria where the value of the asset goes negative.

Let us explore the logic of this proposition. If free disposal of the asset obtains then any path, where $q(t) < 0$ at some finite t, cannot be equilibrium. This is so because once the asset goes negative in value the owner can harvest his y and throw the asset away. However, if the asset is like a nuclear plant that yields earnings of y each period that is perfectly safe, a chain of self-fulfilling beliefs in a world of unlimited liability can get started where the value of shares becomes negative and welfare goes down. This is an example of how limited liability assures *Pareto Optimality*. But Pareto Optimality alone is not enough to eliminate chaotic equilibria as we shall see below.

3.4. A payment of epsilon real earnings on fiat money is efficient

Scheinkman (1977) has shown how introduction of a market for claims to an earnings stream of $y > 0$ each period, no matter how small y may be, eliminates the inefficient equilibria in the Samuelson (1958) and Gale (1973) overlapping generations models. The reason for Scheinkman's result is intuitive, by hindsight. The inefficient equilibria are overaccumulative in that the interest rate is negative enough of the time to fail the Cass (1972) and Benveniste and Gale (1975) efficiency criterion. But introduction of a market for claims to $y > 0$, under limited liability, forces the interest rate to be positive enough of the time to force efficiency by the Cass–Benveniste–Gale criterion.

This finding allows us to state

Proposition.   A payment of $y > 0$ of earnings on fiat money, no matter how small is y, tends to force efficiency of all equilibria in overlapping generations models provided that free disposal or limited liability obtains.

3.5. *The offer curve diagram for an asset market*

The offer curve apparatus can be easily amended to depict equilibria when $y > 0$. Just draw the offer curve of the young through the same endowment point (w_y, w_0) as before, but replace the PPF, R, with $R^y = \{(c_y, c_0): c_y + c_0 = w_y + w_0 + y\}$. Figure 10.3 depicts steady state equilibrium, L, and a sequence of equilibria that converge to the lower steady state L^n where the value of the asset is negative. Recall that free disposal eliminates these and that they are the analogues of Gale's hyperinflationary equilibria when $y = 0$. Also, recall that the case $y = 0$ is the case of pure fiat money. Figure 10.4 depicts three positive steady state equilibria and a continuum of positive

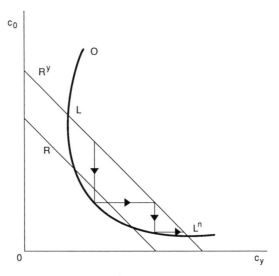

Figure 10.3

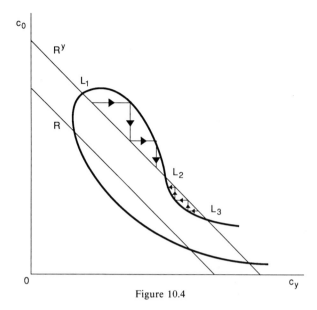

Figure 10.4

equilibria. This shows that $y > 0$ will not get rid of the possibility of a continuùm of equilibria. These equilibria are robust in the sense that they cannot be perturbed away by a small perturbation of tastes and endowments.

It should be straightforward to conduct an exercise much like that in Grandmont (1985) to show that a parameterization of tastes may be found such that, even though $y > 0$, a period doubling cascade can be constructed. Intuitively you would construct an offer curve that bows out to the left around R^y as Grandmont did for case $y = 0$.

We have cited several papers that have established theoretical examples of *chaotic rational expectations equilibria.* More examples are surveyed in Baumol and Benhabib (1988). How convincing are such arguments to skeptical writers such as Sims (1984) and Granger (1987)? Skepticism about deterministic chaos in macroeconomics probably comes from some evidence which we briefly review next.

First, in the U.S., shocks to development along trend such as World War I, World War II, the Great Depression, the two oil shocks, etc, seem to wear off as the economy returns to trend. Even the unit root literature which argues that many shocks are permanent, rather than transitory, seems to be moving toward a consensus that there is more evidence of a return to trend rather than divergence (cf. Cochrane (1988) and references).

Second, savings as a fraction of GNP seems to be a rather stable fraction of GNP over time, known as *Denison's Law*. See P. David and J. Scadding (1974) and references for discussions of the strong evidence supporting Denison's Law.

Third, real interest rates do not move much across time except for the recent Reagan period. A dramatic graph that shows the historical movement of real interest rates is in Rostow (1983, p. 34). Fama (1976) has adduced evidence that the expected real return on T-bills is constant across time. The behavior of nominal and real interest rates will be discussed in section 4 of this chapter.

Fourth, if chaos had a really good chance to appear it would happen in situations where there are production lags and where there are heavy durables with a natural replacement cycle. Automobiles might be a good example. Pent up demand for automobiles after World War II in the U.S. is a natural place to look for cycles and chaos in auto sales. A graph of auto sales in Rostow (1983, p. 98) reveals a relatively smooth path to trend in auto sales after World War II.

In summary, it is difficult to formulate a chaotic model in macroeconomics that is consistent with the existing evidence already mentioned. It is even harder to construct a model so that it is consistent with other stylized facts of the macroeconomy detailed in works such as Tobin (1980), Lucas (1987), and McCallum's review (1986) of evidence for and against the real business cycle paradigm.

As we have said before, it is an irresolvable question whether macroeconomic fluctuations are generated by high dimensional chaos or infinite dimensional, i.e., stochastic processes. What *is* potentially resolvable is whether the fluctuations are generated by a low dimensional deterministic chaotic generator or a stochastic generator. Low dimensional chaos involves *instability* and *overshooting*. While no one denies that business cycles are accompanied by periods of booms and busts the evidence is more consistent with a view that the fluctuations are generated by a deterministic cycle buffeted by noise about trend (an $AR(2)$ process for detrended real GNP for example) or stochastic trends (a unit root process for example).

4. Applications to finance

In the first three sections we outlined some concepts from chaos theory, some concepts from empirical nonlinear science, and applications to macroeconomics. In this section we try to tie these ideas together with applications to finance. Scheinkman and LeBaron (1987) have documented dependence in weekly aggregate stock returns that does not appear to be just autoregressive conditional heteroscedasticity. They get an estimate of the correlation dimension of about six. This estimate is invariant under linear autoregressive versions of the residual diagnostic unlike the case for the macroeconomic data studied by Brock and Sayers (1988). Below we review possible explanations for this finding as well as other evidence for intertemporal dependence in stock returns. An attempt is made to link evidence on dependence in returns to the business cycle but the attempt is only speculative. This is currently an active area of research.

4.1. The choice of time scale on which to look for complex dynamics in finance

In serious confrontation of the theory of complex dynamics with data the issue of appropriate time scale comes up. We saw in section 3 how important the issue of time scale was in the debate on whether chaos was theoretically plausible in macroeconomics. Since business cycles have a modal length of about 3 and one half years, the demonstration that chaotic equilibria exist in a two period overlapping generations model was not a theoretically convincing argument to macroeconometricians. It only serves, at this stage, as a logical possibility. It is important, however, to recognize that some models with borrowing restraints can generate equilibrium dynamics that behave much like the dynamics generated by an overlapping generations model and are capable of generating chaotic fluctuations at business cycle frequencies (Woodford (1987)). But, then, the issue arises whether the degree of tightness of borrowing constraints needed to generate chaos at business cycle frequencies is consistent with empirical evidence on the tightness of borrowing restraints in reality. At this point in time, this issue is not resolved.

The same issue arises in finance. For short time intervals first differences in the logarithm of stock prices should not be very predictable in a frictionless market. Otherwise arbitragers could exploit the dependence and turn a profit over and above the opportunity cost of the funds tied up in the arbitrage position. Let us explain.

Returns on stock i over time period $[t, t+h]$ are defined by,

$$r_{i,t,t+h} = (p_{i,t+h} + y_{i,t,t+h})/p_{i,t} - 1. \tag{4.1}$$

At the minute to minute level Wood et al. (1985) have documented: (i) returns tend to be higher at the opening of the exchange, fall over the first 20-30 min, look unpredictable in the middle, and rise in the last 20-30 min to the close, (ii) trading volume and price volatility follow the same pattern near the opening and the close. Details of market micro structure are very important at this frequency. Measured returns may show spurious dependence due to measurement difficulties such as "bid/ask bounce". See Marsh and Rock (1986) for details. For reasons of measurement error problems as well as a theoretical presumption that chaos should not be likely at the minute to minute frequency, we will not spend any time analyzing stock price dynamics for chaos in this case. Actually, even though the equilibrium theory to be discussed makes it look extremely unlikely that one would ever find evidence of chaos at the minute to minute frequency, an apparent disequilibrium panic like the Monday Massacre of October 19, 1987 might generate evidence of chaotic dynamics. The whole week of October 19-23 was turbulent with the Dow falling from 2178.69 at Monday's open to 1738.74 at Monday's close – a 508 point drop accompanied by a huge volume of trading. The volume of 1.3 billion shares traded during this week was more than the total number of shares traded during all of 1964. Similar patterns emerged in most of the world's major stock exchanges during the same week. Markets seesawed while volume skyrocketed. Incidents like these are worth keeping in mind as we discuss the standard theory of unpredictability of stock prices.

4.2. Are daily and weekly price changes unpredictable?

Sims (1984) gives the standard economic reasoning that price changes must be unpredictable over small time intervals in a frictionless market, such as the stock markets. This is formalized by Sims' (1984).

Definition. A process $\{P(t)\}$ is *instantaneously unpredictable* if and only if, almost surely,

$$E_t[(P(t+v) - E_t[P(t+v)])^2]/E_t[(P(t+v) - P(t))^2] \to 1, \, v \to 0. \quad (4.2)$$

Here E_t is taken w.r.t. the information set I_t. ($\{I_t\}$ is an increasing sequence of sub sigma fields of a master sigma field, I.) In words, "for an instantaneously unpredictable process prediction error is the dominant component of changes over small intervals. Of course, for a martingale (4.3) below with finite second moments, the ratio in (4.2) is exactly 1". Sims points out that, under (4.2), regressions of $P_{t+s} - P_t$ on any variable in I_t have $R^2 \to 0$, $s \to 0$. Under (4.3), $R^2 = 0$. He also points out that (4.2) doesn't rule out predictability over longer time periods. He then argues that this is consistent with empirical evidence in finance. Short periods for Sims are daily to weekly.

The martingale hypothesis is

$$E[P_{t+s} | I_u, u \leq t] = P_t, \qquad s > 0. \tag{4.3}$$

Notice that (4.3) can be obtained from representative agent general equilibrium asset pricing models such as Lucas (1978) and Brock (1982) by making the utility function linear, the subjective discount rate equal to zero, and adjusting P_t for any dividends paid out. In practice (4.3) is adjusted for discounting, $G(t+1)$, and net cash flow, $y(t+1)$, over the period $[t, t+1]$. The discount process $\{G\}$ and the net cash flow process $\{y\}$ can also be random. Malliaris (1981) gives a detailed mathematical description of (4.3) with illustrations from financial economics.

Recall that chaos theory teaches that trajectories generated by chaotic maps are potentially perfectly predictable provided that you can measure the state perfectly. But if you measure the state today with error, then forecasts of the future state become worthless at an exponential rate. Hence, nonlinear dynamicists sometimes say that chaotic dynamics are unpredictable. Yet the financial logic leads us to believe that low dimensional chaotic deterministic generators for stock prices and returns over daily to weekly time periods should be extremely unlikely. After all, if a predictable structure is present, arbitraging on the part of traders should destroy it provided it is easy to be recognized by traders over very short time intervals. This is the intuitive content of the Sims argument.

4.3. Evidence on complex dynamics in stock returns

Scheinkman and LeBaron (1987) have estimated the correlation dimension for 1226 weekly observations on CRSP value weighted U.S. stock returns index for the mid 60s. They find roughly 6. They calculate another estimate of dimension due to Takens (1984) which is also close to 6. Similar results for closing prices over the mid 1970s to the mid 1980s for gold and silver on the London Exchange were reported by Frank and Stengos (1986). They get correlation dimension estimates between 6 and 7 for daily, weekly, and biweekly series.

We examine several stock returns series below: (a) VW = Monthly returns on the Value Weighted New York Stock Exchange index for the mid 20s to the late 70s. (b) EW = Monthly returns on the Equation Weighted New York Stock Exchange index for the same period. (c) BLVW = Weekly returns on the Value Weighted CRSP index used in the Scheinkman and LeBaron (1987) study. Both EW and VW are CRSP indices taken from the Gennotte and Marsh (1986) study. We deliberately make the analysis difficult by estimating correlation dimension and by reporting step wise empirical derivatives of the Grassberger Procaccia diagram. Recall that the Grassberger Procaccia (GP) diagram is $\ln(C_m(e))$ plotted against $\ln(e)$. These empirical derivatives are going to look rough because we lose the inherent smoothing involved in estimating the slope of the *constant slope zone* of the Grassberger Procaccia diagram by regression analysis or by eyeball analysis. We then compare this series of empirical derivatives for the shuffled counterpart.

Put

$$SC(0.9^n) = [\ln(C_m(0.9^n)) - \ln(C_m(0.9^{n-1}))]/[\ln(0.9)]. \qquad (4.4)$$

SC is an estimate of the empirical derivative at 0.9^n. Look at table 10.2.

We have succeeded in replicating the Scheinkman and LeBaron study. The dimension of both halves of the data set is between 6 and 7 when taking into account the roughness of empirical derivatives relative to the estimated empirical slopes of Grassberger Procaccia plots. The dimension of the shuffled series is surely bigger in both halves of the data set. Note however that the difference in behavior between the original series and the shuffled series is smaller for the second half than for the first half. Here *shuffling* refers to the process of creating an IID series with the same stationary distribution as the original series.

By way of comparison we looked at the monthly EW and VW indices. Notice that they display similar behavior to the weekly BLVW data set. This is comforting. Gennotte and Marsh (1986) calculated Grassberger Procaccia plots for this same data set after taking out the January effect and taking out linear structure. They find significant evidence of nonlinear dependence. It is significant because they calculate Brock, Dechert and Scheinkman (1987) statistics for the spread between the Grassberger Procaccia plot for their prewhitened January adjusted data and the Grassberger Procaccia plot for the shuffled data. The Brock, Dechert and Scheinkman statistics were highly significant, especially for EW. It is striking that the

Table 10.2

EW: $N = 696$, $m = 10$

e	0.9^6	0.9^7	0.9^8	0.9^7	0.9^{10}	0.9^{11}	0.9^{12}	0.9^{13}	0.9^{14}	0.9^{15}
SC	2.9	3.4	4.0	5.0	5.6	5.9	6.3	7.1	7.0	8.0
SC_{sf}	5.0	5.6	6.1	6.6	7.1	7.5	8.0	8.3	9.1	9.7

VW: $N = 696$, $m = 10$

e	0.9^6	0.9^7	0.9^8	0.9^9	0.9^{10}	0.9^{11}	0.9^{12}	0.9^{13}	0.9^{14}	0.9^{15}
SC	4.3	5.0	5.6	5.9	7.0	7.1	7.0	7.2	8.7	6.7
SC_{sf}	5.3	6.0	6.6	7.3	7.8	8.6	9.0	9.0	9.0	10.4

BLVW[1:600]: $N = 600$, $m = 10$

e	0.9^6	0.9^7	0.9^8	0.9^9	0.9^{10}	0.9^{11}	0.9^{12}	0.9^{13}	0.9^{14}	0.9^{15}
SC	3.7	4.1	4.2	4.4	4.8	4.9	5.4	6.0	7.1	7.4
SC_{sf}	6.5	7.3	7.6	8.6	7.3	10.7	6.1	11.9	19.7	644.2

BLVW[601:1226]: $N = 626$, $m = 10$

e	0.9^6	0.9^7	0.9^8	0.9^9	0.9^{10}	0.9^{11}	0.9^{12}	0.9^{13}	0.9^{14}	0.9^{15}
SC	5.9	6.5	7.2	7.6	7.8	8.8	8.5	8.5	9.7	14.6
SC_{sf}	6.7	7.2	7.4	7.7	7.7	8.6	10.4	10.1	7.5	645.6

DSE8TBLM: $N = 628$, $m = 10$

e	0.9^6	0.9^7	0.9^8	0.9^9	0.9^{10}	0.9^{11}	0.9^{12}	0.9^{13}	0.9^{14}	0.9^{15}
SC	1.2	1.4	1.6	1.8	1.9	1.9	2.0	1.8	1.7	1.8
SC_{sf}	3.3	3.9	4.4	4.6	4.8	5.2	5.3	5.6	5.9	7.1

KODAK: $N = 720$, $m = 10$

e	0.9^6	0.9^7	0.9^8	0.9^9	0.9^{10}	0.9^{11}	0.9^{12}	0.9^{13}	0.9^{14}	0.9^{15}
SC	5.5	6.1	7.1	7.5	7.9	8.9	7.8	9.1	9.2	9.5
SC_{sf}	6.0	6.6	6.9	8.0	7.3	8.3	10.9	12.7	8.7	3.8

Code for Table: EW, VW, BLVW[1:600], BLVW[601:1226], DSE8TBLM, KODAK equals returns on equal weighted CRISP index, returns on value weighted CRISP index, first 600 returns on S1B's value weighted index, next 626 returns on S1B's value weighted index, residuals of an $AR(8)$ fit to first difference's of tbill returns, and returns on Kodak stock, respectively. N equals number of observations, m equals embedding dimension. All data were divided by the standard deviation and multiplied by 0.2. SC, SC_{sf} denote the empirical slope of the GP diagram for the original series and the shuffled series. This table is drawn from Brock (1987b).

significance of dependence was so high for EW because most of the January effect resides in small firms which loom relatively large in EW compared to VW. But Gennotte and Marsh took out the January effect.

Gennotte and Marsh looked at the subsample January 1942–December 1971. The Brock, Dechert and Scheinkman statistic fell to 2.45 for EW and 1.01 for VW in contrast to 7.23 for EW and 4.39 for VW for the whole sample. Since Gennotte and Marsh fitted best linear models to the data as well as taking out the January seasonality therefore under the null hypothesis of linearity, modulo estimation error, the 5% level of the Brock, Dechert and Scheinkman statistic is around ±2. Therefore the size of the Brock, Dechert and Scheinkman statistic could be looked upon as a rough measure of nonlinearity in these data. It is interesting that the subsample January 1942–December 1971 appears linear.

In contrast with these results (especially for the value weighted indices) the behavior of the monthly returns for the individual stock, such as KODAK appear IID. There is little difference in behavior between the original returns and the shuffled returns. What difference there is seems to be due to the roughness of empirical derivatives.

Contrast this with the behavior of Treasury Bills taken from Ibbotson and Sinquefield (1977, p. 90, Exhibit B8). These data were also used by Gennotte and Marsh (1987) to measure the risk free rate of return. We reduced this series to stationarity by taking first differences. Now test the null hypothesis that first differences of T-bill returns have a low dimensional deterministic chaotic explanation.

We identified best fit linear models by Box–Jenkins methods to eliminate the linear dependence in T-bill returns. Recalling the discussion of the residual diagnostic, this prewhitening does not change the dimension of the underlying dynamics if they are chaotic. The results for DSE8TBLM are typical. We get low dimension of the residuals even after fitting an autoregressive process of order 8 to the first differences of T-bill returns. The dimension appears to be around 2. Furthermore, the dimension of the shuffled counterpart is much larger although it is not equal to the theoretical value which is 10.

We are puzzled by the T-bill results. There seems to be strong evidence consistent with a chaotic explanation. We do not conclude that however because the largest Liapunov exponent has not been estimated and shown to be positive. Also, unlike Swinney's (1985, p. 285) case for the Belousov–Zhabotinski chemical reaction the dynamics have not been reconstructed. All we can say at this stage is that T-bill returns are worthy of further investigation.

There is one thing that the scientist must keep in mind when interpreting this evidence. During the period under scrutiny the government intervened in determining interest rates. There were periods where T-bill rates did not move at all because the government was controlling interest rates. In other periods, the government was more concerned about the growth of the monetary base and less about fluctuations in interest rates. Hence, the dynamics is subject to regime shifts. Shifts in the government posture toward controlling ease of credit and controlling interest rates impact on the short run opportunity cost of funds. This influences stock returns. The market watches the central bank very carefully. Thus government activity in the financial markets makes it even harder to interpret the evidence.

4.4. *What may explain the evidence for nonlinearity*

There are well known anomalies in finance. Financial economists use the term *anomaly* to refer to patterns in returns that appear inconsistent with absence of arbitrage profits after investors are paid the competitive price for systematic risk bearing. It is typical in finance to search for an explanation in terms of systematic movements in risk return tradeoffs. Let us explain. The Capital Asset Pricing Model (CAPM) adjusts returns for one source of risk - covariance with the market as a whole. Arbitrage Pricing Models (APT) adjust returns for a small number, say 3 to 5, of systematic sources of risk. Theory predicts that diversifiable risks bear no price in financial equilibrium and that there is a tradeoff between expected return and systematic risk across portfolios. This tradeoff depends upon the state of the economy. Movements in this tradeoff have the potential for explaining the findings in table 10.1 as well as the Scheinkman and LeBaron findings. Let's take a brief look at this theory.

As a quick idea of how the CAPM and APT models work assume returns on stock i at date t, $\{R_{it}\}$ can be written as a linear factor model:

(LFM.1) $R_{it} = A_{it} + \Sigma B_{kit}\delta_{kt} + e_{it}, \quad i = 1, \ldots, N.$

Here the sum runs from $k = 1, \ldots, K \ll N$; δ, e are random and independent of each other at date t and have conditional mean 0 at each date t; A, B are deterministic at date t. Note that A_{it} is expected returns on asset i at date t conditional on date $t-1$ information. Insert (LFM.1) into the pricing equation below where the discounting process is $\{G\}$ to get

(LFM.2) $1 = E_{t-1}[G(t)R_{it}].$

Assume that $K \ll N$ and the structure in (LFM.1) allows enough diversification opportunities so that the market acts as if $E_{t-1}[G(T)e_{it}] = 0$. Form widely diversified portfolios to diversify away the unsystematic risks $\{e_{it}\}$. Assuming that the $E_{t-1}[G(t)e_{it}]$ terms are zero and rewriting (LFM.2) gives,

(APT/CAPM) $A_{it} = L_{0t} + \Sigma B_{kit}L_{kt}, L_{0t} = 1/E_{t-1}G(t),$

$L_{kt} = -[E_{t-1}(G(T)\delta_{kt})]/[E_{t-1}G(t)].$

The meaning of the (APT/CAPM) equation is intuitive. It states that expected returns on stock i, A_{it}, is the sum of the risk free return, L_{0t} plus the sum over $k = 1$ to K of the price of risk of type k, L_{kt}, times the quantity, B_{kit}, of type k risk borne by stock i. The t subscripts denote that this relationship can shift over time.

The CAPM can be viewed as the special case of one source of systematic risk that cannot be diversified away, i.e., $K = 1$. The APT is the more general case of several sources of undiversifiable risk.

These models are operationalized by constructing indices to proxy for the unobservable to the scientist $\{\delta_{kt}\}$. For the CAPM case $\{\delta_{it}\}$ is proxied by returns minus conditional expectation of returns where the returns are on a wide index such as the New York Stock Exchange index.

Note that $G(t) = bu'(c_t)/u'(c_{t-1})$ for a representative infinitely lived consumer as in Lucas (1978). This is a version of the consumption beta model where returns are predicted to vary with aggregate consumption. In general $G(t)$ is determined by tastes of the public for risk bearing. These tastes may change through time. This movement of tastes for risk bearing impacts on stock prices through the above equations. This will be relevant in trying to interpret some of the evidence.

Evidence for and against the above theory is mixed. Rothschild (1986) reviews some of the evidence that is pertinent here. Systematic risk (i.e., beta risk) as measured by the CAPM helps explain average returns. But so also does own risk. The association between size and average return is as good as the association between measured beta and average return. Factors help explain average returns but they are hard to measure and it is difficult to get a consensus on which factors are most important and how to measure them.

With this background look at some evidence presented in Haugen's (1987) textbook and its references, where excess returns adjusted for risk appear to exist. For the Standard and Poor's Index of 500 stocks, for daily returns over 1962-1968, Monday's return (that is, the return from Friday's close to Monday's open) appears to be negative, Wednesdays and Fridays tend to have higher returns than Tuesdays and Thursdays. These differentials are not large enough to return a profit if you have to pay commissions (Haugen (1987, p. 478)).

Over 1929-1940, January's average return was 6.63%, compared with an average of 0.19% for all other months. This has been confirmed for later periods. Most of it occurs in the first five trading days of January and most of it is in the smaller firms. Stock returns are higher in January for nearly every other country with highly organized stock markets. In January, high beta (large covariance with the aggregate market) stocks produce higher than average rates of return. So the relationship between expected returns and beta also changes in January. The CAPM risk premium for January was 3.02% in comparison with 0.36% for the rest of the months over 1935–1980.

The average daily excess return for January (adjusted for beta risk) over 1963–1979 for the smallest ranking (based on value of a share) 10% of stocks is around 0.5%/day and −0.3%/day for the largest ranking 10% of stocks. The January average daily excess return falls as value increases. It is approximately 0%/day for all other months for all value classes.

It is fair to say that the January effect is striking, robust, and has stimulated a lot of effort in finance to explain it. Most of the research uses a context like APT/CAPM to search for plausible explanations. For example, small firms are a factor. Researchers are looking for a source of systematic risk that differentially impacts upon small firms during the December–January period. We doubt that the January effect can explain the dimension findings of table 10.2. This is so because Gennotte and Marsh (1986) took out the January effect and still got similar results.

4.5. More puzzles and anomalies

It seems risky to construct an explanation for the findings of table 10.1, Scheinkman and LeBaron (1987), and Frank and Stengos (1986) that is dependent upon the consumption beta model. This is so because the consumption beta model is soundly rejected by data; See Ferson and Merrick (1987) and references especially to Hansen and Singleton; see also Prescott and Mehra (1985). The puzzle is not so much that stocks behave oddly w.r.t. theory, that is the CAPM/APT is not wildly rejected across risky portfolios; rather it is the low return of T-bills relative to stocks. This is dramatically vivid on page 3 of Ibbotson and Sinquefield (1977). Cumulation of an initial investment of $1 on common stocks, long term bonds, T-bills, and inflation over 1925–1975 in the U.S. are 90.57, 5.44, 3.25, 3.31 respectively. From 1947–1975 inflation and T-bills march in tandem, yielding a real return on T-bills of about 0 during 1947–1975. Prescott and Mehra (1985) argue that you need ridiculously high risk aversion to reconcile this spread in returns between stocks and T-bills with a consumption beta model. Cochrane (1987) finds it easier to reconcile the equity premium with aggregate marginal rates of transformation than Prescott and Mehra do with aggregate marginal rates of substitution.

Consumption beta models are more consistent with data when nonstationarities and business cycle effects are accounted for (Ferson and Merrick

(1987)). Turn next to evidence of mean reversion in stock returns at the weekly frequency.

Lehman (1987) finds sharp evidence for market inefficiency in the "form of systematic tendencies for current 'winners' and 'losers' in one week to experience sizeable return reversals over the subsequent week in a way that reflects apparent arbitrage profits". Lehman's results appear to contradict many versions of the CAPM/APT equation because his portfolios are wealth free, appear to have no systematic risk in them, but yet earn significantly positive returns when closed out. There is sure to be controversy whether Lehman controlled for all sources of systematic risk. Issues of measurement are paramount in testing financial theories and will probably prevent us from ever getting a decent ("decent" from the point of view of natural science) consensus. Lehman's findings are a potential explanation for the Scheinkman and LeBaron (1987) results.

4.6. Autoregressive conditional heteroscedasticity

Even though returns may not be predictable on average it still may be true that their variances may be predictable. Furthermore, it appears that volatilities move together across financial assets (even exchange rates) at a point in time. Bollerslev fits the model.

$$y_t = y_{t|t-1} + e_t, \ e_t \text{ is distributed } N(0, h_{t|t-1}), \tag{4.5}$$

$$h_{t|t-1} = a_0 + a_1 e_{t-1}^2 + b_1 h_{t-1|t-2}, \tag{4.6}$$

$$y_{t|t-1} = b_0 + \delta h_{t|t-1}^{1/2}. \tag{4.7}$$

Here y_t is monthly returns on the S&P. This is an example of a Generalized Autoregressive Conditional Heteroscedastic (GARCH-M) model with conditional mean, $y_{t|t-1}$, dependent upon current conditional volatility.

The idea is intuitive: Looking at the APT/CAPM formula suggests that aggregate returns should be high on average when volatility is high in order to compensate investors for bearing higher risk. Furthermore, stylized facts dating back to Mandelbrot and others are these: (i) unconditional distributions of stock returns are fat tailed; (ii) volatilities are persistent; (iii) large linear forecast errors tend to come together but appear unpredictable in sign. The GARCH-M class of models is an attempt to parameterize this kind of data in a way to do statistical inference.

Bollerslev's results are:

$$b_0 = -0.0340, \; \delta = 1.2565, \; a_0 = 0.0002, \; a_1 = 0.0561, \; b_1 = 0.8038, \qquad (4.8)$$

$$(0.0220) \quad (0.6892) \quad (0.0001) \quad (0.0340) \quad (0.1066).$$

Asymptotic standard errors are in parenthesis. While the results are not overwhelmingly strong the persistence parameter b_1 for volatility is surely significant. Of course, all this is conditional on the GARCH-M being the correct model for S&P returns. This might be false. Also, we have no idea how fast the distribution converges to the asymptotic distribution.

We continue with more examples in the next section.

5. Miscellaneous applications and exercises

(1) *Evidence of mean reverting fads and long term dependence.* The weekly and monthly levels are a good place at which to search for evidence of complex dynamics in stock returns for several reasons.

First, Shiller's (1984) prominent work on stock prices and social dynamics argues that swings in fashion of say 3–5 years in length could lead to long swings in returns that would be hard to detect in autocorrelation tests performed on weekly or monthly returns.

Second, Summers (1986b) has shown that adding a slowly mean reverting measurement error process (say $z_t = \Phi z_{t-1} + n_t$, $\{n_t\}$ IID with mean 0 and finite variance, with Φ near unity) to the geometric random walk (a random walk in logarithms) leads to a stochastic process that is hard to distinguish from a geometric random walk by autocorrelation function tests.

Third, Fama and French (1986) have shown that a version of the Shiller and Summers process leads to negative autocorrelations in monthly returns at the 3–5 year level and that actual stock returns data have statistically significant negative autocorrelations at the 3–5 year level. One may also view Lehman's (1987) results of mean reversion at the weekly level as consistent with a version of the Shiller and Summers model.

Fourth, at an impressionistically suggestive level, Montroll and Badger (1974) suggest that many fads and popularist movements seem to last for a similar length of time. A reading of Shiller's (1984) list of fads and fashions does not contradict this. Thorp and Mitchell referenced in Montroll and Badger (1974) fit a log normal model to the duration of business cycles across 15 countries over 1790–1925. The fit is quite good. The fitted log normal peaks at a frequency between 3–3.5 years. It is fat tailed to the right however. So 6-8 year cycles are not all that scarce. Nevertheless, it is suggestive that the modal length of business cycles matches Fama and French's 3-5 year interval for negative autocorrelations.

Turn back to Shiller's (1984) suggestive article. Shiller argues that interest in the stock market waxes and wanes much like interest in fashions. He also argues that social pressures influence investors in much the same way that social pressures influence teenage kids (and the rest of us).

Fama and French (1986) present evidence that suggests, in the context of APT/CAPM, that whatever it is that causes the 3-5 year mean reversion in stock returns, it impacts widely across all stock groups. Therefore, the Fama and French evidence is consistent with slow movements in the discounting process, $G(t)$, over time as well as with a Shiller and Summers mean reverting pricing error process.

Lo and MacKinlay (1988) build a statistical test on the observation that variances of kth period differences of a random walk must grow linearly in k. They construct another test for random walks driven by heteroscedastic innovations (ARCH innovations are included). General random walks are vigorously rejected by weekly returns on the CRSP equally weighted index and still are rejected by weekly returns on the CRSP value weighted index over 1962-1985. These rejections are largely due to small stocks. They investigate a version of the Shiller and Summers mean reverting fads model and reject it.

(2) *A wildly speculative story consistent with the evidence.* What are we to make out of the somewhat confusing collection of evidence presented? It appears worthwhile, in view of the evidence that the correlation dimension of stock returns is somewhere between 6 and 7 together with the fairly strong evidence for predictability of stock returns over long intervals like 3-5 years, that a chaos with 3-5 year swings could be consistent with this data. Furthermore, the evidence suggests that it enters the system through $G(t)$ or mean reverting pricing errors or perhaps through mean reversion in the net cash flows of firms. Given Lo and MacKinley's claim to reject the mean reverting pricing error model, movements in $G(t)$ or movements in net cash flow appear to be a good place for chaos to enter stock returns if it enters anywhere. Since returns on nearly risk free assets move like $1/E_{t-1}[G(t)]$ (cf. the APT/CAPM formula) and since T-bills did not move like stock prices, we must proceed cautiously if we are to interpret the evidence in terms of movements in $G(t)$ alone.

One fact that impresses itself quickly on a financial analyst is that the quantity of government paper, including T-bills, is not constant over time. Therefore, even though the surface behavior of T-bills may contradict the story that we are going to propose, the contradiction may be resolved when government activity to control interest rates and when government monetary and fiscal policy is taken into account. It is also important to realize that T-bills may be a close substitute for fiat money. The 1947–1975 Ibbotson and Sinquefield evidence on T-bills and inflation is consistent with the close substitute view. Their evidence from 1925–1946 is not. T-bills cumulated much faster than inflation during this period.

Consider a world where the current quantity of stock market investors is a function of the past history of returns on the market and past history of numbers of investors in the market. Let each investor plan as if they live for two periods and let all active investors have identical tastes to keep the analysis simple.

We have an overlapping generations structure much like those discussed and referenced in Baumol and Benhabib (1988) and Grandmont (1985). The marginal rate of substitution between this period's consumption and next period's consumption determines $G(t+1)$. Holding the quantity supplied of stock fixed at unity for all time and imposing supply of stock = demand for stock, makes $G(t+1)$ a function of the current number of investors this period, $N(t)$, in equilibrium. Modest conditions show that $G(t+1)$ is increasing in the number of active investors, $N(t)$. It seems possible to get chaos or complex dynamics for plausible specifications of $N(t)$. However, the details have not yet been worked out.

(3) *Another story for the evidence: the business cycle.* Swings in the public's tastes for risk bearing may be tied to the business cycle. After all it is known that: (i) fluctuations of real GNP about trend are fit well by low order autoregressive processes such as $AR(2)$'s with near unit roots, (ii) the amplitude (severity) of business cycles is less in the post World War II period in the U.S. than in the pre World War II period. Corporate profits covary with general activity such as real GNP but are more volatile. Profits power the ability to pay dividends on corporate stock.

In order to relate this to mean reverting evidence on the time scale discussed by Fama and French consider investors at the trough of the cycle expecting a rise. Since rises are highly persistent (real GNP about trend is a near unit root $AR(2)$ process) one could expect the stock market to rise and the bull market to last towards the peak of the cycle. Now contrast this with investors at the peak anticipating a fall in economic activity. One would expect a bear market. One would also expect people to be more tolerant of risk bearing when they expect things to get better and stay better relative to trend and vice versa for the fall. Hence this cyclical change in the attitudes toward risk bearing should magnify swings in stock returns over the cycle.

This seems roughly consistent with the evidence but pushes the ultimate roots of swings in stock returns back to swings in economic activity in general.

There is also the problem that this is a consumption beta type of story. The data may not be as hostile to a model where $G(t+1)$ is not forced to be the marginal rate of substitution of a single risk averse infinitely lived agent type as it is in the consumption beta models. The model of Scheinkman and Weiss (1986) generates equations related to CAPM/APT but contains two agent types. It also links swings in asset prices to relative swings in generalized profitability or generalized productivity across the economy.

There is evidence that stock prices are systematically related to business cycle movements. After all, a *pure fads* interpretation of the Fama and French findings is not very attractive. We have the problem of explaining when fads start and when they die. If this is completely random then we have a reconciliation problem with the stock market – business cycle evidence. So we are going to identify "fad" with magnification effects ignited by the business cycle.

Motivated by Shiller's well known work on *excess volatility* of asset prices we are going to look for forces that magnify movements of stock prices from their fundamental values. The fundamentals themselves move over the business cycle. We will entertain the notion that the theory describes a central tendency for stock prices over time. We will look for forces that magnify upswings and downswings so that there are persistent movements from the fundamental that eventually revert back to the fundamental. This is an attempt to capture the mean reverting idea of Shiller, Fama, French and Summers.

With this perspective look at the distillation of the history of speculation by Montroll and Badger (1974). We quote them verbatim.

"We close this historical review of speculational orgies with a brief summary of the mechanism behind practically all these events. We use the words of the stock exchange, but the basic ideas are general and, in fact, can be translated into other examples of public hysteria quite easily. There are eight important steps:

(I) Increasing industrial production and sales (or demand for some commodity such as land) in a period in which there is general optimism causes a rise in price of stock (or of the commodity).

(II) If at the same time private savings and uncommitted cash is increasing, the rise attracts new investors and enlarges the depth of involvement of those already in the market.

(III) This induces larger rises in market prices and attracts less sophisticated people who pay attention only to changes in market prices, essentially ignoring the activity of the companies whose stock they purchase.

(IV) The small down payment (margin, in stocks, binders in Florida real estate, etc.) becomes widely used so that the demand for stock increases more rapidly than the rate at which real money is put into the market. Furthermore, the behavior of the market becomes practically uncoupled from industrial production, or the actual value of the use of the object being invested in. The investor is buying only to sell soon after profits are made.

(V) Success and demand for stock breed enterprises which have nothing to do with production; for example, investment trusts or, in the case of real estate booms, swamp land, etc.

(VI) As values skyrocket, the number of new people entering the speculative orgy decreases. Those already committed become more sensitive. They know they want to get out while they are ahead, but they also become a little greedy so that they stay in as long as there is some rise.

(VII) A small, more knowledgeable, group observes that the original reason for the excitement, industrial production and its future prospects, has not kept up with the inflated values of the stock. They start to sell out.

(VIII) Since new buyers are few, prices go down somewhat as these sales are made. The sensitive people react. As the continuous drop occurs, the installment (or margin) buyers are in trouble. The stock held as security is sold in a market of few buyers and the panic is on.

This, of course, is a simplified model but still it contains most of the main ideas. It should not be difficult to make a mathematical formulation of this mechanism. We hope to discuss such a scheme elsewhere . . . ".

Apparently, Montroll never discussed such a scheme elsewhere. We searched a list of his publications published in a memorial volume by Shlesinger and Weiss (1985) and found no mention of such work in his published papers. We conjecture that Montroll may have found that it is not easy to write down such a model and have its testable implications treated fondly by the data in any way that would command a consensus by fellow scientists. We buttress this conjecture below.

Much has been written in economics on bubbles and excessive movements in asset prices. The excess volatility literature flounders on the fundamental measurement difficulty: the scientist can never capture all the information that the traders have; therefore there will always appear to be excess volatility relative to any fitted model attempting to match measured stock prices to measured fundamentals. In spite of this difficulty we believe that most economists share (yet see the next paragraph) the belief that stock prices are excessively volatile relative to fundamentals. The bubbles literature suffers from similar difficulty.

A review of recent empirical work on bubble testing and excess volatility especially that of Flood, Garber, Shiller, West, is in Flood, Hodrick, and Kaplan (1986). They argue that most of the evidence of bubbles and excess volatility is due to model misspecification and not due to actual self propelled expectation bubbles that diverge from fundamentals like that of the Montroll and Badger scenario.

How can we try to settle this dispute? One thing that Montroll and Badger focused on in their review of the history of speculation as told by economists of a more literary bent (such as J. K. Galbraith's *The Great Crash*) is some measure of the depth of interest in the stock market. Montroll and Badger had no data on the number of people buying stocks so they examined another market, the market for collectible coins. They found a strong positive association between subscriptions to the magazine *Coin World* and movements in coin prices for 1960D small date pennies, 1955 half dollars, and 1950 pennies over the period 1960-1972. The height of the boom in prices followed by the depth of the collapse was especially severe for the 1960D small date pennies.

(4) *An underlying chaotic process driving stock returns.* We have presented evidence from other studies in empirical nonlinear science (Scheinkman and LeBaron (1987), Gennotte and Marsh (1986), Frank and Stengos (1986)) that the dimension of stock returns is between 6 and 7 or, at the minimum, stock returns are nonlinear in the sense that the residuals of best fit linear models are highly dependent.

Our initial computer experiments with simulated Shiller, Fama, French and Summers slow mean reverting processes have failed to detect this kind of dependence with tests based upon methods of Brock, Dechert and Scheinkman like those used above. This appears to be true because as the persistence $\Phi \to 1$ of the mean reverting "pricing error process" of Shiller, Fama, French and Summers, the first difference over a *fixed* time interval of observed log stock price goes in mean square norm to an IID process. Hence, convergence in distribution is implied and the BDS test is fooled. Hence, we do not believe that Shiller, Fama, French and Summers' type of processes account for the evidence of nonlinearity in stock returns in table 10.2.

We do not believe that ARCH or GARCH processes account for all of the nonlinear dependence for several reasons. (i) Scheinkman and LeBaron (1987) argue that simulated ARCH-M processes calibrated to their data do not display the observed pattern of their "S" statistics; (ii) Brock, Dechert and Scheinkman have shown that GARCH processes generate zero bispectra and cite evidence that the bispectrum of stock returns is significantly nonzero; and (iii) Brock (1987b) discusses conflicts between GARCH and ARCH models as currently applied and theory and evidence in macro-economics and finance.

(5) Brock and Sayers (1988) have presented evidence of strong nonlinear dependence in (a) industrial production, (b) civilian employment, (c) unemployment rate, (d) pigiron production. This nonlinearity may have been channeled into stock returns through this equilibration of the market. Real GNP failed to show nonlinear structure but it may have been eliminated by aggregation.

(6) *Multivariate test.* Nothing said here proves that there are chaotic dynamics driving stock returns at business cycle frequencies or that business cycle data are chaotic. But the best fit linear models (after reduction to linearity by units changes, transformation of variables, deseasonalization, and detrending) do not account for all of the temporal dependence in these data. Investigation of dependence of stock returns on variables like measure of the "depth of interest" in the market. Shiller (1984) and Montroll and Badger (1974) deserve as much attention as investigation of dependence upon conditional variance (ARCH and its cousins).

At the very least chaos theory stimulates the researcher to look for *magnification* or *overreactive* effects in data in the search for evidence of the endogenous instability that is characteristic of chaotic dynamics. This new perspective has already led to a new statistical test (Brock, Dechert, and Scheinkman (1987)) for nonlinearity and intertemporal dependence that has good power against alternatives for which many tests have weak power. This test has been generalized to multivariate series by E. Baek (1987) and has been used to test for possible nonlinear dependence missed by Stock and Watson (1987) in bivariate money and industrial production vector autoregressions. Baek's test has excellent size and power characteristics. We confidently predict that ideas from nonlinear science and chaos theory will continue to stimulate useful new methodology in economics even though the evidence for deterministic data generators in economic nature may be weak.

(7) It would be interesting to use the methodology of this chapter to investigate the behavior of volume of trading in equity, futures or options

markets at various time dimensions. For a brief survey of existing theories of trading volume behavior and for random walk tests see Malliaris and Urrutia (1988).

6. Further remarks and references

That low dimensional deterministic dynamics could generate stochastic looking trajectories has been known in mathematics at least since the days of Poincare. Applied scientists did not take much interest in this phenomenon until the piece by Ruelle and Takens (1971) successfully challenged the high dimensional Hopf-Landau view of the transition to turbulence and replaced it with a view that assigns a dominant role to strange attractors of low dimensional nonlinear dynamical systems. This view received a chilly reception in the scientific community until evidence adduced by Swinney (1983, 1985) and others made the case for the presence of strange attractors in data generated by real physical systems. In the meantime, computer simulations demonstrated that a vast variety of stochastic-like paths these models generated will have to confront data with the same success of the received models in order to persuade macroeconometricians. Substantial frictions and market imperfections will have to be present to get around the randomness inherent in the logic of frictionless asset markets.

Interest in the general theory of chaos has even stirred up the world community of intellectuals and literati, especially in Europe. A somewhat controversial example is the output of the Brussels school (e.g., Prigogine and Stengers (1984) and Prigogine (1980)). An October, 1985 conference at the Palais des Academies in Brussels on theoretic ideas on chaos and their applications, attracted such notables as Jonas Salk and Alvin Toffler. Several speakers, at the Brussels conference argued that Western science has been dominated for three centuries by the Newtonian paradigm which Toffler called "the bloodless, cold, machine model taught by classical science". He said, "the new science of instability . . . serves us by shifting the attention of scientists and intellectuals to disorder, instability, diversity, disequilibrium, non-linear relationships, and the importance of time". (Prigogine and Sanglier (1987, p. 330).)

Business Week, August 4, 1986 did a full length article on this topic. One scientist was quoted in *Business Week* as saying that the study of chaos "is as important historically as the discovery of the wheel". Not to be outdone by the Europeans, the American Santa Fe Institute hosted a conference organized by two Nobel Laureates, Kenneth Arrow (Economics) and Philip Anderson (Physics). The proceedings are being published in David Pines (1988). Meanwhile the American National Academy of Sciences National Research Council issued a public research briefing on "Order, Chaos, and Patterns: Aspects of nonlinearity" (NAS (1987)). It is not an exaggeration to say that activity in this area is feverish at the present time. Some early economic applications of chaos are presented in Brock (1985).

This chapter gives a survey of the relevant natural science literature and offers some extensions and adaptations appropriate to economics. It also outlines some preliminary approaches to detecting the presence of noisy nonlinear dynamics in economic data. However, the really exciting work for economics remains to be done. That is to fuse a synthesis between the recent methods used by natural science to test for the presence of nonlinear low dimensional dynamics in data when the noise level is small with the statistically sophisticated methods of social science that can handle a lot more noise in the data but a lot less nonlinearity.

For the reader who wishes to study further the mathematics of nonlinear dynamics and chaos we suggest Guckenheimer and Holmes (1983), Percival (1983), Devaney (1986), Thompson and Stewart (1986), Jordan (1987) and the readings in Holden (1986). For a historical survey see Gleick (1987).

Special acknowledgement. Dee Dechert and José Scheinkman have greatly contributed to the development of ideas in this and other chapters of the book and we are intellectually indebted to them.

MATHEMATICAL REVIEWS

> Mathematics as an expression of the
> human mind reflects the active will,
> the contemplative reason, and the
> desire for aesthetic perfection. Its
> basic elements are logic and intuition,
> analysis and construction, generality
> and individuality.
>
> Courant and Robbins (1941, p. xv)

1. Introduction

This appendix collects numerous definitions and results from analysis, linear algebra, elementary topology and optimization theory to offer the reader a source for a quick reference of mathematical concepts used throughout the book.

The material is covered briefly and several references are supplied for the reader interested in studying specific concepts in more detail.

2. Results from analysis

In chapter 1 and elsewhere, the concepts of continuity, uniform continuity, convergence, uniform convergence, equicontinuity and others are used. The definitions of these concepts follow.

A function f which is defined in some neighborhood of a point c is said to be *continuous* at the point c provided that the function has a definite finite value $f(c)$ at c, and also as x approaches c, $f(x)$ approaches $f(c)$; that is $\lim_{x \to c} f(x) = f(c)$. Alternatively, let f be a function and let c be a number in an open and connected set called the *domain* of f and denoted by D. Then f is continuous at c if, and only if, to each $\varepsilon > 0$ there corresponds a $\delta > 0$ such that $|f(x) - f(c)| < \varepsilon$ whenever $|x - c| < \delta$ and $x \in D$. If a function is continuous at all points of a domain D, then it is said to be *continuous on D*.

Suppose that a function f is defined on a domain D. If for any $\varepsilon > 0$ there exists a number $\delta > 0$ such that $|f(x) - f(c)| < \varepsilon$ when $|x - c| < \delta$ and $x \in D$ holds for all $c \in D$, then we say that $f(x)$ is *uniformly continuous* on D.

Let $\{f_n(x)\}$ be a sequence of real valued functions defined on a domain $D \subset R^n$. We say that $\{f_n(x)\}$ is a *Cauchy sequence* if for any $\varepsilon > 0$ there exists a positive integer n_0 such that whenever $n > m \geq n_0$, $|f_n(x) - f_m(x)| < \varepsilon$ for all x in D.

A sequence $\{f_n(x)\}$ defined on a domain $D \subset R^n$ is *uniformly convergent* to some function $f(x)$ on D if, and only if, for any $\varepsilon > 0$ there is a positive integer n_0 such that, for all x in D, $|f_n(x) - f(x)| < \varepsilon$ whenever $n \geq n_0$.

Next we recall a few important theorems.

Theorem 2.1. The uniform limit of a sequence of continuous functions is a continuous function.

For a proof see A. Friedman (1971, p. 159).

Theorem 2.2. (Taylor's Theorem.) Let $f(x)$ be a function that is continuous and has $n + 1$ first derivatives on an open interval containing the points a and x. Then the value of the function at x is given by

$$f(x) = f(a) + \frac{f'(a)}{1!}(x - a) + \frac{f''(a)}{2!}(x - a)^2 + \cdots$$

$$+ \frac{f^{(n)}(a)}{n!}(x - a)^n + R_n(x, a),$$

where

$$R_n(x, a) = \int_a^x \frac{(x - t)^n}{n!} f^{(n+1)}(t)\, dt,$$

is called the remainder.

For a proof see Friedman (1971, p. 102).

Theorem 2.3. (Fundamental theorem of integral calculus.) If $f(x)$ is continuous in the interval $a \leq x \leq b$, and if $F(x) = \int f(x)\, dx$ is an indefinite integral of $f(x)$, then the definite integral

$$\int_a^b f(x)\,dx = \int_a^b F'(x)\,dx = F(b)-F(a),$$

where the derivative of

$$F(x) = \int_a^x f(u)\,du$$

is

$$dF/dx = F'(x) = f(x).$$

For details see Kamien and Schwartz (1981, p. 253).

Theorem 2.4. (Gronwall's inequality.) If c is a real constant, $f(x) \geq 0$ and $h(x)$ are continuous real functions for $a \leq x \leq b$ which satisfy

$$h(x) \leq c + \int_a^x f(s)h(s)\,ds \quad a \leq x \leq b$$

then

$$h(x) \leq \left(\exp \int_a^x f(s)\,ds\right)c \quad a \leq x \leq b.$$

Theorem 2.5. (Generalized Gronwall inequality.) If ϕ, α are real valued and continuous functions for $a \leq t \leq b$, $\beta(t) \geq 0$ is integrable on $[a, b]$ and

$$\phi(t) \leq \alpha(t) + \int_a^t \beta(s)\phi(s)\,ds \quad a \leq t \leq b$$

then

$$\phi(t) \leq \alpha(t) + \int_a^t \beta(s)\alpha(s)\left(\exp \int_a^t \beta(u)\,du\right)ds, \quad \text{for } a \leq t \leq b.$$

For proofs of these two theorems see Hale (1969, pp. 36–37).

We conclude this section by recalling some simple properties of complex numbers. *Complex numbers* are expressions of the form $a + ib$, where a and b are real numbers and i is the symbol for $\sqrt{-1}$.

Two complex numbers $a + bi$ and $c + di$ are equal if, and only if, $a = c$ and $b = d$.

The sum of two complex numbers $(a + bi) + (c + di)$ is the complex number $(a + c) + (b + d)i$.

The product of two complex numbers $(a + bi)(c + di)$ is the complex number $(ac - bd) + (ad + bc)i$, and the product of a real number x and a complex number $a + bi$ is the complex number $ax + (bx)i$.

Division of two complex numbers $(c + di)/(a + bi)$ is a complex number $x + yi$ where

$$x = (ac + bd)/(a^2 + b^2); \quad y = (ad - bc)/(a^2 + b^2); \quad a^2 + b^2 \neq 0.$$

The absolute value of a complex number $|a + ib|$ equals $\sqrt{a^2 + b^2}$. Finally we give *Euler's Relations*:

$$e^{iz} = \cos z + i \sin z,$$

$$e^{-iz} = \cos z - i \sin z.$$

A standard reference for complex analysis is Churchill (1960).

3. Basic topological concepts

Any real number is called a *point* and the set of all real numbers is called the *real line*. The point 0 (zero) is called the origin of the real line. Given any points a and b, with $a < b$, we call the set of points satisfying $a < x < b$ the *open* interval with endpoints a and b. We denote this open interval by (a, b), or $\{x: a < x < b\}$ or $a < x < b$. Similarly, we define the *closed* interval $[a, b]$, or $\{x: a \leq x \leq b\}$ to be the set of all points satisfying $a \leq x \leq b$. These notations can be generalized in R^n.

A set of real numbers G is said to be *bounded above* if there is a number K such that $x \leq K$ for all $x \in G$. Such a number K is called the *upper bound* of G. The set G is *bounded below* if there is a number L such that $x \geq L$ for all $x \in G$. L is called the *lower bound* of G. If G is bounded above and below, then we say G is *bounded*. This is clearly the case if, and only if, there exists a positive number M such that $|x| \leq M$ for all $x \in G$.

A set G is said to be *unbounded* if it is not bounded. A set G is *compact* if, and only if, it is closed and bounded. Moore (1964) gives an introduction to elementary general topology.

Let $f(x)$ be a function defined on an interval I. Consider the set G of its values $f(x)$, where x varies in I. If G is bounded above then we say that f is *bounded above*. This is the case if, and only if, there exists a constant N such that $f(x) \le N$, for all $x \in I$. If G is a bounded set, then we say that f is a *bounded function* on I. This is the case if, and only if, there exists a positive constant M such that $|f(x)| \le M$ for all $x \in I$. If f is *not* bounded, then we say it is *unbounded*.

A useful result is the following:

Theorem 3.1. Let f be a continuous function on a closed and bounded interval $[a, b]$. Then f is bounded.

For a proof see Friedman (1971, p. 51).

Let F be a family of real valued functions defined on an interval I. F is called *uniformly bounded* if there is a positive constant M such that $|f(x)| \le M$ for all $x \in I$ and f in F. F is called *equicontinuous* on I if for any $\varepsilon > 0$ there is a $\delta > 0$ (independent of x, y, and f) such that $|f(x) - f(y)| < \varepsilon$ whenever $|x - y| < \delta$ for all x and $y \in I$ and for all f in F.

A key result used in the theory of ordinary differential equations is the famous *Ascoli lemma*.

Theorem 3.2. (Ascoli lemma.) Let F be a family of functions which is bounded and equicontinuous at every point of an interval I. Then every sequence $\{f_n\}$ of functions in F contains a subsequence which is uniformly convergent on every compact subinterval of I.

For a proof see Coppel (1965, p. 7).

4. Results from linear algebra

Put rather simply, a *matrix* is a rectangular array of numbers. The numbers in the array are called the entries in the matrix. An $m \times n$ matrix consists of mn elements a_{ij}, with $i = 1, \ldots, m$ and $j = 1, \ldots, n$, written in an array of m rows and n columns. For $m \times n$ matrix A, the *transpose* of A, denoted A^T, is defined to be the $n \times m$ matrix whose first column is the first row of A, whose second column is the second row of A and so on with its final column being the last row of A.

Two matrices A and B with the same number of rows and also the same number of columns may be added or subtracted. For example,

$$C = A + B$$

is defined by

$$c_{ij} = a_{ij} + b_{ij}.$$

Thus, to add two matrices, one simply adds the corresponding entries; to subtract two matrices, one subtracts corresponding entries.

Multiplication of a matrix by a scalar k, is performed by multiplying every element of the matrix by k. Now consider two matrices A and B with A an $m \times p$ matrix and B a $p \times n$ matrix. Matrix multiplication is possible only when the number of columns of A equals the number of rows of B. The product of AB is an $m \times n$ matrix defined by

$$C = AB$$

with

$$c_{ij} = \sum_{k=1}^{p} a_{ik} b_{kj}.$$

It is not in general true that $AB = BA$. In fact, although AB can be formed, the product BA may not be capable of being formed.

Division is not defined for matrix algebra. However, the inverse of a matrix bears the same relationship to that matrix that the reciprocal of a number bears to that number in ordinary algebra. Thus, in matrix algebra the product of a matrix A and its inverse A^{-1} is the identity matrix I, that is $AA^{-1} = I = A^{-1}A$. The identity matrix, denoted by I, is an $n \times n$ matrix with ones as the elements on the main diagonal and zeros elsewhere. A matrix A that does not have an inverse is called *singular*.

We assume that the reader is familiar with the notion of a determinant and we state some simple properties for the determinant of a matrix A denoted by $\det A$. These properties are:

(i) $\det A = \det A^{\mathrm{T}}$
(ii) If A and B are square matrices of the same size then $\det (AB) = (\det A) \cdot (\det B)$.
(iii) A matrix A is invertible if, and only if, $\det A \neq 0$.

If $A = \{x_1, x_2, \ldots, x_n\}$ is a set of vectors, then the vector equation

$$k_1 x_1 + k_2 x_2 + \cdots + k_n x_n = (0, 0, \ldots, 0)$$

has at least one solution, namely $k_1 = k_2 = \cdots = k_n = 0$. If this is the only solution, then A is called a *linearly independent* set. If there are other solutions, then A is called a *linearly dependent* set.

We also offer two more definitions of linear dependence:

(i) A system of equations A, which has

$$\det A = 0$$

and consequently is not invertible, is linearly dependent.

(ii) A set of two or more vectors is linearly dependent if, and only if, at least one of the vectors is a linear combination of the remaining vectors.

If A and B are square matrices, we say that B is *similar* to A if there is an invertible matrix P such that $B = P^{-1}AP$. Note that the equation $B = P^{-1}AP$ can be rewritten as $A = PBP^{-1}$ or $A = (P^{-1})^{-1}BP^{-1}$. Letting $Q = P^{-1}$ yields $A = Q^{-1}BQ$ which says that A is similar to B. Therefore, B is similar to A if, and only if, A is similar to B.

If A is an $n \times n$ matrix, then a nonzero vector x in R^n space is called an *eigenvector* of A if Ax is a scalar multiple of x; that is

$$Ax = \lambda x$$

for some scalar λ. The scalar λ is called a *characteristic value* or an *eigenvalue* of A and x is said to be an *eigenvector* corresponding to λ.

To find the eigenvalues of A we rewrite $Ax = \lambda x$ as $Ax = \lambda Ix$ or equivalently $(\lambda I - A)x = 0$. For λ to be an eigenvalue, there must be a nonzero solution of this equation. However, we have a nonzero solution if, and only if,

$$\det(\lambda I - A) = 0.$$

This last equation is called the *characteristic equation* of A and the polynomial obtained by expanding $\det(\lambda I - A)$ is called the *characteristic polynomial*. An important result is this:

Theorem 4.1. Similar matrices have the same characteristic polynomials and the same characteristic values.

For a proof see Paige and Swift (1961, pp. 279-280).

It is particularly useful if a similar matrix is triangular. A matrix is called *triangular* if it is a square matrix such that all its elements either above or below the main diagonal are zero. The characteristic roots of a triangular matrix are the elements along the principal diagonal. Therefore, for a given matrix A, if it is possible to find a similar triangular matrix, the characteristic roots of A can simply be read off the diagonal of the similar triangular matrix. A special case of a triangular matrix is the diagonal matrix. The square matrix D with elements d_{ij} is called *diagonal* if $d_{ij} = 0$ for all $i \neq j$. A matrix A is called *orthogonal* if $A^T = A^{-1}$. A matrix A is called *symmetric* if $A^T = A$. A key theorem is the following.

Theorem 4.2. If A is a real symmetric matrix it has an orthogonally similar diagonal matrix. If A is a real symmetric matrix it has only real characteristic values. If a square matrix A has *distinct* characteristic roots there is a similarity transformation $P^{-1}AP = D$ where D is diagonal.

For a proof see Paige and Swift (1961, pp. 287–289).

Not all matrices are diagonalizable. It is however possible to get close to a diagonal form using the Jordan canonical form as is explained in chapter 2.

For an $n \times n$ matrix A with elements a_{ij} we define the *trace of* A, denoted by tr A, as

$$\text{tr } A = \sum_{i=1}^{n} a_{ii}.$$

In stability analysis we often use the fact that the trace of a square matrix is the sum of its characteristic roots.

Suppose A is a function of a scalar variable t, in the sense that each entry of A is a function of t. Then

$$\frac{dA}{dt} = \left[\frac{da_{ij}}{dt} \right].$$

It follows that

$$\frac{d}{dt}(AB) = \frac{dA}{dt} B + A \frac{dB}{dt}.$$

The integral of a matrix is defined as

$$\int A \, dt = \left[\int a_{ij} \, dt \right].$$

Suppose ϕ is a scalar function of vector x. Then $d\phi/dx$ is a vector whose ith entry is $\partial\phi/\partial x_i$. Suppose ϕ is a scalar function of matrix A. Then $d\phi/dA$ is a matrix whose (i, j) entry is $\partial\phi/\partial a_{ij}$. Let

$$F_i(x, u) = F_i(x_1, x_2, \ldots, x_r, u_1, u_2, \ldots, u_r), \quad 1 \leq i \leq r,$$

be functions having continuous first derivatives in an open set containing a point (x^0, u^0). The matrix

$$
\begin{bmatrix}
\dfrac{\partial F_1}{\partial u_1} & \dfrac{\partial F_1}{\partial u_2} & \cdots & \dfrac{\partial F_1}{\partial u_r} \\[2ex]
\dfrac{\partial F_2}{\partial u_1} & \dfrac{\partial F_2}{\partial u_2} & \cdots & \dfrac{\partial F_2}{\partial u_r} \\[2ex]
\vdots & \vdots & & \\[1ex]
\dfrac{\partial F_r}{\partial u_1} & \dfrac{\partial F_r}{\partial u_2} & \cdots & \dfrac{\partial F_r}{\partial u_r}
\end{bmatrix}
$$

or briefly $\partial F_i / \partial u_j$ is called the *Jacobian matrix* of $(F_1, \ldots, F_r)$ with respect to $(u_1, \ldots, u_r)$.

The *norm* of a vector x is a real valued function denoted by $|x|$ or $\|x\|$ that satisfies the properties

 (i) $|x| \geq 0$, with $|x| = 0$ if, and only if, $x = 0$,
 (ii) $|\lambda x| = |\lambda||x|$ for any scalar λ,
 (iii) $|x + y| \leq |x| + |y|$.

The three most commonly used norms of a vector $x = (x_1, \ldots, x_n)$ are:

$$
\sup_{1 \leq x_i \leq n} |x_i|; \qquad \sum_{i=1}^{n} |x_i|; \qquad \left[\sum_{i=1}^{n} |x_i|^2 \right]^{1/2}.
$$

For an $m \times n$ matrix A representing a linear mapping from $R^n \to R^m$, we define the induced norm of A to be

$$
|A| = \sup_{|x|=1} |Ax| = \sup_{x \neq 0} \frac{|Ax|}{|x|}.
$$

These topics are presented in detail in Bellman (1970) and Hernstein (1964).

5. On quadratic forms

There is a close connection between the characteristic roots of a matrix and the properties of quadratic forms. Recall that a quadratic equation may be written as

$$
a_{11} x_1^2 + (a_{12} + a_{21}) x_1 x_2 + a_{22} x_2^2
$$

which can be put into matrix form

$$
\begin{bmatrix} x_1 & x_2 \end{bmatrix}
\begin{bmatrix} a_{11} & a_{12} \\ a_{21} & a_{22} \end{bmatrix}
\begin{bmatrix} x_1 \\ x_2 \end{bmatrix}.
$$

With this simple illustration we can define the *quadratic form* as a relation $x^\mathrm{T}Ax$ where A is an $(n \times n)$ matrix with real entries and x is an n-vector. For a quadratic form $Q = x^\mathrm{T}Ax$, for all real $x \neq 0$ we define

(1) Q is *positive definite* if $Q > 0$;
(2) Q is *positive semidefinite* if $Q \geq 0$;
(3) Q is *negative definite* if $Q < 0$;
(4) Q is *negative semidefinite* if $Q \leq 0$;
(5) Q is *indefinite* if $Q \gtreqless 0$.

The basic result of this section is

Theorem 5.1. (1) A quadratic form is positive definite if and only if characteristic roots are all positive. (2) A quadratic form is positive semidefinite if and only if characteristic roots are all nonnegative. (3) A quadratic form is negative definite if and only if characteristic roots are all negative. (4) A quadratic form is negative semidefinite if and only if characteristic roots are all nonpositive. (5) A quadratic form is indefinite if and only if at least one characteristic root is positive and one is negative.

For a proof see Hadley (1961, pp. 255–256).

6. Optimal control

In continuous time the general optimal control problem is stated thus:

$$V(y, t_0) \equiv \max \int_{t_0}^{T} v(x, u, s)\, \mathrm{d}s + B(x(T), T), \qquad (6.1)$$

$$\text{s.t. } \dot{x} = f(x, u, t), \quad x(t_0) = y, \qquad (6.2)$$

where $V: R^n \times R \to R$, $f: R^n \times R^m \times R \to R^n$, $v: R^n \times R^m \times R \to R$, $B: R^n \times R \to R$. Here V is the *state valuation function*, also called the indirect utility function, starting at state y at time t_0; v is the instantaneous utility or payoff when the system is in state $x = x(s) \in R^n$ at time s, and control $u = u(s) \in R^m$ is applied at date s; B is a bequest or scrap value function giving the value of the state $x(T)$ at date T; and $\dot{x} \equiv \mathrm{d}x/\mathrm{d}t = f(x, u, t)$ gives the law of motion of the state. The discrete time version of step size h of (6.1) and (6.2) is analogous with $\dot{x}$ replaced by $(x(t + h) - x(t))/h$ and $\int$ replaced by $\sum$. Under modest regularity conditions the solution to the discrete time problem converges to the solution to the continuous time problem as $h \to 0$. The horizon T may be finite or infinite.

Under regularity assumptions by dynamic programming the value function V satisfies the Hamilton-Jacobi-Bellman (HJB) equation; furthermore the state and costate necessary conditions must be satisfied with $p \equiv V_x$:

(HJB equation) $\qquad -V_t = \max_u H^*(p, x, u, t) \equiv H^{*0}(p, x, t),$ (6.3)

(Hamiltonian definition) $\quad H^*(p, x, u, t) \equiv v + pf,$ (6.4)

(co-state equations) $\qquad \dot{p} = -H^{*0}_x, \dot{x} = H^{*0}_p, x(t_0) = y,$ (6.5)

(terminal conditions) $\qquad V(x, T) = B(x, T), p(T) = B_x(x, T).$ (6.6)

The variable p is called the *costate* variable, *adjoint* variable, or *dual* variable; and the function H^* is called the *Hamiltonian*. These variables are introduced for the same reasons and have the same interpretation that Lagrange-Kuhn-Tucker multipliers have in nonlinear programming. The terminal conditions (6.6) are sometimes called *transversality conditions*.

Equations (6.3)-(6.6) are the workhorses of optimal control theory. We briefly explain their derivation and meaning here following Brock (1987a) and other standard references such as Athans and Falb (1966) or Miller (1979).

Equation (6.1) may be written:

$$V(y, t) = \max\left\{ \int_{t_0}^{t_0+h} v(x, u, x)\, ds + \int_{t_0+h}^{T} v(x, u, s)\, ds + B[x(T), T] \right\}$$

$$= \max\left[\int_{t_0}^{t_0+h} v(x, u, s)\, ds + \max \int_{t_0+h}^{T} v(x, u, s)\, ds + B[x(T), T] \right]$$

$$= \max\left\{ \int_{t_0}^{t_0+h} v(x, u, s)\, ds + V[x(t_0+h), t_0+h] \right\}$$

$$= \max\{v(y, u, t_0)h + V(y, t_0) + V_x(y, t_0)\Delta x + V_t(y, t_0)h + o(h)\}$$

$$= \max\{vh + V(y, t_0) + V_x fh + V_t h + o(h)\}. \tag{6.7}$$

The first equation is obvious; the second follows from the following principle called the *principle of optimality*: to maximize a total sum of payoffs from $x(t_0) = y$ over $[t_0, T]$ you must maximize the subtotal of the sum of payoffs from $x(t_0 + h)$ over $[t_0 + h, T]$; the third follows from the definition of the state valuation function; the fourth follows from the integral mean value theorem and expansion of $V(x(t_0+h), t_0+h))$ in a Taylor series about $x(t_0) = y$ and t_0; the fifth follows from $\Delta x \equiv x(t_0+h) - x(t_0) = fh + o(h)$. Here $o(h)$ is any function of h that satisfies

$$\lim_{h \to 0} o(h)/h = 0.$$

Subtract $V(y, t_0)$ from the LHS and the extreme RHS of the above equation; divide by h and take limits to get (6.3). So (6.3) is nothing but the principle of optimality in differential form.

Equation (6.4) is just a definition. To motivate this definition rewrite equation (1.7), thus putting $p \equiv V_x$.

$$-V_t = \max\{v(y, u, t_0) + pf(y, u, t_0) + o(h)/h\}. \tag{6.8}$$

Observe that the *Hamiltonian function* H^* just collects the terms that contain the control u. The control u must be chosen to maximize H^* along an optimum path. This follows directly from equation (6.7).

The principle that the optimal control u^0 must maximize H^* is important. It is called the *maximum principle*. One chooses the control to maximize the sum of current instantaneous payoff $v(y, u, t_0)$ and future instantaneous value $p\dot{x} = pf(y, u, t_0)$, $p \equiv V_x$. The quantity p, called the *costate* variable, is the marginal value of the state variable. It measures the incremental sum of payoffs from an extra unit of state variable.

Equation (6.5) is easy to derive. The relation $x = H^{*0}_p$ follows from $\dot{x} = f(x, u^0, t)$ and the envelope theorem. The relation $\dot{p} = -H^{*0}_x$ follows from substitution of the derivative of (1.3) wrt x into the expression for $dp/dt = (d/dt)V_x$.

Finally (6.6) is simple. If there is an inequality constraint $x(t) \geq b$ for all t, but $B \equiv 0$, then, the transversality condition, $p(T) = B_x(x, T)$ takes the form $p(T)x(T) = 0$. The condition $p(T)x(T) = 0$ means that nothing of value is left over at the terminal date T. When T is infinite, for a large class of problems the condition takes the form

$$\lim_{T \to \infty} p(T)x(T) = 0 \tag{6.9}$$

and is called the *transversality condition at infinity*. Benveniste and Scheinkman (1982), Araujo and Scheinkman (1983), and Weitzman (1973) show that (6.9) is necessary and sufficient for optimality for a large class of problems.

It is instructive to give a rough heuristic argument to motivate why (6.9) might be necessary for optimality. For any date T with terminal date in (6.1) set equal to infinity, assume the state valuation function $V(y, T)$ is concave in *y*. (Note that t_0 is replaced with T and T is replaced by ∞ in (6.1) here.) Use concavity and $p(T) \equiv V_x(x(T), T)$ to get the bound

$$V(x(T), T) - V(x(T)/2, T)$$
$$\geq V_x(x(T), T)x(T)/2 = p(T)x(T)/2. \tag{6.10}$$

Now suppose that the distant future is insignificant in the sense that $V(z(T), T) \to 0$, $T \to \infty$ for any state path *z*. Then it is plausible to expect that the LHS of (6.10) will go to 0 as $T \to \infty$. If $x(T) \geq 0$ and $p(T) \geq 0$ (more *x* is better than less) then

$$\lim_{T \to \infty} p(T)x(T) = 0$$

which is (6.9).

Examples exist where (6.9) is not necessary for optimality. The idea is that if the distant future is significant then there is no reason to expect the value of leftovers $p(T)x(T)$ to be forced to zero along an optimum path. See Benveniste and Scheinkman (1982), and Araujo and Scheinkman (1983) for the details and references.

In the same manner and for the same reasons as a time series analyst transforms his time series to render it time stationary the dynamic economic modeller searches for a change of units so that (abusing notation) problem (6.1) may be written in the time stationary form

$$V(y, t_0) = \int_{t_0}^{T} e^{-\delta t} v(x, u) \, ds + e^{-\delta T} B[x(T)], \tag{6.11}$$

$$\dot{x} = f(x, u), \quad x(t_0) = y. \tag{6.12}$$

By the change of units $W(y, t_0) = e^{\delta t} V(y, t_0)$, $q = e^{\delta t} p$, $H = e^{\delta t} H^*$ and we may write the optimality conditions (6.3)-(6.6) in the form:

$$\delta W - W_t = \max_u H(q, x, u) = H^0(q, x), \tag{6.13}$$

$$H(q, x, u) \equiv v(x, u) + qf, \tag{6.14}$$

$$\dot{q} = \delta q - H_x^0, \quad \dot{x} = H_q, \quad x(t_0) = y, \tag{6.15}$$

$$W(x, T) = B(x), \quad q(T) = B_x(x). \tag{6.16}$$

When the horizon $T = \infty$, *W* becomes independent of *T* so that $W_t = 0$; the transversality condition becomes

$$\lim_{t \to \infty} e^{-\delta t} q(t)x(t) = 0, \tag{6.17}$$

and (6.17) is *necessary* as well as *sufficient,* for a solution of (6.15) to be optimal. The condition (6.17) determines q_0.

For further details see Mangasarian (1966), Brock (1987a), Arrow and Kurz (1970) or Kamien and Schwartz (1981). Barron et al. (1987) use monotone control methods to solve certain problems in economics. Pindyck (1973), Turnovsky (1974) and B. Friedman (1975) apply control theory to stabilization policies.

Finally, chapters 5, 7, 9 and 10 use elementary notions from measure theory which are presented in Royden (1968).

SELECTED BIBLIOGRAPHY

Abraham, R. and J.E. Marsden (1978), *Foundations of Mechanics*, second edition, Benjamin/Cummings Publishing Company, Reading, Massachusetts.

Aeyels, D. (1981), "Generic Observability of Differentiable Systems", *Society of Industrial and Applied Mathematics Journal on Control and Optimization*, 19, 595-603.

Aghelvi, B.B. and M.S. Khan (1977), "Inflationary Finance and the Dynamics of Inflation: Indonesia, 1951-72", *American Economic Review*, 67, 390-403.

Allen, R.G.D. (1938), *Mathematical Analysis for Economists*, St Martin's Press, New York.

Allingham, M.G. (1974), "Equilibrium and Stability", *Econometrica*, 42, 705-716.

Al-Nowaihi, A. and P.L. Levine (1985), "The Stability of the Cournot Oligopoly Model: A Reassessment", *Journal of Economic Theory*, 35, 307-321.

Anderson, B.O. and J.B. Moore (1971), *Linear Optimal Control*, Prentice-Hall, Englewood Cliffs, New Jersey.

Anderson, T.W. (1971), *The Statistical Analysis of Time Series*, John Wiley & Sons, New York.

Andronov, A.A., E.A. Leontovich, I.I. Gordon and A.G. Maier (1973), *Theory of Bifurcations of Dynamic Systems on a Plane*, John Wiley & Sons, New York.

Antosiewicz, H. (1958), "A Survey of Liapunov's Second Method", *Annals of Mathematical Studies*, 4, 141-166.

Apostol, T.M. (1967), *Calculus, Volume I*, second edition, Blaisdell Publishing Company, New York.

Apostol, T.M. (1969a), *Calculus, Volume II*, second edition, Blaisdell Publishing Company, New York.

Apostol, T.M. (1969b), "Some Explicit Formulas for the Exponential Matrix e^{At}", *American Mathematical Monthly*, 76, 289-292.

Araujo, A.P. and J.A. Scheinkman (1977), "Smoothness, Comparative Dynamics and the Turnpike Property", *Econometrica*, 45, 601-620.

Araujo, A.P. and J.A. Scheinkman (1979), "Notes on Comparative Dynamics", in: J.R. Green and J.A. Scheinkman, eds, *General Equilibrium, Growth, and Trade: Essays in Honor of Lionel McKenzie*, Academic Press, New York, 217-226.

Araujo, A.P. and J.A. Scheinkman (1983), "Maximum Principle and Transversality Condition for Concave Infinite Horizon Economic Models", *Journal of Economic Theory*, 30, 1-16.

Arnold, V.I. (1973), *Ordinary Differential Equations*, MIT Press, Cambridge, Massachusetts.

Arnold, V.I. (1983), *Geometrical Methods in the Theory of Ordinary Differential Equations*, Springer-Verlag, New York.

Arrow, K.J. and L. Hurwicz (1958), "On the Stability of the Competitive Equilibrium, I", *Econometrica*, 26, 522-552.

Arrow, K.J. and M. McManus (1958), "A Note on Dynamic Stability", *Econometrica*, 26, 448-454.

Arrow, K.J. and M. Nerlove (1958), "A Note on Expectations and Stability", *Econometrica*, 26, 297–305.

Arrow, K.J., H.D. Block and L. Hurwicz (1959), "On the Stability of the Competitive Equilibrium, II", *Econometrica*, 27, 82–109.

Arrow, K.J. and M. Kurz (1970), *Public Investment, the Rate of Return, and Optimal Fiscal Policy*, Johns Hopkins Press, Baltimore, Maryland.

Arrow, K.J. and F. Hahn (1971), *General Competitive Analysis*, Holden-Day, San Francisco, California.

Athans, M. and P.L. Falb (1966), *Optimal Control: An Introduction to the Theory and Its Applications*, McGraw-Hill, New York.

Atkinson, F.V. (1958), "On Stability and Asymptotic Equilibrium", *Annals of Mathematics*, 68, 690–708.

Attfield, C.L.E., D. Demery and N.W. Duck (1985), *Rational Expectations in Macroeconomics*, Basil Blackwell, England.

Auerbach, A. (1979), "Wealth Maximization and the Cost of Capital", *Quarterly Journal of Economics*, 93, 433–446.

Averch, H. and L. Johnson (1962), "Behavior of the Firm Under Regulatory Constraint", *American Economic Review*, 52, 1053–1069.

Azariadis, C. and R. Guesnerie (1986), "Sunspots and Cycles", *Review of Economic Studies*, 53, 725–737.

Baek, E. (1987), "Contemporaneous Independence Test of Two IID Series", working paper, Department of Economics, University of Wisconsin, Madison, Wisconsin.

Balasko, Y. (1975), "Some Results on Uniqueness and on Stability of Equilibrium in General Equilibrium Theory", *Journal of Mathematical Economics*, 2, 95–118.

Barbashin, E.A. (1970), *Introduction to the Theory of Stability*, Wolters-Noordhoff, Groningen, Holland.

Barnett, W. and P. Chen (1987), "The Aggregation-Theoretic Monetary Aggregates are Chaotic and Have Strange Attractors", in: W. Barnett, E. Berndt and H. White, eds, *Dynamic Econometric Modeling*, Cambridge University Press, New York.

Barron, E.N., R. Jensen and A.G. Malliaris (1987), "Minimizing a Quadratic Payoff with Monotone Controls", *Mathematics of Operations Research*, 12, 297–308.

Batavia, B., N.A. Lash and A.G. Malliaris (1986), "The Dynamics of Inflation and Economic Policy: The Case of Greece 1953–83", *Greek Economic Review*, 7, 200–217.

Baumol, W. and J. Benhabib (1988), "Chaos: Significance, Mechanism, and Economic Applications", *Journal of Economic Perspectives*, 2.

Baye, M.R. (1985), "A Note on Price Stability and Consumers' Welfare", *Econometrica*, 53, 213–216.

Becker, R.A. (1980), "On the Long-Run Steady State in a Simple Dynamic Model of Equilibrium with Heterogeneous Households", *Quarterly Journal of Economics*, 95, 375–382.

Becker, R.A. (1985), "Capital Income Taxation and Perfect Foresight", *Journal of Public Economics*, 26, 147–167.

Becker, R.A., J.H. Boyd, III and B.Y. Sung (1987), "Recursive Utility and Optimal Capital Accumulation, I: Existence", working paper, Department of Economics, University of Rochester, Rochester, New York.

Bellman, R.E. (1953), *Stability Theory of Differential Equations*, McGraw-Hill, New York.

Bellman, R.E. (1970), *Introduction to Matrix Analysis*, second edition, McGraw-Hill, New York.

Ben-Mizrachi, A., et al. (1984), "Characterization of Experimental (Noisy) Strange Attractors", *Physical Review*, 29A, 975–977.

Benavie, A. (1972), *Mathematical Techniques for Economic Analysis*, Prentice-Hall, Englewood Cliffs, New Jersey.

Bendixson, I. (1901), "Sur les Courbes Définiés par des Equations Differentielles", *Acta Mathematica*, 24, 1–88.

Benettin, G., et al. (1976), "Kolmogorov Entropy and Numerical Experiments", *Physical Review*, 14A, 2338–2345.

Benettin, G., et al. (1980), "Liapunov Characteristic Exponents for Smooth Dynamical Systems: A Method for Computing All of Them", *Meccanica*, 15, 9–20.

Benhabib, J. (1980), "Adaptive Monetary Policy and Rational Expectations", *Journal of Economic Theory*, 23, 261–266.

Benhabib, J. and K. Nishimura (1979), "The Hopf Bifurcation and the Existence and Stability of Closed Orbits in Multisector Models of Optimal Economic Growth", *Journal of Economic Theory*, 21, 421–444.

Benhabib, J. and R.H. Day (1981), "Rational Choice and Erratic Behaviour", *Review of Economic Studies*, 48, 459–471.

Benhabib, J. and T. Miyao (1981), "Some New Results on the Dynamics of the Generalized Tobin Model", *International Economic Review*, 22, 589–596.

Benhabib, J. and K. Nishimura (1981), "Stability of Equilibrium in Dynamic Models of Capital Theory", *International Economic Review*, 22, 275–293.

Benhabib, J. and R.H. Day (1982), "A Characterization of Erratic Dynamics in the Overlapping Generation Model", *Journal of Economic Dynamics and Control*, 4, 37–55.

Benhabib, J. and C. Bull (1983), "The Optimal Quantity of Money: A Formal Treatment", *International Economic Review*, 24, 101–111.

Benhabib, J. and K. Nishimura (1985), "Competitive Equilibrium Cycles", *Journal of Economic Theory*, 35, 284–306.

Bensoussan, A. (1982), *Stochastic Control by Functional Analysis Methods*, North-Holland Publishing Company, New York.

Benveniste, L.M. and D. Gale (1975), "An Extension of Cass' Characterization of Infinite Efficient Production Programs", *Journal of Economic Theory*, 10, 229–238.

Benveniste, L.M. and J.A. Scheinkman (1979), "On the Differentiability of the Value Function in Dynamic Models of Economics", *Econometrica*, 47, 727–732.

Benveniste, L.M. and J.A. Scheinkman (1982), "Duality Theory for Dynamic Optimization Models of Economics: The Continuous Time Case", *Journal of Economic Theory*, 27, 1–19.

Bernfeld, S.R. (1970), "Liapunov Functions and Global Existence Without Uniqueness", *Proceedings of the American Mathematical Society*, 25, 571–577.

Bewley, T.F. (1980a), "The Permanent Income Hypothesis and Long-Run Economic Stability", *Journal of Economic Theory*, 22, 377–394.

Bewley, T.F. (1980b), "The Permanent Income Hypothesis and Short-Run Price Stability", *Journal of Economic Theory*, 23, 323–333.

Bhagwati, J.N., R.A. Brecher and T. Hatta (1987), "The Global Correspondence Principle: A Generalization", *American Economic Review*, 77, 124–132.

Bhatia, N.P. and G.P. Szegö (1967), *Dynamical Systems: Stability, Theory and Applications*, Springer-Verlag, New York.

Bhatia, N.P. and G.P. Szegö (1970), *Stability Theory of Dynamical Systems*, Springer-Verlag, New York.

Bhattacharya, R. and M. Majumdar (1980), "On Global Stability of Some Stochastic Economic Processes: A Synthesis", in: L. Klein, et al., eds, *Quantitative Economics and Development*, Academic Press, New York, 19–43.

Birkhoff, G.D. (1927), *Dynamical Systems*, American Mathematical Society Colloquium Publications, New York.

Birkhoff, G.D. and Q.C. Rota (1978), *Ordinary Differential Equations*, third edition, John Wiley & Sons, New York.

Black, F. (1974), "Uniqueness of the Price Level in Monetary Growth Models with Rational Expectations", *Journal of Economic Theory*, 7, 53-65.

Blad, M.C. (1981), "Exchange of Stability in a Disequilibrium Model", *Journal of Mathematical Economics*, 8, 121-145.

Blanchard, O.J. (1983), "Dynamic Effects of a Shift in Savings: The Role of Firms", *Econometrica*, 51, 1583-1592.

Blatt, J.M. (1978), "On the Econometric Approach to Business-Cycle Analysis", *Oxford Economic Papers*, 30, 292-300.

Blatt, J.M. (1980), "On the Frisch Model of Business Cycles", *Oxford Economic Papers*, 32, 467-479.

Blatt, J.M. (1981), *Dynamic Economic Systems*, M.E. Sharpe, Armonk, New York.

Blinder, A.S. and R. Solow (1973), "Does Fiscal Policy Matter?", *Journal of Public Economics*, 2, 319-338.

Blume, L.E., M.M. Bray and D. Easley (1982), "Introduction to the Stability of Rational Expectations Equilibrium", *Journal of Economic Theory*, 26, 313-317.

Boldrin, M. and L. Montrucchio (1986), "On the Indeterminancy of Capital Accumulation Paths", *Journal of Economic Theory*, 40, 26-39.

Bollerslev, T. (1986), "Generalized Autoregressive Conditional Heteroskedasticity", *Journal of Econometrics*, 31, 307-327.

Borg, G. (1949), "On a Liapunov Criterion of Stability", *American Journal of Mathematics*, 71, 67-70.

Boyce, W.E. and R.C. DiPrima (1986), *Elementary Differential Equations and Boundary Value Problems*, fourth edition, John Wiley & Sons, New York.

Boyd, III, J.H. (1986a), "Recursive Utility and the Ramsey Problem", working paper, Department of Economics, University of Rochester, Rochester, New York.

Boyd, III, J.H. (1986b), "Symmetries, Equilibria and the Value Function", working paper, Department of Economics, University of Rochester, Rochester, New York.

Brauer, F. (1961), "Global Behavior of Solutions of Ordinary Differential Equations", *Journal of Mathematical Analysis and Applications*, 2, 145-158.

Brauer, F. and J.A. Nohel (1967), *Ordinary Differential Equations: A First Course*, W.A. Benjamin, Inc., Reading, Massachusetts.

Brauer, F. and J.A. Nohel (1969), *Qualitative Theory of Ordinary Differential Equations: an Introduction*, W.A. Benjamin, Inc., Reading, Massachusetts.

Braun, M. (1978), *Differential Equations and Their Applications: An Introduction to Applied Mathematics*, second edition, Springer-Verlag, New York.

Braun, M. (1983), *Differential Equations and Their Applications: An Introduction to Applied Mathematics*, third edition, Springer-Verlag, New York.

Bray, M.M. (1982), "Learning, Estimation, and the Stability of Rational Expectations", *Journal of Economic Theory*, 26, 318-339.

Breakwell, J.V., J.L. Speyer and A.E. Bryson (1963), "Optimization and Control of Nonlinear Systems Using the Second Variation", *Society of Industrial and Applied Mathematics Journal on Control and Optimization*, 1, 193-223.

Brillinger, D. and M. Hatanaka (1969), "Harmonic Analysis of Non-stationary Multivariate Economic Processes", *Econometrica*, 37, 131-141.

Brock, W.A. (1970), "On Existence of Weakly Maximal Programmes in A Multi-Sector Economy", *Review of Economic Studies*, 37, 275-280.

Brock, W.A. (1972), "On Models of Expectations That Arise From Maximizing Behavior of Economic Agents Over Time", *Journal of Economic Theory*, 5, 348-376.

Brock, W.A. (1973), "Some Results on the Uniqueness of Steady States in Multi-Sector Models of Optimum Growth When Future Utilities are Discounted", *International Economic Review*, 14, 535-559.

Brock, W.A. (1974), "Money and Growth: The Case of Long Run Perfect Foresight", *International Economic Review*, 15, 750-777.

Brock, W.A. (1975), "A Simple Perfect Foresight Monetary Model", *Journal of Monetary Economics*, 1, 133-150.

Brock, W.A. (1977a), "The Global Asymptotic Stability of Optimal Control: A Survey of Recent Results", in: M.D. Intriligator, ed., *Frontiers of Quantitative Economics, III A*, North-Holland Publishing Company, Amsterdam, 207-237.

Brock, W.A. (1977b), "Differential Games With Active and Passive Variables", in: R. Henn and O. Moeschlin, eds, *Mathematical Economics and Game Theory: Essays in Honor of Oskar Morgenstern*, Springer-Verlag, New York, 34-52.

Brock, W.A. (1982), "Asset Prices in a Production Economy", in: J.J. McCall, ed., *Economics of Information and Uncertainty*, University of Chicago Press, Chicago, Illinois, 1-43.

Brock, W.A. (1985), "Distinguishing Random and Deterministic Systems", *International Conference on Nonlinear Economic Dynamics*, June 17-20, Paris, France.

Brock, W.A. (1986a), "Distinguishing Random and Deterministic Systems: Abridged Version", *Journal of Economic Theory*, 40, 168-195.

Brock, W.A. (1986b), "Applications of Recent Results on the Asymptotic Stability of Optimal Control to the Problem of Comparing Long-Run Equilibria", in: H. Sonnenschein, ed., *Models of Economic Dynamics*, Springer-Verlag, New York, 86-116.

Brock, W.A. (1987a), "Optimal Control and Economic Dynamics", in: J. Eatwell, M. Milgate and P. Newman, eds, *The New Palgrave: A Dictionary of Economic Theory and Doctrine*, Macmillan, London, England.

Brock, W.A. (1987b), "Nonlinearity and Complex Dynamics in Finance and Economics", in: D. Pines, ed., *The Economy as an Evolving Complex System*, Addison-Wesley, New York.

Brock, W.A. (1988a), "Overlapping Generations Models with Money and Transactions Costs", in: B.M. Friedman and F. Hahn, eds, *Handbook of Monetary Economics*, North-Holland Publishing Company, New York.

Brock, W.A. (1988b), "Notes on Nuisance Parameter Problems and BDS Type Tests for IID", working paper, Department of Economics, University of Wisconsin, Madison, Wisconsin.

Brock, W.A. and L. Mirman (1972), "Optimal Economic Growth and Uncertainty: The Discounted Case", *Journal of Economic Theory*, 4, 479-513.

Brock, W.A. and J.A. Scheinkman (1975), "Some Results on Global Asymptotic Stability of Control Systems", working paper, Department of Economics, University of Chicago, Chicago, Illinois.

Brock, W.A. and E. Burmeister (1976), "Regular Economies and Conditions for Uniqueness of Steady States in Optimal Multi-Sector Economic Models", *International Economic Review*, 17, 105-120.

Brock, W.A. and A. Haurie (1976), "On Existence of Weakly Optimal Trajectories Over an Infinite Time Horizon", *Mathematics of Operations Research*, 1, 337-346.

Brock, W.A. and J.A. Scheinkman (1976), "Global Asymptotic Stability of Optimal Control Systems with Applications to the Theory of Economic Growth", *Journal of Economic Theory*, 12, 164-190.

Brock, W.A. and J.A. Scheinkman (1977a), "The Global Asymptotic Stability of Optimal Control With Applications to Dynamic Economic Theory", in: J.D. Pitchford and S.J. Turnovsky, eds, *Applications of Control Theory to Economic Analysis*, North-Holland Publishing Company, Amsterdam, 173-205.

Brock, W.A. and J.A. Scheinkman (1977b), "On the Long-Run Behavior of a Competitive Firm", in: G. Schwodiauer, ed., *Equilibrium and Disequilibrium in Economic Theory*, D. Reidel Publishing Company, Dordrecht, Holland, 397-411.

Brock, W.A. and M. Majumdar (1978), "Global Asymptotic Stability Results for Multi-Sector Models of Optimal Growth Under Uncertainty When Future Utilities are Discounted", *Journal of Economic Theory*, 18, 225-243.

Brock, W.A. and M.J.P. Magill (1979), "Dynamics Under Uncertainty", *Econometrica*, 47, 843-868.

Brock, W.A. and J.A. Scheinkman (1980), "Some Remarks on Monetary Policy in an Overlapping Generations Model", in: J. Kareken and N. Wallace, eds, *Models of Monetary Economics*, Federal Reserve Bank of Minneapolis, 211-232.

Brock, W.A. and S.J. Turnovsky (1981), "The Analysis of Macroeconomic Policies in Perfect Foresight Equilibrium", *International Economic Review*, 22, 179-209.

Brock, W.A. and W.D. Dechert (1985), "Dynamic Ramsey Pricing", *International Economic Review*, 26, 569-591.

Brock, W.A. and W.D. Dechert (1987), "Theorems on Distinguishing Deterministic and Random Systems", in: W. Barnett, E. Berndt and H. White, eds, *Dynamic Econometric Modeling*, Cambridge University Press, New York.

Brock, W.A., W.D. Dechert and J.A. Scheinkman (1987), "A Test for Independence Based on the Correlation Dimension", working paper, Department of Economics, University of Wisconsin, Madison, Wisconsin.

Brock, W.A. and C. Sayers (1988), "Is the Business Cycle Characterized by Deterministic Chaos?", *Journal of Monetary Economics*, 21, 71-90.

Bronson, R. (1973), *Modern Introductory Differential Equations*, McGraw-Hill, New York.

Brown, D. and G. Heal (1980), "Two-Part Tariffs, Marginal Cost Pricing and Increasing Returns in a General Equilibrium Model", *Journal of Public Economics*, 13, 25-49.

Buiter, W.H. (1977), " 'Crowding Out' and the Effectiveness of Fiscal Policy", *Journal of Public Economics*, 7, 309-328.

Buiter, W.H. (1984), "Saddlepoint Problems in Continuous Time Rational Expectations: A General Method and Some Macroeconomic Examples", *Econometrica*, 52, 665-680.

Bunow, B. and G. Weiss (1979), "How Chaotic is Chaos? Chaotic and Other 'Noisy' Dynamics in the Frequency Domain", *Mathematical Biosciences*, 47, 221.

Burganskaya, L.I. (1974), "Stability in the Large of a System of Nonlinear Differential Equations", *Journal of Differential Equations*, 11, 402-404.

Burmeister, E. (1980), *Capital Theory and Dynamics*, Cambridge University Press, Cambridge, England.

Burmeister, E. (1981), "On the Uniqueness of Dynamically Efficient Steady States", *International Economic Review*, 22, 211-219.

Burmeister, E. and A.R. Dobell (1970), *Mathematical Theories of Economic Growth*, Macmillan, London, England.

Burmeister, E. and S.J. Turnovsky (1972), "Capital Deepening Response in an Economy With Heterogeneous Capital Goods", *American Economic Review*, 62, 842-853.

Burmeister, E. and D.A. Graham (1973), "Price Expectations and Stability in Descriptive and Optimally Controlled Macro-Economic Models", *Journal of Electrical Engineers Conference Publication No. 101*, Institute of Electrical Engineers, London, England.

Burmeister, E. and D.A. Graham (1974), "Multi-Sector Economic Models With Continuous Adaptive Expectations", *Review of Economic Studies*, 41, 323–336.

Burmeister, E. and D.A. Graham (1975), "Price Expectations and Global Stability in Economic Systems", *Automatica*, 11, 487–497.

Burmeister, E. and S.J. Turnovsky (1976), "The Specification of Adaptive Expectations in Continuous Time Dynamic Economic Models", *Econometrica*, 44, 879–905.

Burmeister, E. and P.J. Hammond (1977), "Maximin Paths of Heterogeneous Capital Accumulation and the Instability of Paradoxical Steady States", *Econometrica*, 45, 853–870.

Burmeister, E. and N.V. Long (1977), "On Some Unresolved Questions in Capital Theory: An Application of Samuelson's Correspondence Principle", *The Quarterly Journal of Economics*, 91, 289–314.

Burmeister, E. and S.J. Turnovsky (1977), "Price Expectations and Stability in a Short-Run Multi-Asset Macro Model", *American Economic Review*, 67, 213–218.

Burmeister, E. and S.J. Turnovsky (1978), "Price Expectations, Disequilibrium Adjustments, and Macroeconomic Price Stability", *Journal of Economic Theory*, 17, 287–311.

Burton, T.A. (1985), *Stability and Periodic Solutions of Ordinary and Functional Differential Equations*, Academic Press, New York.

Bushaw, D. (1969), "Stabilities of Liapunov and Poisson Types", *Society of Industrial and Applied Mathematics Review*, 11, 214–225.

Calvo, G.A. (1977), "The Stability of Models of Money and Perfect Foresight: A Comment", *Econometrica*, 45, 1737–1739.

Calvo, G.A. (1978a), "On the Time Consistency of Optimal Policy in a Monetary Economy", *Econometrica*, 46, 1411–1428.

Calvo, G.A. (1978b), "Optimal Seignorage from Money Creation", *Journal of Monetary Economics*, 4, 503–517.

Calvo, G.A. (1979), "On Models of Money and Perfect Foresight", *International Economic Review*, 20, 83–103.

Calvo, G. and M. Obstfeld (1988), "Optimal Time-Consistent Fiscal Policy with Finite Lifetimes", *Econometrica*, 56, 411–432.

Carathéodory, C. (1927), *Vorlesungen uber reelle Funktionen*, Leipzig, Germany.

Carr, J. (1981), *Applications of Centre Manifold Theory*, Springer-Verlag, New York.

Cass, D. (1965), "Optimum Growth in an Aggregative Model of Capital Accumulation", *Review of Economic Studies*, 32, 233–240.

Cass, D. (1972), "On Capital Overaccumulation in the Aggregative, Neoclassical Model of Economic Growth: A Complete Characterization", *Journal of Economic Theory*, 4, 200–223.

Cass, D. and K. Shell (1976a), "The Structure and Stability of Competitive Dynamical Systems", *Journal of Economic Theory*, 12, 31–70.

Cass, D. and K. Shell (1976b), "Introduction to Hamiltonian Dynamics in Economics", *Journal of Economic Theory*, 12, 1–10.

Cass, D., M. Okuno and I. Zilcha (1980), "The Role of Money in Supporting the Pareto Optimality of Competitive Equilibrium in Consumption Loan Type Models", in: J. Kareken and N. Wallace, eds, *Models of Monetary Economics*, Federal Reserve Bank of Minneapolis, 13–48.

Cesari, L. (1963), *Asymptotic Behavior and Stability Problems in Ordinary Differential Equations*, second edition, Springer-Verlag, New York.

Chang, F.R. (1982), "A Note on the Stochastic Value Loss Assumption", *Journal of Economic Theory*, 26, 164-170.

Chang, F.R. (1987), "Optimal Growth with Recursive Preferences", working paper, Department of Economics, Indiana University, Bloomington, Indiana.

Chang, F.R. (1988), "The Inverse Optimal Problem: A Dynamic Programming Approach", *Econometrica*, 55, 147-172.

Chang, F.R. and A.G. Malliaris (1987), "Asymptotic Growth Under Uncertainty: Existence and Uniqueness", *Review of Economic Studies*, 54, 169-174.

Chetaev, N.G. (1961), *The Stability of Motion*, Pergamon Press, New York.

Chiang, A.C. (1984), *Fundamental Methods of Mathematical Economics*, third edition, McGraw-Hill, New York.

Churchill, R. (1960), *Complex Variables and Applications*, second edition, McGraw-Hill, New York.

Cochrane, J. (1988), "How Big is the Random Walk in GNP", *Journal of Political Economy*, 96, 893-920.

Cochrane, J. (1987), "A Production Based Asset Pricing: An Empirical Approach to the Link Between Asset Prices and Macroeconomic Fluctuations", working paper, Department of Economics, University of Chicago, Chicago, Illinois.

Coddington, E.A. (1961), *An Introduction to Ordinary Differential Equations*, Prentice-Hall, Englewood Cliffs, New Jersey.

Coddington, E.A. and N. Levinson (1955), *Theory of Ordinary Differential Equations*, McGraw-Hill, New York.

Collet, P. and J. Eckmann (1980), *Iterated Maps on the Internal as Dynamical Systems*, Birkhauser, Basel, Switzerland.

Coppel, W.A. (1965), *Stability and Asymptotic Behavior of Differential Equations*, Heath Mathematical Monographs, Boston, Massachusetts.

Coppel, W.A. (1978), *Dichotomies in Stability Theory, Lecture Notes in Mathematics*, 629, Springer-Verlag, New York.

Courant, R. and H. Robbins (1941), *What is Mathematics?*, Oxford University Press, London, England.

Craine, R. (1987), "Risky Business: The Allocation of Capital", working paper, Department of Economics, University of California at Berkeley.

Crutchfield, J. and N. Packard (1983), "Symbolic Dynamics of Noisy Chaos", *Physica*, 7D, 201-223.

Danthine, J.P. (1978), "Information, Futures Prices, and Stabilizing Speculation", *Journal of Economic Theory*, 17, 79-98.

DasGupta, S. (1985), "A Local Analysis of Stability and Regularity of Stationary States in Discrete Symmetric Optimal Capital Accumulation Models", *Journal of Economic Theory*, 36, 302-318.

DasGupta, P.S. and G.M. Heal (1979), *Economic Theory and Exhaustible Resources*, Cambridge University Press, Oxford, England.

d'Aspremont, C. and J.H. Drèze (1979), "On the Stability of Dynamic Process in Economic Theory", *Econometrica*, 47, 733-737.

Datko, R. (1966), "Global Stability of Second Order Autonomous Differential Equations", *Journal of Differential Equations*, 2, 412-419.

David, P. and J. Scadding (1974), "Private Savings: Ultra-rationality, Aggregation and Denison's Law", *Journal of Political Economy*, 82, 225-249.

Day, R.H. (1982), "Irregular Growth Cycles", *American Economic Review*, 72, 406-414.

Day, R.H. (1983), "The Emergence of Chaos From Classical Economic Growth", *Quarterly Journal of Economics*, 98, 201-213.

Day, R.H. and W.J. Shafer (1983), "Keynesian Chaos", working paper, Department of Economics, University of Southern California, Los Angeles.

Debreu, G. (1974), "Excess Demand Functions", *Journal of Mathematical Economics*, 1, 15-21.

Debreu, G. (1986), "Theoretic Models: Mathematical Form and Economic Content", *Econometrica*, 54, 1259-1270.

DeCanio, S. (1979), "Rational Expectations and Learning From Experience", *Quarterly Journal of Economics*, 93, 47-57.

Dechert, W.D. (1978), "Optimal Control Problems from Second-Order Difference Equations", *Journal of Economic Theory*, 19, 50-63.

Dechert, W.D. (1983), "Increasing Returns to Scale and the Reverse Flexible Accelerator", *Economics Letters*, 13, 69-75.

Dechert, W.D. (1984), "Has the Averch-Johnson Effect Been Theoretically Justified?", *Journal of Economic Dynamics and Control*, 8, 1-17.

Dechert, W.D. and K. Nishimura (1983), "A Complete Characterization of Optimal Growth Paths in an Aggregated Model with a Non-Concave Production Function", *Journal of Economic Theory*, 31, 332-354.

Demsetz, H. (1968), "Why Regulate Utilities?", *Journal of Law and Economics*, 11, 55-65.

Deneckere, R. and S. Pelikan (1986), "Competitive Chaos", *Journal of Economic Theory*, 40, 13-25.

Desai, M. (1973), "Growth Cycles and Inflation in a Model of the Class Struggle", *Journal of Economic Theory*, 6, 527-545.

Devaney, R.L. (1986), *An Introduction to Chaotic Dynamical Systems*, Benjamin/Cummings Publishing Company, Reading, Massachusetts.

Donsimoni, M.P., N.S. Economides and H.M. Polemarchakis (1986), "Stable Cartels", *International Economic Review*, 27, 317-327.

Dornbusch, R. (1976), "Expectations and Exchange Rate Dynamics", *Journal of Political Economy*, 84, 1161-1176.

Duhem, P. (1954), *The Aim and Structure of Physical Theory*, second edition, Princeton University Press, Princeton, New Jersey.

Eckalbar, J.C. (1980), "The Stability of Non-Walrasian Processes: Two Examples", *Econometrica*, 48, 371-386.

Eckhaus, W. (1965), *Studies in Nonlinear Stability Theory*, Springer-Verlag, New York.

Eckmann, J. and D. Ruelle (1985), "Ergodic Theory of Chaos and Strange Attractors", *Reviews of Modern Physics*, 57, 617-656.

Eisner, R. and R.H. Strotz (1963), "Determinants of Business Investments", in: D.B. Suits et al., eds, *Impacts of Monetary Policy*, Prentice-Hall, Englewood Cliffs, New Jersey.

Engle, R. (1982), "Autoregressive Conditional Heteroscedasticity With Estimates of the Variance of U.K. Inflation", *Econometrica*, 50, 987-1007.

Epstein, L.G. (1982), "Comparative Dynamics in the Adjustment-Cost Model of the Firm", *Journal of Economic Theory*, 27, 77-100.

Epstein, L.G. (1987), "The Global Stability of Efficient Intertemporal Allocations", *Econometrica*, 55, 329-356.

Evans, G. (1985), "Expectational Stability and the Multiple Equilibria Problem in Linear Rational Expectation Models", *Quarterly Journal of Economics*, 100, 1217-1233.

Fair, R. (1978), "A Criticism of One Class of Macroeconomic Models with Rational Expectations", *Journal of Money, Credit and Banking*, 10, 411-417.

Fama, E. (1976), *Foundations of Finance*, Basic Books, Inc., New York.

Fama, E. and K. French (1986), "Permanent and Temporary Components of Stock Prices", working paper, Center for Research on Security Prices, Graduate School of Business, University of Chicago, Chicago, Illinois.

Feinstein, C.D. and S.S. Oren (1983), "Local Stability Properties of the Modified Hamiltonian Dynamic System", *Journal of Economic Dynamics and Control*, 4, 387-397.

Feldstein, M. (1976), "Inflation, Income Taxes, and the Rate of Interest: A Theoretical Analysis", *American Economic Review*, 66, 809-820.

Feldstein, M., J. Green, and E. Sheshinski (1978), "Inflation and Taxes in a Growing Economy With Debt and Equity Finance", *Journal of Political Economy*, 86, S53-S70.

Feldstein, M., J. Green, and E. Sheshinski (1979), "Corporate Financial Policy and Taxation in A Growing Economy", *Quarterly Journal of Economics*, 93, 411-432.

Ferson, W. and J. Merrick, Jr. (1987), "Non-stationarity and State-of-the-Business-Cycle Effects in Consumption-Based Asset Pricing Relations", *Journal of Financial Economics*, 18, 127-146.

Finizio, N. and G. Ladas (1978), *Ordinary Differential Equations with Modern Applications*, Wadsworth Publishing Company, Belmont, California.

Fischer, S. (1972), "Keynes-Wicksell and Neoclassical Models of Money and Growth", *American Economic Review*, 62, 880-890.

Fischer, S. (1979), "Capital Accumulation on the Transition Path in a Monetary Optimizing Model", *Econometrica*, 47, 1433-1439.

Fisher, F.M. (1983), *Disequilibrium Foundations of Equilibrium Economics*, Cambridge University Press, Cambridge, England.

Fleming, W.H. (1971), "Stochastic Control for Small Noise Intensities", *Society of Industrial and Applied Mathematics Journal on Control*, 9, 473-517.

Fleming, W.H. and R.W. Rishel (1975), *Deterministic and Stochastic Optimal Control*, Springer-Verlag, New York.

Flood, R.P., R.J. Hodrick and P. Kaplan (1986), "An Evaluation of Recent Evidence on Stock Market Bubbles", working paper #1971, *National Bureau of Economic Research*, Cambridge, Massachusetts.

Frank, M. and T. Stengos (1986), "Measuring the Strangeness of Gold and Silver Rates of Return", working paper, Department of Economics, University of Guelph, Canada.

Friedman, A. (1971), *Advanced Calculus*, Holt, Rinehart and Winston, New York.

Friedman, B.M. (1975), *Economic Stabilization Policy: Methods in Optimization*, North-Holland Publishing Company, Amsterdam.

Friedman, B.M. (1978), "Stability and Rationality in Models of Hyperinflation", *International Economic Review*, 19, 45-64.

Friedman, J.W. (1971), "A Non-cooperative Equilibrium for Super-games", *Review of Economic Studies*, 38, 1-22.

Friedman, M. (1969), *The Optimum Quantity of Money and Other Essays*, Aldine, Chicago.

Friedman, M. (1971), "The Revenue from Inflation", *Journal of Political Economy*, 79, 846-856.

Froehling, H., et al. (1981), "On Determining the Dimension of Chaotic Flows", *Physica*, 3D, 605-617.

Fuchs, G. (1975), "Structural Stability for Dynamical Economic Models", *Journal of Mathematical Economics*, 2, 139-154.

Fuchs, G. (1979), "Is Error Learning Behavior Stabilizing?", *Journal of Economic Theory*, 20, 300-317.

Gale, D. (1963), "A Note on Global Instability of Competitive Equilibrium", *Naval Research Logistics Quarterly*, 10, 81-87.

Gale, D. (1967), "On Optimal Development in a Multi-Sector Economy", *Review of Economic Studies*, 34, 1–18.

Gale, D. (1973), "Pure Exchange Equilibrium of Dynamic Economic Models", *Journal of Economic Theory*, 6, 12–36.

Gallant, A.R. and G. Tauchen (1986), "Seminonparametric Estimation of Conditionally Constrained Heterogeneous Processes: Asset Pricing Applications", working paper, Department of Economics, Duke University, Durham, North Carolina.

Gal'perin, E.A. and N.N. Krasovskii (1963), "On the Stabilization of Stationary Motions in Nonlinear Control Systems", *Journal of Applied Mathematics and Mechanics*, 27, 1521–1546.

Gandolfo, G. (1980), *Economic Dynamics: Methods and Models*, second edition, North-Holland Publishing Company, Amsterdam.

Gantmacher, F.R. (1959), *The Theory of Matrices, I*, Chelsea, New York.

Garcia, G. (1972), "Olech's Theorem and the Dynamic Stability of Theories of the Rate of Interest", *Journal of Economic Theory*, 4, 541–544.

Gaudet, G. (1977), "On Returns to Scale and the Stability of Competitive Equilibrium", *American Economic Review*, 67, 194–198.

Gennotte, G. and T. Marsh (1986), "Variations in Ex Ante Risk Premiums on Capital Assets", working paper, Business School, University of California at Berkeley.

Geweke, J. (1987), "Modelling Nonlinearity with Normal Polynomial Expansions", working paper, Department of Economics, Duke University, Durham, North Carolina.

Gleick, J. (1987), *Chaos: Making a New Science*, American Mathematical Society, Providence, Rhode Island.

Gordon, D.F. and A. Hynes (1970), "On the Theory of Price Dynamics", in: E.S. Phelps et al., eds, *Microeconomic Foundations of Employment and Inflation Theory*, W.W. Norton and Company, Inc., New York, 369–393.

Grandmont, J.M. (1985), "On Endogenous Competitive Business Cycles", *Econometrica*, 53, 995–1045.

Grandmont, J.M. (1986), ed., *Nonlinear Economic Dynamics*, Academic Press, New York.

Granger, C. (1987), "Stochastic or Deterministic Non-Linear Models? A Discussion of the Recent Literature in Economics", working paper, Department of Economics, University of California at San Diego.

Granger, C. and P. Newbold (1977), *Forecasting Economic Time Series*, Academic Press, New York.

Granger, C. and A. Andersen (1978), *An Introduction to Bilinear Time Series Models*, Vandenhoeck and Ruprecht, Gottingen, Germany.

Grassberger, P. and I. Procaccia (1983a), "Measuring the Strangeness of Strange Attractors", *Physica*, 9D, 189–208.

Grassberger, P. and I. Procaccia (1983b), "Estimation of the Kolmogorov Entropy From a Chaotic Signal", *Physical Review A*, 28, 2591–2593.

Gray, J.A. (1984), "Dynamic Instability in Rational Expectations Models: An Attempt to Clarify", *International Economic Review*, 25, 93–122.

Gray, M.R. and S.J. Turnovsky (1979), "The Stability of Exchange-Rate Dynamics Under Perfect Myopic Foresight", *International Economic Review*, 20, 643–660.

Grebogi, C., et al. (1984), "Strange Attractors That Are Not Chaotic", *Physica*, 13D, 261–268.

Green, J.R. (1974), "The Stability of Edgeworth's Recontracting Process", *Econometrica*, 42, 21–34.

Guckenheimer, J. (1978), "Comments on Catastrophe and Chaos", in: S.A. Levin, ed., *Lectures on Mathematics in the Life Sciences*, The American Mathematical Society, Providence, Rhode Island, 10, 1-47.

Guckenheimer, J. (1982), "Noise in Chaotic Systems", *Nature*, 298, 358-361.

Guckenheimer, J. and P. Holmes (1983), *Nonlinear Oscillations, Dynamical Systems, and Bifurcations of Vector Fields*, Springer-Verlag, New York.

Guesnerie, R. (1975), "Pareto Optimality in Non-Convex Economies", *Econometrica*, 43, 1-30.

Hadjimichalakis, M.G. (1971a), "Money, Expectations and Dynamics: An Alternative View", *International Economic Review*, 12, 381-402.

Hadjimichalakis, M.G. (1971b), "Equilibrium and Disequilibrium Growth With Money: The Tobin Models", *Review of Economic Studies*, 38, 457-479.

Hadjimichalakis, M.G. (1973), "On the Effectiveness of Monetary Policy as a Stabilization Device", *Review of Economic Studies*, 40, 561-570.

Hadjimichalakis, M.G. (1979), "Monetary Policy and Stabilization of a Growing Economy", *Greek Economic Review*, 1, 48-60.

Hadjimichalakis, M.G. (1981), "Expectations of the 'Myopic Perfect Foresight' Variety in Monetary Dynamics: Stability and Non-Neutrality of Money", *Journal of Economic Dynamics and Control*, 3, 157-176.

Hadjimichalakis, M.G. and K. Okuguchi (1979), "The Stability of a Generalized Tobin Model", *Review of Economic Studies*, 46, 175-178.

Hadley, G. (1961), *Linear Algebra*, Addison-Wesley, Reading, Massachusetts.

Hahn, F. (1962), "The Stability of the Cournot Oligopoly Solution", *Review of Economic Studies*, 29, 329-331.

Hahn, F. (1966), "Equilibrium Dynamics with Heterogeneous Capital Goods", *Quarterly Journal of Economics*, 80, 633-646.

Hahn, F. (1982), "Stability", in: K.J. Arrow and M.D. Intriligator, eds, *Handbook of Mathematical Economics, Volume II*, North-Holland Publishing Company, Amsterdam.

Hahn, W. (1963), *Theory and Application of Liapunov's Direct Method*, Prentice-Hall, Englewood Cliffs, New Jersey.

Hahn, W. (1967), *Stability of Motion*, Springer-Verlag, New York.

Halanay, S. (1966), *Differential Equations: Stability, Oscillations, Time Lags*, Academic Press, New York.

Hale, J.K. (1969), *Ordinary Differential Equations*, Wiley-Interscience, New York.

Harberger, A.C. (1962), "The Incidence of the Corporation Income Tax", *Journal of Political Economy*, 70, 215-240.

Harris, C.J. and J.F. Miles (1980), *Stability of Linear Systems: Some Aspects of Kinematic Similarity*, Academic Press, New York.

Hartman, P. (1961), "On Stability in the Large for Systems of Ordinary Differential Equations", *Canadian Journal of Mathematics*, 13, 480-492.

Hartman, P. (1964), *Ordinary Differential Equations*, John Wiley & Sons, New York.

Hartman, P. and C. Olech (1962), "On Global Asymptotic Stability of Solutions of Ordinary Differential Equations", *Transactions of the American Mathematical Society*, 104, 154-178.

Hartman, R. (1987), "Monetary Uncertainty and Investment in an Optimizing, Rational Expectations Model with Income Taxes and Government Debt", *Econometrica*, 55, 169-176.

Haugen, R. (1987), *Introductory Investment Theory*, Prentice-Hall, Inc., New Jersey.

Heller, W.P. (1975), "Tâtonnement Stability of Infinite Horizon Models With Saddle-Point Instability", *Econometrica*, 43, 65-80.

Helpman, E. and A. Razin (1982), "Dynamics of a Floating Exchange-Rate Regime", *Journal of Political Economy*, 90, 728-754.

Henderson, J.M. and R.E. Quandt (1971), *Microeconomic Theory: A Mathematical Approach*, second edition, McGraw-Hill, New York.

Herstein, I.N. (1964), *Topics in Algebra*, Blaisdell Publishing Company, New York.

Hestenes, M.R. (1966), *Calculus of Variations and Optimal Control Theory*, John Wiley & Sons, New York.

Hicks, J.R. (1946), *Value and Capital*, second edition, Clarendon Press, Oxford.

Hillier, B. and J.M. Malcomson (1984), "Dynamic Inconsistency, Rational Expectations and Optimal Government Policy", *Econometrica*, 52, 1437-1451.

Hinich, M. (1982), "Testing for Gaussianity and Linearity of a Stationary Time Series", *Journal of Time Series Analysis*, 3, 169-176.

Hinich, M. and D. Patterson (1985), "Evidence of Nonlinearity in Daily Stock Returns", *Journal of Business and Economic Statistics*, 3, 69-77.

Hirota, M. (1981), "On the Stability of Competitive Equilibrium and the Patterns of Initial Holdings: An Example", *International Economic Review*, 22, 461-467.

Hirota, M. (1985), "Global Stability in a Class of Markets with Three Commodities and Three Consumers", *Journal of Economic Theory*, 36, 186-192.

Hirsch, M.W. and C. Pugh (1970), "Stable Manifolds and Hyperbolic Sets", in: S. Chern and S. Smale, eds, *Proceedings of the Symposium in Pure Mathematics XIV, Global Analysis*, American Mathematical Society, Providence, Rhode Island.

Hirsch, M.W. and S. Smale (1974), *Differential Equations, Dynamical Systems and Linear Algebra*, Academic Press, New York.

Holden, A.V. (1986), ed., *Chaos*, Princeton University Press, Princeton, New Jersey.

Homma, M. (1981), "A Dynamic Analysis of the Differential Incidence of Capital and Labour in a Two-Class Economy", *Journal of Public Economics*, 15, 363-378.

Hotelling, H. (1931), "The Economics of Exhaustible Resources", *Journal of Political Economy*, 39, 137-175.

Ibbotson, R. and R. Sinquefield (1977), *Stocks, Bonds, Bills and Inflation: The Past (1926-1976) and The Future (1977-2000)*, Financial Analysts Research Foundation, University of Virginia, Charlottesville, Virginia.

Intriligator, M.D. (1971), *Mathematical Optimization and Economic Theory*, Prentice-Hall, Englewood Cliffs, New Jersey.

Iooss, G. and D.D. Joseph (1980), *Elementary Stability and Bifurcation Theory*, Springer-Verlag, New York.

Irwin, M.C. (1980), *Smooth Dynamical Systems*, Academic Press, New York.

Jordan, D.W. (1987), *Nonlinear Ordinary Differential Equations*, second edition, Oxford University Press, London, England.

Judd, K. (1985), "Short Run Analysis of Fiscal Policy in a Simple Perfect Foresight Model", *Journal of Political Economy*, 93, 298-321.

Kamien, M. and N. Schwartz (1981), *The Calculus of Variations and Optimal Control in Economics and Management*, North-Holland Publishing Company, Amsterdam.

Karlin, S. (1959), *Mathematical Methods and Theory in Games, Programming and Economics, Volume I*, Addison-Wesley, Reading, Massachusetts.

Keenan, D. (1982), "Uniqueness and Global Stability in General Equilibrium Theory", *Journal of Mathematical Economics*, 9, 23-25.

Khalil, H.K. (1980), "A New Test for D-Stability", *Journal of Economic Theory*, 23, 120-122.

King, R., C. Plosser, J. Stock and M. Watson (1987), "Stochastic Trends and Economic Fluctuations", working paper #2229, *National Bureau of Economic Research*, Cambridge, Massachusetts.

Kleidon, A. (1986a), "Variance Bounds Tests and Stock Price Valuation Models", *Journal of Political Economy*, 94, 953–1001.

Kleidon, A. (1986b), "Anomalies in Financial Economics: Blueprint for Change?", *Journal of Business*, 59, S469–S499.

Klevorick, A. (1971), "The 'Optimal' Fair Rate of Return", *Bell Journal of Economics*, 2, 122–153.

Koçak, H. (1986), *Differential and Difference Equations Through Computer Experiments*, Springer-Verlag, New York.

Koopmans, T. (1965), "On the Concept of Optimal Economic Growth", in: *The Econometric Approach to Development Planning*, Rand McNally, Chicago, 225–287.

Krasovskii, N.N. (1963), *Stability of Motion: Applications of Liapunov's Second Method to Differential Systems and Equations with Delay*, Stanford University Press, Stanford, California.

Kuga, K. (1977), "General Saddlepoint Property of the Steady State of a Growth Model with Heterogeneous Capital Goods", *International Economic Review*, 18, 29–58.

Kurz, M. (1968a), "The General Instability of a Class of Competitive Growth Processes", *Review of Economic Studies*, 35, 155–174.

Kurz, M. (1968b), "Optimal Economic Growth and Wealth Effects", *International Economic Review*, 9, 348–357.

Kurz, M. (1969), "On the Inverse Optimal Problem", in: H.W. Kuhn and G.P. Szego, eds, *Mathematical Systems Theory and Economics I*, Springer-Verlag, Berlin.

Kushner, H.J. (1967), *Stochastic Stability and Control*, Academic Press, New York.

Kwakernaak, H. and R. Sivan (1972), *Linear Optimal Control Systems*, Wiley-Interscience, New York.

Kydland, F.E. and E.C. Prescott (1977), "Rules Rather Than Discretion: The Inconsistency of Optimal Plans", *Journal of Political Economy*, 85, 473–491.

Kydland, F.E. and E.C. Prescott (1982), "Time to Build and Aggregate Fluctuations", *Econometrica*, 50, 1345–1370.

Ladde, G.S. and V. Lakshimkantham (1980), *Random Differential Inequalities*, Academic Press, New York.

LaSalle, J.P. (1964), "Recent Advances in Liapunov Stability Theory", *Society of Industrial and Applied Mathematics Review*, 6, 1–11.

LaSalle, J.P. (1968), "Stability Theory for Ordinary Differential Equations", *Journal of Differential Equations*, 4, 57–65.

LaSalle, J.P. (1986), *The Stability and Control of Discrete Processes*, Springer-Verlag, New York.

LaSalle, J.P. and S. Lefschetz (1961), *Stability by Liapunov's Direct Method with Applications*, Academic Press, New York.

Lee, E.B. and L. Markus (1967), *Foundations of Optimal Control Theory*, John Wiley & Sons, New York.

Lefschetz, S. (1962), *Differential Equations: Geometric Theory*, second edition, Wiley-Interscience, New York.

Lefschetz, S. (1965), *Stability of Nonlinear Control Systems*, Academic Press, New York.

Lehman, B. (1987), "Fads, Martingales and Market Efficiency", working paper, School of Business, Columbia University, New York.

Lehnigk, S.H. (1966), *Stability Theorems for Linear Motions: With an Introduction to Liapunov's Direct Method*, Prentice-Hall, Englewood Cliffs, New Jersey.

Leighton, W. (1970), *Ordinary Differential Equations*, third edition, Wadsworth Publishing Company, Belmont, California.

Levhari, D. and N. Liviatan (1972), "On Stability in the Saddle-Point Sense", *Journal of Economic Theory*, 4, 88–93.

Levin, J.J. (1960), "On the Global Asymptotic Behavior of Nonlinear Systems of Differential Equations", *Archives of Rational Mechanics and Analysis*, 6, 65–74.

Levin, J.J. and J.A. Nohel (1960), "Global Asymptotic Stability for Nonlinear Systems of Differential Equations and Applications to Reactor Dynamics", *Archives of Rational Mechanics and Analysis*, 6, 194–211.

Li, T. and J. Yorke (1975), "Period Three Implies Chaos", *American Mathematical Monthly*, 82. 985–992.

Liapunov, A.M. (1949), *Problème Général de la Stabilité du Mouvement*, Princeton University Press, Princeton, New Jersey.

Liapunov, A.M. (1966), *Stability of Motion*, Academic Press, New York.

Lindelof, E. (1894), "Sur l'application des méthodes d'approximations successives a l'etude des integrales reeles des equations differentielles ordinaire", *Journale de Mathematiques Pures et Applique*, 10, 117–128.

Lipschitz, R. (1876), "Sur la possibilité d'intégrer completement un systeme donne d'equations differentielles", *Bulletin des Sciences Mathematiques*, 10, 291–346.

Litterman, R. and L. Weiss (1985), "Money, Real Interest Rates, and Output: A Reinterpretation of Postwar U.S. Data", *Econometrica*, 53, 129–156.

Liviatan, N. and P.A. Samuelson (1969), "Notes on Turnpikes: Stable and Unstable", *Journal of Economic Theory*, 1, 454–475. Reprinted in: R.C. Merton, ed. (1972), *The Collected Scientific Papers of Paul A. Samuelson, Volume III*, MIT Press, Cambridge, Massachusetts, 135–156.

Lo, A. and A.C. Mackinlay (1988), "Stock Market Prices do not Follow Random Walks: Evidence From A Simple Specification Test", *Review of Financial Studies*, 1, 41–66.

Long, J. and C. Plosser (1983), "Real Business Cycles", *Journal of Political Economy*, 91, 39–69.

Lucas, Jr, R.E. (1967), "Optimal Investment Policy and the Flexible Accelerator", *International Economic Review*, 8, 78–85.

Lucas, Jr, R.E. (1975), "An Equilibrium Model of the Business Cycle", *Journal of Political Economy*, 83, 1113–1144.

Lucas, Jr, R.E. (1978), "Asset Prices in an Exchange Economy", *Econometrica*, 46, 1429–1445.

Lucas, Jr, R.E. (1981), *Studies in Business Cycle Theory*, MIT Press, Cambridge, Massachusetts.

Lucas, Jr, R.E. (1982), "Interest Rates and Currency Prices In a Two-Country World", *Journal of Monetary Economics*, 10, 335–359.

Lucas, Jr, R.E. (1986), "Adaptive Behavior and Economic Theory", *Journal of Business*, 59, S401–S426.

Lucas, Jr, R.E. (1987), *Models of Business Cycles*, Basil Blackwell, Oxford, England.

Lucas, Jr, R.E. and E.C. Prescott (1971), "Investment Under Uncertainty", *Econometrica*, 39, 659–681.

Lucas, Jr, R.E. and N.L. Stokey (1983), "Optimal Fiscal and Monetary Policy in an Economy Without Capital", *Journal of Monetary Economics*, 12, 55–93.

Magill, M.J.P. (1972), "Capital Accumulation Under Random Disturbances", working paper, Department of Economics, Indiana University, Bloomington, Indiana.

Magill, M.J.P. (1977a), "Some New Results on the Local Stability of the Process of Capital Accumulation", *Journal of Economic Theory*, 15. 174–210.

Magill, M.J.P. (1977b), "A Local Analysis of N-Sector Capital Accumulation Under Uncertainty", *Journal of Economic Theory*, 15, 211–219.

Magill, M.J.P. (1979), "The Stability of Equilibrium", *International Economic Review*, 20, 577–597.

Magill, M.J.P. and J.A. Scheinkman (1979), "Stability of Regular Equilibria and the Correspondence Principle for Symmetric Variational Problems", *International Economic Review*, 20, 297–315.

Majumdar, M. and T. Mitra (1982), "Intertemporal Allocation With a Non-convex Technology: The Aggregated Framework", *Journal of Economic Theory*, 27, 101–136.

Malliaris, A.G. (1981), "Martingale Methods in Financial Decision Making", *Society of Industrial and Applied Mathematics Review*, 23, 434–443.

Malliaris, A.G. (1982), "A Solvable General Equilibrium Growth Model with Money", *Economic Notes*, 11, 28–43.

Malliaris, A.G. (1983), "Itô's Calculus in Financial Decision Making", *Society of Industrial and Applied Mathematics Review*, 25, 481–496.

Malliaris, A.G. (1984), "A Survey of Itô's Calculus and Economic Analysis", Applications of Stochastic Processes to Finance Conference, *Center of Education and Research Applied to Management*, June 22–23, Nice, France.

Malliaris, A.G. (1987a), "Economic Uncertainty: Its Continuous Time Modeling," in: George Bitros and C. Davos, eds, *Essays in Honor of Professor P. Christodoulopoulos*, Graduate School of Business and Economics, Athens, Greece, 107–121.

Malliaris, A.G. (1987b), "Stochastic Controll", in: J. Eatwell, M. Milgate and P. Newman, eds, *The New Palgrave: A Dictionary of Economic Theory and Doctrine*, Macmillan, London, England, 501–503.

Malliaris, A.G. (1988a), "Approaches to the Cash Management Problem", in: C.F. Lee, ed., *Advances in Financial Planning and Forecasting*, 3, JAI Press, Inc., Greenwich, Connecticut.

Malliaris, A.G. (1988b), "Illustrations of the Quantity Theory of Money: Annual Data 1947–1987", in: W.R. Heilmann, ed., *Fourth Symposium on Money, Banking and Insurance*, University of Karlsruhe, Verlag Versicherungswirtschaft, Karlsruhe, West Germany.

Malliaris, A.G. (1988c), "Illustrations of the Quantity Theory of Money: Further Evidence", working paper, Graduate School of Business, Loyola University of Chicago, Chicago, Illinois.

Malliaris, A.G. and W.A. Brock (1982), *Stochastic Methods in Economics and Finance*, North-Holland Publishing Company, Amsterdam.

Malliaris, A.G. and G. Kaufman (1984), "Duration Based Strategies for Managing Bank Interest Rate Risk", in: H. Göppl and R. Henn, eds, *Third Symposium on Money, Banking, and Insurance*, Volume I, University of Karlsruhe, Verlag Versicherungswirtschaft, Karlsruhe, West Germany, 683–697.

Malliaris, A.G. and J. Urrutia (1988), "Trading Volume in Futures Markets: Theory and Testing", *Second International Conference on Financial Markets, Developments and Reforms*, June 28–30, Paris, France.

Mangasarian, O.L. (1963), "Stability Criteria for Nonlinear Ordinary Differential Equations", *Society of Industrial and Applied Mathematics Journal on Control and Optimization*, 1, 311–318.

Mangasarian, O.L. (1966), "Sufficient Conditions for the Optimal Control of Nonlinear Systems", *Society of Industrial and Applied Mathematics Journal on Control and Optimization*, 4, 139–152.

Mangasarian, O.L. (1969), *Nonlinear Programming*, McGraw-Hill, New York.

Mantel, R.R. (1974), "On the Characterization of Aggregate Excess Demand", *Journal of Economic Theory*, 7, 348-353.

Mantel, R.R. (1976), "Homothetic Preferences and Community Excess Demand Functions", *Journal of Economic Theory*, 12, 197-201.

Marcet, A. and T. Sargent (1988), "The Fate of Systems with Adaptive Expectations", *American Economic Review: Papers and Proceedings*, 78, 168-172.

Markus, L. (1954), "Global Structure of Ordinary Differential Equations in the Plane", *Transactions of the American Mathematical Society*, 76, 127-148.

Markus, L. and H. Yamabe (1960), "Global Stability Criteria for Differential Systems", *Osaka Mathematical Journal*, 12, 305-317.

Marsh, T. and K. Rock (1986), "The Transaction Process and Rational Stock Price Dynamics", working paper, Business School, University of California at Berkeley.

Martin, Jr, R.H. (1973), "Conditional Stability and Separation of Solutions to Differential Equations", *Journal of Differential Equations*, 13, 81-105.

Martin, Jr, R.E. (1983), *Ordinary Differential Equations*, McGraw-Hill, New York.

Mas-Colell, A. (1974), private communication.

Massell, B.F. (1969), "Price Stabilization and Welfare", *Quarterly Journal of Economics*, 83, 284-298.

Massera, J.L. (1949), "On Liapunov's Conditions of Stability", *Annals of Mathematics*, 50, 705-721.

Massera, J.L. (1956), "Contributions to Stability Theory", *Annals of Mathematics*, 64, 182-206.

May, R. (1976), "Simple Mathematical Models with Very Complicated Dynamics", *Nature*, 261, 459-467.

McCallum, B.T. (1977), "Price-Level Stickiness and the Feasibility of Monetary Stabilization Policy With Rational Expectations", *Journal of Political Economy*, 85, 627-634.

McCallum, B.T. (1978), "Price Level Adjustments and the Rational Expectations Approach to Macroeconomic Stabilization Policy", *Journal of Money, Credit and Banking*, 10, 418-436.

McCallum, B.T. (1980), "Rational Expectations and Macroeconomic Stabilization Policy: An Overview", *Journal of Money, Credit and Banking*, 12, 716-746.

McCallum, B.T. (1983), "On Non-Uniqueness in Rational Expectations Models", *Journal of Monetary Economics*, 11, 139-168.

McCallum, B.T. (1986), "Real Business Cycle Models", in: R. Barro, ed., *Handbook of Modern Business Cycle Theory*, Harvard University Press, Cambridge, Massachusetts.

McCann, R.C. (1982), *Introduction to Ordinary Differential Equations*, Harcourt Brace Jovanovich, New York.

McFadden, D. (1967), "The Evaluation of Development Programmes", *Review of Economic Studies*, 34, 25-50.

McKenzie, L.W. (1960), "Matrices with Dominant Diagonals and Economic Theory", in: K.J. Arrow, S. Karlin and P.C. Suppes, eds, *Mathematical Methods in the Social Sciences, 1959: Proceedings of the First Stanford Symposium*, Stanford University Press, Stanford, California, 47-62.

McKenzie, L.W. (1968), "Accumulation Programs of Maximum Utility and the von Neumann Facet", in: J.N. Wolfe, ed., *Value, Capital, and Growth: Papers in Honour of Sir John Hicks*, Edinburgh University Press, Edinburgh, Scotland, 353-383.

McKenzie, L.W. (1982), "A Primal Route to the Turnpike and Liapunov Stability", *Journal of Economic Theory*, 27, 194-209.

McKenzie, L.W. (1983), "Optimal Economic Growth and Turnpike Theorems", in: K.J. Arrow and M.D. Intriligator, eds, *The Handbook of Mathematical Economics, Volume 3*, North-Holland Publishing Company, Amsterdam.

McLure, Jr, C.E. (1975), "General Equilibrium Incidence Analysis: The Harberger Model After Ten Years", *Journal of Public Economics*, 4, 125-161.

Meisters, G. and C. Olech (1988), "A Stronger Form of Olech's Theorem on Globally One-to-One Mappings of the Plane", *The American Mathematical Society Meeting*, Session #237, January 6-9, Atlanta, Georgia.

Metzler, L. (1945), "Stability of Multiple Markets: The Hicks Conditions", *Econometrica*, 13, 277-292.

Michel, A.N. (1970), "Quantitative Analysis of Systems: Stability, Boundedness and Trajectory Behavior", *Archives for Rational Mechanics and Analysis*, 38, 107-122.

Michener, R. (1984), "A Neoclassical Model of the Balance of Payments", *Review of Economic Studies*, 51, 651-664.

Miller, M. (1977), "Debt and Taxes", *Journal of Finance*, 32, 261-275.

Miller, M. and F. Modigliani (1961), "Dividend Policy, Growth, and the Valuation of Shares", *Journal of Business*, 34, 411-433.

Miller, M. and M. Scholes (1978), "Dividends and Taxes", *Journal of Financial Economics*, 6, 333-364.

Miller, M. and M. Scholes (1982), "Dividends and Taxes: Some Empirical Evidence", *Journal of Political Economy*, 90, 1118-1141.

Miller, M. and K. Rock (1985), "Dividend Policy under Asymmetric Information", *Journal of Finance*, 40, 1031-1051.

Miller, R.E. (1979), *Dynamic Optimization and Economic Applications*, McGraw-Hill, New York.

Miller, R.K. (1987), *Introduction to Differential Equations*, Prentice-Hall, Englewood Cliffs, New Jersey.

Miller, R.K. and A.N. Michel (1982), *Ordinary Differential Equations*, Academic Press, New York.

Mitra, T. (1979), "On Optimal Economic Growth With Variable Discount Rates: Existence and Stability Results", *International Economic Review*, 20, 133-145.

Mitra, T. (1987), "On the Existence of a Stationary Optimal Stock for a Multi-Sector Economy with a Non-Convex Technology", working paper, Department of Economics, Cornell University, Ithaca, New York.

Mitra, T. and I. Zilcha (1981), "On Optimal Economic Growth With Changing Technology and Tastes: Characterization and Stability Results", *International Economic Review*, 22, 221-238.

Miyao, T. (1981), *Dynamic Analysis of the Urban Economy*, Academic Press, New York.

Modigliani, F. and M. Miller (1958), "The Cost of Capital, Corporation Finance and the Theory of Investment", *American Economic Review*, 48, 261-297.

Montroll, E. and W. Badger (1974), *Introduction to Quantitative Aspects of Social Phenomena*, Gordon and Breach, Science Publishers, Inc., New York.

Moore, T. (1964), *Elementary General Topology*, Prentice-Hall, Englewood Cliffs, New Jersey.

Morishima, M. (1952), "On the Laws of Change of the Price System in an Economy which Contains Complementary Commodities", *Osaka Economic Papers*, 1, 101-113.

Mortensen, D.T. (1973), "Generalized Costs of Adjustment and Dynamic Factor Demand Theory", *Econometrica*, 41, 657-665.

Mufti, I.H. (1961), "Stability in the Large Systems of Two Equations", *Archives for Rational Mechanics and Analysis*, 7, 119-134.

Mundell, R.A. (1968), *International Economics*, Macmillan, London, England.

Murata, Y. (1977), *Mathematics for Stability and Optimization of Economic Systems*, Academic Press, New York.

Mussa, M. (1976), *A Study in Macroeconomics*, North-Holland Publishing Company, Amsterdam.

Mussa, M. (1978), "On the Inherent Stability of Rationally Adaptive Expectations", *Journal of Monetary Economics*, 4, 307–313.

Mussa, M. (1982), "A Model of Exchange-Rate Dynamics", *Journal of Political Economy*, 90, 74–103.

Muth, J.F. (1961), "Rational Expectations and the Theory of Price Movements", *Econometrica*, 29, 315–335.

Nadiri, M.I. and S. Rosen (1969), "Interrelated Factor Demand Functions", *American Economic Review*, 59, 457–471.

Nadiri, M.I. and S. Rosen (1973), *A Disequilibrium Model of Demand for Factors of Production*, National Bureau of Economic Research, New York.

Nagatani, K. (1970), "A Note on Professor Tobin's 'Money and Economic Growth'", *Econometrica*, 38, 171–175.

National Academy of Sciences (1987), *Report of the Research Briefing Panel on Order, Chaos and Patterns: Aspects of Non-linearity*, National Academy Press, Washington, D.C.

Neftci, S. (1984), "Are Economic Time Series Asymmetric Over the Business Cycle?", *Journal of Political Economy*, 92, 307–328.

Negishi, T. (1962), "The Stability of a Competitive Economy: A Survey Article", *Econometrica*, 30, 635–669.

Neher, P.A. (1971), *Economic Growth and Development: A Mathematical Introduction*, John Wiley & Sons, New York.

Nelson, C. and C. Plosser (1982), "Trends and Random Walks in Macroeconomic Time Series: Some Evidence and Implications", *Journal of Monetary Economics*, 10, 139–162.

Nemytskii, V.V. and V.V. Stepanov (1960), *Qualitative Theory of Differential Equations*, Princeton University Press, Princeton, New Jersey.

Nikaido, H. (1968), *Convex Structures and Economic Theory*, Academic Press, New York.

Nikaido, H. (1970), *Introduction to Sets and Mappings in Modern Economics*, North-Holland Publishing Company, Amsterdam.

Obstfeld, M. (1984), "Multiple Stable Equilibria in an Optimizing Perfect-Foresight Model", *Econometrica*, 52, 223–228.

Obstfeld, M. and K. Rogoff (1983), "Speculative Hyperinflation in Maximizing Models: Can We Rule Them Out?", *Journal of Political Economy*, 91, 675–705.

Obstfeld, M. and A.C. Stockman (1984), "Exchange-Rate Dynamics" in: R.W. Jones and P.B. Kenen, eds, *Handbook of International Economics, Volume II*, North-Holland Publishing Company, Amsterdam.

Oi, W.Y. (1961), "The Desirability of Price Instability Under Perfect Competition", *Econometrica*, 29, 58–64.

Okuguchi, K. (1976), *Expectations and Stability in Oligopoly Models*, Springer-Verlag, New York.

Olech, C. (1963), "On the Global Stability of an Autonomous System on the Plane", *Contributions to Different Equations, Volume I*, 389–400.

Oseledec, V. (1968), "A Multiplicative Ergodic Theorem: Liapunov Characteristic Numbers for Dynamical Systems", *Transactions of the Moscow Mathematical Society*, 19, 197–231.

Paige, L. and J. Swift (1961), *Elements of Linear Algebra*, Blaisdell Publishing Company, New York.

Peano, G. (1890), "Démonstration de l'integrabilité des équations differentielles ordinaires", *Mathematische Annalen*, 37, 182–228.

Pearce, I.F. (1974), "Matrices With Dominating Diagonal Blocks", Journal of Economic Theory, 9, 159-170.

Peixoto, M.M. (1962), "Structural Stability on Two-Dimensional Manifolds", Topology, 1, 101-120.

Percival, I.C. (1983), Introduction to Dynamics, Cambridge University Press, Cambridge, England.

Persson, M., T. Persson and L. Svensson (1987), "Time Consistency of Fiscal and Monetary Policy", Econometrica, 55, 1419-1431.

Phelps, E.S. (1972), Inflation Policy and Unemployment Theory, W.W. Norton & Company, Inc., New York.

Phelps, E.S., et al. (1970), eds, "Microeconomic Foundations of Employment and Inflation Theory, W.W. Norton & Company, Inc., New York.

Phelps, E.S. and S.G. Winter Jr (1970), "Optimal Price Policy Under Atomistic Competition", in: E.S. Phelps et al., eds, Microeconomic Foundations of Employment and Inflation Theory, W.W. Norton & Company, Inc., New York, 309-337.

Picard, E. (1890), "Mémoire sur la théorie des équations aux derivees partielles et la methode des approximations successives", Journale de Mathematiques Pures et Appliqué, 6, 423-441.

Pindyck, R.C. (1973), Optimal Planning for Economic Stabilization: The Application of Control Theory to Stabilization Policy, North-Holland Publishing Company, Amsterdam.

Pines, D. (1988), ed., The Economy as an Evolving Complex System, Addison-Wesley, New York.

Plaat, O. (1971), Ordinary Differential Equations, Holden-Day, San Francisco, California.

Pohjola, M. (1985), "Built-In Flexibility of Progressive Taxation and the Dynamics of Income: Stability, Cycles, or Chaos?", Public Finance, 40, 263-273.

Pontryagin, L.S. (1962), Ordinary Differential Equations, Addison-Wesley, Reading, Massachusetts.

Pontryagin, L.S., V.G. Boltyanskii, R.V. Gamkrelidze and E.F. Mischenko (1962), The Mathematical Theory of Optimal Processes, Wiley-Interscience, New York.

Poterba, J. and L. Summers (1987), "Mean Reversion in Stock Prices: Evidence and Implications", working paper #2343, National Bureau of Economic Research, Cambridge, Massachusetts.

Prescott, E.C. (1973), "Market Structure and Monopoly Profits: A Dynamic Theory", Journal of Economic Theory, 6, 546-557.

Prescott, E.C. and R. Mehra (1980), "Recursive Competitive Equilibrium: The Case of Homogeneous Households", Econometrica, 48, 1365-1379.

Prescott, E.C. and R. Mehra (1985), "The Equity Premium: A Puzzle", Journal of Monetary Economics, 15, 145-161.

Prigogine, I. (1980), From Being to Becoming, W.H. Freeman & Company, New York.

Prigogine, I. and I. Stengers (1984), Order Out of Chaos: Man's New Dialogue With Nature, Bantam Books, New York.

Prigogine, I. and M. Sanglier (1987), Laws of Nature and Human Conduct, G.O.R.D.E.S. Task Force of Research Information and Study on Science, Bruxelles, Belgium.

Purvis, D.D. (1973), "Short-Run Dynamics in Models of Money and Growth", American Economic Review, 63, 12-23.

Purvis, D.D. (1978), "Dynamic Models of Portfolio Behavior: More on Pitfalls in Financial Model Building", American Economic Review, 68, 403-409.

Quirk, J. and R. Saposnik (1968), Introduction to General Equilibrium Theory and Welfare Economics, McGraw-Hill, New York.

Ramsey, F.P. (1928), "A Mathematical Theory of Saving", Economic Journal, 38, 543-559.

Ramsey, J. and H. Yuan (1987), "The Statistical Properties of Dimension Calculations Using Small Data Sets", working paper, Department of Economics, New York University.

Reid, W.T. (1971), *Ordinary Differential Equations*, John Wiley & Sons, New York.

Riley, J.G. (1979), "Informational Equilibrium", *Econometrica*, 47, 331-359.

Roberts, Jr, C.E. (1979), *Ordinary Differential Equations: A Computational Approach*, Prentice-Hall, Englewood Cliffs, New Jersey.

Rockafellar, R.T. (1970a), "Generalized Hamiltonian Equations for Convex Problems of Lagrange", *Pacific Journal of Mathematics*, 33, 411-427.

Rockafellar, R.T. (1970b), "Conjugate Convex Functions in Optimal Control and the Calculus of Variations", *Journal of Mathematical Analysis and Applications*, 32, 174-222.

Rockafellar, R.T. (1973), "Saddle Points of Hamiltonian Systems in Convex Problems of Lagrange", *Journal of Optimization Theory and Applications"*, 12, 367-390.

Rockafellar, R.T. (1976), "Saddle Points of Hamiltonian Systems in Convex Lagrange Problems Having a Nonzero Discount Rate", *Journal of Economic Theory*, 12, 71-113.

Romer, P.M. (1986a), "Increasing Returns and Long-Run Growth", *Journal of Political Economy*, 94, 1002-1037.

Romer, P.M. (1986b), "Increasing Returns, Specialization, and External Economies: Growth as Described by Allyn Young", working paper, Rochester Center for Economic Research, University of Rochester, Rochester, New York.

Romer, P.M. (1987), "Growth Based on Increasing Returns Due to Specialization", *American Economic Review: Papers and Proceedings*, 77, 56-62.

Rostow, W. (1983), *The Barbaric Counter-Revolution: Cause and Cure*, University of Texas Press, Austin, Texas.

Rothschild, M. (1986), "Asset Pricing Theories", in: W. Heller, R. Starr and D. Starrett, eds, *Uncertainty, Information and Communication: Essays in Honor of Kenneth J. Arrow*, Cambridge University Press, New York.

Rouche, N., P. Habets, and M. Laloy (1977), *Stability Theory by Liapunov's Direct Method*, Springer-Verlag, New York.

Roux, J., R. Simoyi, and H. Swinney (1983), "Observation of a Strange Attractor", *Physica*, 8D, 257-266.

Roxin, E.O. (1965a), "Stability in General Control Systems", *Journal of Differential Equations*, 1, 115-150.

Roxin, E.O. (1965b), "On Stability in Control Systems", *Society of Industrial and Applied Mathematics Journal on Control and Optimization*, 3, 357-372.

Roxin, E.O. (1972), *Ordinary Differential Equations*, Wadsworth Publishing Company, Belmont, California.

Royden, H.L. (1968), *Real Analysis*, second edition, Macmillan, London, England.

Ruelle, D. and F. Takens (1971), "On the Nature of Turbulence", *Communications in Mathematical Physics*, 20, 167-192.

Ryder, Jr, H.E. and G.M. Heal (1973), "Optimal Growth With Intertemporally Dependent Preferences", *Review of Economic Studies*, 40, 1-31.

Sakai, H. and H. Tokumaru (1980), "Autocorrelations of a Certain Chaos", *IEEE Transactions Acoustics, Speech Signal and Processes*, V.I. ASSP-28, 588-590.

Samuelson, P.A. (1941), "The Stability of Equilibrium: Comparative Statics and Dynamics", *Econometrica*, 9, 97-120, reprinted in: J.E. Stiglitz, ed., *The Collected Scientific Papers of Paul A. Samuelson, Volume I*, MIT Press, Cambridge, Massachusetts, 539-562.

Samuelson, P.A. (1942), "The Stability of Equilibrium: Linear and Nonlinear Systems", *Econometrica*, 10, 1-25, reprinted in: J.E. Stiglitz, ed., *The Collected Scientific Papers of Paul A. Samuelson, Volume I*, MIT Press, Cambridge, Massachusetts, 565-589.

Samuelson, P.A. (1947), *Foundations of Economic Analysis*, Harvard University Press, Cambridge, Massachusetts.

Samuelson, P.A. (1958), "An Exact Consumption–Loan Model of Interest With or Without the Social Contrivance of Money", *Journal of Political Economy*, 66, 467–482.

Samuelson, P.A. (1971), "On the Trail of Conventional Beliefs about the Transfer Problem", in: J.N. Bhagwati, et al., eds, *Trade, Balance of Payments and Growth: Papers in International Economics in Honor of Charles P. Kindleberger*, North-Holland Publishing Company, Amsterdam, 327–351.

Samuelson, P.A. (1972a), "The General Saddle-Point Property of Optimal-Control Motions", *Journal of Economic Theory*, 5, 102–120.

Samuelson, P.A. (1972b), "The Consumer Does Benefit from Feasible Price Stability", *Quarterly Journal of Economics*, 86, 476–493.

Samuelson, P.A. and R.M. Solow (1956), "A Complete Capital Model Involving Heterogeneous Capital Goods", *Quarterly Journal of Economics*, 70, 537–562.

Sanchez, D.A. (1968), *Ordinary Differential Equations and Stability, Theory: An Introduction*, W.H. Freeman, San Francisco.

Sanchez, D.A. and R.C. Allen, Jr. (1983), *Differential Equations: An Introduction*, Addison-Wesley, Reading, Massachusetts.

Santomero, A.M. and J.J. Siegel (1981), "Bank Regulation and Macro-Economic Stability", *American Economic Review*, 71, 39–53.

Sargent, T. (1981), "Interpreting Economic Time Series", *Journal of Political Economy*, 89, 213–248.

Sargent, T. (1987), *Dynamic Macroeconomic Theory*, Harvard University Press, Cambridge, Massachusetts.

Sargent, T. and N. Wallace (1973), "The Stability of Models of Money and Growth With Perfect Foresight", *Econometrica*, 41, 1043–1048.

Sattinger, D.H. (1973), *Topics in Stability and Bifurcation Theory, Lecture Notes in Mathematics*, Springer-Verlag, New York.

Scarf, H. (1960), "Some Examples of Global Instability of the Competitive Equilibrium", *International Economic Review*, 1, 157–172.

Scarf, H. (1981), "Comment on: 'On the Stability of Competitive Equilibrium and the Patterns of Initial Holdings: An Example' ", *International Economic Review*, 22, 469–470.

Scheinkman, J.A. (1976), "On Optimal Steady States of N-Sector Growth Models When Utility is Discounted", *Journal of Economic Theory*, 12, 11–30.

Scheinkman, J.A. (1977), "Notes on Asset Pricing", working paper, Department of Economics, University of Chicago, Chicago, Illinois.

Scheinkman, J.A. (1978), "Stability of Separable Hamiltonians and Investment Theory", *Review of Economic Studies*, 45, 559–570.

Scheinkman, J.A. (1980), "Discussion", in: J. Kareken and N. Wallace, eds, *Models of Monetary Economics*, Federal Reserve Bank of Minneapolis, 91–96.

Scheinkman, J.A. and L. Weiss (1986), "Borrowing Constraints and Aggregate Economic Activity", *Econometrica*, 54, 23–45.

Scheinkman, J.A. and B. LeBaron (1987), "Nonlinear Dynamics and Stock Returns", working paper, Department of Economics, University of Chicago, Chicago, Illinois.

Schenone, O.H. (1975), "A Dynamic Analysis of Taxation", *American Economic Review*, 65, 101–114.

Schinasi, G.J. (1982), "Fluctuations in a Dynamic, Intermediate-Run IS-LM Model: Applications of the Poincare–Bendixson Theorem", *Journal of Economic Theory*, 28, 369–375.

Seade, J. (1980), "The Stability of Cournot Revisited", *Journal of Economic Theory*, 23, 15-27.

Seierstad, A. and K. Sydsaeter (1987), *Optimal Control Theory With Economic Applications*, North-Holland Publishing Company, Amsterdam.

Senchack, Jr, A.J. (1975), "The Firm's Optimal Financial Policies: Solution, Equilibrium, and Stability", *Journal of Financial and Quantitative Analysis*, 10, 543-555.

Shane, M. (1974), "Capital Markets and the Dynamics of Growth", *American Economic Review*, 64, 162-169.

Shell, K. (1967), ed., *Essays on the Theory of Optimal Economic Growth*, MIT Press, Cambridge, Massachusetts.

Shell, K. (1971), "On Competitive Dynamical Systems", in: H.W. Kuhn and G.P. Szegö, eds, *Differential Games and Related Topics*, North-Holland Publishing Company, Amsterdam, 449-476.

Shiller, R.J. (1978), "Rational Expectations and the Dynamic Structure of Macroeconomic Models", *Journal of Monetary Economics*, 4, 1-44.

Shiller, R.J. (1984), "Stock Prices and Social Dynamics", *Brookings Papers on Economic Activity*, 457-510.

Schlesinger, M. and G. Weiss (1985), *The Wonderful World of Stochastics: A Tribute to Elliot W. Montroll*, North-Holland Publishing Company, New York.

Shub, M. (1986), *Global Stability of Dynamical Systems*, Springer-Verlag, New York.

Sidrauski, M. (1967), "Inflation and Economic Growth", *Journal of Political Economy*, 75, 796-810.

Siegel, J.J. (1976), "Stability of Keynesian and Classical Macroeconomic Systems", *Journal of Monetary Economics*, 2, 257-266.

Simmons, G.F. (1972), *Differential Equations, With Applications and Historical Notes*, McGraw-Hill, New York.

Sims, C. (1984), "Martingale-Like Behavior of Prices and Interest Rates", working paper, Department of Economics, University of Minnesota, Minneapolis, Minnesota.

Skiba, A. (1978), "Optimal Growth With a Convex-Concave Production Function", *Econometrica*, 46, 527-540.

Smale, S. (1967), "Differentiable Dynamical Systems", *Bulletin of the American Mathematical Society*, 73, 747-817.

Smale, S. (1976), "Dynamics in General Equilibrium Theory", *American Economic Review*, 66, 288-294.

Smale, S. (1980), *The Mathematics of Time: Essays on Dynamical Systems, Economic Processes, and Related Topics*, Springer-Verlag, New York.

Smith, G. (1978), "Dynamic Models of Portfolio Behavior: Comment on Purvis", *American Economic Review*, 68, 410-416.

Solow, R.M. (1956), "A Contribution to the Theory of Economic Growth", *Quarterly Journal of Economics*, 70, 65-94.

Sonnenschein, H. (1972), "Market Excess Demand Functions", *Econometrica*, 40, 549-563.

Sonnenschein, H. (1973), "Do Walras' Identity and Continuity Characterize the Class of Community Excess Demand Functions?", *Journal of Economic Theory*, 6, 345-354.

Sonnenschein, H. (1982), "Price Dynamics Based on the Adjustment of Firms", *American Economic Review*, 72, 1088-1096.

Sonnenschein, H. (1986), ed., *Models of Economic Dynamics*, Springer-Verlag, New York.

Stein, J.L. (1980), "The Dynamics of Spot and Forward Prices in an Efficient Foreign Exchange Market with Rational Expectations", *American Economic Review*, 70, 565-583.

Stein, J.L. and K. Nagatani (1969), "Stabilization Policies in a Growing Economy", *Review of Economic Studies*, 36, 165-183.

Stiglitz, J. (1973), "Taxation, Corporate Financial Policy, and the Cost of Capital", *Journal of Public Economics*, 2, 1-34.

Stiglitz, J. (1974), "On the Irrelevance of Corporate Financial Policy", *American Economic Review*, 64, 851-866.

Stiglitz, J. and H. Uzawa (1969), eds, *Readings in the Modern Theory of Economic Growth*, MIT Press, Cambridge, Massachusetts.

Stock, J. (1985), "Estimating Continuous Time Processes Subject to Time Deformation: An Application to Postwar U.S. GNP", working paper, Kennedy School of Government, Harvard University, Cambridge, Massachusetts.

Stock, J. (1986), "Measuring Business Cycle Time", working paper, Kennedy School of Government, Harvard University, Cambridge, Massachusetts.

Stock, J. (1987), "Hysteresis and the Evolution of Postwar U.S. and U.K. Unemployment", working paper, Kennedy School of Government, Harvard University, Cambridge, Massachusetts.

Stock, J. and M. Watson (1987), "Interpreting the Evidence on Money-Income Causality", working paper #2228, *National Bureau of Economic Research*, Cambridge, Massachusetts.

Strauss, A. (1965), "Liapunov Functions and Global Existence", *Bulletin of the American Mathematical Society*, 71, 519-520.

Strauss, A. and J.A. Yorke (1969), "Identifying Perturbations Which Preserve Asymptotic Stability", *Proceedings of the American Mathematical Society*, 22, 513-518.

Stutzer, M. (1980), "Chaotic Dynamics and Bifurcation in a Macro Model", *Journal of Economic Dynamics and Control*, 2, 353-376.

Summers, L. (1986a), "Some Skeptical Observations on Real Business Cycle Theory", *Quarterly Review of the Federal Reserve Bank of Minneapolis*, 10, 23-27.

Summers, L. (1986b), "Does the Stock Market Rationally Reflect Fundamental Values?", *Journal of Finance*, 41, 591-601.

Swinney, H. (1983), "Observations of Order and Chaos in Nonlinear Systems", *Physica*, 7D, 3-15.

Swinney, H. (1985), "Observation of Complex Dynamics and Chaos", in: E.G.D. Cohen, ed., *Fundamental Problems in Statistical Mechanics VI*, North-Holland Publishing Company, Amsterdam.

Takayama, A. (1985), *Mathematical Economics*, second edition, Cambridge University Press, Cambridge, England.

Takens, F. (1980), "Detecting Strange Attractors in Turbulence", in: D. Rand and L. Young, eds, *Dynamical Systems and Turbulence, Lecture Notes in Mathematics*, 898, Springer-Verlag, New York, 366-382.

Takens, F. (1983), "Distinguishing Deterministic and Random Systems", in: G. Barenblatt, G. Iooss and D.D. Joseph, eds, *Nonlinear Dynamics and Turbulence*, Pitman Advanced Publishing Program, Boston, Massachusetts, 315-333.

Takens, F. (1984), "On the Numerical Determination of the Dimension of an Attractor", unpublished manuscript.

Tarr, D.G. (1978), "Expectations and Stability With Gross Complements", *Review of Economic Studies*, 45, 617-620.

Taylor, J.B. (1977), "Conditions for Unique Solution in Stochastic Macroeconomic Models with Rational Expectations", *Econometrica*, 45, 1377-1387.

Taylor, J.B. (1986), "Rational Expectations Models in Macroeconomics", in: K. Arrow and S. Honkapohja, eds, *Frontiers of Economics*, Oxford: Basil Blackwell, England, 391-425.

Thom, R. (1975), *Structural Stability and Morphogenesis: An Outline of a General Theory of Models*, W.A. Benjamin, Inc., Reading, Massachusetts.

Thompson, J.M.T. and H.B. Stewart (1986), *Nonlinear Dynamics and Chaos: Geometrical Methods for Engineers and Scientists*, John Wiley and Sons, New York.

Tillmann, G. (1985), "Existence and Stability of Rational Expectation Equilibria in a Simple Overlapping Generation Model", *Journal of Economic Theory*, 36, 333-351.

Tobin, J. (1965), "Money and Economic Growth", *Econometrica*, 33, 671-684.

Tobin, J. (1969), "A General Equilibrium Approach to Monetary Theory", *Journal of Money, Credit and Banking*, 1, 15-29.

Tobin, J. (1975), "Keynesian Models of Recession and Depression", *American Economic Review*, 65, 195-202.

Tobin, J. (1980), *Asset Accumulation and Economic Activity*, University of Chicago Press, Chicago, Illinois.

Tobin, J. (1986), "The Monetary-Fiscal Mix: Long-Run Implications", *American Economic Review*, 76, 213-218.

Tobin, J. and W. Buiter (1976), "Long-Run Effects of Fiscal and Monetary Policy on Aggregate Demand", in: J. Stein, ed., *Monetarism*, North-Holland Publishing Company, Amsterdam, 273-309.

Treadway, A.B. (1969), "On Rational Entrepreneurial Behaviour and the Demand for Investment", *Review of Economic Studies*, 36, 227-239.

Treadway, A.B. (1971), "The Rational Multivariate Flexible Accelerator", *Econometrica*, 39, 845-855.

Turnovsky, S.J. (1974), "The Stability Properties of Optimal Economic Policies", *American Economic Review*, 64, 136-148.

Turnovsky, S.J. (1976), "The Distribution of Welfare Gains From Price Stabilization: The Case of Multiplicative Disturbances", *International Economic Review*, 17, 133-148.

Turnovsky, S.J. (1977), *Macroeconomic Analysis and Stabilization Policies*, Cambridge University Press, Cambridge, England.

Turnovsky, S.J. (1978), "Macroeconomic Dynamics and Growth in a Monetary Economy: A Synthesis", *Journal of Money, Credit and Banking*, 10, 1-26.

Turnovsky, S.J. (1982), "The Incidence of Taxes: A Dynamic Macroeconomic Analysis", *Journal of Public Economics*, 18, 161-194.

Turnovsky, S.J. and E. Burmeister (1977), "Perfect Foresight, Expectational Consistency, and Macroeconomic Equilibrium", *Journal of Political Economy*, 85, 379-393.

Turnovsky, S.J. and W.A. Brock (1980), "Time Consistency and Optimal Government Policies in Perfect Foresight Equilibrium", *Journal of Public Economics*, 13, 183-212.

Turnovsky, S.J., H. Shalit and A. Schmitz (1980), "Consumer's Surplus, Price Instability, and Consumer Welfare", *Econometrica*, 48, 135-152.

Uzawa, H. (1964), "Optimal Growth in a Two-Sector Model of Capital Accumulation", *Review of Economic Studies*, 31, 1-24.

Uzawa, H. (1974), "On the Dynamic Stability of Economic Growth: The Neoclassical Versus Keynesian Approaches", in: G. Horwich and P.A. Samuelson, eds, *Trade, Stability and Macroeconomics*, Academic Press, New York, 523-553.

Vainberg, M.M. (1973), *Variational Method and Method of Monotone Operators in the Theory of Nonlinear Equations*, John Wiley & Sons, New York.

Varian, H.R. (1977), "The Stability of a Disequilibrium IS-LM Model", *Scandinavian Journal of Economics*, 79, 260-270.

Walras, L. (1954), *Elements of Pure Economics*, translated by W. Jaffe, G. Allen and Unwin, London, England.

Wan, Y.H. (1978), "On the Structure and Stability of Local Pareto Optima in a Pure Exchange Economy", *Journal of Mathematical Economics*, 5, 255-274.

Waugh, F.V. (1944), "Does the Consumer Benefit from Price Instability", *Quarterly Journal of Economics*, 58, 602-614.

Weitzman, M. (1973), "Duality Theory for Infinite Horizon Convex Models," *Management Science*, 19, 783-789.

Wilson, C.A. (1979), "Anticipated Shocks and Exchange Rate Dynamics", *Journal of Political Economy*, 87, 639-647.

Wintner, A. (1946), "Asymptotic Equilibria", *American Journal of Mathematics*, 68, 125-132.

Wolf, A.J., J. Swift, H. Swinney, and J. Vastano (1985), "Determining Liapunov Exponents from a Time Series", *Physica*, 16D, 285-317.

Wood, R., T. McInish and J. Ord (1985), "An Investigation of Transactions Data for New York Stock Exchange Stocks", *Journal of Finance*, 40, 723-741.

Woodford, M. (1987), "Imperfect Financial Intermediaries and Complex Dynamics", working paper, Graduate School of Business, University of Chicago, Chicago, Illinois.

Wu, S.Y. (1979), "An Essay on Monopoly Power and Stable Price Policy", *American Economic Review*, 69, 60-72.

Yoshizawa, T. (1975), *Stability Theory and the Existence of Periodic Solutions and Almost Periodic Solutions*, Springer-Verlag, New York.

Zarnowitz, V. (1985), "Recent Work on Business Cycles in Historical Perspective: Review of Theories and Evidence", *Journal of Economic Literature*, 23, 523-580.

Zubov, V.I. (1964), *Methods of A.M. Liapunov and Their Application*, P. Noordhoff, Groningen, Holland.

INDEX